D0264647

ISBN 1-55009-036-4

9 781550 090369

Thromboembolic Complications during Infancy and Childhood

Thromboembolic Complications during Infancy and Childhood

MAUREEN ANDREW, MD, FRCP

Professor of Pediatrics
McMaster University Medical Center
Hamilton Civic Hospital's Research Center, Hamilton
Director, Children's Thrombophilia Program
The Hospital for Sick Children, Toronto

PAUL T. MONAGLE, MBBS, MSc, FRACP, FRCPA

Head, Haematology Laboratory
Divisional Director Laboratory Services
Women's and Children's Health Care Network
Senior Lecturer, Department of Paediatrics
University of Melbourne, Melbourne, Australia

LuAnn BROOKER, RT

McMaster University Medical Center, Hamilton
The Hospital for Sick Children, Toronto

2000
B.C.Decker Inc.
Hamilton • London

B.C. Decker Inc.
4 Hughson Street South
P.O. Box 620, L.C.D. 1
Hamilton, Ontario L8N 3K7
Tel: 905-522-7017; 1-800-568-7281
Fax: 905-522-7839
E-mail: info@bcdecker.com
Website: http://www.bcdecker.com

ISBN 1–55009–036–4
Printed in Canada by the University of Toronto Press

Sales and Distribution

United States
B.C. Decker Inc.
P.O. Box 785
Lewiston, NY U.S.A. 14092-0785
Tel: 905-522-7017/1-800-568-7281
Fax: 905-522-7839
e-mail: info@bcdecker.com
website: http://www.bcdecker.com

Canada
B.C. Decker Inc.
4 Hughson Street South
P.O. Box 620, L.C.D. 1
Hamilton, Ontario L8N 3K7
Tel: 905-522-7017/1-800-568-7281
Fax: 905-522-7839
e-mail: info@bcdecker.com
website: http://www.bcdecker.com

Japan
Igaku-Shoin Ltd.
Foreign Publications Department
3-24-17 Hongo, Bunkyo-ku,
Tokyo 113-8719, Japan
Tel: 3 3817 5676
Fax: 3 3815 6776
e-mail: fd@igaku.shoin.co.jp

U.K., Europe, Scandinavia, Middle East
Blackwell Science Ltd.
Osney Mead
Oxford OX2 0EL
United Kingdom
Tel: 44-1865-206206
Fax: 44-1865-721205
e-mail: info@blackwell-science.com

Australia
Blackwell Science Asia Pty, Ltd.
54 University Street
Carlton, Victoria 3053
Australia
Tel: 03 9347 0300
Fax: 03 9349 3016
e-mail: info@blacksci.asia.com.au

South Korea
Seoul Medical Scientific Books Co.
C.P.O. Box 9794
Seoul 100-697
Seoul, Korea
Tel: 82-2925-5800
Fax: 82-2927-7283

South America
Ernesto Reichmann, Distribuidora
 de Livros Ltda.
Rua Coronel Marques
335-Tatuape, 03440-000
Sao Paulo-SP-Brazil
Tel/Fax: 011-218-2122

Foreign Rights
John Scott & Co.
International Publishers' Agency
P.O. Box 878
Kimberton, PA 19442
Tel: 610-827-1640
Fax: 610-827-1671

Notice: The authors and publisher have made every effort to ensure that the patient care recommended herein, including choice of drugs and drug dosages, is in accord with the accepted standard and practice at the time of publication. However, since research and regulation constantly change clinical standards, the reader is urged to check the product information sheet included in the package of each drug, which includes recommended doses, warnings, and contraindications. This is particularly important with new or infrequently used drugs.

The authors would like to dedicate
Thromboembolic Complications during Infancy and Childhood
to our children:

Laura, Kate, Sara and Andrew Monagle;
Neal and Anya Brooker;
Michelle and Adam O'Brodovich

and in memory of

Robbie Andrew O'Brodovich (1982-1986)

whose brief life brought so much joy.

PREFACE

The concept idea of writing a book devoted to the subject of thromboembolic disease during infancy and childhood arose from numerous conversations that I have had with pediatricians caring for children with these complications; my own practice at the Hospital for Sick Children, Toronto, Canada; and a paucity of information in the literature. Over the last 30 years tertiary care pediatrics has witnessed unparalleled advances in therapy for children with previously lethal disorders which include prematurity, congenital heart disease, cancer, organ failure, and other diverse illnesses. At the same time we have witnessed the evolution of new diseases secondary to the longer survival and treatment of children with these previously lethal diseases. Thromboembolic events, which are primarily secondary to venous and arterial catheterization or use of prosthetic materials, are among the most frequent and serious secondary complications and require specific strategies for both prevention and treatment. Over the same time frame there has been an explosion of knowledge at the molecular level resulting in the discovery of a genetic basis for several congenital prothrombotic disorders. The latter has resulted in the identification of many asymptomatic children with congenital prothrombotic disorders, and who may be at increased risk for thromboembolic disease in the presence of an acquired risk factor. I have attempted to address many of these issues and to make this book a practical one which clinicians can use to determine a reasonable course of action for the investigation and treatment of thromboembolic disease in pediatric patients.

Apart from the many investigators who have indirectly contributed to the content of this book, there are several people who have directly contributed. I would like to thank Ms. L. Mitchell for her editing of the tables, Dr. G.deVeber who assisted with the chapter on stroke, Ms. P. Vegh and Ms. M. Johnson for their assistance with the chapter on laboratory methods, and Drs. J. Weitz, J. Ginsberg, C. Kearon, F. Ofuso, M. Crawthers, and A. Cochrane for reviewing several chapters for content, particularly in regard to the adult literature. I would also like to thank the rest of my clinical and laboratory research team upon whom I depend upon greatly. Finally, I wish to thank my publisher, B.C. Decker for patience and assistance in bringing this book to fruition. I hope that this book proves useful to physicians caring for children with thromboembolic diseases.

MA
November, 1999

CONTENTS

1 INTRODUCTION

The primary objective of health care during childhood differs from adults in that the impact of successful interventions improves not only the health of our children but of future adults with several decades of life ahead of them. Ideally, the success or failure of therapy should not be measured in 1 or 2 year survival rates, but in the ability of children to grow into normal adults, unimpaired by their primary disease or complications of their therapy. This philosophy has seen the emergence of a new field in pediatric medicine over the last decade, pediatric thrombophilia. The increased aggressiveness of therapy for primary illnesses, aided by massive improvements in available supportive care, has led to the survival of many children who previously would have died. The complications of therapy, often related to life-saving supportive care, such as central venous line (CVL) related thromboembolic events (TEs), are now recognized as significant causes of secondary mortality and morbidity. As pediatricians we need to find management strategies to avoid such complications and ensure that the increased survival of sick children equates with an increased production of normal healthy adults.

Thromboembolic events are recognized as a major health problem in adults.[1] Sustained research efforts have led to clearly defined treatment guidelines for many clinical situations in adults with TEs.[1] However, the avalanche of medical research in this field, like many other fields, has created difficulties. Many studies have conflicting or unequivocal results making clinical decisions uncertain. Without clear methods to assess the relative strengths and weaknesses of individual or collective studies, clinicians are forced into anecdotal or empirical decision making. Clinical practice based on the best available literature and recommendations derived from such literature form the foundation of an approach to health care often referred to as evidence-based medicine.[1] The concept is old, but the recent advances in applied health research have provided reproducible and reliable assessment tools that enable clinicians to assess the evidence in the published literature with more clarity and certainty.

The identification of factors that lead to bias and imprecision in clinical research has facilitated a more rigorous assessment of medical research and has set standards in clinical research design and implementation that are significantly improving the quality of health care research and health care. This is crucial because even the use of rigorous assessment tools of clinical studies will not improve the strength of the clinical recommendations if the quality of the clinical trials being assessed are poor.

Adult TEs have been at the forefront of this evidence-based medicine approach, using advanced strategies to assess methodological rigour of studies, culminating in clinical recommendations. The first American College of Chest Physicians (ACCP) conference was convened in 1986.[2] Initially, five levels of evidence were proposed and three grades of recommendations. This system was modified over the years and, in 1998, the grading system was modified further to emphasize the concepts of clinically important differences and to include the risk ratio of a particular treatment into the grading system. The current approach to grades of recommendation is shown in Table 1–1.[1] The strength of recommendations depends on two factors: the methodological rigour that results in the estimate of treatment effect and the trade-off between benefits and risks. Methodological rigour is classified into three cate-

Table 1–1   Current Approach to Grades of Recommendations

For specified level of expected event rate in untreated patients:

Recommendation

    A: Methods strong, results consistent—randomized controlled trials, no heterogeneity
    1:   Effect clear—clear that benefits do (or do not) outweigh risks

    A: Methods strong, results consistent—randomized controlled trials, no heterogeneity
    2:   Effect equivocal—uncertainty whether benefits outweigh risks

    B: Methods strong, results inconsistent—randomized controlled trials, heterogeneity present
    1:   Effect clear—clear that benefits do (or do not) outweigh risks

    B: Methods strong, results inconsistent—randomized controlled trials, heterogeneity present
    2:   Effect equivocal—uncertainty whether benefits outweigh risks

    C: Methods weak—observational studies
    1:   Effect clear—clear that benefits do (or do not) outweigh risks

    C: Methods weak—observational studies
    2:   Effect equivocal—uncertainty whether benefits outweigh risks

Reproduced with permission of Guyatt GH, Cook DJ, Sackett DL, et al. Grades of recommendations for antithrombotic agents. Chest 1998; 114:441S–4S.

gories: (a) metanalysis or large randomized controlled trials (RCTs) with consistent results, (b) randomized trials with inconsistent results, and (c) observational studies. The trade-off between benefits and risks is either (1) clear, such that most patients, regardless of individual differences, would make the same choice; or (2) less clear, such that individual patients may vary in their choice depending on certain factors. Factors that influence the grade of recommendation are listed in Table 1–2.[3]

In 1986, only 24 percent of the 72 recommendations published in the first ACCP conference were based on grade A evidence.[2] In 1998, 44 percent of the 91 recommendations were grade A. In stark contrast, in 1998, there remained not a single grade A recommendation in the ACCP guidelines for antithrombotic therapy in children.[1,4] Over 90 percent of recommendations were grade C, reflecting the paucity of randomized trials in pediatric TEs, the overabundance of observational studies, and the need to extrapolate many pediatric recommendations from adult data.

There are a variety of reasons for this lack of methodologically sound research in pediatric TEs. First, the relatively recent recognition of this disease entity has not provided sufficient time to organize multi-center trials. Second, the reduced incidence of TEs compared to that seen in adults makes single institutional studies difficult. Third, the reduced incidence also impacts on the availability of funds to support clinical research in children, especially from industry sources that are looking for larger markets to expand into. Fourth, there is a common misconception that children are physiologically and pathologically "little adults." This leads to extrapolation and implementation of adult guidelines without consideration of the vast differences in the hemostatic system between children and adults. Fifth, the diverse and complex nature of the underlying illness in many children affected by TEs increases the difficulty of performing studies. Finally, the special ethical considerations that one must consider when planning research in children have unfortunately led some investigators to erroneously conclude that clinical research is unethical in children.

Although each of the above reasons may have been valid in excusing the previous lack of methodologically sound clinical research in pediatric TEs, this is clearly no longer the case. Pediatric TEs are now recognized as a major cause of secondary mortality and morbidity in pediatric tertiary care hospitals. In spite of the reduced incidence compared to adult TEs, the impact on the lives of children with decades to live is immense. Well-organized networks with the capabilities of performing multi-center trials are now in existence. Recent Federal

Table 1–2 Factors That May Change/Weaken a Recommendation to Treat, Changing from Grade 1 to Grade 2

Issue	Example
Less serious outcome	Preventing postphlebitic syndrome rather than death after myocardial infarction.
Smaller treatment effect	Stroke reduction: ticlopidine versus aspirin in transient ischemic attack (20% relative risk reduction) contrasts with anticoagulation in atrial fibrillation (68% relative risk reduction).
Imprecise estimate of treatment effect	Aspirin in atrial fibrillation (wide confidence interval) versus aspirin for stroke prevention in patients with transient ischemic attacks (narrower confidence interval).
Lower risk of target event	Warfarin in low risk versus high risk patients with atrial fibrillation.
Higher risk of therapy	Difference in risk of serious hemorrhage in warfarin versus aspirin.
Higher costs*	Tissue plasminogen activator versus streptokinase after myocardial infarction.
Varying values	Most young, healthy people will put a high value on prolonging their lives (and thus, incur suffering to do so); the elderly and infirm are likely to vary in the value they place on prolonging their lives (and may vary in the suffering they are ready to experience to do so).

*Costs could potentially affect the grade of recommendation. The greater the costs, the weaker the recommendation to treat. Clinicians may be hesitant to include costs as a factor in the strength of their recommendations. In the fifth ACCP Consensus Conference, costs were not included as a factor but instances were noted in which the cost of an intervention recommended was very high relative to the alternatives.

Reproduced with permission of Guyatt GH, Cook DJ, Sackett DL, et al. Grades of recommendations for antithrombotic agents. Chest 1998; 114:441S–4S.

Drug Administration (FDA) requirements mandate that new therapies and technology acquire specific pediatric data prior to licencing in the United States, encouraging industry to actively support appropriate research in this field. The increased understanding of the physiologic and pathologic differences between the hemostatic system in children and adults has improved the knowledge on which adult therapies can be manipulated to better suit children, and confirmed the need for specific pediatric studies. Similarly, the recognition of the diverse and complex nature of major primary childhood illnesses emphasizes the need for specific well-designed studies, the results of which will be applicable to the patient population in question. Finally, the realization that to continue to treat children without any attempt to improve the level of evidence for that treatment is in fact unethical. Within the confines of good clinical practice and appropriate ethical considerations, we must take the opportunity to conduct methodologically sound research that will improve the health care of the current and future generations of children.

The data presented in this book are the result of an evidence-based approach to the currently available literature. Treatment recommendations and guidelines are based on the best available evidence considering the design and strength of the studies reported. Current, ongoing, well-designed clinical trials are mentioned to alert the reader to the fact that recommendations may change in the near future as better quality information becomes available. Areas where studies are urgently needed are also highlighted. We hope that future editions of this or other books can describe grade A recommendations for the prevention and treatment of TEs in children, reflecting improved standards in applied clinical research in pediatric medicine and ultimately improved health care for our children.

REFERENCES

1. Dalen JE, Hirsch J. Fifth ACCP Consensus Conference on Antithrombotic Therapy. Chest 1998; 114:439S–769S.
2. American College of Chest Physicians and The National Heart and Blood Institute. ACCP-NHLBI National Conference on Antithrombotic Therapy. Chest 1986; 89:1S–106S.
3. Guyatt GH, Cook DJ, Sackett DL, et al. Grades of recommendations for antithrombotic agents. Chest 1998;114:441S–4S.
4. Michelson AD, Bovill E, Monagle P, Andrew M. Antithrombotic therapy in children. Chest 1998;114: 748S–69S.

2 DEVELOPMENTAL HEMOSTASIS: RELEVANCE TO THROMBOEMBOLIC COMPLICATIONS IN PEDIATRIC PATIENTS

The discovery of individual components of hemostasis over the past century has been accompanied by the realization that the hemostatic system in infants and children is profoundly different from adults. Throughout childhood, the hemostatic system is a dynamic, evolving system that has many unique features. Although hemostasis in the young can be considered immature, the hemostatic system must also be considered physiologic because it provides protection from hemorrhagic and thromboembolic events (TEs) in healthy children. Indeed, the hemostatic system throughout childhood has some significant advantages over the adult system. For example, TEs occur so commonly in adults with a variety of medical conditions or following surgical procedures that prophylactic anticoagulant therapy is warranted.[1,2] Anticoagulants are not warranted in children with similar disorders because of the low incidence of TEs. However, the immaturity of the hemostatic system in the very young does leave them vulnerable to some disorders, such as hemorrhagic disease of the newborn secondary to vitamin K (VK) deficiency.[3–10] These examples illustrate the need to fully understand the ontogeny of hemostasis and the effects of aging on hemostasis. An understanding of developmental hemostasis in the broadest sense will optimize the prevention, diagnosis, and treatment of hemostatic problems during childhood and will undoubtedly provide new insights into the pathophysiology of hemorrhagic and thrombotic complications for all ages. In this chapter, the coagulation system, fibrinolytic system, and platelet function are reviewed in general and in the context of developmental hemostasis.

THE COAGULATION SYSTEM

Coagulation Proteins

Under physiologic conditions, blood is maintained in a fluid phase. In response to damage to the vessel wall, platelets, plasma coagulation proteins, and the vessel orchestrate the formation of a hemostatic plug. A schematic outline of blood coagulation is shown in Figure 2–1. The central purpose of coagulant proteins is to generate thrombin from prothrombin. Although blood coagulation can theoretically be initiated by the contact system or by exposure of blood to tissue factor (TF), the latter is the physiologically important activation pathway.[11,12]

Factor VII/Tissue Factor Pathway Factor (F) VIIa binding to TF initiates coagulation as FVIIa-TF ac-

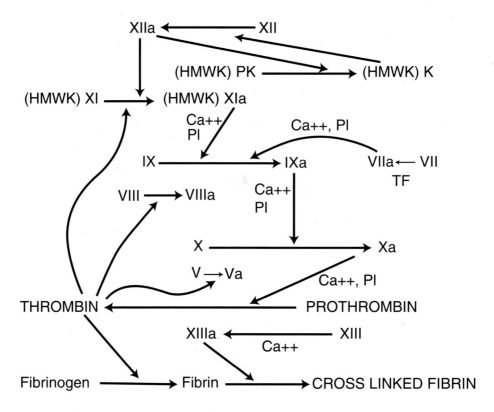

Figure 2–1 Schema of the coagulation system.

XIIa = activated factor XII; HMWK = high molecular weight kininogen; PK = prekallikrein; Ca⁺⁺calcium; P1 = plasminogen; XIa = activated factor XI; IXa = activated factor IX; VIIa = activated factor VII; TF = tissue factor; VIIIa = activated factor VIII; Xa = activated factor X; Va = activated factor V; XIIIa = activated factor XIII.

Reproduced with permission.[352]

tivates both FX[13–15] and FIX.[15] Factor VII (50 kDa, 100 µg/mL) is a VK dependent protein with 10 γ-carboxy glutamic acid residues at the amino terminal region.[16] The latter are critical for the calcium (Ca⁺⁺) mediated binding of VK dependent proteins to coagulant surfaces where thrombin production occurs. Whether the zymogen form of FVII displays some intrinsic enzymatic activity in its native form is still unclear.[17] A likely explanation for the activity observed in FVII comes from the detection of low concentrations of FVIIa within the population of FVII molecules.[18] Factor VII is cleaved to a two chain serine protease by several coagulation enzymes including FXa,[19] FXIIa[20] (cleavage by FXIIa may be of questionable significance), FIXa,[21] and thrombin.[22] Alternatively, FVII bound to TF is converted to FVIIa by low concentrations of FXa, FIXa, or FVIIa.[23] Tissue factor (46 kDa) is an ex-

tracellular lipoprotein anchored to the membranes of cells in which TF is synthesized and can be complexed with a mixture of phospholipids.[24] Tissue factor is produced by several cell types, is present in almost all tissues,[25] and is expressed as a transmembrane protein with a short intracytoplasmic domain.[26,27] Endothelial cells in culture have minimal TF activity, but can be induced to synthesize and express TF on their surfaces.[28–30] Whether TF is pathologically expressed in vivo by endothelium in humans is unknown at this time.[31,32] Under increased shear stress, increased TF expression in endothelium has been observed in vivo.[33] Tissue factor is considered the cell surface receptor for FVIIa where it cleaves its natural substrate.[13–15,34] Patients with no measurable FVII activity have severe bleeding problems, in keeping with the importance of FVIIa/TF activation of coagulation.[35]

Role of Factor XI Factor XIa converts FIX to FIXa[36] and, by acceleration of thrombin generation, has been shown to be a critical component in thrombin-activable fibrinolysis inhibitor (TAFI)-dependent inhibition of fibrinolysis.[37] Activation of FXI occurs either by the action of FXIIa,[38] feedback reaction from the low concentrations of thrombin formed during early stages of coagulation,[39] cleavage by meizothrombin,[40] or autoactivation by FXIa.[38] In vivo, however, it has been suggested that perturbants such as endotoxin only lead to activation of FXI by thrombin (appearance of active thrombin parallels the formation of FXIa, without any markers of prekallikrein or FXII activation being observed).[41] Conversion of FXI to FXIa by thrombin occurs in the presence of polyanions (dextran sulfate) or on activated platelet surfaces.[39] Thrombin activation of FXI on the platelet plasma membrane proceeds optimally by using prothrombin as a cofactor.[42] Alternatively, although activation of FXI by meizothrombin proceeds at a rate similar to that of thrombin and is enhanced by phosphatidylcholine-phosphatidylserine-phosphatidylethanolamine vesicles, reaction of FXI with meizothrombin is unaffected by either dextran sulfate or heparin.[40] Autoactivation of FXI by FXIa is assisted by binding of heparin to lysyl groups (particularly Lys253 on the zymogen).[38] Once formed, FXIa is inhibited irreversibly by antithrombin UFH[38] or reversibly by protease nexin-2.[43] Both inhibition reactions are catalyzed by standard heparin (as well as low molecular weight heparin in the case of antithrombin).[44]

TENase Complexes Factor VIIa proteolytic activation of FX in the presence of TF, Ca^{++}, and a phospholipid surface forms the extrinsic TENase complex. In vivo, phospholipid surfaces are provided by cells, particularly platelets and stimulated endothelial cells. Factor IXa, in the presence of FVIIIa, Ca^{++}, and a phospholipid surface, forms the intrinsic TENase complex. In the intrinsic TENase complex, FVIIIa functions as the cofactor when FIXa activates FX. Factor VIII (265 kDa, 0.1 µg/mL) is converted to FVIIIa by limited cleavage by thrombin and to a lesser extent by FXa.[45,46] The importance of FVIII is evidenced by the severe bleeding disorder

in FVIII deficient patients (Hemophilia A). Factor XIa (150 kDa, 2-7 µg/mL) and FVIIa catalyze the conversion of FIX (55 kDa, 4 µg/mL), a VK dependent protein, to FIXa. The NH$_2$-terminal Gla-domain of FIX has 12 γ-carboxyglutamic acid residues.[47] Inherited deficiencies of FIX constitute Hemophilia B, a serious bleeding disorder.

Prothrombinase Complex The final reaction of the coagulation pathway is catalyzed by the prothrombinase complex that consists of FVa (cofactor), FXa (enzyme), Ca^{++}, and a phospholipid surface. The prothrombinase complex converts prothrombin to thrombin by two peptide bond cleavages in the zymogen giving rise to prothrombin fragment 1.2 (F1.2) and α-thrombin. Both FX (55 kDa, 4-10 µg/mL) and prothrombin (73 kDa, 100 µg/mL) are VK-dependent serine proteases that also bind to negatively charged phospholipids through their γ-carboxyglutamic acid residues.[48,49] The activated form of FV (330 kDa, 4-14 µg/mL), FVa, is the cofactor necessary for prothrombin activation by FXa to proceed at a physiologically relevant rate.[50] FVa functions as a receptor in platelet membranes binding both prothrombin and FX in close proximity.[51–53] Thus, FX and prothrombin bind to surfaces by two separate but complementary mechanisms, that is, FVa and a Ca^{++} dependent process.[54,55]

Thrombin Human α-thrombin consists of an A chain linked by a disulfide bond to a B chain.[56] Three principal functional domains of α-thrombin have been described and consist of the catalytic centre where substrates are cleaved, a substrate recognition exosite necessary for initial interaction with substrates,[57–59] and an anion-binding exosite(s) where polyanions (eg, UFH) bind. Thrombin is a serine protease with many procoagulant functions,[60] including cleaving fibrinopeptides A (FPA) and B (FPB) from fibrinogen resulting in fibrin formation; activating FXI, FVIII,[61] and FV[62,63] to enhance further thrombin generation; activating FXIII, which promotes covalent crosslinking of fibrin,[64] facilitates cell-cell or cell-clot interactions of activated platelets,[65] and activating platelets.[66] In addition, thrombin has multiple anticoagulant and antifibrinolytic functions. As will be described in more detail subsequently, when thrombin binds endothelial cell bound thrombomodulin (TM), the protein C / protein S inhibitory system is activated.[67] Thrombin-TM complexes also activate a recently described plasma procarboxypeptidase, thrombin activable fibrinolysis inhibitor (TAFI).[68–72]

Fibrinogen (340 kDa,1560-4000 µg/mL) consists of two symmetrical half-molecules, each of which has three polypeptide chains termed Aα, Bβ, and γ.[73,74] The two halves are joined by three disulfide bridges between $\gamma(2)$ and A$\alpha(1)$ chains in the central amino-terminal domain (E domain).[75] Cleavage of FPA (Aα1-16) and FPB (Bβ1-14) in the E domain by thrombin initiates fibrin assembly.[76] Fibrin monomers can be considered as tridominal structures with a central E domain and two outer D domains that assemble in an antiparallel, staggered, overlapping manner with noncovalent interactions between E and D domains to form two-stranded fibrils.[77–79] At the same time, the fibrils undergo noncovalent lateral associations to form thicker fibers.[80,81] Activated FXIII (320 kDa, A chain:15 µg/mL, B chain: 21 µg/mL [plasma (FXIII) = 10 µg/mL]) covalently links assembled fibrin by formation of e-(γ-glu) lys isopeptide bonds, initially between γ chains and more slowly between α chains. Cross linking provides structural stability and integrity to an otherwise easily deformable fibrin clot. Several plasma proteins (including α_2-antiplasmin (α_2AP)) also become crosslinked to α chains by FXIIIa.[82] A secondary binding site for thrombin is also present on the E domain and is dependent on the Bβ15-42 sequence.[83,84] This secondary site serves to protect thrombin from its nat-

Table 2–1 Coagulation Screening Tests and Coagulation Factor Levels in Fetuses, Full-Term Infants, and Adults

Parameter	Fetuses (Weeks Gestation)			Newborn (Number = 60)	Adult (Number = 40)
	19-23 (Number = 20)	24-29 (Number = 22)	30-38 (Number = 22)		
PT (sec)	32.5 (19-45)	32.2 (19-44)[†]	22.6 (16-30)	16.7 (12.0-23.5)*	13.5 (11.4-14.0)
PT (INR)	6.4 (1.7-11.1)	6.2 (2.1-10.6)[†]	3.0 (1.5-5.0)*	1.7 (0.9-2.7)*	1.1 (0.8-1.2)
APTT (sec)	168.8 (83-250)	154.0 (87-210)[†]	104.8 (76-128)[†]	44.3 (*35-52)*	33.0 (25-39)
TCT (sec)	34.2 (24-44)*	26.2 (24-28)	21.4 (17.0-23.3)	20.4 (15.2-25.0)[†]	14.0 (12-16)
Fibrinogen(g/L)	0.85 (0.57-1.50)	1.12 (0.65-1.65)	1.35 (1.25-1.65)	1.68 (0.95-2.45)[†]	3.0 (1.78-4.50)
I Ag (g/L)	1.08 (0.75-1.50)	1.93 (1.56-2.40)	1.94 (1.30-2.40)	2.65 (1.68-3.60)[†]	3.5 (2.50-5.20)
IIc (%)	16.9 (10-24)	19.9 (11-30)*	27.9 (15-50)[†]	43.5 (27-64)[†]	98.7 (70-125)
VIIc (%)	27.4 (17-37)	33.8 (18-48)*	45.9 (31-62)	52.5 (28-78)[†]	101.3 (68-130)
IXc (%)	10.1 (6-14)	9.9 (5-15)	12.3 (5-24)[†]	31.8 (15-50)[†]	104.8 (70-142)
Xc (%)	20.5 (14-29)	24.9 (16-35)	28.0 (16-36)[†]	39.6 (21-65)[†]	99.2 (75-125)
Vc (%)	32.1 (21-44)	36.8 (25-50)	48.9 (23-70)[†]	89.9 (50-140)	99.8 (65-140)
VIIIc (%)	34.5 (18-50)	35.5 (20-52)	50.1 (27-78)[†]	94.3 (38-150)	101.8 (55-170)
XIc (%)	13.2 (8-19)	12.1 (6-22)	14.8 (6-26)[†]	37.2 (13-62)[†]	100.2 (70-135)
XIIc (%)	14.9 (6-25)	22.7 (6-40)	25.8 (11-50)[†]	69.8 (25-105)[†]	101.4 (65-144)
PK (%)	12.8 (8-19)	15.4 (8-26)	18.1 (8-28)[†]	35.4 (21-53)[†]	99.8 (65-135)
HMWK (%)	15.4 (10-22)	19.3 (10-26)	23.6 (12-34)[†]	38.9 (28-53)[†]	98.8 (68-135)

Values are the mean, followed in parentheses by the lower and upper boundaries including 95% of the population.

*$p < .05$, [†]$p < .01$

PT = prothrombin time; INR = International Normalized Ratio; sec = seconds; g/L = grams/litre; Ag = antigen; PK = prekallikrein; HMWK = high molecular weight kininogen; n = number.

Reproduced with permission.[100]

ural inhibitors (see subsequent section) and permits the ongoing conversion of other fibrinogen molecules to fibrin.[83,85] During fibrinolysis, the peptides connecting the D and E domains are cleaved with the generation of E and/or D-containing fragments. The D products in these fragments contain cross-linked γ chains (ie, D-dimer, etc).

Coagulation Screening Tests Coagulation screening tests commonly used to provide an overall measurement of the capacity for thrombin generation are the prothrombin time (PT), which provides a measure of the FVIIa/TF pathway, and the activated partial thromboplastin time (APTT), which provides a measure of the contact factor pathway. PT test results are highly dependent on the reagent used (chapter 13) and are now standardized by conversion to the International Normalized Ratio (INR). The INR is the ratio of the patient's PT in seconds divided by the control population PT in seconds, raised to the power of the International Sensitivity Index (ISI).[86] The ISI is a means of correcting for differences in reagent sensitivities to decreased plasma concentrations of the VK dependent

factors.[86] The thrombin clotting time (TCT) is another commonly used coagulation test that measures the rate of fibrin formation in response to exogenously added thrombin. Further aspects of these and other laboratory tests are discussed in chapter 13.

Coagulation Proteins: Infancy and Childhood

Components of hemostasis are synthesized by the fetus and do not cross the placenta from the mother into the fetus. Plasma concentrations of coagulation proteins parallel gestational age (GA) with an initial appearance at approximately 10 weeks GA.[87-100] Samples obtained during fetoscopy provide the best assessment of normal values for fetuses and, potentially, very premature infants[100] (Tables 2-1 and 2-2). In-depth studies of hemostasis following birth, and during infancy and childhood, have only recently been completed. These studies were difficult to conduct because of the practical problems of obtaining blood samples from healthy infants and children, the requirement

Table 2–2 Blood Coagulation Inhibitor Levels in Fetuses, Full-Term Infants, and Adults

Parameter	*Fetuses (Weeks Gestation)*			*Newborns (Number = 60)*	*Adults (Number = 40)*
	19-23 (Number = 20)	*24-29 (Number = 22)*	*30-38 (Number = 22)*		
AT (%)	20.2 (12-31)*	30.0 (20-39)	37.1 (24-55)[†]	59.4 (42-80)[†]	99.8 (65-130)
HCII (%)	10.3 (6-16)	12.9 (5.5-20)	21.1 (11-33)[†]	52.1 (19-99)[†]	101.4 (70-128)
TFPI (%)[‡]	21.0 (16.0-29.2)	20.6 (13.4-33.2)	20.7 (10.4-31.5)[†]	38.1 (22.7-55.8)[†]	73.0 (50.9-90.1)
PC Ag (%)	9.5 (6-14)	12.1 (8-16)	15.9 (8-30)[†]	32.5 (21-47)[†]	100.8 (68-125)
PC Act (%)	9.6 (7-13)	10.4 (8-13)	14.1 (8-18)*	28.2 (14-42)[†]	98.8 (68-125)
Total PS (%)	15.1 (11-21)	17.4 (14-25)	21.0(15-30)[†]	38.5 (22-55)[†]	99.6 (72-118)
Free PS (%)	21.7 (13-32)	27.9 (19-40)	27.0 (18-40)[†]	49.3 (33-67)[†]	98.7 (72-128)
Ratio of Free PS: Total PS	0.82 (0.75-0.92)	0.83 (0.76-0.95)	0.79 (0.70-0.89)[†]	0.64 (0.59-0.98)[†]	0.41 (0.38-0.43)
C4B-BP (%)	1.8 (0-6)	6.1 (0-12.5)	9.3 (5-14)	18.6 (3-40)[†]	100.3 (70-124)

Values are the mean, followed in parentheses by the lower and upper boundaries including 95% of the population.

AT = antithrombin; HCII = heparin cofactor II; TFPI tissue factor pathway inhibitor; PC = protein C; PS = protein S; Ag = antigen; Act = activity.

*p < .05, [†]p < .01

[‡]Twenty samples were assayed for each group but only 10 for 19-23 week old fetuses.

Reproduced with permission.[100]

Table 2–3 Reference Values for Coagulation Tests in Healthy Full-Term Infants during the First Six Months of Life

	Day 1		Day 5		Day 30		Day 90		Day 180		Adult	
	M	B	M	B	M	B	M	B	M	B	M	B
PT (s)	13.0	(10.1-15.9)*	12.4	(10.0-15.3)*	11.8	(10.0-14.3)*	11.9	(10.0-14.2)*	12.3	(10.7-13.9)*	12.4	(10.8-13.9)
INR	1.00	(0.53-1.62)	0.89	(0.53-1.48)	0.79	(0.53-1.26)	0.81	(0.53-1.26)	0.88	(0.61-1.17)	0.89	(0.64-1.17)
APTT (s)	42.9	(31.3-54.5)	42.6	(25.4-59.8)	40.4	(32.0-55.2)	37.1	(29.0-50.1)	35.5	(28.1-42.9)*	33.5	(26.6-40.3)
TCT (s)	23.5	(19.0-28.3)*	23.1	(18.0-29.2)	24.3	(19.4-29.2)*	25.1	(20.5-29.7)*	25.5	(19.8-31.2)*	25.0	(19.7-30.3)
Fibrinogen (g/L)	2.83	(1.67-3.99)*	3.12	(1.62-4.62)*	2.70	(1.62-3.78)	2.43	(1.50-3.79)*	2.51	(1.50-3.87)*	2.78	(1.56-4.00)
FII (U/mL)	0.48	(0.26-0.70)	0.63	(0.33-0.93)	0.68	(0.34-1.02)	0.75	(0.45-1.05)	0.88	(0.60-1.16)	1.08	(0.70-1.46)
FV (U/mL)	0.72	(0.34-1.08)	0.95	(0.45-1.45)	0.98	(0.62-1.34)	0.90	(0.48-1.32)	0.91	(0.55-1.27)	1.06	(0.62-1.50)
FVII (U/mL)	0.66	(0.28-1.04)	0.89	(0.35-1.43)	0.90	(0.42-1.38)	0.91	(0.39-1.43)	0.87	(0.47-1.27)	1.05	(0.67-1.43)
FVIII (U/mL)	1.00	(0.50-1.78)*	0.88	(0.50-1.54)*	0.91	(0.50-1.57)*	0.79	(0.50-1.25)*	0.73	(0.50-1.09)	0.99	(0.50-1.49)
vWF (U/mL)	1.53	(0.50-2.87)	1.40	(0.50-2.54)	1.28	(0.50-2.46)	1.18	(0.50-2.06)	1.07	(0.50-1.97)	0.92	(0.50-1.58)
FIX (U/mL)	0.53	(0.15-0.91)	0.53	(0.15-0.91)	0.51	(0.21-0.81)	0.67	(0.21-1.13)	0.86	(0.36-1.36)	1.09	(0.55-1.63)
FX (U/mL)	0.40	(0.12-0.68)	0.49	(0.19-0.79)	0.59	(0.31-0.87)	0.71	(0.35-1.07)	0.78	(0.38-1.18)	1.06	(0.70-1.52)
FXI (U/mL)	0.38	(0.10-0.66)	0.55	(0.23-0.87)	0.53	(0.27-0.79)	0.69	(0.41-0.97)	0.86	(0.49-1.34)	0.97	(0.67-1.27)
FXII (U/mL)	0.53	(0.13-0.93)	0.47	(0.11-0.83)	0.49	(0.17-0.81)	0.67	(0.25-1.09)	0.77	(0.39-1.15)	1.08	(0.52-1.64)
PK (U/mL)	0.37	(0.18-0.69)	0.48	(0.20-0.76)	0.57	(0.23-0.91)	0.73	(0.41-1.05)	0.86	(0.56-1.16)	1.12	(0.62-1.62)
HMWK (U/mL)	0.54	(0.06-1.02)	0.74	(0.16-1.32)	0.77	(0.33-1.21)	0.82	(0.30-1.46)*	0.82	(0.36-1.28)*	0.92	(0.50-1.36)
FXIII$_a$ (U/mL)	0.79	(0.27-1.31)	0.94	(0.44-1.44)*	0.93	(0.39-1.47)*	1.04	(0.36-1.72)*	1.04	(0.46-1.62)*	1.05	(0.55-1.55)
FXIII$_b$ (U/mL)	0.76	(0.30-1.22)	1.06	(0.32-1.80)	1.11	(0.39-1.73)*	1.16	(0.48-1.84)*	1.10	(0.50-1.70)	0.97	(0.57-1.37)

All factors except fibrinogen are expressed as units per millilitre (U/mL) where pooled plasma contains 1.0 U/mL. All values are expressed as mean (M) followed by the lower and upper boundary encompassing 95% of the population (B). Between 40 to 77 samples were assayed for each value for the newborn. Some measurements were skewed due to a disproportionate number of high values. The lower limit, which excludes the lower 2.5% of the population, has been given.

PT = prothrombin time; s = seconds; g/L = grams/litre; INR = International Normalized Ratio; APTT = activated partial thromboplastin time; TCT = thrombin clotting time; F = factor; vWF = von Willebrand factor; PK = prekallikrein; HMWK = high molecular weight kininogen.

* Values that are indistinguishable from those of the adult.

Table 2–4 Reference Values for Coagulation Tests in Healthy Premature Infants (30-36 Weeks Gestation) during the First Six Months of Life

Coagulation Tests	Day 1 M	Day 1 B	Day 5 M	Day 5 B	Day 30 M	Day 30 B	Day 90 M	Day 90 B	Day 180 M	Day 180 B	Adult M	Adult B
PT (sec)	13.0	(10.6-16.2)*	12.5	(10.0-15.3)*	11.8	(10.0-13.6)*	12.3	(10.0-14.6)	12.5	(10.0-15.0)*	12.4	(10.8-13.9)
INR	1.0	(0.61-1.70)	0.91	(0.53-1.48)	0.79	(0.53-1.11)	0.88	(0.53-1.32)	0.91	(0.53-1.48)	0.89	(0.64-1.17)
APTT (sec)	53.6	(27.5-79.4)†	50.5	(26.9-74.1)	44.7	(26.9-62.5)	39.5	(28.3-50.7)	37.5	(27.2-53.3)	33.5	(26.6-40.3)
TCT (sec)	24.8	(19.2-30.4)	24.1	(18.8-29.4)*	24.4	(18.8-29.9)	25.1	(19.4-30.8)	25.2	(18.9-31.5)	25.0	(19.7-30.3)
Fibrinogen (g/L)	2.43	(1.50-3.73)*†	2.80	(1.60-4.18)*†	2.54	(1.50-4.14)	2.46	(1.50-3.52)	2.28	(1.50-3.60)	2.78	(1.56-4.00)
II (U/mL)	0.45	(0.20-0.77)	0.57	(0.29-0.85)†	0.57	(0.36-0.95)	0.68	(0.30-1.06)	0.87	(0.51-1.23)	1.08	(0.70-1.46)
V (U/mL)	0.88	(0.41-1.44)*†	1.00	(0.46-1.54)*	1.02	(0.48-1.56)*	0.99	(0.59-1.39)	1.02	(0.58-1.46)*	1.06	(0.62-1.50)
VII (U/mL)	0.67	(0.21-1.13)	0.84	(0.30-1.38)	0.83	(0.21-1.45)	0.87	(0.31-1.43)	0.99	(0.47-1.51)*	1.05	(0.67-1.43)
VIII (U/mL)	1.11	(0.50-2.13)	1.15	(0.53-2.05)*†	1.11	(0.50-1.99)	1.06	(0.58-1.88)*†	0.99	(0.50-1.87)*†	0.99	(0.50-1.49)
vWF (U/mL)	1.36	(0.78-2.10)	1.33	(0.72-2.19)	1.36	(0.66-2.16)	1.12	(0.75-1.84)*†	0.98	(0.54-1.58)*	0.92	(0.50-1.58)
IX (U/mL)	0.35	(0.19-0.65)†	0.42	(0.14-0.74)†	0.44	(0.13-0.80)	0.59	(0.25-0.93)	0.81	(0.50-1.20)	1.09	(0.55-1.63)
X (U/mL)	0.41	(0.11-0.71)	0.51	(0.19-0.83)	0.56	(0.20-0.92)	0.67	(0.35-0.99)	0.77	(0.35-1.19)	1.06	(0.70-1.52)
XI (U/mL)	0.30	(0.08-0.52)†	0.41	(0.13-0.69)†	0.43	(0.15-0.71)*	0.59	(0.25-0.93)*	0.78	(0.46-1.10)	0.97	(0.67-1.27)
XII (U/mL)	0.38	(0.10-0.66)†	0.39	(0.09-0.69)†	0.43	(0.11-0.75)	0.61	(0.15-1.07)	0.82	(0.22-1.42)	1.08	(0.52-1.64)
PK (U/mL)	0.33	(0.09-0.57)	0.45	(0.25-0.75)	0.59	(0.31-0.87)	0.79	(0.37-1.21)	0.78	(0.40-1.16)	1.12	(0.62-1.62)
HMWK (U/mL)	0.49	(0.09-0.89)	0.62	(0.24-1.00)†	0.64	(0.16-1.12)†	0.78	(0.32-1.24)	0.83	(0.41-1.25)*	0.92	(0.50-1.36)
XIIIa (U/mL)	0.70	(0.32-1.08)	1.01	(0.57-1.45)*	0.99	(0.51-1.47)*	1.13	(0.71-1.55)*	1.13	(0.65-1.61)*	1.05	(0.55-1.55)
XIIIb (U/mL)	0.81	(0.35-1.27)	1.10	(0.68-1.58)*	1.07	(0.57-1.57)*	1.21	(0.75-1.67)	1.15	(0.67-1.63)	0.97	(0.57-1.37)

All factors except fibrinogen are expressed as units per millilitre (U/mL) where pooled plasma contains 1.0 U/mL. All values are given as a mean (M) followed by the lower and upper boundary encompassing 95% of the population (B). Between 40 and 96 samples were assayed for each value for the newborn. Some measurements were skewed due to a disproportionate number of high values. The lower limit, which excludes the lower 2.5% of the population, has been given (B).

PT = prothrombin time; APTT = activated partial thromboplastin time; TCT = thrombin clotting time; VIII = Factor VIII procoagulant; vWF = von Willebrand factor; PK = prekallikrein; HMWK = high molecular weight kininogen; INR = International Normalized Ratio.

Reproduced with permission.[103]

Table 2–5 Reference Values for Coagulation Tests in Healthy Children Ages 1 to 16 Years as Compared to Adults

	1 to 5 Yrs	6 to 10 Yrs	11 to 16 Yrs	Adult
	M B	M B	M B	M B
PT(s)	11 (10.6-11.4)	11.1 (10.1-12.1)	11.2 (10.2-12.0)	12 (11.0-14.0)
INR	1.0 (0.96-1.04)	1.01 (0.91-1.11)	1.02 (0.93-1.10)	1.10 (1.0-1.3)
APTT(s)	30 (24-36)	31 (26-36)	32 (26-37)	33 (27-40)
Fibrinogen (g/L)	2.76 (1.70-4.05)	2.79 (1.57-4.0)	3.0 (1.54-4.48)	2.78 (1.56-4.0)
Bleeding Time (min)	6 (2.5-10)*	7 (2.5-13)*	5 (3-8)*	4 (1-7)
FII (U/mL)	0.94 (0.71-1.16)*	0.88 (0.67-1.07)	0.83 (0.61-1.04)*	1.08 (0.70-1.46)
FV (U/mL)	1.03 (0.79-1.27)	0.90 (0.63-1.16)*	0.77 (0.55-0.99)*	1.06 (0.62-1.50)
FVII (U/mL)	0.82 (0.55-1.16)*	0.85 (0.52-1.20)	0.83 (0.58-1.15)*	1.05 (0.67-1.43)
FVIII (U/mL)	0.90 (0.59-1.42)	0.95 (0.58-1.32)	0.92 (0.53-1.31)	0.99 (0.50-1.49)
vWF (U/mL)	0.82 (0.60-1.20)	0.95 (0.44-1.44)	1.00 (0.46-1.53)	0.92 (0.50-1.58)
FIX (U/mL)	0.73 (0.47-1.04)*	0.75 (0.63-0.89)*	0.82 (0.59-1.22)*	1.09 (0.55-1.63)
FX (U/mL)	0.88 (0.58-1.16)*	0.75 (0.55-1.01)*	0.79 (0.50-1.17)*	1.06 (0.70-1.52)
FXI (U/mL)	0.97 (0.56-1.50)	0.86 (0.52-1.20)	0.74 (0.50-0.97)	0.97 (0.67-1.27)
FXII (U/mL)	0.93 (0.64-1.29)	0.92 (0.60-1.40)	0.81 (0.34-1.37)*	1.08 (0.52-1.64)
PK (U/mL)	0.95 (0.65-1.30)	0.99 (0.66-1.31)	0.99 (0.53-1.45)	1.12 (0.62-1.62)
HMWK (U/mL)	0.98 (0.64-1.32)	0.93 (0.60-1.30)	0.91 (0.63-1.19)	0.92 (0.50-1.36)
FXIIIa (U/mL)	1.08 (0.72-1.43)*	1.09 (0.65-1.51)*	0.99 (0.57-1.40)	1.05 (0.55-1.55)
FXIIIs (U/mL)	1.13 (0.69-1.56)*	1.16 (0.77-1.54)*	1.02 (0.60-1.43)	0.97 (0.57-1.37)

All factors except fibrinogen are expressed as units/mL (U/mL), where pooled plasma contains 1.0 U/mL. All data are expressed as the mean (M) followed by the upper and lower boundary encompassing 95% of the population (B). Between 20 and 50 samples were assayed for each value for each age group. Some measurements were skewed due to a disproportionate number of high values. The lower limit, which excludes the lower 2.5% of the population, has been given.

s = seconds; g/L = grams/litre; min = minutes; PT = prothrombin time; INR = International Normalized Ratio; APTT = activated partial thromboplastin time; F = factor; vWF = von Willebrand Factor; PK = prekallikrein; HMWK = high molecular weight kininogen.

*Values that are significantly different from adults.

Reproduced with permission.[104]

for a large sample size due to the greater variability in plasma concentrations of coagulation proteins during infancy, and the need for microassays to measure coagulation proteins in small volumes. Although numerous studies have reported plasma concentrations of individual coagulation proteins in newborns, or more commonly in cord blood, only a few studies meet the minimum guidelines published by the neonatal subcommittee of the International Congress on Thrombosis and Hemostasis.[101] In brief, subjects must be described for GA, postnatal age (PA), health, and use of VK. The site from which the sample is drawn must be specified and details of sample handling provided. The methods used for analysis should be described and data analysis provided.

Reference Ranges Comprehensive reference ranges for coagulation proteins from over 400 healthy infants and children are described in Tables 2–3, 2–4, and 2–5. Figure 2–2 shows the influence of age on mean values of several coagulation proteins throughout childhood.[102–105] A large study of fetal samples obtained by fetoscopy from healthy fetuses undergoing diagnostic studies provides an accurate estimation of physiologic values of components of the coagulation system from 19 to 38 weeks GA (Tables 2–1 and 2–2).[100] Three large studies of full-term infants (36 to 40 weeks GA), healthy premature infants (30 to 36 weeks GA), and healthy children (1 to 16 years of age) provide reference ranges for components of the coagulation system throughout childhood (Tables 2–3, 2–4, and 2–5).[102–105] These three population-based studies differ from other reports in that Day 1 samples were obtained from infants not umbilical cords, the same cohort of healthy infants and children was studied longitudinally, each reference range reflects a minimum of 40 samples, and the boundaries reflect 95 percent of the population.[102–105] In many cases, data are grouped for simplicity of presentation because individual analysis did not reveal significant differences between groups of children. Additional composite summaries of results from several studies of cord plasmas and newborn plasmas on Day 1 of life are also available.[101,106,107] However, cord blood may not completely reflect values from infants during the first day of life.

Factor Levels Plasma concentrations of the four contact factors and the four VK-dependent factors are decreased at birth. Factor VII plasma concentrations increase rapidly in both premature and full-term infants, suggesting there must be physiologic events following birth that enhance the maturation of the coagulation system. Plasma concentrations of other coagulation proteins gradually increase toward adult values over the first 6 months of life (Figure 2–2). In contrast, plasma concentrations of the cofactors FV and FVIII at birth are similar or increased compared to adult values (Figure 2–2). Plasma concentrations of von Willebrand Factor (vWF), vWF high molecular–weight multimers, and vWF collagen-binding activity are increased during the first weeks of life.[108–110] The vWF multimeric pattern and collagen-binding activity approximate those observed in adults by 2 to 6 months of life.[109] The increased plasma concentrations of vWF may persist beyond 6 months of age.[104]

Prothrombinase Complex The overall effect of the unique age-dependent features of the coagulation system on the formation of the intrinsic and extrinsic TENase complexes has not been measured directly. However, the rate of thrombin generation by the prothrombinase complex has been measured with a sensitive chromogenic assay.[111–115] Thrombin generation is both delayed and decreased in newborn plasma compared to adult plasma.[111–113,115] Indeed, the degree of impairment is similar to plasma from adults receiving therapeutic amounts of oral anticoagulants (OAs) or UFH (Figure 2–3).[111,115] The amount of thrombin generated is directly proportional to plasma concentrations of prothrombin,[111] while the rate at which thrombin is generated is dependent upon plasma concentrations of all procoagulants (Figure 2–4). The slow rate of thrombin generation in newborns is reflected in prolonged PTs and APTTs.[101–103,105–107] Prolonged PT values in fetal blood also vary depending upon the

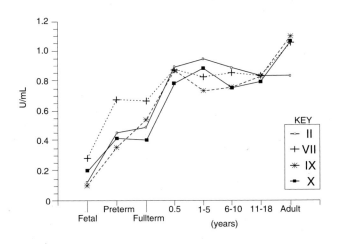

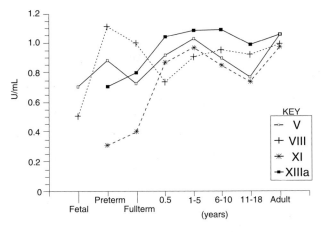

Figure 2–2 Plasma concentrations of selected coagulant proteins over age.

II = factor II; VII = factor; IX = factor IX; V = factor V; VIII = factor VIII; IX = factor XI; XIIIa = activated factor XIII.

Reproduced with permission.[353]

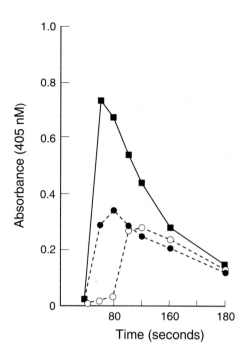

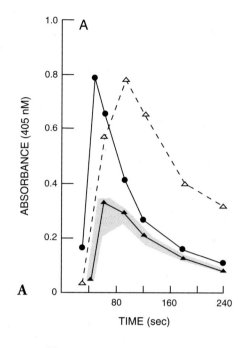

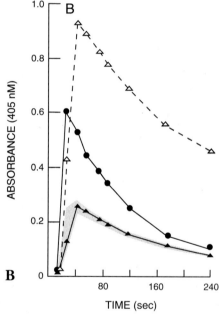

Figure 2–3 Generation of thrombin following activation in the activated partial thromboplastin time system from adults (■), from full-term infants on Day 1 of life (●), and from premature infants on Day 1 of life (○). The amount of thrombin generated was determined by its ability to cleave a chromogenic substrate, resulting in a change in the absorbance at 405 nM.

nM = nanomolar.

Reproduced with permission.[111]

sensitivity of the reagent used[116] (chapter 13). The physiologically slower rate of thrombin generation in newborns may provide protection from TEs. However, in the presence of pathologic conditions, the impaired ability to generate thrombin may result in a greater vulnerability to hemorrhagic complications, such as VK deficiency or disseminated intravascular coagulation (DIC).

"Fetal" Fibrinogen At birth, fibrinogen is present in a "fetal" form characterized by increased sialic acid content compared to "adult" fibrinogen.[117–120] The amino acid composition, and rate of release of FPA by thrombin of fetal fibrinogen, are similar to adult fibrinogen. Two unit TCTs performed without Ca++ in the system are prolonged in newborns, which may reflect differences in polymerization of fibrin produced from the "fetal" fibrinogen.[121] The TCTs in Tables 2–3 and 2–4 are two unit TCTs with Ca++ in the buffering system. These TCTs are

Figure 2–4 Thrombin generation following activation in the activated partial thromboplastin time system (panel A) and relationship to prothrombin concentration (panel B) in cord plasma (▲–▲), adult plasma (●–●), and cord plasma to which specific coagulation factors have been added. The single addition of either of factors IX, X, or contact product to the activated partial thromboplastin time system or X or VII to the prothrombin time system did not alter the amount of thrombin generated ((■) range of mean values). In contrast, the addition of prothrombin (Δ–Δ) to either system increased the amount of thrombin generated to adult levels.

sec = seconds; nM = nanomolar; APTT = activated partial thromboplastin time; PT = prothrombin time.

Reproduced with permission.[111]

not sensitive to "fetal" fibrinogen but are sensitive to UFH and decreased fibrinogen concentrations. The physiologic significance, if any, of "fetal" fibrinogen is not known.

Factor Levels during Childhood Until recently, the coagulation system following the first few months of life was assumed to be the same as for adults. However, closer examination of the coagulation system of 6-month-old infants showed that plasma concentrations of the VK dependent factors and contact factors were still 10 to 20 percent less than adult values (Figure 2–2). These differences, in combination with the very low risk of thrombosis in children, led to the completion of a comprehensive study of the coagulation system throughout childhood.[104] Plasma concentrations of several coagulation proteins, including FII and FVII, remain less than adult values for much of childhood (Figure 2–2).[104]

Thrombin Generation during Childhood The reduced plasma concentrations of coagulant proteins during childhood decrease the capacity to generate thrombin, by approximately 25 percent, compared to adults (Figure 2–5).[122] The reduced capacity to generate thrombin does not likely place children at any increased risk for hemorrhagic complications but may contribute to the mechanism(s) responsible for the low incidence of TEs. Other data support the latter hypothesis. Prothrombin concentrations are directly related to the capacity to generate thrombin in newborns[111] and adults receiving OAs.[111] Within the adult population, the risk of ischemic cardiovascular events, such as acute myocardial infarction, and ischemic cerebrovascular accidents positively correlates with plasma concentrations of FVII.[123] Whether the decreased plasma concentrations of FVII and FII during childhood are in part responsible for the low risk of TEs remains to be shown.

Coagulation Inhibitors

Certain plasma proteins (or inhibitors), endothelial cell surfaces, and fibrin regulate the generation and inhibition of thrombin. The direct inhibitors of thrombin in plasma include antithrombin (AT), α_2-macroglobulin (α_2M), and heparin cofactor II (HCII).[124–126]

Direct Inhibitors of Thrombin Antithrombin (59 kDa, 300 µg/mL), is a single polypeptide chain belonging to the serine proteinase family of inhibitors (serpins). Antithrombin inactivates serine proteases, including thrombin, by forming a 1:1 covalent bond with the active site. Antithrombin-mediated inhibition of thrombin is potentiated by the glycosaminoglycans (GAGs), heparin sulfate (HS) and UFH. Physiologically, endothelial cell surface–associated HS potentiates AT-dependent inhibition of thrombin.[127] Therapeutically, UFH and its low molecular–weight derivatives are the most commonly used anticoagulants for the prevention and initial treatment of TEs. α_2-macroglobulin (180 kDa, 2100 µg/mL), like AT, binds to several serine proteases of blood coagulation, including thrombin.[128,129] However, in adult plasma α_2M inhibits only a small fraction of thrombin compared to AT, and inhibition of thrombin by α_2M is not enhanced by GAGs. When α_2M binds to thrombin, it inhibits the ability of thrombin to cleave protein substrates such as fibrinogen, but not small molecules such as chromogenic substrates. Heparin cofactor II (65.6 kDa 90 µg/mL), like AT, inactivates thrombin, forming a 1:1 covalent bond that completely neutralizes thrombin's activity. However, HCII inhibits only a small fraction of thrombin added to plasma. Inhibition of thrombin by HCII can be potentiated by dermatan sulfate (DS).[130] Dermatan sulfate is present in the subendothelium[131] and to a lesser degree on the surface of endothelial cells. In vivo, the potentiation of HCII inhibition of thrombin by the DS GAG may increase the physiologic importance of this inhibitor.[130] The safety and effectiveness of DS is currently being evaluated in animal models and in man.[132–135]

Protein C / Protein S / Thrombomodulin System In addition to the direct plasma inhibitors of thrombin, there are other, indirect but nevertheless very important, mechanisms that influence the generation and activities of thrombin. First, thrombin itself inhibits coagulation when it binds to the endothelial cell surface receptor, TM.[136,137] Thrombomodulin (60 kDa) is a protein integrated into endothelial cell membranes through a membrane-spanning domain. Thrombomodulin binds to thrombin through an epidermal growth factor (EGF)-like region on TM and at a site on thrombin distant from the active site.[137] Thrombomodulin binding of thrombin may "lift" thrombin away from the surface, thereby potentiating its interaction with protein C.[137] Thrombin bound to TM no longer cleaves fibrinogen, FV, and FVIII, nor activates platelets.[138–140] However, thrombin bound to TM activates the VK dependent inhibitor protein C to its activated form, activated protein C (APC).[136,141] Protein C (62 kDa, 4.0 µg/mL) consists of both a heavy chain (which contains the active site) and a light chain. Activated protein C is a serine protease that inactivates FVa and FVIIIa by

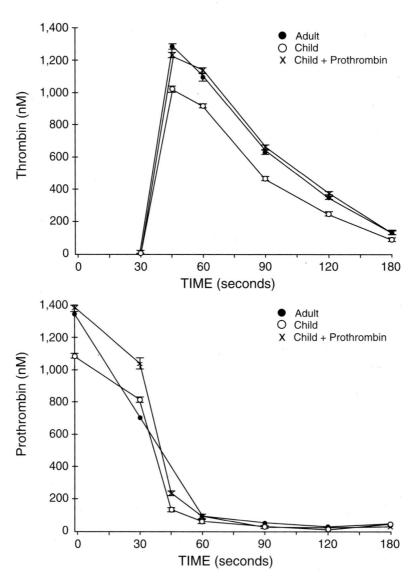

Figure 2–5 The upper panel shows thrombin generation in pooled defibrinated plasmas from healthy children of all ages (1 to 16 years), the same children's plasma supplemented with prothrombin, and adults (20 to 45 years). Plasma from children generated approximately 27 percent less thrombin than plasma from adults. Starting plasma concentrations of prothrombin were decreased by approximately 16 percent in plasma from children compared to adults. Children's plasma supplemented with prothrombin generated similar amounts of thrombin compared to adult plasma. Following activation with activated partial thromboplastin reagent, prothrombin was completely consumed within 60 seconds in all plasmas. The lower panel shows the change in plasma prothrombin concentrations in correspondence to the generation of thrombin shown in the upper panel.

nM = nanomolar.

Reproduced with permission.[122]

limited proteolysis. Activated protein C activity is enhanced by another VK dependent inhibitor, protein S, that functions as a cofactor. Protein S (69 kDa, 25 μg/mL) is a single chain glycoprotein (GP) present in two forms, a free active form and an inactive form that circulates bound to C_4B. Activated protein C is inhibited by at least two plasma inhibitors, protein C inhibitor (PCI)[143] and α_1-antitrypsin (α_1AT).[144] Patients with inherited deficiencies of protein C and protein S are at risk for TEs, usually as adults.

Tissue Factor Pathway Inhibitor A second indirect mechanism for regulating the generation of thrombin is by an inhibitor of the FVIIa / TF pathway, tissue factor pathway inhibitor (TFPI). TFPI (33 kDa) is synthesized by endothelial cells[145,146] and inhibits FVIIa / TF following the generation of FXa.[147–149] Factor Xa binds to TFPI in a Ca^{++}-independent reaction requiring the active site of FXa. Next, the TFPI / FXa complex binds to FVIIa / TF in an FXa-Ca^{++}-dependent reaction.[149,150]

Fibrin Inhibition of Thrombin A third mechanism for regulating thrombin activity is by fibrin itself.[85,151] Thrombin binds to fibrin and is relatively protected from inactivation by plasma antiproteases. Thrombin bound to fibrin can still cleave fibrinogen to fibrin but at a considerably slower rate.[151]

Coagulation Inhibitors: Infancy and Childhood

Thrombin activity is regulated by the same mechanisms during infancy and childhood, however, there are several important physiologic differences in thrombin regulation that likely provide part of the explanation for the decreased risk of TEs in children compared to adults (Tables 2–2, 2–6, and 2–7).

Protective Role of α_2-Macroglobulin Plasma concentrations of AT and HCII are approximately 50 percent of adult values during the first weeks of life (Figure 2–6).[101–107] One anticipates that decreased levels of these inhibitors could markedly impair the inhibition of thrombin and place infants at greater risk of TEs. When measured directly, the inhibition of thrombin is slower in plasma from newborns compared to adults. However, the magnitude of the difference between adult and newborn plasmas is less than predicted (Figure 2–7)[113,114] and is due to increased thrombin inhibition by α_2M in newborn plasma.[114] In contrast to AT and HCII, plasma concentrations of α_2M at birth are increased over adult values and are approximately twice adult values by 6 months of age (see Figure 2–6).[102,103,152] The increased plasma concentrations of α_2M compensate in large part for the decreased plasma concentrations of AT.[102–104,114] Postnatally, average values for plasma concentrations of AT increase to adult val-

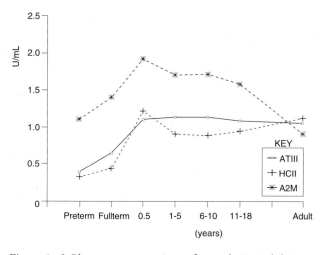
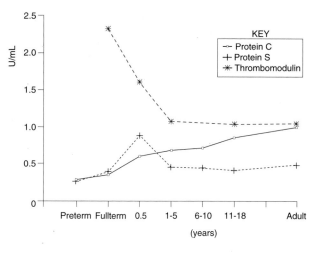

Figure 2–6 Plasma concentrations of coagulation inhibitors over age.

ATIII = antithrombin; HCII = heparin cofactor II; a_2M = α_2-macroglobulin; U/mL = units/mL.

Reproduced with permission.[353]

Table 2–6 Reference Values for the Inhibitors of Coagulation during the First Six Months of Life

	Day 1		Day 5		Day 30		Day 90		Day 180		Adult	
	M	B	M	B	M	B	M	B	M	B	M	B
AT (U/mL)	0.63	(0.39-0.87)	0.67	(0.41-0.93)	0.78	(0.48-1.08)	0.97	(0.73-1.21)*	1.04	(0.84-1.24)*	1.05	(0.79-1.31)
α₂M (U/mL)	1.39	(0.95-1.83)	1.48	(0.98-1.98)	1.50	(1.06-1.94)	1.76	(1.26-2.26)	1.91	(1.49-2.33)	0.86	(0.52-1.20)
C INH (U/mL)	0.72	(0.36-1.08)	0.90	(0.60-1.20)*	0.89	(0.47-1.31)	1.15	(0.71-1.59)	1.41	(0.89-1.93)	1.01	(0.71-1.31)
α₁AT (U/mL)	0.93	(0.49-1.37)*	0.89	(0.49-1.29)*	0.62	(0.36-0.88)	0.72	(0.42-1.02)	0.77	(0.47-1.07)	0.93	(0.55-1.31)
HCII (U/mL)	0.43	(0.10-0.93)	0.48	(0.00-0.96)	0.47	(0.10-0.87)	0.72	(0.10-1.46)	1.20	(0.50-1.90)	0.96	(0.66-1.26)
Protein C (U/mL)	0.35	(0.17-0.53)	0.42	(0.20-0.64)	0.43	(0.21-0.65)	0.54	(0.28-0.80)	0.59	(0.37-0.81)	0.96	(0.64-1.28)
Protein S (U/mL)	0.36	(0.12-0.60)	0.50	(0.22-0.78)	0.63	(0.33-0.93)	0.86	(0.54-1.18)*	0.87	(0.55-1.19)*	0.92	(0.60-1.24)
Healthy Premature Infants (30 to 36 Weeks Gestation)												
AT (U/mL)	0.38	(0.14-0.62)†	0.56	(0.30-0.82)	0.59	(0.37-0.81)†	0.83	(0.45-1.21)+	0.90	(0.52-1.28)†	1.05	(0.79-1.31)
α₂M (U/mL)	1.10	(0.56-1.82)†	1.25	(0.71-1.77)	1.38	(0.72-2.04)	1.80	(1.20-2.66)	2.09	(1.10-3.21)	0.86	(0.52-1.20)
C INH (U/mL)	0.65	(0.31-0.99)	0.83	(0.45-1.21)	0.74	(0.40-1.24)†	1.14	(0.60-1.68)*	1.40	(0.96-2.04)	1.01	(0.71-1.31)
α₁AT (U/mL)	0.90	(0.36-1.44)*	0.94	(0.42-1.46)*	0.76	(0.38-1.12)†	0.81	(0.49-1.13)*†	0.82	(0.48-1.16)*	0.93	(0.55-1.31)
HCII (U/mL)	0.32	(0.10-0.60)†	0.34	(0.10-0.69)	0.43	(0.15-0.71)	0.61	(0.20-1.11)	0.89	(0.45-1.40)*†	0.96	(0.66-1.26)
Protein C (U/mL)	0.28	(0.12-0.44)†	0.31	(0.11-0.51)	0.37	(0.15-0.59)†	0.45	(0.23-0.67)†	0.57	(0.31-0.83)	0.96	(0.64-1.28)
Protein S (U/mL)	0.26	(0.14-0.38)†	0.37	(0.13-0.61)	0.56	(0.22-0.90)	0.76	(0.40-1.12)†	0.82	(0.44-1.20)	0.92	(0.60-1.24)

All values are expressed in units per millilitre (U/mL) where pooled plasma contains 1.0 U/mL. All values are given as a mean (M) followed by the lower and upper boundary encompassing 95% of the population (B). Between 40 and 75 samples were assayed for each value for the newborn. Some measurements were skewed due to a disproportionate number of high values. The lower limits, which exclude the lower 2.5% of the population, have been given (B).

AT = antithrombin; α₂M = α₂-macroglobulin; C INH = C esterase inhibitor; α₁ AT = α-antitrypsin; HCII = heparin cofactor II.

*Values that are indistinguishable from those of the adult. †Values different from those of full-term infants.

Reproduced with permission.[105]

Table 2–7 Reference Values for the Inhibitors of Coagulation in Healthy Children Ages 1 to 16 Years as Compared to Adults

	1 to 5 Yrs		6 to 10 Yrs		11 to 16 Yrs		Adult	
	M	B	M	B	M	B	M	B
AT (U/mL)	1.11 (0.82-1.39)		1.11 (0.90-1.31)		1.05 (0.77-1.32)		1.00 (0.74-1.26)	
α_2M (U/mL)	1.69 (1.14-2.23)*		1.69 (1.28-2.09)*		1.56 (0.98-2.12)*		0.86 (0.52-1.20)	
C INH (U/mL)	1.35 (0.85-1.83)*		1.14 (0.88-1.54)		1.03 (0.68-1.50)		1.00 (0.71-1.31)	
α_1AT (U/mL)	0.93 (0.39-1.47)		1.00 (0.69-1.30)		1.01 (0.65-1.37)		0.93 (0.55-1.30)	
HCII (U/mL)	0.88 (0.48-1.28)*		0.86 (0.40-1.32)*		0.91 (0.53-1.29)*		1.08 (0.66-1.26)	
Protein C (U/mL)	0.66 (0.40-0.92)*		0.69 (0.45-0.93)*		0.83 (0.55-1.11)*		0.96 (0.64-1.28)	
Protein S								
Total (U/mL)	0.86 (0.54-1.18)		0.78 (0.41-1.14)		0.72 (0.52-0.92)		0.81 (0.60-1.13)	
Free (U/mL)	0.45 (0.21-0.69)		0.42 (0.22-0.62)		0.38 (0.26-0.55)		0.45 (0.27-0.61)	

All values are expressed in units per millilitre (U/mL), where for all factors pooled plasma contains 1.0 U/mL, with the exception of free protein S, which contains a mean of 0.4 U/mL. All values are given as a mean (M), followed by the lower and upper boundary encompassing 95% of the population (B). Between 20 and 30 samples were assayed for each value for each age group. Some measurements were skewed due to a disproportionate number of high values. The lower limits, which excludes the lower 2.5% of the population, have been given.

AT = antithrombin; α_2M = α 2-macroglobulin; C INH = C inhibitor; α_1AT = α1-antitrypsin; HCII = heparin cofactor II.

*Values that are significantly different from adults.

Reproduced with permission.[104]

ues by approximately 3 months of age and remain constant throughout the rest of childhood (Figure 2–6). In contrast, plasma concentrations of α_2M remain increased throughout childhood and do not decrease to adult values until the third decade of life (Figure 2–6).[104,152] α_2-macroglobulin inhibition of thrombin remains increased throughout childhood, likely contributing to both the decreased risk of TEs in healthy children (Figure 2–8) as well as in children with heterozygote AT deficiency (chapter 3).[153]

Fetal Anticoagulant In addition to the increased binding of thrombin to α_2M, the quantity of thrombin complexing to HCII is disproportionately increased in plasma from newborns compared to adults (Figure 2–8). The enhanced HCII-thrombin complex formation reflects the presence of a circulating DS proteoglycan (DSPG) that catalyzes thrombin inhibition by HCII.[154] The fetal DSPG circulates in a concentration of 0.29 μg/mL of plasma, has a molecular weight of approximately

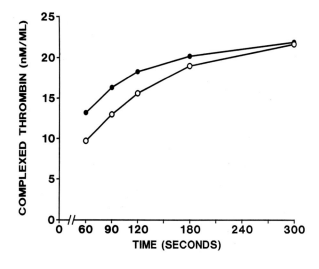

Figure 2–7 Inhibition of ^{125}I-thrombin (25 nanomolar) in adult (●–●) and neonatal (O–O) plasma differs significantly between the two age groups.

nM = nanomolar.

Reproduced with permission from Schmidt B, Mitchell L, Ofosu F, Andrew M. Alpha$_2$-macroglobulin is an important progressive inhibitor of thrombin in neonatal and infant plasma. Thromb Haemost 1989;62:1074–7.

150 kDa, is also present in plasma from pregnant women, and is likely released from the placenta.[155] The DSPG disappears from maternal blood within days of delivery. The length of time that the fetal DSPG circulates in newborns is not known, except that it is still present during the first week of life in sick infants with respiratory distress syndrome (RDS).[113]

Protein C / Protein S / Thrombomodulin System

Similar to adults, thrombin generation in the young is also controlled by the protein C / protein S / TM inhibitor system. Plasma concentrations of protein C and protein S during infancy and childhood are significantly reduced compared to adults (Figure 2–6). The composition of the protein C molecule in neonatal plasma is identical to that seen in adults;

however, there is a twofold increase in single chain protein C in the neonate as compared to the adult form.[156] In neonates, there is an inverse correlation between plasma concentrations of the total protein C antigen and the amount of single chain.[156] Animal studies report an increased glycosylation of fetal protein C compared to adults, which may reflect an altered post-translational processing.[157] The latter may exist as a general process by which certain coagulation proteins are modified during fetal development. There is no evidence that the fetal form of protein C significantly affects its functional activity. Protein S circulates completely in the free, active form in newborns,[158,159] because C_4B binding protein is absent in newborn plasma. The latter likely compensates for decreased plasma concentrations of total protein S (Figure 2–6).

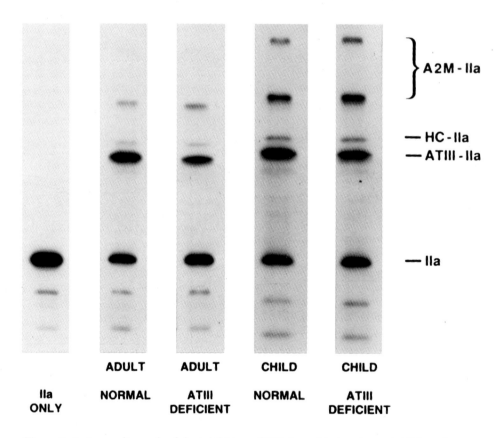

Figure 2–8 Autoradiograph of the inhibition of ^{125}I-thrombin by plasma inhibitors in normal adults, antithrombin deficient adults, normal children, and antithrombin deficient children. α_2-macroglobulin compensates for decreased plasma concentrations of antithrombin in antithrombin deficient children.

IIa = thrombin; ATIII = antithrombin; A_2M = $\alpha_2$macroglobulin; HCII = heparin cofactor II.

Reproduced with permission.[153]

The lower limits of normal for plasma concentrations of protein C and protein S remain decreased throughout early childhood and are important to consider when assessing children for inherited deficiencies of these inhibitors. The lower limit for protein C is 0.40 units/mL until 10 years of age, and 0.55 units/mL until the third decade of life. These values are in keeping with recent age-related differences in plasma protein C concentrations within the healthy adult male population.[160] Similarly, lower limits of normal for plasma concentrations of total protein S are between 0.41 and 0.54 units/mL and approximately 0.20 units/mL for free protein S during early childhood.[102–104] In contrast to protein C and protein S, plasma concentrations of TM are increased during early childhood but decrease to adult values during the teenage years.[161–165]

Other Inhibitors There is limited information on the importance of other inhibitors such as TFPI, α_1AT, and C1 esterase inhibitor (C INH) during childhood. In cord blood, plasma concentrations of TFPI are decreased (64%) compared to adult values[166] whereas plasma concentrations of α_1AT and C INH are similar or increased.[102] Whether the latter provides any additional protection to the young from TEs has not been explored. In summary, there are several novel mechanisms for enhancing thrombin regulation during infancy and childhood.

The Influence of Age on the Vessel Wall and Endothelium

The endothelium maintains an anticoagulant surface that down-regulates blood coagulation. Specifically, endothelial cells accelerate the inactivation of thrombin by AT and HCII through surface-bound GAGs. The endothelial cell receptor, TM, complexes with thrombin resulting in the conversion of protein C to APC, which in turn proteolytically degrades FVa and FVIIIa. The endothelium synthesizes the major initiator of fibrinolysis, tissue plasminogen activator (TPA), and its primary inhibitor, plasminogen activator inhibitor (PAI). In addition, an anticoagulant surface is mediated by lipoxygenase and cyclo-oxygenase metabolites of unsaturated fatty acids synthesized by the endothelium.

The Influence of Age on the Regulation Of Thrombin

Activation of coagulation in vivo with the generation of thrombin can be quantitated by measurement of activation peptides such as F1.2, FPA, and protein C activation peptide, and by enzyme-inhibitor complexes, such as thrombin-AT (TATs), protein C to protein C inhibitor (PCI), and protein C-α_1AT. Blood coagulation is activated at the time of birth as evidenced by increased plasma concentrations of FPA and TATs in cord blood.[167–171] However, this process seems to be well controlled and self limited. Indeed, activation of coagulation during the birth process neither results in significant consumption of circulating plasma coagulation proteins nor clinical morbidity.[88,89] Plasma concentrations of F1.2 and TAT complexes are similar in children and young adults (ages 20 to 40 years).[167,169,171,172] However, with increasing age (over 40), plasma concentrations of F1.2 increase[172] as well as plasma concentrations of FPA and protein C activation peptide.[172] This ex vivo evidence of impaired thrombin regulation in older adults, in combination with in vitro evidence of enhanced regulation of thrombin during childhood, together strongly suggest that the regulation of thrombin deteriorates with age, which parallels an increased risk of TEs.

Mechanisms Responsible for the Influence of Age on the Coagulation System

One of the notable features of the coagulation system in early infancy is that plasma concentrations of coagulation proteins are not all similarly different from adult values. For example, levels of four VK dependent coagulation proteins (FII, FVII, FIX, FX), four contact factors (FII, FXI, PK, HMWK), and four inhibitors (AT, HCII, protein C, protein S) are approximately 50 percent of adult values. In contrast, levels of fibrinogen, FVIII, FV, FXIII, and inhibitors α_2M, α_1AT, and C INH are similar to or increased above adult values. Further, the postnatal pattern of maturation differs for different coagulation proteins. The complexity of the ontogeny of hemostasis suggests that several mechanisms regulate plasma concentrations of coagulation proteins. Potential mechanisms include: 1) altered synthesis and release from cells, 2) faster clearance, 3) consumption during birth, and 4) "fetal" forms for some coagulation proteins.

Production of Coagulation Factors A recent study in rabbits using in situ hybridization reported that fetal liver contains more prothrombin mRNA than does adult liver, and that per microgram of protein extracts of adult and fetal liver, fetal liver contains as much prothrombin as does the adult liver.[173] During development in the mouse, FII mRNA is only detected in embryonic liver after expression of thrombin receptor and TF mRNA.[174] Thus, activators of thrombin generation (TF) and thrombin activatable protein (thrombin receptor) are in place prior to appearance of the zymogen (prothrombin). In addition, a study comparing the increase in plasma AT levels to the increase in hepatic AT mRNA in sheep from the eighth week of gestation until the fourth week after birth concluded that the increase in plasma AT activity was not regulated at the transcriptional level.[175] Production of mRNA for FVII, FVIII, FIX, FX, fibrinogen, AT, and protein C was measured in hepatocytes from 5- to 10-week-old human embryos, fetuses, and from adults.[176] The embryonic-fetal transcripts and adult mRNAs were similar in size, and the nucleotide sequences of FIX and FX mRNAs were identical. However, the expression of mRNA was variable, with adult values for some coagulation proteins and decreased expression for others (Figure 2–9).[176] Concentrations of prothrombin mRNA in newborn and adult rabbit livers are also similar.[177] Studies in human hepatocytes have shown that FV, fibrinogen beta, and albumin may be independently regulated.[178] Furthermore, it was found that glucocorticoids increased FV and fibrinogen mRNAs 1.6 and 5 fold, respectively, without affecting that of albumin, which suggests a possible endocrine role in the control of production of some coagulation factors.[178] Only one study has reported decreased mRNA concentrations for prothrombin in a sheep model.[179] The heterogeneity of findings in the study by Hassan and colleagues suggests that for some proteins secretion from the hepatocyte is impaired

or that proteins are released normally but cleared from the circulation at an increased rate.[176]

Clearance of Coagulation Proteins Faster clearance of at least some coagulation proteins occurs in newborns. Fibrinogen, whether of fetal lamb or adult sheep origin, is cleared more rapidly in healthy newborn lambs than in adult sheep (Figure 2–10).[120] Similarly, premature infants with or without RDS show shortened survivals of fibrinogen compared to healthy adults.[180,181] The half-life of AT is shorter in infants requiring exchange transfusion for hyperbilirubinemia than for healthy adults.[182] An increased basal metabolic rate in newborns contributes in part to the accelerated clearance of these and other proteins.[183]

Consumption of Coagulation Proteins Activation of coagulation occurs at birth with the generation of thrombin. However, it does not cause a significant decrease of plasma concentrations of coagulation proteins in healthy infants, although this may be an important mechanism in asphyxiated infants.[88,89,184]

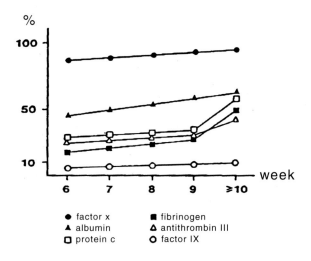

● factor x   ■ fibrinogen
▲ albumin   △ antithrombin III
□ protein c   ○ factor IX

Figure 2–9 Concentrations of factors VII, IX, and X at 7 to 8 weeks of gestation in liver and plasma. Concentrations are expressed as a percentage of adult levels. Liver and plasma concentrations are similar for factor IX but are discordant for factors VII and X, indicating that multiple regulation mechanisms influence the ontogenic biologic availability of coagulation proteins.

F = factor.

Reproduced with permission.[356]

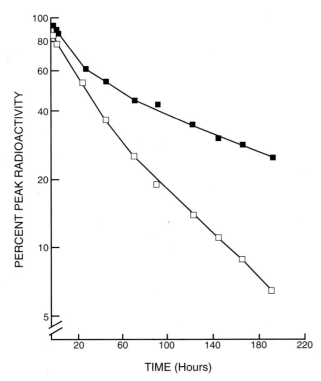

Figure 2–10 The survival curves of radiolabeled fetal lamb fibrinogen in the adult sheep (■, n = 5) and newborn lamb (◻, n = 5). The fetal fibrinogen had a consistently faster turnover in the lamb compared to the sheep. The values are all expressed as the mean with all SEM less than 5%.

Reproduced with permission.[89]

"Fetal" Forms of Coagulation Proteins

"Fetal" Forms of Coagulation Proteins As discussed previously, some coagulation proteins exist in fetal forms. The best characterized in the coagulation system are "fetal" fibrinogen[117–119] and "fetal" protein C.[156] Yet in neither case does the "fetal" form affect the measurement of its plasma concentration when performed with standard assays. Similarly, a unique fetal isoform of AT is described in sheep. This isoform had a 2500 Dalton higher molecular mass compared with the other fetal, neonatal, and adult AT isoform, and disappeared from the circulation between days 2 and 7 after birth. These AT isoforms differ in their carbohydrate moiety.[175]

THE FIBRINOLYTIC SYSTEM

Components of Fibrinolysis

Once a fibrin clot has formed in vivo, it is modified by the fibrinolytic system (Figure 2–11). Components of fibrinolysis interact to generate plasmin from its zymogen form, plasminogen.[185–188] Tissue plasminogen activator and urokinase (u-PA) are the physiologically important activators of fibrinolysis while PAI-1, α_2AP, and secondarily α_2M are important inhibitors.

Profibrinolytic Components Plasminogen (93 kDa, 200 µg/mL) is produced by the liver and circulates in two forms, one with an NH_2-terminal glutamic acid residue (glu-plasminogen) and one with NH_2-terminal lysine, valine, or methionine residues (lys-plasminogen). Glu-plasminogen can be converted to lys-plasminogen, which has a higher affinity for fibrin and increased fibrinolytic activity.[189] Both forms bind to fibrin through specific lysine binding sites that also mediate the interaction of plasminogen with its inhibitor, α_2AP.[190] Plasmin is a two-chain trypsin-like serine protease that cleaves fibrin and fibrinogen in sequential steps resulting in the formation of fibrin/fibrinogen degradation products (FDPs) such as D-dimer, fibrin fragment Bβ 15-42, and fibrinogen fragment Bβ 1-42. When plasmin is bound to fibrin, it is relatively protected from inhibition by α_2AP because

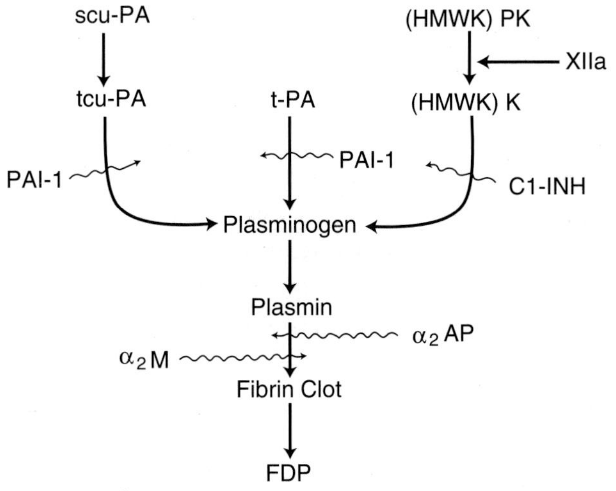

Figure 2–11 Schema of the fibrinolytic system.

scu-PA = single chain urokinase plasminogen activator; HMWK = high molecular weight kininogen; PK = prekallikrein; tcu-PA = two chain urokinase plasminogen activator; t-Pa = tissue plasminogen activator; PAI = plasminogen activator inhibitor; C INH = C inhibitor; α_2M = α_2-macroglobulin; α_2AP = α_2-antiplasmin; FDP = fibrin/fibrinogen degradation products.

Reproduced with permission.[352]

the lysine binding sites that mediate the specific binding of plasmin to fibrin are also necessary for the interaction of plasmin with α_2AP.[191-193] In contrast, plasmin not bound to fibrin is rapidly inhibited by α_2AP.[190,192,194]

Activators of Fibrinolysis Tissue plasminogen activator (60 kDa, 0.01 μg/mL) is the most important plasma activator of plasminogen. Tissue plasminogen activator, a serine protease produced by endothelial cells, circulates complexed to its inhibitor PAI-1 or, to a lesser extent, as free TPA.[195] TPA-PAI-1 complexes have relatively low affinity for fibrin, whereas free TPA has high binding affinity for fibrin, mediated through lysine binding sites. Fibrin promotes interaction between TPA and its substrate plasminogen, thereby enhancing TPA activity.[193,194,196] Urokinase, the predominantly extravascular activator of plasminogen, is a serine protease produced by kidney and other cell types, including endothelial cells, following stimulation.[193,197] Single chain urokinase (scu-PA, 54 kDa, 0.00032 μg/mL) has significant fibrin specificity but relatively low thrombolytic activity until it is converted to its two-chain form (tcu-PA) following limited cleavage by plasmin or kallikrein.[198,199] Two-chain form urokinase has no fibrin specificity and efficiently activates both circulating and fibrin bound plasminogen.[200,201] Plasminogen can be activated by components of the contact system; however, this does not appear to be of physiologic importance.

Inhibitors of Fibrinolysis α_2-antiplasmin (70 kDa, 70 μg/mL), the major inhibitor of plasmin, belongs to the serpin family of inhibitors and is produced in the liver.[193,202] α_2-antiplasmin binds to the active site of plasmin forming a 1:1 stoichiometric complex that has no further activity. α_2-macroglobulin is a less important inhibitor of plasmin than α_2AP in adults. α_2-macroglobulin inhibition of fibrin-bound plasmin is also impaired compared to fluid phase plasmin.[203] The fibrinolytic system is also regulated by PAIs of TPA and u-PA. There are at least four PAIs described in the literature. PAI-1 (54 kDa, 0.005 μg/mL), the major inhibitor of TPA and tcu-PA, is a single chain GP belonging to the serpin family of inhibitors and is produced by endothelial cells.[193,204] Present in plasma during pregnancy, PAI-2 is produced by the placenta. An inhibitor of activated protein C and protease nexin (the fourth PAI), PAI-3 is a nonspecific inhibitor that also inhibits u-PA.[205] A newly described inhibitor of fibrinolysis is TAFI, a plasma procarboxypeptidase, activated by thrombin and in particular thrombin-TM complexes.[70,206,207] Thrombin activable finbinolysis inhibitor (TAFI) probably functions by removing C-terminal lysines from partially degraded fibrin, thereby inhibiting TPA induced fibrinolysis.[70,208] Circulating TAFI is protected from renal excretion by forming a complex with α_2M.[209]

Fibrinolytic Process The initiation and regulation of intravascular fibrinolysis is primarily dependent upon TPA and its inhibition by PAI-1. Free TPA is released by endothelial cells into the circulation and, if fibrin is present, free TPA is adsorbed onto fibrin, which renders it relatively inaccessible to its major inhibitor PAI-1. Fibrin-bound TPA cleaves fibrin-bound plasminogen to plasmin, which proteolytically digests fibrin. In the absence of fibrin, free TPA complexes gradually with PAI-1 and thereby loses its activity.[196] Plasma concentrations of TPA and PAI-1 reflect only a small portion of the fibrinolytic potential. Following a variety of stimuli, endothelial cells release significant amounts of TPA and PAI-1 into the circulation[210,211] and increase the production of these same molecules.[212,213] The overall effect can be either an increase or decrease in fibrinolytic activity. For in vivo studies in humans, one reproducible method of determining fibrinolytic "capacity" is venous occlusion for varying lengths of time (5 to 20 minutes). Numerous studies of adults have documented that both TPA and PAI-1 levels increase with enhanced fibrinolysis being the net effect.[211,214]

Components of the Fibrinolytic System: Infancy and Childhood

Plasminogen and α_2-antiplasmin Although all components of the fibrinolytic system but one are present during infancy and childhood, there are some important developmental differences that impact on the regulation of plasmin (Tables 2–8 and 2–9). Plasma concentrations of plasminogen in cord blood and during the early postnatal period are only 50 percent of adult values.[102–105,215–220] Plasminogen, like fibrinogen, has a fetal form with two glycoforms, but with increased amounts of mannose and sialic acid (Figure 2–12).[221] The same authors reported decreased enzymatic activity as well as decreased binding to cellular receptors for fetal plasminogen.[221] Other investigators have concluded that fetal and newborn plasminogens were identical in function.[222] The latter requires further investigation. Plasma concentrations of α_2AP, the major inhibitor of plasmin, are approximately 80 percent of adult values.[102,103,105,216–219] The importance of plasmin inhibition by α_2M has not been measured in newborn plasma and may well differ from adults, reflecting increased plasma concentrations of α_2M at birth and during early childhood.[102,104,152]

Plasminogen Activators and Inhibitors

In contrast to plasminogen and α_2AP, plasma concentrations of TPA and PAI-1 are significantly increased in plasma from newborns on day one of life compared to adult values. This is in marked contrast to values from cord blood for TPA, u-PA, and PAI-1 that are significantly decreased compared to adult values.[217] Plasma concentrations for PAI-2 are decreased in cord blood and increased in plasma from term newborns.[223]

Childhood

Plasma concentrations of some parameters of fibrinolysis have been measured throughout childhood (Tables 2–8 and 2–9).[104] Although plasma concentrations of plasminogen and α_2AP are similar to adult values by 6 months of life,[105] plasma concentrations of TPA antigen are decreased (50%) and PAI-1 activity increased (50%) throughout childhood into the teenage years (Figure 2–13).[104] A study by Siegbahn and colleagues similarly reported that under basal conditions teenage girls had decreased plasma concentrations of TPA and increased concentrations of PAI-1 compared to adult women.[224]

Activity of the Fibrinolytic System during Infancy and Childhood

There is convincing evidence that

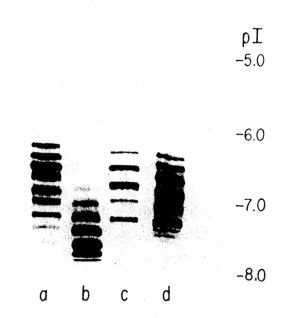

Figure 2–12 Isoelectric focussing gel of plasminogen glycoforms. Lane a: adult plasminogen 1; lane b: adult plasminogen 2; lane c: neonatal plasminogen 1; lane d: neonatal plasminogen 2.

Reproduced with permission.[221]

the fibrinolytic system is transiently activated at birth.[100,102,103,106,107,171,217,225,226] Global tests of fibrinolytic activity such as the whole blood clotting time and euglobulin lysis times are short in cord blood. Further, cord plasma concentrations of Bβ15-42 peptide are increased compared to adult controls.[171] Although activated at birth, the "capacity" of cord plasma to generate plasmin is decreased in vitro compared to adult plasma (Figure 2–14)[217] due primarily to decreased plasma concentrations of plasminogen.[217,227] The decreased capacity to generate plasmin impairs fibrin clot lysis in vitro and may limit therapeutic thrombolysis in vivo.[227] There are no comprehensive studies measuring ex vivo markers of fibrinolysis in healthy children beyond the newborn period. One initial study, which gives reference values for ex vivo markers of fibrinolysis in children, has been reported.[228] However, two studies report that plasma concentrations of PAI-1 levels are increased and TPA levels decreased during childhood compared to adults.[104,224] Further, the fibrinolytic capacity measured following venous stasis induced by cuff occlusion showed a significant reduction in teenage girls compared to older women.[224] Together these data suggest, but do not

Table 2–8 Reference Values for the Components of the Fibrinolytic System during the First Six Months of Life

Healthy Full-Term Infants

	Day 1		Day 5		Day 30		Day 90		Day 180		Adult	
	M	B	M	B	M	B	M	B	M	B	M	B
Plasminogen (U/mL)	1.95 (1.25-2.65)		2.17 (1.41-2.93)		1.98 (1.26-2.70)		2.48 (1.74-3.22)		3.01 (2.21-3.81)		3.36 (2.48-4.24)	
TPA (ng/mL)	9.6 (5.0-18.9)		5.6 (4.0-10.0)*		4.1 (1.0-6.0)*		2.1 (1.0-5.0)*		2.8 (1.0-6.0)*		4.9 (1.4-8.4)	
α_2AP (U/mL)	0.85 (0.55-1.15)		1.00 (0.70-1.30)*		1.00 (0.76-1.24)*		1.08 (0.76-1.40)*		1.11 (0.83-1.39)*		1.02 (0.68-1.36)	
PAI-1 (U/mL)	6.4 (2.0-15.1)		2.3 (0.0-8.1)*		3.4 (0.0-8.8)*		7.2 (1.0-15.3)		8.1 (6.0-13.0)		3.6 (0.0-11.0)	

Healthy Premature Infants (30 to 36 weeks Gestation)

	Day 1		Day 5		Day 30		Day 90		Day 180		Adult	
	M	B	M	B	M	B	M	B	M	B	M	B
Plasminogen (U/mL)	1.70 (1.12-2.48)†		1.91 (1.21-2.61)†		1.81 (1.09-2.53)		2.38 (1.58-3.18)		2.75 (1.91-3.59)†		3.36 (2.48-4.24)	
TPA (ng/mL)	8.48 (3.00-16.70)		3.97 (2.00-6.93)*		4.13 (2.00-7.79)*		3.31 (2.00-5.85)*		3.48 (2.00-5.85)*		4.96 (1.46-8.46)	
α_2AP (U/mL)	0.78 (0.40-1.16)		0.81 (0.49-1.13)†		0.89 (0.55-1.23)†		1.06 (0.64-1.48)*		1.15 (0.77-1.53)*		1.02 (0.68-1.36)	
PAI-1 (U/mL)	5.4 (0.0-12.2)*†		2.5 (0.0-7.1)*		4.3 (0.0-10.9)*		4.8 (1.0-11.8)*†		4.9 (1.0-10.2)*†		3.6 (0.0-11.0)	

For α_2AP, values are expressed as units per millilitre (U/mL) where pooled plasma contains 1.0 U/mL. Plasminogen units are those recommended by the Committee on Thrombolytic Agents. Values for TPA are given as nanograms per millilitre. Values for PAI-1 are given as units per mL where one unit of PAI-1 activity is defined as the amount of PAI-1 that inhibits one international unit of human single chain TPA. All values are given as a mean (M) followed by the lower and upper boundary encompassing 95% of the population (B).

TPA = tissue plasminogen activator; α_2AP = α_2-antiplasmin; PAI-1 = plasminogen activator inhibitor-1.

*Values that are indistinguishable from those of the adult. †Values that are different from those of the full-term infant.

Reproduced with permission.[105]

Table 2–9 Reference Values for the Fibrinolytic System in Healthy Children Ages 1 to 16 Years as Compared to Adults

	1 to 5 Yrs		6 to 10 Yrs		11 to 16 Yrs		Adult	
	M	B	M	B	M	B	M	B
Plasminogen (U/mL)	0.98 (0.78-1.18)		0.92 (0.75-1.08)		0.86 (0.68-1.03)*		0.99 (0.77-1.22)	
TPA (ng/mL)	2.15 (1.0-4.5)*		2.42 (1.0-5.0)*		2.16 (1.0-4.0)*		4.90 (1.40-8.40)	
α_2AP (U/mL)	1.05 (0.93-1.17)		0.99 (0.89-1.10)		0.98 (0.78-1.18)		1.02 (0.68-1.36)	
PAI-1 (U/mL)	5.42 (1.0-10.0)		6.79 (2.0-12.0)*		6.07 (2.0-10.0)*		3.60 (0-11.0)	

For a2AP, values are expressed as units per mL (U/mL), where pooled plasma contains 1.0 U/mL. Values for TPA are given as nanograms/millilitre (ng/mL). Values for PAI-1 are given as units/mL where 1 unit of PAI-1 activity is defined as the amount of PAI-1 that inhibits one international unit of human single-chain TPA. All values are given as mean (M) followed by the lower and upper boundary encompassing 95% of the population (B).

TPA = tissue plasminogen activator; α_2AP = α_2-antiplasmin; PAI-1 = plasminogen activator inhibitor-1.

*Values that are significantly different from adults.

Reproduced with permission.[104]

prove, that fibrinolysis is suppressed during childhood. If true, mechanisms other than enhanced fibrinolysis must be responsible for protecting the young from TEs.

Effect of Age on the Fibrinolytic System in Adults

Basal plasma concentrations of TPA and PAI-1 are also influenced by age within the adult population.[229–237] Although there are some discrepancies between studies, a few generalizations can be made. Between the ages of 20 and 65 years, TPA antigen and TPA-PAI-1 complexes increase in parallel with age[229–232] whereas TPA activity decreases with age.[231,233] In contrast, both PAI-1 antigen and activity increase with age.[231,232] Overall these age dependent changes would be compatible with increased release of TPA and PAI-1 from endothelial cells with the net effect being suppression of fibrinolysis. How these observations link to those made in children is unknown. Thrombin is a potent stimulator of endothelial cell synthesis and release of TPA and to a greater extent PAI-1.[238] Furthermore,

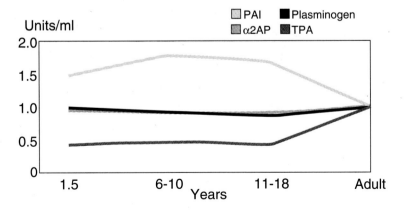

Figure 2–13 Plasma concentrations of components of the fibrinolytic system over age. Tissue plasminogen activator (■), plasminogen activator inhibitor (O), plasminogen (x), α_2-antiplasmin (●).

U/mL = units/mL; TPA = tissue plasminogen activator; PAI = plasminogen activator inhibitor; α_2 AP = α_2-antiplasmin.

Reproduced with permission.[353]

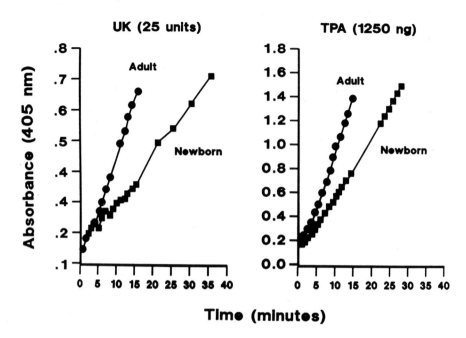

Figure 2–14 Plasmin generation, chromogenic method. Urokinase or tissue plasminogen activator was added to undiluted acid-treated adult (●) and newborn (■) plasma containing S-2251. The change in absorbance over time is shown.

UK = urokinase; TPA = tissue plasminogen activator; nM = nanomolar; ng = nanograms.

Reproduced with permission.[217]

TAFI generation is critically dependent on thrombin generation. Further studies are required before the age-related changes in fibrinolysis can be fully understood.

PLATELETS AND THE VESSEL WALL

Vessel Wall Function

In addition to the fluid phase of hemostasis, there are important cellular components that provide specific physiologic functions. The intact vessel wall provides an important antithrombotic surface under physiologic conditions. The presence of cell surface GAGs, TM, and inhibition of the production of prostacyclin (PGI₂) are some of the antithrombotic mechanisms in place. PG-related GAG molecules within vessel walls are macromolecules with covalently attached GAG chains, either chondroitin sulfate (CS), DS, HS, or keratan sulfate. Many GAG molecules promote AT neutralization of thrombin as well as several other serine proteases. During an adult's lifespan, the vessel wall undergoes an aging process that reflects genetic as well as environmental conditions.

Platelet Structure and Function: General

Structure Platelets are an important cellular component of hemostasis. Platelets are disk-shaped cells produced in the bone marrow and released into the circulation (Figure 2–15). In adults, there are between 150 and 450 x 10⁹/L circulating platelets, with average platelet volumes of 7 to 9 fL. The lifespan of platelets is approximately 7 to 10 days in adults, at which time platelets are removed from the circulation by macrophages in the reticuloendothelial system.[240] The outer surface of platelets contains several adhesive GPs that bind specific adhesive proteins to facilitate platelet-to-surface interactions and platelet-to-platelet aggregation. Under the glycocalyx there is a phospholipid bilayer that provides a procoagulant surface after platelets are activated for thrombin generation[241–246] and an internal membrane system that participates in platelet secretion of granular contents.[247,248] Platelets contain two types of granules, dense bodies and α-granules. Dense bodies contain substances that promote platelet aggregation such as adenosine diphosphate (ADP), serotonin, and Ca^{++}. α-granules contain several substances that have a wide variety of functions, including thrombospondin, an adhesive protein; growth factors such as platelet derived growth factor (PDGF), tissue growth factor beta (TGF-β), and fibroblast growth factor (FGF); platelet factor 4 (PF-4), a substance that interferes with UFH/AT interaction; several coagulation proteins; and β-thromboglobulin, a marker of platelet activation.[249–254]

If the endothelial lining of blood vessels is damaged or removed, platelets adhere to subendothelial layers, undergo shape change, spread over the surface, secrete granular contents, and recruit other platelets into the process of platelet-to-platelet aggregation. During this process thrombin is generated and a stable platelet-fibrin thrombus forms. The following section briefly outlines this complicated process.

Platelet Adhesion Platelet adhesion occurs when platelets contact a damaged vessel wall and spread over components of the subendothelial matrix.[255] Platelet adhesion is promoted by a high shear rate because the distribution of blood cells is not homogeneous. Red cells are concentrated in the middle of the stream while smaller platelets are pushed aside towards the vessel surface. Adhesive proteins mediate bridging between the subendothelium and platelet GPs that belong to the integrin superfamily of adhesion receptors.[256–259] Platelet adhesion to the vessel wall is complex as many adhesive proteins, such as vWF, thrombospondin, fibronectin, and collagen, interact with each other in addition to platelets.[255]

Activation Regulation of platelets is a dynamic process initiated when specific platelet surface re-

ceptors are occupied by a wide variety of extracellular molecules that result in excitatory and/or inhibitory signals.[260–264] These signals can be grouped as strong agonists (thrombin, collagen, prostaglandin endoperoxides, thromboxane A_2 [TXA_2], platelet-activating factor [PAF]), weak agonists (ADP, epinephrine, vasopressin, and serotonin), and antagonists (PGI_2, PGD_2, endothelium-derived relaxing factor [EDRF]). Receptor occupation activates membrane-associated enzymes through receptor-linked changes in signal-transducing GTP-binding regulatory proteins (G proteins).[265,266] These in turn generate intracellular second messengers, phospholipase C (PLC), which promotes platelet activation in a wide variety of ways, and adenyl cyclase, which promotes platelet inhibition by converting intracellular adenosine triphosphate (ATP) into cyclic adenosine

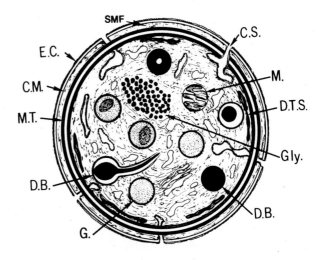

Figure 2–15 Discoid platelet. The diagram summarizes ultrastructural features in thin sections of discoid platelets cut in the equatorial plane. Components of the peripheral zone include the exterior coat (EC), trilaminar unit membrane (CM), and submembrane area containing specialized filaments (SMF) that form the wall of the platelet and line channels of the surface connected canalicular system (SC). The matrix of the platelet interior is the sol-gel zone containing actin microfilaments, structural filaments, the circumferential band of microtubules (MT), and glycogen (Gly). Formed elements embedded in the sol-gel zone include mitochondria (M), granules (G), and dense bodies (DB). Collectively they constitute the organelle zone. The membrane system includes surface connected canalicular system (SC) and the dense tubular system (DTS) that serves as the platelet sarcoplasmic reticulum.

Reproduced with permission.[354]

monophosphate (cAMP), a molecule that antagonizes all Ca^{++}-dependent activation events.[267] Phospholipase C promotes platelet activation by cleaving phosphatidylinositol 4,5-bisphosphate (PIP_2) into inositol 1,4,5-trisphosphate (IP_3) and 1,2-diacylglycerol (DG).[268–270] IP_3 and DG synergistically promote platelet activation by inducing conformational changes in target proteins either directly or indirectly by activation of protein kinases. IP_3 is a Ca^{++} ionophore, thereby increasing cytoplasmic free Ca^{++}, which promotes platelet activation in a number of ways. First, a Ca^{++}/calmodulin-dependent protein kinase catalyzes the phosphorylation of a myosin light chain that is necessary for a functional contractile apparatus.[271] Second, Ca^{++}-dependent proteases promote platelet cytoskeletal reorganization during platelet aggregation.[272] Third, activation of phospholipase A_2 is Ca^{++} dependent and the subsequent platelet response is a consequence of the release and metabolism of arachidonic acid.[273–275]

1,2 Diacylglycerol promotes platelet activation by triggering the translocation of inactive protein kinase C (PKC) from the cytosol to the membrane[276] where it is then activated in the presence of Ca^{++} and phosphatidylserine.[276] The mechanisms by which PKC promotes platelet aggregation and secretion are still not understood completely. PKC promotes Ca^{++}-independent modification of the membrane GPIIb-IIIa complex,[276] modulation of actin polymerization in a cell-free system,[277] and thereby platelet secretion of granules.

PLA_2 releases arachidonic acid (AA) from phosphatidylcholine, phosphatidylethanolamine, and phosphatidylserine in the membrane phospholipid layer.[278,279] Arachidonic acid is subsequently oxidized by two enzyme systems, the cyclo-oxygenase and lipoxygenase pathways.[280,281] In the first system, cyclo-oxygenase converts AA to prostaglandin endoperoxides intermediates (PGG_2, PGH_2) that are converted in turn by thromboxane synthetase to TXA_2, a potent agonist of platelet aggregation. These AA derivatives bind to specific platelet receptors and through a G protein signal transducer directly activate PLC. In the second system, lipoxygenase converts arachidonic acid to hydroxyeicosatetraenoic acid (HETE) that inhibits a number of platelet responses to AA and its derivatives.[282,283]

Shape Change   The metabolic processes initiated by platelet activation result in shape change and platelet aggregation. Shape change is a process whereby platelets change in shape from disks to irregular spheres with extended pseudopods and increased surface to volume area. During this process, the activated platelet plasma membranes internalize ligand-$\alpha IIb\beta 3$ complexes and particulates[284] that are sequestered to the surface-connected canalicular system. This platelet membrane internalization contributes to clot retraction and thrombus development at the sites of injury. Shape change is produced by a reorganization of cytoskeletal proteins and facilitates platelet-to-platelet interaction, or aggregation and release of granular contents.

Secretion   Platelet secretion is a process whereby platelet granules form a cluster and then fuse with membranes of other granules or the open-connected canalicular system.[254] The clustering of granules is dependent on the interaction of actin and myosin filaments that in turn is dependent on Ca^{++}/calmodulin activation of myosin light chain kinase. The fusion of granules is dependent on PKC. Platelet secretion is intimately linked to platelet aggregation.[285] Secretion in response to agonists ADP and epinephrine first requires platelet aggregation that in turn stimulates the metabolism of AA and production of TXA_2. The number of fibrinogen receptors on platelet surfaces is increased by dense granule release of the agonist ADP. Both fibrinogen and vWF are found in the α-granules and are the most important ligands in aggregation. Thrombospondin, released from α-granules, stabilizes the platelet aggregate. Finally, an α-granule membrane protein, P-selectin (formerly known as GMP-140), is present on platelet surfaces following granule secretion.[269,286] The presence of P-selectin on the surface of platelets, at the site of vessel wall injury, has been implicated in increased local adhesion of neutrophils to the vessel surface, which leads to enhanced thrombus formation.[287]

Aggregation Platelet aggregation is dependent on a Ca^{++}-induced conformational conversion of membrane GPIIb/IIIa into a receptor for fibrinogen and other adhesive proteins.[288] Fibrinogen, which binds to GPIIb/IIIa receptors through the carboxy terminus of the γ-chain, is likely of primary importance to platelet aggregation.[289] However, GPIIb/IIIa complexes also bind other adhesive proteins, including fibronectin, vWF, thrombospondin, and vitronectin, which all contain the sequence Arg-Gly-Asp (RGD) that is essential for ligand binding to the GPIIb/IIIa receptor. GPIIb/IIIa receptors are also found on megakaryocytes and endothelial cell surfaces. Release of ADP, serotonin, and Ca^{++} from dense bodies promotes platelet aggregation. Release of the α-granular content promotes a variety of functions that include adhesive proteins that participate in platelet aggregation.

Procoagulant Surface Activated platelets provide significant procoagulant activity by expressing binding sites for specific coagulation proteins.[290,291] Procoagulant activity is induced following an influx of Ca^{++} from plasma and a reorientation of acidic phospholipids (primarily phosphatidylserine) from the inner plasma-membrane bilayer to the outer surface. In addition, platelet membrane vesicles are shed from platelet surfaces and also express binding sites for coagulation proteins thereby promoting the generation of FXa and thrombin.[292]

Vessel Wall and Platelet Function: Infancy and Childhood

Vessel Wall The vessel wall profoundly influences hemostasis due to the procoagulant and anticoagulant properties of endothelial cells and extracellular matrix components. Each of these properties is significantly influenced by age. One of the anticoagulant properties of endothelial cell surfaces is mediated by lipoxygenase and cyclo-oxygenase metabolites of unsaturated fatty acids. Prostacyclin$_2$ production from cord vessels exceeds that of vessels from adults.[293] In a rabbit venous model there is a significant increase in GAGs by mass in inferior vena cavas (IVCs) from pups compared with adult rabbits. The AT-mediated anticoagulant activity of IVC GAGs, especially HS, is increased in pups compared to adult rabbits.[294] In a rabbit arterial model, total PG, CS PG, and HS PG content are increased in the intima and media of aortas from pups compared to adult rabbits. Antithrombin III activity in aortas of pups, due to HS GAGs, is also increased.[295] The increased GAG-mediated vessel wall AT activity in pups compared to adult rabbits suggests that young blood vessels may have greater antithrombotic potential.

When measured directly, thrombin generation in cord plasma is decreased in the presence of human umbilical endothelial cells compared to plastic due to cell surface promotion of AT inhibition of thrombin.[296] Soluble levels of endothelial cell adhesion molecules and selectins are also age dependent, suggesting developmental differences in endothelial cell expression and secretion of these molecules.[297]

Nitric oxide (NO), or EDRF, is a labile humeral agent that modulates vascular tone in fetal and postnatal lungs and contributes to the normal decline in pulmonary vascular resistance at birth. Nitric oxide is a potent inhibitor of platelet adhesion and aggregation, and stimulates disaggregation of platelet aggregates. Nitric oxide likely interacts with PGI$_2$ and other metabolites of the lipoxygenase pathway to modulate platelet function in a synergistic manner.[298]

Platelets In contrast to the vessel wall, there are well-described physiologic differences in the function of cord platelets compared to adult platelets. Until recently, there was little information on the function of platelets taken directly from infants because of the volume of blood required and the technical difficulty of obtaining an adequate sample. Studies with flow cytometry have provided interesting insights into platelet function of the healthy newborn; however, the reduced availability and complexity of flow cytometry has limited the usefulness of this technique in routine clinical practice. For clarification, the terms cord platelets and newborn platelets will be used in the subsequent discussion. Neonatal platelets have been demonstrated to be generally less reactive to physiological agonists, as measured by P-selectin and GPIIb-IIa expression and decrease in surface area by GPIb-IX complex.[299] Platelet hyporeactivity in the neonate is, at least in part, due to a relative defect in a signal transduction pathway.[299] In addition, activation in platelets from term umbilical cord vein blood may be downregulated by decreased platelet activating factor-acetylhydrolase activity in the surrounding plasma (a possible compensatory mechanism to maintain microcirculation within the placenta).[300] In fact, one study was unable to find any increased platelet activation in healthy individuals during the first 3 days of life compared to older children.[301] Apparently conflicting results on cord platelet function likely reflect differences in sample timing, method of collection, the effects of labour, concentrations, and compositions of platelet agonists.

Platelet counts in full-term newborns are not different from adult values with a normal range of 150 to 450 x 10^9/L.[215,302] Values from fetuses between 18 and 30 weeks GA are also within this range, with average values of 250 x 10^9/L.[93] Premature infants may have slightly lower values on average but still well within the adult range. Mean platelet volumes in newborns are also similar to adult values, 7 to 9 fL.[303,304] Platelet survivals have not been studied in healthy full-term infants. However, studies in healthy newborn and adult rabbits suggest that platelet survivals are likely similar in newborns compared to adults.[305] As well, mildly thrombocytopenic infants have platelet survivals that are in the lower range of normal for adults.[306]

Megakaryocyte and Platelet Precursors Cord blood of preterm babies has increased numbers of all megakaryocyte precursors compared to term infants. Term infants, with no evidence of platelet consumption, have increased circulating megakaryotcyte progenitor numbers at birth correlated with platelet numbers, compared to adults.[307] Cord blood megakaryocyte progenitors are exquisitely sensitive to exogenous cytokines. The magnitude of their proliferative and maturational responses to cytokines is related to developmental age.[308] Reticulated platelets are newly synthesized platelets with increased ribonucleic acid content. Reticulated platelet counts are reported as similar to adult levels in healthy neonates greater than 30 weeks GA,

and increased in neonates younger than 30 weeks GA,[309] although another study reports reduced reticulated platelet counts in neonates of all GAs compared to adults.[310] The median level in term babies (0.000145 µg/mL; range 0.000052-0.000237 µg/mL) is similar to that observed in preterm babies (0.000132 µg/mL; 0.000032-0.000318 µg/mL).[311] There is no information on developmental differences of megakaryocyte and platelet precursors during childhood.

Platelet Survival Platelet survival studies using indium oxine labelled platelets are similar in healthy rabbit pups and adult rabbits.[305] Although there are no studies of platelet survival in healthy newborns, studies in thrombocytopenic infants show that the least thrombocytopenic infants have the longest platelet survivals.[306] These studies suggest that platelet survivals in newborns do not likely differ significantly from adults and are 7 to 10 days. There are no studies comparing platelet survival in either healthy or thrombocytopenic children to adults.

Platelet Structure Electron microscopy studies have shown that the number of granules in cord platelets is similar to adult platelets. However, dense granules from cord platelets contain concentrations of serotonin and ADP that are less than 50 percent of adult values. Flow cytometry studies show that, in whole blood samples without added agonist, there are no significant differences between neonates and adults in the platelet binding of monoclonal antibodies that are GPIb or GPIIb-IIIa complex specific. Using a P-selectin-specific monoclonal antibody, neither neonates nor adults have circulating degranulated platelets.[312]

Adhesion Components necessary for platelet adhesion are present in early fetal life. GPIb is present on membranes of fetal platelets in adult amounts.[313] Plasma concentrations of vWF are increased at birth,[102,103,105] with an increase in the functional high molecular weight forms.[109,110] The cord multimeric pattern of vWF appears similar to the forms released by endothelial cells, suggesting that mechanisms for processing the multimeric structure of vWF may not be fully developed at birth. The quantitative and qualitative differences in vWF at birth are likely responsible for enhanced cord platelet agglutination in response to low concentrations of ristocetin[109,110,314] and contribute to the short bleeding time (BT) in newborns.[315–318] The concentrations of vWF decrease to adult levels by 3 months of age and are constant during childhood. In vitro measurements of cord platelet adhesion are not consistently different from adults, although platelet adhesion in newborns has not been assessed with sensitive and reproducible assays, which may explain the conflicting results.

Aggregation Both the receptor, GP IIb/IIIa complexes and ligand, fibrinogen, that mediate platelet aggregation, are present in early fetal life in adult concentrations.[102,103,313] Several investigators have studied cord platelet aggregation in response to a variety of agonists such as epinephrine, collagen, thrombin and arachidonic acid and reported variable differences compared to adult platelets (Figure 2–16). A decreased aggregation response to epinephrine is reproducible and is secondary to decreased numbers of α-adrenergic receptors on cord platelets.[319–321] Whether these receptors are occupied by catecholamines released during birth, or whether there is a delayed maturation of these receptors is not clear.[322] Cord platelets aggregate normally in response to arachidonate[320,323] and produce at least adult levels of thromboxane B_2.[320] Aggregation responses to other agonists are less consistent.[324–327] There are several potential explanations for these discrepant results including inadvertent activation of cord samples during collection,[328] the speed with which samples are processed, the influence of labour, and the use of differing concentrations or composition of platelet agonists. When these variables are controlled, aggregation of cord platelets in response to collagen remains decreased.

Both granular content and secretory ability of cord platelets have been examined for defects that might explain the decreased aggregatory response. Initially, reduced cord platelet aggregation was thought to be due to a physiologic storage pool deficiency based on observations of decreased release of platelet nonmetabolic nucleotides (ATP and ADP) and serotonin.[329–332] However, the differences from adult platelets are small and cord platelets can bind and concentrate exogenous ADP and serotonin in their granules normally.[333] More recent electron microscopy studies show similar numbers of granules in cord and adult platelets.[314,334] Thus a classic storage pool deficiency cannot explain the decreased aggregatory response of cord platelets. Neither does it appear to be a problem with agonist receptors as cord platelets have adult numbers of the collagen receptor GPIa/IIa in addition to other GP receptors.[313,327]

An aspirin-like platelet defect is also not present in cord platelets because they show a normal response to AA and formation of products produced by both the lipoxygenase and cyclo-oxygenase pathway.[320,335–337] When cord platelets are mixed with aspirin treated platelets, both groups of platelets aggregate normally, proving that the prostaglandin pathway is intact in newborn platelets and suggesting that the arachidonic acid from cord platelets results in the release of granular content of adult aspirin-treated platelets.[338]

When compared with adult controls, intracellular Ca^{++} released by the platelets of neonates is significantly impaired in response to collagen and thrombin. However, the Ca^{++} content of the dense tubular system is normal, indicating that the observed impairment in Ca^{++} mobilization in neonates is not due to decreased stores of Ca^{++}.[339] Production of PI_3 and protein phosphorylation are normal,[327] but the production of AA is increased in platelets from newborns compared to adult platelets following stimulation by thrombin.[320] The latter may be due to platelet membranes made more reactive by low levels of vitamin E.[340,341] Recent studies show that clot contraction is similar for cord and adult platelets, suggesting that both fibrinogen receptors and contractile cytoskeletons are intact in cord platelets.[342]

Flow cytometry studies show a reduced TXA_2 production in neonates compared to adults, despite normal binding characteristics of the TXA_2 receptor, which suggests an abnormality in the postreceptor signal transduction pathway.[343] In one study, abnormal platelet aggregation in response to ADP (decreased primary wave and absent secondary wave) was observed in cord platelet rich plasma.[344]

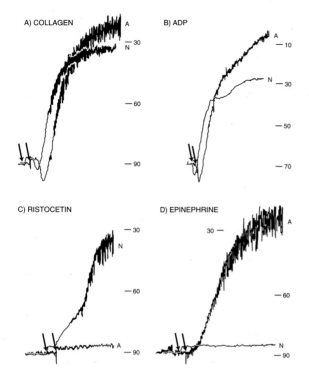

Figure 2–16 Platelet aggregations comparing the response of adult platelets (A) to newborn platelets (N) in response to the following platelet agonists: collagen (A), ADP (B), ristocetin (C), and epinephrine (D).

Reproduced with permission.[355]

However, improved platelet aggregation was seen in newborn platelets drawn 2 hours after birth, with normalization of platelet aggregation at 48 hours.[345] Studies using whole-blood flow cytometry show that, compared with adult platelets, neonatal platelets are hyporeactive to thrombin, a combination of ADP and epinephrine, and a TXA_2 analogue (Figure 2–17).[346,347] The clinical significance of these observations remains unknown.

Platelet Activation during Birth Classically, cord platelets are thought to be in a state of transient dysfunction secondary to platelet activation during birth.[167–169,171] Levels of thromboxane B_2, β-thromboglobulin, and PF-4 are increased in cord blood, suggesting that cord platelets are activated through the prostaglandin pathway and α-granule contents released.[168,169,348] Mechanisms contributing to platelet activation during birth could include thermal changes, stress with adrenergic stimulation, acidosis, hypoxia, and expression of TF.[349] However, recent flow cytometry studies suggest that decreased reactivity of neonatal platelets is not caused by pre-

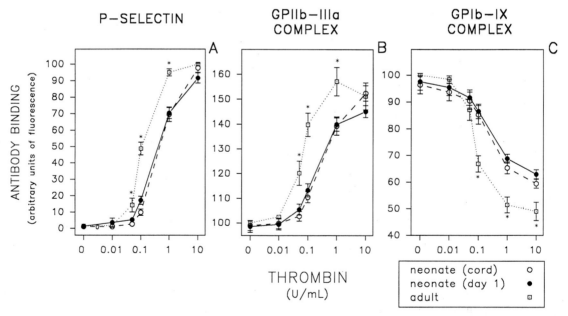

Figure 2–17 Effect of thrombin on the surface expression of P-selectin (A), the glycoprotein IIb-IIIa complex (B), and glycoprotein Ib-IX (C) on neonatal and adult platelets in whole blood. Results were similar for cord and neonatal Day 1 values. Expression of P-selectin and glycoprotein IIb-IIIa complexes were decreased in newborns, whereas glycoprotein Ib-IX expression was relatively preserved in newborns compared with adults following stimulation with thrombin. Data are expressed as mean ± SEM; n = 20. Asterisks indicate $p < 0.05$ for both cord blood and Day 1 neonatal platelets compared with adults platelets.

U/mL = units/mL.

Reproduced with permission.[312]

activation during birth but rather represents a developmental phenomenon.[350] This state of apparent activation has usually resolved by day 10 of life.[351]

REFERENCES

1. Hirsh J, Warkentin TE, Raschkle, et al. Heparin and low-molecular-weight heparin: mechanism of action, pharmacokinetics, dosing considerations, monitoring, efficacy, and safety. Chest 1998;114:489S–510S.
2. Hirsh J, Dalen JE, Anderson DR, et al. Oral anticoagulants: mechanism of action, clinical effectiveness, and optimal therapeutic range. Chest 1998;114:445S–69S.
3. Sutor AH, von Kries R, Cornelissen EAM, et al. Vitamin K deficiency bleeding (VKDB) in infancy. Recommendations by the Perinatal/Pediatric Subcommittee of the International Society of Thrombosis and Haemostasis (ISTH). Thromb Haemost 1999; 81:456–61.
4. Israels LG, Israels ED, Saxena SP. The riddle of vitamin K1 deficit in the newborn. Semin Perinatol 1997; 21:90–6.
5. Andrew, M. The relevance of developmental hemostasis to hemorrhagic disorders of newborns. Semin Perinatol 1997;21:70–85.
6. Jorgensen FS, Fedding P, Vinther S, Andersen GE. Vitamin K in neonates. Peroral versus intramuscular administration. Acta Paediatr 1991;80:304–7.
7. von Kries R. Neonatal vitamin K prophylaxis: the Gordon knot still awaits untying. BMJ 1998;316:161–2.
8. Sutor A, Dagres N, Neiderhoff H. Late form of vitamin K deficiency bleeding in Germany. Klin Padiatr 1995;207:89–97.
9. Von Kries R, Gobel U. Vitamin K prophylaxis and late haemorrhagic disease of newborn (HDN). Acta Paediatr 1992;81:655–7.
10. Sutor, A. Vitamin K deficiency bleeding in infants and children. Semin Thromb Hemost 1995;21:317–29.
11. Mann KG, van't Veer C, Cawthern K, Butenas S. The role of tissue factor pathway in initiation of coagulation. Blood Coagul Fibrinolysis 1998;78:S3–S7.
12. Bauer KA. Activation of the factor VII-tissue factor pathway. Thromb Haemost 1997;78:108–11.
13. Nemerson Y. The reaction between bovine brain tissue factor and factors VII and X. Biochemistry 1966; 501:601–8.
14. Nemerson Y, Repke D. Tissue factor accelerates the activation of coagulation factor VII: the role of a bifunctional coagulation factor. Thromb Res 1985;40:351–8.
15. Rao L, Rapaport S. Activation of factor VII bound to tissue factor: a key early step in the tissue factor pathway of blood coagulation. Proc Natl Acad Sci U S A 1988;85:6687–91.
16. Broze GJ, Majerus P. Purification and properties of human coagulation factor VII. J Biol Chem 1980; 255:1242–7.
17. Zur M, Radcliffe R, Oberdick J, Nemerson Y. The dual role of factor VII in blood coagulation. Initiation and inhibition of a proteolytic system by a zymogen. J Biol Chem 1982;257:5623–31.
18. Kalafatis M, Egan JOq, van't Veer C, et al. The regulation of clotting factors. Crit Rev Eukaryot Gene Expr 1997;7:241–80.
19. Radcliffe R, Nemerson Y. Mechanism of activation of bovine factor VII. Products of cleavage by factor Xa. J Biol Chem 1976;251:4749–802.
20. Radcliffe R, Bagdasarian A, Colman R, Nemerson Y. Activation of bovine factor VII by Hageman factor fragments. Blood 1977;50:611–7.
21. Seligsohn U, Kasper C, Osterud B, Rapaport S. Activated factor VII: presence in factor IX concentrates and persistence in the circulation after infusion. Blood 1978;53:828–37.
22. Radcliffe R, Nemerson Y. Activation and control of factor VII by activated factor X and thrombin. J Biol Chem 1975;250:388–95.
23. Rao LV, Rapaport SI. Cells and the activation of factor VII. Haemostasis 1996;26 Suppl 1:1–5.
24. Guha A, Bach R, Konigsberg W, Nemerson Y. Affinity purification of human tissue factor: interaction of factor VII and tissue factor in detergent micelles. Proc Natl Acad Sci U S A 1986;83:299–302.
25. Astrup T. Assay and content of tissue thromboplastin in different organs. Thromb Diath Haemorrh 1965;14:401–16.
26. Drake T, Morrissey J, Edgington T. Selective cellular expression of tissue factor in human tissues. Implications for disorders of hemostasis and thrombosis. Am J Pathol 1989;134:1087–97.
27. Fleck R, Rao L, Rapaport S, Varki N. Localization of human tissue factor antigen by immunostaining with monospecific, polyclonal anti-human tissue factor antibody. [corrected and republished Thromb Res 1990;59:421–37]. Thromb Res 1990;57:765–82.
28. Nawroth P, Stern D. Modulation of endothelial cell hemostatic properties by tumour necrosis factor. J Exp Med 1986;163:740–5.
29. Bevilacqua M, Pober J, Wheeler M, et al. Interleukin-1 activation of vascular endothelium. Effects on procoagulant activity and leukocyte adhesion. Am J Pathol 1985;121:394–403.
30. Moore K, Andreoli S, Esmon N, et al. Endotoxin enhances tissue factor and suppresses thrombomodulin

expression of human vascular endothelium in vitro. J Clin Invest 1987;79:124–30.

31. Nawroth PP, Waldherr R, Zhang YM, et al. Mechanism of endothelial cell activation. Transplant Proc 1993; 25:2052–3.

32. Stern DM, Esposito C, Gorlach H, et al. Endothelium and regulation of coagulation. Diabetes Care 1991; 14:160–6.

33. Houston P, Dickson MD, Ludbrook V, et al. Fluid shear stress induction of the tissue factor promoter in vitro and in vivo is mediated by Egr-1. Arterioscler Thromb Vasc Biol 1999;19:281–9.

34. Osterud B, Rapaport S. Activation of factor IX by the reaction product of tissue factor and factor VII. Additional pathway for initiating blood coagulation. Proc Natl Acad Sci U S A 1977;74:5260–4.

35. Mariani G, Mazzucconi M. Factor VII congenital deficiency. Clinical picture and classification of the variants. Haemostasis 1983;13:169–77.

36. Roberts HR, Monroe DM, Oliver JA, et al. Newer concepts of blood coagulation. Haemophilia 1998;4: 331–4.

37. von dem Borne PA, Bajzar L, Meijers JC, et al. Thrombin-mediated activation of factor XI results in a thrombin-activable fibrinolysis inhibitor-dependent inhibition of fibrinolysis. J Clin Invest 1997;99: 2323–7.

38. Zhao M, Abdel-Razek T, Sun MF, Gailani D. Characterization of a heparin binding site on the heavy chain of factor XI. J Biol Chem 1998;273:31153–9.

39. Oliver JA, Monroe DM, Roberts HR, Hoffman M. Thrombin activates factor XI on activated platelets in the absence of factor XII. Arterioscler Thromb Vasc Biol 1999;19:170–7.

40. von dem Borne PA, Mosnier LO, Tans G, et al. Factor XI activation by meizothrombin: stimulation by phospholipid vesicles containing both phophatidylserine and phosphatidylethanolamine. Thromb Haemost 1997;78:834–9.

41. Minnema MC, Pajkrt D, Wuillemin WA, et al. Activation of clotting factor XI without detectable contact activation in experimental endotoxemia. Blood 1998;92:3294–301.

42. Baglia FA, Walsh PM. Prothrombin is a cofactor for the binding of factor XI to the platelet surface and for platelet-mediated factor XI activation by thrombin. Biochemistry 1998;37:2271–81.

43. Zhang Y, Scamdura JM, Van Nostrand WE, Walsh PM. The mechanisms by which heparin promotes the inhibition of coagulation factor XIa by protease nexin-2. J Biol Chem 1997;272:26139–44.

44. Mauron T, Lammle B, Wuillemin WA. Influence of low molecular weight heparin and low molecular weight dextran sulfate on the inhibition of coagulation factor XIa by serpins. Thromb Haemost 1998;80: 82–6.

45. Vehar G, Keyt B, Eaton D, et al. Structure of human factor VIII. Nature 1984;312:337–42.

46. Wood W, Capon D, Simonsen C, et al. Expression of active human factor VIII from recombinant DNA clones. Nature 1984;312:330–6.

47. Osterud B, Bouma B, Griffin J. Human blood coagulation factor IX: purification properties and mechanism of activation by factor XI. J Biol Chem 1978; 253:5946–51.

48. Leytus S, Chung D, Kisiel W, et al. Characterization of cDNA coding for human factor X. Proc Natl Acad Sci U S A 1984;81:3699–702.

49. Suttie J, Jackson C. Prothrombin structure, activation and biosynthesis. Physiol Rev 1977;57:1–70.

50. Mann K. Membrane-bound enzyme complexes in blood coagulation. Prog Hemost Thromb 1984;7:1–23.

51. Tracy P. Regulation of thrombin generation at cell surfaces. Semin Thromb Haemost 1988;14:227–33.

52. Tracy P, Peterson J, Nesheim M, et al. Interaction of coagulation factor V and factor Va with platelets. J Biol Chem 1979;254:10354–61.

53. Tracy P, Nesheim M, Mann K. Coordinate binding of factor Va and factor Xa to the instimulated platelet. J Biol Chem 1981;256:743–51.

54. Ofosu FA, Liu L, Feedman J. Control mechanisms in thrombin generation. Semin Thrombos Haemost 1996;22:303–8.

55. Crook M. Platelet prothrombinase in health and disease. Blood Coagul Fibrinolysis 1990;1:167–74.

56. Fenton JI. Structural regions and bioregulatory functions of thrombin. In: Cell proliferation: recent advances. New York: Anonymous Academic Press; 1987;p.133–51.

57. Chang J. Thrombin specificity requirement for apolar amino acids adjacent to the thrombin cleavage site of polypeptide substrate. Eur J Biochem 1985;151: 217–24.

58. Fenton JI, Bing D. Thrombin active-site regions. Semin Thrombos Haemost 1986;12:200–8.

59. Lewis S, Lorand L, Fenton JW II, Shafer J. Catalytic compotence of human α- and γ-thrombin in the activation of fibrinogen and factor XIII. Biochemistry 1987;26:7597–605.

60. Colman RW, Marder VJ, Salzman EW, Hirsh J. Overview of hemostasis. In: Colman RW, Hirsh J, Marder VJ, Salzman EW, editors. Hemostasis and thrombosis: basic principles and clinical practice. Philadelphia: J. B. Lippincott Company; 1994. p. 3–18.

61. Vehar G, Davie E. Preparation and properties of bovine factor VIII (anti-hemophilic factor). Biochemistry 1980;19:401–10.

62. Foster W, Nesheim M, Mann K. The factor Xa-catalyzed activation of factor V. J Biol Chem 1983;258: 13970–7.

63. Suzuki K, Dahlback B, Stenflo J. Thrombin-catalyzed activation of human coagulation factor V. J Biol Chem 1982;257:6556–64.

64. Muszbek L, Adany R, Mikkola H. Novel aspects of blood coagulation factor XIII.I. Structure, distribution, activation, and function. Crit Rev Clin Lab Sci 1996;33:357–421.

65. Devine DB, Bishop PD. Platelet-associated factor XIII in platelet activation, adhesion, and clot stabilization. Semin Thrombos Hemost 1996;22:409–13.

66. McDonagh J. Structure and function of factor XIII. In: Colman RW, Hirsh J, Marder VJ, Salzman EW, editors. Hemostasis and thrombosis: basic principles and clinical practice. Philadelphia: J.B. Lippincott Company; 1994. p. 301–13.

67. Dahlback B. The Protein C Anticoagulant system: inherited defects as basis for venous thrombosis. Thromb Res 1995;77:1–43.

68. Wang W, Boffa MB, Bajzar L, et al. A study of the mechanism of inhibition of fibrinolysis by activated thrombin activable fibrinolysis inhibitor. J Biol Chem 1998;273:27176–81.

69. Bajzar L, Nesheim M, Morser J, Tracey PB. Both cellular and soluble forms of thrombomodulin inhibit fibrinolysis by potentiating the activation of thrombin activable fibrinolysis inhibitor. J Biol Chem 1998; 273:2792–8.

70. Nesheim M, Wang W, Boffa M, et al. Thrombin, thrombomodulin, and TAFI in the molecular link between coagulation and fibrinolysis. Thromb Haemost 1997;78:386–91.

71. Boffa MB, Wang W, Bajzar L, Nesheim ME. Plasma and recombinant thrombin activable fibrinolysis inhibitor (TAFI) and activated TAFI compared with respect to glycosylation, thrombin/thrombomodulin-dependent activation, thermal stability, and enzymatic properties. J Biol Chem 1998;273:2127–35.

72. Kokame K, Zheng X, Sadler JE. Activation of thrombin activable fibrinolysis inhibitor requires epidermal growth factor-like domain 3 of thrombomodulin and is inhibited competitively by protein C. J Biol Chem 1998;273:12135–9.

73. Doolittle, R. The structure and evolution of vertebrate fibrinogen. Ann N Y Acad Sci 1983;408:13–26.

74. Henschen A, Lottspeich F, Kehl M, et al. Covalent structure of fibrinogen. Ann N Y Acad Sci 1983;408: 28–43.

75. Blomback B, Hessel B, Hogg D. Disulfide bridges in NH2-terminal part of human fibrinogen. Thromb Res 1976;8:639–58.

76. Blomback B, Hessel B, Hogg D, et al. A two-step fibrinogen-fibrin transition in blood coagulation. Nature 1978;275:501–5.

77. Budzynski A, Olexa S, Pandya B. Fibrin polymerization sites in fibrinogen and fibrin fragments. Ann N Y Acad Sci 1983;408:301–14.

78. Olexa S, Budzynski A. Evidence for four different polymerization sites involved in human fibrin formation. Proc Natl Acad Sci U S A 1980;77:1374–8.

79. Olexa S, Budzynski A, Doolittle R, et al. Structure of fragment E species from human cross-linked fibrin. Biochemistry 1981;21:6139–45.

80. Carr MJ, Shen L, Hermans J. Mass-length ratio of fibrin fibres from gel permeation and light scattering. Biopolymers 1977;16:1–15.

81. Hantgan R, Fowler W, Erickson H, Hermans J. Fibrin assembly: a comparison of electron microscopic and light scattering results. Thromb Haemost 1980;193: 119–24.

82. Tamaki T, Aoki N. Crosslinking of α_2-plasmin inhibitor and fibronectin to fibrin by fibrin-stabilizing factor. Biochim Biophys Acta 1981;661:280–6.

83. Fenton JI, Olson T, Zabinski M, Wilner GD. Anion-binding exosite of human α-thrombin and fibrin(ogen) recognition. Biochemistry 1988;27: 7106–12.

84. Berliner L, Sugawara Y, Fenton JI. Human α-thrombin binding to non-polymerized fibrin-Sepharose: evidence for an anionic binding region. Biochemistry 1985;24:7005–9.

85. Liu C, Nossel H, Kaplan K. The binding of thrombin by fibrin. J Biol Chem 1979;254:10421–5.

86. Hirsh J. Oral anticoagulant drugs [review article]. N Engl J Med 1991;324:1865–75.

87. Cade J, Hirsh J, Martin M. Placental barrier to coagulation factors: its relevance to the coagulation defect at birth and to haemorrhage in the newborn. BMJ 1969;2:281–3.

88. Kisker C, Robillard J, Clarke W. Development of blood coagulation—a fetal lamb model. Pediatr Res 1981;15:1045–50.

89. Andrew M, O'Brodovich H, Mitchell L. The fetal lamb coagulation system during normal birth. Am J Hematol 1988;28:116–8.

90. Holmberg L, Henriksson P, Ekelund H, Astedt B. Coagulation in the human fetus, comparison with term newborn infants. J Pediatr 1974;85:860–4.

91. Jensen A, Josso S, Zamet P, et al. Evolution of blood clotting factors in premature infants during the first ten days of life: a study of 96 cases with comparison between clinical status and blood clotting factor levels. Pediatr Res 1973;7:638–44.

92. Mibashan R, Rodeck C, Thumpson J, et al. Plasma assay of fetal factors VIIIc and IX for prenatal diagnosis of haemophilia. Lancet 1979;1:1309–11.

93. Forestier F, Daffos F, Galacteros F, et al. Hematological values of 163 normal fetuses between 18 and 30 weeks of gestation. Pediatr Res 1986;20:342–6.

94. Forestier F, Cox WL, Daffos F, Rainaut M. The assessment of fetal blood samples. Am J Obstet Gynecol 1988;158:1184–8.

95. Forestier F, Daffos F, Rainaut M, et al. Vitamin K dependent proteins in fetal hemostasis at mid trimester of pregnancy. Thromb Haemost 1985;53:401–3.

96. Forestier F, Daffos E, Sole Y, Rainaut M. Prenatal diagnosis of hemophilia by fetal blood sampling under ultrasound guidance.Haemostasis 1986;16:346–51.

97. Toulon P, Rainaut M, Aiach M, et al. Antithrombin III (ATIII) and heparin cofactor II (HCII) in normal human fetuses (21st-27th week) [letter]. Thromb Haemost 1986;56:237–8.

98. Barnard D, Simmons M, Hathaway W. Coagulation studies in extremely premature infants. Pediatr Res 1979;13:1330–5.

99. Nossel HL, Lanzkowsky P, Levy S, et al. A study of coagulation factor levels in women during labour and in their newborn infants. Thromb Diath Haemorrh 1966;16:185–97.

100. Reverdiau-Moalic P, Delahousse B, Bardos GBP, et al. Evolution of blood coagulation activators and inhibitors in the healthy human fetus. Blood 1996;88:900–6.

101. Hathaway W, Corrigan J. Report of scientific and standardization subcommittee on neonatal hemostasis. Thromb Haemost 1991;65:323–5.

102. Andrew M, Paes B, Milner R, et al. Development of the human coagulation system in the full-term infant. Blood 1987;70:165–72.

103. Andrew M, Paes B, Milner R, et al. Development of the human coagulation system in the healthy premature infant. Blood 1988;72:1651–7.

104. Andrew M, Vegh P, Johnston M, et al. Maturation of the hemostatic system during childhood. Blood 1992;80:1998–2005.

105. Andrew M, Paes B, Johnston M. Development of the hemostatic system in the neonate and young infant. J Pediatr Hematol Oncol 1990;12:95–104.

106. Corrigan J. Normal hemostasis in fetus and newborn: coagulation. In: Polin R, Fox W, editors. Fetal and neonatal physiology. Philadelphia: W.B. Saunders; 1992. p. 1368–71.

107. Hathaway WE, Bonnar J. Hemostatic disorders of the pregnant woman and newborn infant. New York: Elsevier Science Publishing Co.; 1987.

108. Thomas KB, Sutor AH, Altinkaya N, et al. von Willebrand factor-collagen binding activity is increased in newborns and infants. Acta Paediatr 1995;84:697–9.

109. Katz JA, Moake JL, McPherson PD, et al. Relationship between human development and disappearance of unusually large von Willebrand factor multimers from plasma. Blood 1989;73:1851–8.

110. Weinstein M, Blanchard R, Moake J, et al. Fetal and neonatal von Willebrand factor (vWF) is unusually large and similar to the vWF in patients with thrombotic thrombocytopenia purpura. Br J Haematol 1989;72:68–72.

111. Andrew M, Schmidt B, Mitchell L, et al. Thrombin generation in newborn plasma is critically dependent on the concentration of prothrombin. Thromb Haemost 1990;63:27–30.

112. Vieira A, Ofosu F, Andrew M. Heparin sensitivity and resistance in the neonate: an explanation. Thromb Res 1991;63:85–99.

113. Shah J, Mitchell L, Paes B, et al. Thrombin inhibition is impaired in plasma of sick neonates. Pediatr Res 1992;31:391–5.

114. Schmidt B, Mitchell L, Ofosu F, Andrew M. Alpha$_2$-macroglobulin is an important progressive inhibitor of thrombin in neonatal and infant plasma. Thromb Haemost 1989;62:1074–7.

115. Schmidt B, Ofosu F, Mitchell L, et al. Anticoagulant effects of heparin in neonatal plasma. Pediatr Res 1989;25:405–8.

116. Pinto M, Mitchell L, McCusker P, Andrew M. Standardization of prothrombin times in newborns. J Pediatr 1993;123:310–2.

117. Witt I, Muller H, Kunter LJ. Evidence for the existence of fetal fibrinogen. Thromb Diath Haemorrh 1969;22:101–9.

118. Hamulyak K, Nieuwenhuizen W, Devillee PP, Hemker HC. Re-evaluation of some properties of fibrinogen purified from cord blood of normal newborns. Thromb Res 1983;32:301–20.

119. Galanakis DK, Mosesson MW. Evaluation of the role of in vivo proteolysis (fibrinogenolysis) in prolonging the thrombin time of human umbilical cord fibrinogen. Blood 1976;48:109–18.

120. Andrew M, Mitchell L, Berry L, et al. Fibrinogen has a rapid turnover in the healthy newborn lamb. Pediatr Res 1988;23:249–52.

121. Gralnick HR, Gilvelber H, Abrams E. Dysfibrinogenemia associated with hepatoma. Increased carbohydrate content of the fibrinogen molecule. N Engl J Med 1978;299:221–6.

122. Andrew M, Mitchell L, Vegh P, Ofosu F. Thrombin regulation in children differs from adults in the absence and presence of heparin. Thromb Haemost 1994;72:836–42.

123. Hultin MB. Fibrinogen and factor VII as risk factors in vascular disease. In Progress in Hemostasis and Thrombosis. Prog Hemostas Thromb 1991;215–41.

124. Shapiro S, Anderson D. Thrombin inhibition in normal plasma. In: Lundblad R, Fenton J, Mann K, editors.

Chemistry and biology of thrombin. Ann Arbor, MI: Ann Arbor Science Publishing; 1977. p. 361–74.

125. Downing M, Bloom J, Mann K. Comparison of the inhibition of thrombin by three protease inhibitors. Biochemistry 1978;17:2649–53.

126. Takada A, Koide T, Takada Y. Interaction of thrombin with antithrombin III and α_2 macroglobulin in the plasma. Thromb Res 1979;16:59–68.

127. Rosenberg RD, Rosenberg JS. Natural anticoagulant mechanisms. J Clin Invest 1984;74:1–6.

128. Rinderknecht M, Drokas M. Role of α_2-macroglobulin in haemostatic balance. Nature 1972;239:116.

129. Fischer A. Respective roles of ATIII and α_2M in thrombin inactivation. Thromb Haemost 1981;45:51–4.

130. Tollefsen DM, Petska CA, Monafo WJ. Activation of heparin cofactor II by dermatan sulfate. J Biol Chem 1983;258:6713–6.

131. Heinegard D, Bjorne-Persson A, Coster L, et al. The core proteins of large and small interstitial proteoglycans from various connective tissues from distinct subgroups. Biochem J 1985;230:181–94.

132. Fernandez F, Van Ryn J, Ofosu FA, et al. The hemorrhagic and antithrombotic effects of dermatan sulphate. Br J Haematol 1986;64:309–17.

133. Merton R, Thomas D. Experimental studies on the relative efficacy of dermatan sulfate and heparin as antithrombotic agents. Thromb Haemost 1987;58:839–42.

134. Maggi A, Abbadini M, Pagella P, et al. Antithrombotic properties of dermatan sulfate in a rat venous thrombosis model. Haemostasis 1987;17:329–35.

135. Hoppensteadt D, Racanelli A, Walenga J, Fareed J. Comparative antithrombotic and hemorrhagic effects of dermatan sulfate, heparin sulfate and heparin. Semin Thrombos Hemost 1989;15:378–85.

136. Esmon CT, Owen WG. Identification of an endothelial cell cofactor for thrombin-catalyzed activation of protein C. Proc Natl Acad Sci U S A 1981;78:2249–54.

137. Esmon N. Thrombomodulin. Prog Hemost Thromb 1989;9:29–55.

138. Esmon C, Esmon N, Harris K. Complex formation between thrombin and thrombomodulin inhibits both thrombin-catalyzed fibrin formation and factor V activation. J Biol Chem 1982;257:7944–51.

139. Hofsteenge J, Taguchi H, Stone S. Effect of thrombomodulin on the kinetics of the interaction of thrombin with substrates and inhibitors. Biochemistry 1986;237:243–51.

140. Esmon N, Carroll R, Esmon C. Thrombomodulin blocks the ability of thrombin to activate platelets. J Biol Chem 1983;258:12238–42.

141. Esmon N, Owen W, Esmon C. Isolation of a membrane-bound cofactor for thrombin-catalyzed activation of protein C. J Biol Chem 1982;257:859–64.

142. Suzuki K, Nishioka J, Kusmoto H, Hashimoto S. Protein S is essential for the activated protein C-catalysed inaction of platelet-associated factor Va. J Biochem 1983;96:455–60.

143. Suzuki K, Nishioka J, Kusumoto H, Hashimoto S. Mechanism of inhibition of activated protein C by protein C inhibitor. J Biochem 1984;95:187–95.

144. van der Meer FJM, van Tilburg NH, Van Wijngaarden A, et al. A second plasma inhibitor of activated protein C: alpha-1-antitrypsin. Thromb Haemost 1989;62:756–62.

145. Bajaj M, Kuppuswamy M, Saito H, et al. Cultured normal human hepatocytes do not synthesize lipoprotein-associated coagulation inhibitor: evidence that endothelium is the principal site of its synthesis. Proc Natl Acad Sci U S A 1990;87:8869–73.

146. Novotny W, Girard T, Miletich J, Broze GJ. Purification and characterization of the lipoprotein-associated coagulation inhibitor from human plasma. J Biol Chem 1989;264:18832–7.

147. Wun T, Kretzmer K, Girard T, et al. Cloning and characterization of a cDNA coding for the lipoprotein-associated coagulation inhibitor shows that it consists of three tandem Kunitz-type inhibitory domains. J Biol Chem 1988;263:6001–4.

148. Rao L, Rapaport S. Studies of a mechanism inhibiting the initiation of the extrinsic pathway of coagulation. Blood 1987;69:645–51.

149. Broze GJ, Warren L, Novotny W, et al. The lipoprotein-associated coagulation inhibitor that inhibits factor VII-tissue factor complex also inhibits Xa: insight into its possible mechanism of action. Blood 1988;71:335–43.

150. Warn-Cramer B, Rao L, Maki S, Rapaport S. Modifications of extrinsic pathway inhibitor (EPI) and factor Xa that affect their ability to interact and to inhibit factor VIIa/tissue factor: evidence for a two-step model of inhibition. Thromb Haemost 1988;60:453–6.

151. Weitz J, Hudoba M, Massel D, et al. Clot-bound thrombin is protected from inhibition by heparin-antithrombin III but is susceptible to inactivation by antithrombin III independent inhibitors. J Clin Invest 1990;86:385–91.

152. Ganrot P, Schersten B. Serum α_2-macroglobulin concentration and its variation with age and sex. Clin Chim Acta 1967;15:113–20.

153. Mitchell L, Piovella F, Ofosu F, Andrew M. Alpha$_2$-macroglobulin may provide protection from thromboembolic events in antithrombin III deficient children. Blood 1991;78:2299–304.

154. Andrew M, Mitchell L, Paes B, et al. An anticoagulant dermatan sulphate proteoglycan circulates in the pregnant women and her fetus. J Clin Invest 1992;89:321–6.

155. Delorme M, Xu L, Berry L, et al. Anticoagulant dermatan sulfate proteoglycan (Decorin) in the term human placenta. Thromb Res 1998;90:147–53.

156. Greffe BS, Marlar RA, Manco-Johnson M. Neonatal protein C: molecular composition and distribution in normal term infants. Thromb Res 1989;56:91–8.

157. Manco-Johnson M, Spedale S, Peters M, et al. Identification of a unique form of protein C in the ovine fetus: developmentally linked transition to the adult form. Pediatr Res 1995;37:365–72.

158. Moalic P, Gruel Y, Body G, et al. Levels and plasma distribution of free and c_4b-BP-bound Protein S in human fetuses and full-term newborns. Thromb Res 1988;49:471–80.

159. Schwarz HP, Muntean W, Watzke H, et al. Low total protein S antigen but high protein S activity due to decreased c_4b-binding protein in neonates. Blood 1988;71:562–5.

160. Tait R, Walker I, Islam S, et al. Age related changes in protein C activity in healthy adult males. Thromb Haemost 1991;65:326–7.

161. Knofler R, Hofmann S, Weissbach G, et al. Molecular markers of the endothelium, the coagulation and the fibrinolytic systems in healthy newborns. Semin Thromb Hemost 1998;24:453–61.

162. Yurdakok M, Yigit S, Aliefendioglu D, et al. Plasma thrombomodulin levels in early respiratory distress syndrome. Turk J Pediatr 1998;40:85–8.

163. Distefano G, Romeo MG, Betta P, et al. Thrombomodulin serum levels in ventilated preterm babies with respiratory distress syndrome. Eur J Pediatr 1998;157:327–30.

164. Yurdakok M, Yigit S. Plasma thrombomodulin, plasminogen activator and plasminogen activator inhibitor levels in preterm infants with or without respiratory distress syndrome. Acta Paediatr 1997;86:1022–3.

165. Nako Y, Ohki Y, Harigaya A, et al. Plasma thrombomodulin level in very low birthweight infants at birth. Acta Paediatr 1997;86:1105–9.

166. Warr T, Warn-Cramer B, Rao L, Rapaport S. Human plasma extrinsic pathway inhibitor activity: I. Standardization of assay and evaluation of physiologic variables. Blood 1989;74:201–6.

167. Yuen PMP, Yin JA, Lao TTH. Fibrino peptide A levels in maternal and newborn plasma. Eur J Obstet Gynecol 1989;30:239–44.

168. Suarez CR, Gonzalez J, Menendez C, et al. Neonatal and maternal platelets: activation at time of birth. Am J Hematol 1988;29:18–21.

169. Suarez CR, Menendez CE, Walenga JM, Fareed J. Neonatal and maternal hemostasis. Value of molecular markers in the assessment of hemostatic status. Semin Thromb Hemost 1984;10:280–4.

170. Schmidt B. Antithrombin III deficiency in neonatal respiratory distress syndrome. Blood Coagul & Fibrinolysis 1994;5:S13–S64.

171. Suarez CR, Walenga J, Mangogna LC, Fareed J. Neonatal and maternal fibrinolysis: activation at time of birth. Am J Hematol 1985;19:365–72.

172. Bauer K, Weiss L, Sparrow D, et al. Aging-associated changes in indices of thrombin generation and protein C activation in humans. J Clin Invest 1987;80:1527–34.

173. Cohen L, McKinnell J, Puglisi V, et al. Prothrombin synthesis in the adult and fetal liver. Thromb Hemost 1997;78:1468–72.

174. Soifer SJ, Peters KG, O'Keefe J, Coughlin SR. Disparate temporal expression of the prothrombin and thrombin receptor genes during mouse development. Am J Pathol 1994;144:60–9.

175. Niessen RWLM, Lamping RJ, Peters M, et al. Fetal and neonatal development of antithrombin III plasma activity and liver messenger RNA levels in sheep. Pediatr Res 1996;39:685–91.

176. Hassan H, Leonardi C, Chelucci C, et al. Blood coagulation factors in human embryonic-fetal development: preferential expression of the FVII/tissue factor pathway. Blood 1990;76:1158–64.

177. Karpatkin M, Blei F, Hurlet A, et al. Prothrombin expression in the adult and fetal rabbit liver. Pediatr Res 1991;30:266–9.

178. Mazzorana M, Baffet G, Kneip B, et al. Expression of coagulation factor V gene by normal adult human hepatocytes in primary culture. Br J Haematol 1991;78:229–35.

179. Kisker CT, Perlman S, Bohlken D, Wicklund D. Measurement of prothrombin mRNA during gestation and early neonatal development. J Lab Clin Med 1988;112:407–12.

180. Feusner JH, Slichter SJ, Harker LA. Acquired haemostatic defects in the ill newborn. Br J Haematol 1983;53:73–84.

181. Karitzky D, Kleine N, Pringsheim W, Kunzer W. Fibrinogen turnover in the premature infant with and without idiopathic respiratory distress syndrome. Acta Paediatr 1971;60:465–70.

182. Schmidt B, Wais U, Pringsheim W, Kunzer W. Plasma elimination of antithrombin III is accelerated in term newborn infants. Eur J Pediatr 1984;141:225–7.

183. Pencharz PB, Steffee WP, Cochran W, et al. Protein metabolism in human neonates: nitrogen-balance studies, estimated obligatory losses of nitrogen and whole-body turnover of nitrogen. Clin Sci Mol Med 1977;52:485–98.

184. Andrew M, O'Brodovich H, Mitchell L. The fetal lamb coagulation system during birth asphyxia. Am J Hematol 1988;28:201–4.

185. Nesheim M. Fibrinolysis and the plasma carboxypeptidase. Curr Opin Hematol 1998;5:309–13.

186. Ridker PM. Fibrinolytic and inflammatory markers for arterial occlusion: the evolving epidemiology of thrombosis and hemostasis. Thromb Haemost 1997; 78:53–9.

187. Humphries SE, Panaloo A, Montgomery HE, et al. Gene-environment interaction in the determination of levels of haemostatic variables involved in thrombosis and fibrinolysis. Thromb Haemost 1997;78: 457–61.

188. Lijen HR. Pathophysiology of the plasminogen/plasmin system. Int J Clin Lab Res 1996;26:1–6.

189. Wallen P, Wiman B. Characterization of human plasminogen. I. On the relationship between different molecular forms of plasminogen demonstrated in plasma and found in purified preparation. Biochim Biophys Acta 1970;221:20–30.

190. Wiman B, Wallen P. The specific interaction between plasminogen and fibrin. A physiological role of the lysine binding site in plasminogen. Thromb Res 1977;10:213–22.

191. Wiman B, Collen D. On the kinetics of the reaction between human antiplasmin and plasmin. Eur J Biochem 1978;84:573–84.

192. Wiman B, Collen D. Molecular mechanism of physiological fibrinolysis. Nature 1978;272:549–50.

193. Collen D, Lijnen HR. Basic and clinical aspects of fibrinolysis and thrombolysis. Blood 1991;78: 3114–24.

194. Collen D. On the regulation and control of fibrinolysis. Thromb Haemost 1980;43:77–89.

195. Pennica D, Holmes W, Kohr W, et al. Cloning and expression of human tissue-type plasminogen activator cDNA in E. coli. Nature 1983;301:214–21.

196. Wun T, Capuano A. Initiation and regulation of fibrinolysis in human plasma at the plasminogen activator level. Blood 1987;69:1354–62.

197. Holmes W, Pennica D, Blaber M, et al. Cloning and expression of the gene for pro-urokinase in Escherichia coli. Biotechnology 1985;3:923–4.

198. Collen D, Zamarron C, Lijnen H, Hoylaerts M. Activation of plasminogen by pro-urokinase. II. Kinetics. J Biol Chem 1986;261:1259–66.

199. Lijnen H, Zamarron C, Blaber M, et al. Activation of plasminogen by pro-urokinase. I. Mechanism. J Biol Chem 1986;261:1253–8.

200. Lijnen H, Van Hoef B, De Cock F, Collen D. The mechanism of plasminogen activation and fibrin dissolution by single chain urokinase-type plasminogen activator in a plasma milieu in vitro. Blood 1989;73: 1864–72.

201. Declerck P, Lijnen H, Verstreken M, et al. A monoclonal antibody specific for two chain urokinase-type plasminogen activator. Application to the study of the mechanism of clot lysis with single-chain urokinase-type plasminogen activator in plasma. Blood 1990;75:1794–800.

202. Holmes W, Nelles L, Lijnen H, Collen D. Primary structure of human alpha$_2$-antiplasmin, a serine protease inhibitor (serpin). J Biol Chem 1987;262: 1659–64.

203. Anonick P, Gonias S. Soluble fibrin preparations inhibit the reaction of plasmin with α_2-macroglobulin. Biochem J 1991;275:53–9.

204. Pannekoek H, Veerman H, Lambers H, et al. Endothelial plasminogen activator inhibitor (PAI): a new member of the serpin gene family. EMBO J 1986; 5:2539–44.

205. Heeb M, Espana F, Geiger M, et al. Immunological identity of heparin-dependent plasma and urinary protein C inhibitor and plasminogen activator inhibitor III. J Biol Chem 1987;262:15813–6.

206. Redlitz A, Nicolini FA, Malycky JL, et al. Inducible carboxypeptidase activity: a role in clot lysis in vivo. Circulation 1996;93:1328–30.

207. Bajzar L, Morser J, Nesheim M. TAFI, or plasma procarboxypeptidase B, couples the coagulation and fibrinolytic cascades through the thrombin-thrombomodulin complex. J Biol Chem 1996;271:16603–8.

208. Bajzar L, Manuel R, Nesheim ME. Purification and characterization of TAFI, a thrombin-activable fibrinolysis inhibitor. Thromb Haemost 1995;270: 14477–84.

209. Valnickova Z, Thogersen IB, Christensen S, et al. Activated human plasma carboxypeptidase B is retained in the blood by binding to alpha$_2$-macroglobulin and pregnancy zone protein. J Biol Chem 1996;271: 12937–43.

210. Kluft C, Jie A, Lowe G, Blamey S. Association between postoperative hyper-response in t-PA inhibition and deep vein thrombosis. Thromb Haemost 1986;56: 107–8.

211. Angles-Cano E, Arnoux D, Boutiere B. Release pattern of the vascular plasminogen activator and its inhibitor in human post-venous occlusion plasma as assessed by a spectrophotometric solid-phase fibrin t-PA activity assay. Thromb Haemost 1987;58:843–9.

212. Levin E, Marotti K, Santell L. Protein kinase C and the stimulation of tissue plasminogen activator release from human endothelial cells. Dependence on the elevation of messenger RNA. J Biol Chem 1989; 264:16030–6.

213. van Hinsbergh V, Kooistra T, Kookwijk P. Regulation of plasminogen activator production by endothelial cells: role in fibrinolysis and local proteolysis. Int J Radiat Biol 1991;60(1-2):261–72.

214. Falkon L, Gari M, Borrell M, Fontcuberta J. The release of plasminogen activators (t-PA and u-PA) and plas-

minogen activator inhibitor (PAI-1) after venous stasis. Blood Coagul and Fibrinolysis 1992;3:33–8.

215. Aballi A, de Lamerens S. Coagulation changes in the neonatal period and in early infancy. Pediatr Clin North Am 1962;9:785–817.

216. Corrigan J. Neonatal thrombosis and the thrombolytic system. Pathophysiology and therapy. J Pediatr Hematol Oncol 1988;10:83–91.

217. Corrigan J, Sluth J, Jeter M, Lox C. Newborn's fibrinolytic mechanism: components and plasmin generation. Am J Hematol 1989;32:273–8.

218. Kolindewala JK, Das BK, Dube B, Bhargava B. Blood fibrinolytic activity in neonates: effect of period of gestation, birth weight, anoxia and sepsis. Indian J Pediatr 1987;24:1029–33.

219. Runnebaum IB, Maurer SM, Daly L, Bonnar J. Inhibitors and activators of fibrinolysis during and after childbirth in maternal and cord blood. J Perinat Med 1989;17:113–9.

220. Ambrus C, Jung O, Ambrus J, et al. The fibrinolysin system and its relationship to disease in the newborn. J Pediatr Hematol Oncol 1979;1:251–60.

221. Edelberg JM, Enghild JJ, Pizzo SV, Gonzalez-Gronow M. Neonatal plasminogen displays altered cell surface binding and activation kinetics. Correlation with increased glycosylation of the protein. J Clin Invest 1990;86:107–12.

222. Summaria L. Comparison of human normal, full-term, fetal and adult plasminogen by physical and chemical analyses. Haemostasis 1989;19:266–73.

223. Astedt B, Lindoff C. Plasminogen activators and plasminogen activator inhibitors in plasma of premature and term infants. Acta Paediatr 1997;86:111–3.

224. Siegbahn A, Ruusuvaara L. Age dependence of blood fibrinolytic components and the effects of low-dose oral contraceptives on coagulation and fibrinolysis in teenagers. Thromb Haemost 1988;60:361–4.

225. Markarian M, Githens J, Jackson J, et al. Fibrinolytic activity in premature infants. Relationship of the enzyme system to the respiratory distress syndrome. Am J Dis Child 1967;113:312–21.

226. Ekelund H, Hedner U, Nilsson I. Fibrinolysis in newborns. Acta Paediatr 1970;59:33–43.

227. Andrew M, Brooker L, Paes B, Weitz J. Fibrin clot lysis by thrombolytic agents is impaired in newborns due to a low plasminogen concentration. Thromb Haemost 1992;68:325–30.

228. Ries M, Klinge J, Rauch R. Age-related reference values for activation markers of the coagulation and fibrinolytic systems in children. Thromb Res 1997;85:341–4.

229. Ranby M, Bergsdorf N, Nilsson T, et al. Age dependence of tissue plasminogen activator concentrations in plasma, as studied by an improved enzyme-linked immunosorbent assay. Clin Chem 1986;32:2160–5.

230. Sherry S, Marder V. Thrombosis, fibrinolysis, and thrombolytic therapy: a perspective. Prog Cardiovasc Dis 1991;34(2):89–100.

231. Hashimoto Y, Kobayashi A, Yamazaki N, et al. Relationship between age and plasma t-PA, PA-inhibitor and PA activity. Thromb Res 1987;46:625–33.

232. Aillaud M, Pignol F, Alessi M, et al. Increase in plasma concentration of plasminogen activator inhibitor, fibrinogen, von Willebrand factor, factor VIII: C and in erythrocyte sedimentation rate with age. Thromb Haemost 1986;55:330–2.

233. Krishnamurti C, Tang D, Barr C, Alving B. Plasminogen activator and plasminogen activator inhibitor activities in a reference population. Am J Clin Pathol 1988;89:747–52.

234. Takada Y, Takada A. Plasma levels of t-PA, free PAI-1 and a complex of t-PA with PAI-I in human males and females at various ages. Thromb Res 1989;55:601–9.

235. Takada A, Takada Y, Urano T, et al. Fluctuations of euglobulin lysis time, tissue plasminogen activator, and free and total plasminogen activator inhibitor levels in plasma in daytime. Thromb Res 1990;57:13–20.

236. Kluft C, Jie F, Rijken D, Verheijen J. Daytime fluctuations in blood of tissue-type plasminogen activator (t-PA) and its fast-acting inhibitor (PAI-1). Thromb Haemost 1988;59:329–32.

237. Rosing D, Brakman P, Redwood D, et al. Blood fibrinolytic activity in man. Diurnal variation and the response to varying intensities of exercise. Circ Res 1970;27:171–84.

238. van Hinsbergh V, Sprengers E, Kooistra T. Effect of thrombin on the production of plasminogen activators and PA inhibitor-1 by human foreskin microvascular endothelial cells. Thromb Haemost 1987;57:148–53.

239. Rao GH, Rao AS, White JG. Aspirin in ischemic heart disease. An overview. Indian Heart J 1993;45:73–9.

240. Harker L. Platelet survival time: its measurement and use. In: Progress in Hemostasis and Thrombosis. New York: Grune & Stratton; 1978. p. 321–47.

241. Morin R. The role of phospholipids in platelet function. Ann Clin Lab Sci 1980;10:463–73.

242. Marcus A. The role of lipids in platelet function: with particular reference to the arachidonic acid pathway. J Lipid Res 1978;19:793–826.

243. Gachet C, Hechler B, Leon C, et al. Activation of ADP receptors and platelet function. Thromb Haemost 1997;78:271–5.

244. Levy-Toledano S, Gallet C, Nadal F, et al. Phosphorylation and dephosphorylation mechanisms in platelet function: a tightly regulated balance. Thromb Haemost 1997;78:226–33.

245. Schmitz G, Rothe G, Ruf A, et al. European working group on clinical cell analysis: consensus protocol for

the flow cytometric characterization of platelet function. Thromb Haemost 1998;79:885–9.

246. Cox D. Methods for monitoring platelet function. Am Heart J 1998;135:S160–9.

247. White J, Gerrard J. Interaction of microtubules and microfilaments in platelet contractile physiology. In: Gabinani G, Jasmin G, Cantini M, editors. Methods and achievements in experimental pathology. Basel: Karger; 1979. p. 1–39.

248. Ikeda Y, Steiner M. Phosphorylation and protein kinase activity of platelet tubulin. J Biol Chem 1979;254: 66–74.

249. Files J, Malpass T, Yee E. Studies of human platelet α-granule release in vivo. Blood 1981;58:607–18.

250. Nurden A, Kunicki T, Dupuis D. Specific protein and glycoprotein deficiencies in platelets isolated from two patients with the gray platelet syndrome. Blood 1982;59:709–18.

251. Barber A, Kaser-Glanzmann R, Jakabova M. Characterization of chondroitin 4-sulfate proteoglycan carrier for heparin neutralizing activity (PF4) released from human blood platelets. Biochim Biophys Acta 1972;286:312–29.

252. Dawes J, Smith R, Pepper D. The release, distribution and clearance of human β-thromboglobulin and platelet factor 4. Thromb Res 1978;12:851–61.

253. Lawler J, Slayter H, Coligan J. Isolation and characterization of a high molecular weight protein from human blood platelets. J Biol Chem 1978;253: 8609–16.

254. Hardisty R. Disorders of platelet secretion. Baillieres Clin Haematol 1989;2:673–93.

255. de Groot P. Platelet adhesion. Br J Haematol 1990;75: 308–12.

256. Ikeda H. Cell adhesion molecule. Jap J Clin Med 1998; 56:2493–9.

257. Tsai WB, Horbett TA. The role of fibronectin in platelet adhesion to plasma preadsorbed polystyrene. J Biomater Sci Polym Ed 1998;10:163–81.

258. Ginsberg M, Loftus J, Plow E. Cytoadhesion, integrins and platelets. Thromb Haemost 1988;59:1–6.

259. Sixma J, Nievelstein P, Houdijk W, et al. Adhesion of blood platelets to isolated components of the vessel wall. Ann N Y Acad Sci 1987;509:103–17.

260. De Chrisofaro R, De Candia E. Thrombin interaction with platelet GpIb: structural mapping and effects on platelet interaction. Int J Mol Med 1999;3: 363–71.

261. Igarashi Y, Yatomi Y. Sphingosine 1-phosphate is a blood constituent released from activated platelets, possibly playing a variety of physiological and pathophysiological roles. Acta Biochim Pol 1998;45: 299–309.

262. Puri RN. Phospholipase A2: its role in ADP- and thrombin-induced platelet activation mechanisms. Int J Biochem Cell Biol 1998;30:1107–22.

263. Ferroni P, Pulcinelli FM, Lenti L, Fazzaniga PP. Is soluble P-selectin determination a more reliable marker of in vivo platelet activation than CD62P flow cytometry analysis? Thromb Haemost 1998;81:472–3.

264. Kroll, M. Schafer A. Biochemical mechanisms of platelet activation. Blood 1989;74:1181–95.

265. Casey P, Gilman A. G protein involvement in receptor-effector coupling. J Biol Chem 1988;263:2577–80.

266. Neer E, Clapham D. Roles of G protein subunits in transmembrane signalling. Nature 1988;333:129–34.

267. Feinstein M, Zavoico G, Halenda S. Calcium and cyclic AMP: antagonistic modulators of platelet function. In: Longenecker G, editor. The platelets - physiology and pharmacology. San Diego: Academic Press; 1985. p. 237–55.

268. Berridge M. Inositol trisphosphate and diacylglycerol: two interacting second messengers. Annu Rev Biochem 1987;56:159–93.

269. Majerus P, Connolly T, Deckmyn H, et al. The metabolism of phosphoinositide-derived messenger molecules. Science 1986;234:1519–26.

270. Siess W. Molecular mechanisms of platelet activation. Physiol Rev 1989;69:58–178.

271. Hathaway D, Adelstein R. Human platelet myosin light chain kinase requires the calcium-binding protein calmodulin for activity. Proc Natl Acad Sci U S A 1979;76:1653–7.

272. Fox J, Goll D, Reynolds C, Phillips D. Identification of two proteins (actin-binding protein and p235) that are hydrolyzed by endogenous Ca+-dependent protease during platelet aggregation. J Biol Chem 1985;260:1060–6.

273. Billah M, Lapetina E, Cuatrecasas P. Phospholipase A2 and phospholipase C activities of platelets. J Biol Chem 1980;255:10227–31.

274. Rittenhouse S, Horne W. Ionomycin can elevate intraplatelet Ca2+ and activate phospholipase A2 without activating phospholipase C. Biochem Biophys Res Commun 1984;123:393–7.

275. Puri RM. Phospholipase A2: its role in ADP- and thrombin-induced platelet activation mechanisms. Int J Biochem Cell Biol 1998;30:1107–22.

276. Nishizuka Y. Studies and perspectives of protein kinase C. Science 1986;233:305–12.

277. Halenda S, Rehm A. Thrombin and C-kinase activators potentiate calcium-stimulated arachidonic acid release in human platelets. Biochem J 1987;248: 471–5.

278. Chang J, Musser J, McGregor H. Phospholipase A2: function and pharmacological regulation. Biochem Pharmacol 1987;36:2429–36.

279. Prescott S, Majerus P. The fatty acid composition of phosphatidylinositol from thrombin-stimulated human platelets. J Biol Chem 1981;256:579–82.

280. Lagarde M. Metabolism of fatty acids by platelets and the functions of various metabolites in mediating platelet function. Prog Lipid Res 1988;27:135–52.

281. Needleman P, Turk J, Jakschik B, et al. Arachidonic acid metabolism. Annu Rev Biochem 1986;55:69–102.

282. Aharony D, Smith J, Silver M. Regulation of arachidonate-induced platelet aggregation by the lipoxygenase product, 12-hydroperoxyeicosatetraenoic acid. Biochim Biophys Acta 1982;718:193–200.

283. Croset M, Lagarde M. Stereospecific inhibition of PGH2-induced platelet aggregation by lipoxygenase products of icosaenoic acids. Biochem Biophys Res Commun 1983;112:878–83.

284. Leistikow EA. Platelet internalization in early thrombogenesis. Semin Thromb Hemost 1996;22:289–94.

285. George J, Shattil S. The clinical importance of acquired abnormalities of platelet function. N Engl J Med 1991;324:27–39.

286. Larsen E, Celi A, Gilbert G, et al. PADGEM protein: a receptor that mediates the interaction of activated platelets with neutrophils and monocytes. Cell 1989;59:305–12.

287. Merhi Y, Provost P, Chauvet P, et al. Selectin blockade reduces neutrophil interaction with platelets at the site of deep arterial injury by angioplasty in pigs. Arterioscler Thromb Vasc Biol 1999;19:372–7.

288. Ginsberg M, Loftus J, Plow E. Platelet and adhesion receptor superfamily. In: Jamieson G, editor. Platelet membrane receptors: molecular biology, immunology, biochemistry, and pathology. Proceedings of the American Red Cross Society held in Washington, D.C., October 22-27, 1987. New York: Liss, AR; 1988.p. 171–95.

289. Colman R, Cook J, Niewiarowski S. Mechanisms of platelet aggregation. In: Colman RW, Hirsh J, Marder VJ, Salzman EW, editors. Hemostasis and thrombosis: basic principles and clinical practice. Philadelphia: J.B. Lippincott Company; 1994. p. 508–23.

290. Sims P, Wiedmer T, Esmon C, et al. Assembly of the platelet prothrombinase complex is linked to vesiculation of the platelet plasma membrane: studies in Scott syndrome: an isolated defect in platelet procoagulant activity. J Biol Chem 1989;264:17049–57.

291. Comfurius P, Senden J, Tilly R, et al. Loss of membrane phospholipid asymmetry in platelets and red cells may be associated with calcium-induced shedding of plasma membrane and inhibition of aminophospholipid translocase. Biochim Biophys Acta 1990;1026:153–60.

292. Walsh P. Platelet-coagulant protein interactions. In: Coleman R, Hirsh J, Marder V, Salzman EW, editors. Hemostasis and thrombosis: basic principles and clinical practice. Philadelphia: J.P. Lippincott; 1994. p. 629–51.

293. Jacqz EM, Barrow SE, Dollery CT. Prostacyclin concentrations in cord blood and in the newborn. Pediatrics 1985;76:954–7.

294. Nitschman E, Berry L, Bridge L, et al. Morphological and biochemical features affecting the antithrombotic properties of the inferior vena cava in adult rabbits and rabbit pups. Pediatr Res 1998;43:1–6.

295. Nitschmann E, Monagel P, Andrew M. Morphological and biochemical features affecting the antithrombotic properties of the aorta of adult rabbits and rabbit pups. Thromb Haemost 1998;79:1034–40.

296. Ling Xu, Delorme M, Berry L, et al. Alpha$_2$-macroglobulin remains as important as antithrombin III for thrombin regulation in cord plasma in the presence of endothelial cell surfaces. Pediatr Res 1995;37:373–8.

297. Nash MC, Wade AM, Shah V, Dillon MJ. Normal levels of soluble E-selectin, soluble intercellular adhesion molecule-1 (sICAM-1), and soluble vascular adhesion molecule (sVCAM-1) decrease with age. Clin Exp Immunol 1996;103:167–70.

298. Cheung PY, Salas E, Schulz R, Radomski MW. Nitric oxide and platelet function: implications for neonatology. Semin Perinatol 1997;21:409–17.

299. Michelson AD. Platelet function in the newborn. Semin Thromb Hemost 1998;24:507–12.

300. Ohshige A, Yoshimura T, Maeda T, et al. Increased platelet-activating factor-acetylhydrolase activity in the umbilical venous plasma of growth-restricted fetus. Obstet Gynecol 1999;93:180–3.

301. Irken G, Mutafoglu UK, Olgun N, et al. Platelet activation during the early neonatal period. Biol Neonate 1998;73:166–71.

302. Beverley DW, Inwood MJ, Chance GW, et al. "Normal" haemostasis parameters: a study in a well-defined inborn population of preterm infants. Early Hum Dev 1984;9:249–57.

303. Arad ID, Alpan G, Sznajderman SD, Eldor A. The mean platelet volume (MVP) in the neonatal period. Am J Perinatol 1986;3:1–3.

304. Kipper S, Sieger L. Whole blood platelet volumes in newborn infants. J Pediatr 1982;101:763–6.

305. Castle V, Coates G, Mitchell L, et al. The effect of hypoxia on platelet survival and site of sequestration in the newborn rabbit. Thromb Haemost 1988;59:45–8.

306. Castle V, Coates G, Kelton J, Andrew M. Indium oxine platelet survivals in the thrombocytopenic infant. Blood 1987;70:652–6.

307. Deutsch VR, Olson TA, Nagler A, et al. The response of cord blood megakaryocyte progenitors to IL-3, IL-6

and aplastic canine serum varies with gestational age. Br J Haematol 1995;89:8–16.

308. Murray NA, Roberts IA. Circulating megakaryocytes and their progenitors (BFU-MK and CFU-MK) in term and preterm neonates. Br J Haematol 1995; 89:41–6.

309. Peterec SM, Brennan SM, Rinder HM, et al. Reticulated platelet values in normal and thrombocytopenic neonates. J Pediatr 1996;129:269–74.

310. Joseph MA, Adams D, Maragos J, Saving KL. Flow cytometry of neonatal platelet RNA. J Pediatr Hematol Oncol 1996;18:277–81.

311. Murray NA, Watts TL, Roberts IA. Endogenous thrombopoietin levels and effect of recombinant human thrombopoietin on megakaryocyte precursors in term and preterm babies. Pediatr Res 1998;43: 148–51.

312. Rajasekhar D, Kestin A, Bednarek F, et al. Neonatal platelets are less reactive than adult platelets to physiological agonists in whole blood. Thromb Haemost 1994;72:957–63.

313. Gruel Y, Boizard B, Daffos F, et al. Determinations of platelet antigens and glycoproteins in the human fetus. Blood 1986;68:488–92.

314. Ts'ao C, Green D, Schultz K. Function and ultrastructure of platelets of neonates; enhanced ristocetin aggregation of neonatal platelets. Br J Haematol 1976; 32:225–33.

315. Andrew M, Paes B, Bowker J, Vegh P. Evaluation of an automated bleeding time device in the newborn. Am J Hematol 1990;35:275–7.

316. Feusner JH. Normal and abnormal bleeding times in neonates and young children utilizing a fully standardized template technique. Am J Clin Pathol 1980;74:73–7.

317. Andrew M, Castle V, Saigal S, et al. Clinical impact of neonatal thrombocytopenia. J Pediatr 1987;110: 457–64.

318. Andrew M, Castle V, Mitchell L, Paes B. A modified bleeding time in the infant. Am J Hematol 1989;30: 190–1.

319. Corby D, O'Barr T. Decreased alpha-adrenergic receptors in newborn platelets: Cause of abnormal response to epinephrine. Dev Pharmacol Ther 1981;2: 215–25.

320. Stuart M, Dusse J, Clark A, Walenga R. Differences in thromboxane production between neonatal and adult platelets in response to arachidonic acid and epinephrine. Pediatr Res 1984;18:823–6.

321. Alebouyeh M, Lusher J, Ameri M, et al. The effect of 5-hydroxytryptamine and epinephrine on newborn platelets. Eur J Pediatr 1978;128:163–8.

322. Jones CR, McCabe R, Hamilton CA, Reid JL. Maternal and fetal platelet responses and adrenoreceptor binding characteristics. Thromb Haemost 1985;53:95–8.

323. Ahlsten G, Ewald U, Tuvemo T. Arachidonic acid induced aggregation of platelets from human cord blood compared with platelets from adults. Biol Neonate 1985;47:199–204.

324. Barradas MA, Mikhailidis DP. An investigation of maternal and neonatal platelet function. Biol Res Pregnancy Perinatol 1986;7:60–5.

325. Gader AMA, Bahakim H, Jabber FA, et al. Dose-response aggregometry in maternal/neonatal platelets. Thromb Haemost 1988;60:314–8.

326. Andrews NP, Pipkin FB, Hepinstall S. Blood platelet behaviour in mothers and neonates. Thromb Haemost 1985;53:428–32.

327. Israels S, Daniels M, McMillan E. Deficient collagen-induced activation in the newborn platelet. Pediatr Res 1990;27:337–43.

328. Ahlsten G, Ewald G, Tuvemo T. Cord blood platelet aggregation: quality control by a two-sample technique. Ups J Med Sci 1983;88:9–15.

329. Corby DG, Zuck TF. Newborn platelet dysfunction: a storage pool and release defect. Thromb Haemost 1976;36:200–7.

330. Stuart MJ. The neonatal platelet: evaluation of platelet malonyl dialdehyde formation as an indicator of prostaglandin synthesis. Br J Haematol 1978;39: 83–90.

331. Stuart MJ. Inherited defects of platelet function. Semin Hematol 1975;12:233–53.

332. Stuart MJ. Deficiency of plasma PGI2-like regenerating activity in neonatal plasma. Reversal by vitamin E in vitro. Pediatr Res 1981;15:971–3.

333. Whaun JH. The platelet of the newborn infant: adenine nucleotide metabolism and release. Thromb Haemost 1980;43:99–103.

334. Saving K, Aldag J, Jennings D, et al. Electron microscopic characterization of neonatal platelet ultrastructure: effects of sampling techniques. Thromb Res 1991;61:65–80.

335. Stuart MJ, Allen JB. Arachidonic acid metabolism in the neonatal platelet. Pediatrics 1982;69:714–8.

336. Stuart MJ. The neonatal platelet: evaluation of platelet malonyl dialdehyde formation as an indicator of prostaglandin synthesis. Br J Haematol 1978;39: 83–90.

337. Walenga RW, Sunderji SG, Stuart MJ. Formation of hydroxyeicosatetraenoic acids (HETE) in blood from adults versus neonates: reduced production of 12-HETE in cord blood. Pediatr Res 1988;24:563–7.

338. Weiss JH, Aledort MK, Kochwa S. The effect of salicylate on the hemostatic properties of platelets in man. J Clin Invest 1968;47:2169–80.

339. Gelman B, Setty BN, Chen D, et al. Impaired mobilization of intracellular calcium in neonatal platelets. Pediatr Res 1996;39:692–6.

340. Stuart MJ, Dusse J. In vitro comparison of the efficacy of cyclooxygenase inhibitors on the adult versus neonatal platelet. Biol Neonate 1985;47:265–9.

341. Stuart MJ, Oski FA. Vitamin E and platelet function. J Pediatr Hematol Oncol 1979;1:77–81.

342. Israels SJ, Gowen B, Gerrard JM. Contractile activity of neonatal platelets. Pediatr Res 1987;21:293–5.

343. Israels SJ, Odaibo FS, Robertson C, et al. Deficient thromboxane synthesis and response in platelets from premature infants. Pediatr Res 1997;41: 218–23.

344. Hicsonmez G, Prozorova-Zamani V. Platelet aggregation in neonates with hyperbilirubinemia. Scand J Haematol 1980;24:67–70.

345. Landolfi R, De Cristofaro R, Ciabattoni G, et al. Placental-derived PGI_2 inhibits cord blood platelet function. Haematologica 1988;73:207–18.

346. Michelson AD. Flow cytometry: a clinical test of platelet function. Blood 1996;87:4925–36.

347. Michelson AD. Platelet activation by thrombin can be directly measured in whole blood through the use of the peptide GPRP and flow cytometry: methods and clinical applications. Blood Coagul Fibrinolysis 1994;5:121–31.

348. Kaplan KL, Owen J. Plasma levels of β-thromboglobulin and platelet factor IV as indices of platelet activation in vivo. Blood 1981;57:199–202.

349. Salva AM, Ibe BO, Cliborn E, et al. Hypoxia attenuates metabolism of platelet activating factor by fetal and newborn lamb lungs. J Lipid Res 1996;37:783–9.

350. Grosshaupt B, Muntean W, Sedimayr P. Hyporeactivity of neonatal platelets is not caused by preactivation during birth. Eur J Pediatr 1997;156:944–8.

351. Gatti L, Guarneri D, Caccamo ML, et al. Platelet activation in newborns detected by flow-cytometry. Biol Neonate 1996;70:322–7.

352. Andrew M, Brooker LA. Blood component therapy in neonatal hemostatic disorders. Transfus Med Rev 1995;9:231–50.

353. Andrew M. Developmental hemostasis: relevance to thromboembolic complications in pediatric patients. Thromb Haemost 1995;74(1 Suppl):415–25.

354. White JG, Gerrard JM. Platelet function and its disorders. In: Coleman RW, Hirsh J, Marder VJ, Salzman EW, editors. Hemostasis and thrombosis: basic principles and clinical practice. Philadelphia: J.B. Lippincott Company; 1982. p. 343–63.

355. Andrew M. Platelets in newborns: physiology and pathology. In: Luban N, editor. Transfusion sciences. Elmsford, N Y: Pergamon Press; 1991. p. 207–30.

356. Andrew M. Developmental hemostasis: relevance to newborns and infants. In: Nathan DG, Oski FA, eds. Hematology of infancy and childhood. Philadelphia:WB Saunders;1998.p.114–157.

3

CONGENITAL PROTHROMBOTIC DISORDERS: PRESENTATION DURING INFANCY AND CHILDHOOD

Over 140 years ago, Virchow identified hypercoagulability as a predisposing factor for thromboembolic events (TEs).[1] The term *thrombophilia* was first used to describe members of a family with increased prevalence of venous thromboembolic events (VTEs) and a deficiency of the important natural inhibitors of coagulation, antithrombin III, now known as antithrombin (AT). Subsequently, several congenital abnormalities of hemostasis that predispose to TEs were discovered and the molecular defects delineated. However, optimal strategies for prevention and treatment of TEs secondary to congenital prothrombotic disorders remain to be defined for adults and for children. Patients with single gene defects for recognized congenital prothrombotic disorders rarely present with a first TE during childhood, unless they also have an acquired risk factor that unmasks the defect. In contrast, patients who are homozygous or double-heterozygous for one or more genetic lesion linked to congenital prothrombotic disorder will frequently present with clinical symptoms as newborns or young children.

In children presenting with a first TE, acquired problems and not congenital prothrombotic disorders are more frequently the cause, similar to adults. However, congenital prothrombotic disorders may first present during early infancy, and must be seriously considered, particularly in otherwise healthy infants and children. At the time of initial evaluation, a careful history, physical examination, and laboratory evaluation are required. The interpretation of laboratory results is a particular problem for pediatricians, because the normal physiologic values in children for many coagulation proteins overlap with values considered pathologic in adults.[2-5] The availability of comprehensive reference ranges for components of hemostasis, with reliable upper and lower normal limits, has helped to resolve this issue (Chapter 2).[2-6]

The clinical dilemma for treatment of children with congenital prothrombotic disorders is that although there is a lifelong risk of TEs, and anticoagulant treatment is very effective in preventing TEs, anticoagulants are associated with significant morbidity. Critical questions for the treatment of children with congenital prothrombotic disorders are (1) Which congenital prothrombotic disorders contribute to TEs during childhood; (2) Is long-term prophylactic therapy ever indicated in asymptomatic children; (3) Is intermittent anticoagulation therapy indicated in the presence of an acquired risk factor for TEs; (4) What is the optimal duration of treatment following a first TE during childhood; and (5) What is the risk of recurrent TEs following cessation of treatment for a first TE? This chapter summarizes the available information on these issues and provides guidelines for prophylaxis and treatment of TEs in children with congenital prothrombotic disorders.

GENERAL INFORMATION

Establishing Association between Abnormal Laboratory Test Results and Thromboembolic Events

Although abnormal laboratory test results frequently are linked to TEs, they may not be causally linked to TEs. Well-designed clinical trials such as cross-sectional family studies, case-control studies, and historic or prospective cohort studies are required to establish if there is an association between an abnormal laboratory test result and TEs. Cross-sectional analyses measure the biochemical or molecular abnormality in question in family members who may or may not have had a TE. Case-control studies measure the biochemical or molecular abnormality in question in a group of patients and a group of matched controls. Retrospective cohort studies test individuals with confirmed TEs and compare the incidence of TEs in individuals with and without an abnormality. Prospective cohort studies follow a group of patients having a laboratory abnormality and also a group of matched controls without the abnormality and determine the incidence of TEs over time. Most available information on the contribution of congenital prothrombotic disorders in adults is from cross-sectional family studies.

The magnitude of effect of risk factors on the incidence of a disease may be described in a number of ways. Attributable risk refers to the difference in risk for those patients exposed to a risk factor in question compared to unexposed patients. This implies that the risk factor is a cause and not just a marker of disease. Attributable risk also gives information about the actual incidence of the disease or complication. Relative risk is the number of times that exposed subjects are more likely to develop the outcome of interest, compared to unexposed subjects. Relative risk does not provide information about the incidence or magnitude of absolute risk. However, it does provide a measure of the strength of the association between exposure and disease. Calculation of population risk considers both the risk related to exposure and the prevalence of exposure in a population of interest.

Congenital Prothrombotic Disorders Established to Contribute to Thromboembolic Disease

Clinically significant relationships have been confirmed between TEs and deficiencies of AT, protein C, and protein S, as well as the presence of factor FV Leiden (FV:Q[506]) prothrombin gene Gln Arg, 20210A, and some dysfibrinogenemias in adults.[7] These are aberrations in the natural anticoagulant systems that occur in plasma and at the endothelial cell level; they usually are associated with venous rather than arterial TEs, and commonly first occur in the presence of acquired risk factors such as surgery, pregnancy, immobilization, and dehydration. Congenital deficiencies of AT, protein C, and protein S have been recognized for some years, but prevalence is low, even among patients with familial thrombosis. In contrast, the recent discoveries of FV Leiden and prothrombin gene 20210A have substantially increased the likelihood of identifying an inherited predisposing factor in patients with TEs. A genetic abnormality predisposing to TEs can now be identified in up to one-third of unselected adult patients with VTEs, and more than one-half of adult patients with familial thrombosis.[7-9] The overall increase in risk of TEs for adults with one of these abnormalities is approximately tenfold, compared to that of adults without an abnormality (Table 3–1).[7,10] The ability to diagnose these congenital prothrombotic disorders has permitted accurate family studies, early diagnosis, and strategies focused on prevention of TEs in afflicted adults. There is accumulating evidence that multiple coexisting defects are present in adults with the most marked tendency to develop TEs.

Congenital Disorders That Might Contribute to Thromboembolic Disease

The less well-characterized congenital prothrombotic disorders that might contribute to TEs include abnormalities in the fibrinolytic system, such as plasminogen deficiency,[11-22] tissue plasminogen activator (TPA) deficiency,[23-26] increased plasminogen activator-1 (PAI-1),[27,28] and increased histidine-rich glycoprotein (HRGP).[29,30] Other less well-characterized congenital prothrombotic disorders are heparin factor II (HCII) deficiency[31] and decreased FXII concentrations (Table 3–2).[7,10,32,33]

Prevalence of Congenital Prothrombotic Disorders in General Population

The true prevalence of congenital prothrombotic disorders in the general population is not known, because not all con-

Table 3–1 Odds Ratios for Prevalence of Thrombotic Disease in Various Heterozygous Abnormalities

Type of Abnormality	Number of Families	Prevalence of History of Thrombosis		
		Heterozygous(%)	Normal (%)	OR*
AT deficiency type 1	28	85/192 (44)	6/248 (2)	13.7
AT deficiency type 2	13	15/68 (22)	0/73 (0)	9.8
Protein C deficiency	13	50/113 (44)	21/230 (9)	11.9
Protein S deficiency	15	40/71 (56)	3/69 (4)	10
Dysfibrinogenemia	10	10/25 (40)	0/14 (0)	18

AT = antithrombin.
*Odds ratio.
Data from van den Belt.[10] Reproduced with permission.[7]

genital prothrombotic disorders have been identified. The prevalence of protein C deficiency, AT deficiency, FV Leiden, and prothrombin gene 20210A has been determined in healthy adults and is summarized in Table 3–3.[7,8,34–47] In Caucasians, the prevalence of protein C deficiency is 0.3%, AT deficiency is 0.04%, FV Leiden is 5%, and prothrombin gene 20210A is 2%. There are no studies of sufficient size to estimate the prevalence of protein S deficiency among healthy adults. The prevalence of congenital prothrombotic disorders varies in different populations. For example, the prevalence of FV Leiden varies from approximately 5% in the Caucasian population to less than 1% in the African and Asian populations.[41,48]

Prevalence of Congenital Prothrombotic Disorders in Unselected Adults with a First Thromboembolic Event   The prevalence of protein C deficiency, protein S deficiency, AT deficiency, FV Leiden, and prothrombin gene 20210A increases in

unselected adults with their first TE (Table 3–4).[38,49,50] Among consecutive patients with objectively confirmed deep vein thrombosis (DVT), the prevalence of deficiencies of protein C, protein S, and AT combined is approximately 5%, compared to a 20% prevalence for activated protein C resistance (APCR).[38,49–51]

Prevalence of Congenital Prothrombotic Disorders in Selected Adult Populations   Table 3–5 presents the prevalence of congenital prothrombotic disorders in selected adult populations (i.e., those with a familial history of TE. Prevalences exceed those in unselected adult populations, with or without a first DVT.[52–55] There is some variability between studies, which likely reflects the use of different criteria to identify populations of selected adults. These criteria included adults who experienced a first TE at a young age; adults with recurrent TEs; adults with recurrent TEs in the absence of any classic risk factors for VTE; and adults with positive

Table 3–2 Odds Ratios for Thrombotic Disease in Various Heterozygous Abnormalities

Type of Abnormality	Number of Families	Prevalence of History of Thrombosis		
		Heterozygotes (%)	Normal (%)	OR*
Plasminogen	20	1/90 (1)	0/33 (0)	2.6
Impaired fibrinolysis	18	29/54 (54)	18/55 (33)	1.7
HCII deficiency	4	3/15 (20)	2/16 (13)	0.8
Increased HRGP	5	4/8 (50)	8/36 (22)	3.5

HC = heparin cofactor; HRGP = histidine rich glycoprotein.
*Odds ratio.
Data from van den Belt.[10] Reproduced with permission.[7]

Table 3–3 Prevalence of Protein C and Antithrombin Deficiencies, Factor V:Q^{506} Mutation and Prothrombin Gene 20210A in the Normal Adult Population

Author	Number	Protein C Deficiency %	Antithrombin Deficiency %	Factor V:Q^{506} Mutation %	Prothrombin Gene 20210A %
Meade et al[34]	–	–	0.05	–	–
Tait et al[35]	9669	0.2	0.03	–	–
Miletich et al[36]	5422	0.4	–	–	–
Svensson et al[37]	190	–	–	7	–
Rosendahl et al[38]	474	–	–	3	–
Ridker et al[39]	704	–	–	6	–
Poort et al[46]	463	–	–	–	2
Cumming et al[47]	164	–	–	–	1.2
Makris et al[8]	150	–	–	–	0.7
Weighted mean		0.3	0.04	5	1

Reproduced with permission.[7]

family histories. Prevalences for deficiencies of protein C, protein S, and AT in selected adult populations are higher by 5% to 10% compared to unselected adult populations.[40] The prevalence for APCR is approximately 50%, thus emerging as the most frequent congenital prothrombotic risk factor for VTEs.[52–55] In consecutive patients with DVT and positive family histories, congenital prothrombotic disorders occur in at least one of every four adults.[49]

Summary Table 3–6 compares the prevalences of congenital prothrombotic disorders in the general population to that in unselected adults with their first DVT and in selected adults with DVT.[7]

Clinical Presentation of Congenital Prothrombotic Disorders Venous TEs are the most common clinical presentation of single gene congenital prothrombotic disorders and occur in the presence or absence of other acquired risk factors. The most suggestive features for the presence of a congenital prothrombotic disorder include a positive family history; recurrent TEs; an early age for a first event; the absence of a significant acquired insult; and occurrence in an unusual site. Pregnancy, particularly in the postpartum period, may precipitate TEs in women with a congenital prothrombotic disorder.

Congenital Prothrombotic Disorders Presenting During Childhood The subsequent sections discuss the clinical presentation, diagnosis, and treatment of each of the congenital prothrombotic disorders that may present during childhood.

Table 3–4 Prevalence of Protein C, Protein S, and Antithrombin Deficiencies, Factor V Mutation and *Prothrombin Gene 20210A in Unselected Patients with Episodes of Thrombosis

Author	Number	Protein C Deficiency %	Protein S Deficiency %	Antithrombin Deficiency %	Factor V:Q^{506} Mutation %
Heijboer et al[49]	277	3	2	1	–
Koster et al[50]	474	–	1	1	–
Rosendahl et al[38]	471	3	–	–	20
Mean		3	1.5	1	20

*To date, there is no information on the prevalence of the prothrombin gene 20210A in non-selected patients.
Reproduced with permission.[7]

Table 3–5 Prevalence of Congenital Thrombophilic Disorders in Selected Patients with Both Venous Thromboembolism and Familial Thrombotic History

Author	Number	Protein C Deficiency %	Protein S Deficiency %	Antithrombin Deficiency %	Factor V:Q^{506} Mutation or APCR %	Prothrombin Gene 20210A %
Briet et al[52]	113	8	13	4	–	–
Scharrer et al[53]	158	9	6	5	–	6
Ben-Tal et al[54]	107	6	3	7	–	6
Griffin et al[55]	112	–	–	–	52	8
Mean		7.9	7.2	5.3	52	7

Reproduced with permission.[7]

ACTIVATED PROTEIN C RESISTANCE

General Information

Anticoagulant activities of the protein C/protein S pathway Protein C is a serine protease of molecular weight 62 kDa. It is synthesized by the liver and circulates in plasma at a concentration of 4.0 ug/mL.[56] Protein C is an inactive proenzyme that is rapidly converted to an active enzyme (APC) following limited cleavage by thrombin bound to thrombomodulin (TM), a receptor located on vascular endothelial cells.[57,58] APC is a natural anticoagulant that proteolyzes two cofactors: FVIIIa, which impairs the conversion of FX to FXa, and FVa, which impairs the conversion of prothrombin to thrombin.[56,59,60] In 1993, Dahlback et al reported a previously unrecognized congenital prothrombotic disorder that was characterized by a poor response to APC.[61] In normal individuals, APTT values are prolonged by APC inactivation of FVa and FVIIIa, which impairs the generation of thrombin. In patients with APCR, APTT values are significantly shortened and can be corrected by the addition of normal plasma.[61]

Genetics APCR is an autosomal dominant trait due primarily to a mutant of FV known as FV Leiden. APCR is the single most common congenital prothombotic disorder.[37,62–64] Bertina et al[63] showed that the molecular basis of APCR is a single G-A mutation at nucleotide 1765 (CGA-CAA) within the FV gene, which results in replacement of arginine at position 506 by glutamine (Arg506Gln). This mutation renders FVa relatively resistant to cleavage and, therefore, inactivation by APC.[63,65,66] APC inactivates purified FVaArg506Gln approximately 10 times slower than it does FVa.[67] More than 95% of all APCR cases are caused by FV Leiden.[68] The explanation for the APCR phenotype in the remaining 5% of cases is unclear.[68] APCR is now recognized as the most common congenital prothrombotic disorder in Caucasians. Thrombosis-free survival in patients with APCR is influenced by the presence of heterozygosity or homozygosity, the patient's age, the presence of a second congenital prothrombotic disease, and perhaps the APC ratio.

Table 3–6 Summary of Prevalence of Inherited Thrombophilic Disorders in Different Populations

Population	Protein C Deficiency %	Protein S Deficiency %	Antithrombin Deficiency %	Factor V:Q^{506} Mutation %	Prothrombin Gene 20210A %
Normal population	0.3	–	0.04	5	1
Unselected patients with thrombosis	3	1.5	1	20	–
Patients with thrombosis and suspected thrombophilia	7.9	7.2	5.3	52	7

Reproduced with permission.[7]

Laboratory testing The original functional test for APCR was a modified APTT that measured the anticoagulant response to the addition of a standard amount of APC.[69] The original APTT-based assay for APCR was influenced by the patient's plasma concentrations of FV and FVIII, the APTT reagent, instrumentation, and effects of oral anticoagulants (OAs).[70] The dependence on the patient's plasma concentrations of FV and FVIII is of particular importance in infants, since they have increased plasma concentrations of FVIII and decreased concentrations of FV. Dilution of the patient's plasma with pooled plasma was used in an attempt to correct for these variables, but was only partially successful. APTT assays were subsequently performed with a patient's plasma diluted with FV-deficient instead of normal plasma.[67,69] This allowed testing of patients receiving OAs or having a lupus anticoagulant (LA).[67] Results of both the original and modified APTT assays for APCR are expressed as a ratio, calculated by dividing APTT values obtained in the presence of added APC by APTT values obtained in the absence of added APC.[62] Ratios less than 2.2 are usually considered abnormal.[62] A chromogenic assay that measures the capacity of APC to limit the generation of FXa by inactivating FVIIIa in plasma is also available.[71]

Screening for the FV Leiden mutation at a molecular level involves isolation of deoxyribonucleic acid (DNA) from peripheral blood leukocytes and amplification of the region of the FV gene that spans the mutation by the polymerase chain reaction (PCR). The amplified DNA is then digested with restriction endonucleases, and the resultant fragments electrophoresed on an agarose gel. The number and size of the fragments indicate whether an individual is normal or is heterozygous for or homozygous for the FV Leiden abnormality.[68]

Heterozygous Activated Protein C Resistance

Prevalence in general population

The prevalence of heterozygous FV Leiden varies among different ethnic populations, ranging from less than 1% in African and Asian populations to approximately 5% in the Caucasian population (Table 3–7).[7,40,41] The risk of heterozygous adults developing a TE by mid-adult life is approximately 20%.[34] Additional genetic and clinical risk factors are important co-determinants for the development of TEs. The risk for females is greater than for males, since pregnancy, oral contraceptive use, and post-menopausal estrogen levels also are risk factors that contribute to development of TEs.[72–74]

Prevalence in adults with first thromboembolic event Based on case-control studies, the risk of TEs in adult heterozygous carriers of FV Leiden is five- to tenfold greater.[9,75] The prevalence of FV Leiden in adults with TEs is higher, being approximately 20% in unselected patients and 40% to 60% in selected adults referred to coagulation centers.[9,34,39,62,75,76] Development of TEs in patients with FV Leiden is age-dependent, with younger patients preferentially affected. The Leiden Thrombophilia Study reported the presence of APCR in 21% of adults between 54 and 70 years of age who developed TEs and in 42% of adults less than 25 years of age.[51] The Physicians' Health Study reported the presence of APCR in 11.6% of older males newly presenting with TEs.[39]

Prevalence in adults with second thromboembolic event The prevalence of FV Leiden in adults with a second TE is likely higher, even though there is disagreement between reports. The Physicians' Health Study reported a four- to fivefold increase in recurrent TE in the presence of FV Leiden;[77] two smaller, retrospective studies found no increased rate of recurrent TE.[78,79]

Unusual presentations APCR has been reported in association with Budd-Chiari syndrome,[80] HIT,[81] warfarin-induced skin necrosis,[82] pregnancy,[83–85] and oral contraceptive use.[86]

Table 3–7 Prevalence of Factor V Leiden Mutation in Population Studies

Population	Prevalence
Swedish	7%*
Canadian	5.3%†
Dutch	5%*
Southern Europe	3%
Northern Europe	2%
African and Asian	< 1%*, < 1%

*From Rees;[40] †From Lee;[41] From Rosendahl.[194]
Reproduced with permission.[7]

Homozygous Activated Protein C Resistance

Prevalence of homozygosity for FV Leiden is between 0.02% and 0.12% of the Caucasian population.[38] The mean age for TEs in homozygotes is approximately 25 years (range 10–40), and the risk is increased compared to normals 50 to 100 fold.[9,62,75,87] However, homozygous FV Leiden is a considerably more benign thrombotic disorder than those caused by homozygous deficiencies of protein C or protein S.[88–95] The relatively benign course of homozygous FV Leiden suggests that either the Arg-Gln mutation does not render the FVa molecule absolutely resistant to inactivation by APC, or that additional mechanisms regulate FVa activity in vivo. In addition, inactivation of FVIIIa by APC is preserved in patients with FV Leiden, whereas in patients with deficiencies of protein C or protein S, inactivation of FVIIIa is dysfunctional.[65]

Activated Protein C Resistance Combined with Other Congenital Prothrombotic Disorders

General information The high prevalence of FV Leiden has facilitated studies on the risk of TEs in the presence of multiple congenital prothrombotic disorders. Family studies of APCR in combination with deficiencies of protein C, protein S, and AT show that the combined presence of these defects significantly increases the risk for TEs relative to a single gene defect only. The following sections provide information on APCR in combination with deficiencies of protein C, protein S, and AT in adults.

Activated protein C resistance and protein C deficiency Koeleman et al studied 48 patients with protein C deficiency and a previous DVT for the presence of FV Leiden.[96] The FV Leiden mutation was present in nine symptomatic probands for an incidence of 19%, significantly higher than expected in the general population (2%).[63] Further evidence for an increased risk of thrombosis in patients with both gene defects comes from detailed studies of six families. A significantly higher percentage of carriers for both defects suffered from TEs (73%) compared to carriers of only one defect (31% for protein C gene mutation; 13% for FV Leiden mutation).[96] These observations support the view that there is an increased risk of TEs conferred by coexistence of heterozygous protein C deficiency and heterozygous APCR.[97]

Activated protein C resistance combined with protein S deficiency There are a few reports on coexistence of APCR and protein S deficiency in the same patients,[98,99] and the small number of patients limits the strength of the interpretation. In general, patients with combined deficiencies present with TEs at an earlier age than other family members with only APCR or protein S deficiency. Zoller et al evaluated 18 unrelated families with inherited protein S deficiency for APCR;[98] they reported that 27% of family members with both defects had a history of TEs versus 19% who had either the APCR mutation or protein S deficiency.[96,97] Koeleman et al evaluated 16 unrelated patients with protein S deficiency for APCR.[99] Eighty percent of individuals with both the FV Leiden mutation and protein S deficiency had experienced a TE, which is similar to the percentage of patients with APCR and protein C deficiency (73%).[96,97] The penetrance of thrombotic disease in protein S deficient carriers of the FV Leiden mutation is therefore high. Of three patients with only protein S deficiency, two developed TEs; of seven with only the FV mutation, three developed TEs. The mean age of disease onset of symptomatic protein S deficient carriers of the FV Leiden mutation was 27 years (10–60 years), which is similar to that found for subjects with both protein C deficiency and APCR.[96] The age of disease onset of two symptomatic individuals with only protein S deficiency was 18 and 25 years and of two symptomatic carriers of the APCR mutation 63 and 70 years.[99]

Activated protein C resistance combined with other congenital prothrombotic disorders The combination of APCR with other congenital prothrombotic disorders or combinations of disorders is summarized in Table 3–8.[98–100] Recent studies have reported that the risks of thrombosis in homocystinuria is increased if individuals also have the FV Leiden mutation.[101] Chaturvedi et al, in a series of 28 Caucasian patients under the age of 55 with cerebral ischemic events, reported that 9 had APCR, of which 5 had additional prothrombotic disorders.[102] Lewandowski et al assessed the frequency of additional prothrombotic disorders in family members of 14 symptomatic heterozygous carriers of FV Leiden.[100] They reported that combined congenital prothrombotic disorders were present in 6 of the 14 families (4 protein S deficiency, 1 prothrombin gene 20210A, 1 AT deficiency). Sixty-three percent (7 of 11) of combined defect carriers (mean age 48.5 years) and 59% (24 of 42) of heterozygous FV Leiden carriers (mean age 52.2 years) were symptomatic at the time of the report. Salomon et al assessed the prevalence of single and combined congenital prothrombotic factors in 162 patients referred for evaluation because they had idiopathic VTE.[103] The prevalences of heterzygotes and homozygotes for FV Leiden were 40.1% of patients versus 3.9% of controls. Two or more polymorphisms were detected in 17% (27 of 162) of patients and less than 1% (3 of 336) of controls. Beauchamp et al assessed three families with protein S deficiency and reported that of the five members with TEs, three had FV Leiden.[104] Mustafa et al assessed 29 symptomatic patients with protein C or protein S deficiency who were also tested for FV Leiden.[105] Forty percent (6 of 15) of patients with protein C deficiency also had FV Leiden. Twenty-nine percent (4 of 15) of patients with protein S deficiency also had FV Leiden. The age at first TE was significantly lower in the 10 patients with a combined genetic defect (mean age 18.4 ± 6.6 years) than in those patients with a single genetic defect (mean age 32.6 ± 10.4 years). Spontaneous recurrence was similar in patients with either single and combined defects. In individuals with a combined defect, thrombosis-free survival time was significantly shorter than in individuals with a single defect. A case report by Inbal et al describes two children who presented with purpura fulminans after disseminated intravascular coagulation (DIC), one of which was triggered by a varicella infection. Both were found to have the FV Leiden and protein S deficiency.[106] A case report by Kahn describes a 20-year-old patient who developed early onset preeclampsia and postpartum DVT and was found to be protein S deficient and to have the FV Leiden mutation.[107]

Other There is a strong interaction between FV Leiden, oral contraceptive use, and hyperhomocystinemia.[86,108] FV Leiden also occurs in young individuals with arterial thrombosis.[109]

Activated Protein C Resistance in Children

Reference values Age-dependent differences in plasma concentrations of multiple coagulant factors result in a decreased capacity to generate thrombin during childhood. This is manifest, in part, as prolonged APTT values (Chapter 2). The altered physiologic status of the coagulation system in the young has made it necessary to determine age-related reference ranges for APC ratios throughout childhood (Table 3–9).[110–113] The interpretation of these results depends on whether APC ratios were compared to the presence of FV Leiden and whether a modified APC assay with dilutions of FV-deficient plasma was used.[113,114] In the study by Mandel et al, FV Leiden mutation heterozygotes had APC ratios less than 2.2.[110] Seven patients known to have heterozygote FV Leiden, but not included in the study, also had APC ratios less than 2.2 by the same method. No APC ratios were identified between 2.2 and the cutoff point of 2.8 in the patient cohort. The authors recommended that any child with an APC ratio less than 2.8 should have DNA analysis for the FV Leiden mutation. Uttenreuther-Fischer et al reported mean APCR ratios in neonates were 3.02, compared to 2.33 to 2.73 in all other age groups up to 18 years.[111] However, the neonatal samples were from cord blood, there were few children less than 1 year of age, and the FV Leiden mutation was not determined in this study.

Table 3–8 Percent of Thrombotic Events in Patients with Multiple Inherited Thrombophilic Disorders

Thrombophilic Disorders Tested	Number	Two Thrombophilic Disorders %	One Thrombophilic Disorder %
Protein S, Factor V Leiden*	18	27	19
Protein S, Factor V Leiden†	16	80	55
Factor V Leiden, Protein S, Prothrombin gene 20210A, AT‡	55	63	59

*From Zoller;[87] †From Koeleman;[99] ‡From Lewandowski.[100]

Sifontes et al analyzed 115 cord blood samples, 108 of which were normal by FV PCR analysis.[112] They used a modified APCR ratio. Normal adults had a mean ratio of 1.15 (range 0.76–1.94); normal cord blood samples had a mean ratio of 1.13 (range 0.73–1.9); and the seven samples that were heterozygous for FV Leiden had a mean functional APC ratio of 0.38 (SD 0.10, range 0.21–0.49). In summary, there was no overlap between APCR in newborns without FV Leiden and those heterozygous for the mutation.

The most comprehensive study to determine normal APCR ranges in children is that by Brandt et al.[113] These authors used samples obtained from 169 normal children prior to elective surgery. APCR was determined and expressed as both (1) APC-sensitivity ratio (APC-SR), which is the ratio of the clotting time with APC to the clotting time without APC, and (2) normalized APC-SR (nAPC-SR), which is the ratio of the patient's APC-SR to the APC-SR of the normal plasma pool. Plasma samples also were diluted 1:4 with FV-deficient plasma and reported as FDAPC-SR and nFDAPC-SR, or the patient ratio and the ratio of patient to normal plasma pool respectively. FV Leiden analysis was performed on all patients by PCR of genomic DNA from peripheral blood leucocytes. Seven children (4.1%) were heterozygotes for the Leiden mutation, with no homozygotes. Sensitivity, specificity, positive predictive values, and negative predictive values were calculated for each method. Cutoff points were derived from the 95th percentile of the entire cohort and from 2 SDs below the mean of samples known to be negative for the FV Leiden mutation. The former is clinically more useful, since patients in a study are usually of unknown genotype; this cutoff is thus a more appropriate discriminatory test. Results from this study indicate that sensitivity and positive predictive value are greatly improved when APC ratios are determined using samples diluted in FV-deficient plasma. In contrast, Giordano et al found predilution had different effects on APC ratios in a series of 85 thalassemic patients of median age 17 years.[115] Assays using both undiluted samples and sample diluted 1:5 with FV-deficient plasma were 100% sensitive, but specificity was 81% with undiluted plasma versus 97% with diluted plasma. Mean APC ratios re-ported by Brandt et al were reduced when FV-deficient plasma was used to dilute samples,[113] an effect that may be more pronounced in samples from neonates than from older children. Nowak-Gottl et al reported a median APC ratio of 3.1 (range 2.3–4.5) in 21 healthy neonates when the samples were diluted 1:1 with FV-deficient plasma, versus 2.8 (range 2.05–3.5) when the same samples were diluted 1:11 with FV-deficient plasma.[116] However, the same study found a median APCR of 2.8 in children 1 to 3 months old, irrespective of whether samples were diluted 1:1 or 1:11 with FV-deficient plasma. In samples from children 6 months to 6 years of age with severe sepsis, APC ratios were reduced when the samples were diluted 1:1 (median 2.3, range 1.8–2.8), likely reflecting increased FVIII concentrations. However, APC ratios from the same samples were increased when the samples were diluted 1:11 (median 2.8, range 2.1–3.9). APC ratios in samples from children with heterozygous FV Leiden did not change significantly with dilution at 1:1 or 1:11 with FV-deficient plasma (median 1.7 and 1.6; range 1.2–2.0 and 1.2–2.3 respectively). In a similar study, the same authors compared APCR in 120 healthy infants versus 24 infants with septicemia.[114] APC ratios were determined using undiluted samples and samples diluted 1:5 and 1:11 with FV-deficient plasma. Using a cutoff value of 2.0, concordance with DNA analysis was found only by use of the 1:11 dilution for the healthy infants. Undiluted samples and samples diluted 1:5 resulted in both false negatives and false positives in the septic children. The dilution effects reported for septic patients have also been reported for children with acute lymphoblastic leukemia (ALL).[116,117]

Interaction of activated protein C resistance and fibrinolytic system during childhood There is evidence for activation of the fibrinolytic system in children with FV Leiden. Plasma concentrations of D-Dimer, TPA, PA1,[118,119] TM,[120] and TATs[121] are increased in children with FV Leiden, while plasma concentrations of protein C do not differ from age-matched controls.[120] Because plasma concentrations of protein C and protein S are decreased, and FV and FVIII concentrations are increased or within the adult range during early childhood, an imbalance exists, which may result in activation of the coagulation and fibrinolytic systems. Stress testing by ve-

Table 3–9 Age-Related Reference Ranges for Activated Protein C Ratios

Author	Number	Method	Age	APCR Mean ± SD (Range)	Sensitivity (%)	Specificity (%)
Mandel et al[101]	100	Diluted in FVDP	Not stated	3.4 ± 0.32 (1.9–4.1)	100	100
Sifontes et al[112]	115	Diluted in FVDP	cord blood	1.13 ± 0.22 (0.73–1.9)	100	100
Brandt et al[113]	169	No dilution	3 mos–16 yr	3.02 ± 0.45 (ND)	29	96
		No dilution: APCR normalized to APCR of normal pooled plasma	3 mos–16 yr	1.01 ± 0.16 (ND)	57	97
		Diluted in FVDP	3 mos–16 yr	2.35 ± 0.22 (ND)	100	100
		Diluted in FVDP: APCR normalized to APCR of normal pooled plasma	3 mos–16 yr	1.03 ± 0.05 (ND)	100	99

APCR = activated protein C resistance; FVDP = factor V deficient plasma; ND = not determined; SD = standard deviation.

nous occlusion was performed in 60 children with FV Leiden; the children had a poor fibrinolytic response compared with age-matched healthy controls. TPA activities were significantly reduced and PAI-1 activity was significantly increased in the children with FV Leiden. One explanation is that the FV gene mutation impairs fibrinolytic activity through poor regulation of thrombin generation, which results in increased activity by the thrombin-activable fibrinolysis inhibitor (TAFI).[119]

Incidence in children with thromboembolic events Children with homozygous or heterozygous FV Leiden usually have their first vascular insult following puberty.[119,122] Simioni et al described studies of 80 families, in which 224 individuals carried the FV Leiden mutation and 154 did not.[123] Carriers under age 15 years were observed for a total of 3265 observation years; there were no VTEs. In contrast, carriers over age 15 years, who were observed for a total of 6114 observations, had 17 VTEs among them, for a yearly incidence of 0.28%. When TEs occurred during early infancy and childhood, an acquired risk factor that unmasked the congenital prothrombotic state was usually present.

Incidence in children with more than one congenital prothrombotic disorder Children

may co-inherit multiple prothrombotic conditions. In comprehensive studies of families with AT deficiency and the FV Leiden mutation, Van Boven et al reported that the median age of a first TE was 26 years in family members with isolated AT deficiency and 16 years in family members with both AT deficiency and the FV Leiden mutation.[124]

Incidence in children with acquired disorders Fourteen publications, most of which are case series or case-control studies, that have examined the frequency of the FV Leiden mutation in children with TEs in a variety of clinical situations are summarized in Table 3–10.[116,117,125–127,129–132,134–138] The contribution of APCR to TEs in children is dependent on the underlying disorder and the type of TE. Nowak-Gottl et al reported that 60% of patients with venous TEs and FV Leiden also had additional clinical risk factors.[116] The incidence of FV Leiden was found to vary, depending on the site of the TE. The majority of the children in the study had TEs in the portal venous system, renal veins, and the superior vena cava. Some studies suggest that the risk of TEs secondary to the presence of the FV Leiden are age-dependent and highest during early infancy and the teen years. There are numerous case reports of severe TEs in neonates with FV

Leiden. One infant presented shortly after birth with progressive purpuric skin lesions and microvascular hemorrhagic thrombosis in the brain. The child was treated with fresh frozen plasma (FFP) and had complete resolution of the skin lesions with no long-term complications.[133] Another infant had a life-threatening cerebellar thrombotic event during the second day of life.[134] A term infant with heterozygous FV mutation had a life-threatening inferior vena cava TE during the first 24 hours of life and no other risk factors for TEs.[135] Another neonate, heterozygous for APCR, developed an RVT.[136] The overall thrombogenicity of the FV mutation seems to be aggravated by additional thrombogenic risk factors, such as protein C or protein S deficiency, infection, and anoxia at birth.[134] No studies have provided information about the impact of FV Leiden on risk of recurrent TEs.

Age distribution The age distribution of children with APCR and TEs shows a predominance of infants under 1 year old and a second peak in the teenage years (Figure 3–1).[116,117,137,138]

Underlying diseases The most common underlying disorders in children with FV Leiden who develop TEs are presented in Figure 3–2, based on 10 publications that describe 84 children.[65,117,133–135,139–141] Spontaneous thrombosis occurred in 33% (28 of 84) of children, of which 25% (7 of 28) were homozygous for APCR. The most common acquired risk factors were presence of central venous lines (CVLs), congenital heart disease (CHD), cancer, sepsis, and other causes, in descending order of frequency.

Central nervous system thromboembolism Eight studies were identified that assessed the relationship between childhood stroke (arterial ischemic stroke [AIS] and sinovenous thrombosis [SVT]) and FV Leiden mutation. Results of these studies are summarized in Table 3–11.[126,138,142–145, 147,148] There have also been a number of case reports of FV Leiden in children with stroke.[139,149,150] In many studies, there were coexistent clinical risk factors. Zenz et al reported that five of six patients with AIS and FV Leiden mutation had additional risk factors.[149] Nowak-Gottl et al reported that 9 of 14 children with AIS had additional clinical risk factors.[145] The same authors reported that three of

three children with FV Leiden and SVT and one of five with Leiden and AIS had additional clinical risk factors. Age was an important covariate in this study; 0 of 11 neonates had FV Leiden, compared to 6 of 22 older children. No studies have determined if the presence of FV Leiden mutation alters the risk of further cerebrovascular events.

Specific disease states In addition to arterial and venous TEs, FV Leiden mutation has been implicated in several other childhood disease states. Debus et al reported that 6 of 24 children with porencephaly were heterozygous for FV Leiden and 16 of the 24 children had a prothrombotic abnormality.[151] Nelson et al and Thorarensen et al reported the mutation in children with cerebral palsy.[152,153] Association between FV Leiden mutation and Legg-Calvé-Perthes disease has also been reported. Arruda et al described FV Leiden in 4.9% of 61 children with Legg-Calvé-Perthes compared to 0.7% of controls;[154] Glueck et al reported 12% Leiden positivity in 64 children with Legg-Calvé-Perthes versus 1% of controls.[155] An association between occular involvement in Behçet's disease and FV Leiden has also been reported.[156] There are isolated case reports of association of FV Leiden with varicella-induced purpura fulminans, Banti syndrome, cutis marmorata telangiectasia congenita, hypereosinophilia syndrome, neonatal intracranial hemorrhage, retinal artery occlusion, Noonan syn-

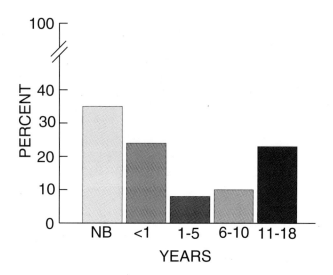

Figure 3–1 Age distribution of children with activated protein C resistance and thromboembolic events, based on a literature review.

Table 3–10 Frequency of Factor V Leiden Mutation in Children with Thrombosis

Author	Location of TE or Patient Population Type	Heterozygote (%)	Homozygote(%)
Nowak-Gottl et al[116]	ALL	3/3 (100%)	0/3 (0%)
Hausler et al[129]	non CVL TE	2/8 (25%)	0 (0%)
Gurgey et al[134]	VTE§/ATE	15/63 (23%)	5/63 (8%)
Aschka et al[117]	VTE/ATE	29/125 (23%)	3/125 (2%)
Sifontes et al[338]	VTE	3/14 (21%)	0 (0%)
Sifontes et al[125]	non CNS TE	5/34 (15%)	0 (0%)
Hagstrom et al[126]	non CNS TE	4/32 (13%)	0/32 (0%)
Sifontes et al[127]	Cancer	1/32 (3%)	0/32 (0%)
Fabri et al[130]	VTE	0/6 (0%)	0/6 (0%)
Seixas et al[131]	PVT	0/20 (0%)	0/20 (0%)
Ong	CPB	0/9 (0%)	0/9 (0%)

TE = thromboembolic event; ALL = acute lymphoblastic leukomia; CVL = central venous lines; VTE = venous thromboembolic event; ATE = arterial thromboembolic event; CNS = central nervous system; PVT = portal vein thrombosis; CPB = cardiopulmonary bypass.

drome with TIAs, DIC secondary to infection, and AIS in children with hemophilia.[106,149,157–163] One study failed to show an association between FV Leiden and migraines.[162]

Skin lesions characterized by microvascular thrombosis have been reported in patients with congenital APCR and acquired APCR. The patient with FV Leiden developed recurrent leg ulcerations in early childhood and also had an intermittent FXIII deficiency, which may have been responsible for slow wound healing.[164,165] Children with severe meningococcal infection characterized by extensive microvascular thrombosis, consumption coagulopathy, and secondary hemorrhages were evaluated for the FV Leiden mutation.[166] Their median age was 7 years (range 0.6–59.7 years). Only three patients were heterozygous for the FV Leiden mutation, an incidence similar to that of the general population. Two of four patients with protein C levels below 30% who were homozygous or compound heterozygous for protein C gene mutations also bore the FV Arg 506 to Gln mutation. The absence of severe TEs during infancy in these two patients suggests that APCR, caused by a heterozygous state of the Arg 506 to Gln genotype, might not increase the risk for thrombosis markedly in the neonatal or childhood period for patients with very low protein C levels. In such cases, the clinical presentation of homozygous FV Leiden mutation is relatively benign.[167]

Prevention and treatment The cumulative risk of venous TEs in heterozygous adult carriers of the FV Leiden mutation is low. A large cross-sectional study of 15,109 patients reported that only 5.7% of affected patients will have had at least one episode of venous TE by the age of 65.[168] Similarly, Ridker et al, in a nested case control study performed as part of a large prospective study of male physicians, reported that the rate of venous TEs in patients less than 50 years old was similar in those

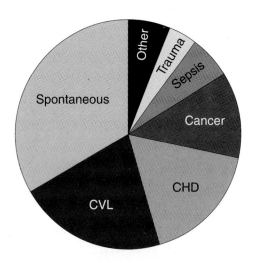

Figure 3–2 Most frequent associated risk factors for thromboembolic events in children with activated protein C resistance.

Table 3–11 Frequency of Factor V Leiden Mutation in Children with Stroke

Author	Thrombosis Location	FV Leiden Heterozygote (%)	FV Leiden Homozygote (%)
Nowak-Gottl et al[145]	AIS	3/4 (75)	0/20 (0)
	SVT	5/16 (31)	
Nowak-Gottl et al[145]	AIS	4/14 (29)	1/14 (7)
Vielhaber et al[147]	SVT	6/32 (19)	3/32 (9)
Zenz et al[149]	AIS	5/33 (15)	1/33 (3)
Hagstrom et al[126]	AIS	6/47 (13)	0/47 (0)
Ganesan et al[143]	AIS	6/67 (9)	0/67 (0)
McColl et al[142]	AIS	2/37 (5)	0 (0)
deVeber et al[148]	AIS/SVT	0/22 (0)	0/22 (0)

AIS = arterial ischemic stroke; SVT = sinovenous thrombosis.

with or without FV Leiden.[169] The relative risk for venous thrombosis in adults with FV Leiden has been estimated to be between 2.2 to 4.2.[170,171] If a similar relative risk applies to children, the extremely low frequency of spontaneous TEs during childhood means that the absolute risk remains minimal. It is therefore unlikely that the detection of the FV 1691 G—A mutation in asymptomatic children would have therapeutic consequences. Over 95% of TEs in children occur in those with major clinical risk factors. Whether all children with clinical risk factors for TEs (CVL, cancer, CHD) should be screened for FV Leiden is unclear. In high-risk situations such as major vascular manipulation, anticoagulation is used routinely, regardless of the presence of additional risk factors. In low-risk situations, anticoagulation of all FV 1691 G—A positive children may not be beneficial, and risks could outweigh any benefits. Before definite recommendations for prophylactic action in asymptomatic children with FV Leiden are made, prospective studies are required.[172] In the absence of such, one approach is to consider prophylactic anticoagulation therapy in very high-risk situations such as cardiac catheterization in small infants, treatment with L-asparaginase, or major orthopedic surgery after the onset of puberty.[137] A second approach is to use careful observation and intervene at the time of onset of symptoms of TEs.

There are currently no data to support a different therapeutic approach to children with TEs. There are case reports describing use of throm-bolytic therapy, low molecular weight heparin (LMWH), unfractionated heparin (UFH), and various durations of OA therapy.[65,127,132,135,136,139,141,173] However, the small number of cases and the marked heterogeneity of the underlying diseases, thrombosis site, and symptom duration make useful interpretation of this data impossible.

Homozygous activated protein C resistance Between 1966 and 1999, homozygous APCR was reported in 15 children.[65,76,117,132,134,174–176] Of 15 homozygous children, three had a PE, three had venous TE, two had cerebral TEs, one had Budd-Chiari, one had Legg-Calvé-Perthes disease, and one had meningococcal purpura fulminans. In four, the location of thrombosis could not be determined. A connection between severity of the TE and homozygosity was not obvious.

PROTHROMBIN GENE VARIANT 20210 GLN-ARG

General Information

Prothrombin Prothrombin is produced in the liver as a single chain glycoprotein with a molecular weight of 72,000 daltons. Prothrombin is the precursor molecule of thrombin, a critical enzyme in hemostasis, which has several coagulant activities including activation of FV, FVIII, and platelets and conversion of fibrinogen to fibrin (Chapter 2). Deficiencies of prothrombin resulting in a bleeding diathesis were first described in 1939 by Quick et al.[177] Several molecular variants of prothrombin that result in congenital bleeding disorders have since been described. Thrombin also has anticoagulant properties that occur when thrombin binds to TM, a receptor for thrombin located on the surface of endothelial cells. Thrombin bound to TM cleaves protein C to the active form, APC, which results in proteolysis of FVa and FVIIIa (Chapter 2). In the late 1990s, a molecular variant of prothrombin that resulted in TEs was described, prothrombin 20210A.[46]

Prothrombin gene variant 20210 Gln—Arg In 1996, Poort et al sequenced the prothrombin genes of probands from 28 families with unexplained thrombophilia and identified a G to A transition at nucleotide position 20210A in the 3'-untranslated region of the gene.[46] In the families described, prothrombin 20210A was linked to the presence of TEs. In a subsequent population-based patient control study (Leiden Thrombophilia Study), heterozygosity for the prothrombin 20210A allele was shown to confer a relative risk for thrombosis of 2.8% (95% CI, 1.4–5.6), making prothrombin 20210A the second most commonly inherited defect linked to TEs.[46] Individuals heterozygous for the prothrombin 20210A allele had significantly increased plasma concentrations of prothrombin (1.32 U/mL) compared to homozygous individuals (1.05 U/mL).[8,46,178–181] The increased plasma concentrations of prothrombin are hypothesized to be responsible for the increased risk of thrombosis secondary to prothrombin 20210A, similar to how the population-based studies showed that increased plasma concentrations of fibrinogen and FV are linked to TEs.

Laboratory testing Although increased plasma concentrations of prothrombin are present in individuals with prothrombin 20210A, the width of the normal range for plasma concentrations of prothrombin excludes this measure as a specific screening test. The mechanism by which the prothrombin gene variant causes increased plasma concentrations of prothrombin levels remains unknown.

The first detection of prothrombin 20210A was based on amplification of a 345-bp fragment of exon 14 of the prothrombin gene (Chapter 13).[182] More recent methods use allele-specific primers for the 20210G and 20210A alleles and have the advantage that the PCR with a restriction enzyme is not required.[46,180,183,184]

Heterozygous Prothrombin Gene 20210A
Prevalence in general population Prothrombin 20210A is at present the second most prevalent prothrombotic polymorphism associated with venous TEs. Similar to FV Leiden, the most prevalent prothrombotic polymorphism, prevalence of prothrombin 20210A differs according to the ethnicity of the population. Prevalence is approximately 2% in the Caucasian population[8,9,46,47,185] and 4% to 5% in Mediterranean populations (Italy, Israel, and Greece), but the allele is rare among nonwhite ethnic groups.[180,181,183,184,186–192] There may be some heterogeneity of the prothrombin 20210A prevalence among Caucasians that requires further delineation.[193]

Prevalence in adults with thromboembolic events Seven studies that provide reliable estimates of the incidence of prothrombin 20210A in adults with TEs are summarized in Table 3–12.[46,47,185,194–197] Prevalences reported range from 4.3% to 19.5%; this variability reflects differences between the studies with regard to the type of TE, inclusion of first or recurrent TEs, and inclusion of patients with variable family histories. Among unselected patients with venous TEs, prothrombin variant 20210A is present in 5.0% to 6.2% of individuals.[8,9,46,47,185] Similar to other congenital prothrombotic disorders, individuals with prothrombin 20210A may present with TEs in unusual locations, such as mesenteric veins and retinal veins.[198–202] The risk of recurrent TEs in individuals with prothrombin 20210A may be as high as 20%.[196,203–205]

Homozygous Prothrombin Gene 20210A
The vast majority of individuals with prothrombin 20210A are heterozygotes. Although homozygous individuals with prothrombin 20210A exist, only a few have been described.[178,179,206–208] Affected individuals usually present in early adult life with severe clinical manifestations and are identified after referral for evaluation for a congenital prothrombotic disorder.[206] Although the presentation of homozygous prothrombin 20210A is relatively severe, it is considerably more benign than for those individuals homozygous for deficiencies of AT, protein C, and protein S. Interestingly, several identified individuals with homozygous prothrombin 20210A

have FV Leiden or acquired risk factors that appear to trigger the TEs.

Prothrombin Gene 20210A Combined with Other Congenital Prothrombotic Disorders Co-inheritance of prothrombin 20210A with other congenital prothrombotic disorders increased the risk of TEs.[8] Individuals with prothrombin 20210A who had TEs were significantly more likely to have FV Leiden or a deficiency of AT or protein C. Co-inheritance of prothrombin 20210A increased the risk of TEs in patients with these other forms of thrombophilia; 8% of 101 unrelated individuals with TEs had prothrombin 20210A, in addition to deficiencies of either protein C, protein S, AT, or FV Leiden. There is some evidence that the combination of prothrombin 20210A and protein C deficiency may be more severe than other combinations.[209] The presence of prothrombin 20210A in combination with other congenital prothrombotic disorders likely increases the risk of recurrent TEs.[108,197]

Salomon et al reported that individuals heterozygous for FV Leiden alone had an odds ratio of 12.4, whereas individuals with both FV Leiden and prothrombin 20210A had an odds ratio of 45.6.[197] Prothrombin 20210A appears to interact with acquired risk factors such as oral contraceptive use in a similar fashion to FV Leiden. Martinelli et al reported that the odds ratio for individuals with the prothrombin 20210A increased from 10 to 145 in women receiving oral contraceptives.[203] Preliminary data suggest that prothrombin variant does not play a major role in the occurrence of thrombosis in primary antiphospholipids syndrome.[210] There is some evidence suggesting that prothrombin 20210A increases the risk of developing TEs in pregnant women[211] and in individuals with other well-established environmental risk factors such as trauma, immobilization, and surgery.

Prothrombin Gene 20210A and Arterial Thrombosis The relationship between prothrombin 20210A and arterial thrombotic disease is not as well defined as for VTEs. Many published studies are limited by small sample sizes and heterogeneous underlying diseases.[180,194,212] The available information suggests that prothrombin 20210A is not likely a major risk factor for arterial thrombosis, but may have a role in some patient populations. Of some relevance to children, the presence of prothrombin 20210A in young women may be a risk factor for myocardial infarction in the presence of an acquired risk factor such as smoking.[109] In another study, prothrombin 20210A was present in 5.1% of adults with coronary heart disease but in only 1.96% of healthy neonates.[213] Recent studies have assessed the interaction of prothrombin 20210A with migraine and arterial vascular disease in either the coronary or cerebral arteries.[180,214,215] Further studies are necessary to clarify the interrelationship between prothrombin 20201A and arterial thrombotic disease.

Table 3–12 Prevalence of Prothrombin 20210A Allele in Venous Thrombosis Patients

Author	Prevalence Number (%)	Risk of Thrombosis Relative to Normal Patients Odds Ratio (95% CI)
Arruda et al[194]	116 (4.3)	6.6 (1.12–49)
Brown et al[185]	504 (5.0)	2.0 (1.0–4.0)
Cumming et al[47]	219 (5.5)	4.7 (1.4–4.0)
Hillarp et al[195]	99 (7.1)	4.2 (1.3–13.6)
Poort et al[46]	471 (6.2)	2.8 (1.4–5.6)
De Stefano et al[196]	273 (8.0)	3.4 (1.2–9.3)
Salomon et al[197]	136 (19.8)	3.8 (1.4–7.4)

CI = confidence interval.
Reproduced with permission.[623]

Prothrombin Gene 20210A in Children

Reference values for prothrombin concentrations Prothrombin plasma concentrations are reduced to approximately 50% of adult levels at birth and during the first month of life. By 3 months of age, prothrombin concentrations increase to 80% of adult values and remain reduced by approximately 10% to 20% throughout childhood, reaching adult levels during late teenage years (Figure 3–3).[2,3,5]

Only one study to date has examined prothrombin concentrations in children with prothrombin 20210A mutation. Balasa et al studied 187 children aged 6 months to 16 years, with at least 10 children of each year of age.[216] Seven children (4%) were heterozygous for the prothrombin 20210A mutation; there were no homozygotes. The mean (± SD) prothrombin concentrations for children with wild type prothrombin were 91% (± 14) and 98% (± 19) for heterozygotes. These values were not significantly different. The percentage of children with prothrombin levels > 95th percentile of the wild type population was 6% for those with wild type prothrombin and 29% for those heterozygous for prothrombin 20210A. Sensitivity of this cutoff point was 14% and specificity 97%. The authors concluded that a significant relationship between increased prothrombin levels and the prothrombin 20210A mutation did not exist in children. Given that the proposed mechanism of increased thrombotic risk for this mutation is increased plasma concentrations of prothrombin, whether the physiologically reduced prothrombin levels throughout childhood can confer protection from thrombosis is unknown.

Absolute risk for thromboembolic events in children with prothrombin 20210 mutation As with other congenital prothrombotic disorders, the majority of affected patients do not develop thromboembolic complications until adult life. There are currently no data to suggest that the prothrombin 20210 mutation significantly alters the absolute risk of thrombosis in childhood.

Attributable or relative risk for thromboembolic events in children with prothrombin 20210A The total number of children with heterozygous prothrombin 20210A and TEs reported in the literature is less than 10,[217,218] and there are

no children with homozygous prothrombin 20210A and TEs. The youngest child in these case reports was an 18-month-old infant who had spontaneous spinal cord infarction.[217] There are no prevalence studies in children with non-CNS VTE. De Stefano et al reported four children with sinovenous thrombosis, one of whom had prothrombin 20210A.[207] McColl et al studied 37 children with AIS.[142] One heterozygote for the 20210A mutation was identified, giving an OR of 1.2 (95%, CI 0.1–10.7). Similarly, Zenz et al found the mutation in 1 of 26 Austrian children with AIS.[144] The prevalence was 3.85% (95%, CI 0.1–21.4), which was not different from the normal population. Becker et al, in a study of 33 children with AIS, also failed to find any relationship between prothrombin 20210A mutation and childhood stroke.[219]

Fabri et al reported the presence of prothrombin 20210A in 2 of 53 children with nephrotic syndrome.[129] Neither of these children had a TE, but three unaffected children did. Finally, Nowak-Gottl et al reported six children with prothrombin 20210A among 301 children with ALL.[220] Thirty-two children had a TE, and the presence of a congenital prothrombotic disorder reduced the overall

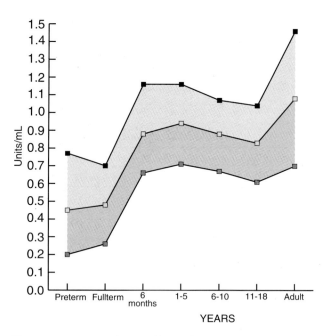

Figure 3–3 Mean values and boundaries encompassing 95% of physiologic values for plasma concentrations of prothrombin over age.

thrombosis-free survival in this study.[220] Further studies are required to determine the role of the prothrombin mutation as a significant etiologic factor in childhood thrombosis.

Antithrombin Deficiency

General Information

Historic perspective Morawitz first used the term "antithrombin" to describe the inhibitory effect of plasma on the clotting activity of thrombin.[221] Howell and Holt in 1918 first recognized the dependency of the antithrombin activity on UFH.[222] Quick and Brinkhous in 1938 and 1939, respectively, labelled the plasma component as a "heparin cofactor."[223,224] Astrup and Darling in 1943 delineated the separate features of progressive antithrombin activity in the absence of UFH and the heparin cofactor activity that rapidly led to loss of thrombin activity in the presence of UFH. Abildgard in 1968 isolated an alpha 2 globulin that had both antithrombin and heparin cofactor activity.[225] Finally, Rosenberg and Damus showed that the progressive antithrombin and heparin cofactor were activities of a single glyoprotein, antithrombin III.[226] Egeberg in 1965 first described the association between an increased risk of TEs and deficiencies of antithrombin III.[227] Antithrombin III was renamed antithrombin (AT) by the Scientific Subcommittee of the International Society of Thrombosis and Haemostasis.

Antithrombin AT is produced in the liver as a single-chain glycoprotein, with a molecular weight of approximately 60 kDa and a plasma concentration of 125 ug/mL (Chapter 2).[228,229] AT is a serine protease inhibitor and inactivates thrombin as well as FXa, FIXa, FXIa, and FXIIa.[228,229] AT forms a 1:1 covalent bond with these proteases where the interaction takes place between the active center serine of the enzyme and the arginine reactive site in AT. The inhibition of serine proteases by AT is markedly accelerated physiologically by proteoglycans on the surface of endothelial cells and present in the vessel wall. Therapeutically, UFH promotes the formation of ternary complexes with AT and reduces the half-time of thrombin inhibition in plasma from 40 seconds to 10 milliseconds.[230] Similar rate enhancements have been observed for the inactivation of FXa and FIXa.[230]

Genetic variants The pattern of inheritance of AT deficiency is autosomal dominant with two major types.[231] Type 1 AT deficiency is characterized by decreased plasma concentrations of AT antigen and AT anticoagulant activities, indicating that the protein is not being produced by the mutant allele.[232] Type II AT deficiency is characterized by decreased AT activity but normal plasma concentrations of AT antigen.[233] Practically, this means that plasma concentrations of AT activity are significantly reduced, whereas plasma concentrations of AT are normal. Type II AT deficiency can be further subdivided into two subtypes: those affecting the UFH-binding site and those that reduce the neutralizing capacity of AT for thrombin activity in the absence of UFH.[234] A database of mutations is available.[234]

The gene coding for AT has been localized to chromosome Iq23-25 and has been completely elucidated.[235–237] The AT gene consists of seven exons and six introns spanning over 19 dB. Several molecular defects have been characterized.[235–237] In general, in type I deficiencies the AT gene remains grossly intact, with mutations associated with TEs comprised of small insertions, deletions, or point mutations within the gene.[234,238,239]

Laboratory testing Laboratory assays for AT consist of both functional and immunologic assays. There are two main types of functional assays for AT, a clot-based assay[240–244] or chromogenic assay.[245–250] The clot-based assay has essentially been replaced by the chromogenic assay. The chromogenic assays assess the inhibition of either exogenous thrombin or FXa. There are several commercial kits available for the measurement of AT by chromogenic assay (Chapter 13). Measurement of AT is slightly problematic in patients receiving UFH as plasma concentrations may be slightly decreased. Plasma concentrations of AT can be measured immunologically by commercially available ELISA assays or by in-house Laurell rocket or Mancini radial immunoassays using commercially available antibodies to AT. Variant AT with an increased affinity to UFH can be measured by crossed immunoelectrophoresis in the presence of UFH.[251]

Heterozygous Deficiency of Antithrombin

Prevalence in general population Initial reports described the prevalence of AT deficiency at 1:200 to 1:5000 but were based upon a functional assay that did not detect the AT activity by HCII.[42,49,252,253] Subsequent reports that used an assay that detected AT/HCII activity reported a prevalence in the general population at approximately 1:250.[252] The risk of heterozygote adults developing a TE by mid-adult life is approximately 50%.[7] Additional genetic and clinical risk factors are likely important code-terminants for the development of TEs.

Prevalence in adults with thromboembolic events Heterozygous AT deficiency is well described and usually presents with VTE in young adults, either spontaneously or following relatively minor acquired risk factors for VTE. Data from family surveys show that the median age of presentation of individuals with heterozygous AT deficiency is 24 years, and that 67% of affected individuals have their first episode prior to 35 years of age.[254] A first TE before the age of 16 is not uncommon in at least one member of afflicted families and about 50% of families have members with a first TE before the age of 15.[254,255] Deficiencies of Type I and the Type II patients with decreased AT and heparin cofactor activities have similar incidences of TEs.[256–261] Type II patients with normal progressive AT activity and decreased AT/heparin cofactor activity rarely develop TEs.[256–261]

The frequency of symptomatic AT deficiency in adults is estimated at between 1:2000[253] and 1:5000.[42,49] In unselected adults with a history of VTEs, the frequency is 1.1%[49] and in selected patients is 2.4%, based upon an analysis of 1750 reported cases.[262–265] There is some evidence that the specific genetic defect of the AT molecule may confer different risks for TE.[266] AT deficiency appears to confer a greater risk of TEs compared to most other congenital prothrombotic disorders including both protein C and protein S deficiency, particularly during pregnancy.[50,267] Whether some forms of AT deficiency result in an increased mortality compared to other congenital prothrombotic disorders is debated.[268,269]

Antithrombin Deficiency Combined with Other Congenital Prothrombotic Disorders Co-inheritance of AT deficiency with other congenital prothrombotic disorders increases the risk of TEs. The likelihood of TEs is substantially increased in patients who are heterozygous for both conditions.[122]

Antithrombin Deficiency in Children

Reference values for antithrombin Reference values for plasma concentrations of AT are available for fetuses,[4] premature infants,[3] full-term infants,[2] and throughout childhood (Figure 3–4).[2,3,5] In general, plasma concentrations of AT are decreased at birth and achieve average values within the adult range by 3 months of age, remaining relatively constant thereafter.

Absolute risk for thromboembolic events in children with antithrombin deficiency In contrast to adults, venous TEs secondary to heterozygous AT deficiency are rare during childhood and usually occur following a significant acquired risk factor for venous TE.[270] In large case series, AT deficiency and other physiologic anticoagulant deficiencies contributed to less than 5% of all venous TEs in pediatric patients.[271] A comprehensive family study reported a negligible incidence of VTE in AT-deficient heterozygotes prior to 15 years of age compared to an annual incidence of 0.87% in heterozygotes greater than 15 years of age.[123] Acquired forms of AT deficiency secondary to diseases such as nephrotic syndrome or liver disease are also linked to the development of VTE during childhood.[272] From 1966 to 1999, there were 57 children reported in the literature with heterozygous AT deficiency and TEs.[147,148,273–297]

Attributable or relative risk for thromboembolic events in children with antithrombin deficiency Few studies have included significant numbers of patients with AT deficiency. Nowak-Gottl[298] described 186 children with VTE compared to 186 age- and disease-matched controls. The OR for AT deficiency was 10.4; however, the small numbers meant that the 95% CI were wide (1.2–90). Aschka found only one child with AT deficiency in 125 children with TEs.[117] Veilhaber reported that 1 of 32 children with SVT had AT deficiency.[147] Similarly, Hagstrom reported a frequency of 1.8% in CNS thrombosis in children but found no cases of AT deficiency in a series of non-CNS thrombosis.[126] A number of other recent cohort studies have failed to identify AT deficiency in children with both arterial and venous TEs.[127,132,145,299] Those studies that reported higher frequencies of AT deficiency did not distinguish between acquired and inherited deficiency.[148]

Age distribution The age distribution of children with AT deficiency and TEs shows a predominance of infants less than 1 year of age (44%) and a second peak in the teenage years (29%).

Type of thromboembolic event Of the 55 cases reported in the literature in which the site of the TE was documented, the majority of children with AT deficiency had venous (n = 41) rather than arterial (n = 14) thrombosis. Occasionally, these children had TEs in unusual locations, such as coronary artery or portal vein thrombosis.

Treatment Treatment options used included UFH (seven), coumadin (nine with four placed on coumadin for life), danazol (five), FFP (five), AT concentrates (two), dialysis (two), LMWH (one), platelets (one), urokinase (one), and surgery (one).

Clinical outcome Clinical outcomes were reported in 23 children. Nine completely recovered, six were thrombosis free on coumadin, three have hemiparesis, one had only a partial resolution of the thrombus, and three died.

Antithrombin Deficiency in Neonates

Clinical presentation Eight publications identified 10 newborns with heterozygous AT deficiency and a TE.[274,278,279,285,286,292,297,300] The clinical presentation was diverse, reflected the site of the thrombus, and did not include purpura fulminans. TEs occurred in arterial or venous vessels and in a variety of unusual locations including the CNS and coronary arteries that resulted in myocardial infarction. One infant developed severe aortic and vena caval thrombosis that was fatal.

Treatment Four infants received AT concentrates: three therapeutically[278,286] and one prophylactically.[295] In one infant, a detailed assessment of the response to AT concentrates was available (Figure 3–5).[295] A bolus of 52 units/kg of AT concentrate (Hoechst Co., Germany) increased the plasma concentration of AT from 0.10 units/mL to 0.75 units/mL at 1 hour and to 0.18 units/mL at 36 hours.[295] A second bolus of 104 units/kg of AT con-

centrate resulted in a 90-minute value of 1.48 units/mL and 24-hour value of 0.19 units/mL. The infant was then treated with a continuous infusion of 2.1 units/kg/hour of AT concentrate that maintained a plasma concentration of AT of 0.40 to 0.50 units/mL. AT plasma concentrations in the other affected newborns were less than 0.30 units/mL.

Homozygous antithrombin deficiency Homozygous AT deficiency is extremely rare, presents within the first 10 years of life, causes severe TEs, which may be venous or arterial, and is associated with plasma concentrations of AT levels that are less than 10%.[252] From 1966 to 1999, there were seven children reported in the literature with homozygous AT deficiency who had TEs.[288,301–303] Ages at first presentation with TEs were 5 months, 1 week,[301] 3 weeks,[302] 9 years, and 10 years.[288] The ages of two brothers found to be compound heterozygotes were not reported. A description of the presentation of the TEs was provided in four children.[301] A 5-month-old girl suffered from right-sided hemiparesis, and an MRI revealed occlusion of the left middle cerebral artery and a large left-side cerebral infarct. Treatment of the child was not described. At age 14 months, she went on to develop IVC and external iliac thrombosis, and at that time was treated with urokinase for 3 weeks in total, followed by

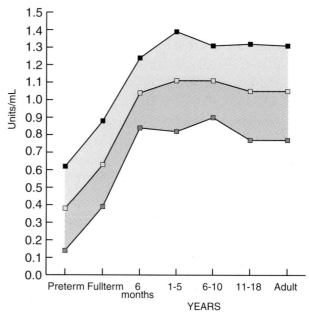

Figure 3–4 Mean values boundaries encompassing 95% of physiologic values for plasma concentrations of antithrombin over age.

long-term OAs. Follow-up MRI and venography showed complete dissolution of the iliac vein thrombus; however, the IVC remained completely occluded.[305] The second infant developed a DVT and an IVC thrombus at the age of 1 week. Recurrent DVT of the legs at age 13 years was diagnosed by venography and the patient subsequently maintained on long-term OAs.[301] The third patient presented at 9 years of age with spontaneous, complete occlusion of the IVC.[301] At least two children died within 3 weeks of birth.[302]

Protein C Deficiency

General Information

Historic perspective Stenflo in 1976 first identified protein C as a vitamin K-dependent protein with an unknown function.[304] Subsequently, Kisiel et al in 1977 showed that this protein was a serine protease that expressed anticoagulant activities when activated.[305,306] Seegers et al in 1976 showed that the anticoagulant activities of this serine protease were identical to a previously reported autoprothrombin IIa.[307,308] Since 1981, several hundred families with protein C deficiency have been reported.[309]

Protein C Protein C is produced in the liver, has a molecular weight of 62 kDa, and a plasma concentration of 4.0 ug/mL.[304,305,310–315] Activated protein C (APC) functions as an inhibitor by inactivating FVa and FVIIIa by limited proteolysis.[57,60] Protein C is converted to APC by thrombin bound to an endothelial cell surface receptor, TM.[58,316] Thrombin bound to TM no longer cleaves fibrinogen, FV, and FVIII or activates platelets.[58,59] However, thrombin bound to TM activates the vitamin K-dependent inhibitor protein C to its activated form, APC.[58,317] APC activity is enhanced by another vitamin K-dependent inhibitor, protein S, that functions as a cofactor. Patients with inherited deficiencies of protein C and protein S are at risk for TEs, usually as adults.

Genetic variants The pattern of inheritance of protein C deficiency is autosomal dominant with two major types.[318–321] Type 1 protein C deficiency is the most common and is characterized by decreased plasma concentrations of both protein C activity and antigen to approximately 50% of nor-mal.[318] Type I protein C deficiency consists of two subtypes. The first subtype is characterized by decreased activity in clot-based assays but normal activity in chromogenic assays.[318] The latter may be due to a decreased capacity of APC to interact with platelet membranes[318] or APC's substrates, FVa and FVIIIa. The second subtype is characterized by decreased activity in both clot-based and chromogenic assays.[319–321] For the latter, the activation of protein C to APC by the thrombin/TM complex is normal but without proteolytic activity, suggesting that the mutations reside near the serine reactive center.[252] Type 11 protein C deficiency is characterized by decreased protein C activity but normal plasma concentrations of protein C. Type I deficiencies are more common than type II mutations.

The gene coding for protein C has been localized to chromosome 2, position q14-q21, and has been completely elucidated.[305,322–324] The protein C gene consists of nine exons and eight introns spanning over 11 kB.[325,326] A database of mutations is available.[331] The gene defects include both nonsense and missense mutations, with the majority being point mutations that affect CpG dinucleotides.[327]

Laboratory testing Laboratory assays for protein C can be considered as functional and immunologic. There are two main types of functional assays that are dependent upon different endpoints: a clot-based assay and a chromogenic assay.[252] The two functional assays can distinguish between two subtypes of type I protein C deficiency.[252]

Measurement of protein C is problematic in patients receiving OAs because OAs decrease plasma activity and, to a lesser extent, plasma concentrations of vitamin K-dependent proteins, including protein C. One approach is to use a ratio of protein C antigen to prothrombin or FX antigen to identify patients with a type I deficiency state.[252] However, the accuracy of the latter approach is uncertain. Patients must be stable on OAs, and the intensity of OA therapy influences the interpretation of the results.[252] Another approach is to compare results from activity assays for protein C and FVII.[252] A more reliable approach is to measure protein C activity in patients who are switched to either UFH or LMWH.[252] OAs should be discontinued for a minimum of 1 week and ideally for a longer period of time prior to measuring protein C activity and antigen.

Heterozygous Deficiency of Protein C

Prevalence in general population The prevalence of type I protein C deficiency in healthy blood donors is 1:200 to 1:300.[36] However, none of the participants in the latter study had a personal or family history of TEs.[36] Similarly, parents of infants with homozygous protein C deficiency rarely have a history of TEs.[167,252] These observations indicate that other parameters modify the phenotypic expression of heterozygous protein C deficiency.

Prevalence in adults with thromboembolic events The risk of TEs appears not to be different for the different types of protein C deficiency (type I and II) or for the large number of mutations identified in protein C deficiency.[327] Family studies report that the risk of VTE is approximately 10 fold greater than for the general population and that approximately 50% of affected individuals will have experienced at least one TE by the age of 40.[328,329]

Protein C Deficiency in Children

Reference values for protein C At birth, plasma concentrations of protein C are very low and

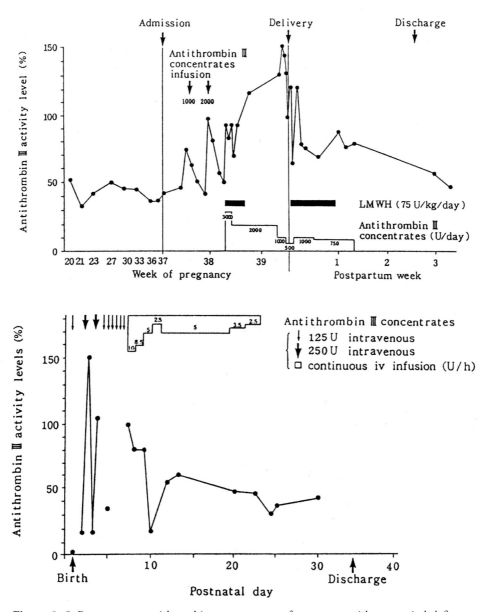

Figure 3–5 Response to antithrombin concentrates of a neonate with congenital deficiency of antithrombin treated with antithrombin concentrates.

remain decreased during the first 6 months of life.[2,3,5] A "fetal" form of protein C differs from the adult form by a twofold increase in single-chain protein C.[330] Plasma concentrations of protein C remain decreased throughout early childhood with approximately 40% of children having levels of protein C in the range at which spontaneous thrombotic disorders occur in heterozygous adults (Figure 3–6).[5] The latter is important to consider when evaluating children for heterozygote protein C deficiency. Although total amounts of protein S are decreased at birth, functional activity is similar to adult values because protein S is completely present in the free, active form, due to the absence of C4B binding protein.[331,332] The influence of age on endothelial cell expression of TM has not been determined; however, plasma concentrations of TM are increased several fold at birth and remain increased throughout childhood.[333] Whether the overall activity of the protein C/protein S system varies with age is unknown.

Absolute risk for thromboembolic events in children with heterozygous protein C deficiency A number of large studies have confirmed that heterozygous protein C deficiency does not usually present with thrombosis during childhood. De Stefano et al[231,334] reported the mean age of first thrombosis in heterozygote protein C deficiency to be during early adult life. Family studies have also reported a negligible incidence of VTE in heterozygotes prior to 15 years of age.[123]

Attributable or relative risk for thromboembolic events in children with heterozygous protein C deficiency Despite the low absolute risk, there are numerous case series and cohort studies suggesting increased prevalence of protein C heterozygosity in children with TEs (Table 3–13). The majority of these children had clinical risk factors that "unmasked" the congenital defect. Studies that failed to find increased heterozygote protein C deficiency in children with TEs are also summarized in Table 3–13.[144,146,147,151,172,335–338]

Age distribution The age range of the children described in studies summarized in Table 3–13 varies from neonates to teenagers. The diagnosis of heterozygote protein C deficiency in neonates is particularly difficult as physiologic values for protein C at birth may be as low as 12% of adult levels. Whether many of the patients reported represented true inherited protein C deficiency or transient acquired reduction in protein C levels is difficult to ascertain. Occasionally, patients were labelled as protein C deficient when the values were actually normal for age.

Treatment The antithrombotic treatment used was infrequently recorded; however, it usually followed adult guidelines. Clinical outcomes were also rarely reported.

Table 3–13 Frequency of Heterozygote Protein C Deficiency in Patients with Thrombosis

Author	Location of TE and Patient Population	Heterozygote (%)
Debus et al[151]	Porencephaly	6/24 (25)
Nowak-Gottl et al[138]	AIS	3/14 (21)
Veihaber et al[147]	SVT	6/32 (19)
Nowak-Gottl et al[145]	AIS/SVT	11/72 (15)
deVeber et al[148]	SVT/AIS	6/89 (7)
Nuss et al[299]	PE	1/14 (7)
Uttenreuther et al[111]	VTE	2/37 (5)
Toumi et al[337]	VTE	2/44 (5)
Sifontes et al[338]	VTE	0/14 (0)
Hagstrom et al[126]	AIS/non CNS VTE	0/85 (0)
Ganesan et al[143]	AIS	0/67 (0)

TE = thromboembolic event; AIS = arterial ischemic stroke; SVT = sinovenous thrombosis; PE = pulmonary embolism; VTE = venous thromboembolism; CNS = central nervous system.

Homozygous Protein C Deficiency

General information Homozygous protein C deficiency is a rare but life-threatening disorder. An international database of mutations in the protein C gene lists only 17 cases and approximately 25 further kindreds are reported in the literature.[36,54,88–95,339–361] The classic presentation of homozygous protein C deficiency is of neonatal purpura fulminans. Purpura fulminans is an acute, lethal syndrome of DIC with rapidly progressive hemorrhagic necrosis of the skin due to dermal vascular thrombosis.[362–364] Protein C levels in these patients are usually undetectable. However, homozygote protein C deficiency can also present with TEs during later childhood. Children with delayed presentation had detectable levels of protein C ranging from 0.02 to 0.23 units/mL. Frequently, there was no family history of TEs in these children with late presentation of homozygous protein C deficiency. Only approximately half of the children reported with homozygous protein C deficiency and late clinical presentation have been confirmed by DNA analysis to be true homozygotes.

Neonatal homozygous protein C deficiency The classic clinical presentation of homozygous protein C deficiency consists of cerebral and/or ophthalmic damage that occurred in utero, purpura fulminans within hours or days of birth, and, on rare occasions, large-vessel thrombosis. The skin lesions start as small ecchymotic sites that increase in a radial fashion and become purplish black with bullae and then necrotic and gangrenous (Figure 3–7).[363,364] The lesions occur mainly on the extremities but can occur on the buttocks, abdomen, scrotum, and scalp. They also occur at pressure points, at sites of previous punctures, and at previously affected sites. The neurologic complications have resulted in mental retardation and delayed psychomotor development. The eye involvement consists of vitreous or retinal hemorrhage secondary to thrombosis, resulting in partial or complete blindness. These infants also have severe diffuse DIC with secondary hemorrhagic complications. The clinical presentation of newborns with homozygous protein S deficiency is similar to homozygous protein C deficiency.[88] Diagnosing homozygote infants with PC deficiency depends upon the appropriate clinical

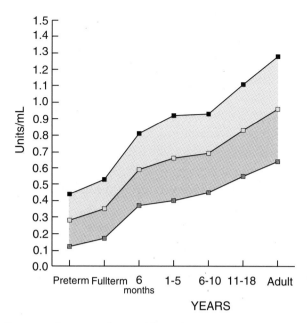

Figure 3–6 Mean values and boundaries encompassing 95% of physiologic values for plasma concentrations of protein C over age.

picture, a PC level that is essentially unmeasurable, and confirmation of a heterozygote state in the parents. The presence of decreased plasma concentrations of PC in the absence of clinical manifestations and family history cannot be considered diagnostic of homozygous PC deficiency as physiologic levels can be as low as 0.12 units/mL.

Initial treatment Neonatal purpura fulminans due to homozygous protein C deficiency is usually not anticipated, and urgent therapy is required. Numerous forms of therapy have been used and include FFP, protein C concentrate, cryoprecipitate, UFH, aspirin, sulfinpyrazone, corticosteroids, vitamin K, aprotinin, and AT concentrates. Protein C replacement therapy is the "physiologic treatment" for purpura fulminans and is recommended in the acute neonatal phase. However, few hospitals have a ready stock of protein C concentrate. Most frequently, the initial treatment is 10 to 20 mL/kg of FFP every 12 hours.[350,354] The plasma protein C levels achieved with these doses of FFP varied from 15% to 32% at 30 minutes after infusion and 4% to 10% at 12 hours.[350] Although FFP may restore protein C levels sufficiently to stop the purpura fulminans, many infants will not tolerate the volume required for ongoing replacement. Second, FFP is not virally inactivated. Protein C concentrate avoids both of these problems, and when available is usually substituted for FFP. Doses of protein C concentrate administered in the literature have ranged from 20 to 60 units/kg. A dose of 60 units/kg resulted in peak protein C levels above 0.60 units/mL.[365] Replacement of protein C was continued until the clinical lesions resolved, which was usually 6 to 8 weeks. In addition to the clinical course, plasma D-dimer concentrations were useful for monitoring the effectiveness of protein C replacement.

Long-term treatment strategies The modalities used for long-term management of infants with homozygous protein C deficiency included OAs and protein C replacement (FFP, protein C concentrate). Liver transplantation was performed successfully in at least one child.[366] Currently, the majority of children are treated with OAs with or without intermittent FFP. The dose of OAs depends on the weight of the child and the amount necessary to remain free of thrombotic complications. A validated protocol for introducing and monitoring OAs in children is now available (Chapter 10).[367,368] When therapy with OA is initiated, the infant should continue receiving protein C replacement until the INR is therapeutic to avoid skin necrosis. The recommended therapeutic range for the INR is 2.5 to 4.5. The risks associated with OAs include bleeding with high INRs and re-current purpuric lesions with low INRs. These children require frequent monitoring of their INR values, often weekly, to avoid these complications. Bone growth and development should also be monitored as the long-term effects of OAs on bone growth in children are not known.

Protein C concentrates Protein C concentrate is purified from vapour-heated PCCs by passage through a monoclonal antibody-coated column. The eluate is subjected to ion exchange, ultra and difiltration before vapour heat treatment. The concentrate is considerably safer than FFP in terms of risk of viral transmission. The major difficulty in the long-term use of protein C replacement therapy, apart from the cost, has been the need for long-term intravenous access. Protein C replacement therapy two to three times per week essentially converts a homozygote protein C deficient into a "severe heterozygote" in terms of circulating protein C levels. The presence of a CVL in this scenario is a strong stimulus for thrombotic complications and would usually necessitate OA as well. A number of authors have recently reported giving protein C concentrate subcutaneously as sole therapy to avoid the need for CVLs.[369,370] Doses of 250 units/kg subcutaneously every third day maintained adequate levels for 48 hours with peak levels at 12 hours post dose.

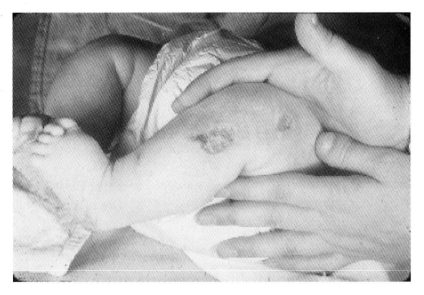

Figure 3–7 Clinical features of purpura fulminans in a neonate with homozygous protein C deficiency.

Late presentations of homozygous protein C deficiency Homozygous protein C deficiency may present with large-vessel thrombosis during childhood or early adult life. At least one patient with homozygous protein C deficiency is asymptomatic at 38 years of age.[347] The cases reported to date are summarized in Table 3–14. Grundy has confirmed homozygous status of a further four of these patients; each had the same nucleotide mutation resulting in a valine for alanine substitution at position 259 (based on Foster numbering system).[326,344] Thus, only 10 patients are confirmed as homozygotes by DNA analysis. Whether the remainder of patients represent double heterozygotes or true homozygotes is unknown.[339,342,347,351,371–375]

Clinical presentation The majority of patients presented with a spontaneous large-vessel thrombosis. Frequently, the possibility of homozygous protein C deficiency was considered when skin necrosis developed in response to initiation of OA therapy.

Therapy Therapeutic options include initial antithrombotic therapy with UFH or LMWH, followed by long-term oral anticoagulation, protein C replacement therapy, or long-term LMWH therapy. Protein C replacement was used in a number of patients during acute TEs or to treat acute skin necrosis. The difficulties of long-term replacement therapy are similar to those discussed for therapy of neonatal homozygote patients. Intravenous doses of 100 U/kg per day were necessary to maintain protein C levels above 20% at 24 hours (Figure 3–8).[360] Warfarin is the most commonly used therapy; however, 40% of patients developed skin necrosis while on warfarin. Skin necrosis is probably secondary to an imbalance between procoagulant and anticoagulant factors. High INRs, which reduce prothrombin levels substantially, may be required to avoid skin necrosis. Table 3–15 shows the protein C and prothrombin levels at various INR values for a homozygote with baseline levels of 0.07 U/mL. This patient developed skin necrosis whenever the INR fell below 3.5. Approximately 20% of patients suffered recurrent TEs during OA therapy, which contributed to alternative therapy being considered. LMWH has been used successfully in a number of patients. Twice-daily LMWH at therapeutic doses (1 mg/kg enoxaparin) were reported to give equivalent suppression of the thrombin antithrombin complexes (TATs) as therapeutic warfarin (INR 2-3) (Figure 3–9).[360] One patient developed a thrombosis during long-term therapy with prophylactic enoxaparin at a dose of 1 mg/kg/day. The effect of long-term therapy with LMWH on bone density is uncertain, especially at therapeutic doses, and careful monitoring is suggested (Figure 3–10).[360]

Protein S Deficiency

General Information

Anticoagulant activities Protein S is a single-chain glycoprotein that is a vitamin K-dependent inhibitor with a molecular weight of 69 kD and a plasma concentration of 25 ug/mL. Protein S circulates in two forms: a free active form and an inactive form that circulates bound to C_4B.[376] Protein S functions by enhancing the proteolytic activity of APC against FVa and FVIIIa.[377] The protein S enhancement of APC is dependent on the presence of membranes.[378] Protein S can reverse the FXa-mediated protection of FVa from proteolysis by APC.[379] When bound to C_4B, protein S is unable to act as a cofactor for APC.[380]

Protein S deficiency Since the initial reports in 1984, protein S deficiency has been identified in many families with TEs.[381,382] There are two main types of protein S deficiency. In type I or the classic form, plasma concentrations of total protein S antigen, free protein S antigen, and protein S functional activity are significantly decreased.[381,382] In type II, total protein S antigen plasma concentrations are normal but concentrations of free protein S and protein S activity are reduced to less than 50% of normal.[383,384] The latter may reflect a molecular abnormality in either protein S or C4b-binding protein that causes a shift in free protein S to the bound form.[383,384] There are some families with normal plasma concentrations of both total and free protein S, but the free protein S is not functional. Unexpectedly, there are some families where both type I and type II deficiencies are present, suggesting that other events influence the presence and form of protein S in plasma. Whether the various forms of pro-

Table 3–14 Late Presentations of Homozygous Protein C Deficiency

Author	First TE (year)	Protein C Ag/Act (%)	Therapy	Complications of Therapy	Comments
Yamamoto et al[623]	31	< 5	unknown	–	292 Gly to Ser
Melissari et al[374]	11	< 5/5	OA	TE	–
	29	7	OA	Skin necrosis	LMWH 3 Y
	13	16/14	OA	–	LMWH
	20	7.5/5	OA	–	–
	17	< 5/14	OA	TE	–
	20	6/5	OA	TE, skin necrosis	LMWH 3 Y
Tuddenham et al[351]	7M	< 1	OA	–	–
	10 M	–	OA	–	–
Conard[375]	17	16/10	OA	Skin necrosis	168 Pro to Leu
	24	23/22	OA	Skin necrosis	267 Ala to Thr
Pescatore et al[339]	45	20/20	OA	Skin necrosis	301 Gly to Ser LMWH 2 Y
Tripodi[347]	28	18/9	OA	–	–
		12/10	none	–	38 yrs old
Sharon[371]	25	10/5	OA	–	–
	11	12/9	OA	–	–
Manabe et al[372]	14	< 5	OA	–	–
Samama et al[373]	17	16/8	OA	Skin necrosis	–
Monagle et al[360]	9	7/7	OA/PPC	VTE skin necrosis	–
	Asymptomatic sibling	7/7	LMWH since 6 years	VTE at 11 year	–

TE = thromboembolic event; AO = oral anticoagulant; LMWH = low molecular weight heparin; PPC = protein C concentrates; VTE = venus thromboembolic event.

tein S deficiency result in the same or differing risks for TEs is unknown at this time.

Genetics The gene for protein S is located on chromosome 3 near the centromere[323,385] and consists of two separate genes designated PROS 1 and PROS 2, formerly alpha and beta respectively.[386–388] The two genes share a high degree of sequence identity. However, only the PROS 1 gene is transcriptionally active,[323,387,388] whereas the PROS 2 gene represents a pseudogene. The PROS 1 gene is more than 80 kilobases in length and contains 14 introns and 15 exons.

Laboratory testing Protein S can be measured by either functional or immunologic assays. All functional assays are based upon the capacity of protein S to function as a cofactor for APC proteolysis of FVa and FVIIIa in clot-based assays that are sensitive to plasma concentrations of protein S. Russell's viper venom or FXa is commonly used to initiate the assay rather than APTT reagents due to the differing sensitivities of APTT reagents to concentrations of protein S in samples, which limits their accuracy.[389–391] For the clot-based assays, protein S-deficient plasma is required and can be prepared by either immunodepletion or aluminum hydroxide adsorption of plasma with subsequent supplementation with purified prothrombin and APC.[391]

There are several immunologic assays that can be used to quantitate free and bound protein S.[392,393] The free and bound forms of protein S can be separated by either electrophoresis or by precipitation with polyethylene glycol.[383,393,394] Detection and quantitation of the amount of free protein S can be

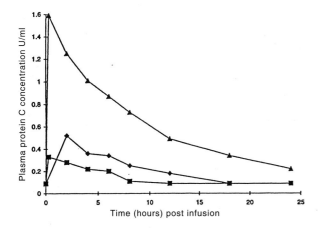

Figure 3–8 Plasma protein C levels after intravenous infusion of protein C concentrate to the proband plotted against time in hours. Doses infused on separate occasions were 40(■), 40(◆), and 100(▲) units/kg. Reproduced with permission.[360]

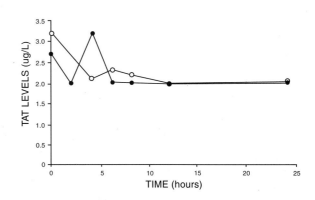

Figure 3–9 Comparison of 24-hour thrombin-antithrombin levels in twice-daily low molecular weight heparin (○) versus warfarin (●) therapy in proband, showing equivalent suppression. Reproduced with permission.[360]

determined by enzyme-linked immunosorbent assays,[395–397] Laurell rockets,[383] radioimmunoassay,[398–400] and crossed immunoelectrophoresis.[394] Measurements of plasma concentrations of protein S are problematic in patients receiving OAs.[391,99,401] Reduced ratios of protein S antigen to prothrombin antigen have been used; however, the reliability of this approach is uncertain and repeat measurements in the absence of OAs are advised.[402]

Heterozygous Deficiency of Protein S

Prevalence in general population The prevalence of protein S deficiency in the general population is uncertain and confounded by several variables including increasing plasma concentrations with age, more variable concentrations in females, and several families with APCR who were misclassified as protein S deficient.[403–405]

Prevalence in adults with thromboembolic events Similarly, the prevalence of protein S defi-

ciency in adults with TEs is uncertain because there are no formal, large-family studies assessing the relative risk of protein S deficiency for TEs and determining the molecular defect. However, the available evidence supports the conclusion that protein S deficiency increases the risk of thrombosis. The documented cases of homozygous protein S deficiency that appear to be as severe as homozygous protein C deficiency also support the latter conclusion.

Risk of thromboembolic events There are several reports of TEs in families with protein S deficiency. Engesser et al[406] analyzed 136 members of 12 families with hereditary protein S deficiency. A total of 55% had VTE and in 77% it was recurrent. The mean age of the first event was 28 years with a range from 15 to 68 years. At age 35, the probability of being free of thromboembolism was 32%. Although in general protein S deficiency-associated TEs do not occur until the teenage years, several cases of TEs have been reported in children as

Table 3–15 Plasma Protein C and Factor II Levels for Various INR Values While on Oral Anticoagulation Therapy

International Normalized Ratio	Factor II (Units/mL)	Protein C (Units/mL)
4.1	0.15	<0.01
3.4	0.12	<0.01
2.8	0.2	<0.01
1.3	0.68	0.07

INR = international normalized ratio.
Reproduced with permission.[360]

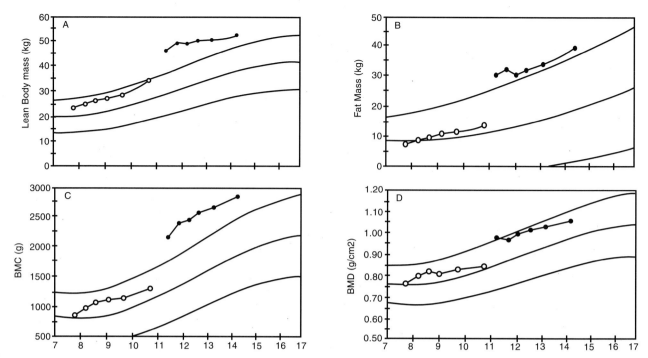

Figure 3–10 Lean body mass (*A*), fat mass (*B*), bone mineral content (*C*), and bone mineral density (*D*), for the proband (●) and sibling (○) as a function of age. Normal centiles (95th, 50th, 5th) are indicated. Although proband shows initial decrease in bone mineral density concurrent with twice-daily low molecular weight heparin therapy, normal growth resumes on daily therapy. Reproduced with permission.[360]

young as 2[407] or 3 years of age.[408,409] In individuals with heterozygous protein S deficiency, there is no relationship between plasma concentrations of protein S and age of onset of TEs, except for homozygous protein S deficiency, which presents at birth with purpura fulminans.

There is considerable heterogeneity in the severity of the TEs, which can be venous or arterial and occur in relatively unusual locations. In a small study of 34 patients with protein S deficiency, 25% had arterial thrombosis.[390] The incidence of protein S deficiency in patients who have had a stroke, particularly young patients, is increased compared to the general population and individuals with VTE.[410–414]

Disorders characterized by abnormal protein S plasma concentrations During pregnancy, plasma concentrations of total protein S are physiologically reduced to approximately 70% of normal and one-third of women have values less than the lower border of normal.[415,416] Plasma concentrations of C4b-binding protein are either unchanged or increased, which causes a shift of free protein S to complex formation, further reducing values for free protein S

and potentially increasing the risk for TEs.[415,417] Plasma concentrations of protein S return to normal values within a few days following delivery.[417] Oral contraceptives also reduce plasma concentrations of total protein S, as well as free protein S, with values between 75% and 84% of normal.[403,417–419] Patients with nephrotic syndrome usually have decreased plasma concentrations of total protein S[420–424] while free protein S values may be constant, increased, or decreased.[420–424] Patients with a lupus anticoagulant usually have normal plasma concentrations of total protein S[425–428] but reduced free protein S levels.[424,430] Liver disease results in moderately reduced total and free protein S levels.[401,431,432] In inflammatory diseases, free protein S levels are often decreased because plasma concentrations of C4b-binding protein, an acute phase reactant, are increased.[433,434]

Protein S Deficiency in Children

Reference values for protein S Protein S circulates completely in the free, active form in newborns,[331,332] because C4b-binding protein is absent in newborn plasma. The latter likely compensates for decreased plasma concentrations of total protein

S. The lower limits of normal for plasma concentrations of total protein S are between 0.41 to 0.54 units/mL and approximately 0.20 units/mL for free protein S during early childhood.[5] Figure 3–11 provides age-related reference ranges for protein S.

Absolute risk for thromboembolic events in children with heterozygous protein S deficiency The majority of cohort and family studies report that, similar to other inherited prothrombotic abnormalities, most patients with the heterozygous form of protein S deficiency do not suffer thromboembolic complications until adult life.[231,334,407,435]

Attributable or relative risk for thromboembolic events in children with heterozygous protein S deficiency Interpretation of the pediatric literature is difficult for a number of reasons. First, protein S deficiency frequently occurs as an acquired abnormality following infection, in particular varicella infection, in children.[436] Many papers do not clearly distinguish between congenital and acquired protein S deficiency. Second, recent literature has continued to highlight the difficulties in assaying protein S levels (Chapter 13). The lack of standardized assay procedures in addition to the inconsistent use of age-related reference ranges further complicates analysis of the current data for children. From 1966 to 1999, there were 40 case reports of children with heterozygous protein S deficiency and TEs during childhood. Of these, 21 were VTE and 11 arterial; 5 children had both venous and arterial thrombosis and in 3 children the site of thrombosis was not clear.[407,437–446] Thrombotic events included arterial ischemic stroke, cerebral sinus thrombosis, peripheral arterial and venous thrombosis, intracardiac and portal vein thrombosis. In addition, children were reported with primary pulmonary hypertension and purpura fulminans associated with intercurrent infection.

Over recent years, a number of cohort studies have examined the role of congenital prothrombotic disorders, including protein S deficiency in children with TEs (Table 3–16). Interestingly, a number of cohort studies that identified significant frequencies of other congenital prothrombotic disorders failed to identify protein S deficiency in their patient population. These negative studies included populations of children with AIS, SVT, VTE, arterial thrombosis, and CVL-related DVT.

Clinical presentation and therapy Children with symptomatic heterozygous protein S deficiency ranged from newborn to late adolescence in age. Many of the children had spontaneous TEs or TEs associated with minimal acquired clinical stimuli. The therapy used and the clinical outcome were not different from that seen in general for thrombosis in children. One paper reported reduced bone mineral density in children with protein S deficiency; however, whether this was related to the disease or the therapy is unknown.[446]

Homozygous protein S deficiency There are a small number of newborns described with homozygous protein S deficiency.[88,447–454] In addition, some children with compound heterozygous mutations have also been described. The first child reported in 1990 to have homozygote protein S deficiency and purpura fulminans has since been reported to actually be a compound heterozygote.[450] The majority of homozygotes or compound heterozygotes presented with purpura fulminans similar to that seen in homozygous protein C deficiency. The opthalmic complications have been described in detail and are similar to severe retinopathy of prematurity.[453] One paper has reported homozygous protein S deficiency presenting in adult life.[451] The plasma concentration of protein S in infants presenting with purpura fulminans is less than 1%.

Treatment There is no specific protein S concentrate available so treatment of purpura fulminans secondary to homozygous protein S deficiency requires either FFP or cryoprecipitate, which contains similar amounts of protein S.[88] A pharmacokinetic study was performed following the infusion of 10 mL/kg of FFP.[88] The recovery of protein S at 2 hours was 0.23 units/mL and at 24 hours 0.14 units/mL with the protein S entirely in the C4b-bound fraction on crossed immunoelectrophoresis. The approximate half-life of protein S in this infant was 36 hours. Long-term treatment strategies are similar to infants with protein C deficiency.

Hyperhomocysteinemia

General Information
Physiologic function Homocysteine is a sulphur-containing amino acid that is not a normal dietary constituent but is solely derived from methion-

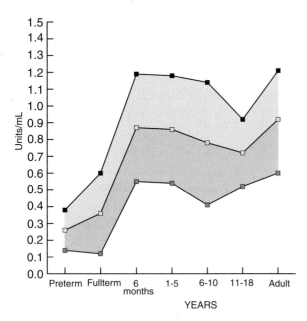

Figure 3–11 Mean values and boundaries encompassing 95% of physiologic values for plasma concentrations of total protein S over age.

ine. The metabolism of homocysteine is at the intersection of two metabolic pathways involving transsulfuration and remethylation (Figure 3–12).[455] In the transsulfuration pathway, homocysteine condenses with serine to form cystathionine in a reaction catalyzed by cystathionine B-synthase (CBS). Cystathionine is subsequently hydrolyzed to form cysteine and α-ketobutyrate. The transsulfuration pathway both synthesizes cysteine and catabolizes excess homocysteine not required in the remethylation pathway.

In the remethylation pathway, homocysteine acquires a methyl group from either N-5-methyltetrahydrofolate (MTHF) or betaine to form methionine, a process that is dependent on the cofactor vitamin B_{12}. Methionine is activated by adenosine triphosphate (ATP) to form S-adenosylmethionine or SAM, which is a universal methyl donor and is subsequently hydrolyzed to regenerate homocysteine. Under physiologic conditions, cellular homocysteine is exported, resulting in low plasma concentrations of homocysteine (10 umol/L).[456] Increased plasma concentrations of homocysteine indicate that the intracellular homocysteine metabolism is abnormal and characterized by increased exportation out of cells, which limits intracellular toxicity but exposes the vasculature to the adverse effects of hyperhomocysteinemia.

Hyperhomocysteinemia is a proven independent risk factor for atherosclerotic vascular disease affecting coronary, cerebral, and peripheral arteries.[457–459] Hyperhomocysteinemia induces its prothrombotic state by adversely affecting the vessel wall, the coagulation system, and platelet function.[457–459] Homocysteine promotes vascular smooth muscle cell growth, oxidizes low-density lipoprotein (LDL), and may adversely affect platelet function. Hyperhomocysteinemia can be secondary

Table 3–16 Prevalence of Protein S Deficiency in Children with Thromboembolic Events

Author	Population	Number	Frequency of Heterozygote Protein S Deficiency	Comments
de Veber[148]	AIS/SVT	87	10/87	Free protein S
Ganesan[143]	AIS	67	1/67	
Sifontes[132]	DVT	14	36173	Spontaneous
Hagstrom[126]	AIS	56	1/56	
	DVT	34	6/34	Majority in patients with spontaneous DVT
Nuss[299]	PE	13	36231	
Bonduel[146]	AIS	3010	3/30	
	SVT		1/10	
Koh[626]	AIS	37	5/37	
Ashka[117]	Arterial TE and venous TE	125	6/125	
Debus[151]	Porencephaly	24	36242	

AIS = arterial ischemic stroke; SVT = sinovenous thrombosis; DVT = deep vein thrombosis; CNS = central nervous system; PE = pulmonary embolism; TE = thromboembolic events.

to either a genetic defect or an acquired nutritional deficiency of vitamin B_6 and vitamin B_{12}.[460,461]

Genetic variants Genetic causes of hyperhomocysteinemia are a deficiency of CBS,[462] a deficiency of 5,10-methylenetetrahydrofolate reductase (MTHFR),[463] and the recently identified thermolabile variant of MTHFR.[464–466]

Cystathionine-B-synthase deficiency: The classic severe form of hyperhomocysteinemia, which is also characterized by homocystinuria, is due to a homozygous deficiency of CBS that results in markedly increased fasting plasma homocysteine concentrations in the range of 400 umol/L.[467] There are several mutations of CBS that can cause homocystinuria, some of which are responsive to treatment with large dosages of vitamin B_6.[468–473]

5,10-methylenetetrahydrofolate reductase deficiency: Homozygous deficiencies of MTHFR or other enzymes necessary for the synthesis of methylated vitamin B_{12}, although very rare, also cause markedly increased plasma homocysteine concentrations.[466,474–479] Patients with MRHFR deficiency also have decreased plasma concentrations of methionine.

Thermolabile variant of 5,10-methylenetetrahydrofolate reductase: Kang et al reported hyperhomocysteinemia and low folate concentrations in a variant of MTHFR that was characterized by thermolability associated with decreased activity.[466] Subsequent studies showed that the thermolabile variant of MTHFR was autosomal recessive, due to a single point mutation, present in approximately 5% of the population and in nearly one-third of patients with premature arterial disease.[480–482] Similar to other congenital prothrombotic disorders, there is evidence that the prevalence of thermolabile MTHFR varies significantly in populations with different racial backgrounds.[465,483,484]

Plasma folate concentrations appear to influence plasma concentrations of homocysteine in individuals with thermolabile MTHFR. Decreased plasma concentrations of folate are linked to increased concentrations of homocysteine with the reverse also being true.[464,466,484] Homozygotes for the thermolabile MTHFR likely have an increased folate requirement compared to individuals with a normal genotype.

Nutritional causes of hyperhomocysteinemia Several studies have convincingly shown that there is an inverse correlation between plasma concentrations of homocysteine and both folate and vitamin B_{12}.[454,466]

Laboratory testing Measurement of plasma homocysteine following overnight fasting is necessary for this diagnosis and age-related normal values are available.[485] An oral methionine loading test with pre- and post-methionine plasma homocysteine levels increases the sensitivity of plasma homocysteine testing. For homozygous homocystinuria, plasma amino acid assays are an adequate screen.

Heterozygous State

Prevalence in adults with arterial disease In 1969, the relationship between severe hyperhomocysteinemia and arterial disease was reported in a patient with autopsy evidence of atherosclerosis and precocious arterial thrombosis in a homocystinuric patient.[486] In 1976, a subsequent study showed that following a methionine load there were increased plasma concentrations of homocysteine-cysteine mixed disulfide in patients with coronary artery disease compared to controls.[487] Numerous studies followed showing that mildly increased homocysteine plasma concentrations (31%) present a risk factor for coronary artery disease,[459,486,488–491] cerebrovascular disease,[457,492–495] and peripheral artery disease.[459,496,497]

Prevalence in adults with venous thromboembolic disease Although historically, arterial TEs have been associated with homocystinuria, recent studies have shown that approximately 50% of TEs are venous (Table 3–17).[462,498,499,628–635] Event free survival analysis shows that patients with moderate hyperhomocysteinemia have a 1.7 greater chance of developing TEs and an increased incidence of recurrent TEs.[498]

Hyperhomocysteinemia combined with other congenital prothrombotic disorders The possibility that co-inheritance of hyperhomocysteinemia and other congenital prothrombotic disorders could synergistically interact to increase the risk for TEs was evaluated in seven large kindreds in which at least one member had homozygous homocystinuria.[499] TEs occurred in 6 of 11 individuals with homocystinuria before the age of 8 years and all 6 patients also had APCR. Conversely, of four patients with homocystinuria who did not have activated protein C resistance, none had thrombosis occurring before the age of 17 years. The investigators

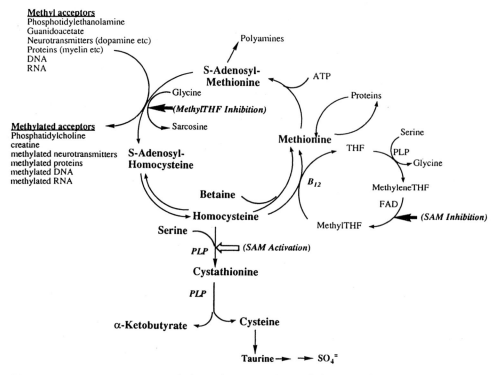

Figure 3–12 Homocysteine metabolic pathways. In the methylation pathway, homocysteine acquires a methyl group either from betaine, a reaction that occurs mainly in the liver or from 5-methyltetrahydrofolate, a reaction that occurs in all tissues and is vitamin B_{12} dependent. In the transsulfuration pathway, homocysteine condenses with serine to form cystathionine in a reaction that is catalyzed by cystathionine-β-synthase and requires pyridoxal-5'-phosphate.

Reproduced with permission.[455]

concluded that the combination of homocystinuria and activated protein C resistance conveys a substantial risk for thrombosis.[101]

Hyperhomocystinemia in Children

Reference values for homocysteine Fasting total plasma homocysteine levels have recently been determined for children. Balasa et al studied fasting morning blood samples from 197 children aged 6 months through 16 years admitted for elective day surgery.[216] Homozygosity for MTHFR C667T genotype was present in 11% of Caucasian children and 3% of African-American children in this patient cohort. Children homozygous for the MTHFR C677T genotype were more likely to have homocysteine levels greater than the 95th percentile. Mean homocysteine levels were 8.4 ± 8.0 for homozygote C667T children compared to 5.9 ± 5.4 for "wild type" normals.

Absolute risk of thrombosis for children with increased homocysteine levels There is insufficient evidence at present to make conclusions about the role of increased homocysteine levels or the MTHFR polymorphism in either venous or arterial thrombosis in children. The high frequency of the MTHFR polymorphism in Caucasian populations, in contrast to the low incidence of TEs in children, suggests that in the absence of significant clinical risk factors, this abnormality is not associated with an increased absolute risk of thrombosis.

Attributable or relative risk of thrombosis for children with increased homocysteine levels McColl et al described a cohort of 37 children with AIS in whom 7 were homozygote for the MTHFR mutation and 13 were heterozygote.[142] The study reported an OR of 1.7 (95% CI: 0.6–4.5) for AIS in the presence of MTHFR. Veilhaber described increased homocysteine levels in only 1 of 32 children with SVT.[147] Fabri found no relationship between the presence of MTHFR and thrombosis in patients with nephrotic syndrome.[130]

HOMOCYSTEINURIA

Genetic defect Homocystinuria is an inborn error of methionine metabolism secondary to CBS deficiency. CBS catalyzes the conversion of homocysteine and serine to cystathionine. The incidence of homocystinuria is 0.5–1/100,000, with affected individuals usually presenting during early childhood. The disease is inherited as an autosomal recessive, with the gene mapped to chromosome 21q22. The pathologic finding is massive accumulation of homocysteine resulting in ocular, musculoskeletal, central nervous system, and vascular manifestations.

Clinical presentation Individuals with homocystinuria usually present during childhood, after the age of 3 years, with the presenting feature being ectopic lens. The musculoskeletal changes resemble those seen in Marfan syndrome. Over 50% have progressive mental retardation and psychiatric disorders. Thromboembolism occurs in 12% to 27% of untreated patients by the age of 15 years. The thrombosis involve large or small vessels, arteries, or veins in any part of the body but especially the brain. There is also an increased risk of TEs after surgical procedures.

Treatment Management consists of a specific diet and replacement with B$_6$ and betaine, which lowers homocysteine levels by remethylating homocysteine to methionine. Aggressive management and reduction of serum homocysteine levels can avoid most of the thromboembolic complications.

Dysfibrinogenemia

General Information

Fibrinogen Fibrinogen is synthesized by hepatocytes and has a molecular weight of 340 kD and a plasma concentration of approximately 3.5 g/L. Each fibrinogen molecule is comprised of two symmetric half-molecules, each of which has three polypeptide chains termed A-alpha, Bß, and y-yammoto (Chapter 2). Cleavage of fibrinogen to fibrin has three phases that are relevant to the testing for dysfibrinogenemias: (1) thrombin proteolyzes fibrinogen to form fibrin by cleaving fibrinopeptide A (FPA) and fibrinopeptide B (FPB) from the Aα and

Table 3–17 Relationship between Homocysteine and Thrombosis

Author	Thrombosis Type	Age (years)	Patients %	Controls %	Odds Ratio (95% CI)
Brattstrom et al[630]	Venous	< 50	14.5	5	3.1 (0.4–27.7)
Amundsen et al[628]	Deep vein	< 56	5.7	2.6	2.3 (0.1–68.5)
			5.7	2.5	2.3 (0.1–68.5)
Bienvenu et al[629]	Arterial + venous	< 58	36	4	13.2 (2.82–83.0)
Falcon et al[631]	Juvenile venous	< 40	8.8	0	00 (1.16–00)
			18.8	2.5	9.1 (1.38–194)
Fermo et al[632]	Venous + arterial	< 45	8.9	5	1.9 (0.5–6.6)
			21.8	5	5.3 (1.7–17.1)
den Heijer et al[498]	Deep vein	44	10	5	2.5 (1.2–5.2)
Cattaneo et al[633]	Deep vein	–	13.5	6.7	2.2 (0.8–6.0)
Simioni et al[634]	Deep vein	62	25	11.5	2.6 (1.1–5.9)
den Heijer et al[635]	Recurrence thrombosis	62P	25	10	2.0 (1.5–2.7)
		51C	24	10	2.6 (1.9–3.6)
Petri et al[499]	Atherothrombotic lupus	38	15	10	3.49 (0.97–12.54)

CI = confidence interval.
Reproduced with permission.[7,10]

Bß chains; (2) fibrin self-assembles to form an organized polymeric structure; and (3) fibrin strands are cross-linked by FXIIIa.

Genetic variant Approximately 45 different dysfibrinogenemias that predispose to TEs have been described. Dysfibrinogenemias are usually autosomal recessive disorders and consanguinity is commonly present in severely affected individuals. Hypodysfibrinogenemias are more complicated and can be either dominant or recessive in inheritance. The majority of dysfibrinogenemias associated with thrombophilia are listed in Table 3–18, with each mutant named after the city of origin of the patient initially affected.[500] The majority of dysfibrinogenemias have single amino acid substitutions.[500]

Functional abnormalities The mechanism by which dysfibrinogenemias occurs appears to be decreased biosynthesis rather than increased utilization. The relationship between the defective fibrinogen molecule and the phenotype of TEs is still poorly understood. In general, there are two functional abnormalities in dysfibrinogenemias associated with TEs. The first involves impaired binding of thrombin to the abnormal fibrin[501–505] and the second involves defective fibrinolysis due to impaired assembly of TPA and plasminogen activation on the abnormal fibrin.[508–512] Impaired thrombin binding is mainly associated with mutations involving the N-termini while defective fibrinolysis is most commonly associated with a truncation of the Aα chain C-termini.[500] Fibrinogens New York, Naples, and Pamplona impair thrombin binding to fibrinogen, resulting in an excess of free thrombin, which can cleave normal fibrinogen and induce platelet aggregation.[503–532] Abnormal TPA-mediated plasminogen activation is characteristic of fibrinogen Nijmegen, Ijmuiden, Dusart, Chapel Hill III, and Pamplona.[507–513,523,524] Fibrinogen Ijmuiden is also associated with abnormal FPB release.[524] In some mutants, defective polymerization leads to thin fibrin fibers with small pores that may be resistant to plasmic digestion. Congenital dysfibrinogenemias may also be associated with abnormal interactions with platelets and defective calcium binding.

Delayed wound healing and wound dehiscence, as reported for fibrinogens Paris I, Cleveland, and Caracas I, may be due to abnormal factor XIIIa-mediated cross-linking, which results in decreased clot strength. Recurrent spontaneous abortions (mainly in the first trimester) associated with bleeding or thrombosis also occur. The mechanism by which dysfibrinogenemia causes infertility or spontaneous abortion is unknown.

Laboratory testing Coagulation tests that use the appearance of a fibrin clot as the endpoint may be abnormal in the presence of dysfibrinogenemias, particularly if there is an associated hypofibrinogenemia. A prolonged PT or APTT is usually the first indicator that a dysfibrinogenemia is present, with the PT being somewhat more sensitive than the APTT. Either a sensitive thrombin clotting time (TCT), which is performed in the absence of calcium with low concentrations of thrombin, a reptilase time or ancrod time is a more sensitive assay to detect dysfibrinogenemias.[533,534] Fibrinogen plasma concentrations measured as clottable protein may be decreased[533,534] but normal when measured immunologically. The discrepancy between clottable and immunologic assays measuring fibrinogen is characteristic for dysfibrinogenemias. The physiologic "fetal" fibrinogen that is uniformly present at birth also prolongs sensitive TCTs and reptilase times, and must be considered when interpreting results for these tests. More sensitive assays that directly measure release of FPA/FPB and polymerization can be used to further characterize the defect. The specific defects resulting in hypofibrinogenemia, with or without associated hypofibrinogenemia, are classed according to whether they result in abnormal release of FPA/FPB, impair fibrin assembly, or cross-linking by FXIII.

Heterozygous State

Prevalence The prevalence of dysfibrinogenemias in the general population is not precisely known due to its rarity. The prevalence of dysfibrinogenemias in adults with TEs is not exactly known because studies are hindered by the low frequency of dysfibrinogenemia in cohorts of patient with TEs. One estimate is that dysfibrinogenemias occur in 0.8% of adults presenting with TEs.[535]

Clinical presentation The clinical presentation is varied and consists of venous thrombosis, PE, arterial occlusion, and bleeding. Approximately 50% of individuals with dysfibrinogenemia do not have clinical symptoms, bleeding occurs in 28%, thrombosis in 20%, and both in the remaining 2%.[500] Some dysfibrinogenemias are associated with impaired wound healing and spontaneous abortion.[533,536] The most common clinical presentations are at birth with umbilical cord bleeding or local bleeding following puncture sites performed for routine neonatal screening.[500] During childhood, bleeding in the form of epistaxis, menorrhagia, gastrointestinal hemorrhage, and hemarthrosis may all occur.[500] Often a relatively mild acquired insult such as trauma can induce bleeding, particularly if the fibrinogen plasma concentration is less than 50 mg/dL.[500] ICH is the most frequent cause of death and may occur at any age.[500] TEs are also a cause of death and may be precipitated by fibrinogen infusions.[500]

Homozygous State The homozygous state of dysfibrinogenemias associated with TEs is rarely described. Homozygous members of the fibrinogen Naples I kindred suffered juvenile arterial stroke, thrombotic abdominal aortic occlusions, and postoperative deep venous thrombosis.[503,504]

Dysfibrinogenemias Combined with Other Congenital Prothrombotic Disorders Fibrinogen Cedar Rapids is a heterozygous dysfibrinogenemia associated with TEs during pregnancy.[526] Co-inheritance of FV Leiden was present in individuals with fibrinogen Cedar Rapids who developed TEs but absent in family members who had the fibrinogen defect but did not have FV Leiden.[526] The exact mechanism by which two coexisting conditions contribute to the thrombophilic state is not clear, but such conditions may ultimately be found in certain families with thrombophilia, especially those with variable clinical expression of TEs such as fibrinogens Kumamoto, Melun I, Kaiserslautern, and Giessen IV.[500]

Table 3–18 Dysfibrinogenemias Associated with Thrombophilia

Molecular Defect	Name	Hypofibrinogenimia	Bleeding	Thrombophilia
AαR19G	Aarhus I, Kumamoto	0	0	Yes
Aα451insert/453 stop-albumin	Miulano III	0	0	Yes
Aα461 stop-albumin	Marburg I	Yes	0	Yes
AαS532C	Caracas V	0	Yes	Yes
AαR5546C-albumin	Dusart, Chapel Hill III	0	0	Yes
BβR14C	Ijmuiden	0	0	Yes
Bβ9-72del	New York I	0	0	Yes
BβR44C	Nijemegen	0	0	Yes
BβR44C	Naples I	0	0	Yes
Bβchain	Oslo I	0	0	Yes
γR275C	Bologna I, Cedar Rapids	0	0	Yes
γR275H	Haifi I, Barcelona III, Bergamo II	0	0	Yes
γG292V	Baltimore I	0	0	Yes
γN308K	Bicetre II	0	0	Yes
γD318G	Giessen IV	0	0	Yes
Yes γdel319N,320D	Vlissengen	0	0	Yes
γD364V	Melun I	0	0	Yes
γK380N	Kaiserslautern	0	0	Yes
Unknown	Malmoe I	Yes	0	Yes

Reproduced with permission.[500]

Lipoprotein Disorders

General Information

Lipids Lipids present in plasma consist of cholesterol, cholesteryl esters, phospholipids, and triglycerides. *Cholesterol* is comprised of 27 carbon atoms arranged in a sterol nucleus of four rings and a tail. Cholesterol is stored within cells in the form of *cholesteryl esters,* which are comprised of a fatty acid with an ester bond at the third carbon of cholesterol. Approximately one-third of cholesterol in humans is derived from diet and two-thirds by in vivo synthesis. *Fatty acids* are long chains of carbon atoms that are classified according to the bonding of hydrogen atoms. Unsaturated fatty acids have no hydrogen atoms, saturated fatty acids have all available carbons occupied by hydrogen atoms, and polyunsaturated fatty acids have two or more carbons occupied by hydrogen atoms. Fatty acids are important components of triglycerides and phospholipids. *Triglycerides* are lipids characterized by a three-carbon basic structure (glycerol) to which fatty acids bind through ester bonds. Triglycerides can be either synthesized in specific cell types or derived from diet. *Phospholipids* are lipids that, similar to triglycerides, frequently have a glycerol basic structure but to which two fatty acids and a phosphorus containing molecule are bound.

Lipoproteins Lipoproteins are spherical in shape with a surface comprised of apolipoproteins, phospholipids, and cholesterol and a core comprised of triglycerides and cholesteryl esters. There are four major groups of lipoproteins that are classified, primarily, by their density and consist of chylomicrons, very low-density lipoproteins (VLDL), low-density lipoproteins (LDL), and high-density lipoproteins (HDL). *Apolipoproteins* are critically important for solubilizing lipids in plasma and function as cofactors or receptors in lipid metabolism. The nucleotide sequence for many apoproteins is known and has facilitated our understanding of dyslipoproteinemias.

Genetic variants Hyperlipidemia is a major risk factor for atherosclerotic vascular disease in adults. There is considerable evidence that hypercholesterolemic adults have abnormal levels during childhood, which has led to a major effort to detect affected children, in the belief that early intervention will be of benefit.[537,538,539] However, the age at which intervention should optimally commence remains unknown, as is the outcome of intervention therapy.

Hyperlipidemias in Children

Reference values for plasma concentrations of lipids and lipoproteins Plasma concentrations of both lipids (cholesterol, triglyceride) and lipoproteins (HDL, LDL, and VLDL) during childhood are provided in Table 3–19. Plasma concentrations of both lipids and lipoproteins are relatively stable throughout childhood, with a few exceptions. Plasma concentrations of total triglycerides increase in the second decade of life with males having levels higher than females, and HDL significantly decreases in young male teenagers. Abnormal single measurements of lipids and lipoproteins in children are not necessarily diagnostic of a specific acquired or inherited lipid disorder.

Screening The issue of whether there are significant benefits from universal screening for lipid disorders, either acquired or congenital, remains unresolved. A causal relationship between relatively mild hyperlipidemia during childhood and coronary artery disease in adults has not been conclusively demonstrated. However, there is evidence that cholesterol deposits are present in coronary arteries in some children, who are completely asymptomatic by 10 years of age. Screening for lipid disorders should be considered in children if one of their parents has a cholesterol concentration exceeding 240 mg/dL, or there is a family history of premature cardiovascular disease and/or xanthomas are present.

Laboratory testing Screening using an umbilical cord sample is feasible if one of the parents has familial hypercholesterolemia (FH). In other situations, screening becomes accurate after approximately 2 years of age. Ideally, samples should be obtained following a 12-hour fast and as either serum or into EDTA. Although the simplest screening procedure is to measure total cholesterol, measurement of total cholesterol, total triglyceride, and HDL cholesterol with subsequent calculation of LDL cholesterol is preferable.

Secondary versus congenital hyperlipidemias
The causes of secondary hyperlipidemia during childhood due to specific diseases include glycogen storage disease, congenital biliary atresia, hypothyroidism, diabetes mellitus, and the nephrotic syndrome. However, exogenous risk factors such as certain medications (oral contraceptives, prednisone, etc.) are likely equally as important. A diagnosis of primary hyperlipidemia is made only following exclusion of potential secondary causes.

Common Clinical Presentations of Hyperlipidemias Arterial thrombosis secondary to clinically significant hyperlipidemias can present with myocardial ischemia, cerebrovascular disease, and peripheral artery disease during childhood.

Myocardial infarction The classic hyperlipidemic state associated with myocardial infarction in childhood is homozygous FH.[540] Cerebrotendinous xanthomatosis and phytosterolemia are other rare familial sterol storage disorders associated with premature atherosclerosis and may cause myocardial infarction during childhood.[541] None of the other primary hyperlipidemic syndromes are associated with myocardial ischema in childhood.[542,543]

Cerebrovascular disease There are a number of retrospective studies that have failed to demonstrate any role for hyperlipidemia in childhood stroke.[544] Studies in homozygous FH show that atherosclerosis in the cerebral circulation lags many years behind aortic and coronary artery disease.[545-547] Postulated reasons for the lack of cerebrovascular disease include differences in shear stress, endothelial glycosaminoglycans (GAGs) composition, and protection from hypertension by the universal presence of aortic stenosis in these patients.[545,546,548] Glueck et al identified a small cohort of children in whom decreased HDL levels and increased TG levels were associated with otherwise unexplained stroke.[549,550] However, they identified the same abnormalities in children with migraines.[551]

Peripheral arterial disease Arteriosclerosis is associated with spontaneous hand and digital ischemia in some teenagers and young adults.[552] However, an associated hyperlipidemic state is not necessarily present.[552] Patients with homozygous FH may develop peripheral atherosclerosis, but it is rarely clinically significant.[553]

Classification of Congenital Dyslipoproteinemia Historically, patients with hyperlipidemia were classified into five major groups according to plasma lipoprotein patterns based on the relative concentrations of various fractions of cholesterol such as LDL, HDL (inversely), and lipoprotein (a) (Lpa).[537,538,542] However, these lipoprotein patterns were not diagnostic for a given genotype and more recent studies have focused on defining the underlying biochemical defects responsible for a given phenotype. The following section discusses only some of the more

Table 3–19 Physiologic Concentration of Lipids during Childhood

Lipid	Sex	Concentration (Range) at Age:			
		0–4 years	5–9 years	10–14 years	15–19 years
Cholesterol (mg/dL)	Female	156 (112–200)	164 (126–205)	160 (124–201)	158 (120–203)
	Male	155 (144–203)	160 (121–203)	158 (119–202)	150 (113–197)
Triglycerides (mg/dL)	Female	64 (34–112)	60 (32–105)	75 (37–131)	75 (39–132)
	Male	56 (29–99)	56 (30–101)	66 (32–125)	78 (37–148)
HDL cholesterol (mg/dL)	Female	-	53 (36–73)	52 (37–70)	52 (35–74)
	Male	-	56 (38–75)	55 (37–74)	46 (30–63)
LDL cholesterol (mg/dL)	Female	-	100 (68–140)	97 (68–136)	96 (59–137)
	Male	-	93 (63–129)	97 (64–133)	94 (62–130)
VLDL cholesterol (mg/dL)	Female	-	10 (1–24)	11 (2–23)	12 (2–24)
	Male	-	8 (0–18)	10 (1–22)	13 (2–26)

HDL = high-density lipoproteins; LDL = low-density lipoproteins; VLDL = very low-density lipoproteins; mg/dL = milligrams/decaliter.

common congenital dyslipoproteinemias that are associated with arterial and, in some rarer circumstances, venous thrombosis in children.

Familial hypercholesterolemia Familial hypercholesterolemia is the most commonly recognized and best understood disorder of lipoprotein metabolism in childhood.[554] Inheritance of FH is autosomal dominant with an incidence of 1 in 500 for heterozygotes and 1 in 1 million for homozygotes.

Clinical presentation of homozygotes: FH is expressed at birth and affected children present with significantly increased serum cholesterol concentrations at birth, cutaneous xanthomata, and coronary artery disease within the first decade of life.[555,556] They develop a classic pattern of atherosclerosis that involves the aortic root leading to aortic stenosis, and coronary artery ostia leading to obstruction.[540,557] Distal coronary arteries are often pristine until adult life. Receptor negative patients have more severe disease than receptor defective patients[543] and males are often more severely affected than females.[558] Death from acute myocardial infarction has been described as early as 18 months of age, and survival beyond the third decade is rare.[557,559–561]

Diagnosis of homozygotes: FH is due to absent or defective LDL receptors, which results in increased serum concentrations of LDL by approximately sixfold and decreased HDL cholesterol concentrations.[562]

Treatment of homozygotes: Plasmapheresis and LDL apheresis are usually required to maintain reduced serum concentrations of LDL cholesterol because diet and drug therapy are frequently ineffective.[554,558,563]

Heterozygotes: In FH heterozygotes, serum concentrations of total and LDL cholesterol are increased by approximately threefold. Clinical evidence of ischemic heart disease does not usually become apparent until early adult life. However, 66% of asymptomatic teenagers with a positive family history and 25% of teenagers with a negative family history have abnormal cardiac stress thallium scans, which have a significant correlation with angiographic abnormalities in individuals with FH.[564,565] If a parent is identified to have FH, FH heterozygotes can be detected reliably at birth using umbilical cord blood where cord serum LDL cholesterol concentrations exceed the 95th percentile or 41 mg/dL.[556] For heterozygotes greater than 1 year of age, total and LDL cholesterol concentrations are usually well above the 99th percentile.

Familial defective apolipoprotein B100 Homozygous familial defective apolipoprotein B100 is secondary to a substitution of glutamine for arginine at position 3500 in the apoB-100 polypeptide.[566] Patients heterozygous for this disorder have moderate increases in serum concentrations of LDL cholesterol due to defective removal of LDL from plasma by LDL receptors.[567,568] Apolipoprotein B100 may occur in as many as 1:500 people but is only responsible for a small proportion of premature CAD. Homozygous familial defective apolipoprotein B100 has a similar clinical presentation compared to homozygous FH.[569,570]

Increased concentrations of Lp(a) Lp(a) is a large lipoprotein with a lipid composition similar to LDL. However, Lp(a) is comprised of two proteins, apoB-100 and a large glycoprotein called apo(a), which is attached to apoB-100 through a disulfide bond. The primary structure of the apo(a) polypeptide is similar to plasminogen.[571] Increased serum concentrations of Lp(a) are inherited, expressed during childhood, and a significant risk factor for CAD in early adult life, similar to heterozygous FH.[572,573] If a parent has increased serum concentrations of Lp(a) level, the children should be tested, usually by an immunochemical method.

Treatment of Hyperlipidemias

Treatment Regardless of the screening approach selected a nutritious well-balanced, low-saturated fat, low-cholesterol diet should be recommended for all healthy children above the age of 2 years, along with encouraging regular aerobic exercise and avoidance of obesity and cigarette smoking.

Diet The first form of therapy for children with hyperlipidemias is diet containing decreased amounts of total fat, saturated fat, and cholesterol and somewhat enriched in unsaturated fat. The intake of complex carbohydrates is increased and that of simple sugars is decreased. The American Heart Association Dietary Treatment of Hyperlipidemia has been developed for children over 2 years of age.

Response to diet In children with metabolic disorders of LDL metabolism (e.g., FH) the serum total and LDL cholesterol concentrations decrease by about 10% to 15%.[562,574] Only approximately 20% of children with heterozygous FH decrease their serum total and LDL cholesterol concentrations to less than 230 and 170 mg/dL, respectively.

Drug therapy Approximately 80% of children with heterozygous and homozygous FH require drugs in addition to diet to decrease serum concentrations of total and LDL cholesterol significantly.[575] Cholestryamine and colestipol, both anion-exchange resins that bind bile acids and prevent their reabsorption through the enterohepatic circulation, are at present the drugs of choice.[576] The side effects of bile acid sequestrants occur less frequently in children compared to adults and usually consist of transient gastric fullness.[575]

Congenital Disorders That May Contribute to Thromboembolic Disease

An association between other hemostatic abnormalities and familial thromboembolic disease has been proposed for several other proteins, but the evidence is not conclusive at this time. The following section briefly discusses the evidence for abnormalities in the fibrinolytic system, tissue factor pathway inhibitor (TFPI), and TM, as well as decreased plasma concentrations of FXII and increased plasma concentrations of FVIII.

Fibrinolytic System

Plasminogen Deficiency
Plasminogen Plasminogen is synthesized by the liver, has a molecular weight of 93 kDa, a plasma concentration of approximately 20 mg/dL, and circulates in plasma in two forms characterized by differing amino terminal regions (Chapter 2). Plasminogen is converted proteolytically to plasmin by either tissue plasminogen activator or urokinase plasminogen activator. Plasmin is a two-chain trypsin-like serine protease that cleaves fibrin and fibrinogen (Chapter 2). Congenital plasminogen deficiency is classified into two types: type I, in which plasma concentrations of plasminogen are decreased in parallel with functional activity, and type II, in which plasma concentrations of plasminogen are normal while the functional activity is decreased.

Histidine-rich glycoprotein (HRG) is a nonenzymatic protein that forms a 1:1 complex with plasminogen in plasma by binding to its lysine binding sites. If plasma concentrations of HRG are increased, plasma concentrations of plasminogen are reduced, which theoretically could predispose to this.

Genetic variant Both deficiencies of plasminogen and some dysplasminogenemias appear to cause TEs in some families.[577,578] Family studies suggest that plasminogen deficiency is inherited in an autosomal recessive pattern.[579] The genetic variants of plasminogen that are linked to TEs are a homozygous point mutation at position 1511 (G to T) leading to a stop codon (TAA) at position 460. This mutation abolishes the catalytic domain of plasmin.

Laboratory testing Plasminogen can be measured using assays that measure either activity or antigen concentration. Usually, the functional assay is a chromogenic assay with several commercial kits being available. A variety of assays are available to measure plasma concentrations of plasminogen and include nephelometry, immunoblotting, and Laurel rockets (Chapter 13).

Plasminogen Deficiency in Adults
Prevalence in general population The prevalence of plasminogen deficiency in the general population is approximately 0.4%, which is slightly less than in some cohorts of patients with TEs (1%–3%).[580]

Prevalence in adults with venous thrombotic disease Heterozygous plasminogen deficiency may or may not be associated with VTE in adults.[14,581–583] In a recent retrospective analysis of 20 families, heterozygotes of type I plasminogen deficiencies were found to experience significantly more TEs than their normal family members but later in life.[578]

If plasminogen deficiency is causal to TEs, then increased plasma concentrations of HRG leading to a secondary decrease in plasminogen concentrations could theoretically also cause an increased rate of TEs. Although several families with thrombophilia and increased plasma concentrations of HRG levels have been reported, a causal relationship has not been proven.[584,585]

Plasminogen Deficiency in Children

Heterozygous plasminogen deficiency Heterozygous plasminogen deficiency has been described in some children with stroke.[148]

Homozygous plasminogen deficiency Homozygous plasminogen deficiency is an extremely rare but devastating disease characterized by a specific constellation of presenting symptoms.

Clinical presentation: Pseudomembranous conjunctivitis was first described in 1847 by Bouisson[586] and the term "conjunctivits lignosa" introduced by Borel in 1933.[587] Ligneous conjunctivitis is characterized by acute or chronic recurrent conjunctivitis in which the conjunctival membranes acquire a wood-like consistency (Figure 3–14).[579,588] Individuals with homozygous plasminogen deficiency usually present within days to weeks of birth with ligneous conjunctivitis. Chronic obstruction of the eye with concurrent corneal involvement leads to blindness in most affected individuals in the absence of treatment. Other presenting clinical symptoms include frequent nasopharyngitis, tracheobronchial obstruction, otitis media, vulvovaginitis, and defective wound healing.[588,598–604] Unexpectedly, large-vessel thrombosis rarely occurs.

Pathophysiology: Plasmin's activities include the degradation and subsequent removal of fibrin from all body fluids. In the eye, the absence of plasmin results in fibrin-rich viscous or membranous material remaining, the invasion of inflammatory cells and fibroblasts, and a wood-like appearance of the conjunctival lesions that occurs as the fibrin dries. In the tracheobronchial tree, fibrin deposits impair the function of the ciliary system with subsequent increased bacterial growth and multiple sinobronchial infections.[588,599] In the ear, fibrin deposits result in frequent middle ear infections.[596] In the central nervous system, fibrin deposition in the ventricular system can impair circulation, resulting in hydrocephalus.[596] A knockout mouse model was developed and showed that plasminogen-deficient mice developed signs of ligneous conjunctivitis, defective wound healing, and internal hydrocephalus.[597–599] The clinical presentation and findings in the knockout mouse model convincingly show the central role of plasminogen deficiency in this disease. The mechanisms preventing large-vessel thrombosis in humans and in the mouse model are speculative and include the presence of other enzymes that can cleave fibrin.

Treatment: Treatment has historically focused primarily on the ligneous conjunctivitis with usual therapies for the management of other clinical symptoms. Various forms of therapy that have been used include hyaluronidase eye drops, corticosteroids, cyclosporine, and antiviral agents, all of which have been generally disappointing.[589–598,600] A combination of determining that plasminogen deficiency was responsible for ligneous conjunctivitis and the development of purified, freeze-dried concentrates of lys-plasminogen (Immuno, Vienna, Austria) has offered a new and effective treatment for this disease. The pharmacokinetics of purified plasminogen concentrates have been assessed in a small number of patients. In one patient, following the initiation of a continuous infusion of lys-plasminogen at a dose of 1000 CU per 24 hours, the plasma concentration of plasminogen was within the normal range within 24 hours. Following the achievement of plasminogen concentrations between approximately 35% and 80%, plasma concentrations of TATs, fibrin monomer, and D-Dimer, which were increased, decreased into the normal range (Figure 3–14).[596] In at least one case, replacement therapy with lys-plasminogen led to rapid regression of the pseudomembranes and normalization of respiratory tract secretions and wound healing (Figure 3–13).[596] Interruption of therapy for even 48 hours resulted in the reappearance of the ligneous conjunctivits. Some authors reported that plasminogen replacement did not alter the clinical course.[599] However, the successful treatment with plasminogen concentrates was secondary to the use of replacement therapy at doses of 2 to 10 times those used previously[599] and over several months.

Tissue plasminogen activator deficiency Decreased plasma concentrations of TPA in the presence of normal concentrations of TPA's main inhibitor, PAI-1, could theoretically be a cause of congenital thromboembolic disease. The evidence linking decreased plasma concentrations of TPA, in either a basal or stimulated setting, with TEs is weak at this time.[23–26,601–603]

Heparin Cofactor Deficiency

Heparin cofactor II HCII is synthesized by the liver and has a molecular weight of 65.6 kD and a plasma concentration of approximately 90 ug/ml.[31,604] HCII, similar to AT, inactivates thrombin forming a 1:1 covalent bond that completely neutralizes thrombin's activity. However, HCII inhibits only a small fraction of thrombin added to plasma compared to AT, which is the major inhibitor of thrombin.[31] Inhibition of thrombin by HCII can be potentiated by dermatan sulphate (DS) as well as heparan sulfate and heparin.[605,606] In contrast to AT, HCII has a narrow specificity and, of all of the coagulation proteins, HCII only inhibits thrombin.

Genetic variant The genetic defects in HCII that are linked to TEs are HCII Oslo (an Arg 189 to His point mutation)[607] and HCII Awaji (an altered amino acid sequence from position 89 and terminate at [107]).[608] HCII Oslo likely influences DS binding site and is analogous to certain defects in type II AT deficiency that alter heparin binding.

Laboratory testing The activity of HCII can be measured using an antithrombin dermatan sulfate cofactor activity using an amidolytic assay (Stachrom HCII, Diagnostica Stago, Asnieres-sur-Seine, France). HCII can also be measured immunologically using a Laurell rocket immunoelectrophoresis assay using a polyclonal specific antibody (Enzyme Research laboratoris, South Bend, Indiana, USA).

Heparin Cofactor II Deficiency in Adults

Prevalence in general population The prevalence of heterozygous HCII deficiency in the general population is not precisely known due to its rarity. Large studies of patients with TEs compared to healthy volunteers report that the prevalence of HCII deficiency is very similar, with values of 0.7% and 0.9%, respectively.[609,610]

Prevalence in adults with venous thrombotic disease A definitive role for HCII deficiency in thrombophilia has yet to be firmly established. While several pedigrees with heterozygous HCII deficiency associated with thrombosis have been reported,[31,609–618] other studies have suggested that the prevalence of this deficiency is similar in healthy subjects and patients with VTE.[31] The current opinion is that heterozygous HCII deficiency itself may

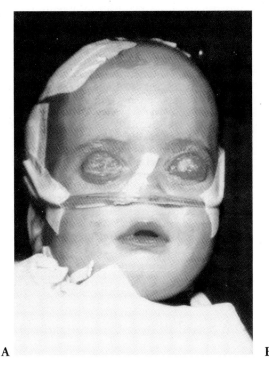 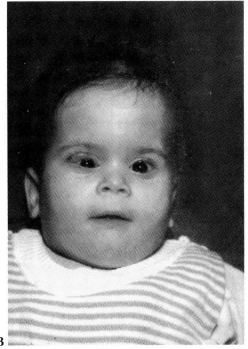

A   B

Figure 3–13 *A,* Initial appearance of a child with homozygous plasminogen deficiency, showing the typical features of ligneous conjunctivitis. *B,* Same patient after 7 months of replacement therapy with Lys-plasminogen.[605]

not be a significant risk factor for VTE at an early age, but may, under certain conditions, form an additional risk factor.

Children A comprehensive search of the literature did not identify a single patient with HCII who presented during infancy or childhood with VTE or other forms of thrombotic disease.

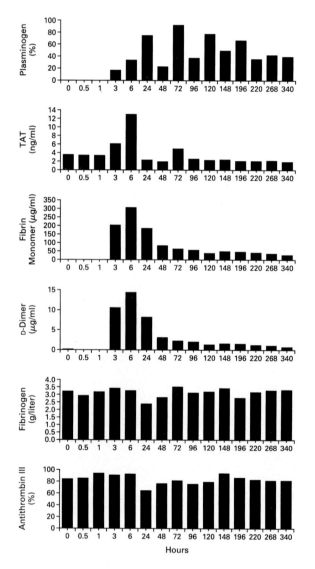

Figure 3–14 Levels of plasminogen, thrombin-antithrombin (TAT) complex, fibrin monomer, D-dimer, fibrinogen, and antithrombin during the initial 340 hours of continuous intravenous Lys-plasminogen replacement therapy. Hours are shown on a nonlinear scale indicating when measurements were made. Plasminogen and antithrombin III levels are expressed as percentages of normal values. Reproduced with permission.[596]

Tissue Factor Pathway Inhibitor (TFPI)

Another potential risk factor for TEs is a deficiency of TFPI. Tissue factor pathway inhibitor is synthesized by endothelial cells, has a molecular weight of 33 kDa, and inhibits FVIIa/tissue factor (TF) following the generation of FXa. The potential presence of abnormal TFPI has been investigated in several symptomatic probands of families with TEs and no genetic abnormalities identified.[614,615] The results are mixed with the most convincing link between decreased plasma concentrations of TFPI and congenital prothrombotic disorders being a single mucleotide substitution in exon 7 (536 C—T).[614]

Thrombomodulin

Thrombomodulin, a transmembrane protein synthesized by endothelial cells, functions as a receptor for thrombin and, thereby, as a cofactor for the activation of protein C. Theoretically, decreased expression of TM by endothelial cells could predispose to TEs. Unfortunately, plasma concentrations of TM may not reflect endothelial expression of TM and therefore may not provide a mechanism for identifying patients who potentially have defects in TM that predispose to TEs. The TM gene has now been assessed in cohorts of symptomatic probands with family histories of TEs and at least four different mutations.[535,616–618] To date, there is no convincing evidence linking defects in TM expression with congenital prothrombotic disorders.

Decreased Plasma Concentrations of Factor XII deficiency

Original studies from Mannhalter et al suggested an increased high frequency of heterozygotes for FXII deficiency in cohorts of thrombophilic patients.[32] However, subsequent studies have not supported these initial findings.[33]

Increased Plasma Concentrations of FVIII

Recently, a large patient/control study reported that increased plasma concentrations of FVIII were linked to congenital thromboembolic disease.[619]

The hereditability of this phenotype and the eventual underlying molecular defects have not been reported so far.

Critical Issues for Diagnosis and Treatment of Children with Congenital Prothrombotic Disorders

Which Congenital Prothrombotic Disorders Contribute to Thromboembolic Events during Childhood? There is convincing evidence that the presence of FV Leiden, prothrombin 20210A, some dysfibrinogenemias and some hyperlipidemic states, and deficiencies of AT, protein C, and protein S contribute to the development of TEs during childhood. However, acquired risk factors are significantly more important as causes for TEs compared to congenital prothrombotic disorders alone in children, a finding similar to adults. In addition, acquired risk factors are present in the majority of children with a congenital prothrombotic disorder who develop TEs during childhood.

Is long-term prophylactic therapy ever indicated in asymptomatic children? In general, long-term continuous prophylactic therapy is probably not indicated for the vast majority of children with congenital prothrombotic disorders. The rationale for this position is that only a very small minority of children with congenital prothrombotic disorders develop TEs and the risk of long-term anticoagulant therapy likely outweighs the efficacy of this approach. However, each child should be considered individually in the context of the specific congenital prothrombotic disorder and family history.

Is Intermittent Anticoagulation Therapy Indicated in the Presence of an Acquired Risk Factor for Thromboembolic Events? For children with a congenital prothrombotic disorder and who have had a previous TE, intermittent anticoagulation therapy in the presence of a newly acquired risk factor for TEs is likely indicated. For children with a congenital prothrombotic disorder who have not had a previous TE, they should be considered on an individual basis. The risk of the particular congenital defect, the strength of the acquired risk factor, and the risk of bleeding should all be considered. Noninvasive screening of sites in which the thrombus would likely occur is another option, particularly if the risk of bleeding is a concern.

What Is the Optimal Duration of Treatment following a First Thromboemoblic Event during Childhood? The optimal duration of treatment following a first TE in children with a congenital prothrombotic disorder is unknown and each child needs to be considered individually. The information required to make a decision includes the specific congenital defect(s), the initial and continued presence of an acquired risk factor that "uncovered" the congenital defect, the extensiveness and location of the TE, the potential seriousness of recurrent thrombosis, and the risk of complications from anticoagulant therapy. One general approach is to treat for 3 to 6 months in children who have a clear acquired risk factor that is no longer present, and the thrombus was either not very extensive or at least partially resolved. Lifelong anticoagulant therapy is likely indicated in children with a congenital prothrombotic disorder and a second TE.

What Is the Risk of Recurrent Thromboembolic Events following Cessation of Treatment for a First Thromboembolic Event? The risk of recurrent TEs following cessation of treatment for a first TE is unknown in children. In the absence of a congenital prothrombotic disorder, the risk of recurrent TEs is approximately 10% to 20% during childhood with a follow-up of only a few years. Probably the risk for recurrent TEs in children with both a congenital prothrombotic disorder is at least as great. However, individuals may live for several years to decades prior to another TE and long-term anticoagulants may not be necessary.

How Should Children with a Congenital Prothrombotic Disorder and Thromboembolic Events Be Treated? The same therapeutic approach can be used regardless of whether a congenital prothrombotic disorder is present (Chapters 9, 10, and 11). Further adjuvent therapy is necessary in some conditions such as homozygous protein C or protein S deficiency, and antithrombin concentrates should be considered in children with AT deficiency who are not responding to anticoagulant therapy.

REFERENCES

1. Virchow R. Phlogose und Thrombose in Gefasssystem. In: Virchow R, ed. Gesammelte Abhandlungen zur wissenschafteichen medicin. Frankfurt: Von Meidinger, 1856.
2. Andrew M, Paes B, Milner R, et al. Development of the human coagulation system in the full-term infant. Blood 1987;70:165–72.
3. Andrew M, Paes B, Milner R, et al. Development of the human coagulation system in the healthy premature infant. Blood 1988;72:1651–7.
4. Reverdiau-Moalic P, Delahousse B, et al. Evolution of blood coagulation activators and inhibitors in the healthy human fetus. Blood 1996;88:900–6.
5. Andrew M, Vegh P, Johnston M, et al. Maturation of the hemostatic system during childhood. Blood 1992; 80:1998–2005.
6. Reverdiau-Moalic P, Delahousse B, Bardos GBP, et al. Evolution of blood coagulation activators and inhibitors in the healthy human fetus. Blood 1996;88: 900–6.
7. Hirsh J. Approach to patients with inherited thrombophilia. Hamilton, ON, BC Decker, 1998.
8. Makris M, Preston FE, Beauchamp NJ, et al. Co-inheritance of the 20210A allele of the prothrombin gene increases the risk of thrombosis in subjects with familial thrombophilia. Thromb Haemost 1997;78: 1426–9.
9. Price DT, Ridker PM. Factor V Leiden mutation and the risks for thromboembolic disease. Ann Intern Med 1997;127:895–903.
10. van den Belt A, Prins M, Huisman M, Hirsh J. Familial thrombophilia: a review analysis. Clin Appl Thromb/Hemost 1996;2:227–36.
11. Mayer K, Hartmann H, Immel A. Congenital heterozygote hypoplasminogenemia as a risk factor for thrombosis. Fibrinolysis 1988;2:37–8.
12. Tabernero MD, Gonzalez-Sarmiento R, Tomas JF, Alberca I. Plasminogen deficiency in a Spanish family. Fibrinolysis 1988;2:40–1.
13. Dolan G, Greaves M, Preston FE. Type I plasminogen deficiency and thrombovascular disease in three kindreds. Fibrinolysis 1988;2:39–40.
14. Girolami A, Marafioti F, Rubertelli M, Capellato MG. Congenital heterozygous plasminogen deficiency associated with a severe thrombotic tendency. Acta Haematol 1986;75:54–7.
15. Mannucci PM, Kluft C, Trass DW. Congenital plasminogen deficiency associated with venous thromboembolism: therapeutic trial with stanozolol. Br J Haematol 1986;63:753–9.
16. Scharrer IM, Wohl RC, Hach V. Investigation of a congenital abnormal plasminogen, Frankfurt I, and its relationship to thrombosis. Thromb Haemost 1986;55:396–401.
17. Hasegawa DK, Tyler BJ, Edson JR. Thrombotic disease in three families with inherited plasminogen deficiency. Blood 1982;60:213a.
18. Lottenberg R, Dolly FR, Kitchens CS. Recurring thromboembolic disease and pulmonary hypertension associated with severe hypoplasminogenemia. Am J Hematol 1985;19:181–93.
19. Aoki N, Moroi M, Sakata Y, et al. Abnormal plasminogen. A hereditary molecular abnormality found in a patient with recurrent thrombosis. J Clin Invest 1978;61:1186–95.
20. Wohl RC, Summaria L, Chediak J, et al. Human plasminogen variant Chicago III. Thromb Haemost 1982;48:146–52.
21. Soria J, Soria C, Bertrand O, et al. Plasminogen Paris 1 congenital abnormal plasminogen and its incidence in thrombosis. Thromb Res 1983;32:229–38.
22. Kazama M, Tahara C, Suzuki Z. Abnormal plasminogen, a case of recurrent thrombosis. Thromb Res 1981;21:517–22.
23. Jorgensen M, Mortensen JZ, Madsen AG, et al. A family with reduced plasminogen activator activity in blood associated with recurrent venous thrombosis. Scand J Haematol 1982;29:217–23.
24. Petaejae J, Myllylae G, Rasi V, Vahtera E. Reduced tissue plasminogen activator release and normal plasminogen activator inhibitor level in a family with recurrent venous thrombosis. Thromb Haemost 1987; 58:38a.
25. Petaejae J, Myllyllae G, Rasi V. Familial clustering of defective release of TPA. Thromb Haemost 1989;62: 442a.
26. Stead NW, Bauer KA, Kinney TR. Venous thrombosis in a family with defective release of vascular plasminogen activator and an elevated plasma factor VIII/von Willebrand's factor. Am J Med 1983;74:33–4.
27. Jorgensen M, Bonnevie-Nielsen V. Increased concentration of the fast-acting plasminogen activator inhibitor in plasma associated with familial thrombosis. Br J Haematol 1987;65:175–80.
28. Engesser L, Brommer EJP, Kluft C, Briet E. Elevated plasminogen activator inhibitor (PAI), a cause of thrombophilia? A study in 203 patients with familial or sporadic venous thrombophilia. Thromb Haemost 1989;62:673–80.
29. Souto JC, Gari M, Mateo J, et al. Congenital histidine-rich glycoprotein deficiency and familial thrombophilia: a new case. Thromb Haemost 1995;73: 952a.
30. Shigekiyo T, Kanazuka M, Azuma H, et al. Congenital deficiency of histidine-rich glycoprotein: failure to identify abnormalities in routine laboratory assays of

hemostatic function, immunologic function and trace elements. J Lab Clin Med 1995;125:719–23.

31. Bertina RM, van der Linden IK, Engesser L, et al. Hereditary heparin cofactor II deficiency and the risk of development of thrombosis. Thromb Haemost 1987;57:196–200.

32. Halbmayer WM, Mannhalter C, Feichtinger C, et al. The prevalence of factor XII deficiency in 103 orally anticoagulated outpatients suffering from venous and/or arterial thromboembolism. Thromb Haemost 1992;68:258–90.

33. Koster T, Rosendahl FR, Briet E, Vandenbroucke JP. John Hagemann's factor and deep vein thrombosis. Br J Haematol 1994;87:422–4.

34. Meade TW, Dyer S, Howarth DJ. Antithrombin III and procoagulant activity: sex differences and effects of the menopause. Br J Haematol 1990;323:1512–6.

35. Tait RC, Walker ID, Davidson JF. Antithrombin III activity in healthy blood donors: age- and sex-related changes and the prevalence of asymptomatic deficiency. Br J Haematol 1990;74:77–81.

36. Miletich J, Sherman L, Broze GJ. Absence of thrombosis in subjects with heterozygous protein C deficiency. N Engl J Med 1987;317:991–6.

37. Svensson P, Dahlback J. Resistance to activated protein C as a basis for venous thrombosis. N Engl J Med 1994;330:517–22.

38. Rosendahl FR, Koster T, Vandenbrouke JP, Reitsma PH. High risk of thrombosis in patients homozygous for Factor V Leiden (activated protein C resistance). Blood 1995;85:1504–1508.

39. Ridker PA, Hennekens CH, Lindpaintner K. Mutation in the gene coding for coagulation factor V and the risk of myocardial infarction, stroke, and venous thrombosis in apparently healthy men. N Engl J Med 1994;332:912–7.

40. Rees DC, Cox M, Clegg JB. World distribution of factor V Leiden. Lancet 1995;346:1133–4.

41. Lee DH, Henderson P, Blajchman M. Prevalence of factor V Leiden in a Canadian blood donor population. Can Med Assoc J 1996;155:285–9.

42. Tait RC, Walker ID, Perry DJ, et al. Prevalence of antithrombin deficiency in the healthy population. Br J Haematol 1994;87:106–12.

43. Tait RC, Walker ID, Islam SI, et al. Influence of demographic factors on antithrombin III activity in a healthy population. Thromb Haemost 1993;70:218–25.

44. Tait RC, Walker ID, Islam SIA, et al. Influence of demographic factors on antithrombin III activity in a healthy population. Br J Haematol 1993;84:476–80.

45. Tait RC, Walker ID, Reitsma PH, et al. Prevalence of protein C deficiency in the healthy population. Thromb Haemost 1995;73:87–93.

46. Poort SR, Rosendahl FR, Reitsma PH, Bertina RM. A common genetic variation in the 3'-untranslated region of the prothrombin gene is associated with elevated plasma prothrombin levels and an increase in venous thrombosis. Blood 1996;88:3698–3703.

47. Cumming AM, Keeney S, Salden A, et al. The prothrombin gene G20210A variant: prevalence in a UK anticoagulant clinic population. Br J Haematol 1997;98:353–5.

48. Rees CD, Cox M, Clegg JB. World distribution of factor V Leiden. Lancet 1995;346:1133–4.

49. Heijboer H, Brandjes D, Buller H, et al. Deficiencies of coagulation-inhibiting and fibrinolytic proteins in outpatients with deep-vein thrombosis. N Engl J Med 1990;323:1512–6.

50. Koster T, Rosendahl F, Briet E, et al. Protein C deficiency in a controlled series of unselected outpatients: an infrequent but clear risk factor for venous thrombosis (Leiden Thrombophilia Study). Blood 1995;85:2756–61.

51. Koster T, Rosendahl FR, de Ronde F, et al. Venous thrombosis due to poor response to activated protein C: Leiden Thrombophilia Study. Lancet 1993;342:1503–6.

52. Briet E, Engesser L, Brommer EJP, et al. Thrombophilia: its causes and a rough estimate of its prevalence. Thromb Haemost 1987;58:39–40.

53. Scharrer I, Hach-Wunderle V, Heyland H, Kuhn C. Incidence of defective TPA release in 158 unrelated young patients with venous thrombosis in comparison to protein C, protein S, ATIII, fibrinogen, and plasminogen deficiency. Thromb Haemost 1987;58:72–3.

54. Ben-Tal O, Zivelin A, Seligsohn U. The relative frequency of hereditary thrombotic disorders among 107 patients and thrombophilia in Israel. Thromb Haemost 1989;61:50–4.

55. Griffin JH, Evatt B, Wideman C, Fernandez JA. Anticoagulant protein C pathway defective in majority of thrombophilic patients. Blood 1999;1989–93.

56. Esmon CT. Molecular events that control the protein C anticoagulant pathway. Thromb Res 1993;70:29–35.

57. Esmon CT, Owen WG. Identification of an endothelial cell cofactor for thrombin-catalyzed activation of protein C. Proc Natl Acad Sci U S A 1981;78:2249–54.

58. Esmon N, Owen W, Esmon C. Isolation of a membrane-bound cofactor for thrombin-catalyzed activation of protein C. J Biol Chem 1982;257:859–64.

59. Esmon C. The protein C anticoagulant pathway. Arterioscler Thromb 1992;12:135–45.

60. Dahlback B. The protein C anticoagulant system: inherited defects as basis for venous thrombosis. Thromb Res 1995;77:1–43.

61. Dahlback B, Carlsson M, Svensson PJ. Familial thrombophilia due to a previously unrecognized mechanism characterized by poor anticoagulant response

to activated protein C. Proc Natl Acad Sci U S A 1993;90:1004–8.

62. Dahlback B. Inherited thrombophilia: resistance to activated protein C as a pathogenic factor of venous thromboembolism. Blood 1995;85:607–14.

63. Bertina RM, Koeleman BPC, Koster T, et al. Mutation in blood coagulation factor V associated with resistance to activated protein C. Nature 1994;369:64–6.

64. Dahlback B, Hildebrand B. Inherited resistance to activated protein C is corrected by anticoagulant cofactor activity found to be a property of factor V. Proc Natl Acad Sci U S A 1994;91:1396–1400.

65. Greengard JS, Eichinger S, Griffin JH, Bauer KA. Brief report: variability of thrombosis among homozygous siblings with resistance to activated protein C due to an Arg-Gln mutation in the gene for factor V. N Engl J Med 1994;331:1559–62.

66. Sun X, Evatt B, Griffin JH. Blood coagulation Factor Va abnormality associated with resistance to activated protein C in venous thrombophilia. Blood 1994;83:3120–5.

67. Griffin JH, Heeb MJ, Kojima Y, et al. Activated protein C resistance: molecular mechanisms. Thromb Haemost 1995;74:444–8.

68. Perry DJ, Pasi KJ. Resistance to activated protein C and factor V Leiden. QJM 1997;90:379–85.

69. Montaruli B, Schinco P, Pannocchia A, et al. Use of modified functional assays for activated protein C resistance in patients with basally prolonged APTT. Thromb Haemost 1997;78:1042–8.

70. Laffan MA, Manning R. The influence of factor VIII on measurement of activated protein C resistance. Blood Coagul Fibrinolysis 1996;7:761–5.

71. Varadi K, Moritz B, Lang H, et al. A chromogenic assay for activated protein C resistance. Br J Haematol 1995;90:884–91.

72. Meschia JF, Biller J, Witt T, et al. Is hormone replacement a risk factor for ischemic stroke in women with factor V Leiden mutation? Arch Neurol 1998;55:1137–9.

73. Glueck CJ, McMahon RE, Bouquot JE, et al. Heterozygosity for the Leiden mutation of the factor V gene, a common pathoetiology for osteonecrosis of the jaw, with thrombophilia augmented by exogenous estrogens. J Lab Clin Med 1997;130:540–3.

74. Glueck CJ, Wang P, Fontaine RN, et al. Effect of exogenous estrogen on atherothrombotic vascular disease risk related to the presence or absence of the factor V Leiden mutation (resistance to activated protein C). Am J Cardiol 1999;84:549–54.

75. van der Meer FJ, Koster JP, Vandenbroucke E, et al. The Leiden Thrombophilia Study (LETS). Thromb Haemost 1997;78:631–5.

76. Samama MM, Trossaert M, Horellou MH, et al. Risk of thrombosis in patients homozygous for factor V Leiden. Blood 1995;86:4700–2.

77. Ridker PM, Miletich JP. Factor V Leiden and risks of recurrent idiopathic venous thromboembolism. Circulation 1995;332:912–3.

78. Rintelen C, Pabinger I. Probability of recurrence of thrombosis in patients with and without Factor V Leiden. Thromb Haemost 1996;75:229–30.

79. Eichinger S, Pabinger I, Stumpflen A, et al. The risk of recurrent venous thromboembolism in patients with and without factor V Leiden. Thromb Haemost 1997;77:624–8.

80. Denninger MH, Beldjord K, Durand F, et al. Budd-Chiari syndrome and factor V Leiden mutation. Lancet 1995;345:525–6.

81. Gardyn J, Sorkin P, Kluger Y, et al. Heparin-induced thrombocytopenia and fatal thrombosis in a patient with activated protein C resistance. Am J Hematol 1995;50:292–5.

82. Makris M, Bardhan G, Preston FE. Warfarin-induced skin necrosis associated with activated protein C resistance. Thromb Haemost 1996;75:523–4.

83. Rai RS, Regan L, Chitolie A, et al. Placental thrombosis and second trimester miscarriage in association with activated protein C resistance. Br J Obstet Gynecol 1996;103:842–4.

84. Rai R, Regan L, Hadley E, et al. Second-trimester pregnancy loss is associated with activated protein C resistance. Br J Haematol 1996;92:489–90.

85. Dizon Townson DS, Nelson JM, Easton K, Ward K. The factor V Leiden mutation may predispose women to severe preeclampsia. Am J Obstet Gynecol 1996;175:902–5.

86. Vandenbroucke JP, Koster T, Briet E, et al. Increased risk of venous thrombosis in oral contraceptive users who are carriers of factor V Leiden mutation. Lancet 1994;344:1453–7.

87. Zoller B, Svensson P, He X, Dahlback B. Identification of the same factor V gene mutation in 47 out of 50 thrombosis-prone families with inherited resistance to activated protein C. J Clin Invest 1994;94:2521–4.

88. Mahasandana C, Suvatte V, Chuansumvita A, et al. Homozygous protein S deficiency in an infant with purpura fulminans. J Pediatr 1990;117:750–3.

89. Tarras S, Gadia C, Meister L, et al. Homozygous protein C deficiency in a newborn: clinicopathologic correlation. Arch Neurol 1988;45:214–6.

90. Branson H, Katz J, Marble R, Griffin J. Inherited protein C deficiency and coumarin-responsive chronic relapsing purpura fulminans in a newborn infant. Lancet 1983;2:1165–8.

91. Seligsohn U, Berger A, Abend M, et al. Homozygous protein C deficiency manifested by massive venous

thrombosis in the newborn. N Engl J Med 1984; 310:559–62.

92. Sills R, Marlar R, Montgomery R, et al. Severe homozygous protein C deficiency. J Pediatr 1984;105: 409–13.

93. Estelles A, Garcia-Plaza I, Dasi A, et al. Severe inherited "homozygous" protein C deficiency in a newborn infant. Thromb Haemost 1984;52:53–6.

94. Marciniak E, Wilson H, Marlar R. Neonatal purpura fulminans: a genetic disorder related to the absence of protein C in blood. Blood 1985;65:15–20.

95. Yuen P, Cheung A, Hsiang J, et al. Purpura fulminans in a Chinese boy with congenital protein C deficiency. Pediatrics 1986;77:670–6.

96. Koeleman B. Activated protein C resistance as an additional risk factor for thrombosis in protein C deficient families. Blood 1994;84:1031–5.

97. Gandrille S, Greengard JS, Alhenc-Gelas M, et al. Incidence of activated protein C resistance caused by Arg 506 Gln mutation in factor V in 113 unrelated symptomatic protein C deficient patients. Blood 1995;86:219–24.

98. Zoller B, Berntsdotter A, Carcia de Frutos P, Dahlback B. Resistance to activated protein C as an additional genetic risk factor in hereditary deficiency of protein S. Blood 1995;85:3518–23.

99. Koeleman BPC, van Rumpt D, Hamulyak K, et al. Factor V Leiden: an additional risk factor for thrombosis in protein S deficient families. Thromb Haemost 1995;74:580–3.

100. Lewandowski K, Rozek M, Turowiecka Z, Markiewicz WT. Combined hemostatic defects in family members of symptomatic carriers of Leiden mutations of factor V. Pol Arch Med Wewn 1998;99:211–7.

101. Mandel H, Brenner V, Berant M, et al. Coexistence of hereditary homocystinuria and factor V Leiden—effect on thrombosis. N Engl J Med 1996;334:763–8.

102. Chaturvedi S, Dzieczkowski J. Multiple hemostatic abnormalities in young adults with activated protein C resistance and cerebral ischemia. J Neurol Sci 1998;159:209–12.

103. Salomon O, Steinberg DM, Zivelin A, et al. Single and combined prothrombotic factors in patients with idiopathic venous thromboembolism: prevalence and risk assessment. Arterioscler Thromb Vasc Biol 1999;19:511–8.

104. Beauchamp NJ, Daly ME, Cooper PC, et al. Molecular basis of protein S deficiency in three families also showing independent inheritance of factor V Leiden. Blood 1996;88:1700–7.

105. Mustafa S, Mannhalter C, Rintelen C, et al. Clinical features of thrombophilia in families with gene defects in protein C or protein S combined with factor V Leiden. Blood Coagul Fibrinolysis 1998;9:85–9.

106. Inbal A, Kenet G, Zivelin A, et al. Purpura fulminans induced by disseminated intravascular coagulation following infection in 2 unrelated children with double heterozygosity for Factor V Leiden and protein S deficiency. Thromb Haemost 1997;77:1086–9.

107. Kahn SR. Severe preeclampsia associated with coinheritance of factor V Leiden mutation protein S deficiency. Obstet Gynecol 1998;91:812–4.

108. De Stefano V, Zappacosta B, Persichilli S, et al. Prevalence of mild hyperhomocysteinaemia and association with thrombophilic genotypes (factor V Leiden and prothrombin G20210A) in Italian patients with venous thromboembolic disease. Br J Haematol 1999;106:564–8.

109. Rosendahl FR, Siscovick DS, Schwartz SM, et al. Factor V Leiden (resistance to activated protein C) increases the risk of myocardial infarction in young women. Blood 1997;89:2817–21.

110. Mandel K, Leaker M, Sparling C, et al. Activated protein C resistance screening in children [abstract]. Blood 1997;90:120b.

111. Uttenreuther-Fisher MM, Ziemer S, Gaedicke G. Resistance to activated protein C (APCR): reference values of APC-ratios for children. Thromb Haemost 1996;76:813–21.

112. Sifontes MT, Nuss R, Hunger SP, et al. Correlation between the functional assay for activated protein C resistance and factor V Leiden in the neonate. Pediatr Res 1997;42:776–8.

113. Brandt G, Gruppo R, Glueck CJ, et al. Sensitivity, specificity, and predictive value of modified assays for activated protein C resistance. Thromb Haemost 1998;79:567–70.

114. Nowak-Gottl U, Kohlhase B, Vielhaber H, et al. APC resistance in neonates and infants: adjustment of the APTT-based method. Thromb Res 1996;81: 665–70.

115. Giordano P, Del Vecchio GC, Altomare M, et al. Resistance to activated protein C in thalassemic patients: an underlying cause of thrombosis. Eur J Haematol 1998;61:123–7.

116. Nowak-Gottl U, Koch D, Aschka B, et al. Resistance to activated protein C (APCR) in children with venous or arterial thromboembolism. Br J Haematol 1996; 92:992–8.

117. Aschka I, Aumann V, Bergmann F, et al. Prevalence of factor V Leiden in children with thromboembolism. Eur J Pediatr 1996;155:1009–14.

118. Nowak-Gottl U, Vielhaber H, Schneppenheim R, Koch HG. Coagulation and fibrinolysis in children with APC-resistance: a population-based study. Fibrinolysis 1996;10:25–7.

119. Nowak-Gottl U, Binder M, Dubbers A, et al. Arg 506 to Gln mutation in the factor V gene causes poor fibrinolytic response in children after venous occlusion. Thromb Haemost 1997;78:1115–8.

120. Nowak-Gottl U, Vielhaber H. Elevated levels of soluble thrombomodulin in plasma from children with the

Arg 506 mutation in the factor V gene. Eur J Haematol 1997;58:51–5.

121. Simioni P, Scarano L, Gavasso S, et al. Prothrombin fragment 1+2 and thrombin-antithrombin complex levels in patients with inherited APC resistance due to factor V Leiden mutation. Br J Haematol 1996;92:435–41.

122. Seligsohn U, Zivelin A. Thrombophilia as a multigenic disorder. Thromb Haemost 1997;78:297–301.

123. Simioni P, Sanson BJ, Prandoni P, et al. Incidence of venous thromboembolism in families with inherited thrombophilia [abstract]. Thromb Haemost 1999; 81:198–202.

124. Van Boven HH, Reitsma PH, Rosendahl FR, et al. Factor V Leiden (FV R506Q) in families with inherited antithrombin deficiency. Thromb Haemost 1996;75: 417–21.

125. Sifontes MT, Nuss R, Hunger SP, et al. Activated protein C resistance and the factor V Leiden mutation in children with thrombosis. Am J Hematol 1998;57: 29–32.

126. Hagstrom JM, Walter J, Bluebond-Langner R, et al. Prevalence of the factor V Leiden mutation in children and neonates with thromboembolic disease. J Pediatr 1998;133:777–81.

127. Sifontes MT, Nuss R, Hunger SP, et al. The factor V Leiden mutation in children with cancer and thrombosis. Br J Haematol 1997;96:484–9.

128. Gurgey A. Clinical manifestations in thrombotic children with factor V Leiden mutation. Pediatr Hematol Oncol 1999;16:233–7.

129. Hausler M, Duque D, Merz U, et al. The clinical outcome after inferior vena cava thrombosis in early infancy. Eur J Pediatr 1999;158:416–20.

130. Fabri D, Belangero VM, Annichino-Bizzacchi JM, Arruda VR. Inherited risk factors for thrombophilia in children with nephrotic syndrome. Eur J Pediatr 1998;157:939–42.

131. Seixas CA, Hessel G, Ribeiro CC, et al. Factor V Leiden is not common in children with portal vein thrombosis. Thromb Haemost 1997;77:258–61.

132. Sifontes MT, Nuss R, Jacobson LJ, et al. Thrombosis in otherwise well children with the factor V Leiden mutation. J Pediatr 1996;128:324–8.

133. Pipe SW, Schmaier A, Nichols WC, et al. Neonatal purpura fulminans in association with factor V R506Q mutation. J Pediatr 1996;128:706–9.

134. Gurgey A, Mesci L, Renda Y, et al. Factor V Q506 mutation in children with thrombosis. Am J Hematol 1996;53:37–9.

135. Kodish E, Potter C, Kirschbaum N, Foster P. Activated protein C resistance in a neonate with venous thrombosis. J Pediatr 1995;127:645–8.

136. Haffner D, Wuhl E, Zieger B, et al. Bilateral renal venous thrombosis in a neonate associated with resistance to activated protein C. Pediatr Nephrol 1996;10:737–9.

137. Nowak-Gottl U, Schneppenheim R, Vielhaber H. APC resistance in childhood thromboembolism: diagnosis and clinical aspects. Semin Thromb Hemost 1997; 23:253–8.

138. Nowak-Gottl U, Auberger K, Gobel U, et al. Inherited defects of the protein C anticoagulant system in childhood thromboembolism. Eur J Pediatr 1996; 155:921–7.

139. Simioni P, de Ronde H, Prandoni P, et al. Ischemic stroke in young patients with activated protein C resistance. A report of three cases belonging to three different kindreds. Stroke 1995;26:885–90.

140. Nowak-Gottl U, Koch HG, Kohlhash B, et al. Resistence to activated protein C (APCR) in children with venous or arterial thromboembolism. Br J Haematol 1996;92:992–8.

141. Eckhof-Donovan S, Schneppenheim R, Krogmann O, et al. Massive femoral and pelvic thrombosis in a boy with activated protein C resistance. Thromb Haemost 1995;(Suppl):862a.

142. McColl MD, Chalmers EA, Thomas A, et al. Factor V Leiden, prothrombin 20210 G—A and the MTHFR C677T mutation in childhood stroke. Thromb Haemost 1999;81:690–4.

143. Ganesan V, McShane MA, Liesner R, et al. Inherited prothrombotic states and ischaemic stroke in childhood. J Neurol Neurosurg Psychiatry 1998;65: 508–11.

144. Zenz W, Bodo Z, Plotho J, et al. Factor V Leiden and prothrombin gene G20210A variant in children with ischemic stroke. Thromb Haemost 1998;80:763–6.

145. Nowak-Gottl U, Strater R, Dubbers A, et al. Ischaemic stroke in infancy and childhood: role of Arg 506 to Gln mutation in the factor V gene. Blood Coagul Fibrinolysis 1996;7:684–8.

146. Bonduel M, Sciuccati G, Hepner M, et al. Prethrombotic disorders in children with arterial ischemic stroke and sinovenous thrombosis. Arch Neurol 1999;56:967–71.

147. Vielhaber H, Ehrenforth S, Koch HG, et al. Cerebral venous sinus thrombosis in infancy and childhood: role of genetic and acquired risk factors of thrombophilia. Eur J Pediatr 1998;157:555–60.

148. deVeber G, Monagle P, Chan A, et al. Prothrombotic disorders in infants and children with cerebral thromboembolism. Arch Neurol 1998;55:1539–43.

149. Zenz W, Bodo Z. Resistance to activated protein C/factor V Leiden mutation (APCR-F-V-LM) in children with stroke [abstract]. Thromb Haemost 1997; (Suppl):PS-408a.

150. Gruppo RA, DeGrauw TJ, Palasis S, et al. Strokes, cutis marmorata telangiectatica congenital, and factor V Leiden. Pediatr Neurol 1998;18:342–5.

151. Debus O, Koch HG, Kurlemann G, et al. Factor V Leiden and genetic defects of thrombophilia in childhood porencephaly. Arch Dis Child Fetal Neonatal Educ 1998;78:F121–4.

152. Nelson KB, Dambrosia JM, Grether JK, Phillips TM. Neonatal cytokines and coagulation factors in children with cerebral palsy. Ann Neurol 1998;44:665–75.

153. Thorarensen O, High K, Clancy RR, Younkin DP. Factor V Leiden mutation: a previously unrecognized cause of neonatal stroke and infantile hemiplegia. Neurology 1996;46:A167–8.

154. Arruda VR, Belangero WD, Ozelo MC, et al. Inherited risk factors for thrombophilia among children with Legg-Calvé-Perthes disease. J Pediatr Orthop 1999;19:84–7.

155. Glueck CJ, Glueck HI, Greenfield D, et al. Protein C and S deficiency, thrombophilia, and hypofibrinolysis: pathophysiologic causes of Legg-Calve Perthes disease. Pediatr Res 1994;35(4 Pt 1):383–8.

156. Verity DH, Vaughan RW, Madanat W, et al. Factor V Leiden mutation is associated with ocular involvement in Behcet disease. Am J Ophthalmol 1999;128:352–6.

157. Woods CR, Johnson CA. Varicella purpura fulminans associated with heterozygosity for factor V Leiden and transient protein S deficiency. Pediatrics 1998;102:1208–10.

158. Stankovics J, Nafy A, Mehes K, Melegh B. Umbilical venous catheterization and development of Banti syndrome: the possible role of the factor V Leiden mutation. Eur J Pediatr 1998;157:696–7.

159. Gumruk F, Gurgey A, Altay C. A case of hypereosinophilic syndrome associated with factor V Leiden mutation and thrombosis. Br J Haematol 1998;101:208–9.

160. Melegh B, Stankovics J, Kis A, et al. Increased prevalence of factor V Leiden mutation in neonatal intracranial hemorrhage. Eur J Pediatr 1998;157:261–2.

161. Talmon T, Scharf J, Mayer E, et al. Retinal arterial occlusion in a child with factor V Leiden and thermolabile methylenetetrahydrofolate reductase mutations. Am J Ophthalmol 1997;124:689–91.

162. Haan J, Kapelle L, de Ronde H, et al. The factor V Leiden mutation (R506Q) is not a major risk factor for migranous cerebral infarction. Cephalalgia 1997;17:605–7.

163. Olcay L, Gurgey A, Topaloglu H, et al. Cerebral infarction associated with Factor V Leiden mutation in a boy with hemophilia. Am J Hematol 1997;56:189–90.

164. Hackenjos K, Bek M, Schopf E, Vanscheidt W. Recurrent ulcerations on both legs since early childhood due to a factor V gene mutation. Dermatology 1996;194:297–98.

165. Peus D, von Schmiedeberg S, Pier A, et al. Coagulation factor V gene mutation associated with activated protein C resistance leading to recurrent thrombosis, leg ulcers, and lymphedema: successful treatment with intermittent compression. J Am Acad Dermatol 1996;71:306–9.

166. Westendorp RGJ, Reitsma PH, Bertina RM. Inherited prethrombotic disorders and infectious purpura. Thromb Haemost 1996;76:899–901.

167. Miletich J, Prescott S, White R, et al. Inherited predisposition to thrombosis. Cell 1993;72:477–80.

168. Rodeghiero F, Tosetto A. Activated protein C resistance and factor V Leiden mutation are independent risk factors for venous thromboembolism. Ann Intern Med 1999;130:643–50.

169. Ridker PM, Glynn RJ, Miletich J, et al. Age-specific incidence rates of venous thromboembolism among heterozygous carriers of factor V Leiden mutation. Ann Intern Med 1997;126:528–31.

170. Ridker PM, Hennekens CH, Lindpainter K, Stampfer MJ, et al. Mutation in the gene coding for coagulation factor V and the risk of myocardial infarction, stroke, and venous thrombosis in apparently healthy men. N Engl J Med 1995;95:912–7.

171. Middeldorp S, Henkens CM, Koopman MM, et al. The incidence of venous thromboembolism in family members of patients with factor V Leiden mutation and venous thrombosis. Ann Intern Med 1998;128:15–20.

172. Uttenreuther-Fischer MM, Vetter B, Hellmann C, et al. Paediatric thromboembolism: the influence of non-genetic factors and the role of activated protein C resistance and protein C deficiency. Eur J Pediatr 1997;156:277–81.

173. Gurgey A, Buyukpamukcu M, Baskut C, et al. Portal vein thrombosis in association with factor V Leiden mutation in a patient with hepatocellular carcinoma. Med Pediatr Oncol 1997;29:224–5.

174. Gurakan F, Gurgey A, Bakkaloglu A, Kocak N. Homozygous factor V Leiden mutation in a child with Budd-Chiari syndrome. J Pediatr Gastroenterol Nutr 1999;28:516–7.

175. Sackesen C, Secmeer G, Gurgey A, et al. Homozygous factor V Leiden mutation in a child with meningococcal purpura fulminans. Pediatr Infect Dis J 1998;17:87–8.

176. Gruppo R, Glueck CJ, Wall E, et al. Legg-Perthes disease in three siblings, two heterozygous and one homozygous for the factor V Leiden mutation. J Pediatr 1998;132:885–8.

177. Quick AJ, Grossman G. Concentration of prothrombin in blood of babies (3 to 7 days old). Proc Soc Exp Biol Med 1939;40:647–8.

178. Corral J, Zuazu I, Rivera H, et al. Clinical and analytical relevance of the combination of prothrombin

20210A/A and factor V Leiden. Results from a large family. Br J Haematol 1999;105:560–3.

179. Kyrle PA, Mannhalter C, Beguin S. Clinical studies and thrombin generation in patients homozygous or heterozygous for the G20210A mutation in the prothrombin gene. Arterioscler Thromb Vasc Biol 1998;18:1287–91.

180. Ferraresi P, Marchetti G, Legnani C. The heterozygous 20210G/A prothrombin genotype is associated with early venous thrombosis in inherited thrombophilias and is not increased in frequency in artery disease. Arterioscler Thromb Vasc Dis 1997;17:2418–22.

181. Simioni P, Tormene D, Manfrin D. Prothrombin antigen levels in symptomatic and asymptomatic carriers of the 20210A prothrombin variant. Br J Haematol 1998;103:1045–50.

182. Degen SJF, Davie EW. Nucleotide sequence of the gene for human prothrombin. Biochem 1987;26: 6165–77.

183. Von Depka Prondzinski M, Eisert R, Oberkannis C, et al. Thrombosis and prothrombin G—A mutation detected by rapid PCR and allele specific hybridization. Blood 1997;90.

184. Hessner MJ, Luhm RA, Pearson SL, et al. Prevalence of prothrombin G20210A, factor V G1691A (Leiden), and methylenetetrahydrofolate reductase (MTHFR) C677T in seven different populations determined by muliplex allele-specific PCR. Thromb Haemost 1999;81:733–8.

185. Brown K, Luddinton R, Williamson D, et al. Risk of venous thromboembolism associated with a G to A transition at position 20210 in the 3' untranslated region of the prothrombin gene. Br J Haematol 1997;98:907–9.

186. Rahimy MC, Krishnamoorthy R, Ahouignan G, et al. The 20210A allele of prothrombin is not found among sickle cell disease patients from West Africa. Thromb Haemost 1998;79:444–5.

187. Isshiki I, Murata M, Watanabe G, Ikeda Y. Frequencies of prothrombin 20210 G—A mutation may be different among races — studies on Japanese population with various forms of thrombotic disorders and healthy subjects. Blood Coagul Fibrinolysis 1998;9:105–6.

188. Miyata T, Kawasaki H, Fujimura H, et al. The prothrombin gene G20210A mutation is not found among Japanese patients with deep vein thrombosis and healthy individuals. Blood Coagul Fibrinolysis 1998;9:451–2.

189. Zivelin A, Rosenberg N, Faier S. A single genetic origin for the common prothrombotic G20210A polymorphism in the prothrombin gene. Blood 1998;92: 1119–24.

190. Dilley A, Austin H, Hooper WC, et al. Prevalence of the prothrombin 20210G—A variant in blacks: infants, patients with venous thrombosis, patients with my-ocardial infarction, and control subjects. J Lab Clin Med 1998;132:452–5.

191. Hooper WC, Dilley A, Austin H, et al. Absence of mutations at APC cleavage sites Arg 306 in factor V and Arg 336, Arg 562, in factor VIII in African-Americans. Thromb Haemost 1998;79:236–7.

192. Dilley A, Austin H, Hooper WC, et al. Relation of three genetic traits to venous thrombosis in an African-American population. Am J Epidemiol 1998;147:30–5.

193. Rosendahl FR, Doggen CJM, Zivelin A. Geographic distribution of the 20219G to prothrombin variant. Thromb Haemost 1998;79:706–8.

194. Arruda VD, Bizzacchi JM, Goncalves MS, Costa FF. Prevalence of the prothrombin gene variant (20210A) in venous thrombosis and arterial disease. Thromb Haemost 1997;78:1430–3.

195. Hillarp A, Zoller B, Svensson PJ, Dahlback B. The 20210A allele of the prothrombin gene is a common risk factor among Swedish outpatients with verified deep venous thrombosis. Thromb Haemost 1997;78: 990–2.

196. De Stefano V, Chiusolo P, Paciaroni K, et al. Prevalence of the factor II G20210GA mutation in symptomatic patients with inherited thrombophilia. Thromb Haemost 1998;80:342–3.

197. Salomon O, Zivelin A, Dardik R, et al. Risk assessment of single, double and triple prothrombotic polymorphisms in patients with idiopathic venous thromboembolism. Arterioscler Thromb Vasc Biol 1999; 19:511–8.

198. Zuazu I, Sanchez I, Fernandez MC, et al. Portal and mesenteric venous thrombosis in a patient heterozygous for the 20210A allele of the prothrombin gene. Haematologica 1998;83:1129–30.

199. Bucciarelli P, Franchi F, Alatri A, et al. Budd-Chiari syndrome in a patient heterozygous for the G20210A mutation of prothrombin. Thromb Haemost 1998;79:445–6.

200. De Stefano V, Chiusolo P, Paciaroni K. Hepatic vein thrombosis in a patient with mutant prothrombin 20210A allele. Thromb Haemost 1998;80:519–20.

201. Darnige L, Jezequel P, Amoura Z, et al. Mesenteric venous thrombosis in two patients heterozygous for the 20210A allele of the prothrombin gene. Thromb Haemost 1998;80:703–4.

202. Albisinni R, Coppola A, Loffredo M, et al. Retinal vein occlusion and inherited conditions predisposing to thrombophilia. Thromb Haemost 1998;80:702–3.

203. Martinelli I, Sacchi E, Landi G, et al. High risk of cerebral vein thrombosis in carriers of a prothrombin gene mutation and in users of oral contraceptives. N Engl J Med 1998;338:1793–7.

204. Rosendahl FR, Vos HL, Poort SL, Bertina R. Prothrombin 20210A variant and age at thrombosis. Thromb Haemost 1998;79:444–5.

205. De Stefano V, Martinelli I, Mannucci PM, et al. The risk of recurrent deep venous thrombosis among heterozygous carriers of both factor V Leiden and the G20210A prothrombin mutation. N Engl J Med 1999;341:801–6.

206. Howard TE, Marusa M, Channell C, Duncan A. A patient homozygous for a mutation in the prothrombin gene 3'-untranslated region associated with massive thrombosis. Blood Coagul Fibrinolysis 1997;8:316–9.

207. De Stefano V, Chiusolo P, Paciaroni K. Prothrombin G20210A mutant genotype is a risk factor for cerebrovascular ischemic disease in young patients. Blood 1998;91:3562–5.

208. Gonzalez-Ordonez AJ, Medina-Rodriguez JM, Fernandez-Alvarez CR, et al. A patient homozygous for mutation 20210A in the prothrombin gene with venous thrombosis and transient ischemic attacks of thrombotic origin. Haematologica 1998;83:1050–1.

209. Arkel YS, Ku DH, Gibson DL, Lau X. Ischemic stroke in a young patient with protein C deficiency and prothrombin gene mutation G20210A. Blood Coagul Fibrinolysis 1998;9:757–60.

210. Bentolila S, Ripoli L, Drouet L, et al. Lack of association between thrombosis in primary antiphospholipid syndrome and the recently described thrombophilic 3'-untranslated prothrombin gene polymorphism. Thromb Haemost 1997;78:1415–21.

211. Grandone E, Marglione M, Colaizzo M. Genetic susceptibility to pregnancy-related venous thromboembolism: roles of factor V Leiden, prothrombin G20210A, and methylenetetrahydrofolate reductase C677T mutations. Am J Obstet Gynecol 1998;179:1324–8.

212. Corral J, Gonzalez R, Lozano ML, et al. The venous thrombosis risk factor 20210A allele of the prothrombin gene is not a major risk factor for arterial thrombotic disease. Br J Haematol 1997;99:304–7.

213. Watzke HH, Schuttrumpf J, Graf S, et al. Increased prevalence of a polymorphism in the gene coding for human prothrombin in patients with coronary heart disease. Thromb Res 1997;87:521–6.

214. Corral J, Iniesta JA, Gonzalez-Conegero R, et al. Migraine and prothrombotic genetic risk factors. Cephalagia 1998;18:257–60.

215. Martinelli I, Franchi F, Akwan S, et al. The transition G to A at position 20210 in the 3'-untranslated region of the prothrombin gene is not associated with cerebral ischemia. Blood 1997;90:3806–7.

216. Balasa V, Gruppo RA, Glueck CJ, et al. The relationship of mutations in the MTHFR, prothrombin, and PAI-1 genes to plasma levels of homocysteine, prothrombin, and PAI-1 in children and adults. Thromb Haemost 1999;81:739–44.

217. Young G, Krohn KA, Packer RJ. Prothrombin G20210A mutation in a child with spinal cord infarction. J Pediatr 1999;134:777–9.

218. Stier C, Potzsch B, Muller-Berghaus G, et al. Severe thrombophilia in a pediatric patients with end-stage renal disease: detection of the prothrombin gene G20210A mutation. Nephrol Dial Transplant 1998;13:2130–2.

219. Becker S, Heller C, Gropp F, et al. Thrombophilic disorders in children with cerebral infarction. Lancet 1998;352:1756–7.

220. Nowak-Gottl U, Wermes C, Junker R, et al. Prospective evaluation of the thrombotic risk in children with acute lymphoblastic leukemia carrying the MTH-FRTT677 genotype, the prothrombin G20210A variant, and further prothrombotic risk factors. Blood 1999;93:1595–9.

221. Morawitz P. Die Chemie der Blutgerinnung. Ergeb Physiol 1905;4:307–8.

222. Howell WH, Holt E. Two new factors in blood coagulation: heparin and pro-antithrombin. Am J Physiol 1918;47:328–9.

223. Brinkhous KM, Smith HP, Warner ED, Seegers WH. The inhibition of blood clotting: an unidentified substance which acts in conjunction with heparin to prevent the conversion of prothrombin into thrombin. Am J Physiol 1939;125:683–7.

224. Quick AJ. The normal antithrombin of the blood and its relation to heparin. Am J Physiol 1938;123:712–3.

225. Abildgaard U. Highly purified antithrombin III with heparin cofactor activity prepared by disc electrophoresis [abstract]. Scand J Clin Lab Invest 1968;21:89–90.

226. Rosenberg RD. The purification and mechanism of action of human antithrombin-heparin cofactor. J Biol Chem 1973;248:6490–505.

227. Egeberg O. Inherited antithrombin deficiency causing thrombophilia. Thromb Diath Haemorrh 1965;13:516–7.

228. Bjork I, Danielsson A, Fenton JW, Jornwall H. The site in human antithrombin for functional proteolytic cleavage by human thrombin. FEBS Lett 1981;126:257–60.

229. Lane DA, Caso R. Antithrombin: structure, genomic organization, function, and inherited deficiency. In: Tuddenham EGD, ed. The molecular biology of coagulation. London: Bailliere Tindall; 1989: 961.

230. Bjork I, Olson ST, Shore JD. Molecular mechanisms of the accelerating effect of heparin on the reactions between anti-thrombin and clotting proteinases. In: Lane DA, Lindahl U, eds. Heparin: chemical and biological properties, clinical applications. London: Edward Arnold; 1989; p. 229.

231. De Stefano V, Finazzi G, Mannucci PM. Inherited thrombophilia: pathogenesis, clinical syndromes, and management. Blood 1996;87:3531–44.

232. Lane DA. Antithrombin III: a database of mutations. Thromb Haemost 1991;66:2265–6.

233. Finazzi G, Cacci R, Barbui T. Different prevalence of thromboembolism in the subtypes of congenital antithrombin deficiency: review of 404 cases. Thromb Haemost 1987;58:1094–5.

234. Lane DA, Olds RJ, Boisclair M, et al. Antithrombin III mutation database: first update. Thromb Haemost 1993;70:361–9.

235. Bock SC, Harris JF, Balazs I, Trent JM. Assignment of the human antithrombin III structural gene to chromosome 1q23–25. Cytogenet Cell Genet 1985;39:67–9.

236. Bock SC, Marrinan JA, Radziejewska E. Antithrombin III Utah: proline 407 to leucine mutation in a highly conserved region near the inhibitor reactive site. Biochem 1988;27:6171–8.

237. Olds RJ, Lane DA, Chowdhury V, et al. Complete nucleotide sequence of the antithrombin gene: evidence for homologous recombination causing thrombophilia. Biochem 1993;32:4216–24.

238. Daly M, Perry DJ, Harper PL, et al. Type I antithrombin deficiency: five novel mutations associated with thrombosis. Blood Coagul Fibrinolysis 1996;7:139–43.

239. Bock SC, Prochownik EV. Molecular genetic survey of 16 kindreds with hereditary antithrombin III deficiency. Blood 1987;70:1273–8.

240. Abilgaard U, Gravem K, Godal HC. Assay of progressive antithrombin in plasma. Thromb Diath Haemorrh 1970;24:244–5.

241. Biggs R, Denson K, Akman N, Barrett R, et al. Antithrombin III, antifactor Xa and heparin. Br J Haematol 1970;19:283–4.

242. Hensen A, Loeliger EA. Antithrombin III—its metabolism and function in blood coagulation. Throm Diath Haemorrh 1963;9:1–2.

243. Marciniak E, Farley CH, DeSimone PA. Familial thrombosis due to antithrombin deficiency. Blood 1974;43:219–20.

244. von Kaulla E, von Kaulla KN. Antithrombin III and diseases. Am J Clin Pathol 1967;48:69–70.

245. Abildgaard U, Lie OR, Odegard OR. A simple amidolytic method for the determination of functionally active antithrombin III. Scand J Clin Lab Invest 1976;36:109–10.

246. Abildgaard U, Lie M, Odegard O. Antithrombin (heparin cofactor) assay with "new" chromogenic substrates (S 2238 and Chromozym TH). Thromb Res 1977;11:549–53.

247. Blomback M, Blomback B, Olsson P, Svendsen L. THe. Thromb Res 1974;5:621–2.

248. Mitchell GA, Hudson PM, Huseby RM, et al. Fluorescent substrate assay for antithrombin III. Thromb Res 1978;12:219–20.

249. Odegard OR, Lie M, Abilgaard U. Heparin cofactor activity measured with an amidolytic method. Thromb Res 1975;6:287–94.

250. Vinazzer H. Photometric assay of antithrombin III with a chromogenic substrate. Haemostasis 1975;4:101–2.

251. Lane DA, Flynn A, Ireland H, et al. Antithrombin III Northwick Park: demonstration of inactive high MW complex with increased affinity for heparin. Br J Haematol 1987;65:451–2.

252. Bauer K. Rare hereditary coagulation factor abnormalities. In: Nathan DG, Oski FA, eds. Hematology of infancy and childhood. 5th ed. Philadelphia: WB Saunders, 1998: 1660–75.

253. Abildgaard U. Antithrombin and related inhibitors of coagulation. In: Poller L, ed. Recent advances in blood coagulation. Edinburgh: Churchill Livingstone, 1981: 151.

254. Thaler E, Lechner K. Antithrombin III deficiency and thromboembolism. Clin Haematol 1981;10:369–90.

255. Hirsh J, Piovella F, Pini M. Congenital antithrombin III deficiency. Incidence and clinical features. Am J Med 1989;87:34S–8S.

256. Sakuragawa N, Takahashi K. Antithrombin III Toyama: a hereditary abnormal antithrombin III of a patient with recurrent thrombophlebitis. Thromb Res 1983;31:305–6.

257. Chasse JF, Esnard F. An abnormal plasma antithrombin with no apparent affinity for heparin. Thromb Res 1984;34:297–8.

258. Fischer AM, Cornu P. Antithrombin II Alger: a new homozygous ATIII variant. Thromb Haemost 1986;55:218–9.

259. Okajima K, Ueyama H. Homozygous variant of antithrombin III that lacks affinity for heparin, ATIII Ku. Thromb Haemost 1989;61:20–1.

260. Owen MC, Borg JY. Heparin binding defect in a new antithrombin III variant: Rouen 47 Arg to His. Blood 1987;69:1275–6.

261. Borg JY, Owen MC. Proposed heparin binding site in antithrombin based on arginine 47: a new variant Rouen-II, 47 Arg to Ser. J Clin Invest 1988;81:1292–3.

262. Tabernero MD, Tomas JF, Alberca I, et al. Incidence and clinical characteristics of hereditary disorders associated with venous thrombosis. Am J Hematol 1991;36:249–59.

263. Malm J, Laurell M, Nilsson I, Dahlback B. Thromboembolic disease—critical evaluation of laboratory investigation. Thromb Haemost 1992;68:7–13.

264. Pabinger I, Brucker S, Kyrle PA, et al. Hereditary deficiency of antithrombin III, protein C, and protein S: prevalence in patients with a history of venous thrombosis and criteria for rational patient screening. Blood Coagul Fibrinolysis 1992;3:547–53.

265. Melissari E, Monte G, Lindo VS, et al. Congenital thrombophilia among patients with venous thromboembolism. Blood Coagul Fibrinolysis 1992;3:749–58.

266. De Stefano V, Leone G. Mortality related to thrombosis in congenital antithrombin III deficiency. Lancet 1991;337:847–8.

267. Conard J, Horellou MH, Van Dreden P. Thrombosis and pregnancy in congenital deficiencies in ATIII, protein C, or protein S: study of 78 women. Thromb Haemost 1990;63:319–30.

268. Rosendahl FR, Heijboer H. Mortality related to thrombosis in congenital antithrombin III deficiency. Lancet 1991;337:1545–6.

269. Cosgriff TM, Bishop DT, Hershgold EJ, et al. Familial antithrombin III deficiency: its natural history, genetics, diagnosis and treatment. Medicine 1983;62:209–20.

270. Andrew M, Brooker L. Blood component therapy in neonatal hemostatic disorders. Transfus Med Rev 1995;9:231–50.

271. Andrew M, David M, Adams M, et al. Venous thromboembolic complications (VTE) in children: first analyses of the Canadian Registry of VTE. Blood 1994;83:1251–7.

272. Andrew M, Brooker L. Hemostatic complications in renal disorders of the young. Pediatr Nephrol 1996;10:88–99.

273. Bromberg WD, Firlit CS. Fibrinolytic therapy for renal vein thrombosis in the child. J Urol 1990;143:86–8.

274. Bjarke B, Herin P, Blomback M. Neonatal aortic thrombosis. A possible clinical manifestation of congenital antithrombin III deficiency. Acta Paediatr Scand 1974;63:297–301.

275. Mitchell L, Piovella F, Ofosu F, Andrew M. Alpha-2-macroglobulin may provide protection from thromboembolic events in antithrombin III deficient children. Blood 1991;78:2299–2304.

276. De Stefano V, Leone G, Carolis M, et al. Antithrombin III in fullterm and preterm newborn infants: three cases of neonatal diagnosis of AT III congenital defect. Thromb Haemost 1987;57:329–31.

277. De Stefano V, Di Donfrancesco A, De Carolis S, et al. Neonatal diagnosis of antithrombin III congenital defect in a premature newborn. Br J Haematol 1987;65:117–24.

278. Schander K, Niesen M, Rehm A, et al. Diagnose und Therapie eines kongenitalen Antithrombin III Manglas in der neonatalen Periode. Blut 1980;40:68.

279. Brenner B, Fishman A, Goldsher D, et al. Cerebral thrombosis in a newborn with a congenital deficiency of antithrombin III. Am J Hematol 1988;27:209–11.

280. Leone G, Valori VM, Storti S, Myers TJ. Inferior vena cava thrombosis in a child with familial antithrombin III deficiency. Thromb Haemost 1980;436:74.

281. Mazza JJ. Antithrombin III (AT III) deficiency spanning four generations. Thromb Haemost 1991;66:737–8.

282. Howarth DJ, Samson D, Stirling Y, Seghatchian MJ. Antithrombin III "Northwick Park": A variant antithrombin normal affinity for heparin but reduced heparin cofactor activity. Thromb Haemost 1985;53:314–9.

283. Egeberg O. Inherited antithrombin deficiency causing thrombophilia. Thromb Diath Haemorrh 1965;13:516–30.

284. Beukes CA, Heyns ADP. A South African family with antithrombin III deficiency. S Afr Med J 1980;58:528–30.

285. Peeters S, Vandenplas Y, Jochmans K, et al. Myocardial infarction in a neonate with hereditary antithrombin III deficiency. Acta Paediatr 1993;82:610–3.

286. Soutar R, Burrows P, Marzinotto V, et al. Overtight nappy precipitating iliac vein thrombosis in antithrombin III deficient neonate. Arch Dis Child 1993;69:599.

287. Jochmans K, Lissens W, Vervoort R, et al. Antithrombin-Gly 424 Arg: a novel point mutation responsible for type I antithrombin deficiency and neonatal thrombosis. Blood 1994;83:146–51.

288. Olds RJ, Lane DA, Ireland H, et al. Novel point mutations leading to type I antithrombin deficiency and thrombosis. Br J Haematol 1991;78:408–13.

289. Creagh MD, Roberts IF, Clark DJ, Preston FE. Familial antithrombin III deficiency and mycoplasma pneumoniae pneumonia. J Clin Pathol 1991;44:870–1.

290. Eyster ME, Parker ME. Treatment of familial antithrombin III deficiency with danazol. Haemostasis 1985;15:119–25.

291. Vomberg PP, Breederveld C, Fleury P, et al. Cerebral thromboembolism due to antithrombin III deficiency in two children. Neuropediatrics 1987;18:42–4.

292. Winter J, Fenech A, Ridley W, et al. Familial antithrombin III deficiency. QJM 1982;204:373–95.

293. Seguin J, Weatherstone K, Nankervis C. Inherited antithrombin III deficiency in the neonate. Arch Pediatr Adolesc Med 1994;148:389–93.

294. Draaisma J, Rotteveel J, Meekma R, Geven W. Neonatal dural sinus thrombosis. Tijdschr Kinder 1991;59:64–7.

295. Shiozaki A, Arai T, Izumi R, et al. Congenital antithrombin III deficient neonate treated with antithrombin III concentrates. Thromb Res 1993;70:211–16.

296. Sas G, Blasko G, Banhegyi J, et al. Abnormal antithrombin III (Antithrombin III "Budapest") as a cause of a familial thrombophilia. Thromb Diath Haemorrh 1974;32:105–15.

297. Newman RS, Spear GS, Kirschbaum N. Postmortem DNA diagnosis of factor V Leiden in a neonate with systemic thrombosis and probable antithrombin deficiency. Obstet Gynecol 1998;92:702–5.

298. Nowak-Gottl U, Junker R, Hartmeier M, et al. Increased lipoprotein (a) is an important risk factor for venous thromboembolism in childhood. Circulation 1999;100:743–8.

299. Nuss R, Hays T, Chudgar U, Manco Johnson M. Antiphospholipid antibodies and coagulation regulatory protein abnormalities in children with pulmonary emboli. J Pediatr Hematol Oncol 1997;19:202–207.

300. Jochmans K, Lissens W, Vervoort R, et al. Antithrombin-Gly 424 Arg: a novel point mutation responsible for Type 1 antithrombin deficiency and neonatal thrombosis. Blood 1994;83:146–51.

301. Chowdhury V, Lane DA, Mille B, et al. Homozygous antithrombin deficiency: report of two new cases (99 Leu to Phe) associated with arterial and venous thrombosis. Thromb Haemost 1994;72:198–202.

302. Hakten M, Deniz U, Ozbay G, Ulutin ON. Two cases of homozygous antithrombin III deficiency in a family with congenital deficiency of ATIII. In: Senzinger H, Vinazzer H, eds. Thrombosis and haemorrhagic disorders. Proceedings of the 6th International Meeting of the Danubian League against Thrombosis and Haemorrhagic Disorders. Wurtzburg, Germany: Schmitt and Meyer, 1989: 177.

303. Vidaud D, Sirieix ME, Alhenc-Gelas M, et al. A double heterozygosity in 2 brothers with antithrombin (ATIII) deficiency due to the association of Arg 47 to His mutation with a 9 base pair (bp) deletion in exon VI. Thromb Haemost 1991;65:838.

304. Stenflo J. A new vitamin K-dependent protein. J Biol Chem 1976;251:355–63.

305. Kisiel W, Canfield WM, Ericsson LH, Davie EW. Anticoagulant properties of bovine plasma protein C following activation by thrombin. J Biol Chem 1977;16:5824–31.

306. Kisiel W. Human plasma protein C. Isolation, characterization, and mechanism of activation by alpha-thrombin. J Clin Invest 1979;64:761–9.

307. Seegers WH, Novoa E, Henry RL, Hassouna HI. Relationship of "new" vitamin K dependent protein C and "old" autoprothrombin II-A. Thromb Res 1976;8:543–52.

308. Marciniak E. Inhibitor of human blood coagulation elicited by thrombin. J Lab Clin Med 1972;79:921–34.

309. Griffin JH. Deficiency of protein C in congenital thrombotic disease. J Clin Invest 1981;68:1370–3.

310. Tait R, Walker I, Islam S, et al. Age-related changes in protein C activity in healthy adult males. Thromb Haemost 1991;65:326–7.

311. Long GL, Belagaje RM, MacGillivray RTA. Cloning and sequencing of liver cDNA coding for bovine protein C. Proc Natl Acad Sci U S A 1984;81:5653–6.

312. Beckman J, Schmidt RK, Santerre F, et al. The structure and evolution of a 461 amino acid human protein C precursor and its messenger RNA, based on the DNA sequence of cloned human liver cDNAs. Nucleic Acids Res 1985;13:5233–47.

313. Foster DC, Yoshitake S, Davie EW. Characterization of cDNA coding for human protein C. Proc Natl Acad Sci U S A 1984;81:4766–70.

314. Dahlback B, Stenflo J. The protein C anticoagulant system. In: Stamatoyannopoulos G, Nienhuis AW, eds. The molecular basis of blood diseases. Philadelphia: WB Saunders, 1994:599–628.

315. Marlar RA, Kressin DC, Madden RM. Contribution of plasma proteinase inhibitors to the regulation of activated protein C in plasma. Thromb Haemost 1993;69:16–20.

316. Esmon N. Thrombomodulin. Prog Haemost Thromb 1989;9:29–55.

317. Hofsteenge J, Taguchi H, Stone S. Effect of thrombomodulin on the kinetics of the interaction of thrombin with substrates and inhibitors. Biochem 1986;237:243–251.

318. Broekmans AW, Bertina RM. Protein C. In: Poller L, ed. Recent advances in blood coagulation. New York: Churchill Livingstone, 1985:117–137.

319. Bertina RM, Brokemans AW. The use of a functional and immunologic assay for plasma protein C in the study of the heterogeneity of congenital protein C deficiency. Thromb Haemost 1984;51:1–2.

320. Comp PC, Nixon RR, Esmon CT. Determination of functional levels of protein C, an antithrombotic protein, using thrombin-thrombomodulin complex. Blood 1984;63:15–16.

321. D'Angelo SV, Comp PC, Esmon CT, D'Angelo A. Relationship between protein C antigen and anticoagulant activity during oral anticoagulation and in selected disease states. J Clin Invest 1985;77:416–25.

322. Rocchi M, Roncuzzi L, Santamaria R, et al. Mapping through somatic cell hybrids and cDNA probes of protein C to chromosome 2, factor X to chromosome 13 and alpha-1-acid glycoprotein to chromosome 9. Hum Genet 1986;74:30–3.

323. Long GL, Marshall A, Gardner JC, Naylor SL. Genes for human vitamin K-dependent protein C and S are located on chromosomes 2 and 3 respectively. Somat Cell Mol Genet 1988;14:93–8.

324. Kato A, Miura O, Sumi Y, Aoki N. Assignment of the human protein C gene (PROC) to chromosome 2q14–q21 by in situ hybridization. Cytogenet Cell Genet 1988;47:45–7.

325 Plutsky J, Hoskins JA, Long GL, Crabtree GR. Evolution and organization of the human protein C gene. Proc Natl Acad Sci U S A 1987;83:546–50.

326. Foster. The nucleotide sequence of the gene for human protein C. Proc Natl Acad Sci U S A 1985;82:4673–7.

327. Reitsma P, Bernardi F, Doing R, et al. Protein C deficiency: a database of mutations, 1995 update on behalf of the Subcommittee on Plasma Coagulation Inhibitors of the Scientific and Standardization Committee of the ISTH. Thromb Haemost 1995;73:876–9.

328. Bovill E, Bauer K, Dickerman J, et al. The clinical spectrum of heterozygous protein C deficiency in a large New England kindred. Blood 1989;73:712–7.

329. Allaart C, Poort S, Rosendahl F, et al. Increased risk of venous thrombosis in carriers of hereditary protein C deficiency defect. Lancet 1993;341:134–8.

330. Greffe BS, Marlar RA, Manco-Johnson M. Neonatal protein C: molecular composition and distribution in normal term infants. Thromb Res 1989;56:91–8.

331. Moalic P, Gruel Y, Body G, et al. Levels and plasma distribution of free and c_4b-BP-bound pmrotein S in human fetuses and fullterm newborns. Thromb Res 1988;49:471–80.

332. Schwarz HP, Muntean W, Watzke H, et al. Low total protein S antigen but high protein S activity due to decreased c_4b-binding protein in neonates. Blood 1988;71:562–5.

333. Menashi S, Aurousseau MH, Gozin D, et al. High levels of circulating thrombomodulin in human foetuses and children. Thromb Haemost 1999;81:906–9.

334. De Stefano V, Leone G, Mastrangelo S, et al. Clinical manifestations and management of inherited thrombophilia: retrospective analysis and follow-up after diagnosis of 238 patients with congenital deficiency of antithrombin III, protein C, protein S. Thromb Haemost 1994;72:352–8.

335. Nowak-Gottl U, Dubus O, Findeisen M, et al. Lipoprotein (a): its role in childhood thromboembolism. Pediatr 1997;99:E11.

336. Nuss R, Hays T, Chudgar U, Manco-Johnson M. Antiphospholipid antibodies and coagulation regulatory protein abnormalities in children with pulmonary embolism. J Pediatr Hematol Oncol 1997;19:202–7.

337. Toumi NH, Khaldi F, Ben Becheur S, et al. Thrombosis in congenital deficiencies of ATIII, protein C, or protein S: a study of 44 children. Hematol Cell Therapy 1997;39:295–9.

338. Sifontes MT, Nuss R, Jacobson LJ, et al. Thrombosis in otherwise well children with the factor V Leiden mutation. J Pediatr 1996;128:324–8.

339. Pescatore P, Horellou H, Conard J, et al. Problems of oral anticoagulation in an adult with homozygous protein C deficiency and late onset of thrombosis. Thromb Haemost 1993;69:311–5.

340. Marlar R, Sills R, Groncy P, et al. Protein C survival during replacement therapy in homozygous protein C deficiency. Am J Hematol 1992;41:24–31.

341. Deguchi K, Tsukada T, Iwasaki E, et al. Late-onset homozygous protein C deficiency manifesting cerebral infarction as the first symptom at age 27. Intern Med 1992;31:922–5.

342. Yamamoto K, Matsushita T, Sugiura I, et al. Homozgous protein C deficiency: identification of a novel missense mutation that causes impaired secretion of the mutant protein C. J Lab Clin Med 1992;119:682–9.

343. Auberger K. Evaluation of a new protein C concentrate and comparison of protein C assays in a child with congenital protein C deficiency. Ann Hematol 1992;64:146–51.

344. Grundy C, Melissari E, Lindo V, et al. Late-onset homozygous protein C deficiency. Lancet 1991; 338(8766):575–6.

345. Ozkutlu S, Saraclar M, Atalay S, et al. Two-dimensional echocardiographic diagnosis of tricuspid valve noninfective endocarditis due to protein C deficiency (lesion mimicking tricuspid valve myxoma). Jap Heart J 1991;32:139–45.

346. Marlar R, Neumann A. Neonatal purpura fulminans due to homozygous protein C or protein S deficiencies. Semin Thromb Haemost 1990;16:299–309.

347. Tripodi A, Franchi F, Krachmalnicoff A, Mannucci P. Asymptomatic homozygous protein C deficiency. Acta Haematol 1990;83:152–5.

348. Petrini P, Segnestam K, Ekelund H, Egberg N. Homozygous protein C deficiency in two siblings. Pediatr Hematol Oncol 1990;7:165–75.

349. Marlar R, Adcock D, Madden R. Hereditary dysfunctional protein C molecules (type II): assay characterization and proposed classification. Thromb Haemost 1990;63:375–9.

350. Marlar R, Montgomery R, Broekmans A. Report on the diagnosis and treatment of homozygous protein C deficiency. Report of the Working Party on Homozygous Protein C Deficiency of the ISTH Subcommittee on Protein C and Protein S. Thromb Haemost 1989;61:529–31.

351. Tuddenham E, Takase T, Thomas A, et al. Homozygous protein C deficiency with delayed onset of symptoms at 7 to 10 months. Thromb Res 1989;53:475–84.

352. Hartman R, Manco-Johnson M, Rawlings J, et al. Homozygous protein C deficiency: early treatment with warfarin. Am J Pediatr Hematol Oncol 1989;11:395–401.

353. Vukovich T, Auberger K, Weil J, et al. Replacement therapy for a homozygous protein C deficiency-state using a concentrate of human protein C and S. Br J Haematol 1988;70:435–40.

354. Gladson C, Groncy P, Griffin J. Coumarin necrosis, neonatal purpura fulminans, and protein C deficiency. Arch Dermatol 1987;123:1701a–6a.

355. Casella J, Bontempo F, Markel H, et al. Successful treatment of homozygous protein C deficiency by hepatic transplantation. Lancet 1988;1(8583):435–8.

356. Manco-Jonhson M, Marlar R, Jacobson L, et al. Severe protein C deficiency in newborn infants. J Pediatr 1988;113:359–63.

357. Peters C, Casella J, Marlar R, et al. Homozygous protein C deficiency: observations on the nature of the molecular abnormality and the effectiveness of warfarin therapy. Pediatrics 1988;81:272–6.

358. Rappaport E, Speights V, Helbert B, et al. Protein C deficiency. South Med J 1987;80:240–2.

359. Marlar R, Montgomery R, Broekmans A, and the Working Party. Diagnosis and treatment of homozygous protein C deficiency: report of the working party on Homozygous Protein C and Protein S, International Committee on Thrombosis and Haemostasis. J Pediatr 1989;114:528–34.

360. Monagle P, Andrew M, Halton J, et al. Homozygous protein C deficiency: description of a new mutation and successful treatment with low molecular weight heparin. Thromb Haemost 1998;79:756–61.

361. Hattenbach LO, Beeg T, Kreuz W, Zubcov A. Ophthalmic manifestation of congenital protein C deficiency. J Aapos 1999;3:188–90.

362. Auletta M, Headington J. Purpura fulminans: a cutaneous manifestation of severe protein C deficiency. Arch Dermatol 1988;124:1387–91.

363. Adcock D, Brozna J, Marlar R. Proposed classification and pathologic mechanisms of purpura fulminans and skin necrosis. Semin Thromb Haemost 1990;16:333–40.

364. Adcock D, Hicks M. Dermatopathology of skin necrosis associated with purpura fulminans. Semin Thromb Haemost 1990;16:283–92.

365. Dreyfus M, Magny J, Bridey F, et al. Treatment of homozygous protein C deficiency and neonatal purpura fulminans with a purified protein C concentrate. N Engl J Med 1991;325:1565–8.

366. Walker JF. Protein C deficiency in liver disease. Ann Clin Lab Sci 1990;20:106–12.

367. Streif W, Andrew M, Marzinotto V, et al. Analysis of warfarin therapy in pediatric patients: a prospective cohort study. Blood 1999; in press.

368. Andrew M, Marzinotto, V, Brooker L, et al. Oral anticoagulant therapy in pediatric patients: a prospective study. Thromb Haemost 1994;71:265–9.

369. Sanz-Rodriguez C, Gil-Fernandez JJ, Zapater P, et al. Long-term management of homozygous protein C deficiency: replacement therapy with subcutaneous purified protein C concentrate. Thromb Haemost 1999;81:887–90.

370. Minford AM, Parapia LA, Stainforth C, Lee D. Treatment of homozygous protein C deficiency with subcutaneous protein C concentrate. Br J Haematol 1996;93:215–6.

371. Sharon C. Homozygous protein C deficiency with moderately severe clinical symptoms. Thromb Res 1986;41:483–8.

372. Manabe S, Matsuda M. Homozygous protein C deficiency combined with heterozygous dysplasminogenemia in a 21-year-old thrombophilic male. Thromb Res 1985;39:333–41.

373. Samama M. Successful progressive anticoagulation in a severe protein C deficiency and previous skin necrosis at the initiation of oral anticoagulant treatment. Thromb Haemost 1984;51:132–3.

374. Melissari E, Kakkar V. Congenital severe protein C deficiency in adults. Br J Haematol 1989;72:222–228.

375. Conard J. Homozygous protein C deficiency with late onset and recurrent coumarin induced skin necrosis. Lancet 1992;339:743–4.

376. Suzuki K, Nishioka J, Kusmoto H, Hashimoto S. Protein S is essential for the activated protein C-catalysed inaction of platelet-associated factor Va. J Biochem 1983;96:455–60.

377. Walker FJ. Regulation of activated protein C by a new protein. A possible function for bovine protein S. J Biol Chem 1980;255:5521–4.

378. Walker FJ. Regulation of activated protein C by protein S: the role of phospholipid in factor Va inactivation. J Biol Chem 1981;256:11128–31.

379. Solymoss S, Tucker MM, Tracey PB. Kinetics of inactivation of membrane-bound factor Va by activated protein C. Protein S modulates factor Xa protection. J Biol Chem 1988;263:14884–90.

380. Dahlback B. Inhibition of protein Ca function of human and bovine protein S by C4b binding protein. J Biol Chem 1986;261:12022–7.

381. Schwarz HP, Fischer M, Hopmeier P, et al. Plasma protein S deficiency in familial thrombotic disease. Blood 1984;64:1297–1300.

382. Broekmans AW, Bertina RM, Reinalda Poot J, et al. Hereditary protein S deficiency and venous thromboembolism. A study in 3 Dutch families. Thromb Haemost 1985;53:273–7.

383. Comp R, Doray D, Patton D, Esmon C. An abnormal plasma distribution of protein S occurs in functional protein S deficiency. Blood 1986;67:504–5.

384. Comp PhC, Esmon CT. Recurrent thromboembolism in patients with a partial deficiency of protein S. N Engl J Med 1984;311:1525–8.

385. Ploos van Amstel HK, Zanden AL, van der Bakker E, et al. Two genes homologous with human protein S cDNA are located on chromosome 3. Thromb Haemost 1987;58:982–3.

386. Schmidel KD, Tatro AV, Phelps LG, et al. Organization of the human protein S genes. Biochem 1990;26:7845–52.

387. Ploos van Amstel HK, Reitsma PH, van der Logt PE, Bertina RM. Intron-exon organization of the active human protein S gene PS alpha and its pseudogene PS beta. Biochem 1990;29:7853–60.

388. Edenbrandt CM, Lundwall A, Wydro R, Stenflo J. Molecular analysis of the gene for vitamin K dependent protein S and its pseudogene. Biochem 1990;29:7861–7.

389. Han P, Pradham M. A simple functional protein S assay using PROTAC. Clin Lab Haematol 1990;12:201–8.

390. Wiesel ML, Charmantier JL, Freyssinet JM, et al. Screening of protein S deficiency using a functional assay in patients with venous and arterial thrombosis. Thromb Res 1990;58:461–8.

391. van de Waart P, Preissner KT, Bechtold JR, Muller-Berghaus G. A functional test for protein S activity in plasma. Thromb Res 1987;48:427–37.

392. Graves-Hoagland R, Walker FJ. Protein S and thrombosis. Ann Clin Lab Sci 1989;19:208–15.

393. Comp PC, Nixon RR, Cooper MR, Esmon CT. Familial protein S deficiency is associated with recurrent thrombosis. J Clin Invest 1984;74:2082–8.

394. Edson JU, Vogt JM, Huesman DA. Laboratory diangosis of inherited protein S deficiency. Am J Clin Pathol 1990;94:176–86.

395. Krachmainicoff A, Tobesi S, Valsecchi C, et al. A monoclonal antibody to human protein S used as the capture antibody for measuring total protein S by enzyme immunoassay. Clin Chem 1990;36:43–6.

396. Deutz-Terlouw P, Ballering L, Wijngaarden A, Bertina R. Two ELISA's for the measurement of protein S, and their use in the laboratory diagnosis of protein S deficiency. Clin Chim Acta 1989;186:321.

397. Woodhams BJ. The simultaneous measurement of total and free protein S by ELISA. Thromb Res 1988;50:213–20.

398. Bertina RM, van Wijngaarden A, Reinalda-Poot J, et al. Determination of plasma protein S: the protein cofactor of activated protein C. Thromb Haemost 1985;53:268–72.

399. Poort SR, Deutzterlouw PP, van Wijngaarden A, Bertina RM. Immunoradiometric assay for the calcium stabilized conformation of human protein S. Thromb Haemost 1988;58:998–1004.

400. Fair DS, Revak DJ. Quantitation of human protein S in the plasma of normal and warfarin-treated individuals by radioimmunoassay. Thromb Res 1984;36:527–35.

401. Kobayashi I, Amemiya N, Endo T, et al. Functional activity of protein S determined with use of protein C activated by venom activator. Clin Chem 1989;35:1648–9.

402. Hirsh J, Dalen JE, Anderson DR, et al. Oral anticoagulants: mechanism of action, clinical effectiveness, and optimal therapeutic range. Chest 1998;114:445S–69S.

403. Boerger LM, Morris PC, Thurnau GR, et al. Oral contraceptives and gender affect protein S status. Blood 1987;69:692–4.

404. Miletich JP, Broze GJ. Age and gender dependence of total protein S antigen in the normal adult population. Blood 1988;72:371a.

405. Faioni EM, Franchi F, Asti D, et al. Resistance to activated protein C in nine thrombophilic families: interference in a protein C functional assay. Thromb Haemost 1993;70:1067–71.

406. Engesser L, Brockmans AW, Briet E, et al. Hereditary protein S deficiency: clinical manifestations. Ann Intern Med 1987;106:677–682.

407. De Stefano, V, Leone G, Ferrelli R, et al. Severe deep vein thrombosis in a 2-year-old child with protein S deficiency. Thromb Haemost 1987;58:1089.

408. Mannucci P, Tripodi A, Bertina R. Protein S deficiency associated with "juvenile" arterial and venous thromboses. Thromb Haemost 1986;55:440.

409. Israels SJ, Seshia SS. Childhood stroke associated with protein C or S deficiency. J Pediatr 1987;111:5624.

410. Sacco RL, Owen J, Mohr JP, et al. Free protein S deficiency: a possible association with cerebrovascular occlusion. Stroke 1989;20:1657–61.

411. Schafer HP, von Felton A. Protein S deficiency in young patients with thrombotic brain infarction. Schweiz Med Wochenschr 1989;119:489–92.

412. Moreb J, Kitchens CS. Acquired functional protein S deficiency, cerebral venous thrombosis, and coumarin skin necrosis in association with antiphospholipid syndrome: report of two cases. Am J Med 1989;87:207–10.

413. Davous P, Horellou MH, Samama M. Cerebral infarction and familial protein S deficiency. Stroke 1990;21:1760–1.

414. Girolami A, Simioni P, Lazzro AR, Cordiano I. Severe arterial cerebral thrombosis in a patient with protein S deficiency. Moderately reduced total and markedly reduced free protein S: a family study. Thromb Haemost 1989;61:144–7.

415. Comp PC, Thurnau GR, Welsh J, Esmon CT. Functional and immunologic protein S levels are decreased during pregnancy. Blood 1986;68:881–5.

416. Lao TT, Yuen PMP, Yin JA. Protein S and protein C levels in Chinese women during pregnancy, delivery, and the puerperium. Br J Obstet Gynaecol 1989;96:881–6.

417. Malm JL, Laurell M, Dahlback B. Changes in the plasma levels of vitamin K dependent protein C and S and of C4b binding protein during pregnancy and oral contraception. Br J Haematol 1988;68:437–44.

418. Huisveld IA, Hospers JEH, Meijers JCM, et al. Oral contraceptives reduce total protein S but not free protein S. Thromb Res 1987;45:109–114.

419. Gilabert J, Fernanadez JA, Espana F, et al. Physiological coagulation inhibitors (protein S, protein C and antithrombin III) in severe preeclamptic states and in users of oral contraceptives. Thromb Res 1988;49:319–29.

420. Vaziri ND, Alikhani S, Patel B, et al. Increased levels of protein C activity, protein C concentration and free protein S in nephrotic syndrome. Nephron 1988;49:20–3.

421. Vaziei ND, Shah GM, Winer RL, et al. Coagulation and cascade, fibrinolytic system, antithrombin III, protein C and protein S in patients maintained on continuous ambulatory peritaoneal dialysis. Thromb Res 1989;53:173–80.

422. Rostoker G, Pech MA, Lagrue G. Proteins C and S of coagulation: new markers of thrombotic risk in nephrotic syndrome. Pathol Biol 1988;36:297–9.

423. Allon M, Soffer O, Evatt B, et al. Protein S and C antigen levels in proteinuric patients: dependence on

type of glomerular pathology. Am J Hematol 1989; 31:96–101.

424. Gouault-Heilmann M, Gadelha Parente T, Levent M, et al. Total and free protein S in nephrotic syndrome. Thromb Res 1988;48:37–42.

425. Eldrup-Horgensen J, Brace L, Flanigan DP, et al. Lupus-like anticoagulant and lower extremity arterial occlusive disease. Circulation 1989;80:11154–5.

426. Tsakiris DA, Settas L, Makris PE, Marbet GA. Lupus anticoagulant—antiphospholipid antibodies and thrombophilia. Relation to protein C-protein S-thrombomodulin. J Rheumatol 1990;17:785–9.

427. Amer L, Kisiel W, Searles RP, Williams RC. Impairment of the protein C anticoagulant pathway in a patient with systemic lupus erythematosus, anticardiolipin antibodies and thrombosis. Thromb Res 1990;57:247–58.

428. Marciniak E, Romond EH. Impaired catalytic function of activated protein C: a new in vitro manifestation of lupus anticoagulant. Blood 1989;74:2426–32.

429. Stankiewicz AJ, Steiner M, Lally EV, Kaplan SR. Abnormally high level of C4b binding protein and deficiency of free fraction of protein S in a patient with systemic lupus erythematosis and recurrent thromboses. J Rheumatol 1991;18:82–7.

430. Hasselaar P, Derksen R, Blokziul L. Risk factors for thrombosis in lupus patients. Ann Rheum Dis 1989; 48:933–40.

431. D'Angelo A, Vigano-D'Angelo S, Esmon CT, Comp PC. Acquired deficiencies of protein S. J Clin Invest 1988;81:1445–54.

432. Takahashi H, Tatewaki W, Wada K, Shibatga A. Plasma protein S in disseminated intravascular coagulation, liver disease, collagen disease diabetes, mellitus, and under oral anticoagulant therapy. Clin Chim Acta 1989;182:195–208.

433. Harper PL, Jarvis J, Jennings I, et al. Changes in the natural anticoagulants following bone marrow transplantations. Bone Marrow Transplant 1990;5:39–42.

434. Tsuchida A, Thomson NM, Salem HH, et al. Serial monitoring show plasma protein C and free protein S levels are decreased during human acute renal allograft rejection. Transplant Proc 1990;22:2134–6.

435. Simioni P, Zanardi S, Saracino A. Occurrence of arterial thrombosis in a cohort of patients with hereditary deficiency of clotting inhibitors. J Med 1992;23:61–74.

336. Manco Johnson MJ, Nuss R, Key N, et al. Lupus anticoagulant and protein S deficiency in children with postvaricella purpura fulminans or thrombosis. J Pediatr 1996;128:319–23.

437. Blanco A, Bonduel M, Penalva L, et al. Deep vein thrombosis in a 13-year-old boy with hereditary protein S deficiency and a review of the pediatric literature. Am J Hematol 1994;45:330–4.

438. Witt O, Pereira PL, Tillmann W. Severe cerebral venous sinus thrombosis and dural arteriovenous fistula in an infant with protein S deficiency. Childs Nerv Sys 1999;15:128–30.

439. Zimmerman AA, Watson RS, Williams JK. Protein S deficiency presenting as an acute postoperative arterial thrombosis in a four-year-old child. Anesth Anal 1999;88:535–7.

440. Charuvanji A, Laothamatas J, Torcharus K, Srivimonmas S. Moyamoya disease and protein S deficiency: a case report. Pediatr Neurol 1997;17:171–3.

441. Zoller B, He X, Dahlback B. Homozygous APC-resistance combined with inherited type I protein S deficiency in a young boy with severe thrombotic disease. Thromb Haemost 1995;73:743–5.

442. Simioni P, Battistella PA, Drigo P, et al. Childhood stroke associated with familial protein S deficiency. Brain Dev 1994;16:241–5.

443. Horowitz I, Galvis A, Gomperts E. Arterial thrombosis and protein S deficiency. J Pediatr 1992;121:934–7.

444. Prats J, Garaizar C, Zuazo E, et al. Superior sagittal sinus thrombosis in a child with protein S deficiency. Neurology 1992;42:2303–4.

445. O'Sullivan J, Chatuverdi R, Bennett MK, Hunter S. Protein S deficiency: early presentation and pulmonary hypertension. Arch Dis Child 1992;67:960–1.

446. Pan EY, Gomperts ED, Millen R, Gilsanz V. Bone mineral density and its association with inherited protein S deficiency. Thromb Res 1990;58:221–31.

447. Pegelow CH, Ledford M. Severe protein S deficiency in a newborn. Pediatrics 1992;89:674–5.

448. Gomez E, Ledford MR, Pegelow CH, et al. Homozygous protein S deficiency due to a one base pair deletion that leads to a stop codon in exon III of the protein S gene. Thromb Haemost 1994;71:723–6.

449. Marlar RA, Neuman A. Neonatal purpura fulminans due to homozygous protein C or protein S deficiencies. Semin Thromb Hemost 1990;16:299–309.

450. Mahasandana C, Suvatte V, Marlar RA, et al. Neonatal purpura fulminans associated with homozygous protein S deficiency [letter]. Lancet 1990;335:61–2.

451. Hui CH, Lam CC, Sze CS. A family of protein S deficiency including two adults with homozygous deficiency. Thromb Haemost 1997;78:1158–9.

452. Mahadandana C, Veerakul G, Tanphaichitr VS, et al. Homozygous protein S deficiency: 7 year follow-up. Thromb Haemost 1996;76:1122–3.

453. Mintz-Hittner HA, Miyashiro MJ, Knight-Nanan DM, et al. Vitreoretinal findings similar to retinopathy of prematurity in infants with compound heterozygous protein S deficiency. Ophthalmology 1999;106:1525–30.

454. Pung-Amritt P, Poort SR, Vos HL, et al. Compound heterozygosity for one novel and one recurrent mutation in a Thai patient with severe protein S deficiency. Thromb Haemost 1999;81:189–92.

455. D'Angelo A, Selhub J. Homocysteine and thrombotic disease. Blood 1997;90:1–11.

456. Christensen B, Refsum H, Vintermyr O, Ueland PM. Homocysteine export from cells cultured in the presence of physiological or superfluous levels of methionine: methionine loading of nontransformed, transformed, proliferating, and quiescent cells in culture. J Cell Biol 1991;146:52–3.

457. Boers GHJ. Heterozygosity for homocystinuria in premature peripheral and cerebral occlusive arterial disease. N Engl J Med 1985;313:709–15.

458. Genest JJ. Plasma homosyteine levels in men with premature coronary artery disease. J Am Coll Cardiol 1990;16:1114–9.

459. Clarke R. Hyperhomocysteinemia: an independent risk factor for vascular disease. N Engl J Med 1991;324:1149–55.

460. Selhub J, Jacques PF, Wilson PWF, et al. Vitamin status and intake as primary determinants of homocysteinemia in an elderly population. JAMA 1993;270:2693–8.

461. Chauveau P, Chadefaux B, Coude M, et al. Increased plasma homocysteine concentration in patients with chronic renal failure. Miner Electrol Metab 1992;18:196–8.

462. Mudd SH, Skovby F, Levy HL, et al. The natural history of homocysteinuria due to cystathionine b-synthase deficiency. Am J Hum Genet 1985;37:1–31.

463. Wada Y, Narisawa K, Arakawa T. Infantile type of homocysteinuria with 5, 10-methylenetetrahydrofolate reductase deficiency. Monogr Hum Genet 1978;9:140–6.

464. Jacques PF, Bostom AG, Williams RR, et al. Relation between folate status, a common mutation in methylenetetrahydrofolate reductase, and plasma homocysteine concentrations. Circulation 1996;93:7–9.

465. Kluijtmans LA, van den Heuvel LP, Boers GH, et al. Moleclar genetic analysis in mild hyperhomocysteinemia: a common mutation in the methylenetetrahydrofolate reductase gene is a genetic risk factor for cardiovascular disease. Am J Hum Genet 1996;58:35–41.

466. Kang SS, Zhou J, Wong PWK, et al. Intermediate homocysteinemia: a thermolabile variant of methylenetetrahydrofolate reductase. Am J Hum Genet 1988;43:414–5.

467. Mudd SH, Leby HL, Skorby F. Disorders of transulfuration. In: Scriver CR, Beaudet AL, Sly W, Vall DL, eds. The metabolic and molecular basis of inherited disease. 7th Ed. New York: McGraw-Hill, 1995:1279–1327.

468. Fowler B, Kraus J, Packman S, Rosenberg LE. Homocysteinuria: evidence for three distinct classes of cystathionine-b-synthase mutants in cultured fibroblasts. J Clin Invest 1978;61:645–6.

469. Barber GW, Spaeth GL. The successful treatment of homocystinuria with pyridoxine. J Pediatr 1969;75:463–4.

470. Kozich V, Kraus JP. Screening for mutations by expressing cDNA segments in E coli: homocystinuria due to cystathionine b-synthase deficiency. Hum Mutat 1992;1:113–4.

471. Hu FL, Gu Z, Kozich V, et al. Molecular basis of cystathionine b-synthase deficiency in pyridoxine responsive and nonresponsive homocystinuria. Hum Mol Genet 1993;2:1857–1858.

472. Sebastio G, Sperandeo MP, Panico M, et al. The molecular basis of homocystinuria due to cystathionine-b-synthase deficiency in Italian families and report of four novel mutations. Am J Hum Genet 1995;56:1324–5.

473. Sperando MP, Panico M, Pepe A, et al. Molecular analysis of patients affected by homocystinuria due to cystathionine-b-synthase deficiency: report of a new mutation in exon 8 and a deletion in intron 11. J Inherit Metab Dis 1995;18:211–2.

474. Levy HL, Mudd SH, Schulman JD, et al. A derangement in B12 metabolism associated with homocystinemia, cystathioninemia, hypomethioninemia and methylmalonic aciduria. Am J Med 1970;48:390–91.

475. Goodman SI, Moe PG, Hammond KB, et al. Homocystinuria with methylmalonic aciduria: two cases in a sibship. Biochem Med 1970;4:500–1.

476. Mudd SH, Levy HL, Morrow G. Deranged B12 metabolism: effects on sulfur aminoacid metabolism. Biochem Med 1970;4:193–4.

477. Mudd SH, Uhlendorf BW, Freeman JM, et al. Homocystinuria associated with decreased methylenetetrahydrofolate reductase deficiency. Biochem Biophys Res Commun 1972;46:905–6.

478. Shih VE, Salam MZ, Mudd SH, et al. A new form of homocystinuria due to 5, 10-methylenetetrahydrofolate reductase deficiency. Pediatr Res 1972;6:395–6.

479. Kanwar YS, Manaligod JR, Wong PWK. Morphologic studies in a patient with homocystinuria due to 5, 10-methylenetetrahydrofolate reductase deficiency. Pediatr Res 1976;10:598–609.

480. Engbersen AMT, Franken DG, Boers GHJ. Thermolabile 5, 10-methylenetetrahydrofolate reductase as a cause of mild hyperhomocysteinemia. Am J Hum Genet 1995;56:142–3.

481. Frosst P, Blom H, Milos R, et al. A candidate genetic risk factor for vascular disease: a common mutation methylenetetrahydrofolate reductase. Nat Genet 1995;10:111–3.

482. Goyette P, Frosst P, Rosenblatt DS, Rozen R. Human methylenetetrahydrofolate reductase: isolation of cDNA, mapping and mutation identification. Nat Genet 1994;7:195–6.

483. Motulsky A. Nutritional ecogenetics: homcoystiene-related arteriosclerotic vascular disease, neural tube defects, and folic acid. Am J Hum Genet 1996;58:17–8.

484. de Franchis R, Mancini FP, D'Angelo A, et al. Elevated total plasma homocyteine (tHcy) and 677CT mutation of the 5, 10-methylenetetrahydrofolate reductase gene in thrombotic vascular disease. Am J Hum Genet 1996;59:262–3.

485. Vilaseca MA, Moyano D, Ferrer I, Artuch R. Total homocysteine in pediatric patients. Clin Chem 1997; 43:690–2.

486. Murphy-Cuthorian DR, Wexman MP, Grieco AJ, et al. Methionine intolerance: a possible risk factor for coronary artery disease. J Am Coll Cardiol 1985; 6:725–6.

487. Wilken DEL, Wilcken B. The pathogenesis of coronary artery. J Clin Invest 1976;57:1079–80.

488. Kang SS, Wong PWK, Cook HY, et al. Protein-bound homocyst(e)ine. A possible risk factor for coronary artery disease. J Clin Invest 1986;77:1482–3.

489. Israelsson B, Brattstrom LE, Hultberg BL. Homocysteinemia and myocardial infarction. Atherosclerosis 1988;71:227–8.

490. Olszewski AJ, Szostak WB. Homocysteine content of plasma proteins in ischemic heart disease. Atherosclerosis 1988;69:109–110.

491. Ubbink JG, Vermack WJH, Bennett JM, et al. The prevalence of homocysteinemia and hypercholesterolemia in angiographically defined coronary artery disease. Klin Wochenschr 1991;69:527–8.

492. Araki A, Sako Y, Fukushima Y, et al. Plasma sulphydryl-containing amino acids in patients with cerebral infarction and in hypertensive subjects. Atherosclerosis 1989;79:139–40.

493. Coull BM, Malinow MR, Beamer N, et al. Elevated plasma homocyst(e)ine concentration as an independent risk factor for stroke. Stroke 1990;21:572–6.

494. Brattstrom L, Lindgren A, Israelsson B, et al. Hyperhomocysteinaemia in stroke…prevalence, cause, and relationships to type of stroke and stroke risk factors. Eur J Clin Invest 1992;22:214–5.

495. Brattstrom L, Hardebo JE, Hultberg B. Moderate homocysteinemia. A possible risk factor for arteriosclerotic cerebrovascular disease. Stroke 1984;15:1012–3.

496. Malinow MR, Kang SS, Taylor LM, et al. Prevalence of hyperhomocysteinemia in patients with peripheral arterial occlusive disease. Circulation 1989;79:1180–1.

497. Taylor LM, DeFrang RD, Harris EJ, Porter JM. The association of elevated plasma homocysteine with progression of symptomatic peripheral arterial disease. J Vasc Surg 1991;13:128–36.

498. den Heijer M, Blom HJ, Gerrits WBJ, et al. Is hyperhomocysteinaemia a risk factor for recurrent venous thrombosis? Lancet 1995;345:882–5.

499. Petri M, Roubenoff R, Dallal GE, et al. Plasma homocysteine as a rick factor for atherothrombotic events

in systemic lupus erythematosus. Lancet 1996;348:1120–1.

500. Mosesson MW. Dysfibrinogenemia and thrombosis. Semin Thromb Hemost 1999;25:311–9.

501. Liu CY, Koehn JA, Morgan FJ. Characterization of fibrinogen New York I. A dysfunctional fibrinogen with a deletion of Bb9-72 corresponding exactly to exon 2 of the gene. J Biol Chem 1985;260:4390–6.

502. Liu CY, Wallen P, Handley DA. Fibrinogen New York I: the structural, functional, and genetic deficits and an hypothesis of the role of fibrin in the regulation of coagulation and fibrinolysis. In: Lane D, Henschen A, Jasani M, eds. Fibrinogen, fibrin formation, and fibrinolysis. Berlin: Walter de Gruyter, 1986:79–90.

503. Di Minno G, Martinez J, Cirillo F. A role for platelets and thrombin in the juvenile stroke of two siblings with defective thrombin-adsorbinhg capacity of fibrin(ogen). Arterioscler Thromb 1991;11:785–96.

504. Koopman J, Haverkate F, Lord ST, et al. Molecular basis of fibrinogen Naples associated with defective thrombin binding and thrombophilia. Homozygous substitution of Bb68 Ala—Thr. J Clin Invest 1992;90:238–44.

505. Yamaguchi FI, Sugo T, Hashimoto Y. Fibrinogen Kumamoto with an AaArg19—Gly substitution associated clinically with thrombosis. Fibrinolysis 1996;10:23a.

506. Koopman J, Haverkate F, Grimbergen J, et al. Fibrinogen Marburg: a homozygous case of dysfibrinogenemia, lacking amino acid A-alpha-461—610 (lys461—AAA StopTAA). Blood 1992;80:1972–9.

507. Collet JP, Soria J, Mirshahi M. Dusart syndrome: a new concept of the relationship between fibrin clot architecture and fibrin clot degradability. Hypofibrinolysis related to an abnormal clot structure. Blood 1993;82:2462–9.

508. Soria J, Soria C, Caen JP. A new type of congenital dysfibrinogenemia with defective fibrin lysis-Dusard syndrome: possible relationship to thrombosis. Br J Haematol 1983;53:575–86.

509. Lijnen HR, Soria J, Soria C, et al. Dysfibrinogenemia (fibrinogen Dusard) associated with impaired fibrin-enhanced plasminogen activation. Thromb Haemost 1984;51:108–9.

510. Koopman J, Haverkate F, Grimbergen J. Molecular basis for fibrinogen Dusart (A alpha544 Arg—Cys) and its association with abnormal fibrin polymerization and thrombophilia. J Clin Invest 1993;91:1637–43.

511. Siebenlist KR, Mosesson MW, DiOrio JP. The polymerization of fibrinogen dusart (Aalpha554 Arg—Cys) after removal of carboxy-terminal regions of A alpha chains. Blood Coagul Fibrinolysis 1993;4:61–5.

512. Mosesson MW, Siebenlist KR, Hainfeld JF. The relationship between the fibrinogen D domain self-association/cross-linking site (yXL) and the fibrinogen Dusart abnormality (A alphaR544C-albumin).

Clues to thrombophilia in the "Dusart Syndrome". J Clin Invest 1996;97:2342–50.

513. Ebert R. Index of variant human fibrinogens. Boca Raton, FL: CRC Press, 1994.

514. Furlan M, Steinmann C, Jungo M. A frameshift mutation in exon V of the Aa-chain gene leading to truncated Aa-chains in the homozygous dysfibrinogen Milano III. J Biol Chem 1994;269:33129–34.

515. Furlan M, Steinmann C, Lammle B. Binding of calcium ions and their effect on clotting of fibrinogen Milano III, a variant with truncated Aa-chain. Blood Coagul Fibrinolysis 1996;7:331–5.

516. Sugo T, Nakamikawa C, Takebe M. Factor XIIIa cross-linking of the Marburg fibrin: formation of a alpha-m, gamma-n-heteromultimers and the alpha-chain linked albumin-γ-complex, and disturbed protifibril assembly resulting in acquisition of plasmin resistance relevant to thrombophilia. Blood 1998;91:3282–8.

517. Haverkate F, Samama M. Familial dysfibrinogenemia and thrombophilia: report on a study of the SSC Subcommittee on Fibrinogen. Thromb Haemost 1995;73:151–61.

518. Arocha-Pinango CL, Torres A, Marchi R. A new thrombotic dysfibrinogenemia present in several members of a Venezuelan family. Thromb Haemost 1987; 58:149a.

519. Marchi R, Archa-Pinango CL, Gil F. Electron microscopy studies of 7 patients with dysfibrinogenemia and some of their relatives. Rev Iberoamer Thromb Hemost 1990;3:185–90.

520. Beck EA, Charache P, Jackson DP. A new inherited coagulation disorder caused by an abnormal fibrinogen ("Fibrinogen Baltimore"). Nature 1965;208:143–5.

521. Koopman J, Haverkate F, Briet E, Lord ST. A congenitally abnormal fibrinogen (Vlissingen) with a 6-base deletion in the γ-chain gene, causing defective calcium binding and impaired fibrin polymerization. J Biol Chem 1991;266:13456–61.

522. Galanakis DK, Spitzer SG, Scharrer I, Peerschke EI. Impaired platelet aggregation support by two dysfibrinogens: a γ319–320 deletion and a γ310 Met—Thr substitition. Thromb Haemost 1993;69:2564a.

523. Wada Y, Lord ST. A correlation between thrombotic disease and a specific fibrinogen abnormality (Aalpha 554 Arg—Cys) in two unrelated kindred, Dusart and Chapel Hill III. Blood 1994;84:3709–14.

524. Koopman J, Haverkate F, Grimbergen J. Abnormal fibrinogens Ijmudiden (BbArg14—Cys) and Nijmegen (BbArg44—Cys) form disulfide-linked fibrinogen-albumin complexes. Proc Natl Acad Sci U S A 1992; 89:3478–82.

525. Engesser L, Koopman J, de Munk G. Fibrinogen Nijmegen: congenital dysfibrinogenemia associated with impaired TPA mediated plasminogen activation and decreased binding of TPA. Thromb Haemost 1988;60:113–20.

526. Mosesson MW, Siebenlist KR, Olson JD. Thrombophilia associated with dysfibrinogenemia (fibrinogen Cedar Rapids [γR275c]) and a heterozygous factor V Leiden defect. Thromb Haemost 1997;(Suppl):382a.

527. Brook JG, Tabori S, Tatarsky I, et al. Fibrinogen "Haifa"—a new fibrinogen variant. Haemostasis 1983;13:277–81.

528. Borrell M, Garf M, Coll C. Abnormal polymerization and normal binding of plasminogen and TPA in three new dysfibrinogenemias: Barcelona III and IV (γ275Arg—His) and Villajoyosa (γ275Arg—Cys). Blood Coagul Fibrinolysis 1995;6:198–206.

529. Reber P, Furlan M, Henschen A. Three abnormal fibrinogen variants with the same amino acid substitution (γ275Arg—His): fibrinogens Bergamo II, Essen and Perugia. Thromb Haemost 1986;56:401–6.

530. Bentolila S, Samama MM, Conard J, et al. Association of dysfibrinogenemia and thrombosis. Apropos of a family (fibrinogen Melun) and review of the literature. Ann Intern Med 1995;146:575–80.

531. Brennan SO, Loreth RM, George PM. Oligosaccharide configuration of fibrinogen Kaiserslautern: electrospray ionization analysis of intact γ chains. Thromb Haemost 1998;80:263–5.

532. Ridgway HJ, Brennan SO, Loreth RM, George PM. Fibrinogen Kaiserslautern (γ380 Lys to Asn): a new glycosolated variant with delayed polymerization. Br J Haematol 1997;99:562–9.

533. Bertina RM, Koeleman BP, Koster T, et al. Mutation in blood coagulation factor V associated with resistance to activated protein C. Nature 1994;369:64–7.

534. Spraggon G, Everse SJ, Doolittle RF. Crystal structures of fragment D from human fibrinogen and its crosslinked counterpart from fibrin. Nature 1997; 389:455–62.

535. Krakow W, Endres GF, Siegel BM, Scheraga HA. An electron microscopic investigation of the polymerization of bovine fibrin monomer. J Mol Biol 1972; 71:95–103.

536. Haverkate F, Samama M. Familial dysfibrinogenemia and thrombophilia. Report on a study of the SSC Subcommittee on Fibrinogen. Thromb Haemost 1995;73:151–61.

537. Pandya BV, Cierniewski CS, Budzyski AZ. Conservation of human fibrinogen conformation after cleavage of the Bb chain NH2 terminus. J Biol Chem 1985;260:2994–3000.

538. Fallat RW, Tsang RC, Glueck CJ. Hypercholesterolemia and hypertriglyceridemia in children. Prev Med 1974;3:390–405.

539. Haber C, Kwiterovich PO. Dyslipoproteinemia and xanthomatosis. Pediatr Dermatol 1984;1:261–80.

540. Orth-Gomer K, Mittleman MA, Schenk-Gustafsson K, et al. Lipoprotein (a) as a determinant of coronary heart disease in young women. Circulation 1997;95: 329–34.

541. Haitas B, Baker SG, Meyer TE, et al. Natural history and cardiac manifestations of homozygous familial hypercholesterolaemia. QJM 1990;76:731–40.

542. Salen G, Horak I, Rothkopf M, et al. Lethal atherosclerosis associated with abnormal plasma and tissue sterol composition in sitosterolemia with xanthomatosis. J Lipid Res 1985;26:1126–33.

543. West RJ, Lloyd JK. Hypercholesterolemia in childhood. Adv Pediatr 1979;26:1–34.

544. Sprecher DL, Schaefer EJ, Kent KM, et al. Cardiovascular features of homozygous familial hypercholesterolemia. Analysis of 16 patients. Am J Cardiol 1984;54:20–30.

545. Janaki S, Baruah JK, Jayaram SR, et al. Stroke in the young: a four year study, 1968 to 1972. Stroke 1975;6:318–20.

546. Postiglione A, Nappi A, Brunetti A, et al. Relative protection from cerebral atherosclerosis of young patients with homozygous familial hypercholesterolemia. Atherosclerosis 1991;90:23–30.

547. Rubba A, Mercuri M, Faccenda F, et al. Premature carotid atherosclerosis: does it occur in both familial hypercholesterolemia and homocystinuria? Ultrasound assessment of arterial intima-media thickness and blood flow velocity. Stroke 1994;25:943–50.

548. Mabuchi H. Causes of death in patients with familial hypercholesterolemia. Atherosclerosis 1986;61:1–6.

549. Allen JM, Thompson GR, Myant NB, et al. Cardiovascular complications of homozygous familial hypercholesterolaemia. Br Heart J 1980;44:361–8.

550. Glueck CJ. Pediatric victims of unexplained stroke and their families: familial lipid and lipoprotein abnormalities. Pediatrics 1982;69:308–16.

551. Daniels S. Cerebrovascular arteriosclerosis and ischemic childhood stroke. Stroke 1982;13:360–4.

552. Gluek CJ, Bates SR. Migraine in children: association with primary and familial dyslipoproteinemias. Pediatrics 1986;77:316–23.

553. Guarda LA, Borrero JL. Hand and digital ischemia due to arteriosclerosis and thromboembolization in young adults: pathologic features with clinical correlations. Med Pathol 1990;3:654–8.

554. Rubba P. Extracoronary atherosclerosis in familial hypercholesterolemia. Atherosclerosis 1988;71:205–13.

555. Goldstein J, Brown M. Familial hyercholesterolemia. In: Stanbury JB, ed. Metabolic basis of inherited disease. New York: McGraw-Hill, 1989.

556. Kwiterovich PO, Frederickson DS, Levy RI. Familial hypercholesterolemia (one form of familial type) J Clin Invest 1974;53:1237–8.

557. Kwiterovich PO, Levy RI, Fredrickson DS. Neonatal diagnosis of familial type II hyperlipoproteinemia. Lancet 1973;i:118–9.

558. Rose V, Wilson G, Steiner G. Familial hypercholesterolemia: report of coronary death at age 3 in a homozygous child and prenatal diagnosis in a heterzygous sibling. J Pediatr 1982;100:757–9.

559. Hoeg JM. Familial hypercholesterolemia. What the zebra can teach us about the horse. JAMA 1994;271:543–6.

560. Goldstein J, Brown M. The LDL receptor defect in familial hypercholesterolemia. Med Clin North Am 1982;66:335–62.

561. Williams ML. Death of a child as a result of familial hypercholesterolaemia. Med J Aust 1989;150:93–94. [published erratum appears in Med J Aust 1989, 150:228].

562. Clemens P, Beisiegel U, Steinhagen-Thiessen E. Family study in familial hypercholesterolemia with a receptor-negative homozygous 9-year-old boy. Helv Paediatr Acta 1986;41:173–82.

563. Kwiterovich PO. Pediatric implications of heterozygous familial hypercholesterolemia. Screening and dietary treatment. Arteriosclerosis 1989;9:I111–20.

564. Leonard JV, Clarke M, Macartney FJ, Slack J. Progression of atheroma in homozygous familial hypercholesterolemia during regular plasma exchange. Lancet 1981;2:811–2.

565. Hegele RA, Connelly PW, Cullen-Dean G, Rose V. Elevated plasma lipoprotein(a) associated with abnormal stress thallium scans in children with familial hypercholesterolemia. Am J Cardiol 1993;70:1109–12.

566. Mouratidis B. Detection of silent coronary artery disease in adolescents and young adults with familial hypercholesterolemia by single photon emission computed tomography thallium-201 scanning. Am J Cardiol 1992;70:1109–12.

567. Soria LF, Ludwig EA, Clarke RG. Association between a specific apolipoprotein mutation and familial defective apolipoprotein B-100. Proc Natl Acad Sci U S A 1989;86:587–8.

568. Vega GL, Grundy SM. In vivo evidence for reduced binding of low density lipoprotein to receptors as a cause of primary moderate hypercholesterolemia. J Clin Invest 1986;78:141–2.

569. Innerarity TL, Weisgraber KF, Arnold KS. Familial defective apolipoprotein B-100 low density lipoproteins with abnormal receptor binding. Proc Natl Acad Sci U S A 1987;84:6919–20.

570. Rubinsztein DC, Rall FJ, Seftel HC, et al. Characterization of six patients who are double heterozygotes for familial hypercholesterolemia and familial defective apo B-100. Arterioscler Thromb 1993;13:1076–81.

571. Rauh G. Familial defective apolipoprotein B-100: clinical characteristics of 54 cases. Atherosclerosis 1992;92:233–41.

572. McLean JW, Tomlinsson JE, Kuang WL. cDNA sequence of human apolipoprotein (a) in homologous to plasminogen. Nature 1987;330:132–3.

573. Utermann G, Menzel HJ, Kraft HG. Lp(a) glycoprotein phenotype: inheritance and relation to Lp(a)

lipoprotein concentrations in plasma. J Clin Invest 1987;80:458–9.

574. Breslow JL. Genetic basis of lipoprotein disorders. J Clin Invest 1989;84:373–4.

575. Kwiterovich P, Beaty T, Bachorik P. Pediatric hyperlipoproteinemia: the phenotypic expression of hyperapobetalipoproteinemia in young probands and their parents. In: Widholm K, Naito NK, eds. Recent aspects of diagnosis and treatment of lipoprotein disorders: impact on the prevention of atherosclerotic disease. New York: Alan R Liss, 1988: 89.

576. Kwiterovich PG. Bile acid sequestrant resin therapy in children. In: Fears R, ed. Pharmacological control of hyperlipidemia. Barcelona: Prous Science Publishers, 1986.

577. Kwiterovich PG. Beyond cholesterol: the Johns Hopkins complete guide for avoiding heart disease. Baltimore: The Johns Hopkins Press, 1989.

578. Dolan G, Preston FE. Familial plasminogen deficiency and thromboembolism. Fibrinolysis 1988;2:26–34.

579. Santori MT, Patrassi GM, Theodoridis P, Perin A. Heterozygous type I plasminogen deficiency is associated with an increased risk for thrombosis. Blood Coagul Fibrinolysis 1994;5:889–93.

580. Bateman JB, Pettit TH, Isenberg SJ, Simons KB. Ligneous conjunctivitis: an autosomal recessive disorder. J Pediatr Ophthalmol Strabismus 1986;23:137–40.

581. Tait RC, Walker ID, Islam SIA, et al. Plasminogen levels and putative prevalence of deficiency in 4500 blood donors. Br J Haematol 1991;77:10–1.

582. Tait RC, Walker ID, Conkie JA, et al. Isolated familial plasminogen deficiency may not be a risk factor for thrombosis. Thromb Haemost 1996;76:1004–8.

583. Shigekiyo T, Uno Y, Tomonari A. Type I plasminogen deficiency is not a risk factor for thrombosis. Thromb Haemost 1992;67:189–92.

584. Sartori MT, Patrassi GM, Theodoridis P, et al. Heterozygous type I plasminogen deficiency is associated with an increased risk for thrombosis: a statistical analysis in 20 kindreds. Blood Coagul Fibrinolysis 1994;5:889–93.

585. Engesser L, Kluft C, Briet E, Brommer EJ. Familial elevation of plasma histidine-rich glycoprotein in a family with thrombophilia. Br J Haematol 1987;67:355–8.

586. Castaman G, Ruggeri M, Burei F, Rodeghiero F. High levels of histidine-rich glycoprotein and thrombotic diathesis. Thromb Res 1993;69:297–305.

587. Bouisson M. Ophthalmie sur-aigue avec formation de pseudomembranes à la surface de la conjunctive. Ann Ocul 1847;17:100–4.

588. Borel MG. Un nouveau syndrome palpebral. Bull Soc Fr Ophthal 1933;46:168–80.

589. Eagle RC, Brooks JS, Katowitz JA, et al. Fibrin as a major constituent of ligneous conjunctivitis. Am J Ophthal 1986;101:493–4.

590. Hidayat AA, Riddle PJ. Ligneous conjuncitivis: a clinicopathologic study of 17 cases. Ophthalmology 1987;94:949–59.

591. Chambers JD, Blodi FC, Golden B, McKee AP. Ligneous conjunctivitis. Trans Am Acta Ophthal Otolaryngol 1969;73:996–1004.

592. Cooper TJ, Kazdan JJ, Cutz E. Ligneous conjunctivitis with tracheal obstruction: a case report with light and electron microscopy findings. Can J Ophthalmol 1979;14:57–62.

593. Firat T. Ligneous conjunctivitis. Am J Ophthalmol 1974;78:679–88.

594. Francois P, Victoria-Troncoso V. Treatment of ligneous conjunctivitis. Am J Ophthalmol 1968;65:674–8.

595. Marcus DM, Walton D, Donshik P, et al. Ligneous conjunctivitis with ear involvement. Arch Ophthalmol 1990;108:514–9.

596. Scurry J, Planner R, Fortune DW, et al. Ligneous (pseudomembranous) inflammation of the female genital tract: a report of 2 cases. J Reprod Med 1993; 38:407–12.

597. Schott D, Dempfle CE, Beck P, et al. Therapy with a purified plasminogen concentrate in an infant with ligneous conjunctivitis and homozygous plasminogen deficiency. N Engl J Med 1998;339:1679–186.

598. Mingers AM, Heimburger N, Zeithler P, et al. Homozygous type I plasminogen deficiency. Semin Thromb Hemost 1997;23:259–69.

599. Schuster V, Mingers AM, Seidenspinner S, et al. Homozygous mutations in the plasminogen gene of two unrelated girls with ligneous conjuctivitis. Blood 1997;90:958–66.

600. Mingers AM, Heimburger N, Lutz E. Familiarer homozygoter und heterozygoter Typ I plasminogenmangel. In: Scharrer I, Schramm W, eds. Hamophilie-Symposium; Hamburg. Berlin: Springer-Verlag, 1996: 96–104.

601. Schwartz GS, Holland EJ. Induction of ligneous conjunctivitis by conjunctival surgery. Am J Ophthalmol 1995;120:253–4.

602. Tezzon F, Ferrari G, Sharbaro V, et al. Deep cerebral venous thrombosis and hereditary tissue plasminogen activator (TPA) deficiency. Ital J Neurol Sci 1994;15:507–12.

603. Latham B, Kathoy EA, Barrett O, Gonzalez MF. Deficient tissue plasminogen activator release and normal tissue plasminogen activator inhibitor in a patient with recurrent deep vein thrombosis. Am J Med 1990;88:199–200.

604. Patrassi GM, Sartori MT, Viero ML, et al. Venous thrombosis and tissue plasminogen activator release deficiency: a family study. Blood Coagul Fibrinolysis 1991;2:231–5.

605. Jaffe EA, Armellino A, Tollefsen DA. Biosynthesis of functionally active heparin cofactor II by a human

hepatoma-derived cell line. Biochem Biophys Res Commun 1985;132:368–74.

606. Tollefsen DM, Pestka CA, Monafo WK. Activation of heparin cofactor II by dermatan sulfate. J Biol Chem 1983;260:3501–5.

607. Gralnick HR, Gilvelber H, Abrams E. Dysfibrinogenemia associated with hepatoma. Increased carbohydrate content of the fibrinogen molecule. N Engl J Med 1978;299:221–6.

608. Blinder MA, Andersson TR, Abildgaard U, Tollefsen DM. Heparin cofactor II Oslo: mutation of Arg180 to His decreases the affinity for dermatan sulphate. J Biol Chem 1989;264:5128–33.

609. Kondo S, Tokunaga F, Kario K, et al. Molecular and cellular basis for type I heparin cofactor II deficiency (heparin cofactor Awaji). Blood 1996;78:1006–12.

610. Simioni P, Lazarro AR, Corer E, et al. Constitutional heparin cofactor II deficiency and thrombosis: report of six patients belonging to two separate kindreds. Blood Coagul Fibrinolysis 1990;1:351–6.

611. Sie P, Dupouy D, Pichon J. Constitutional heparin cofactor II deficiency associated with recurrent thrombosis. Lancet 1985;2:414–6.

612. Tran TH, Marbet GA, Duckert F. Association of hereditary heparin cofactor II deficiency with thrombosis. Lancet 1985;2:413–4.

613. Simioni P, Lazzaro AR, Coser E, et al. Hereditary heparin cofactor II deficiency and thrombosis: report of six patients belonging to two separate kindreds. Blood Coagul Fibrinolysis 1990;1:351–6.

614. Weisdorf DJ, Edson JR. Recurrent venous thrombosis associated with inherited deficiency of heparin cofactor II. Br J Haematol 1990;77:125–6.

615. Kleesick K, Schmidt M, Gotting C, et al. The 536C—T transition in the human tissue factor pathway inhibitor (TFPI) gene is statistically associated with a higher risk for venous thrombosis. Thromb Haemost 1999;82:1–5.

616. Ariens RA, Alberio G, Moia M, Mannucci PM. Low levels of heparin-releasable tissue factor pathway inhibitor in young patients with thrombosis. Thromb Haemost 1999;81:203–7.

617. Ohlin AK, Marlar RA. The first mutation identified in the thrombomodulin gene in a 45-year-old man presenting with thromboembolic disease. Blood 1995;85:330–6.

618. Olin AK, Marlar RA. Mutations in the thrombomodulin gene associated with thromboembolic disease. Thromb Haemost 1995;73:1096–7.

619. Norlund L, Zoller B, Ohlin AK. A novel thrombomodulin gene mutation in a patient suffering from sagittal sinus thrombosis. Thromb Haemost 1997;78:1164–6.

620. Koster T, Blann AD, Briet E, et al. Role of clotting factor VIII in effect of von Willebrand factor on occurrence of deep vein thrombosis. Lancet 1995;345:152–5.

621. Bertina RM. The prothrombin 20210 G to A variation and thrombosis. Curr Opin Hematol 1998;5:339–42.

622. The NINDS t-PA Stroke Study Group. Intracerebral hemorrhage after intravenous t-PA therapy for ischemic stroke. Stroke 1997;28:2109–18.

623. Yamamoto K, Matsushita T, Sugiura I, et al. Homozygous protein C deficiency: identification of a novel missense mutation that causes impaired secretion of the mutant protein C. J Lab Clin Med 1986;119:682–9.

624. Jensen A, Josso S, Zamet P, et al. Evolution of blood clotting factors in premature infants during the first ten days of life: a study of 96 cases with comparison between clinical status and blood clotting factor levels. Pediatr Res 1973;7:638–44.

625. Abbondanzo S, Gootenberg J, Lofts R, McPherson R. Intracranial hemorrhage in congenital deficiency of factor XIII. Am J Pediatr Hematol Oncol 1988;10:65–8.

626. Johnson C, Snyder M, Weaver R. Effects of fresh frozen plasma infusions on coagulation screening tests in neonates. Arch Dis Child 1982;57:950–2.

627. Koh S, Chen LS. Protein C and S deficiency in children with ischemic cerebrovascular accident. Pediatr Neurol 1997;17:319–21.

628. Amundsen T, Ueland PM, Waage A. Plasma homocystein levels in patients with deep venous thrombosis. Arterioscler Thromb Vasc Biol 1995;15:1321–3.

629. Bienvenu T, Ankri A, Chadfaux B, et al. Elevated total plasma homocysteine, a risk factor for thrombosis. Thromb Res 1993;70:123–4.

630. Brattstrom L, Lingren A, Israelsson B, et al. Homocysteine and cystein: determinants of plasma levels in middle-aged and elderly patients. J Int Med 1994;236:631–4.

631. Falcon CR, Cattaneo M, Panzeri D, et al. High prevalence of hyperhomocysteineia in patients with juvenile thrombosis. Arterioscler Thromb 1994;14:1080–3.

632. Fermo I, D'Angelo SV, Paroni et al. Prevalence of moderate hyperhomocysteinemia in patients with early onset venous and arterial occlusive disease. Ann Intern Med 1995;123:747–53.

633. Cattaneo M, Martinelli I, Mannucci PM. Hyperhomocysteinemia as a risk factor for deep venous thrombosis. N Engl J Med 1996;335:974–5.

634. Simioni P, Prandoni P, Burlina A, et al. Hyperhomocysteinemia and deep venous thrombosis: a case control study. Thromb Haemost 1996;76:883–6.

635. den Jeijer M, Koster T, Blum HJ, et al. Hyperhomocysteinemia as a risk factor for deep venous thrombosis. N Engl J Med 1996;334:759–62.

4 EPIDEMIOLOGY OF VENOUS THROMBOEMBOLIC EVENTS

Unlike venous thromboembolic events (VTE) in adults, VTE in pediatric patients is usually a secondary complication of a primary illness or therapy. As survival for major childhood illnesses such as congenital heart disease (CHD) and cancer improves, the incidence of VTE is increasing dramatically. In critically ill children, the diagnosis of VTE requires a high index of clinical suspicion. The epidemiology of VTE in pediatric and neonatal patients is significantly different to that of adults. Age-related changes in the hemostatic system are responsible for many differences, in both etiology and response to therapy. Throughout this chapter, differences in the epidemiology that impact on the diagnosis and management of pediatric patients with VTE are highlighted. The management guidelines for VTE in adults frequently are extrapolated to VTE in pediatric patients, although they may not be optimal for children. Ongoing studies likely will result in specific guidelines for pediatric patients in the near future. This chapter discusses peripheral VTE only and does not include pulmonary embolism (PE) (see Chapter 5), VTE of the central nervous system (CNS) (see Chapter 7), or VTE in specific locations (see Chapter 8).

Several sources of information on the epidemiology of VTE in pediatric patients were used for this chapter, including comprehensive reviews of the literature, population-based registries,[1–5] and an international registry (1-800-NO-CLOTS).[6] Reports prior to 1980 were not systematically included because medical practice has changed considerably, profoundly influencing the epidemiology of VTE in children.

VENOUS THROMBOEMBOLIC EVENTS: AN OVERVIEW

Age and Incidence of Venous Thromboembolic Events

Estimates of the incidence of VTE support the generally accepted view that the frequency of VTE in pediatric patients is significantly less than for adults (Figure 4–1).[1–8] The Canadian Registry of VTE in children reported an incidence of 0.07 per 10,000 and an incidence of 5.3 per 10,000 per hospital admission.[1,3] An international registry of VTE in newborns reported an incidence of 0.24 per 10,000 ad-

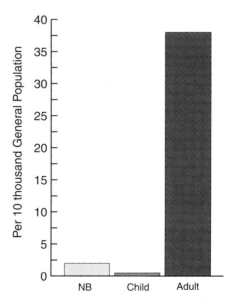

Figure 4–1 The frequency of venous thromboembolism in newborns and children is slightly less than for adults.

NB = newborn.

missions to the neonatal intensive care unit (NICU).[2] A German prospective nationwide 2-year registry study reported the incidence of symptomatic neonatal thromboembolism to be 0.51 per 10,000 births, with approximately half of the cases being venous and half arterial.[5] Children less than 1 year of age and teenagers are at greatest risk for VTE (Figure 4–2, A and B)[1,3,8] If newborns are included, the first year of life clearly is the time of greatest risk for VTE during childhood.[2] Comparable incidences of VTE in the adult population have been estimated at 2.5% to 5.0%.[9–11]

There are other comparisons that can be drawn between pediatric and adult patients that illustrate the age dependency of VTE. First, a comprehensive review of the French and English literature revealed only 308 cases of VTE in children since 1975 compared to many thousands for adult patients.[8] Second, prophylactic anticoagulation is indicated in adult patients following acquired risk factors for

VTE, such as hip or knee replacements, because the incidence of VTE in these patients ranges between 40% and 60%.[12–14] Prophylactic anticoagulation is not used in pediatric patients following lower limb or scoliosis surgery, and the rate of clinically apparent VTE in this population is less than 1%.[15] Third, patients with congenital prothrombotic disorders rarely present with their first VTE until early adulthood.[16] In summary, pediatric patients are relatively protected from VTE compared to adults, reflecting several age-dependent mechanisms (see Chapter 2).

Relation between Gender and Venous Thromboembolic Events in Children

The gender distribution of VTE appears to be similar in pediatric patients. For adults, there may be a slight predominance of females between the years of 20 and 39, reflecting effects of the use of oral contraceptives and pregnancy.[11,17]

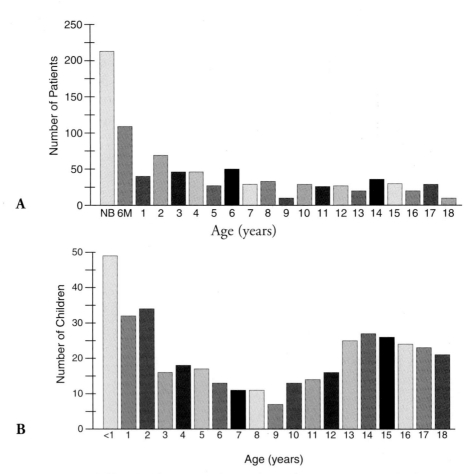

Figure 4–2 Children less than 1 year of age and teenagers are at greatest risk of venous thromboembolism. *A,* from 1-800-NO CLOTS; *B,* from the Canadian registry.

Underlying Disorders

Similar to adults, the three essential criteria predisposing to VTE during childhood include abnormalities in the vessel wall, disturbances of blood flow, and alterations in blood coagulability (Virchow's triad).[18] Intravascular catheters damaging vessel walls, thrombosed chorionic vessels embolizing to fetal vessels, or local thrombi associated with a patent ductus are examples of vessel wall abnormalities.[19] Disturbed blood flow can be secondary to the presence of large bore catheters in small veins, increased blood viscosity,[19] and polycythemia.[19] In newborns, poor deformability of physiologically large red cells also may increase blood viscosity.[20] Finally, activation of both the coagulation and fibrinolytic systems, frequently secondary to shock or infection, extracorporeal circulation, and endothelial damage from central venous line (CVL) placement are linked to VTE in pediatric patients.[19,21,22]

Idiopathic VTE occur in less than 1% of newborns and in less than 5% of children compared to approximately 40% of adults.[1–3,8] Underlying diseases for newborns with VTE usually are life-threatening and include diseases associated with prematurity, birth asphyxia, presence of CVLs, and systemic infection.[2] Underlying diseases for infants and children with VTE also are serious and include cancer, major trauma or surgery, CHD, systemic lupus erythematosus (SLE), renal failure, and other disorders (Figure 4–3, A and B).[1,3,19,21,23] The majority of pediatric patients have several risk factors for VTE.[21] The Canadian Childhood Thrombophilia Registry reported that only 4% of VTE in children was idiopathic, 12% of children had only one risk factor, and 84% had two or more risk factors (Figure 4–4).[3] The proportion of idiopathic VTE in the lower limbs is increased.[7,8,24–27] Studies that reported increased rates of idiopathic VTE have included both venous and arterial thrombosis in any location, including the CNS. Thrombotic events in the CNS frequently are idiopathic or secondary to disorders that influence the percentage of idiopathic thrombosis if included in estimates of thrombosis in any location.

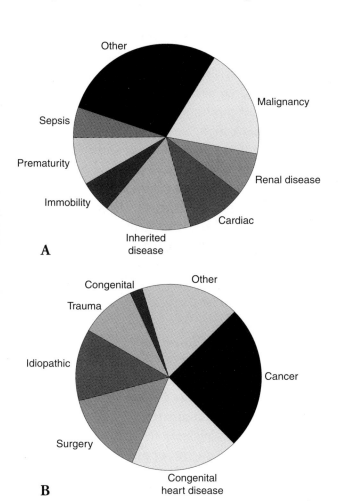

A

B

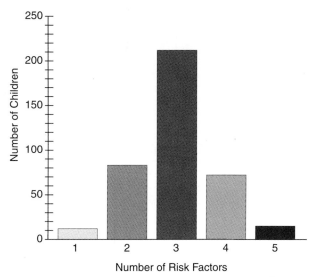

Figure 4–3 The underlying diseases in children with venous thromboembolism. *A,* from 1-800- NO CLOTS; *B,* from the Canadian registry.

Figure 4–4 The number of risk factors in children with deep vein thrombosis and/or pulmonary embolism.

The predisposing causes of VTE in children are changing. For example, prior to the early 1970s, ventriculoatrial shunts, infection, and CHD were the leading causes of VTE in children.[8,28-32] Ventriculoatrial shunts currently are rarely used because they cause right atrial thrombi and continuous microembolization to the lung with subsequent pulmonary hypertension.[28] In contrast, cancer, a leading cause of VTE in the 1990s, was an infrequent cause of VTE in children prior to the late 1960s, because the survival rate was poor. Irrespective of the underlying medical problem and age, the presence of CVL currently is the single most important risk factor for VTE in pediatric patients of all ages. Central venous lines are associated with over 90% of neonatal VTE and over 66% of childhood VTE (Figure 4–5).[1-4] Because of the importance of CVL-related VTE, this topic is considered separately, in a subsequent section.

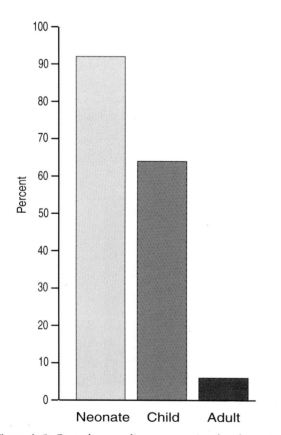

Figure 4–5 Central venous lines are associated with over 90% of deep vein thrombosis in neonates and 60% of children.

Congenital Prothrombotic Disorders

Homozygous deficiencies of protein C and protein S classically present during the neonatal period, although heterozygous deficiencies usually do not become apparent until after puberty (see Chapter 3). The contribution of heterozygous protein C and protein S deficiency or other congenital prothrombotic disorders to VTE in pediatric patients is uncertain, because relevant testing is not routinely performed and some congenital prothrombotic disorders, such as activated protein resistance (APCR) or factor F V Leiden, and prothrombin gene 20210A only recently have been characterized.[1] For the majority of children, an acquired risk factor for VTE unmasks the congenital disorder.[1,5,8,21,33-47]

The reported incidence of congenital prothrombotic disorders in children with VTE varies from 10% to over 60%.[33-51] In children with cancer and VTE, the reported incidences are 3%[52] and 83%.[53] The variability in incidence reflects small sample sizes, variability in study design, differing definitions of prothrombotic disorders, and different patient selection. Screening for congenital prothrombotic disorders in children with VTE probably is worthwhile, regardless of the presence or absence of acquired risk factors. At this time, uniform screening of children with major illnesses, or who require CVLs, for congenital prothrombotic disorders, to provide prophylactic therapy, cannot be recommended. The contribution of congenital prothrombotic disorders to VTE in pediatric patients remains to be clarified (see Chapter 3).

Location

Deep venous thrombosis (DVT) occurs in the upper venous system in 80% of newborns and in 60% of children, compared to less than 2% of adults.[3,4,54] The sole reason for the increased frequency of DVT in the upper venous system is CVL.[1-4,8] Because of the importance of CVL-related DVT, DVT in children can be classified as either non-CVL related or CVL related.[1-4,8] Figure 4–6 provides a schema of the deep venous system in the upper half of the body, and Figure 4–7 provides

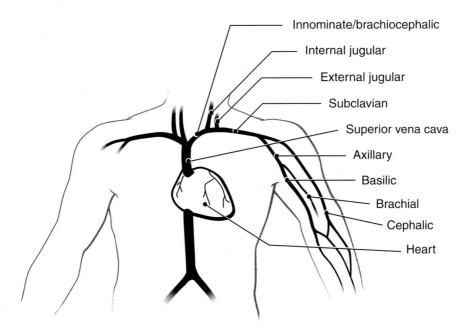

Figure 4–6 Schema of the deep venous system in the upper half of the body. Reproduced with permission.[55]

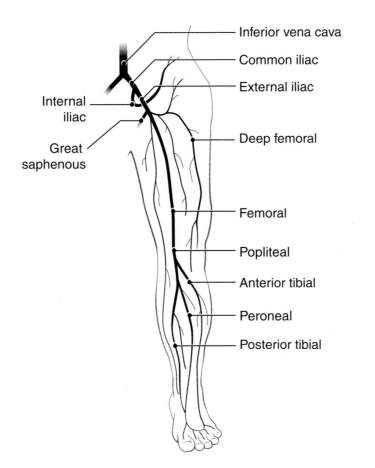

Figure 4–7 Schema of the deep venous system in the lower half of the body. Reproduced with permission.[55]

a schema of the deep venous system in the lower half of the body.[55]

CENTRAL VENOUS LINE-RELATED VENOUS THROMBOEMBOLIC EVENTS

Historic Perspective

Intravenous therapy with peripheral catheters began in 1945.[56] Once mechanical problems were overcome, sepsis and septic thrombophlebitis became the most serious complications and were directly related to the duration of peripheral catheter placement.[57,58] As medicine advanced, other significant drawbacks of peripheral catheters became apparent, such as the reduced ability to infuse hyperosmolar solutions and use of aggressive chemotherapeutic regimens for the treatment of cancer.

Cannulation of jugular or subclavian veins facilitated the use of long lines that permitted more effective therapy, but sepsis rates persisted as a significant problem. Cuffed, tunneled Silastic catheters, as pioneered by Broviac and colleagues and adapted by Hickman and coworkers, revolutionized the management of pediatric patients requiring prolonged central venous access, particularly for chemotherapy and total parenteral nutrition (TPN).[59–61] These CVLs were tunneled under the skin and required exit-site care, flushing, and some activity restrictions. An early study showed that Broviacs were significantly better than plastic CVL for duration of patency and reduced risk of infection.[62,63] However, CVLs also caused iatrogenic complications of which infection and VTE were the most important.

The next advance was totally implantable subcutaneous ports, which have all of the advantages of external venous CVLs, plus they have minimal maintenance requirements, are not easily visible, and likely have a lower rate of septic complications.[64,65] Most recently, thin long lines (or "spaghetti" lines) threaded from the antecubital fossa are being used, particularly in newborns requiring sustained venous access.[66–69] Despite widespread use and importance of CVLs, there are no well-designed trials comparing different devices for their risk of infection and thrombosis.

Indications for Central Venous Lines

Currently, CVLs are critically important for modern medical management of pediatric patients with a variety of diseases. Central venous lines usually are placed for cardiac catheterization (CC), in neonatal and pediatric intensive care units (PICU), and for long-term supportive care of children requiring TPN, chemotherapy, and long-term blood products or antibiotics. In large tertiary care pediatric centers, approximately 1000 to 2000 children per year have CVLs placed. Despite the frequency of CVL insertion, few institutions have appropriate follow-up programs to accurately monitor potential long-term complications.

Pathogenesis of Central Venous Line-Related Thrombi

Central venous lines are thrombogenic because their surfaces are foreign, they damage vessel walls, blood flow is disrupted, and some substances infused are damaging to vessels. The occurrence of CVL-related DVT likely is influenced by many parameters, such as the ratio of the CVL-to-vessel diameter, length of time in place, specific use, and catheter material.

Catheter Materials and Thrombogenicity There are no well-designed clinical trials that compare the clinical thrombogenicity of different catheter materials. However, catheter thrombogenicity has been assessed using several techniques, including the number and size of thrombi detected radiographically, catheter occlusion rate, platelet adhesion, and ability to bind fibrinogen.[70–75] The thrombogenicity of polyethylene, silicone, and polyurethane catheters was compared in a prospective study of 52 patients. The incidence of CVL-related DVT was highest for polyethylene catheters (70%), and significantly less for silicone (20%) and polyurethane catheters (17%).[76] Another series of studies confirmed that polyethylene catheters are the most thrombogenic, but found no significant differences between silicone elastomer, polyurethrane, and polyvinylchloride catheters.[70–73]

Several approaches to minimizing catheter surface thrombogenicity have been assessed. Precoating catheters with albumin was ineffective for the prevention of VTE.[77] Ion beam pretreatment of catheter surfaces may reduce their thrombogenicity.[78] Heparin bonding of catheters was assessed in several studies and likely provides some protection from VTE.[73,79–85] However, protection from VTE offered by heparin bonding of catheters should not be overestimated, particularly when catheters are left in place for more than 24 hours.[86]

Pathologic Classification of Central Venous Line-Related Thrombosis

Three types of CVL-related thrombotic complications are described in the literature: (1) clots at the tip of CVLs that impair infusion or withdrawal of blood, (2) fibrin sleeves that are not adherent to vessel walls but may occlude CVLs, and (3) CVL-related deep venous thrombi that adhere to vessel walls with partial or complete obstruction of vessels in which the CVL is located.[87] The relation between these three forms of CVL-related DVT is unknown, because the most commonly used diagnostic tests cannot assess the presence of all forms of CVL-related thrombi. The following discussion refers to CVL-related DVT, as distinct from fibrin sheaths or CVL-tip clots.

Epidemiology of Central Venous Line-Related Thrombosis

Clinical Classification Central venous line-related DVT can be classified clinically as either asymptomatic or symptomatic. However, in many cases, the classification of CVL-related DVT as asymptomatic is a misnomer. Whereas acute symptoms may be unusual, chronic symptoms, as described subsequently, frequently are encountered and clinically are important.

Clinical Symptoms The clinical symptoms of acute CVL-related DVT include swelling, pain, and discoloration of the related limb, swelling of the face, PE,[1,3,4,88–97] chylothorax,[88,98–100] chylopericardium,[101] and superior vena cava (SVC) syndrome.[1,3,4,88,90,98,102,103] Fatal PEs do occur secondary to CVL-related DVT, although possibly less frequently than from DVT in the lower limbs.[4,54,88,90,91,93–97] High-risk patient populations include smaller children and those receiving TPN[88,104–108] or hemodialysis.[109,110]

Central venous line-related DVT more commonly presents with chronic symptoms, which include repeated loss of patency requiring local thrombolytic therapy, repeated requirement for CVL replacement, CVL-related sepsis, and prominent collateral circulation in the skin over the chest, back, neck, and face (Figure 4–8).[1,3] These collaterals can progress, resulting in significant long-term complications.

Diagnosis The diagnosis of CVL-related DVT is highly dependent upon the diagnostic test used to investigate CVLs that are blocked. The available radiographic tests include lineograms, ultrasound, and venography. Lineograms are performed by injecting dye into the CVL and should not be confused with venography, which is performed by injecting dye into a vein in a limb. Lineograms are useful for delineating the location of the tips of CVLs, and clots present at the tip of CVLs. However, lineograms cannot be relied upon to detect significant DVT along the intravascular length of CVLs (Figure 4–9). Problematic issues with ultrasound detection of CVL-related DVT include the presence of the clavicle, which "hides" part of the distal subclavian vein from view; the inability to distinguish large collaterals from "true" large veins in the upper system (i.e., subclavian artery); and the inability to compress veins in a central location, owing to the presence of the thoracic cage. Compression is the feature of ultrasound that has been validated against venography for the detection of DVT in the lower venous system in adults.[111–119] In summary, ultrasound and lineograms are relatively insensitive for the detection of DVT in children owing to the predominance of DVT in subclavian veins, innominate veins, and the SVC. One study in adults that compared ultrasound to venography concluded that ultrasound was as sensitive and specific as venography.[120] However, all patients had extensive involvement of axillary veins, where com-

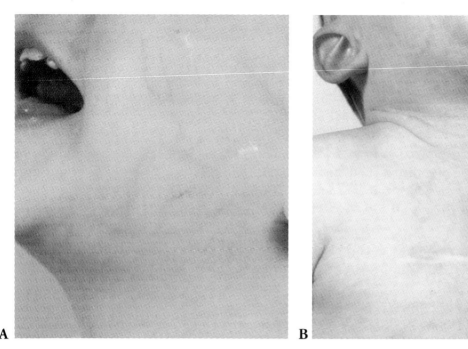

A   B

Figure 4–8 Central venous line-related collateral circulation in two children. *A*, on the face; *B*, on the upper chest. To view these figures in color, refer to CD-Rom.

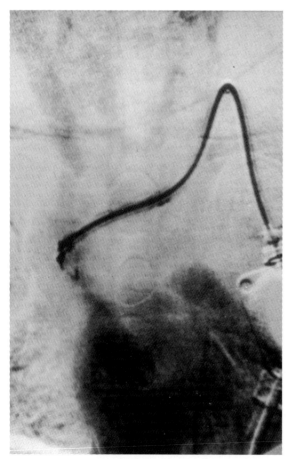

Figure 4–9 Lineogram with a clot at the tip. Reproduced with permission. [55]

pression by ultrasound could be assessed. Axillary veins rarely are involved in upper system DVT in children because CVLs usually are placed through the jugular vein into the proximal subclavian vein and into the SVC. Other diagnostic techniques for DVT include spiral computed tomography (CT) and magnetic resonance imaging (MRI); however, neither has been validated against venography in children. [121,122]

Clinical Significance of Asymptomatic Radiographically Detected Central Venous Line-Related Thrombosis

Recent trends in the management of VTE in adults have focused on clinically "symptomatic" thrombosis as distinct from clinically "asymptomatic" thrombosis but detected through either screening or incidental radiologic studies. There are several reasons why radiologically detected CVL-related DVTs in children are of clinical importance and differ from asymptomatic DVT in adults. First, there is increasing evidence that CVL-related DVT is associated with CVL-related sepsis. In a recent meta-analysis by Randolph et al, prophylactic unfractionated heparin (UFH)-reduced CVL-related

DVT (relative risk [RR] = 0.43; 95% confidence interval [CI] = 0.23–0.78) (Figure 4–10)[85], bacterial colonization (RR = 0.18; 95% CI = 0.06–0.60), and probably CVL-related bacteremia (RR = 0.26; 95% CI = 0.07–1.03).[85] Second, CVL-related DVT are associated with PE, which may be fatal.[4] Approximately 30% of adults with cancer who are receiving long-term TPN via CVLs are reported to have high probability ventilation-perfusion (V/Q) scans. Central venous line-related upper limb DVTs in adults are associated with rates of PE that range from 7% to 12%.[89,123] Central venous line-related DVTs are the most common source for PE in children.[1,3,4] As discussed in Chapter 5, PE in children

frequently is not diagnosed during life due to the subtlety of the symptoms and the presence of primary illnesses that can cause sudden cardiorespiratory deterioration. Third, many children with CVLs have significant right-to-left intracardiac shunts that increase the risk of stroke from CVL-related DVT. Fourth, the long-term consequences of CVL-related DVT only now are becoming apparent. Chronic venous obstruction and collateral development are associated with an increased risk of postphlebitic syndrome (PPS) and loss of future venous access that may be important in children requiring organ transplantation in the future. Recent case reports have documented sudden death associated with rupture

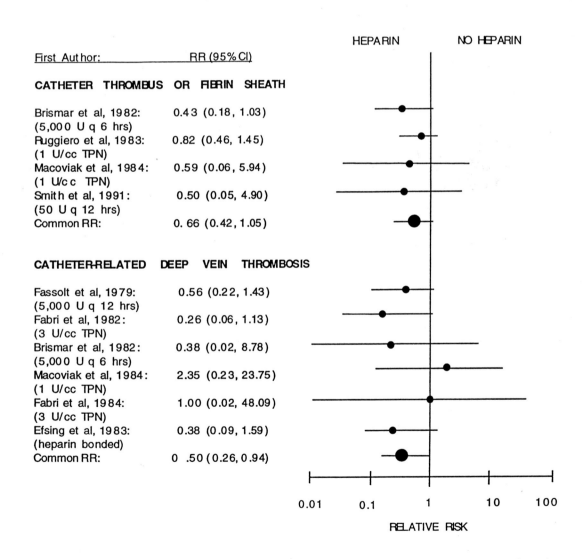

Figure 4–10 Effect of heparin on central venous catheter-related thromboembolic complications from the literature summarized in the meta-analysis by Randolph.

Reproduced with permission.[85]

of an intrathoracic collateral vessel thought to be attributable to a CVL placed many years previously.

Incidence of Central Venous Line-Related Deep Venous Thrombosis in Adults

The incidence of CVL-related DVT almost certainly has been underestimated in the past, in part owing to failure to recognize the clinical significance of chronic or subtle symptoms. The most important factors in determining the incidence of CVL-related DVT are the study design and the selected diagnostic test. For adults, the incidence of CVL-related DVT ranges from 0.7%, based upon the presence of overt clinical symptoms (SVC syndrome or arm swelling), to 22%, based upon the presence of a blocked CVL.[64,124–130] In two studies, 82 adults were screened with venography or Doppler ultrasonography, and the incidence of CVL-related DVT was 38% and 76%, respectively.[126,131] More recently, in a prospective cohort study in adults with cancer, venograms were performed on days 8 and 30, and then every 2 months until CVL removal. The venograms detected DVT in 64% of patients at day 8, 65% at day 30, and 66% at day 105. Acute clinical symptoms developed in 6% of this cohort.[125] Similarly, in the control arm of a randomized controlled trial (RCT) in adults with CVLs, 62% had venographically demonstrated DVT at 90 days following CVL insertion.[126]

Incidence of Central Venous Line-Related Thrombosis in Children

The proportion of acute DVT related to CVLs in infants, children, and adults is shown in Figure 4–5. Central venous lines are responsible for the majority of DVT during childhood. The reported incidence of CVL-related DVT in children is integrally linked to clinical awareness and choice of radiographic test. Radiographic tests used to detect CVL-related DVT include ultrasound, lineograms, venography, and V/Q scans.

Clinical Detection There are numerous cohort studies using "clinical endpoints" that report CVL-related DVT between 1% and 10%.[90,132–146] Recent studies of peripheral long lines report an incidence of clinical DVT of 0.3% to 0.4%.[67] A prospective cohort study of 89 children with femoral vein catheters placed in the PICU reported that 9.5% of children developed clinically evident swelling of the instrumented leg attributable to DVT. The same authors conducted a review of femoral vein CVL complications within the literature and reported a thrombotic rate of 10% based upon clinical symptoms. A population-based registry of CVL-related DVT used the total number of admissions per center during the time of the registry to calculate an incidence of clinically evident CVL-related DVT of 3.5 per 10,000 pediatric hospital admissions.[4] However, there was no uniform diagnostic testing, and this figure likely underestimates the true incidence.

Ultrasonography and Echocardiography The incidence of CVL-related DVT in children over 1 year of age detected by ultrasound ranges from 1% to 44% (Table 4–1).[96,147–155] The median incidence of CVL-related thromboembolic events (TE) diagnosed by ultrasound or echocardiography was 35% in studies with the most rigorous designs (randomized, crossover, or cross-sectional),[96,147,148] but less in prospective cohorts. The incidence of CVL-related DVT in infants less than 1 year of age detected by ultrasound ranges from 2% to 19% (Table 4–2).[88,90,156–161] The median incidence of CVL-related TE diagnosed by either ultrasound or echocardiography was 14% in prospective cohort studies and 7% in retrospective studies.[88,90,156–161] The study design profoundly influenced the reported incidence of CVL-related DVT based on ultrasound or echocardiography. For example, a cross-sectional study in children with cancer and long-term CVLs used echocardiography to detect thrombi and reported an incidence of right atrial thrombosis of 9%.[151] In a prospective cohort, 18% of patients in an intensive care setting with CVLs in place for 48 hours developed CVL-related DVT.[149]

Lineograms Lineograms are performed by injecting contrast material through a CVL and can establish the location of the tip of a CVL and detect CVL rupture with extravasation of dye. Lineograms can-

Table 4–1 Incidence of Thromboembolic Events in Children Over 1 Year of Age with Central Venous Lines as Diagnosed by Ultrasound or Echocardiography

Author	Year	Study Design	Number of Cases	Purpose	Incidence of TE (%)
Krafte-Jacobs et al[147]	1995	RCT	25 25	Supportive care	44* 8†
Dollery et al [96]	1994	CS	34	Total parenteral nutrition	35
Smith et al [148]	1991	CO	14	Chemotherapy	14
Beck et al [149]	1998	PC	93	Supportive care	18
Shefler et al[150]	1995	PC	61	Supportive care	10
Korones et al [151]	1996	PC	156	Chemotherapy	9
Stenzel et al[153]	1989	PC	395	Supportive care	1
Moukarzel et al[152]	1991	R	50	Total parenteral nutrition	4
Ross et al[154]	1989	R	350	Total parenteral nutrition	5
Babcock[155]	1991	R	52	Supportive care	19

TE = thrombolic events; RCT = randomized controlled trial; CS = cross-sectional study; CO = cross-over study; PC = prospective cohort; R = retrospective.

*Standard catheters, †Heparin-bonded catheters

not detect large-vessel thrombi along the course of the CVL. The incidence of CVL-related DVT in infants and children detected by lineograms ranges from 4% to 23% (Table 4–3).[141,162–165] The median incidence of CVL-related TEs diagnosed by lineograms was 22% in prospective cohort studies and only 8% in retrospective studies.[141,162–165] The design of the study profoundly influences the reported incidence. For example, in a cross-sectional study in children with cancer and long-term CVLs, the reported incidence of right atrial thrombosis was 9%.[151] In a prospective cohort, 18% of patients

Table 4–2 Incidence of Thromboembolic Events in Infants Less Than 1 Year of Age with Central Venous Lines as Diagnosed by Ultrasound or Echochocardiography

Author	Year	Number of Cases	Catheter Purpose	Incidence of TE (%)
Prospective cohort study				
Pipus et al[156]	1994	46	Total parental nutrition	17
Mehta et al[157]	1992	42	Supportive care	14
Marsh et al[158]	1988	56	Total parental nutrition	2
Retrospective study				
Sadiq et al[159]	1987	52	Total parental nutrition	19
Schiff[160]	1993	69	Supportive care	12
Mollitt et al[88]	1983	117	Nutrition	7
Wever et al[161]	1995	218	Care	6
Mulvihill[90]	1984	294	Nutrition	5

TE = thromboembolic events.

Table 4–3 Incidence of Thromboembolic Events in Children with Central Venous Lines as Diagnosed by Lineograms

Author	Year	Number of Cases	Catheter Purpose	Incidence of TE (%)
Prospective cohort study				
Bagnall et al[162]	1989	254	Chemotherapy	23
Moore et al[163]	1985	25	Total parental nutrition	20
Retrospective study				
Haire et al[164]	1990	225	Chemotherapy	10
Effmann et al[141]	1978	57	Total parental nutrition	8
Curnow et al[165]	1985	274	Total parental nutrition	4

TE = thromboembolic events.

in an intensive care setting, with CVLs in place for 48 hours, developed CVL-related DVT detected by Doppler ultrasound (95% CI = 10%, 26%).[149]

Venography Venograms are performed by injecting dye through a peripheral vein of a limb, which delineates the deep veins draining a limb. Studies using venography to detect DVT in children are rare. In a cross-sectional study of children receiving home TPN, 66% of children had evidence of extensive CVL-related DVT that was characterized by extensive collateral circulation.[166] In a Canadian registry, 34% of children had their DVT diagnosed by venography.[3]

Salonvaara et al evaluated 44 clinically symptomatic newborns with venography. Deep venous thrombosis was found in 10 of 44 (23%).[167] Medeiros et al evaluated 13 children with hemo-

philia and reported that one patient (8%) had a small nonocclusive thrombus on the same side as his functioning catheter and a second child had minimal narrowing of the subclavian vein at the site of a prior CVL.[168]

Incidence of Central Venous Line-Related Pulmonary Embolism

The incidence of CVL-related PE is unknown, and studies in the literature almost certainly provide an underestimation. The median incidence of CVL-related PE was 31% in two cross-sectional studies, 34% in two prospective cohort studies, and 35% in two retrospective studies (Table 4–4).[4, 93–97] Two cross-sectional studies used V/Q scans to detect PE in children.[94,96] The study by Dollery et al reported a mortality from PE of 12%.[96]

Table 4–4 Incidence of Pulmonary Embolism in Infants and Children with Central Venous Lines

Author	Year	Study Design	Number of Cases	Catheter Purpose	Incidence of TE (%)
Ament[93]	1995	PC	12	Total parental nutriton	50
Hoyer et al[94]	1986	CS	26	Supportive care	28
Massicotte et al[4]	1998	PC	39	Chemotheraoy Congenital heart disease	16
Pollard et al[95]	1995	R	21	Total parental nutrition	57
Dollery et al[96]	1994	CS	34	Total parental nutrition	35
Uderzo et al[97]	1995	R	452	Chemotherapy	4

PE = pulmonary embolism; PC = prospective cohort CS = case series; R = retrospective.

Incidence of Central Venous Line-Related Thrombosis Detected by Loss of Patency

There are numerous studies in children of all ages that report the incidence of loss of CVL patency.[132–134,136,139,140,142,169–199] The incidence of loss of CVL patency in children over 1 year of age ranges from 1% to 74% (Table 4–5).[132–136,152,169–172,174–189] The median incidence of temporary loss of CVL patency restored primarily with urokinase (UK) was 26%.[169,174–179,183,184,186–188] The median incidence of loss of CVL patency resulting in treatment for DVT by CVL removal was 5%.[132–136,152,170–172,180–182,185,189] The incidence of loss of CVL patency in children less than 1 year of age ranges from 10% to 30% (Table 4–6).[88,90,139–145,156–161,165,167,191–202] The median incidence of temporary loss of CVL patency resolved primarily with local instillations of UK in infants was 15%.[192,193,195,196] The median incidence of loss of CVL patency with an associated TE was 9%.[89,139–145, 167, 194, 197–200] The median incidence of CVL-associated TE detected by echocardiography, ultrasound, venography, or autopsy was 8%.[87,156–161,165,191,201,202] The relatively uniform median incidence, regardless of diagnostic test, suggests that the incidence of clinically important CVL-related TE is approximately 10% for infants.

Significance of the Duration of Central Venous Line Insertion

Older studies reported a significant relation between CVL duration in vivo and the incidence of CVL-related DVT.[135,154,159,162,163,169,174,193,203] However, these studies relied on clinical diagnosis to screen for CVL-related DVT, and clinical symptoms likely occur much later than initial clot formation. Shefler et al reported a cohort of 56 children in PICUs with femoral vein catheters, in which 10% developed CVL-related DVT detected by ultrasound.[150] No DVT was detected before 6 days duration of CVL insertion. In contrast, a number of studies report that the majority of DVT develop within days of CVL insertion. DeCicco et al, in a consecutive cohort of 127 adults with cancer, performed venography at day 8 and day 30, and then twice monthly until CVL removal.[125] In the 95 evaluable patients in whom more than one venogram was performed, the incidence of CVL-related DVT was 64%, 65%, and 66% on days 8, 30, and 105, respectively (days represent mean day of study following CVL insertion). All venograms were independently graded as to the extent of the DVT, and the grades did not change with time.[125] A separate study using serial Doppler ultrasound in children with CVLs in PICUs demonstrated that almost all CVL-related DVT occurred within 4 days of CVL insertion.[149] These clinical studies support the hypothesis that short-term and long-term CVLs are potent causes of CVL-related DVT. The results are consistent with the concept that the procedure of CVL insertion is associated with disruption to the endothelial surface, which may precipitate thrombus formation. Over time, the CVL surface becomes endothelialized, which likely reduces the thrombogenic potential.

CENTRAL VENOUS LINES IN SPECIFIC PATIENTS OR DISEASES

Newborns and Small Infants

Central venous lines in newborns are placed either through the umbilical vein into the inferior vena cava (IVC), into the upper venous system through peripheral veins in the arm ("long lines"), or into the upper venous system through the major vessels, usually the jugular vein. Currently, long lines are used extensively in premature and older infants who require TPN for a few weeks to months of life.[66,68,69,204,205] Little is known about the precision and accuracy of noninvasive imaging techniques that commonly are used to make the diagnosis of long line-related DVT.[206]

Umbilical Venous Lines in Newborns The median incidence of umbilical vein catheterization (UVC)-related TE that necessitated removal of the UVC was 2.5% based upon loss of patency and 29% based upon detection of UVC-related TE using ultrasound, echocardiography, and autopsy (Table 4–7).[137,138,201,207–210] The appropriate placement of UVC is critical to the prevention of serious organ impairment. Portal vein thrombosis and he-

Table 4–5 Incidence of Thromboembolic Events and Infection in Children with Central Venous Lines as Diagnosed by Loss of Catheter Patency

Author	Year	Study Design	Number of Cases	Catheter Purpose	Incidence of TE (%)	Incidence of INF (%)
Patency Restored with Urokinase						
Barzaghi et al[186]	1995	PC	38	Chemotherapy	74	18
Gleason-Morgan et al[178]	1991	R	24	Supportive care	63	33
Biagi et al[187]	1997	RCT	73	Chemotherapy	40	24
					26	29
Schwartz et al[177]	1990	RCT	21	Chemotherapy	29	25
			24		38	5
Kohli-Kumar et al[184]	1992	R	79	Chemotherapy	27	45
Kovesi[188]	1997	R	74	Chemotherapy	26	36
Stockwell et al[169]	1983	R	24	Chemotherapy	25	42
Hockenberry et al[174]	1989	R	82	Chemotherapy	22	5
Atkinson et al[176]	1990	PC	142	Chemotherapy	18	NR
Springer et al[175]	1984	R	26	Total parental nutrition	16	4
Uderzo et al[183]	1992	PC	55	Chemotherapy	15	31
Dawson et al[179]	1991	R	231	Chemotherapy	9	NR
Patency Loss Treated by CVL Removal						
Moukarzel et al[185]	1994	R	27	Total parental nutrition	24	NR
Vargas et al[172]	1987	R	234	Total parental nutrition	18	32
Sellden et al[181]	1991	PC	158	Chemotherapy	13	70
Krul et al[170]	1986	R	42	Chemotherapy	10	5
Moukarzel et al[152]	1991	R	38	Total parental nutrition	10	NR
Golladay[133]	1986	PC	31	Chemotherapy	6	3
Weber et al[132]	1983	R	116	Total parental nutrition Chemotherapy	6	6
Chua[189]	1998	R	57	Supportive care	4	32
Darbyshire et al[134]	1985	PC	49	Chemotherapy	2	12
Newman et al[171]	1986	PC	115	Supportive care	2	5
Mirro et al[135]	1989	PC	286	Chemotherapy	2	NR
Casado-Flores et al[180]	1991	PC	322	Supportive care	2	NR
Brown et al[182]	1991	PC	44	Total parental nutrition	2	NR
Gauderer[136]	1985	PC	146	Total parental nutrition Chemotherapy	1	NR

TE = thromboembolic events; INF = infection; PC = prospective cohort; R = retrospective; RCT = randomized controlled trials; NR = not reported.

Table 4–6 Incidence of Thromboembolic Events and Infection in Infants with Central Venous Lines, with All Diagnostic Techniques

Author	Year	Study Design	Number of Cases	Catheter Purpose	Diagnosis	Incidence of TE (%)	Incidence of INF (%)
Patency restored with Urokinase							
Grisoni et al[193]	1986	R	107	Supportive care	P	21	19
Sherman et al[192]	1983	R	55	Supportive care	P	15	4
Mactier et al[195]	1986	R	42	Total parenteral nutrition	P	14	12
Lally et al[196]	1986	R	86	Total parenteral nutrition	P	12	21
Patency loss associated with TE							
Abdullah et al[198]	1990	R	63	Total parenteral nutrition and supportive care	P	30	NR
Chathas et al[197]	1990	R	478	Total parenteral nutrition	P	23	5
Salonvaara et al[167]	1999	PC	44	Supportive care	P	23	9
Durand et al[194]	1986	PC	53	Total parenteral nutrition	P	15	8
Hogan and Pulito[199]	1992	R	92	Supportive care	P	14	22
Fonkalsrud et al[139]	1982	R	118	Total parenteral nutrition	P	10	2
Ogata et al[140]	1984	R	40	Supportive care	P	10	30
Effmann et al[141]	1978	R	82	Total parenteral nutrition	P	8	NR
Roberts and Gollow[200]	1990	R	65	Supportive care	P	8	11
Goutail-Flaud et al[142]	1991	R	587	Supportive care	P	6	4
Mulvihill and Fonkalsrud[90]	1984	R	294	Total parenteral nutrition Nutrition	P	5	NR
Warner et al[143]	1987	R	22	Total parenteral nutrition	P	4	9
Valk et al[144]	1995	PC	138	Supportive care	P	4	1
Dolcourt and Bose[145]	1982	PC	15	Supportive care	P	0	0
Thromboembolisms Detected by Echocardiography, Ultrasound, Venograph, or Autopsy							
Sadiq et al[159]	1987	R	52	Total parenteral nutrition	ECHO VENO	19	58
Pippus et al[156]	1994	PC	46	Total parenteral nutrition	US	17	59
Tanke et al[201]	1994	PC	92	Supportive care	US, ECHO	17	NR
Mehta et al[157]	1992	PC	42	Supportive care	US	14	2
Schiff and Stonestreet[160]	1993	R	69	Supportive care	ECHO	12	21
Loeffet et al[191]	1982	R	119	Total parenteral nutrition	US VENO, A	8	7
Mollit et et al[88]	1983	R	117	Total parenteral nutrition	US	7	NR
Wever et al[161]	1995	R	218	Supportive care	US	6	62
Curnow et al[165]	1985	R	274	Total parenteral nutrition	ECHO VENO	4	1
Marsh et al[158]	1988	PC	56	Total parenteral nutrition	US	2	NR
Vain et al[202]	1978	R	39	Supportive care	A	13	NR

PC = prospective cohort; P = patency; ECHO = echocardiography; VENO = venography; US = ultrasound; A = autopsy; NR = not reported.

Table 4–7 Incidence of Thromboembolic Events in Infants with Umbilical Vein Catheters for the Purpose of Supportive Care

Author	Year	Design	Number of Cases	Diagnosis	Incidence (%)
UVC removed owing to loss of patency					
Storme et al[138]	1999	PC	108	Patency	3
Khilnani et al[137]	1991	RCT	43	Patency	2
UVC removed owing to detection of TE					
Yadav et al[207]	1993	PC	22	Ultrasound	54
Wigger et al[208]	1970	R	33	Autopsy	33
Roy et al[209]	1997	PC	48	Echocardiogram	6
					29
Tanke et al[201]	1994	PC	92	Ultrasound Echocardiogram	17
Raval et al[210]	1995	R	62	Echocardiogram	14

UVC = umbilical venous catheter; PC = prospective cohort; RCT = randomized controlled trials; R = retrospective; TE = thromboembolic event.

patic necrosis can be caused by UVC not placed beyond the ductus venosus, particularly when hyperosmolar solutions are infused.[211,212] However, appropriate placement of UVC in sick neonates is associated with a low risk of portal vein thrombosis, with a reported incidence of 1.3%.[213] The incidence of long-term consequences of UVC is uncertain because there are no comprehensive follow-up studies reported in the literature. However, there are case reports of portal hypertension,[214–216] splenomegaly,[216,217] gastric and esophageal varices,[217] and hypertension.[218]

Central Venous Lines in Newborns and Young Infants Many reported studies group newborns and infants less than 1 year of age together, which necessitates a joint analysis and limits the information available on separate age groups. Table 4–6 summarizes the studies reporting the incidence of CVL-related DVT based on loss of CVL patency,[90,139–145,167,192–200] or objective tests.[88,156–161,165,191,201,202] The importance of diagnostic evaluation is illustrated in the study by Chathas et al, in which 7 of 478 catheters were considered to cause CVL-related DVT. However, 101 catheters were removed nonelectively because of CVL tips "clotting." These infants were not assessed with objective tests to ascertain if there were CVL-related DVT present.

Pediatric Populations that Require Long-Term Central Venous Lines

There are several diseases in children in which CVLs form a critically important part of routine care. The primary disease processes, and their respective therapies, undoubtedly have significant impact on the epidemiology of CVL-related DVT and on potential benefits of antithrombotic therapies. The following section summarizes literature specific to CVL-related VTE in common disease processes in children.[65,135,154,162,169,174,179,219–221]

Cancer Cancer in adults is a frequent cause of DVT unrelated to CVLs.[4] However, cancer in children is a relatively rare cause of DVT in the absence of CVLs. The incidence of all childhood cancers in North America currently is estimated at 1.31 per 10,000 children. Of these children, approximately 80% have CVLs placed to administer direct and supportive therapy. The exact incidence of CVL-related DVT in children with cancer is not known, but essentially all cases of DVT are directly related to CVLs. The reported incidence of loss of patency ranges from 1% to 74%. Many publications report incidences of CVL-related DVT between 1% and 11% based upon clinical symptoms of SVC obstruction   or   arm   swelling   (Table

4–8).[132–134,136,169,170,173,174,179,181,183,184,186–188] The median incidence of temporary loss of CVL patency was 26% (see Table 4–8),[169,174,179,183,184,186–189] of associated TE first detected by loss of patency was 6%,[132–136,170,181] and of associated TE detected by lineogram, ultrasound, or V/Q scans was 14% (see Table 4–8).[97,148,151,162,164] A recent study using spiral CT in 25 children previously treated for cancer, in whom CVLs had been removed at least 2 months previously, reported venous occlusion in 12% (95% CI = 4%, 31%).[222] Proportionally, children with cancer constitute almost 50% of patients with CVL-related DVT reported in the Canadian registry.[4]

Total Parenteral Nutrition Children requiring long-term TPN form the second largest group of patients requiring long-term CVLs. The reported frequency of CVL-related DVT in children receiving home TPN ranges from 1% to 80%[105,135,157,159,162,163,169,174,219–221,223] with the lowest frequencies reflecting the clinical diagnosis of SVC syndrome and highest frequencies reflecting venographic evidence of DVT (Table 4–9).[88,90,93,95,96,105,132,136,139,141,152,154,156,158,159,163,165,172,174,175,182,185,190,191,193–198] The median incidence of temporary loss of CVL patency was 15%,[139,174,175,193,195,196] of associated TE presenting with loss of patency 17%,[132,136,152,172,182,185,190,194,197,198] and of associated

Table 4–8 Central Venous Line-Related Thromboembolic Events in Children with Cancer

Author	Year	Study Design	Number of Cases	Diagnosis	Incidence of TE (%)
Barzaghi et al[186]	1995	PC	38	Patency	74
Biagi et al[187]	1997	RCT	73	Patency	40
					26
Kohli-Kumar et al[184]	1992	R	79	Patency	27
Kovesi and Kardos[188]	1997	R	74	Patency	26
Stockwell et al[169]	1983	R	24	Patency	25
Hockenberry et al[174]	1984	R	82	Patency	22
Uderzo et al[183]	1992	PC	55	Patency	15
Dawson et al[179]	1991	R	231	Patency	9
Sellden et al[181]	1991	PC	158	Patency	13
Krul et al[170]	1986	R	42	Patency	10
Weber et al[132]	1983	R	116	Patency	6
Golladay and Mallitt[133]	1986	PC	31	Patency	6
Darbyshire et al[134]	1985	PC	49	Patency	2
Mirro et al[135]	1989	PC	286	Patency	2
Gauderer and Stellato[136]	1985	PC	146	Patency	1
Bagnal et al[162]	1984	PC	254	Lineogram	23
Smith et al[148]	1991	RCT	14	Ultrasound	14
Haire et al[164]	1990	R	225	Lineogram	10
Korones et al[151]	1996	PC	156	Ultrasound	9
Uderzo et al[97]	1995	R	452	Ventilation-perfusion	4

TE = thromboembolic events; PC = prospective cohort; RCT = randomized controlled trial; R = retrospective; P = patency.

Table 4–9 Central Venous Line-Related Thromboembolic Events in Children Receiving Total Parenteral Nutrition

Author	Year	Study Design	Number of Cases	Diagnosis	Incidence of TE (%)
Temporary loss of CVL patency					
Hockenberry et al[174]	1989	R	82	Patency	22
Grisoni et al[193]	1986	R	107	Patency	21
Springer et al[175]	1989	R	26	Patency	16
Mactier et al[195]	1986	R	42	Patency	14
Lally et al[196]	1987	R	86	Patency	12
Fonkalsrud et al[139]	1982	R	298	Patency	9
TE-associated loss of patency					
Marzinotto et al[105]	1993	CS	12	Venography	66
Abdullah et al[198]	1990	R	63	Patency	30
Moukarzel et al[185]	1994	R	27	Patency	24
Chathas et al[197]	1990	R	478	Patency	23
Moukarzel et al[152]	1991	R	38	Patency	20
Vargas et al[172]	1987	R	234	Patency	18
Durand et al[194]	1986	PC	53	Patency	15
Fonkalsrud et al[190]	1982	R	94	Patency	12
Weber et al[132]	1983	R	116	Patency	6
Brown et al[182]	1983	PC	44	Patency	2
Gauderer et al[136]	1985	PC	146	Patency	1
TE detected by ultrasound, ventilation/perfusion, linogram, or venography					
Pollard et al[95]	1995	R	21	Ultrasound	57
Ament and Newth[93]	1995	CS	12	Ventilation/ perfusion	50
Dollery et al[96]	1994	CS	34	Ultrasound	35
Moore et al[163]	1985	PC	25	Linogram	20
Sadiq et al[159]	1987	R	52	Ultrasound	19
Pippus et al[156]	1994	PC	46	Ultrasound	17
Loeff et al[191]	1982	R	119	Ultrasound Venography Autopsy	8
Effman et al[141]	1978	R	57	Linogram	8
Moukarzel et al[152]	1991	R	90	Ultrasound	7
Mollitt et al[88]	1983	R	117	Ultrasound	7
Ross et al[154]	1989	R	350	Ultrasound	5
Mulvihill and Fonkalsrud[90]	1984	R	294	Ultrasound	5
Curnow et al[165]	1985	R	274	Linogram	4
Marsh et al[158]	1988	PC	56	Ultrasound	2

TE = thromboembolic events; R = retrospective; PC = prospective cohort; CS = cross-sectional.

TE detected by lineograms, ultrasound, venography, or V/Q scans at 8%.[88,90,93,95,96,141,152,154,156,158,159,163,165,191] There are three cross-sectional studies that were designed to determine the incidence of CVL-related VTE in children requiring long-term TPN. In the first study, the frequency of CVL-related DVT assessed by venography in 12 children was 66%.[105] For most children, there was extensive obliteration of the venous system, including the SVC, innominate, and subclavian veins. Extensive collaterals had developed and drained the venous circulation of the arms and head. These same 12 children were never suspected to have DVT, only blocked CVLs. Prior to the venograms, multiple ultrasounds and lineograms were performed and did not identify the extensive VTEs.[105]The main clinical finding, which had not been described previously, was dilated superficial veins in the skin on the side of the CVL (see Figure 4–8).

In the second study, a combination of V/Q scans and echocardiograms was used to screen for VTE in 34 patients.[96] Echocardiograms and lung perfusion scans were done in 34 children and adolescents with gut failure who had received TPN for 2 months to 9 years. Major thrombotic emboli were found in 12 patients (35%), and 4 died as a direct result.[96]

In the third study, 12 children on TPN were prospectively studied with V/Q scans for evidence of PE. Half of the children had findings consistent with PE, but none had clinical symptoms.[93] These frequencies are similar to those reported in adult patients requiring TPN, in whom the incidence of CVL-related DVT ranges from 2.7% to 71%.[124,127–129] The wide range of incidence for CVL-related DVT in adults also reflects the difference between clinically symptomatic and radiographically detected DVT.

The incidence of CVL-related DVT in children requiring home TPN may be particularly high for several reasons: (1) the CVLs are required for prolonged durations, on the order of several years; (2) the CVLs are accessed on a daily basis; (3) the TPN solution itself is likely procoagulant for several reasons (the amino acid and hypertonic dextrose components of TPN are able to strongly induce en-

dothelial cell and monocyte or macrophage procoagulant activity expression in vitro);[88,105–107,224] (4) the concentration of calcium is high, which may enhance local coagulation factor assembly, resulting in increased local generation of thrombin. Thus, patients receiving TPN may be at greater risk for CVL-related DVT compared to patients not receiving TPN. The contribution of short-term use of TPN to CVL-related DVT in children remains to be determined.

Hemodialysis Another group of patients who require CVLs is small children requiring hemodialysis.[225] As in adults, TE related to venous access for hemodialysis present a major management problem.[110,226] At least 30% of percutaneous accesses for hemodialysis are revised because of TE.[227] In children, peritoneal dialysis frequently is preferred, because of the difficulties associated with maintaining percutaneous access (see Chapter 8).[227–231]

Other Childhood Diseases Requiring Long-Term Central Venous Lines Other childhood diseases where CVLs are critically important to the delivery of effective primary care include cystic fibrosis, chronic infections, and hemophilia. Children with cystic fibrosis require frequent courses of intravenous antibiotics, and, usually, by their teenage years have limited venous access. A recent retrospective review, in conjunction with an incomplete cross-sectional survey using Doppler ultrasound, identified symptomatic CVL-related DVT in 9% of patients and asymptomatic DVT in a further 10% of children with cystic fibrosis and totally implantable vascular access devices ("portacaths").[232,233] Small series of patients with hemophilia requiring CVLs for regular factor VIII infusions have documented CVL-related DVT as a complication.[234,235]

Pediatric Populations Requiring Short-Term Central Venous Lines

Pediatric Intensive Care Central venous lines frequently are used for relatively short periods of time to manage patients in PICUs. A number of venous sites, including internal jugular, subclavian veins, and femoral veins, are accessed either percutaneously or with venous cutdown procedures. Table 4–10 summarizes the few reports on thrombotic complications in these patients.[147,149,150,180] The incidence of CVL-related TE in children in the PICU was 2%, based on loss of patency requiring removal of the CVL. In contrast, ultrasound showed a 10% to 44% incidence of CVL-related TE. In a RCT of patients admitted to a PICU, 50 patients were allocated to receive a femoral catheter that was either a standard CVL or a heparin-bonded CVL.[147] Of the 50 patients, 13 (26%) had VTE: 11 (44%) of the 25 patients in the standard catheter group, in comparison with 2 (8%) of the 25 patients in the heparin-bonded catheter group (p = .004). In addition, there was a significantly higher incidence of positive blood culture results among patients in the standard catheter group (24% vs 0%; p = .009). Positive catheter blood culture results were obtained in 38% of patients with CVL-related DVT versus 3% without CVL-related DVT (p = .001). Clinical evidence of DVT was present in 69% of patients with proven CVL-related DVT compared to 27% of patients without CVL-related DVT (p = .007).[147]

Burns Children with extensive burns require relatively short-term TPN to bring caloric and nitrogen intake up to levels necessary for metabolic equilibrium.[236] Thrombotic complications occur in these patients and may be more frequent when fluid status is poorly controlled.

Cardiac Catheterization Children undergoing investigation and treatment for cardiac anomalies frequently require angiographic studies that necessitate short-term venous catheters, usually through the femoral vein. In a series of 17 patients having catheter ablation,[122] magnetic resonance angiography was performed routinely 12 to 70 hours after catheterization, 22% of children had evidence of venous obstruction; however, none was symptomatic.[122] In a case series of 22 children who developed IVC, internal iliac, or femoral vein thrombosis after balloon angiography, no symptoms were apparent immediately after the procedure.[237]

Diagnosis, Management, and Outcome

Diagnosis Venography remains the gold standard diagnostic test for the detection of upper venous system CVL-related DVT. In contrast to venography of a lower limb, unilateral upper limb venography may not give a clear picture of the central veins, owing to washout from the contralateral venous system. Bilateral upper limb venography avoids washout of contrast in the central venous system and gives optimal radiographs, which is particularly helpful for the detection of DVT in the upper venous system (Figure 4–11).

Ultrasound is limited, owing to the fact that compression in the upper central veins is not feasible, and compression is the feature of ultrasound that has been shown to be sensitive and specific for the detection of DVT in the lower venous system.[112,114,118,238–240] Other limitations of ultrasound are that large collateral vessels may be mistaken for the normal vasculature and that the distal end of the clavicle may obscure the distal subclavian vein. Interpretation of ultrasound usually is considerably easier when it is read in conjunction with a

Table 4–10 Central Venous Line-Related Thromboembolic Events in Children in the Intensive Care Unit

Author	Year	Study Design	Diagnosis	Number of Cases	Incidence of TE (%)
Krafte-Jacobs et al[147]	1995	PC	Ultrasound	25	44*
				25	8+
Shefler et al[150]	1995	PC	Ultrasound	56	10
Casado-Flores et al[180]	1991	PC	Patency	322	2
Beck et al[149]	1998	PC	Ultrasound	93	18

TE = thromboembolic events; PC = prospective cohort.

*Standard catheter, +heparin-bonded catheters.

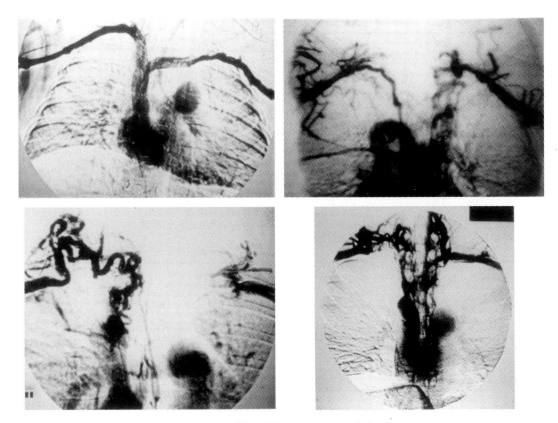

Figure 4–11 Normal venogram (upper left) and three examples of abnormal venograms. Reproduced with permission.[167]

venogram, and subsequent ultrasounds are a non-invasive way to monitor response to therapy or progress of disease. Ultrasound is valuable for the detection of DVT in the internal jugular veins, which often are not imaged by upper limb venography in the absence of brachiocephalic or SVC obstruction. Ultrasound also may be useful for peripheral long lines that have substantial components of the CVL within the brachial and axillary veins.

Lineograms have little role in detecting CVL-associated DVT. Lineograms are valuable for determining the location of CVL tips and CVL leakage (see Figure 4–9). Lineograms also are helpful in diagnosing CVL-tip thrombosis and CVL fibrin sheaths when backflow is a problem. Magnetic resonance imaging and spiral CT scan have yet to be critically compared to venography for the detection of DVT in children. However, they may both offer viable alternatives to venography. Femoral venous CVL-related DVT is readily detected using ultrasound, although extension into the IVC may be

missed. A high index of suspicion is required for early diagnosis.

Blockage of a Central Venous Line When a CVL blocks, patency is usually restored with simple measures or local instillation of UK (Tables 4–11 and 4–12).[135,233,241,242] Recent concerns regarding the preparation of UK have limited its use in North America (see Chapter 11). If a CVL remains blocked, it is removed, usually without evaluation with objective tests for DVT. One can argue that this approach is appropriate if there are no clinically important ramifications. However, this is not likely the case. For example, replacement of CVLs requires repeated anesthesia and surgery, with eventual loss of vessel patency in the upper venous system necessitating entry from the lower system. In addition, these children are at risk for clinically symptomatic DVT, recurrent DVT, or the long-term complication of PPS. In general, if a CVL fails to function properly after two doses of UK, or

Table 4–11 Protocol for Treatment of Blocked Central Venous Lines or TPA

	Blood-Related Blockage	Chemical-Related Blockage
Indications	Blood sampling Blood administration Blood backup in infusion line	Infusion line running the sudden unexplained occlusion
Initial Action	1. Attempt to aspirate	1. Attempt to aspirate
	2. Flush with 0.9% NaCl	2. Flush with 0.9% NaCl
	3. Follow guidelines Table 4–12	3. Follow HC guidelines (Table 4–12)
	4. If able to flush line, but unable to get blood return, proceed to diagnostic workup if clinically indicated	4. If no blood return, follow urokinase guidelines
		5. If able to flush line, but no blood return, proceed to diagnostic workup if clinically indicated
	5. If unable to flush line, contact the surgery unit	6. If unable to flush line, contact the surgery unit

HC = hydrochloric acid; NaCl = sodium chloride.

Reproduced with permission.[260]

Table 4–12 Guidelines for Local Instillation of Hydrochloric Acid or Urokinase

Treatment	Central Venous Catheter		Subcutaneous Port
	Single-Lumen	Double-Lumen	
HC (0.1M)	2ml x 2–4 hr*	2ml/lumen x 2–4 hr*	3ml x 2–4 hr*
Urokinase (5000 μ/ml) undiluted	2ml x 2– hr* If unsuccessful in obtaining blood return, repeat above once in 24 hr	2ml/lumen x 2–4hr* If unsuccessful in obtaining blood return, repeat above once in 24 hr	3ml x 2–4 hr* If unsuccessful in obtaining blood return, repeat above once in 24 hr
TPA ≤ 10kg	0.5 mg diluted in 0.9% NaCl to volume required to fill line	0.5 mg per lumen diluted in 0.9% NaCl to fill volume of line Treat 1 lumen at a time	0.5 mg diluted with 0.9% NaCl to 3 mL
TPA ≥ 10kg	1.0 mg in 1.0 mL 0.9% NaCl Use amount required to fill volume of line, to maximum of 2 mL = 2 mg	1.0 mg/mL Use amount required to volume of line, to maximum of 2 mL = 2 mg per lumen Treat 1 lumen at a time	2.0 mg diluted with 0.9% NaCl to 3 mL

After 2–4 hr instillation of each drug, withdraw drug. If possible, flush the catheter with 0.9% sodium chloride, attempt to aspirate blood.

TPA = tissue plasminogen activator.

Reproduced with permission.[260]

blocks for a second time, the patient should be actively investigated for a CVL-related DVT.

Management of Central Venous Line-Related Deep Vein Thrombosis
The aims of treatment of CVL-related DVT are to prevent immediate and potential long-term complications. Immediate complications are venous obstruction and PE, which are potentially fatal (see Chapter 5). Long-term complications are similar to those for all DVT and include recurrent thrombosis, PPS, and complications of anticoagulant therapy. These outcomes are discussed subsequently. Currently, there is no convincing evidence to suggest that CVL-related DVT can be considered benign.

The treatment of CVL-related DVT is similar to treatment of non-CVL-related DVT and consists of initial therapy with either UFH or low molecular-weight heparin (LMWH) followed by approximately 3 months of either oral anticoagulants (OAs) or LMWH (see Chapters 9 and 10). Systemic dose thrombolytic therapy may have a role in some patients with acute, serious symptoms, such as SVA syndrome (see Chapter 11). For many children, thrombolytic therapy would not be expected to be successful because the DVT has gradually occurred over a prolonged period of time and is relatively resistant to thrombolytic therapy.

Removal of a CVL that is associated with large-vessel DVT (as distinct from fibrin sheath or tip clot) is an individual decision that depends on a number of factors. If the CVL is not functional, then removal is inevitable and may be helpful. However, consideration should be given to initial anticoagulant therapy prior to CVL removal. This may salvage the CVL functionally and may minimize the risk of embolic complications. Pulmonary embolism occurring at the time of or immediately after CVL removal has been documented but clinically is uncommon. Some authors have reported, and advocated, transesophageal echocardiography during CVL removal, to monitor for embolization and hence allow rapid treatment. The validity of this approach remains unproven. If a patient is known to have a right-to-left intracardiac shunt, then anticoagulant therapy prior to CVL removal is suggested. In general, thrombolytic therapy is not recommended in the presence of right-to-left shunts as lysis may induce arterial emboli.

If a CVL is still functional despite an associated DVT, factors that need to be considered prior to removal include the need for ongoing therapy, the availability of other venous access, the degree of venous obstruction, and the response to initial anticoagulant therapy. In many situations, initial aggressive anticoagulant therapy enables safe preservation of crucial venous access. Patients with previous CVL-related DVT should be considered for ongoing secondary anticoagulant prophylaxis for as long as they have a CVL in situ. Another alternative is to cease therapy after 3 months and follow with regular ultrasound. Further studies are required to determine the optimal duration and intensity of therapy for CVL-related VTE.

Prophylaxis for Central Venous Line-Related Thrombosis A successful approach to the problem of DVT in high-risk adult patients has been pro-phylactic anticoagulation with low doses of UFH, LMWH, or OAs. Randomized controlled trials have convincingly and repeatedly shown that the risk reduction for DVT related to hip and knee surgery is reduced from approximately 50% to 10%.[244-247] A RCT of low-dose OAs (1 mg) compared to placebo in adults with CVLs showed that the incidence of DVT, based on venography, was safely reduced from 37% to 9.5%.[131] A similar study comparing 2500 IU Fragmin, a LMWH, subcutaneously daily to no therapy in adults with cancer and a Port-A-Cath® (Sims Dettec Inc., St. Paul, MN), showed a reduction in venographically identified thrombosis at 90 days from 62% to 6% (RR = 6.75; 95% CI = 1.05–43.58).[126]

Currently, most children with CVLs regularly receive prophylactic therapy with UFH in the form of CVL flushes with UFH-containing solutions, or low-dose UFH infusions (1-3 U/mL) concurrently with TPN or other infusions (see Chapter 9). For children with long-term CVLs who are predominantly outpatients, CVLs are flushed for a minimum of once every 4 to 6 weeks. However, the currently recognized incidence of clinically significant CVL-related DVT occurs despite this form of prophylaxis, and the question of whether more aggressive thromboprophylaxis is warranted remains unanswered.

The complexity of the primary illness in most children with CVL-related DVT, and the intensity of their therapy, whether medical or surgical, increases the potential for bleeding complications from prophylactic anticoagulation. In addition, OAs or subcutaneous LMWH therapy are more difficult to administer in small children (see Chapters 9 and 10). Current RCTs aimed at assessing the safety and validity of prophylactic anticoagulation in children with CVLs will provide the information needed that will allow clinicians to make rational decisions in this area.

NONCENTRAL VENOUS LINE-RELATED THROMBOSIS

Non-CVL-related DVT can occur in any venous system, but lower extremities present the most common site of symptomatic DVT. The venous drainage of the lower limb is depicted in Figure

4–7. The proximal venous system, which is the clinically important system for DVT, includes the iliac veins, the superficial and common femoral veins, and popliteal vein. Calf veins, which do not contribute to clinically important DVT unless they extend into the proximal venous system, include the anterior and posterior tibial and peroneal veins. Spontaneous axillary DVT is rare in children but does occur. Venous thromboembolic events in other specific sites or organ systems are discussed in Chapter 8.

Spontaneous Lower Limb Deep Venous Thrombosis

Incidence A review of the French and English literature identified 203 cases of DVT in the lower extremity.[8] The incidence of lower extremity DVT was approximately 1.2 cases per 10,000 hospital admissions.[7,8] Although there are isolated reports documenting the occurrence of asymptomatic lower extremity DVT in pediatric patients, the incidence is unknown. The incidence of lower extremity DVT continues to increase with age throughout adult life. Although the incidence of DVT and PE in adult patients is influenced by geographic and ethnic variations,[9,248] these data are not available for pediatric patients. Female and male children appear to be affected equally.[8]

Clinical Presentation The clinical manifestations of lower extremity DVT are leg pain, inguinal or abdominal pain, swelling, reddish or purple discoloration, occasionally fever, and PE without leg symptoms. A delay in diagnosis and treatment can contribute to the extent of the DVT and the severity of the clinical presentation. Asymptomatic deep venous thrombi also have been discovered during the investigation of PE and PPS.[24,25]

Diagnosis of Lower Extremity Thrombosis

The clinical diagnosis of lower extremity DVT in children is likely as nonspecific as in adults. In a retrospective review of venograms performed for clinically suspected DVT in children, only 18% of venograms were positive for DVT.[249] In children,

the radiographic diagnosis of lower extremity DVT is less problematic than the diagnosis of upper extremity DVT. Limitations still include the small size of the patients, serious underlying diseases that limit transportation to radiology, and lack of validated noninvasive diagnostic radiographic tests.

Radiographic Evaluation of Deep Venous Thrombosis Radiographic techniques used to diagnose DVT in the lower extremities can be considered as either invasive (i.e., venography) or noninvasive (i.e., Doppler ultrasound). In adults, venography remains the reference test against which the sensitivity (ability to diagnose true positive cases) and specificity (ability to exclude true negative cases) of other tests are compared. Compression ultrasound is sensitive and specific for the diagnosis of proximal DVT in the lower extremity in adults but not for calf vein clots.[111–114,116–119] Ultrasound is an attractive alternative to venography for children and may have acceptable sensitivity and specificity. There are no studies evaluating the sensitivity and specificity of ultrasound compared to venography in children with lower extremity clots. The small size of the vessels during infancy may affect the sensitivity and specificity of the technique. The percentage of abnormal ultrasounds that revert to normal following lower limb DVT in children is not known. If ultrasound does not revert to normal, venography may be required to distinguish between recurrent DVT and PPS in the lower extremity. Figure 4–12 shows the relative proportion of different objective tests used to diagnose both CVL and non-CVL-related DVT in pediatric patients.[1] The incidence of congenital prothrombotic disorders likely is increased in these children compared to the general population of children who develop CVL-related DVT.

Spontaneous Axillary Vein Thrombosis

Spontaneous axillary vein DVT in children is rare and usually occurs in teenagers. The symptoms are similar to those seen in adults and include swelling, pain, and erythema of the arm. Frequently, patients give a history of having commenced a new sport recently, in which they are using their arms more

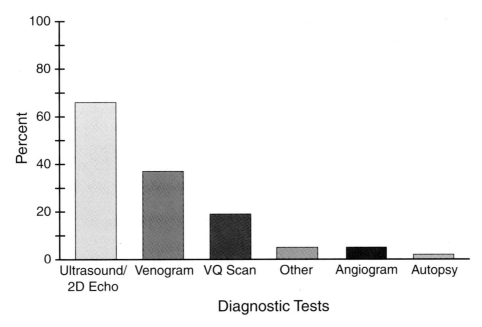

Figure 4–12 Relative proportion of different objective tests used to diagnose both central venous line and noncentral venous line-related deep vein thrombosis in pediatric patients.

VQ = ventilation / perfusion scan; 2D Echo = echocardiography.

strenuously. The diagnosis can be confirmed with ultrasound.[115] Pulmonary embolism can occur from an axillary vein DVT.[89]

Axillary vein DVT in children may be associated with an intrathoracic mass lesion, a congenital thoracic inlet obstruction, or a hypercoaguable condition. Appropriate imaging and hematologic testing should be performed in all cases to exclude these precipitating conditions. Treatment guidelines are similar to those for other venous DVT and are discussed in detail in subsequent chapters.

COMPLICATIONS OF VENOUS THROMBOEMBOLIC EVENTS

Complications of VTE can be classified as immediate or long term and apply equally to CVL- and non-CVL-related DVT. Serious immediate complications include death from extension into the heart or lung (PE),[4,93–97] nonlethal PE,[88] chylothorax,[8,88,98–100] and SVC syndrome.[88,90,98,102,103,250] Long-term complications include recurrent DVT,[1] PPS,[1] long-term anticoagulation therapy with its associated risk of bleeding, and hemorrhage from ruptured collateral varices. Repeated CVL-induced DVT also may result in loss of CVL patency, repeat

anesthesia with surgical placement of CVLs, and eventual loss of vessel patency in the upper venous system, necessitating entry from the lower venous system. For adults, only one-third to one-half of occluded veins recanalize[54,251] and PPS occurs at least as frequently, if not at a higher rate than in lower limbs (20–40%).[54,252,253]

Pulmonary Embolism

The frequency of PE in children is unknown but likely is underestimated. Children with PE often have multiple risk factors for DVT, which may consist of clinical diseases, therapies, or underlying hypercoagulable conditions. The most important clinical risk factor identified is the presence of CVL-related DVT. The clinical features of PE in children often are subtle or are masked by their primary illnesses. Increased diagnostic suspicion is required to prevent mortality and morbidity from undiagnosed PE. Currently, the most common method of diagnosis for PE in children is autopsy, highlighting the lack of clinical suspicion in most instances. Diagnostic strategies for PE in children are extrapolated from studies in adults. The positive and negative predictive values of a number of investigations may be reduced in children, owing to age-dependent physiologic and pathophysiologic differences. Anticoagulation is the mainstay of therapy for children with PE, based mostly on data extrapolated from data in adults (see Chapter 5). The outcome for children with PE is uncertain; however, the mortality probably is similar to that reported in adults with PE (see Chapter 5).

Recurrent Venous Thromboembolic Events

In adults the incidence of recurrent VTE is 4% to 7%.[254–256] The only long-term follow-up data that can provide an estimate on the incidence of recurrent DVT in children are from the Canadian registry. In the first 405 patients (mean follow-up 2.86 yr), recurrent VTE occurred in approximately 8% of children.[1,4] Children of all ages, with or without CVLs and with diverse underlying primary problems, were and are at risk for recurrent VTE, which may be either systemic or in the form of new PE. The incidence of recurrent VTE will inevitably increase with age.

Postphlebitic Syndrome

For adults, only one-third to one-half of occluded veins recanalize, and PPS occurs in approximately 20% of patients.[257] Postphlebitic syndrome, a serious long-term outcome of DVT, is caused by incompetent perforating valves and blood flow directed from the deep system into the superficial system, leading to edema and impaired viability of subcutaneous tissues. Physiologically, the fibrinolytic system is suppressed during childhood, which may predispose children to an increased incidence of PPS compared to adults.[258,259] Symptoms of PPS include swelling, pain, pigmentation, induration of the skin, and ulceration (Figure 4–13).[55] In adults, PPS could potentially occur over several decades. Symptoms of PPS may occur early or be delayed as long as 5 to 10 years after the initial event. The timing of presentation of PPS in children is unknown but, in general, the diagnosis of PPS is a clinical diagnosis; however, the diagnosis is assisted by demonstrating venous reflux, which can readily be detected with ultrasound. Initial follow-up data from the Canadian registry (mean duration, 2.86 yr) suggest the frequency of clinically detected PPS in children is approximately 10% to 12%.[3,4] The frequency likely will increase with increased

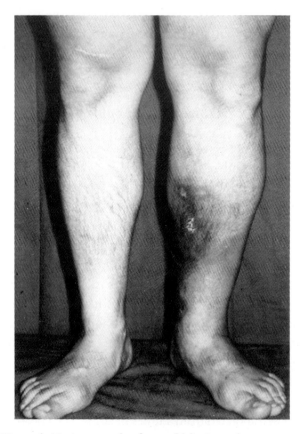

Figure 4–13 An example of post-phlebetic syndrome.

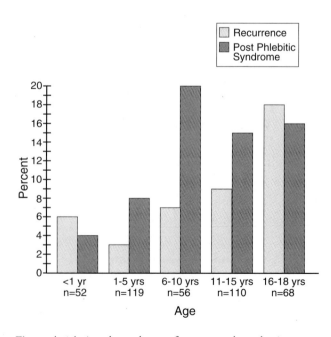

Figure 4–14 Age dependency of recurrent thrombotic events and postphlebitic syndrome in children.

Suspected Deep Vein Thrombosis

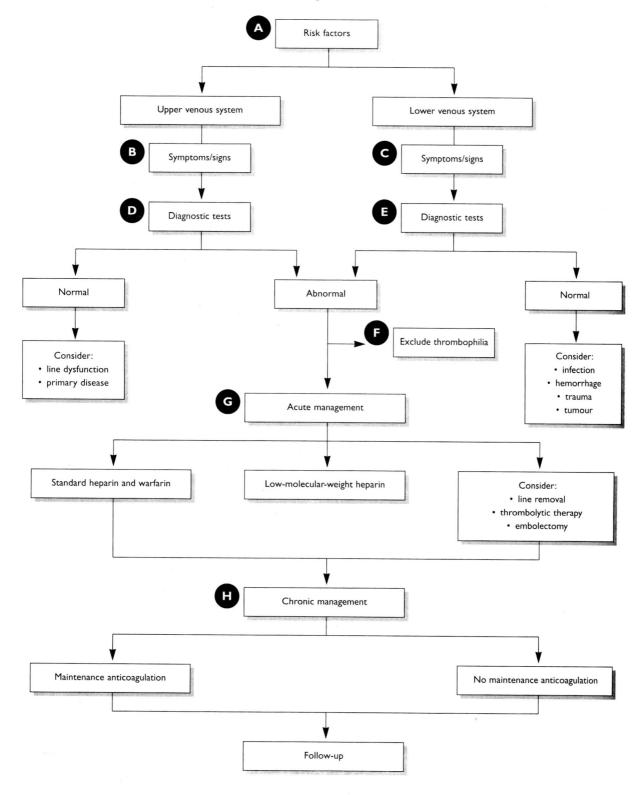

Figure 4–15 Outline of a practical approach to venous thrombotic disease in children.

duration of follow-up. The increased proportion of upper limb DVT in children compared to adults may delay the presentation of PPS, because the effects of gravity are less pronounced. The occurrence of PPS was increased in older children, although whether this represents chance, a difference in clinical detection rates, or a true protective mechanism in infants is unknown (Figure 4–14). The frequency and severity of PPS likely are related to the extent and recurrence of DVT.[1] Further prospective studies are required to verify the incidence and determine predisposing features for PPS in children.

Mortality

Although relatively uncommon, death from VTE occurs in children. In the Canadian registry, the all-causes mortality was 65 of 405 children (16%). Mortality directly attributable to DVT or PE occurred in nine children (2.2%), all of whom had CVL-related DVT.[3] Cause of death was either PE or extension of DVT into the heart.[1] Figure 4–15 provides a schema for the diagnosis and treatment of children with VTE.

REFERENCES

1. Andrew M, David M, Adams M, et al. Venous thromboembolic complications (VTE) in children: first analyses of the Canadian Registry of VTE. Blood 1994;83:1251–7.
2. Schmidt B, Andrew M. Neonatal thrombosis: report of a prospective Canadian and international registry. Pediatrics 1995;96:939–43.
3. Monagle P, Adams M, Mahoney M, et al. Long-term outcome of pediatric thromboembolic disease: a report from the Canadian Childhood Thrombophilia Registry. Pediatr Res 1999 (in press).
4. Massicotte MP, Dix D, Monagle P, et al. Central venous catheter related thrombosis (CVL-related DVT) in children: analysis of the Canadian Registry of Venous Thromboembolic Complications. J Pediatr 1998;133:770–6.
5. Nowak-Gottl U, von Kries R, Gobel U. Neonatal symptomatic thromboembolism in Germany: two year survey. Arch Dis Child Fetal Neonatal Educ 1997;76:F163–7.
6. Andrew M, Massicotte MP, deVeber G, et al. 1-800-NO-CLOTS: a quaternary care solution to a new tertiary care disease: childhood thrombophilia [abstract]. Thromb Haemost 1997;77:727.
7. Wise RC, Todd JK. Spontaneous, lower-extremity venous thrombosis in children. Am J Dis Child 1973;126:766–9.
8. David M, Andrew M. Venous thromboembolism complications in children: a critical review of the literature. J Pediatr 1993;123:337–46.
9. Coon W, Willis P, Keller J. Venous thromboembolism and other venous disease in the Tecumseh Community Health Study. Circulation 1973;48:839–46.
10. Gjores J. The incidence of venous thrombosis and its sequelae in certain districts in Sweden. Acta Chir Scand 1956;206(Suppl):1–10.
11. Clagett GP, Anderson FA, Heit JA, et al. Prevention of venous thromboembolism. Chest 1998;114(Suppl):531S–60S.
12. Planes A, Vochelle N, Mansat C. Prevention of deep vein thrombosis after total hip replacement by enoxaparin: one daily injection of 40 mg versus two daily injections of 20 mg. Thromb Haemost 1987;1(Suppl):415a.
13. Hull R, Delmore T, Hirsh J, et al. Effectiveness of an intermittent pulsatile elastic stocking for the prevention of calf and thigh vein thrombosis in patients undergoing elective knee surgery. Thromb Res 1979;16:37–45.
14. Leclerc J, Desjardins L, Geerts W, et al. A randomized trial of enoxaparin for the prevention of deep vein thrombosis after major knee surgery. Thromb Haemost 1991; 65(Suppl):753a.
15. Uden A. Thromboembolic complications following scoliosis surgery in Scandinavia. Acta Orthop Scand 1979;50:175–8.
16. Andrew M, Brooker LA. Blood component therapy in neonatal hemostatic disorders. Transfus Med Rev 1995;9:231–50.
17. Collins R, Scrimgeour A, Yusuf S, Peto R. Reduction in fatal pulmonary embolism and venous thrombosis by perioperative administration of subcutaneous heparin: overview of results of randomized trials in general, orthopedic, and urologic surgery. N Engl J Med 1988;318:1162–73.
18. Virchow R. Phlogose und Thrombose in Gefasssystem. In: Virchow R, ed. Gesammelte Abhandlungen zur wissenschafteichen Medicin. Frankfurt: Von Meidinger, 1856.
19. Andrew M. Acquired disorders in children. In: Nathan DG, Oski FA, eds. Hematology: of infancy and childhood. Philadelphia: WB Saunders, 1998: 1677–717.
20. Aarts PAMM, Bolhuis PA, Sakariassen KS, et al. Red blood cell size is important for adherence of blood platelets to artery subendothelium. Blood 1983; 62:214–20.
21. Michelson AD, Bovill E, Monagle P, Andrew M. Antithrombotic therapy in children. Chest 1998;114(Suppl):748S–69S.

22. Andrew M, Schmidt B. Hemorrhagic and thrombotic complications in children. In: Colman R, Hirsh J, Marder V, Salzman E, eds. Hemostasis and thrombosis: basic principles and clinical practice. Philadelphia: JB Lippincott; 1994:989–1022.

23. Andrew M. Developmental hemostasis: relevance to newborns and infants. In: Nathan DG, Oski FA, eds. Hematology: of infancy and childhood. Philadelphia: WB Saunders;1998:114–57.

24. Marcinski A, Barral V, Sauvegrain J. Acquired deep venous thrombosis in children. Pediatric Radiol 1985;15:300–6.

25. Norotte G, Glorion C, Rigault P, et al. Complications thromboemboliques en orthopedie pediatrique. Recueil "multicentrique" de 33 observations. Chir Pediatr 1989;30:193–8.

26. Robin M, Boyer C. Causes des thromboses veineuses de l'enfant et de l'adolescent en dehors de la periode neonatale. Arch Fr Pediatr 1987; 44:467–72.

27. Nguyen LT, Laberge JM, Guttman FM, Albert D. Spontaneous deep vein thrombosis in childhood and adolescence. J Pediatr Surg 1986; 21:640–3.

28. Noonan J, Ehmke D. Complications of ventriculovenous shunts for control of hydrocephalus. Report of three cases with thromboemboli to the lungs. N Engl J Med 1963; 269:70–4.

29. Tyler H, Clark D. Cerebrovascular accidents in patients with congenital heart disease. AMA Arch Neurol Psychol 1957; 77:483–9.

30. Jones DRB, Macintyre IMC. Venous thromboembolism in infancy and childhood. Arch Dis Child 1975; 50:153–5.

31. Nachbur B, Baumgartner G, Huser HJ. Deep thrombophlebitis of the lower extremities in children. VASA 1979;8:53–9.

32. Janin Y, Becker J, Wise L, et al. Superior vena cava syndrome in childhood and adolescence: a review of the literature and report of three cases. J Pediatr Surg 1982;17:290–5.

33. De Stefano V, Leone G, Carolis M, et al. Antithrombin III in fullterm and preterm newborn infants: three cases of neonatal diagnosis of AT III congenital defect. Thromb Haemost 1987; 57:329–31.

34. Mannucci PM, Tripodi A, Bertina RM. Protein S deficiency associated with "juvenile" arterial and venous thromboses. Thromb Haemost 1986; 55:440.

35. Ehrenforth S, Koch HG, Rehan M, et al. Multicentre evaluation of combined prothrombotic defects associated with thrombophilia in childhood [abstract]. Blood 1997; 90:470.

36. Manco-Johnson MJ. Disorders of hemostasis in childhood: risk factors for venous thromboembolism. Thromb Haemost 1997; 78:710–14.

37. Miletich J, Prescott S, White R, et al. Inherited predisposition to thrombosis. Cell 1993; 72:477–80.

38. Andrew M, Michelson AD, Bovill T, et al. The prevention and treatment of thromboembolic disease in children: a need for thrombophilia programs. Am J Pediatr Hematol Oncol 1997; 19:7–22.

39. Nowak-Gottl U, Debus O, Findeisen M, et al. Lipoprotein (a): its role in childhood thromboembolism. Pediatrics 1997; 99:E11.

40. Nowak-Gottl U, Schneppenheim R, Vielhaber H. APC resistance in childhood thromboembolism: diagnosis and clinical aspects. Semin Thromb Haemost 1997; 23:253–8.

41. Nowak-Gottl U, Strater R, Dubbers A, et al. Ischaemic stroke in infancy and childhood: role of Arg506 to Gln mutation in the factor V gene. Blood Coagul Fibrinolysis 1996; 7:684–8.

42. Nowak-Gottl U, Dubbers A, Kececioglu D, et al. Factor V Leiden, protein C, and lipoprotein (a) in catheter-related thrombosis in childhood: a prospective study. J Pediatr 1997; 131:608–12.

43. Kohlhase B, Kececioglu D, Nowak-Gottl U. Intracardiac thrombus associated with resistance to activated protein C. Cardiol Young 1998; 8:116–18.

44. Nowak-Gottl U, Vielhaber H, Schneppenheim R, Koch HG. Coagulation and fibrinolysis in children with APC-resistance: a population based study. Fibrinolysis 1996; 10:25–7.

45. Nowak-Gottl U, Auberger K, Gobel U, et al. Inherited defects of the protein C anticoagulant system in childhood thrombo-embolism. Eur J Pediatr 1996; 155:921–7.

46. Nowak-Gottl U, Koch D, Aschka B, et al. Resistance to activated protein C (APCR) in children with venous or arterial thromboembolism. Br J Haematol 1996; 92:992–8.

47. Aschka I, Aumann V, Bergmann F, et al. Prevalence of factor V Leiden in children with thromboembolism. Eur J Pediatr 1996; 155:1009–14.

48. Nuss R, Hays T, Manco-Johnson MJ. Childhood thrombosis. Pediatrics 1995; 96:291–4.

49. Toumi NH, Khaldi F, Ben Becheur S, et al. Thrombosis in congenital deficiencies of ATIII, protein C, or protein S: a study of 44 children. Hematol Cell Ther 1997; 39:295–9.

50. Gurgey A, Mesci L, Renda Y, et al. Factor V Q506 mutation in children with thrombosis. Am J Hematol 1996; 53:37–9.

51. Kohlhase B, Veilhaber H, Kehl HG, et al. Thromboembolism and resistance to activated protein C in children with underlying cardiac disease. J Pediatr 1996; 128:324–8.

52. Sifontes MT, Nuss R, Hunger SP, et al. The factor V Leiden mutation in children with cancer and thrombosis. Br J Haematol 1997; 96:484–9.

53. Nowak-Gottl U, Aschka I, Koch GH, et al. Resistance to activated protein C (APCR) in children with acute lymphoblastic leukemia: the need for a prospective

multicentre study. Blood Coagul Fibrinolysis 1995; 6:761–4.

54. Lindblad B, Bergqvist D. Aggressive or conservative treatment in subclavian vein thrombosis. In: Eklof B, Gjores J, Thulesius O, Bergqvist D, eds. Controversies in the management of venous disorders. London: Butterworth & Co., 1989:141–58.

55. Andrew M, deVeber G. Blood clots and strokes: a guide for parents and little folks. Hamilton, ON: B.C. Decker Inc., 1998.

56. Meyers I. Intravenous catheterzation. Am J Nurs 1945; 45:930–1.

57. Smits H, Freedman LR. Prolonged venous catheterization as a cause of sepsis. N Engl J Med 1967; 276: 1229–33.

58. Feld R, Leers WD, Curtic JE. Intravenous catheter infection study: a prospective trial in patients with neoplastic disease. Med Pediatr Oncol 1975; 1:175–81.

59. Broviac JW, Cole JJ, Scribner BH. A silicone rubber atrial catheter for prolonged parenteral alimentation. Surg Gynecol Obstet 1973; 136:602–6.

60. Hickman RO, Buckner CD, Clift RA, et al. A modified right atrial catheter for access to the venous system in marrow transplant recipients. Surg Gynecol Obstet 1979; 148:871–5.

61. Sanders JE, Hickman RO, Aker S, et al. Experience with double lumen right atrial catheters. JPEN J Parenter Enteral Nutr 1982; 6:95–9.

62. Ladefoged K, Jarnum I. Long-term parenteral nutrition. BMJ 1978; 2:262–6.

63. Larson EB, Wooding M, Hickman RO. Infectious complications of right atrial catheters used for venous access in patients receiving intensive chemotherapy. Surg Gynecol Obstet 1981;153: 369–73.

64. Strum S, McDermed J, Korn A, Joseph C. Improved methods for venous access: the Port-A-Cath, a totally implanted catheter system. J Clin Oncol 1986; 4:596–603.

65. Ingram J, Weitzman S, Greenberg ML, et al. Complications of indwelling venous access lines in the pediatric hematology patient: a prospective comparison of external venous catheters and subcutaneous ports. Am J Pediatr Hematol Oncol 1991; 13:130–6.

66. Wilson-Storey D. Just a 'wee prick' with a needle. J R Coll Surg Edinb 1996; 41:412–13.

67. Dubois J, Gavel L, Tapiero B, et al. Peripherally inserted central venous catheters in infants and children. Radiology 1997; 204:622–6.

68. Racadio JM, Johnson ND, Doellman DA. Peripherally inserted central venous catheters: success of scalp-vein access in infants and children. Radiology 1999; 210:858–60.

69. Crowley JJ, Pereira JK, Harris LS, Becker CJ. Peripherally inserted central catheters: experience in 523 children. Radiology 1997; 204:617–21.

70. Linder LE, Curelaru I, Gustavsson B, et al. Material thrombogenicity in central venous catheterization: a comparison between soft antebrachial catheters of silicone elastomere and polyurethane. JPEN J Parenter Enteral Nutr 1984; 8:399–406.

71. Curelaru I, Gustavsson B, Hultman E, et al. Material thrombogenicity in central venous catheterization. III. A comparison between soft polyvinylchloride and soft polyurethane elastomere, long antebrachial catheters. Acta Anaesthesiol Scand 1984; 28:204–8.

72. Curelaru I, Gustavsson B, Hansson AH, et al. Material thrombogenicity in central venous catheterization. II. A comparison between plain silicon elastomere and plain polyethylene, long, antebrachial catheters. Acta Anaesthesiol Scand 1983; 27:158–64.

73. Bennegard K, Curelaru I, Gustavsson B, et al. Material thrombogenicity in central venous catheterization. I. A comparison between uncoated and heparin-coated long antibrachial polyethylene catheters. Acta Anaesthesiol Scand 1982; 26:112–20.

74. Ahlsten G, Ewald U, Tuvemo T. Maternal smoking reduces prostacyclin formation in human umbilical arteries. A study on strictly selected pregnancies. Acta Obstet Gynecol Scand 1986; 65:645–9.

75. Andrew M, Kelton JG. Neonatal thrombocytopenia. Clin Perinatol 1984; 11:359–91.

76. Pottecher T, Forrler M, Picardat P, et al. Thrombogenicity of central venous catheters: prospective study of polyethylene, silicone, and polyurethane catheters with phlebography or post mortem examination. Eur J Anaesthesiol 1984; 1:361–5.

77. Bailly AL, Laurent A, Lu H, et al. Fibrinogen binding and platelet retention: relationship with the thrombogenicity of catheters. J Biomed Mater Res 1996; 30:101–8.

78. Bambauer R, Schiel R, Mestres P, et al. Scanning electron microscopic investigation of catheters for blood access. Blood Purif 1996; 14:249–56.

79. Appelgren P, Ransjo U, Bindslev L, Larm O. Does surface heparinisation reduce bacterial colonisation of central venous catheters? Lancet 1995; 345:130–1.

80. Appelgren P, Ransjo U, Bindslev L, et al. Surface heparinization of central venous catheters reduces microbial colonization in vitro and in vivo: results from a prospective, randomized trial. Crit Care Med 1996; 24:1482–9.

81. Downs JB, Chapman RL, Hawkins F. Prolonged radial artery catheterization. An evaluation of heparinized catheters and continous irrigation. Arch Surg 1974; 108:671–3.

82. Hoar PF, Wilson RM, Mangano DT. Heparin bonding reduces thrombogenicity of pulmonary artery catheters. N Engl J Med 1980; 305:993–5.

83. Mangano DT. Heparin bonding and long-term protection against thrombogenesis. N Engl J Med 1982; 307:894–5.

84. Jackson J, Truog W, Watchko J, et al. Efficacy of thromboresistant umbilical artery catheters in reducing aortic thrombosis and related complications. J Pediatr 1987; 110:102–5.

85. Randolph AG, Cook DJ, Gonzales CA. Benefit of heparin in central venous and pulmonary artery catheters: a meta-analysis of randomized controlled trials. Chest 1998; 113:165–71.

86. Mollenholt P, Eriksson I, Andersson T. Thrombogenicity of pulmonary-artery catheters. Intensive Care Med 1987; 13:57–9.

87. Williams EC. Catheter-related thrombosis. Clin Cardiol 1990; 13(4 Suppl 6):VI34–6.

88. Mollitt DL, Golladay ES. Complications of TPN catheter-induced vena caval thrombosis in children less than one year of age. J Pediatr Surg 1983; 18:462–7.

89. Marie I, Levesque A, Cailleux N, et al. Deep venous thrombosis of the upper limbs. Rev Med Interne 1998; 19:399–408.

90. Mulvihill SJ, Fonkalsrud EW. Complications of superior versus inferior vena cava occlusion in infants receiving central total parenteral nutrition. J Pediatr Surg 1984; 19:752–7.

91. Rockoff MA, Gang DL, Vacanti JP. Fatal pulmonary embolism following removal of a central venous catheter. J Pediatr Surg 1984; 19:307–9.

92. Derish MR, Smith DW, Frankel LR. Venous catheter thrombus formation and pulmonary embolism in children. Pediatr Pulmonol 1995; 20:349–54.

93. Ament J, Newth CJ. Deep venous lines and thromboembolism. Pediatr Pulmonol 1995; 20:347–8.

94. Hoyer PF, Gonda S, Barthels M, et al. Thromboembolic complications in children with nephrotic syndrome. Acta Paediatr Scand 1986; 75:804–10.

95. Pollard A, Sreeram N, Wright JG, et al. ECG and echocardiographic diagnosis of pulmonary thromboembolism associated with central venous lines. Arch Dis Child 1995; 73:147–50.

96. Dollery CM, Sullivan ID, Bauraind O, et al. Thrombosis and embolism in long-term central venous access for parenteral nutrition. Lancet 1994; 344:1043–5.

97. Uderzo C, Faccini P, Ravelli A, et al. Pulmonary thromboembolism in childhood leukemia: 8-years experience in a pediatric hematology center. J Clin Oncol 1995; 13:2805–12.

98. Le Coultre C, Oberhansli I, Mossaz A, et al. Postoperative chylothorax in children: differences between vascular and traumatic origin. Presented at the 37th Annual International Congress of the British Association of Paediatric Surgeons July 25–27, 1990.

99. Kramer SS, Taylor GA, Garfinkel DJ, Simmons MA. Lethal chylothoraces due to superior vena caval thrombosis in infants. Am J Radiol 1981; 137:559–63.

100. Dhande V, Kattwinkel J, Alford B. Recurrent bilateral pleural effusions secondary to superior vena cava obstruction as a complication of central venous catheterization. Pediatrics 1983; 72:109–13.

101. Kurekci E, Kaye R, Koehler M. Chylothorax and chylopericardium: a complication of a central venous catheter. J Pediatr 1998; 132:1064–6.

102. Graham LJ, Gumbiner CH. Right atrial thrombus and superior vena cava syndrome in a child. Pediatrics 1984; 73:225–8.

103. Bertrand M, Presant CA, Klein L, Scott E. Iatrogenic superior vena cava syndrome. A new entity. Cancer 1984; 54:376–8.

104. Ryan JAJ, Abel RM, Abbott WM, et al. Catheter complications in total parenteral nutrition. A prospective study of 200 consecutive patients. N Engl J Med 1974; 290:757–61.

105. Marzinotto V, Adams M, Pencharz P, et al. Catheter-related thrombosis in children receiving home TPN: incidence, diagnosis, management [abstract]. Thromb Haemost 1993; 69:1079.

106. Wakefield A, Cohen Z, Craig M, et al. Thrombogenicity of total parenteral nutrition solutions: I. Effect on induction of monocyte/macrophage procoagulant activity. Gastroenterology 1989; 97:1210–19.

107. Wakefield A, Cohen Z, Rosenthal A, et al. Thrombogenicity of total parenteral nutrition solutions: II. Effect on induction of endothelial cell procoagulant activity. Gastroenterology 1989; 97:1220–8.

108. Montemurr P, Lattanzio A, Chetta G, et al. Increased in vitro and in vivo generation of procoagulant activity (tissue factor) by mononuclear phagocytes after intralipid infusion in rabbits. Blood 1985; 65:1391–5.

109. Franzone AJ, Tucker BL, Brennan LP, et al. Hemodialysis in children. Arch Surg 1971; 102:592–3.

110. Idriss FS, Nikaidok LR, King R, Swenson O. Arteriovenous shunts for hemodialysis in infants and children. J Pediatr Surg 1971; 6:639–44.

111. Cogo A, Lensing AW, Prandoni P, Hirsh J. Distribution of thrombosis in patients with symptomatic deep vein thrombosis. Implications for simplifying the diagnostic process with compression ultrasound. Arch Intern Med 1993; 153:2777–80.

112. Biondetti PR, Vigo M, Tomasella G, Prandoni P. Diagnosis of deep venous thrombosis of the legs: accuracy of ultrasound using vein compression. Radiol Med (Torino)1990; 80:463–8.

113. Wells PS, Hirsh J, Anderson DR, et al. Comparison of the accuracy of impedance plethysmography and compression ultrasonography in outpatients with clinically suspected deep vein thrombosis. A two-centre paired-design prospective trial. Thromb Haemost 1995; 74:1423–7.

114. Cogo A, Lensing AW, Prandoni P, et al. Comparison of real-time ultrasound B-mode ultrasonography and Doppler ultrasound with contrast venography in the

diagnosis of venous thrombosis in symptomatic out-patients. Thromb Haemost 1993; 70:404–7.

115. Miller N, Satin R, Tousignant L, Sheiner JM. A prospective study comparing duplex scan and venography for diagnosis of lower-extremity deep vein thrombosis. Cardiovasc Surg 1996; 4:505–8.

116. Heijboer H, Cogo A, Buller HR, et al. Detection of deep vein thrombosis with impedance plethysmography and real-time compression ultrasonography in hospitalized patients. Arch Intern Med 1992; 152:1901–3.

117. Prandoni P, Lensing AW. New developments in noninvasive diagnosis of deep vein thrombosis of the lower limbs. Ric Clin Lab 1990; 20:11–17.

118. Kraaijenhagen RA, Lensing AW, Lijmer JG, et al. Diagnostic strategies for the management of patients with clinically suspected deep vein thrombosis. Curr Opin Pulm Med 1997; 3:268–74.

119. Lensing AW, Doris CI, McGrath FP, et al. A comparison of compression ultrasound with color Doppler ultrasound for the diagnosis of symptomless postoperative deep vein thrombosis. Arch Intern Med 1997; 157:765–8.

120. Prandoni P, Polistena P, Bernardo E, et al. Upper extremity deep venous thrombosis. Arch Intern Med 1997; 157:57–62.

121. Rose SC, Gomes AS, Yoon HC. Magnetic resonance angiography for mapping potential central venous sites in patients with advanced occlusive disease. Am J Roentgenol 1996; 166:1181–7.

122. Miga DE, McKellar LF, Denslow S, et al. Incidence of femoral vein occlusion after catheter ablation in children: evaluation with magnetic resonance angiography. Pediatr Cardiol 1997; 18:204–7.

123. Hingorani A, Ascher E, Lorenson E, et al. Upper extremity deep venous thrombosis and its impact on morbidity and mortality rates in a hospital-based population. J Vasc Surg 1997; 26:853–60.

124. Brismar B, Hardstedt C, Malmborg AS. Bacteriology and phlebography in catheterization for parenteral nutrition. Acta Chir Scand 1980; 146:115–19.

125. DeCicco M, Matovic M, Balestreri L, et al. Central venous thrombosis: an early and frequent complication in cancer patients bearing long-term silastic catheter. A prospective study. Thromb Res 1997; 86:101–13.

126. Monreal M, Alastrue A, Rull M, et al. Upper extremity deep venous thrombosis in cancer patients with venous access devices: prophylaxis with a low molecular weight heparin (Fragmin). Thromb Haemost 1996; 75:251–3.

127. Padberg FT, Ruggiero J, Blackburn GL, Bistrian BR. Central venous catheterization for parenteral nutrition. Ann Surg 1981; 193:264–70.

128. Valerio D, Hussey JK, Smith FW. Central vein thrombosis associated with intravenous feeding: a prospec-

tive study. JPEN J Parenter Enteral Nutr 1981; 5:240–2.

129. Wolfe BM, Ryder MA, Nishikawa RA, et al. Complications of parenteral nutrition. Am J Surg 1986; 152: 93–9.

130. Pieters PC, Dittrich J, Prasadu U, Berman W. Acute Budd-Chiari syndrome caused by percutaneous placement of a transhepatic inferior vena cava catheter. J Vasc Interv Radiol 1997; 8:587–90.

131. Bern MM, Lokich JJ, Wallach SR, et al. Very low doses of warfarin can prevent thrombosis in central venous catheters. A randomized prospective trial. Ann Intern Med 1990; 112:423–8.

132. Weber T, West K, Grosfeld J. Broviac central venous catheterization in infants and children. Am J Surg 1983; 145:202–4.

133. Golladay E, Mollitt D. Percutaneous placement of a venous access port in a pediatric patient population. J Pediatr Surg 1986; 21:683–4.

134. Darbyshire P, Weightman N, Speller D. Problems associated with indwelling central venous catheters. Arch Dis Child 1985; 60:129–34.

135. Mirro JJ, Rao BN, Stokes DC, et al. A prospective study of Hickman/Broviac catheters and implantable ports in pediatric oncology patients. J Clin Oncol 1989; 7:214–22.

136. Gauderer M, Stellato T. Subclavian Broviac catheters in children: technical consideration in 146 consecutive placements. J Pediatr Surg 1985; 20:402–5.

137. Khilnani P, Goldstein B, Todres ID. Double lumen umbilical venous catheters in critically ill neonates: a randomized prospective study. Crit Care Med 1991; 19:1348–51.

138. Storme L, Ouali M, Ganga-Zandzou PS, et al. Use of double lumen umbilical vein catheters in a neonatal intensive care unit. Arch Pediatr 1999; 6:386–90.

139. Fonkalsrud E, Ament M, Berquist W, Burke M. Occlusion of the vena cava in infants receiving central venous hyperalimentation. Surg Gynecol Obstet 1982; 154:189–92.

140. Ogata E, Schulman S, Raffensperger J, et al. Caval catheterization in the intensive care nursery: a useful means for providing parenteral nutrition to the extremely low birth-weight infant. J Pediatr Surg 1984; 19:258–62.

141. Effmann E, Ablow R, Touloukian R, Seashore J. Radiographic aspects of total parenteral nutrition during infancy. Radiology 1978; 127:195–201.

142. Goutail-Flaud MF, Shabarek FM, Berg A, et al. Central venous catheter-related complications in newborns and infants: a 587 case survey. J Pediatr Surg 1991; 26:645–50.

143. Warner B, Gorgone P, Schilling S, et al. Multiple purpose central venous access in infants less than 1,000 grams. J Pediatr Surg 1987; 22:820–2.

144. Valk WJC, Liem KD, Geven WB. Seldinger technique as an alternative approach for percutaneous insertion of hydrophilic polyurethane central venous catheters in newborns. J Parenter Enteral Nutr 1995; 19:151–5.

145. Dolcourt JL, Bose CL. Percutaneous insertion of silastic central venous catheters in newborn infants. Pediatrics 1982; 70:484–6.

146. Johnson EM, Saltzman DA, Suh G, et al. Complications and risks of central venous catheter placement in children. Surgery 1998; 124:911–16.

147. Krafte-Jacobs B, Sivit C, Majia R, Pollack M. Catheter-related thrombosis in critically ill children: comparison of catheters with and without heparin bonding. J Pediatr 1995; 126:50–4.

148. Smith SM, Dawson SM, Hennessey R, Andrew M. Maintenance of the patency of indwelling central venous catheters: is heparin necessary. Am J Pediatr Hematol Oncol 1991; 13:141–3.

149. Beck C, Dubois J, Grignon A, et al. Incidence and risk factors of catheter related deep vein thrombosis in a pediatric intensive care unit: a prospective study. J Pediatr 1998; 133:237–41.

150. Shefler A, Gillis J, Lam A, et al. Inferior vena cava thrombosis as a complication of femoral vein catheterisation. Arch Dis Child 1995; 72:343–5.

151. Korones DN, Buzzard CJ, Asselin BL, Harris JP. Right atrial thrombi in children with cancer and indwelling catheters. J Pediatr 1996; 128:841–6.

152. Moukarzel A, Azancot-Benisty A, Brun P, et al. M-mode and two-dimensional echocardiography in the routine follow-up of central venous catheters in children receiving total parenteral nutrition. J Parenter Enteral Nutr 1991; 15:551–5.

153. Stenzel J, Green T, Fuhrman B, et al. Percutaneous central venous catheterization in a pediatric intensive care unit: a survival analysis of complications. Crit Care Med 1989; 17:984–8.

154. Ross PJ, Ehrenkranz R, Kleinman CS, Seashore JH. Thrombus associated with central venous catheters in infants and children. J Pediatr Surg 1989; 24:253–6.

155. Babcock DS. Sonographic evaluation of suspected pediatric vascular diseases. Pediatr Radiol 1991; 21:486–9.

156. Pippus KG, Giacomantonio JM, Gillis DA, Rees EP. Thrombotic complications of saphenous central venous lines. J Pediatr Surg 1994; 29:1218–19.

157. Mehta S, Connors AFJ, Danish EH, Grisoni E. Incidence of thrombosis during central venous catheterization of newborns: a prospective study. J Pediatr Surg 1992; 27:18–22.

158. Marsh D, Wilkerson S, Cook L, Pietsch J. Right atrial thrombus formation screening using two-dimensional echocardiograms in neonates with central venous catheters. Pediatrics 1988; 81:284–6.

159. Sadiq H, Devaskar S, Keenan K, Weber T. Broviac catheterization in low birth weight infants: incidence and treatment of associated complications. Crit Care Med 1987; 15:47–50.

160. Schiff DE, Stonestreet BS. Central venous catheters in low birth weight infants: incidence of related complications. J Perinatol 1993; 13:153–8.

161. Wever M, Liem K, Geven W, Tanke R. Urokinase therapy in neonates with catheter-related central venous thrombosis. Thromb Haemost 1995; 73:180–5.

162. Bagnall HA, Gomperts E, Atkinson JB. Continuous infusion of low-dose urokinase in the treatment of central venous catheter thrombosis in infants and children. Pediatrics 1989; 83:963–6.

163. Moore RA, McNicholas KW, Naidech H, et al. Clinically silent venous thrombosis following internal and external jugular central venous cannulation in pediatric cardiac patients. Anesthesiology 1985; 62:640–3.

164. Haire WD, Lieberman RP, Edney J, et al. Hickman catheter-induced thoracic vein thrombosis. Cancer 1990; 66:900–8.

165. Curnow A, Idowu J, Behrens E, et al. Urokinase therapy for silastic catheter-induced intravascular thrombi in infants and children. Arch Surg 1985; 120:1237–40.

166. Andrew M, Marzinotto V, Pencharz P, et al. A cross-sectional study of catheter-related thrombosis in children receiving total parenteral nutrition at home. J Pediatr 1995; 126:358–63.

167. Salonvaara M, Riikonen P, Kekomaki R, Heinonen K. Clinically symptomatic central venous catheter-related deep venous thrombosis in newborns. Acta Paediatr 1999; 88:642–6.

168. Medeiros D, Miller KL, Rollins NK, Buchanan GR. Contrast venography in young haemophiliacs with implantable central venous access devices. Haemophilia 1998; 4:10–15.

169. Stockwell M, Adams M, Andrew M, et al. Central venous catheters for out-patient management of malignant disorders. Arch Dis Child 1983; 58:633–5.

170. Krul E, van Leeuwen E, Vos A, Voute P. Continuous venous access in children for long-term chemotherapy by means of an implantable system. J Pediatr Surg 1986; 21:689–90.

171. Newman BM, Jewett TC, Karp MP, Cooney DR. Percutaneous central venous catheterization in children: first-line choice for venous access. J Pediatr Surg 1986; 21:685–8.

172. Vargas JH, Ament ME, Berquist WE. Long-term home parenteral nutrition in pediatrics: ten years of experience in 102 patients. J Parenter Enteral Nutr 1987; 6:24–32.

173. Shulman RJ, O'Brien Smith E, Rahman S, et al. Single- vs. double-lumen central venous catheters in pediatric oncology patients. Am J Dis Child 1988; 142:893–5.

174. Hockenberry MJ, Schultz WH, Bennett B, et al. Experience with minimal complications in implanted catheters in children. Am J Pediatr Hematol Oncol 1989; 11:295–9.

175. Springer JC, Azizkhan RG, Mesrobian HGJ. Continuous venous access in children with urological diseases. J Urol 1989; 141:364–6.

176. Atkinson JB, Bagnall HA, Gomperts E. Investigational use of tissue plasminogen activator (t-PA) for occluded central venous catheters. JPEN J Parenter Enteral Nutr 1990; 14:310–11.

177. Schwartz C, Hendrickson KJ, Roghmann K, Powell K. Prevention of bacteremia attributed to luminal colonization of tunneled central venous catheters with vancomycin-susceptible organisms. J Clin Oncol 1990; 8:1591–7.

178. Gleason-Morgan D, Church JA, Bagnall-Reeb H, Atkinson J. Complications of central venous catheters in pediatric patients with acquired immunodeficiency syndrome. Pediatr Infect Dis J 1991; 10:11–14.

179. Dawson S, Pai MKR, Smith S, et al. Right atrial catheters in children with cancer: a decade of experience in the use of tunnelled, exteriorized devices at a single institution. Am J Pediatr Hematol Oncol 1991; 13:126–9.

180. Casado-Flores J, Valdivielso-Serna A, Perez-Jurado L, et al. Subclavian vein catheterization in critically ill children: analysis of 322 cannulations. Intensive Care Med 1991; 17:350–4.

181. Sellden H, Lannering B, Marky I, Nilsson K. Long-term use of central venous catheters in paediatric oncology treatment. Acta Anaesthesiol Scand 1991; 35:315–19.

182. Brown R, Millar A, Knobel J, Cywes S. Central venous catheters. Technique and experience at a Red Cross War Memorial Children's Hospital, Cape Town, 1987–1990. S Afr Med J 1991; 80:11–13.

183. Uderzo C, D'Angelo P, Rizzari C, et al. Central venous catheter-related complications after bone marrow transplantation in children with hematological malignancies. Bone Marrow Transplant 1992; 9:113–17.

184. Kohli-Kumar M, Rich A, Pearson A, et al. Comparison of saphenous versus jugular veins for central venous access in children with malignancy. J Pediatr Surg 1992; 27:609–11.

185. Moukarzel A, Haddad I, Ament M, et al. 230 patient years of experience with home long-term parenteral nutrition in childhood: natural history and life of central venous catheters. J Pediatr Surg 1994; 29:1323–7.

186. Barzaghi A, Dell'Orto M, Rovelli A, et al. Central venous catheter clots: incidence, clinical significance and catheter care in patients with hematologic malignancies. Pediatr Hematol Oncol 1995; 12:243–50.

187. Biagi E, Arrigo C, Dell'Orto MG, et al. Mechanical and infective central venous catheter-related complications: a prospective non-randomized study using Hickman and Groshong catheters in children with hematological malignancies. Support Care Cancer 1997; 5:228–33.

188. Kovesi T, Kardos M. Durability of tunnelled central venous catheters in children with malignant diseases. Paediatr Anaesth 1997; 7:353–6.

189. Chua MC, Chan IL. Use of central venous lines in paediatrics: a local experience. Ann Acad Med Singapore 1998; 27:358–62.

190. Fonkalsrud EW, Berquist W, Burke M, Ament ME. Long-term hyperalimentation in children through saphenous central venous catheterization. Am J Surg 1982; 143:209–11.

191. Loeff D, Matlak M, Black R, et al. Insertion of a small central venous catheter in neonates and young infants. J Pediatr Surg 1982; 17:944–9.

192. Sherman M, Vitale D, McLaughlin G, Goetzman B. Percutaneous and surgical placement of fine silicone elastomer central catheters in high-risk newborns. JPEN J Parenter Enteral Nutr 1983; 7:75–8.

193. Grisoni E, Mehta S, Connors A. Thrombosis and infection complicating central venous catheterization in neonates. J Pediatr Surg 1986; 21:772–6.

194. Durand M, Ramanathan R, Martinelli B, Tolentino M. Prospective evaluation of percutaneous central venous silastic catheters in newborn infants with birth weights of 510 to 3920 grams. Pediatrics 1986; 78:245–50.

195. Mactier H, Alroomi LG, Young DG, Raine PAM. Central venous catheterization in very low birthweight infants. Arch Dis Child 1986; 61:449–53.

196. Lally KP, Hardin WD, Boettcher M, et al. Broviac catheter insertion: operating room or neonatal intensive care unit. J Pediatr Surg 1987; 22:823–4.

197. Chathas MK, Paton JB, Fisher DE. Percutaneous central venous catheterization. Am J Dis Child 1990; 144:1246–50.

198. Abdullah F, Dietrich KA, Pramanik AK. Percutaneous femoral venous catheterization in preterm infants. J Pediatr 1990; 117:788–91.

199. Hogan L, Pulito A. Broviac central venous catheters inserted via the saphenous or femoral vein in the NICU under local anesthesia. J Pediatr Surg 1990; 27:1185–8.

200. Roberts J, Gollow I. Central venous catheters in surgical neonates. J Pediatr Surg 1990; 25:632–4.

201. Tanke RB, van Megen R, Daniels O. Thrombus detection on central venous catheters in the neonatal intensive care unit. Angiology 1994; 45:477–80.

202. Vain N, Georgeson K, Cha C, Swarner O. Central parenteral alimentation in newborn infants: a new tech-

nique for catheter placement. J Pediatr 1978; 93:864–6.

203. Effeney D, Friedman MB, Gooding GA. Iliofemoral venous thrombosis: real-time ultrasound diagnosis, normal criteria, and clinical application. Radiology 1984; 150:787–92.

204. Simmons JR, Buzdar AU, Ota DM, et al. Complications associated with indwelling catheters. Med Pediatr Oncol 1992; 20:22–5.

205. Obaido F, Fajardo CA, Cronin C. Recovery of intralipid from lumbar puncture after migration of saphenous vein catheter. Arch Dis Child 1992; 67:1201–3.

206. Schmidt B. The etiology, diagnosis, and treatment of thrombotic disorders in newborn infants: a call for international and multi-institutional studies. Semin Perinatol 1997; 21:86–9.

207. Yadav S, Dutta AK, Sarin SK. Do umbilical vein catheterization and sepsis lead to portal vein thrombosis? A prospective, clinical, and sonographic evaluation. J Pediatr Gastroenterol Nutr 1993; 17:392–6.

208. Wigger H, Bransilver BR, Blanc WA. Thromboses due to catheterization in infants and children. J Pediatr 1970; 76:1–11.

209. Roy M, Turner-Gomes S, Gill G, et al. Incidence and diagnosis of neonatal thrombosis associated with umbilical venous catheters [abstract]. Thromb Haemost 1997; 78:724.

210. Raval NC, Gonzales E, Bhat AM, et al. Umbilical venous catheters: evaluation of radiographs to determine position and associated complications of malpositioned umbilical venous catheters. Am J Perinatol 1995; 12:201–4.

211. Scott JM. Iatrogenic lesions in babies following umbilical vein catheterization. Arch Dis Child 1995; 40:426.

212. Enger E, Jacobsson B, Sorensen SE. Tissue toxicity of intravenous solutions. A phlebographic and experimental study. Acta Pediatr Scand 1976; 65:248–52.

213. Schwartz DS, Gettner PA, Konstantino MM, et al. Umbilical venous catheterization and the risk of portal vein thrombosis. J Pediatr 1997; 131:760–2.

214. Oski FA, Allen DM, Diamond LK. Portal hypertension: a complication of umbilical vein catheterization. Pediatrics 1963; 31:297.

215. Obladen M, Ernst D, Feist D. Portal hypertension in children following neonatal umbilical disorders. J Perinat Med 1975; 3:101–4.

216. Tizard JPM. Portal hypertension following exchange transfusion through the umbilical vein. Proc Soc Exp Biol Med 1962; 55:772.

217. Vos LJM, Potocky V, Broker FWL, et al. Splenic vein thrombosis with oesophageal varices: a late complication of umbilical vein catheterization. Ann Surg 1974; 180:152–6.

218. Evans DJ, Silverman M, Bowley NB. Congenital hypertension due to unilateral renal vein thrombosis. Arch Dis Child 1981; 56:306–8.

219. Pegelow CH, Narvaez M, Toledano SR, et al. Experience with a totally implantable venous device in children. Am J Dis Child 1986; 140: 69–71.

220. Shulman RJ, Rahman S, Mahoney D, et al. A totally implanted venous access system used in pediatric patients with cancer. J Clin Oncol 1987; 5:137–40.

221. Harvey WH, Pick TE, Reed K, Solenberger RI. A prospective evaluation on the Port-A-Cath implantable venous access system in chronically ill adults and children. Surg Gynecol Obstet 1989; 169:495–500.

222. Wilimas JA, Hudson M, Rao B, et al. Late vascular occlusion of central lines in pediatric malignancies. Pediatrics 1998; 101:E7.

223. Poole MA, Ross MN, Haase GM, Odom LF. Right atrial catheters in pediatric oncology: a patient/parent questionnaire study. Am J Pediatr Hematol Oncol 1991; 13:152–5.

224. Montemurro P, Lattanzio A, Chetta G, et al. Increased in vitro and in vivo generation of procoagulant activity (tissue factor) by mononuclear phagocytes after intralipid infusion in rabbits. Blood 1985; 65:1391–5.

225. Mahan JD, Mauer SM, Nevins TE. The Hickman catheter: a new hemodialysis access device for infants and small children. Kidney Int 1983; 24:694–7.

226. Franzone A, Tucker B, Brennan L, et al. Hemodialysis in children. Arch Surg 1971; 102:592–3.

227. Bunchman TE. Pediatric hemodialysis: lessons from the past, ideas for the future. Kidney Int Suppl 1996; 53:S64–7.

228. Sharma A, Zilleruelo G, Abitbol C, et al. Survival and complications of cuffed catheters in children on chronic hemodialysis. Pediatr Nephrol 1999; 13:245–8.

229. Vasmant D, Bourquelot P, Bensman A, et al. Value of the Hickman catheter in pediatric nephrology. Presse Med 1986; 15:429–32.

230. Lumsden AB, MacDonald MJ, Allen RC, Dodson TF. Hemodialysis access in the pediatric patient population. Am J Surg 1994; 168:197–201.

231. Zobel G, Rodl S, Urlesberger R, et al. Continuous renal replacement therapy in critically ill patients. Kidney Int 1998; 66:S169–73.

232. Deerojanawong J, Sawyer SM, Fink AM, et al. Totally implantable venous access devices in children with cystic fibrosis: incidence and type of complications. Thorax 1998; 53:285–9.

233. Morris J, Occhionero M, Gauderer M, et al. Totally implantable vascular access devices in cystic fibrosis: a four-year experience with fifty-eight patients. J Pediatr 1990; 117:82–5.

234. Perkins JL, Johnson VA, Osip JM, et al. The use of implantable venous access devices (IVADs) in children with hemophilia. J Pediatr Hematol Oncol 1997; 19:339–44.

235. Blanchette VS, Al-Musa A, Stain AM, et al. Central venous access devices in children with hemophilia: an update. Blood Coagul Fibrinol 1997; 8(Suppl 1):S11–4.

236. Popp MB, Law EJ, MacMillan BG. Parenteral nutrition in the burned child: a study of twenty-six patients. Ann Surg 1973; 179:219–25.

237. Mathews RA, Park SC, Neches WH, et al. Iliac venous thrombosis in infants and children after cardiac catheterization. Cathet Cardiovasc Diagn 1979; 5:67–74.

238. Barnes CL, Nelson CL, Nix ML, et al. Duplex scanning versus venography as a screening examination in total hip arthroplasty patients. Clin Orthop 1991; 271:180–9.

239. Wells PS, Hirsh J, Anderson DR, et al. Accuracy of clinical assessment of deep vein thrombosis. Lancet 1995; 345:1326–30.

240. Wells PS, Lensing AW, Davidson BL, et al. Accuracy of ultrasound for the diagnosis of deep venous thrombosis in asymptomatic patients after orthopedic surgery. A meta-analysis. Ann Intern Med 1995; 122:47–53.

241. Kellam B, Fraze D, Kanarek K. Clot lysis for thrombosed central venous catheters in pediatric patients. J Perinatol 1987; 7:242–4.

242. Winthrop AL, Wesson DE. Urokinase in the treatment of occluded central venous catheters in children. J Pediatr Surg 1984; 19:536–8.

243. Sivaram CA, Craven P, Chandrasekaran K. Transesophageal echocardiography during removal of central venous line associated thrombus in superior vena cava syndrome. Am J Card Imaging 1996; 10:266–9.

244. Turpie A, Levine M, Hirsh J, et al. A randomized controlled trial of PK10169 low molecular weight heparin for the prevention of deep vein thrombosis in patients undergoing elective hip surgery. N Engl J Med 1986; 315:925–9.

245. Levine M, Hirsh J, Gent M, et al. Prevention of deep vein thrombosis after elective hip surgery: a randomized trial comparing low molecular weight heparin with standard unfractionated heparin. Ann Intern Med 1991; 114:545–51.

246. Spiro T, Enoxaparin Clinical Trials Group. A randomized trial of enoxaparin administered postoperatively for the prevention of deep vein thrombosis following elective hip replacement [abstract]. Thromb Haemost 1991; 65(Suppl):927.

247. Francis C, Marder V, Evarts C, Yaukookbodi S. Two-step warfarin therapy: prevention of postoperative venous thrombosis without excessive bleeding. JAMA 1983; 249:374–8.

248. Sandritter W, Beneke G. Pathology of vein diseases. Internist (Berlin) 1967; 8:377–83.

249. Perlmutt L, Fellows KE. Lower extremity deep vein thrombosis in children. Pediatr Radiol 1983; 13:266–8.

250. Tanaka K, Takao M, Yada I, et al. Alterations in coagulation and fibrinolysis associated with cardiopulmonary bypass during open heart surgery. J Cardiothorac Anesth 1989;3:181–8.

251. Swinton NW Jr., Edgett JW Jr., Hall RJ. Primary subclavian-axillary vein thrombosis. Circulation 1968; 38:737–45.

252. Tilney NI, Griffiths HJG, Edwards EA. Natural history of major venous thrombosis of the upper extremity. Arch Surg 1970; 101:792–6.

253. Painter TD, Karpf M. Deep venous thrombosis of the upper extremity, five years experience at a university hospital. Angiology 1984; 35:743–9.

254. Hull R, Raskob G, Hirsh J, et al. Continuous intravenous heparin compared to intermittent subcutaneous heparin in the initial treatment of proximal vein thrombosis. N Engl J Med 1986; 315:1109–14.

255. Gallus A, Jackaman J, Tillett J, et al. Safety and efficacy of warfarin started early after submassive venous thrombosis or pulmonary embolism. Lancet 1986; 2:1293–6.

256. Hull R, Raskob G, Rosenbloom D. Heparin for 5 days as compared with 10 days in the initial treatment of proximal venous thrombosis. N Engl J Med 1990; 322:1260–4.

257. Franzeck UK, Schalch I, Bollinger A. On the relationship between changes in the deep veins evaluated by duplex sonography and the post thrombotic syndrome 12 years after deep vein thrombosis. Thromb Haemost 1997; 77:1109–12.

258. Andrew M, Vegh P, Johnston M, et al. Maturation of the hemostatic system during childhood. Blood 1992; 80:1998–2005.

259. Siegbahn A, Ruusuvaara L. Age dependence of blood fibrinolytic components and the effects of low-dose oral contraceptives on coagulation and fibrinolysis in teenagers. Thromb Haemost 1988; 60:361–4.

260. Andrew M, deVeber G. Pediatric thromboembolism and stroke protocols. Hamilton, ON: B.C. Decker Inc., 1997.

5 PULMONARY EMBOLISM IN CHILDHOOD

Pulmonary embolism (PE) is a serious complication in adult patients, with considerable morbidity and mortality.[1,2] Several large, well-designed clinical trials have focused on the prevention, diagnosis, and optimal management of PE in adult patients.[3–7] In contrast, the literature on PE in pediatric patients is comprised of case reports and case series, with only a few hundred patients reported in the entire world literature. The epidemiologic features of PE in pediatric patients are poorly described and there are few specific or validated guidelines for the diagnosis or management of PE in children.[8–16]

Over the past two decades, dramatic improvements in tertiary care pediatrics has occurred, resulting in the survival of pediatric patients with diseases that were previously lethal.[17] Paradoxically, the survival of critically ill children has led to new secondary complications that were previously very rare.[17] Thromboembolic events (TEs), which include PE, are one of the most frequent and serious secondary complications, occurring disproportionately in children successfully treated for congenital heart disease (CHD) and cancer.[8] The cause of the increasing incidence of PE in children is likely multifactoral. However, the single most important contributing risk factor is central venous lines (CVLs).[14,17,18] Central venous lines are essential for the provision of supportive care for critically ill children by facilitating the administration of fluids, nutrition, and life saving drugs in patients in whom adequate venous access would not be possible. Second in importance to CVLs as a risk factor for PE is the use of extracorporeal circulation techniques that sustain pediatric patients through acute reversible cardiorespiratory insults that were previously lethal.

For the following chapter on PE, Medline searches of the literature were conducted from 1966 to 1998 using combinations of key words and supplemented by additional references located through the bibliographies of listed articles. All articles were evaluated for the strength of the study design using standardized criteria.[19] Results from studies with stronger study designs were prioritized over results from studies with weaker designs. Information on the epidemiology, diagnosis, treatment, and outcome of PE in children is presented. Future studies, required to improve the diagnosis and management of PE in children, are discussed.[8–12,15]

EPIDEMIOLOGIC FEATURES OF PULMONARY EMBOLUS

The earliest described case of PE in childhood dates back to 1861, when Löschner reported a PE in an 8-year-old child.[20] Despite this, over 130 years later, the number of cases of PE in children reported in the literature number only in the few 100s, restricted mostly to case reports and series. The epidemiologic features of PE in pediatric patients is discussed under the following headings: incidence, etiology and risk factors, clinical presentation, diagnosis, and treatment.

Incidence

Compared to adults, the incidence of PE in children is decreased.[9–15,17,18] The physiologic mechanism(s) contributing to the protective effects for TEs in children are discussed in Chapter 2. The precise incidence of PE in pediatric patients is unknown but is increasing and reflects the evolution of serious secondary complications in children surviving previously lethal diseases. Retrospective autopsy studies have reported overall incidences of PE in children between 0.05 and 4.2 percent.[9–15] The variation in results likely reflects patient selection and the variable techniques (macroscopic versus microscopic) used to detect PE. The largest retrospective chart review reported an incidence of PE of 78 per 100,000 hospitalized adolescents.[11] The only published prospective cohort study reported an incidence of symptomatic PE of 8.6 per 100,000 hospital admissions of children between 1 month and 18 years of age.[17] Clinical studies likely provide a minimal estimate of the incidence of PE in children due to a decreased index of suspicion and absence of standardized diagnostic techniques. Table 5–1 summarizes the available information on the incidence of PE in children with specific diseases.

Etiology and Risk Factors

Risk factors for PE in children can be classified into two broad groups: congenital or acquired prothrombotic disorders and clinical diseases/therapies. Children who develop PE usually have several risk factors that include both congenital and acquired conditions and clinical disease states.

Congenital and Acquired Prothrombotic Conditions

There are no reports that specifically assess the contribution of congenital and acquired prothrombotic

Table 5–1   Incidence of Pulmonary Embolism in Selected Diseases During Childhood

Author	Year	Study Type	Total Number	Specific Disease	Diagnostic Method	Incidence PE (%)
Sanerkin et al[70]	1966	R	330	Newborns	Histology	14
Raman et al[117]	1971	P	30 adults and children	Guillain-Barré syndrome	V/Q scans	33
Egli et al[57]	1973	R	3377	Nephrotic	Clinical	1.8
Hoyer et al[56]	1986	R	26	Asymptomatic Nephrotic	Routine V/Q scans	27
Desat et al[49]	1989	R	178	Fatal burns	Autopsy	1.7
Piat et al[63]	1989	R	32	VA shunts	Clinical	3
Hsu et al[48]	1991	XS	62	Pre-cardiac transplant	V/Q scans, angiography	31
Marraro et al[58]	1991	P	205	Acute leukemia	Digital angiography	3.5
Uderzo et al[43]	1993	R	67	BMT for leukemia	Clinically indicated angiography	4.5
McBride et al[50]	1994	R	28692	Trauma	Clinical	0.000069
Dollery et al[97]	1994	XS	34	Long-term TPN	Routine perfusion scans/CXR	32
Nuss et al[16]	1995	R	61	Thrombosis	Clinically indicated V/Q	20
Derish et al[14]	1995	R	21	ICU deaths	Histology	24
Massicotte et al[18]	1998	P	244	CVL-related thrombosis	Clinically indicated V/Q	18

PE = pulmonary embolism; n = number; TPN = total parenteral nutrition; CXR = chest x-ray; V/Q = ventilation-perfusion scan; CVL = central venous line; ICU = intensive care unit; BMT = bone marrow transplant; VA shunts = ventriculo-atrial shunt; R = retrospective; P = prospective; XS = cross-sectional.

Reproduced with permission from Monagle P, Peters M, Andrew M. Pulmonary embolism in childhood. In: van Beek E, Oudkerk M, ten Cate JW, editors. Pulmonary embolism: epidemiology, diagnosis, and treatment. Oxford: Blackwell Scientific Publishers; 1998.

conditions to PE as distinct from venous thromboembolic events (VTE) in children. Congenital prothrombotic disorders linked with VTE are discussed in detail in Chapter 3 and include deficiencies of protein C, protein S, antithrombin (AT), and plasminogen; dysfibrinogenemias; Factor V Leiden; and prothrombin gene 20210 mutation. The most common acquired prothrombotic disorder linked with VTE in pediatric patients is the presence of antiphospholipid antibodies.[21–30] Congenital prothrombotic disorders have also been identified in children with PE, although the magnitude of the contribution is uncertain but likely significant.[30–34] Similar to adults, the most frequently identified congenital prothrombotic abnormality in children with VTE is the Factor V Leiden mutation.[34] The newly described prothrombin 20210 mutation is a weak risk factor for VTE in adults with an unknown role in pediatric VTE.[35]

A number of retrospective studies and registries have reported incidences of congenital and acquired hypercoagulable conditions in 60 to 77 percent of children with thrombosis.[8] Frequently, multiple abnormalities were detected. However, all of the registries reported incomplete testing of their total cohorts, raising the possibility of selection bias for those children most likely to have congenital prothrombotic conditions. This could result in an overestimation of the true incidence of hypercoagulable conditions in children with VTE. Further, well-designed prospective studies are necessary to determine the incidence more accurately. However, testing for congenital or acquired prothrombotic conditions in children with PE can be recommended at this time, even in the setting of obvious clinical risk factors. The presence of congenital or acquired prothrombotic disorders is important and likely impacts on the risk of recurrent VTE and treatment decisions.

Clinical Diseases and Therapies

Pulmonary embolism is an extension of deep venous thrombosis (DVT) in the extremities that results in some similar epidemiologic features. In contrast to adults in whom 95 percent of PE comes from DVT in the lower limbs,[1–7] PE in children frequently comes from DVT in the upper or central venous systems.[14,17,18] Central venous line-related DVTs are the most common source for PE in children.[14,17,18] In a prospective, population-based registry of VTE in children, the incidence of PE was approximately 18 percent in children with CVL related DVT.[14,17,18] However, in general, children with significant clinical symptoms were investigated for PE, suggesting that the incidence of 18 percent is an underestimate. In the same registry, of the children investigated for PE, the incidence of PE was over 75 percent. Pulmonary embolism may occur while CVLs are in situ, during removal of CVLs, or from residual thrombis following CVL removal.[14,17,18,36] Pulmonary embolism may also occur following thrombolysis of CVL-related right atrial thrombosis.[37]

Other clinical situations in which children develop PE independent of CVLs include cancer,[38–41] bone marrow transplantation,[42,43] CHD,[12,44–46] cardiac bypass and extracorporeal circulation,[47] cardiomyopathy awaiting heart transplantation,[48] major burns,[49] trauma,[50] surgery[51] (especially for large vascular hemangioma),[52,53] nephrotic syndrome,[54–57] leukemia,[43,58] thalassemia major,[59] liver transplantation,[60] sepsis,[61] homocystinuria,[62] and ventriculoatrial shunts.[63] Ventriculoatrial shunts have been replaced by ventriculoperitoneal shunts in part due to the incidence of PE. Neonates may develop PE in these and other clinical situations.[8,64–70]

The frequency of CVL-related DVT/PE in children is sufficient to warrant clinical trials of prophylactic anticoagulant therapy. Studies reporting on the incidence of PE in other clinical scenarios are uniformly small case series with inherent biases that preclude definitive conclusions about the incidence of PE. Large prospective studies are required to determine if the incidence of PE in these other clinical scenarios warrants prophylactic trials or just early identification.

In addition to PE comprised of embolized fibrin thrombi, PE in pediatric patients may comprise other pathologic or iatrogenic materials[71] such as teflon,[72] Intralipid,[73,74] right ventricular myxoma,[75,76] fat, air,[77–79] tumor,[39–41] (especially Wilms' tumor),[38,39,41] brain tissue,[13,14,80] necrotic liver tissue,[81] and bone marrow.[42,43] The specific clinical situation is critically important in identifying the possibility of PE secondary to non-fibrin materials. Unlike PE comprised of fibrin, anticoagulation is not likely necessary in PE comprised of other materials.

Clinical Presentation

Autopsy studies over the last three decades have clearly shown that the clinical diagnosis of PE is rarely made in pediatric patients during life.[8–10,12–14,21] In children, PE frequently presents with minimal symptoms that can be attributed to other co-morbid conditions, or are clinically silent. In one retrospective series, only 50 percent of children had clinical symptoms attributable to PE. However, the diagnosis of PE was considered in only 15 percent of these children.[9] Other case series also report on the subtlety of symptoms of PE in children.[8–10,12,21,56] The clinical symptoms of PE in pediatric patients are usually similar to those in adults and reflect in part the size of the embolus and the general condition of the patient. However, some younger patients are unable to verbalize the symptoms, in which case the diagnosis is dependent on the clinicians assessment of changes in the respiratory status of their patients. Respiratory distress of some type is the most consistent feature.[12,21] Dyspnea, pleuritic chest pain, hemoptysis, shortness of breath, cough, cyanosis, acute right heart failure, hypotension, increasing oxygen requirements, fever, arrhythmias, pallor, and sudden collapse are all linked to the clinical presentation in children with acute PE.[9,11,12,15,38,49,51,55,82] Unfortunately, sudden death may be the initial presentation of PE but may also indicate that more subtle symptoms of PE were not correctly identified.[13,14] Recurrent acute PE may remain undetected until a child presents with chronic pulmonary hypertension or cardiac failure.

The clinical symptoms of PE are not specific and are often similar to clinical symptoms of the underlying disorder, or concurrent illnesses, that cause respiratory deterioration. Examples include sepsis or cardiac failure in critically ill children. Pulmonary embolism should be considered in the differential diagnosis of cardiorespiratory deterioration in all critically ill children.

DIAGNOSIS

The following section discusses the radiographic tests used to diagnose PE and provides a diagnostic approach to PE in pediatric patients. Historically, the diagnosis of PE in children was made primarily by autopsy.[9] Increasing awareness of the clinical symptoms of PE in pediatric patients has increased ante mortem diagnosis. Radiographic tests used to diagnose PE include pulmonary angiogram, ventilation-perfusion (V/Q) scan, magnetic resonance imaging (MRI), Spiral CT (helical computerized tomography), echocardiogram, and others. The clinical utility of these radiographic tests has been studied extensively in adults resulting in useful diagnostic approaches to patients with suspected PE.[3–6] Currently, the diagnostic approach validated in adult patients is extrapolated to children even though there may be important differences in the specificity and sensitivity of specific investigations or diagnostic strategies in children.

Pulmonary Angiography

Pulmonary angiography is the gold standard radiographic test for the diagnosis of PE (Figure 5–1).[83] Pulmonary angiography requires selective catheterization of the pulmonary arteries and injection of radio-opaque contrast media.[5] Pulmonary angiography can be problematic in pediatric patients for a variety of reasons that include technical difficulties in small children, a lack of experience by pediatric radiologists who perform the test infrequently, the presence of complex CHD, and the presence of critical illnesses that increase the risk for complications from the procedure. In adults, the morbidity and mortality from pulmonary angiography are 3 percent and 0.2 percent, respectively,[84] with the presence of severe pulmonary hypertension accounting for most of the fatal complications.[83] The mortality and morbidity in pediatric patients are unknown but present. In order to minimize the risks of pulmonary angiography, it should be restricted to tertiary care pediatric centers where there is adequate experience in catheterizing small children and performing the test. The interpretation of pulmonary

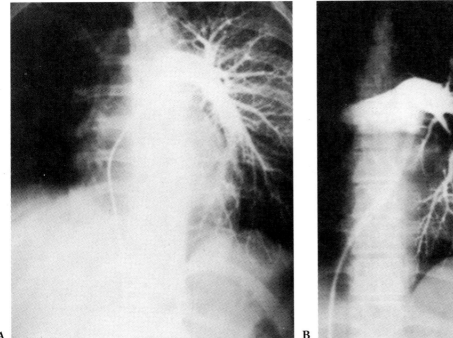
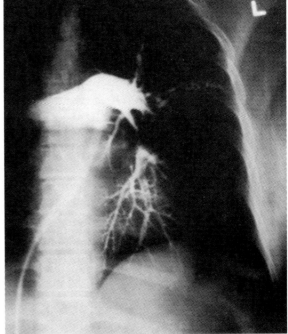

Figure 5–1   *A,* A normal pulmonary angiogram. *B,* Filling defects in major branches of the left pulmonary artery.

Reproduced with permission from Andrew M, deVeber G. Blood clots and strokes: a guide for parents and little folks. Hamilton: B.C. Decker Inc.; 1998.

angiography can also be problematic in children due to the presence of complex CHD and unusual pulmonary disorders as well as a variety of acquired diseases that may influence the interpretation of the angiogram. Pulmonary angiography may be insensitive for small peripheral PE that can be detected by perfusion scanning.[5]

Ventilation-Perfusion Scans

Historically, perfusion scans alone were used for the diagnosis of PE. The introduction of ventilation scans, in combination with perfusion scans, significantly increased the sensitivity and specificity of V/Q scans for the detection of PE. Currently, a V/Q scan is the most frequently used diagnostic test for PE in both adult and pediatric patients (Figure 5–2).

Ventilation scanning is performed by the inhalation of a radioactive gas, most commonly xenon 133 or technetium 99 (^{99}Tc; eg, Technegas), which is then distributed throughout the lung resulting in images that reflect the ventilated areas of the

lung.[3–5] Doses of the isotope based on age and weight are available and result in minimal radiation exposure to critical organs as a result of the procedure.[85] Ventilation scans can be performed in older children in a manner similar to adults that requires holding their breath. In young infants and neonates reliable images can be obtained through continuous tidal breathing with little or no cooperation.[85]

Perfusion scanning is performed by injecting particles labeled with radioactive isotope, most commonly ^{99}Tc Macroaggregated Albumin (MAA).[86] The mean particle size is 30 microns and, when injected intravenously, ^{99}Tc labeled MAA particles temporarily block approximately 1 in 1,000 pulmonary capillaries and precapillary arterioles. The average particle size guarantees first pass entrapment in the lungs, with their distribution reflecting regional pulmonary blood flow. The biological half life of the labeled MAA is 2 to 9 hours and scintillation counts provide images reflecting pulmonary blood flow. Perfusion scanning is very safe in patients of all ages; however, the technique of

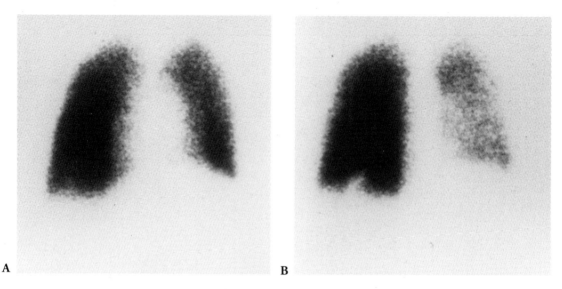

A   B

Figure 5–2   *A,* A normal ventilation scan. *B,* An abnormal perfusion scan.

Reproduced with permission from Andrew M, deVeber G. Blood clots and strokes: a guide for parents and little folks. Hamilton: B.C. Decker Inc.; 1998.

temporary obstruction of capillaries used for perfusion scanning has important implications for children.[85] Adult lungs contain over 290×10^9 capillaries and the number of particles injected ranges from 2×10^5 to 10^6. Neonates have significantly reduced numbers of pulmonary capillaries that increase rapidly during early infancy. Adult levels are probably reached around the end of the first decade. The injection of 2×10^5 to 10^6 particles of MAA into a neonate could cause increased occlusion of capillaries and potentially cause severe hypoxia. High specific activity ^{99}Tc labeled particles in age-related doses should be used to minimize this risk.[85] The mean particle size should be kept below 50 microns. The risk of perfusion scan induced hypoxia is accentuated in children with severe diffuse pulmonary disease and advanced pulmonary hypertension.[85] Severe pulmonary hypertension results in arterial thickening and reduction in vessel lumen size such that higher order arterioles may be occluded by the MAA particles.[87] Although such adverse reactions are exceptionally rare, a fatal reaction has been reported in a 7-year-old child. A similar theoretical concern exists in children with right to left cardiac shunts.[85] The MAA particles may pass across the shunt and be lodged in the cerebral circulation.[88] In an experimental model, animals, in which high dose MAA was injected directly into the internal carotid arteries, developed acute and chronic cerebral changes. This risk remains theoretical as cerebral hypoxia secondary to perfusion scanning has never been demonstrated clinically in a child.

The classification of V/Q scans in children is directly extrapolated from results in adults and can be categorized as high, intermediate, or low probability for PE (Table 5–2). The sensitivity and specificity of V/Q scans for the detection of PE has not been assessed in children and there are some unique underlying diseases that may influence the interpretation of V/Q scans. For example, V/Q scans may be difficult to interpret in children with CHD characterized by imbalanced pulmonary blood flow between the left and right lungs, or even within each lung.[88] Children with left to right shunts may have variable distribution of the isotope due to the mixture of arterial blood in the pulmonary arteries.[88] Coexistent peripheral pulmonary artery stenosis may be confused with multiple PE.[89]

Pulmonary Arterial Flow Studies

This technique is an extension of nuclear angiocardiography and is useful for indicating obstruction of the central pulmonary arteries. ^{99m}Tc-diethylene-triamine pentaacetic acid is the usual radionucleotide. The method is not widely used.[83]

Table 5–2 Criteria for Ventilation-Perfusion Scan Diagnosis of Pulmonary Embolism

Hull[5]	PIOPED[3]	PISA-PED[4] Perfusion Scans Only
High probability 1 or more segmental V/Q mismatch or large subsegmental mismatch	High probability 2 or more large (> 75%) segmental V/Q mismatches 2 or more moderate (25–75%) segmental V/Q mismatches and 1 large mismatch 4 or more moderate segmental mismatches	PE +ve: abnormal scan consistent with PE Single or multiple wedge shaped perfusion defects of any size
Non high probability 1 or more matched V/Q defects or small subsegmental mismatch	Indeterminate probability Not high or low Low probablility Nonsegmental perfusion defects Single moderate V/Q mismatch/normal CXR Any perfusion defect with larger CXR abnormality Large or moderate matched defects 3 or more small segmental perfusion defects with normal CXR	PE -ve: abnormal scan not compatible with PE Single or multiple perfusion defects that are not wedge shaped
	Very low probability 3 or less small segmental perfusion defects with normal CXR	Near normal Perfusion defects smaller or equal in size to CXR abnormalities
Normal No ventilation or perfusion defects	Normal No perfusion defects	Normal No perfusion defects

PIOPED = Prospective Investigation of Pulmonary Embolism Diagnosis; PISA-PED = Prospective Investigative Study of Acute Pulmonary Embolism Diagnosis; V/Q = ventilation/perfusion scan; +ve = positive; -ve = negative; CXR = chest x-ray.

Reproduced with permission from Monagle P, Peters M, Andrew M. Pulmonary embolism in childhood. In: van Beek E, Oudkerk M, ten Cate JW, editors. Pulmonary embolism: epidemiology, diagnosis, and treatment. Oxford: Blackwell Scientific Publishers; 1998.

Magnetic Resonance Imaging and Helical Computerized Tomography

Magnetic resonance imaging and Spiral CT are potentially useful techniques for evaluating abnormalities of the pulmonary vasculature but must be regarded as investigational and not definitive tests for the diagnosis of PE in children at this time. MRI and Spiral CT are currently being evaluated in adults, and no studies in children have been published.[90,91]

Echocardiography

Echocardiographic diagnosis of PE can be useful for the direct imaging of PE in the central pulmonary arteries.[92] Indirect indices of more peripheral PE provided by echocardiography include increased right ventricular volume or pressure.[92] However, the presence of structural cardiac defects or a past history of cardiovascular disease makes these findings

Table 5–3 Electrocardiogram Abnormalities Possibly Associated with Pulmonary Embolism in Children

S > 1.5 mm in I and aVL or R/S < 1

Q in III and aVF, but not II

Negative T in III, aVF, V1–V5

Right bundle branch block

ST elevation in V1

Upright T waves in V1

QRS < 5 mm in all limb leads

Transition in V5 or V6

Frontal QRS > 90°

Indeterminate axis

Right atrial hypertrophy

Atrial arrhythmia

Reproduced with permission from Monagle P, Peters M, Andrew M. Pulmonary embolism in childhood. In: van Beek E, Oudkerk M, ten Cate JW, editors. Pulmonary embolism: epidemiology, diagnosis, and treatment. Oxford: Blackwell Scientific Publishers; 1998.

less specific. Echocardiography is of value in detecting intracardiac thrombi, which, if present, provides indirect evidence for the diagnosis of PE.

Electrocardiograms

Table 5–3 provides a list of electrocardiogram (ECG) abnormalities caused by PE. Although ECGs can be useful adjunctive screening tools for PE, the findings are nonspecific.[92] The same ECG changes are present in children with some forms of CHD as well as acquired cardiac conditions. In addition, normal age-related changes in ECG may make interpretation of these abnormalities difficult. The presence of multiple abnormalities on ECG has been suggested to increase the diagnostic specificity of ECG, although this approach has not gained widespread acceptance.[92,93]

D-dimers

D-dimers are increasingly used in the diagnosis of TEs in adults and are particularly useful for their negative predictive value.[94] There are no similar studies in children with VTEs. However, the usefulness of D-dimers in the diagnosis of VTE in pediatric patients is likely to be considerably less than for adults because the majority of children with VTE have serious systemic illnesses such as cancer or cardiac disease that would result in positive D-dimers.

Additional Studies

Additional investigations, such as blood gas analysis and chest radiography, lack both sensitivity and specificity for PE. However, these tests do provide useful information about the cardiorespiratory system.[2]

Diagnostic Strategy for Pulmonary Embolism in Children

The accurate diagnosis of PE in children is important because the presence of PE necessitates treatment with anticoagulants to prevent the risk of mortality. The absence of PE eliminates the need for anticoagulants, which spares children being exposed to an unnecessary risk of bleeding. With the exception of pulmonary angiography, no single investigation can reliably diagnose PE in the majority of clinical circumstances. Pulmonary angiography is infrequently used in pediatric patients due to the invasiveness, high cost, and limited availability of the technique.[2]

A combination of clinical probability of PE and V/Q scans provides a sensitive and specific approach to the diagnosis of PE in adults. The central concept is that clinical signs and symptoms in a patient are important and can influence the pretest probability of PE.[95] The subsequent results of a diagnostic test, such as V/Q scans, do not tell us whether a PE is present but they do modify the pretest probability yielding the post-test probability of PE. The direction and magnitude of this change in probability are due to the specific properties of the investigation being used. Previously, the terms sensitivity (proportion of people with the disease in whom the test is positive) and specificity (proportion of people without the disease in whom the test is negative) were used to describe the clinical utility of investigations. A more simple and useful measure of the accuracy with which a test identifies the disease in question is the likelihood ratio (LR).[95] Likelihood ratios indicate by how much a given test result will increase or decrease the pretest probability. Although the calculation of post-test probability from pretest probability and LR involves conversion of proportions to and from odds, the use of this principle is greatly simplified by published nomograms.[95]

The pretest probability has been shown to have a major influence on the diagnostic process for patients with suspected PE. Although some of the guidelines for pretest clinical probability of PE in adults will apply to children, there are many age and disease dependent differences in the risk for PE that necessitate separate guidelines for children. For example, a child with a CVL-related DVT is probably a high clinical-risk patient, regardless of the presence or absence of clinical symptoms. Increasing appreciation of the subtle signs associated with PE in children and current ongoing studies will hopefully improve the clinical accuracy of predicting PE in children.

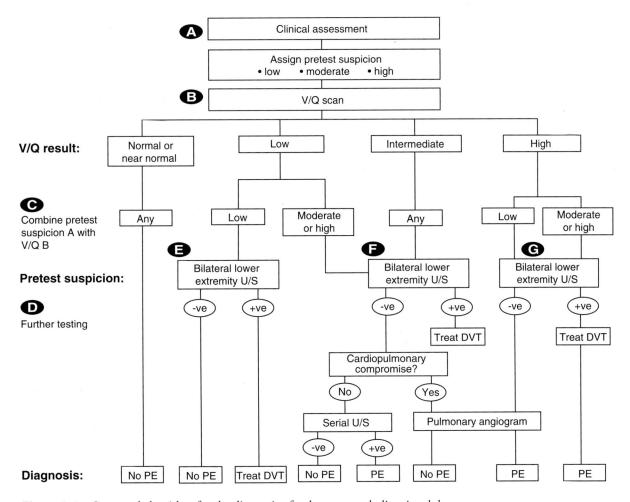

Figure 5–3   Suggested algorithm for the diagnosis of pulmonary embolism in adults.

Ventilation-perfusion scanning is the most frequently used, and useful, noninvasive radiographic technique for the investigation of PE in children. In adult patients, if the clinical probability of PE is thought to be intermediate or high, then a high-probability V/Q scan confirms the diagnosis and further testing is not required. If the clinical probability of PE is low and the V/Q scan is low-probability, then the diagnosis of PE is unlikely. In the setting of an intermediate scan, or high clinical suspicion yet a low-probability scan, then further information is required. Adult algorithms for this scenario frequently involve the use of lower limb venography (Figure 5–3) or Doppler ultrasound to detect any DVT, the source of emboli. Prospective studies evaluating the combination of pretest clinical probability with V/Q scans for the diagnosis of PE in children will be required to validate this promising approach.

Even in the absence of prospective studies, a practical approach to the diagnosis of PE in children is possible using the same principles as for adults. Figure 5–4 provides a suggested algorithm for diagnosing PE in children. In children with suspected PE, a V/Q scan should be performed whenever feasible. If the V/Q scan is high probability for PE, this can be generally accepted as diagnostic for PE and anticoagulant therapy should be instituted. If the V/Q scan is normal, this can be generally accepted as diagnostic for the absence of PE. If the V/Q scan is indeterminate, further tests are required. If a CVL is in place in the upper venous system, a venogram (Figure 5–5) and compression ultrasound of the jugular veins should be performed. If a thrombus is detected, anticoagulation therapy should be instituted. If the CVL is in the lower venous system, ultrasound can be used to screen for DVT. If the ultrasounds are normal, either follow-up ultrasounds

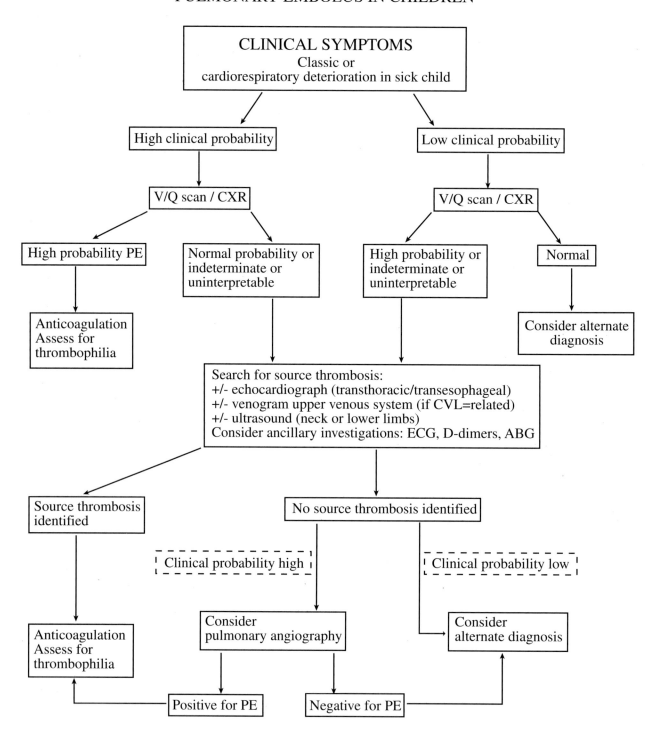

Figure 5–4   Suggested algorithm for the diagnosis of PE in children.

V/Q = ventilation perfusion scan; CXR = chest X-ray; PE = pulmonary embolism; CVL = central venous line; ECG = electrocardiogram; ABG = analysis blood gas.

Reproduced with permission from Monagle P, Peters M, Andrew M. Pulmonary embolism in childhood. In: van Beek E, Oudkerk M, ten Cate W, editors. Pulmonary embolism: epidemiology, diagnosis, and treatment. Oxford: Blackwell Scientific Publishers; 1998.

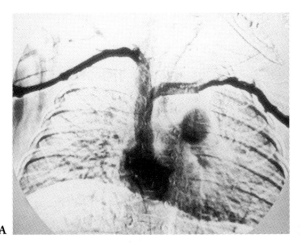
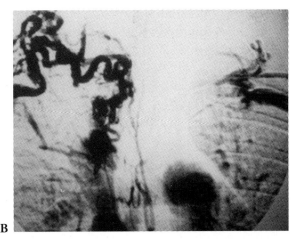

A   B

Figure 5–5   *A,* A venogram done on a child, showing the normal vascular architecture of the upper system. *B,* An abnormal venogram of the upper system.

Reproduced with permission from Andrew M, deVeber G. Blood clots and strokes: a guide for parents and little folks. Hamilton: B.C. Decker Inc.; 1998.

or bilateral venograms should be considered depending on the strength of the clinical concern for PE. Serial testing is usually not required for venogram negative patients. In addition, an echocardiogram should be considered, particularly if there is underlying congenital or acquired heart disease.

Other tests are used to detect DVT but may be insensitive for certain locations. For example, ultrasound is relatively insensitive for DVT in the proximal subclavian, innominate vein, and superior vene cava but likely quite sensitive for DVT in the jugular veins, axillary veins, and proximal veins draining the lower limbs. The differential sensitivity

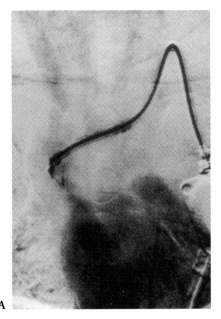
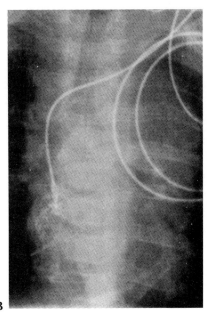

A   B

Figure 5–6   *A,* A normal lineogram in a child with a central venous catheter. *B,* A central venous line with a clot at its tip.

Reproduced with permission from Andrew M, deVeber G. Blood clots and strokes: a guide for parents and little folks. Hamilton: B.C. Decker Inc.; 1998.

by location for ultrasound likely reflects the ability or lack thereof to compress veins. Lineograms (contrast injected through a CVL) are also insensitive in diagnosing CVL-related DVT except if there is a clot at the tip of the CVL (Figure 5–6).[96,97] Electrocardiogram and D-dimers may add further useful information but are unlikely to positively confirm the diagnosis of PE.

If the V/Q scan is uninterpretable due to abnormal pulmonary blood flow secondary to cardiac disease, either structural or functional, then the demonstration of a source thrombosis associated with clinical symptoms of PE is usually enough to warrant a positive diagnosis and subsequent therapy. In some instances, pulmonary angiography is necessary to establish the diagnosis.

Evaluation for Congenital or Acquired Prothrombotic Conditions

When the diagnosis of PE is conclusive, pediatric patients should generally be evaluated for the presence of congenital or acquired prothrombotic disorders, even in the presence of definitive acquired risk factors for PE. Table 5–4 provides suggested minimal investigations for prothrombotic disorders. Indefinite oral anticoagulant (OA) therapy with an international normalized ratio (INR) of 2.0 to 3.0, low-dose anticoagulant therapy (INR < 2.0), or close monitoring are options for children with a continuing risk factor following initial therapy.

TREATMENT

General Information

Treatment of acute PE is comprised of general supportive care and specific therapy for the PE. Supportive care consists of adequate cardiorespiratory support and is not discussed further. Specific management for PE includes one or more of the following interventions: unfractionated heparin (UFH) or low-molecular-weight heparin (LMWH), OAs, thrombolytic therapy, a filter, and embolectomy.

The extent and resolution of the initial PE is important when considering indefinite therapy with anticoagulants. For example, children with extensive PE that does not resolve following an extended period of treatment may have little pulmonary reserve, increasing the risk of death from further PE.

Unfractionated Heparin

As for adult patients, anticoagulation remains the mainstay of therapy for PE in pediatric patients.[98] Guidelines for anticoagulation therapy for PE in pediatric patients are similar to those for any VTE, with initial therapy comprised of intravenous UFH (or LMWH). The recommended therapeutic range for activated partial thromboplastin time (APTT) values in children with PE are extrapolated from adults and consist of APTT values that reflect an UFH concentration of 0.2 to 0.4 units/mL (by protamine titration) or 0.35 to 0.7 units/mL (by an anti-factor Xa assay).[99] Because APTT reagents have differing sensitivities to UFH, coagulation laboratories must standardize their therapeutic UFH range (Chapter 9).[99] In pediatric patients, APTT values correctly predict plasma concentrations of UFH for approximately 70 percent of values.[100] A modified nomogram for adjusting UFH has been validated for children (Chapter 9).[100,101] Treatment with UFH should be continued for a minimum of 5 days and longer if the PE or DVT is extensive. In general, pediatric patients with PE require 7 to 10 days of UFH with OA therapy deferred until at least 5 days of UFH with therapeutic APTT values is completed.

Table 5–4   Suggested Hypercoagulable Screen for Children with Pulmonary Embolism

Known thrombophilic conditions
    Protein C deficiency
    Protein S deficiency
    Antithrombin deficiency
    Activated protein C resistance/factor V Leiden mutation
    Prothrombin gene 20210 mutation
    Antiphospholipid antibodies/lupus anticoagulant
    Dysfibrinogenemia

Possible thrombophilic conditions
    Elevated lipoprotein (a)
    Elevated serum homocysteine
    Plasminogen deficiency
    Increased histidine-rich glycoprotein
    Heparin cofactor II deficiency

Reproduced with permission from Monagle P, Peters M, Andrew M. Pulmonary embolism in childhood. In: van Beek E, Oudkerk M, ten Cate JW, editors. Pulmonary embolism: epidemiology, diagnosis, and treatment. Oxford: Blackwell Scientific Publishers; 1998.

Oral Anticoagulation Therapy

Oral anticoagulation therapy with either warfarin, phenprocoumon, or acenocoumarol is one option for the 3 to 6 months of anticoagulation required for the treatment of PE following initial therapy with UFH.[98] OAs should be overlapped with UFH for a minimum of 5 days. For some patients, UFH and OA therapy can be started together and UFH therapy discontinued on day 6 if the INR is therapeutic (INR 2.0 to 3.0) for 2 consecutive days. However, for extensive PE, 7 to 10 days of UFH therapy should be considered and the initiation of OA therapy delayed. Long-term OA therapy should be continued for a minimum of 3 months, or longer for extensive PE. If OAs are used, the target INR range is 2.0 to 3.0. Validated nomograms for adjusting OA therapy in children have been published (Chapter 10).[98]

Low-Molecular-Weight Heparin

Clinical trials in adults have established that LMWHs offer several advantages over UFH that may benefit children (Chapter 9).[102] Dosing guidelines for two LMWHs are established in children and neonates (Chapter 9).[103,104] The target therapeutic anti-factor Xa range is 0.50 to 1.0 units/mL when the sample is taken 4 to 6 hours following the morning dose. Current studies are examining the efficacy and safety of LMWH for three months versus UFH followed by OA therapy for the treatment of DVT/PE in children (Chapter 9). The outcome of these studies will further define the role of LMWH in the treatment of PE in pediatric patients.

Thrombolytic Therapy

In most adults with PE thrombolytic therapy is not indicated because their clinical outcome with anticoagulant therapy alone is good and thrombolytic therapy is associated with increased cost and risk of bleeding. Thrombolysis is usually only considered in adults with massive PE, where syncope, hypotension, severe hypoxemia, or heart failure are present.[102] Similarly, patients with submassive embolism but severe underlying cardiac or respiratory disease may derive lifesaving benefit from thrombolytic therapy.[2] The guidelines for the use of thrombolytic therapy in adults with PE are based on randomized controlled trials assessing the efficacy and safety of thrombolytic therapy.[1,2] Corresponding studies in pediatric patients have not been conducted. Guidelines for adults with PE are not likely optimal for pediatric patients because of age dependent differences in the fibrinolytic system, which influences the response to thrombolytic agents.[105–108] Also, the risk of hemorrhagic complications from thrombolytic agents may also differ from adults, with an increased risk in the premature infant. The risk/benefit ratio of thrombolytic therapy for PE in pediatric patients remains unknown. Several case reports and small case series have reported successful thrombolysis in children using urokinase (UK) or tissue plasminogen activator (TPA).[37,49,109,110] The thrombolytic agents were administered either by local pulmonary artery–directed catheters or systemic intravenous infusions and were generally used in combination with UFH therapy. The optimal dose and duration of thrombolytic therapy is unknown, and there is a wide range of published dose schedules, usually supported by only individual case reports (Chapter 11). The bleeding risk from thrombolytic therapy in children depends on the underlying clinical disease and likely the duration of thrombolytic therapy (Chapter 11). There are no trials that have compared therapy with thrombolytic agents to anticoagulation alone in pediatric patients. Currently, thrombolytic therapy cannot be generally recommended as first line therapy for PE in all pediatric patients. The decision to use thrombolytic therapy should be individualized and considered in children with large, new PE, particularly if the PE is hemodynamically compromising. Concurrent anticoagulation therapy with either UFH or LMWH should be considered. Guidelines for thrombolytic therapy in pediatric patients are provided in Chapter 11.

Embolectomy

Embolectomy has been used successfully in pediatric patients as young as 6 days old and often following major cardiac surgery.[61,111,112] For example, embolectomy following Fontan surgery is used when the cause of obstructed pulmonary blood flow is not clear and exploratory surgery is required. Other circumstances in which embolectomy should be considered is in the presence of massive PE with severely compromised pulmonary circulation. Embolectomy should always be followed by an appropriate period of anticoagulation due to the substantial risk of recurrent TEs.

Caval Filters

Caval filters are commonly used in adults as secondary prophylaxis to prevent PE when anticoagulation therapy is contraindicated or has failed to prevent further PE. Caval filters can be used in children, although obviously decreasing age and size increases the technical challenge. However, the usefulness of caval filters in children is limited because the majority of DVT associated with PE are not in the lower limbs. Safe placement of a filter to prevent PE from a central venous or intracardiac TE associated with a CVL is usually impossible. Case reports of successful and failed caval filters in children have been published.[50,113,114] In contrast to adults, temporary filters are often used in children and removed when the source of PE is gone or anticoagulation therapy can be used.[113]

Primary Prophylaxis for Pulmonary Embolism

The role of primary anticoagulant prophylaxis in children at risk for TEs and subsequent PE is unknown. International trials that will determine the potential benefit of prophylactic anticoagulation in children with CVLs, systemic lupus erythematosus (SLE), or following Fontan surgery are underway and will begin to delineate the optimal role of prophylactic anticoagulation therapy in the prevention of PE.

OUTCOME

Some authors have suggested that the mortality from PE may be decreased in pediatric patients compared to adult patients due to a superior physiologic tolerance to PE.[1,9] However, the Canadian Childhood Thrombophilia Registry recently reported its experience with CVL-related DVT. Of the 39 children

diagnosed with PE, 20 percent died as a result of the PE. Half of the children who died received no treatment, whereas half died despite aggressive therapy. The majority of survivors received antithrombotic therapy. Very few children in the registry were investigated for PE, so the results are likely biased towards the more severe PE. Nevertheless, the PE-related mortality in this study is consistent with adult estimates of mortality in untreated PE. Chronic pulmonary hypertension and resultant cardiac failure are well-described clinical presentations of multiple undiagnosed PE in children.[114,115] The recurrence rate for PE in children is uncertain but likely depends on the underlying risk factors, the effectiveness of primary antithrombotic treatment, and the duration of therapy. There are no data on the long-term effects of PE on pulmonary function in children. Further studies are required to accurately determine the long-term sequelae of PE in children.

CONCLUSION

1. The frequency of PE is probably underestimated in children.
2. Children with PE often have multiple risk factors for thrombotic events, which may consist of clinical diseases, therapies, and underlying hypercoagulable conditions. The most important clinical risk factor identified is the presence of CVL-related thrombosis.
3. The clinical features of PE in children are often subtle or masked by their primary illness. Increased diagnostic suspicion is required to prevent mortality and morbidity from undiagnosed PE.
4. Diagnostic strategies for PE in children are extrapolated from studies in adults. The positive and negative predictive values of a number of investigations may be reduced in children due to physiologic and pathophysiologic differences between children and adults.
5. Anticoagulation is the mainstay of therapy for children with PE, based mostly on extrapolation from data in adults. Until such time as specific studies in children provide more relevant treatment guidelines, therapy needs to be individualized.

6. The outcome for children with PE is uncertain; however, the mortality probably is similar to that reported in adults with PE.0

REFERENCES

1. Carson J, Kelley M, Duff A, et al. The clinical course of pulmonary embolism. N Engl J Med 1992;326:1240–5.
2. Hirsh J, Hoak J. Management of deep vein thrombosis and pulmonary embolism: a statement for healthcare professionals. From the Council on Thrombosis (in consultation with the Council on Cardiovascular Radiology), American Heart Association. Circulation 1996;93:2212–45.
3. PIOPED Investigators. Value of the ventilation/perfusion scan in acute pulmonary embolism. Results of the prospective investigation of pulmonary embolism diagnosis. JAMA 1990;263:2753–9.
4. The PISA-PED Investigators. Invasive and noninvasive diagnosis of pulmonary embolism: preliminary results of the prospective investigative study of acute pulmonary embolism diagnosis (PISA-PED). Chest 1995;107:33S–8S.
5. Hull RD, Hirsh J, Carter CJ, et al. Pulmonary angiography, ventilation perfusion lung scanning and venography for clinically suspected pulmonary embolism with abnormal perfusion lung scan. Ann Intern Med 1983;98:891–9.
6. Hull RD, Raskob GB, Coates G, et al. A new noninvasive management strategy for patients with suspected pulmonary embolism. Arch Intern Med 1989;149:2549–55.
7. Hull RD, Raskob GB, Ginsberg JS, Panju AA. A noninvasive strategy for the treatment of patients with suspected pulmonary embolism. Arch Intern Med 1994;154:289–97.
8. Monagle P, Peters M, Andrew M. Pulmonary embolism in childhood. In: van Beek E, Oudkerk M, ten Cate JW, editors. Pulmonary embolism: epidemiology, diagnosis, and treatment. Oxford: Blackwell Scientific Publishers; 1998.
9. Buck JR, Connor RH, Cook WW, et al. Pulmonary embolism in children. J Pediatr Surg 1981;16:385–91.
10. Emery JL. Pulmonary embolism in children. Arch Dis Child 1962;37:591–5.
11. Bernstein D, Coupey S, Schonberg S. Pulmonary embolism in adolescents. Am J Dis Child 1986;140:667–71.
12. Jones RH, Sabiston DC. Pulmonary embolism in childhood. Monogr Surg Sci 1966;3:35–51.
13. Byard RW, Cutz E. Sudden and unexpected death in infancy and childhood due to pulmonary thromboembolism. Arch Pathol Lab Med 1990;114:142–4.
14. Derish MR, Smith DW, Frankel LR. Venous catheter thrombus formation and pulmonary embolism in children. Pediatr Pulmonol 1995;20:349–54.
15. Mathew D, Levin M. Pulmonary thromboembolism in children. Intensive Care Med 1986;12:404–6.
16. Nuss R, Hays T, Manco-Johnson M. Childhood thrombosis. Pediatrics 1995;96:291–4.
17. Andrew M, David M, Adams M, et al. Venous thromboembolic complications (VTE) in children: first analyses of the Canadian Registry of VTE. Blood 1994;83:1251–7.
18. Massicotte MP, Dix D, Monagle P, et al. Central venous catheter related thrombosis (CVL-related DVT) in children: analysis of the Canadian Registry of Venous Thromboembolic Complications. J Pediatr 1998;133:770–6.
19. Guyatt GH, Cook DJ, Sackett DL, et al. Grades of recommendations for antithrombotic agents. Chest 1998;114:441S–4S.
20. Löschner. Phlebitis venae cruralis sinistrae, peri-et myocarditis, embolia et oedema pulmonum. Jahrb f Kenderh 1861;4:66.
21. David M, Andrew M. Venous thromboembolism complications in children: a critical review of the literature. J Pediatr 1993;123:337–46.
22. Kwong T, Leonidas JC, Ilowite NT. Asymptomatic superior vena cava thrombosis and pulmonary embolism in an adolescent with SLE and antiphospholipid antibodies. Clin Exp Rheumatol 1994;12:215–7.
23. Nuss R, Hays T, Chudgar U, Manco-Johnson M. Antiphospholipid antibodies and coagulation regulatory protein abnormalities in children with pulmonary embolism. J Pediatr Hematol Oncol 1997;19:202–7.
24. Berube C, David M, Laxer R, et al. The relationship of antiphospholipid antibodies to thromboembolic disease in systemic lupus erythematosus in children: a cross-sectional study. Pediatr Res 1998;44:351–6.
25. Manco-Johnson MJ, Nuss R. Lupus anticoagulant in children with thrombosis. Am J Hematol 1995;48:240–3.
26. Montes de Oca MA, Babron MC, Bletry O, et al. Thrombosis in systemic lupus erythematosus: a French collaborative study. Arch Dis Child 1991;66:713–7.
27. Pelkonen P, Simell O, Rasi V, Vaarala O. Venous thrombosis associated with lupus anticoagulant and anticardiolipin antibodies. Acta Paediatr Scand 1988;77:767–72.
28. St Clair W, Jones B, Rogers JS, et al. Deep venous thrombosis and a circulating anticoagulant in systemic lupus erythematosus. Am J Dis Child 1981;135:230–2.
29. Bernstein ML, Salusinsky Sternbach M, Bellefleur M, Esseltine DW. Thrombotic and hemorrhagic com-

plications in children with the lupus anticoagulant. Am J Dis Child 1984;138:1132–5.

30. Sternberg TL, Bailey MK, Lazarchick J, Brahen NH. Protein C deficiency as a cause of pulmonary embolism in the perioperative period. Anesthesiology 1991;74:364–6.

31. Miletich J, Prescott S, White R, et al. Inherited predisposition to thrombosis. Cell 1993;72:477–80.

32. Sifontes MT, Nuss R, Hunger SP, et al. The factor V Leiden mutation in children with cancer and thrombosis. Br J Haematol 1997;96:484–9.

33. Sifontes MT, Nuss R, Jacobson LJ, et al. Thrombosis in otherwise well children with the factor V Leiden mutation. J Pediatr 1996;128:324–8.

34. Sifontes MT, Nuss R, Hunger SP, et al. Activated protein C resistance and the factor V Leiden mutation in children with thrombosis. Am J Hematol 1988;57:29–32.

35. Hillarp A, Zoller B, Svensson PJ, Dahlback B. The 20210 A allele of the prothrombin gene is a common risk factor among Swedish outpatients with verified deep venous thrombosis. Thromb Haemost 1997;78:990–2.

36. Rockoff M, Gang DL, Vancanti JP. Fatal pulmonary embolism following removal of a central venous catheter. J Pediatr Surg 1984;19:307–9.

37. Zureikat GY, Martin GR, Silverman NH, Newth CJL. Urokinase therapy for a catheter-related right atrial thrombus and pulmonary embolism in a 2-month-old infant. Pediatr Pulmonol 1986;2:303–6.

38. Bulas DI, Thompson R, Reaman G. Pulmonary emboli as a primary manifestation of Wilm's tumour. Am J Roentgenol 1991;56:155–6.

39. Zakowski M, Edwards RH, McDonough ET. Wilms' tumor presenting as sudden death due to tumor embolism. Arch Pathol Lab Med 1990;114:605–8.

40. Booth A, Tweed CS. Fatal pulmonary embolism due to osteogenic sarcoma in a child. Clin Radiol 1989;40:533–5.

41. Akyon MG, Arslan G. Pulmonary embolism during surgery for a Wilms' tumour (nephroblastoma). Case report. Br J Anaesth 1981;53:903–5.

42. Allen BT, Day DL, Dehner LP. CT demonstration of asymptomatic pulmonary emboli after bone marrow transplantation. Case report. Pediatr Radiol 1987;17:65–7.

43. Uderzo C, Marraro G, Riva A, et al. Pulmonary thromboembolism in leukaemic children undergoing bone marrow transplantation. Bone Marrow Transplant 1993;11:201–3.

44. Olson M, Driscoll DJ, Edwards WD, et al. Pulmonary microthrombi. Caveat for successful modified Fontan operation. J Thorac Cardiovasc Surg 1993;106:739–44.

45. Rosenthal TN, Bulbul ZR, Friedman AH, et al. Thrombosis of the pulmonary artery stump after distal ligation. J Thorac Cardiovasc Surg 1985;110:1563–5.

46. Svane S. Primary thrombosis of pulmonary artery in a child wtih tetralogy of Fallot. Br Heart J 1977;39:815–9.

47. Fink SM, Bockman DE, Howell CG, et al. Bypass circuits as the source of thromboemboli during extracorporeal membrane oxygenation. J Pediatr 1989;115:621–4.

48. Hsu D, Addonizio L, Hordof A, Gersony W. Acute pulmonary embolism in pediatric patients awaiting heart transplantation. J Am Coll Cardiol 1991;17:1621–5.

49. Desat MH, Linares HA, Herndon DN. Pulmonary embolism in burned children. Burns 1989;15:376–80.

50. McBride WJ, Gadowski GR, Keller MS, Vane DW. Pulmonary embolism in pediatric trauma patients. J Trauma 1994;37:913–5.

51. Goodman NW, Falkner MJ. Massive introperative pulmonary embolism in a child. Br J Anaesth 1987;59:1059–62.

52. Eberhard DA. Two-year-old boy with *Proteus* syndrome and fatal pulmonary thromboembolism. Pediatr Pathol 1994;14:771–9.

53. Machin GA, Kent S. Pulmonary thromboembolism from a large hemangioma in a 4-week-old infant. Pediatr Pathol 1989;9:73–8.

54. Zimmerman RL, Novek S, Chen JT, Roggli V. Pulmonary thrombosis in a 10-year-old child with minimal change disease and nephrotic syndrome. Am J Clin Pathol 1994;101:230–6.

55. Jones GL, Hebert D. Pulmonary thrombo-embolism in the nephrotic syndrome. Pediatr Nephrol 1991;5:56–8.

56. Hoyer PF, Gonda S, Barthels M, et al. Thromboembolic complications in children with nephrotic syndrome. Acta Paediatr Scand 1986;75:804–10.

57. Egli F, Elminger P, Stalder G. Thrombosis as a complication of nephrotic syndrome. Helv Paediatr Acta 1973;30:20–1.

58. Marraro G, Uderzo C, Marchi P, et al. Acute respiratory failure and pulmonary thrombosis in leukemic children. Cancer 1991;3:696–702.

59. Landing BR, Nadorra R, Hyman CB, Ortega JA. Pulmonary lesions of thalassemia major. Perspec Pediatr Pathol 1987;11:82–96.

60. Gossey S, van Obbergh L, Weynand B, et al. Platelet aggregates in small lung vessels and death during liver transplantation. Lancet 1991;338:532–4.

61. Gorlach G, Hager K, Mulch J, et al. Surgical therapy of pulmonary thrombosis due to candidiasis in a premature infant. J Cardiovasc Surg 1986;27:341–3.

62. Brandstetter Y, Weinhouse E, Splaingard ML, Tang TT. Cor pulmonale as a complication of methylmalonic

acidemia and homocystinuria. Am J Med Genet 1990;36:167–71.

63. Piat JH, Hoffman HJ. Cor pulmonale: a lethal complication of ventriculoatrial CSF diversion. Childs Nervous System 1989;5:29–31.

64. Plotz RD. Neonatal pulmonary microaggregates and thrombi. Lack of correlation with blood transfusion. Am J Clin Pathol 1987;87:380–3.

65. Mirkin LD, Wong RC. Intrauterine infarction of a pulmonary segment in a full term newborn. A case report. Am J Clin Pathol 1993;100:701–3.

66. Clapp S, Bedard M, Farooki ZQ, Arciniegas E. Pulmonary artery thrombus associated with the ductus arteriosus. Am Heart J 1986;111:796–7.

67. Wesley JR, Keens TG, Miller SW, Platzker AC. Pulmonary embolism in the neonate: occurrence during the course of total parenteral nutrition. J Pediatr 1978;93:113–5.

68. Levin DL, Weinberg AG, Perkin RM. Pulmonary microthrombi syndrome in newborn infants with unresponsive persistent pulmonary hypertension. J Pediatr 1983;102:299–303.

69. Szymonowicz W, Preston H, Yu VY. The surviving monozygotic twin. Arch Dis Child 1986;61:454–8.

70. Sanerkin NG, Edwards P, Jacobs J. Pulmonary thrombo-embolic phenomena in the newborn. J Pathol Bacteriol 1966;91:569–74.

71. Williams RA. High incidence of pulmonary foreign body embolism. Pediatr Pathol 1992;12:479–80.

72. Weingarten J, Kauffman SL. Teflon embolization to pulmonary arteries. Ann Thorac Surg 1977;23:371–3.

73. Hulman G, Levene M. Intralipid microemboli. Arch Dis Child 1986;61:702–3.

74. Mughal MZ, Robinson MJ, Duckworth W. Neonatal fat embolism and agglutination of Intralipid. Arch Dis Child 1984;59:1098–9.

75. Gonzalez A, Altieri PI, Marquez EU, et al. Massive pulmonary embolism associated with a right ventricular myxoma. Am J Med 1980;69:795–8.

76. Parker K, Embry J. Sudden death due to tricuspid valve myxoma with massive pulmonary embolism in a 15-month old male. J Forensic Sci 1997;42:524–6.

77. Fenton TR, Bennett S, McIntosh N. Air embolism in ventilated very low birthweight infants. Arch Dis Child 1988;63:641–3.

78. Lee SK. Pulmonary vascular air embolism in the newborn. Arch Dis Child 1989;64:507–10.

79. Leicht CH, Waldman J. Pulmonary air embolism in the pediatric patient undergoing central catheter placement: a report of two cases. Anesthesiology 1986;64:519–21.

80. Pillay SV. Pulmonary embolism of cerebral tissue in a neonate. A case report. S Afr Med J 1980;58:498.

81. Brooks SE, Taylor E, Golden MH, Golden BE. Electron microscopy of herpes simplex hepatitis with hepato-cyte pulmonary embolization in Kwashiorkor. Arch Pathol Lab Med 1991;115:1247–9.

82. Nichols MM, Tyson KR. Saddle embolus occluding pulmonary arteries. Am J Dis Child 1978;132:926.

83. Hackbarth R, Kulms L, Sarniak A. Central pulmonary embolism with normal ventilation perfusion scan: diagnosis by nuclear pulmonary artery flow studies. Ann Emerg Med 1991;20:95–7.

84. Mills SL, Jackson DC, Older RA. The incidence, etiologies and avoidance of complications of pulmonary angiography in a large series. Radiology 1980;136:295–9.

85. Papanicolaou N, Treves S. Pulmonary scintigraphy in pediatrics. Semin Nucl Med 1980;10:259-285.

86. Ryan KL, Fedullo PF, Davis GB. Perfusion scan findings understate the severity of angiographic and hemodynamic compromise in chronic thromboembolic pulmonary hypertension. Chest 1988;93:1180–5.

87. Vincent WR, Goldberg SJ, Desilets D. Fatality immediately following rapid infusion of macroaggregates of ^{99m}Tc albumin (MAA) for lung scan. Radiology 1968;91:1180–4.

88. Mishkin F, Knote J. Radioisotope scanning of the lungs in patients with systemic pulmonary anastomoses. Am J Roentgenol Radium Ther Nucl Med 1968;102:267–73.

89. Hurley RJ, Wesselhoeft H, James AE. Use of nuclear imaging in the evaluation of pediatric cardiac disease. Semin Nucl Med 1972;2:353–72.

90. Meaney JFM, Weg JG, Chenvert TL, et al. Diagnosis of pulmonary embolism with magnetic resonance angiography. N Engl J Med 1997;335:1422–7.

91. van Rossum AB, Treurniet FE, Kieft GJ, et al. Role of spiral volumetric computed tomography scanning on the assessment of patients with clinical suspicion of pulmonary embolism and an abnormal ventilation/perfusion lung scan. Thorax 1996;51:23–8.

92. Pollard AJ, Sreeram N, Wright JG, et al. ECG and echocardiographic diagnosis of pulmonary thromboembolism associated with central venous catheters. Arch Dis Child 1995;73:147–50.

93. Dollery CM, Sullivan I, Bull K, Milla P. ECG and echocardiographic diagnosis of pulmonary thromboembolism associated with central venous lines (letter). Arch Dis Child 1996;75:169.

94. Demers C, Ginsberg J, Johnston M, et al. D-dimer thrombin-antithrombin III complexes in patients with clinically suspected pulmonary embolus. Thromb Haemost 1992;67:408–12.

95. Jaeschke R, Guyatt GH, Sackett DL, Evidence-Based Medicine Working Group. III. How to use an article about a diagnostic test. B. What are the results and will they help me in caring for my patients. JAMA 1994;271:703–7.

96. Andrew M, Marzinotto V, Pencharz P, et al. A cross-sectional study of catheter-related thrombosis in children receiving total parenteral nutrition at home. J Pediatr 1995;126:358–63.

97. Dollery CM, Sullivan ID, Bauraind O, et al. Thrombosis and embolism in long-term central venous access for parenteral nutrition. Lancet 1994;344:1043–5.

98. Michelson AD, Bovill E, Monagle P, Andrew M. Antithrombotic therapy in children. Chest 1998; 114:748S–69S.

99. Hirsh J. Heparin. N Engl J Med 1991;324:1565–74.

100. Andrew M, Marzinotto V, Blanchette V, et al. Heparin therapy in pediatric patients: a prospective cohort study. Pediatr Res 1994;35:78–83.

101. Cruickshank M, Levine M, Hirsh J, et al. A standard heparin nomogram for the management of heparin therapy. Arch Intern Med 1991;151:333–7.

102. Ginsberg JS. Management of venous thromboembolism. N Engl J Med 1996;335:1816–28.

103. Massicotte P, Adams M, Marzinotto V, et al. Low molecular weight heparin in pediatric patients with thrombotic disease: a dose finding study. J Pediatr 1996;128:313–8.

104. Massicotte MP, Adams M, Leaker M, Andrew M. A nomogram to establish therapeutic levels of the low molecular weight heparin (LMWH), clivarine in children requiring treatment for venous thromboembolism (VTE) [abstract]. Thromb Haemost 1997;77(Suppl):282.

105. Andrew M, Paes B, Milner R, et al. Development of the human coagulation system in the full-term infant. Blood 1987;70:165–72.

106. Andrew M, Paes B, Johnston M. Development of the hemostatic system in the neonate and young infant. Am J Pediatr Hematol Oncol 1990;12: 95–104.

107. Andrew M, Vegh P, Johnston M, et al. Maturation of the hemostatic system during childhood. Blood 1992; 80:1998–2005.

108. Andrew M, Paes B, Milner R, et al. Development of the human coagulation system in the healthy premature infant. Blood 1988;72:1651–7.

109. Beitzke A, Zobel G, Zenz W, et al. Catheter-directed thrombolysis with recombinant tissue plasminogen activator for acute pulmonary embolism after Fontan operation. Pediatr Cardiol 1996;17:410–2.

110. Pyles LA, Pierpont ME, Steiner ME, et al. Fibrinolysis by tissue plasminogen activator in a child with pulmonary embolism. J Pediatr 1990;116:801–4.

111. Putnam JB, Lemmer JH, Rocchini AP, Bove EL. Embolectomy for acute pulmonary artery occlusion following Fontan procedure. Ann Thorac Surg 1988;45:335–6.

112. Moreno-Cabral RJ, Breitweser JA. Pulmonary embolectomy in the neonate. Chest 1983;84:502–4.

113. Khong PL, John PR. Technical aspects of insertion and removal of an inferior vena cava IVC filter for prophylactic treatment of pulmonary embolus. Pediatr Radiol 1997;27:239–41.

114. Soares EA, Landell GA, de Oliveira JA. Subacute cor pulmonale in children: report of two cases. Pediatr Pulmonol 1992;12:52–7.

115. McMahon D, Aterman K. Pulmonary hypertension due to multiple emboli. J Pediatr 1978;92:841–5.

116. Andrew M, deVeber G. Blood clots an strokes: a guide for parents and little folks. Hamilton, (ON): B.C. Decker Inc.; 1998.

117. Raman TK, Blake JA, Harris TM. Pulmonary embolism in Landry-Guillain-Barré-Strohl syndrome. Chest 1971;60:555–7.

6

ARTERIAL THROMBOEMBOLIC COMPLICATIONS IN PEDIATRIC PATIENTS

Arterial thromboembolic events (TEs) in children are, with few exceptions, iatrogenic complications that occur in children being treated for serious primary diseases. The majority of arterial injuries occur in association with arterial catheters, arteriography, and needling procedures to obtain blood samples.[1,2] The clinically significant incidence of TEs following these procedures is not surprising since the vessels are usually very small and the children very ill.[2] Arterial TEs usually require urgent treatment, owing to pending organ or limb loss, and present management dilemmas because of the limited information on optimal treatment. The diagnostic and therapeutic approaches to arterial TEs during childhood are frequently extrapolated from adult guidelines. In doing so, clinicians assume that the epidemiology and results of treatment for arterial TEs are similar in children and adults, which is unlikely. A Medline search of the literature from 1966 to 1998 was performed and is the basis of this following chapter. Arterial TEs are classified as either catheter related or non-catheter related, with the former being relatively common and the latter relatively rare.

CATHETER-RELATED ARTERIAL THROMBOEMBOLIC COMPLICATIONS

Arterial catheterizations are performed in children for diagnostic, therapeutic, and monitoring purposes. There are three main types of arterial catheterizations performed: (1) peripheral arterial catheters in the intensive care setting; (2) umbilical artery catheterization (UAC) in newborns; and (3) cardiac catheterization (CC) in children with congenital heart disease (CHD) or acquired conditions. Typical complications of arterial catheters at all locations are TEs, stenosis, and infection.

Mechanisms

Several mechanisms likely contribute to TE following arterial catheterizations including activation of the coagulation system induced by catheter surfaces, damaged endothelial cell surfaces, or intimal injuries at sites of introduction of arterial catheters. Activation of the coagulation system generates thrombin, which results in fibrin formation and activation of platelets, which may form occlusive thrombi or simply coat catheters. Subsequently, when catheters are removed, the platelet-fibrin coat may strip off as the catheter is withdrawn through the small entry-site hole in the artery leaving a fully or partially occluding thrombus.[3-6] On occasion, the introduction of guide wires or catheters may cause subintimal dissection and intimal flap formation, with subsequent thrombus formation.[7] Arterial spasm may occur when catheters are introduced into arteries or manipulated, which disrupts blood flow, contributing to thrombus formation.[7,8] Some substances infused through arterial catheters are thrombogenic.[9,10]

Several strategies for decreasing the thrombogenicity of arterial catheters have been evaluated. First, the composition of catheters was altered.[11-13] Catheters constructed of polyurethane and silicone elastomere appear to be less thrombogenic than polyvinyl chloride catheters.[11-13] A second strategy for reducing the thrombogenicity of catheters was altering their surface properties. Precoating catheters with albumin was ineffective for the prevention of TE.[14] Bonding catheters with unfractionated heparin (UFH) was assessed in several studies in adults and may reduce the incidence of TEs if catheters are in place for very short periods of time.[15,16] Unfractionated heparin bonded UACs for newborns, as compared to polyvinyl chloride UACs, did not reduce the incidence of aortic TE assessed by ultrasound.[11] Protection from TE offered by UFH-bonded catheters should not be overestimated, particularly when catheters are left in place for over 24 hours.[16]

Peripheral Arterial Catheters

Figure 6–1 shows the arterial supply to the body. The radial artery is the most common site of entry for peripheral artery catheters in children. The dorsalis pedis and posterior tibial arteries are used occasionally, usually when there is no access via the radial arteries.[17]

The reasons for cannulating peripheral arteries in modern pediatric intensive care units (ICUs) are for the purposes of blood gas analyses, continuous monitoring of oxygen saturation and blood pressure, and to facilitate repetitive blood sampling. Occlusion of peripheral arterial catheters is problematic because of the need to replace them and the potential ischemic insult to the involved limb, which frequently is the hand. Prior to the placement of a radial artery catheter, assessment of arterial flow to the hand via the ulnar artery is important and can be clinically assessed by the Allen test, which consists of simultaneous pressure to radial and ulnar arteries sufficient to obstruct flow to the hand.[18] Pressure on the ulnar artery is released and subsequent flow to the hand assessed.[18] The incidence of TEs of peripheral arterial catheters in the absence of UFH is influenced by catheter material[11-13,15,16] duration of placement,[19] diameter,[19] length,[20] solutions infused,[20] concentration of UFH,[21] and arterial site.[20]

Incidence and Prevention of Arterial Catheter-Related Thromboembolic Events in Adults

Table 6–1 summarizes the studies that assess the incidence of TEs of peripheral arterial catheters in adults.[19,20,22,23] The incidence of peripheral artery catheter-related TEs in adults is reported in four studies that also assess the role of UFH in maintaining catheter patency (see Table 6–1). Early studies showed that intermittent flushes of UFH did not provide adequate prevention of loss of peripheral

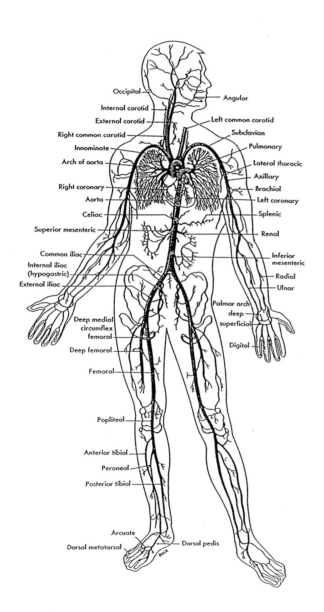

Figure 6–1 Anatomy of the arterial blood supply to the body.

Table 6–1 Thrombotic Complications of Peripheral Arterial Catheters in Adults

Author	Design	Intervention	Number	Duration of Patency	Loss of Patency (%)
Downs et al[19]	RCT	UFH-B	10	122 ± 16 h	
		Teflon	10	166 ± 20 h*	NR
Clifton et al[23]	RCT	UFH 12 u/h	151	86% at 96 h*	2.0*
		NaCl	108	52% at 40 h	8.0
AACN Nurses[20]	RCT	UFH	2573	90% at 72 h*	6.2*
		NaCl	2464	79% at 72 h	12.0
Kulkarni et al[22]	RCT	UFH 2 u/mL	40	92% at 96 h*	7.5*
		NaCl	38	74% at 96 h	19.0

RCT = randomized controlled trial; UFH = unfractionated heparin; AACN = American Association of Critical Care Nurses; NaCl = sodium chloride; NR = not reported; B = bonded.

*$p < 0.05$.

arterial catheter patency. Subsequent studies compared continuous infusions of fluids that either contained or did not contain UFH and showed that continuous infusions of UFH preserved arterial catheter patency.[19,20,22,23] The following provides a summary of the key studies that describe the benefits of low-dose UFH infusions for the preservation of peripheral arterial catheter patency in adults. Downs et al compared UFH-bonded (UFH-B) polyethylene catheters to Teflon catheters with all patients receiving 6 units per hour of UFH.[19] The results showed that Teflon catheters were more thrombogenic than polyethylene catheters, even when the latter were UFH bonded. Clifton et al compared saline flushes to UFH for the prevention of occlusion of peripheral arterial catheters in 259 patients.[23] Following 96 hours, 86% of catheters flushed with UFH-supplemented saline were patent whereas only 52% of catheters flushed with saline alone were patent at 40 hours. The American Association of Critical Care Nurses (AACN) Thunder Project evaluated UFH and non-UFH flush solutions in 5037 adults in a randomized, multicenter trial.[20] Unfractionated heparin-flushed catheters had a probability of remaining patent of 0.97 (97% chance) at 24 hours, decreasing to a probability of 0.90 by 72 hours. Nonheparinized catheters had a probability of remaining patent of 0.93 (93%) at 24 hours, dropping to a probability of 0.79 (79%) at 72 hours. Arterial pressure-monitoring catheters maintained with UFH flush solutions had a signif-

icantly greater probability of remaining patent over time compared to catheters maintained with non-UFH flush solutions.[20] Kulkarni et al compared UFH to saline for the prevention of occlusion of peripheral arterial catheters in 78 adults. Following 96 hours, 92% of catheters flushed with UFH-supplemented saline were patent as compared to 74% of catheters flushed with saline alone.[22]

Incidence and Prevention of Arterial Catheter-Related Thromboembolic Events in Children
The incidence of peripheral artery catheter-related TEs in children has been reported in three studies, some of which also assessed the role of specific interventions to maintain catheter patency (Table 6–2).[21,24,25] Butt et al assessed a flow rate of 2 mL per hour and 1 mL per hour in 319 patients and reported that there was no significant difference for duration of catheter patency.[21] However, increasing the concentration of UFH from 1 to 5 units/mL (n = 154) significantly prolonged catheter patency.[21] Sellden et al assessed intermittent versus continuous flushing with UFH-containing solutions in 338 patients less than 1 year of age with radial arterial catheters.[24] Catheters were removed because of malfunction in 76% of patients receiving intermittent flushes compared to 52% of patients receiving continuous infusions of UFH.[24] In a randomized controlled trial (RCT), Rais-Bahrami et al evaluated premature catheter removal in 60 newborns with peripheral arterial catheters.[25] Patency of peripheral

Table 6–2 Thrombotic Complications of Peripheral Arterial Catheters in Children

Author	Design	Intervention	Number	Duration of Patency	Loss of Patency (%)
Butt et al[21]	RCT	UFH 1 u/mL 1 mL/h	164	33.5 h	NR
		UFH 1 u/mL 2 mL/h	152	40.8 h	
		UFH 5 u/mL 5 mL/h	154	43.5 h*	
Rais-Bahrami et al[25]	RCT	UFH-D 1 u/mL	3030	39 h*	NR
		UFH-NaCl 1 u/mL		107 h	
Sellden et al[24]	R	UFH-I 12.5 u/mL	296	2.8 d*	76*
		UFH-C 5.0 u/mL	42	6.3 d	52

UFH = unfractionated heparin; I = intermittent; C = continuous; RCT = randomized controlled trial; R = retrospective; D = dextrose; NaCl = sodium chloride; NR = not reported.

*$p < 0.05$.

arterial catheters was prolonged in infants receiving UFH normal saline flushes compared to UFH dextrose flushes.[25] Heulitt et al compared solutions containing or not containing papaverine in 239 children, ages 3 weeks to 18 years;[26] 93% of catheters receiving papaverine-supplemented solutions were patent as compared to 78% of catheters without papaverine supplementation.[26] Tarry et al identified 44 cases of peripheral arterial TEs secondary to catheterization in children with nephrotic syndrome.[27] Among these patients, TEs were caused by vessel trauma secondary to attempted blood sampling in nine cases (20%).[27]

Clinical Presentation and Diagnosis   Careful monitoring of temperature, color, and capillary refill time of the hand or foot is important for early detection of arterial catheter-related TEs. Thromboembolic events in the radial artery usually do not result in loss of the entire hand unless the ulnar artery is absent.[28] Acute impairment of arterial blood flow to the hand or foot is characterized by diminished or absent pulses, a prolonged capillary refill time, and a cool, pale hand or foot. Doppler ultrasound usually is used to provide confirmation of the TE.

Prevention   Based upon current evidence, low-dose UFH therapy administered, preferably by continuous infusion, can be recommended to prolong patency of peripheral arterial catheters.[19–25]

Treatment   When peripheral catheter-related TEs occur, the catheter needs to be removed immediately in most circumstances.[19–23,25] Anticoagulants and thrombolytic agents commonly are used, but there is essentially no information on optimal use of these agents in children with peripheral arterial TEs. Chapters 9, 10, and 11 provide further information on the use of anticoagulation and thrombolytic agents in children.

Umbilical Artery Catheterizations

Arterial access in sick premature newborns is necessary for blood gas analyses, continuous monitoring of oxygen saturation and blood pressure, and to facilitate repetitive blood sampling. In newborns, the umbilical artery is the most commonly chosen site, because of size and ease of access (Figure 6–2). Complications of UAC placement include TE, vasospasm, bleeding, infection, and hypertension.[10,29] Thromboembolic events associated with UACs include necrotizing enterocolitis secondary to mesenteric artery occlusion, embolic events to the lower limbs, and embolic events to the central nervous system (CNS) via a right-to-left shunt, such as a patent foramen ovale.

Position of Umbilical Artery Catheter Tips There has been considerable debate as to the best position for UAC tips. In general, positions are considered as

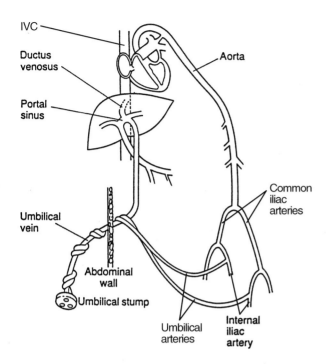

Figure 6–2 Anatomy of the umbilical artery and its course into the aorta.

"high," with UAC tips between T6 and T10, and "low," with UAC tips between L3 and L5. High UACs are reported to function better with fewer complications.[30–37] However, the complications may be more serious, since a local thrombus may affect the celiac, mesenteric, and renal arteries. The clinical relevance of these TEs is uncertain and major artery TEs can still occur with UACs in a low position.[38–40] In a large retrospective survey of UAC practices, with 117 respondents, 44% expressed a preference for high and 44% for low positioning of UAC tips; 12% had no preference.[41] Two RCTs assessed the relation between placement of UAC tip (high or low) and both blockage and necrotizing enterocolitis (Table 6–3).[37,42] The Umbilical Artery

Catheter Trial Study Group reported no significant difference in the incidence of necrotizing enterocolitis or intracranial hemorrhage (ICH) or death, between high or low placement of UACs (see Table 6–3).[37] In a randomized study of 308 patients with UACs by Kempley et al, the incidence of necrotizing enterocolitis was not influenced by high or low placement of UACs within the aorta.[42] Umbilical artery catheters with tips high in the aorta were in place for longer periods of time compared to UACs low in the aorta, which also were associated with an increased rate of lower limb blanching and cyanosis.[42] At this time, there is no convincing evidence that the location of the tip of UACs influences the incidence of TEs.[30,41–45]

Diagnosis The gold standard test for the diagnosis of UAC-related TEs is contrast angiography,[46] which, unfortunately, rarely is feasible. A low index of suspicion is apparent, as evidenced by a disturbingly large proportion of aortic TEs diagnosed at autopsy.[39,46,47] Noninvasive imaging techniques, such as Doppler ultrasound, are attractive because of their ease of performance at the bedside. However, the validity of these techniques has not been established. The need to critically assess these diagnostic tests was illustrated in a study where real-time ultrasound failed to visualize aortic TEs in four patients, three of whom had complete aortic obstruction by contrast angiography.[48]

Incidence The reported incidence of UAC-related TEs reflects, in large part, the choice of diagnostic tool. The five forms of diagnosis of UAC-related TEs include clinical symptoms (Table 6–4), loss of patency (Table 6–5), ultrasound (Table 6–6), angiography (Table 6–7), and autopsy (Table 6–8).

Table 6–3 Positioning of Umbilical Artery Catheters

Author	Design	Position	Number	Blockage (%)	Necrotizing Enterocolitis (%)
UACT Group[37]	RCT	High	481	4.8	2.5
		Low	489	3.1	2.0
Kempley et al[42]	RCT	High	162	1.2	6.7
		Low	146	8.2	6.6

UACT = Umbilical Artery Catheter Trial; RCT = randomized controlled trial.

*p < .05.

Clinical Presentation The clinical presentation of UAC TEs varies depending on the extent of the thrombosis and involvement of other arteries. The majority of infants are clinically asymptomatic or with minor symptoms, whereas a small percentage have major symptoms of severe ischemia to the legs and selected organ dysfunction. The incidence of major clinical symptoms secondary to UACs is approximately 1% to 5% of catheterized infants (Table 6–4).[11,44,49–52]

Table 6–4 Incidence of Thromboembolism in Children with Umbilical Artery Catheters as Assessed by Clinical Signs

Author	Design	Intervention	Number	Clinical	Incidence (%)
Alpert et al[49]	R	No UFH	507	Major	1
O'Neill et al[50]	R	No UFH	4000	Major	1
Stringel et al[44]	R	NR	100	Major	3
			100	Minor	32
Caeton et al[51]	R	NR	100	Major	5
				Minor	46
Jackson et al[11]	RCT	UHF-B	61	Minor	17
		PVC	64	Minor	17
Cohen et al[52]	R	No UFH	166	Minor	1.2

UFH = unfractionated heparin; B = bonded; PVC = polyvinyl chloride; R = retrospective; RCT = randomized controlled trial; NR = not reported.

Table 6–5 Incidence of Thromboembolism in Children with Umbilical Artery Catheters as Assessed by Catheter Patency

Author	Design	Intervention	Number	Incidence
Rajani et al[54]	RCT	UFH 1 u/mL	32	12.5%*
		D/NaCI	30	63.3%
David et al[55]	RCT	UFH 1 u/mL	23	13%*
		D/NaCI	26	58%
Bosque et al[56]	RCT	UFH-C 1 u/mL	18	0%*
		UFH-I 1 u/mL	29	13.8%
Jackson et al[11]	RCT	UFHB-PU	61	NR
		PVC	64	
Horgan et al[57]	RCT	UFH 1 u/mL	59	4%*
		No UFH	52	19%
Horgan et al[57]	RCT	UFH 1 u/mL	59	16 TE
		No UFH	52	18 TE
UCACT Group[37]	RCT	NR	970	3.9%
Ankola et al[58]	RCT	UFH 0.25 u/mL	15	13%*
		D/NaCl	15	73%
Kempley et al[42]	RCT	No UFH	308	4.5%
Fletcher et al[30]	PC	NR	582	8.2%
Hall et al[53]	R	No UFH	80	8.8%

UFH = unfractionated heparin; UFHB-PU = unfractionated heparin bonded polyurethane; PVC = polyvinyl chloride; UFH-C = unfractionated heparin-continuous; UFH-I = unfractionated heparin-intermittent; RCT = randomized controlled trial; PC = prospective cohort; R = retrospective; TE = thromboembolic event; D = dextrose; NaCl = sodium chloride; NR = not reported.

*$p < .05$.

Table 6–6 Incidence of Thromboembolism in Children with Umbilical Artery Catheters as Assessed by Ultrasound

Author	Design	Intervention	Number	Incidence (%)	Clinically Asymptomatic (%)
Oppenheimer et al[59]	PC	UFH	71	14	17
Seibert et al[60]	PC	NR	81	26	29
Horgan et al[57]	CC	UFH	59	27	NR
		D	52	35	
Jackson et al[11]	RCT	UFHB-PU	61	22	NR
		PVC	64	36	

PC = prospective cohort; CC = case control; UFH = unfractionated heparin; D = dextrose; NR = not reported; RCT = randomized controlled trial; UFHB-PU = unfractionated heparin bonded polyurethane catheters; PVC = polyvinylchloride.

Table 6–7 Incidence of Thromboembolism in Children with Umbilical Artery Catheters as Assessed by Angiography

Author	Design	Intervention	Number	Incidence (%)
Olinsky et al[66]	PC	NR	30	30
Neal et al[34]	PC	UFH 2 u/mL	64	28
Mokrohisky et al[31]	PC	UFH 2 u/mL	73	28
Saia et al[67]	PC	NR	38	26
Goetzman et al[62]	PC	No UFH	98	24
Wesstrom[33]	PC	LEH	71	0
		SEH		26
		LSH		33
		SSH		64

PC = prospective cohort; LEH = long end-hole catheters; SEH = short end-hole catheters (SHE), long side-hole catheters; SSH = short side-hole catheters; NR = not reported; u/mL = units per millilitre; UFH = unfractionated heparin.

Loss of Patency   There are nine studies that assessed the incidence of UAC-related aortic TEs, based on loss of UAC patency (see Table 6–5).[11,30,37,42,53–58] All studies were either prospective studies or RCTs in which the potential benefits of UFH were assessed. The incidence of loss of patency ranged from 13% to 73% in the absence of UFH and from 0% to 13% in the presence of UFH.

Ultrasound   Four studies assessed the incidence of UAC-related aortic TEs using ultrasound (see Table 6–6).[11,57,59,60] All studies prospectively used ultrasound to screen for UAC-related aortic TEs and attempted to identify risk factors. The incidence of ultrasound-detected TE ranged from 14% to 36%, with a wide variation in the percentages of clinically symptomatic TEs. The latter likely reflected differing definitions of clinical symptoms, such as

loss of patency versus arterial compromise to a limb. Jackson et al evaluated heparin-bonded catheters versus the catheter in standard use.[11] Outcome was assessed by ultrasound (Doppler sphygmomanometer) at 3 and 11 days of age. On day 3, ultrasound disclosed aortic TEs in five (6%) patients. By day 11, 22% and 36% of the two groups showed TEs. There was no significant difference between the two groups of patients. Most of the ultrasound-detected UAC aortic TEs appeared to be sleeve clots. Ultrasound also has been used extensively to confirm the presence and management of UAC-related aortic TEs.[48,61–63]

Some studies assessed the influence of UACs on flow in large arteries that branch from the aorta into critical organs. Shah et al studied blood flow velocity in the superior mesenteric artery in 32 premature infants with UACs, using duplex pulsed

Table 6–8 Incidence of Thromboembolism in Children with Umbilical Artery Catheters as Assessed by Autopsy

Author	Design	Intervention	Number	Incidence (%)
Henriksson et al[68]	R	NR	18	28
Tooley[39]	R	UFH	123	23
Joseph et al[47]	R	NR	129	19
Wigger et al[69]	R	UR	116	17
Marsh et al[70]	R	NR	165	9

R = retrospective; UFH = unfractionated heparin; NR = not reported.

Doppler ultrasound.[64] Insertion and removal of UACs, aspiration of blood from UACs, and bolus infusion of fluids into the UACs did not diminish blood flow velocity or increase vascular resistance in the superior mesenteric artery. Glickstein et al used two-dimensional echocardiography (2D ECHO) with pulsed Doppler to evaluate renal blood flow velocities in premature newborns with and without UACs.[65] They concluded that even in the absence of clinical symptoms, UAC-related aortic TEs caused abnormalities in renal hemodynamics.

Angiography In six prospective angiographic studies, the incidence of UAC-related TE ranged from 0% to 64% (Figure 6–3)(see Table 6–7).[31,33,34,62,66,67]

Autopsy Only five autopsy studies since 1970 were identified (see Table 6–8).[39,47,68–70] Four of the five autopsy studies were published in the 1970s[39,68–70] and one in the 1980s.[47] None were reported in the 1990s. The incidence of UAC-related TEs ranged from 9% to 28% with the most recent study reporting an incidence of 19%.[47]

Prevention Placement of UACs is one of the very few instances where UFH prophylaxis is used in newborns to maintain vessel patency and prevent symptomatic TEs. The effectiveness of low-dose UFH infusions was evaluated in seven well-designed studies (Table 6–9).[11,54–58] Patency, which likely is linked to the presence of local TEs, was prolonged by the use of low-dose UFH.[54–58] Local TEs, detected by ultrasound, were not decreased in two studies; however, the power was insufficient to detect a difference of 20%.[11,57] Unfractionated heparin-bonded UACs were compared to polyvinyl chloride catheters in a RCT comprising 125 neonates.[11] The results showed that UFH-bonded UACs did not significantly reduce the incidence of clinical complications or prolongation of patency.[11] The lack of efficacy for UFH-bonded UACs may reflect a longer duration in vivo than for catheters previously assessed in adults.[15]

Relationship between Heparin Prophylaxis and Intracranial Hemorrhage Three studies assessed the relation between low-dose UFH infusions and ICH (Table 6–10).[45,71,72] In the first study, a retro-

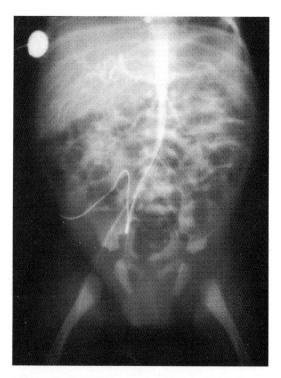

Figure 6–3 Angiogram showing thrombosis secondary to an umbilical artery catheter.

Table 6–9 Clinical Trials Assessing Heparin's Capacity to Reduce Catheter-Related Thrombotic Complications

Reference	Design	Intervention	Number	Outcome	
				Event (P or TE)	Bleeding
Rajani et al[54]	RCT	UFH	32	4 P*	NR
		No UFH	30	19 P	NR
David et al[55]	RCT	UFH	2626	3 P*	0-
		No UFH		15 P	0-
Bosque et al[56]	RCT	UFH-C	1819	0 P	NR
		UFH-I		8 P	NR
Jackson et al[11]	RCT	UFHB-PU	6164	13 TE	NR
		PVC		23 TE	NR
Horgan et al[57]	RCT	UFH	5952	16 TE	NR
		No UFH		18 TE	NR
Horgan et al[57]	RCT	UFH	5952	2 P*	NR
		No UFH		10 P	NR
Ankola et al[58]	RCT	UFH	1515	2 P*	4 ICH
		No UFH		11 P	5 ICH

RCT = randomized controlled trial; UFH = unfractionated heparin; P = patency; TE = thromboembolic event; UFHB-PU = unfractionated heparin bonded-polyurethane; PVC = polyvinyl chloride; C = continuous; I = intermittent; ICH = intracranial hemorrhage; NR = not reported.

*p < .05.

spective case-control study, UFH was implicated as a risk factor for ICH in low birthweight infants.[71] However, this study was retrospective, the 95% confidence interval around the odds ratio of 3.9 was large (1.4–11.0), and the magnitude of the risk was uncertain.[71] In a second study, the association of UFH exposure with ICH among very low birthweight infants was assessed in a clinical trial that was designed to assess UAC placement.[45] The authors reported that infants with ICH received increased concentrations of UFH (83.5 units/kg/d) compared to infants without ICH (59.4 units/kg/d).[45] An odds ratio of 1.96 with a 95% confidence interval of 1.32 to 2.91 was reported. A recent RCT trial of 113 infants who received either 1 unit/ml UFH (n = 55) or no UFH (n = 58) in their infusate reported that there was no difference in the incidence of ICH.[72] In the same study, the influence of UFH on the coagulation system also was assessed, and no differences were detected that were attributable to

Table 6–10 Heparin and the Risk of Intracranial Hemorrhage in Premature Infants with an Umbilical Artery Catheter

Author	Design	Intervention	Number	Outcome ICH	Death
Lesko et al[71]	R	UFH	88%*	n = 66	NR
		No UFH	52%	n = 254	NR
Malloy et al[45]	R	83.5 u UFH/kg/d	2696	30%*	NR
		59.4 u UFH/kg/d	13	70%	NR
Chang et al[72]	RCT	UFH 1 u/mL	55	36%	9%
		No UFH	58	32%	17%

UFH = unfractionated heparin; R = retrospective; RCT = randomized controlled trial; CC = case control; ICH = intracranial hemorrhage; NR = not reported.

*p < .01.

*No significant difference.

UFH.[72] A survey of American nurseries in 1986 reported that 75% of nurseries used UFH prophylaxis in concentrations between 0.01 and 2.0 units/mL.[73] At this time, the evidence implicating UFH as a cause of ICH is weak.

Treatment

Therapeutic options for newborns with UAC-related TEs depend on the extent of the TE, compromise of limb or organ, and risk of serious bleeding. Anticoagulant and thrombolytic therapy are important therapeutic modalities for clinically significant UAC-related TEs. Chapters 9, 10, and 11 discuss the use of anticoagulant and thrombolytic therapy in detail.

Outcome Symptomatic, acute UAC-related TEs frequently threaten organ or limb viability with a potentially lethal outcome.[69,70] Long-term morbidity may manifest as hypertension,[52,63,65,74,75] abnormal renal function,[63,65,74] or discrepancies in leg measurements,[42,49,50,75,76] with claudication.[77,78] There are several studies that assessed long-term consequences of UAC-related TEs. The conclusions of these studies differ, reflecting study designs, inclusion of control populations, objective testing, and the outcome parameters measured.[30,43,47,49–52,63, 65,74–76,78–84]

The long-term outcome of UAC-related TEs has been assessed in only two large case series. Seibert et al prospectively studied 81 neonates and reported that 26% of infants developed TEs detected by ultrasound.[60] Newborns were asymptomatic in 29% of cases; 24% had hematuria as their only presenting symptom. During follow-up, one-third of infants had blood pressures greater than the 95th percentile for age. One had a 1-cm discrepancy in leg-length and seven had a 5- to 2-cm discrepancy between legs in either thigh or calf circumference. No evidence of residual clot was seen on ultrasound. Long-term morbidity consisted of renovascular hypertension and leg-growth abnormalities. Caplan et al also identified no aortic abnormalities by scintigraphy, ultrasound, or both in 15 children with neonatal aortic TEs monitored for 5 to 58 months.[74] Others have monitored patients for similar or shorter intervals.[43,79,85] Payne et al followed

10 newborns with aortic TEs diagnosed by follow-up ultrasound.[63] Thromboembolism was suspected by ultrasound on the first day of examination in 92%. Resolution of a TE was evaluated by ultrasound in all surviving patients. Follow-up ultrasound 1 to 3 years after discharge showed persistent abnormalities in one patient. Paraplegia and gangrene of the extremities associated with UAC-related TEs have been reported.[78,80,84,86] The long-term outcome of UAC-related TEs remains uncertain at this time and is an important area of research, because the conclusions likely will influence initial prophylaxis and management.

Cardiac Catheterization

Arterial Anatomy of the Upper and Lower Limb
Figure 6–1 shows the arterial supply to the leg and arm. The superficial femoral artery is the most common site of entry for CCs in children. The superficial femoral artery is an end artery with relatively poor collateral circulation from the profunda femoral artery around the knee.[87–89]

Brachial Artery Thrombosis
The brachial artery in the arm is used rarely for CC, usually in older children, and when access is not available through a femoral artery.[90–92] The incidence of brachial artery-related TEs may be increased compared to the femoral route, particularly in small patients. A study by Real et al of 25 children after CC reported that 83% of patients who had a femoral arteriotomy and all who had a brachial arteriotomy developed circulatory impairment identifiable by oscillometry following the arterial repair.[90] Mansfield et al studied arterial injuries in children and young adults (ages 2–25 yr) who had undergone a CC.[91] There were 8 injuries of the brachial artery, 4 injuries of the axillary artery, and 17 of the superficial femoral artery. Stanger et al did a prospective study of 1160 CCs in neonates and children.[92] Of 178 children having a brachial arteriotomy, 9.1% had catheter complications. Of 660 children having femoral arteriotomy, 4% had catheter complications. Although patients undergoing brachial arteriotomy were much older than those undergoing femoral arteriotomy, the incidence of complications was more than twice the incidence of complications following

femoral arteriotomies. Particularly striking was the incidence of brachial artery complications in patients with coarctation of the aorta (16%).

Femoral Artery Thrombosis Traditionally, CCs were performed only for diagnostic purposes. By the mid 1980s, the indications for interventional CCs expanded to include many therapeutic procedures.[93] Interventional CCs currently are used for the following purposes: balloon dilations for aortic valvuloplasty,[93–101] balloon dilation of native coarctation,[102–107] recurrent coarctation,[96,108,109] other aortic arch obstructions,[110] subaortic stenosis[111,112] and supra-aortic stenosis,[113] balloon dilation of Blalock-Taussig (BT) shunts,[114] transaortopulmonary shunt dilation of peripheral pulmonary artery stenosis,[115] retrograde balloon mitral valvuloplasty,[116] and retrograde balloon dilation of pulmonary venous obstruction following the Mustard operation.[93,117]

One serious complication of femoral artery catheterization is local thrombus formation in the ileofemoral system, which usually begins at the puncture site and extends proximally or distally for variable distances. The subsequent injury may range from a mild decrease in pulse strength as a result of partial obstruction by a thrombus, to severe ischemia and potential loss of limb secondary to significant interruption of arterial blood flow. The risk of severe vascular complications is linked to technical difficulties and increased catheter-to-artery size ratios. Arterial spasm usually resolves within a few hours following CC, and most TEs resolve following treatment with UFH or by thrombolytic therapy. Arterial spasm or TEs that rapidly resolve are usually of little concern. However, vessel injury or TEs resulting in chronic vascular insufficiency can cause serious long-term complications, including decreased growth of the affected extremity leading to leg-length discrepancy, vascular insufficiency leading to compartment syndrome or claudication, and loss of arterial access that may be needed for future diagnostic or interventional procedures.

Incidence The incidence of femoral artery TEs following CCs is influenced by several parameters of which balloon dilations, the use of prophylactic anticoagulation with UFH, size and age, repeated

catheter manipulations, and increased hematocrit are the most important.[4,21,118,119] Arterial complications following CC are six times more likely to occur when balloon angiography or valvotomy is performed. An intentional arterial "tear" is created during insertion of balloon catheters, and thrombi form to occlude the opening upon removal of catheters. The large size and irregular bumpy surface of the balloons may contribute to increased intimal trauma, cause spasm, and result in TEs.[7] Patient size, hemodynamic status, technique, and total time of arterial cannulation all interplay in the risk of TEs.[120] The use of larger French-sized catheters is also associated with a high incidence of femoral artery TEs.

Prophylactic Anticoagulation In the absence of prophylactic UFH, symptomatic femoral artery TEs following a diagnostic CC occur in approximately 40% of children less than 10 years of age and in less than 5% of older children.[7,118,121–125] Currently, UFH prophylaxis is used extensively, and the incidence of symptomatic femoral artery TEs is between 0.8% and 7.3%.[17,92,120,122,126–131]

Size and Age The increased risk of femoral artery TEs in small children reflects, in part, the catheter-to-vessel diameter ratio and may be diminished by the use of smaller catheters introduced through a femoral sheath. In addition, small children are particularly vulnerable to volume deficit, dehydration, hypotension, and subsequent low flow states, which can further increase the incidence of TEs.[124,132]

Repeated Catheter Manipulations Repeated catheter manipulations, which may be necessary to pass a catheter from the aorta to the left ventricle, and balloon dilatation, which causes significant disruption of the endothelium, also increase the incidence of femoral artery TEs.[7,118,120,122,133,134]

Clinical Presentation and Diagnosis Careful monitoring of distal pulses following CC is important for early detection of impaired flow and the presence of a thrombus. Acute impairment of arterial blood flow to a limb is characterized by diminished or absent pulses, a prolonged capillary refill time, and a cool, pale limb. Bedside objective tests include decreased blood flow as assessed by hand-held Doppler, and decreased blood pressure in excess of 10 mmHg compared to the other leg. Contrast angiography is the most accurate diagnostic test, but frequently is not practical in the acute situation.

Prevention Five RCTs were identified that addressed the issue of prophylactic anticoagulation for children undergoing CC (Table 6–11).[4,17,118,119,135] Aspirin (15 mg/kg for 5 doses) was compared to placebo in 95 children and did not demonstrate a significant benefit.[135] Unfractionated heparin (100 units/kg as a bolus) was compared to placebo and showed a reduction in TEs from 40% to 8% in children less than 10 years of age.[118] In the same study, the incidence of TEs in older children was similar, at 5%, for both the placebo and UFH therapies.[118] Based on the conclusions from this one well-designed study, UFH in doses of 100 to 150 units/kg is the most common form of prophylaxis for children undergoing CC. A study published in 1981 compared the use of 10 units/mL of UFH in the flush solution, which totaled approximately 100 units/kg by the end of the procedure, to an initial bolus of 100 units/kg of UFH.[4] There was no difference in the incidence of TEs; however, 75% of patients were older than 5 years of age, which may have contributed to the overall low risk of TEs.[4] A study published in 1997 compared the effect of two dosages of UFH on the incidence of arterial TEs in 366 children (17 d–11 yr, mean age, 39.5 ± 40.9 mo) following CC.[119] The incidence of TEs was similar, at 9.8%, in the 50 IU/kg UFH group and 9.3% in the 100 IU/kg group. Of the patients with arterial TEs, 23 responded to intravenous UFH and 12 required thrombolytic therapy. Clinical trials assessing optimal dosing of prophylactic anticoagulants in the context of current catheter use are needed.

Many centers monitor activity of UFH by an activated whole blood clotting time (ACT), which increases by approximately threefold following an initial dose of 100 units/kg of UFH.[136,137] However, ACT values are influenced by age, the presence of cyanotic CHD, which may have an associated coagulopathy, and technique.[137] Further boluses of UFH commonly are administered if the CC is prolonged, or if ACT values decrease below levels of approximately three times baseline.[136,137]

Outcomes Related to Thrombotic Occlusion Following Cardiac Catheterization Outcomes related to TEs following CC can be considered as short and long term. Short-term consequences of CC-related TEs include threatened limb viability and the morbidity of intervention with anticoagulants or thrombolytic therapy. Long-term consequences of femoral artery TEs likely reflect the effectiveness of initial therapy and include leg length discrepancies, muscle wasting, claudication, and loss of arterial access, which is important for chil-

Table 6–11 Thromboembolic and Bleeding Complications Following Cardiac Catheterization

Author	Design	Intervention	Number	Outcome (%)
Freed et al[135]	RCT	Aspirin 15 mg/kg	37	22
		Placebo	58	24
Freed et al[118]	RCT	UFH 1 mg/kg	40	8*
		Placebo	37	41
Rao et al[4]	RCT	UFH 100 u/mL	5660	11
		Placebo		17
Girod et al[17]	C	UFH 100 u/kg bolus	6943	1
		UFH 150 u/kg + u/kg/h	8124	1
Saxena et al[119]	RCT	UFH 50 u/kg	1831	10
		UFH 100 u/kg	83	9

UFH = unfractionated heparin; RCT = randomized controlled trial; C = cohort.

*$p < .05$.

dren who require multiple CCs.[138] If additional TEs of the profunda femoral artery occur, claudication and shortness might also occur in the thigh. Ischemia is enhanced during rapid growth, such as occurs in the first year of life and during puberty.[138]

Late complications of femoral artery catheterization can be clinically important. In a study by Taylor et al,[139] 58 children who were less than 5 years old at the time of catheterization were evaluated 5 to 14 years later using arterial duplex scanning and lower extremity bone length radiographs. Arterial occlusion was present in 33% of patients. The mean ankle–brachial index in the catheterized limbs was 0.79 and leg-growth retardation was present in 8% of children. In a study by Celermajer et al,[88] over 30% of previously catheterized children and adolescents presented with vascular access problems at subsequent catheterizations due to an occluded vessel, a stenosed vessel, or scar tissue. The practical implications of difficult access include prolonged access time, prolonged total catheter duration, and significant discomfort for patients studied under local anesthesia. In a study by Hurwitz et al, recatheterization was performed in 48 children, 6 months to 9 years after the initial study.[126] There was complete occlusion of the femoral artery in 4 of 48 (8%) patients with extensive hypogastric collateralization reconstituting the femoral artery approximately 3 to 4 cm below the inguinal ligament.[126]

Treatment Options for the treatment of acute arterial TEs following CC consist of anticoagulants, thrombolytic therapy, embolectomy, and reconstructive surgery.

Anticoagulants The general practice in the majority of children's hospitals is to initiate therapy with UFH, because approximately 70% of TEs resolve without exposing children to the greater risks of thrombolytic therapy, embolectomy, or surgical reconstruction.[120] Depending upon the time interval from UFH administration during CC, UFH is initiated either with a bolus of 75 to 100 units/kg or as a continuous infusion. On average, infants less than 2 months of age have increased requirements of UFH per body weight (28 units/kg/hr) compared to older children who require, on average, 20 units/kg/hr. Unfractionated heparin therapy is discussed in detail in Chapter 9.

Thrombolytic therapy If the arterial occlusion does not resolve, thrombolytic therapy usually is preferred over embolectomy because of the poor outcome of embolectomy in very small children.[120] Table 6–12 summarizes the available information on the use of thrombolytic therapy in children with femoral artery TEs following CC. Streptokinase (SK), urokinase (UK), and tissue plasminogen activator (TPA) all have been used to treat femoral artery TEs in children.[120,127,129–131,140–142] In general, treatment of femoral artery TEs usually is effective in preventing tissue ischemia, claudication, or amputation (see Chapter 11).

Embolectomy In general, embolectomy should be avoided in small children if thrombolytic therapy is not contraindicated because of the risks of reocclusion. For a balloon embolectomy, a catheter of appropriate size is introduced through the previous arteriotomy site and then passed retrograde through the thrombus up and into the external and common iliac arteries. The balloon is in-

Table 6–12 Thrombolytic Therapy for Femoral Artery Thrombosis due to Cardiac Catheterization

Author	Agent	Age	Number	Infusion Dose	Successful Outcome (%)
Wessel et al[127]	SK	2 d–40 mo	16	1000 u/mL	87
Ino et al[120]	SK	3 d–55 mo	11	1–2000 u/mL	100
	UK			4000 u/mL	
Kirk et al[140]	SK	3 d–34 mo	14	750–1000 u/mL	100
Brus et al[130]	SK	0.02–1.5 yr	9	1–2000 u/mL	100
Kothari et al[131]	SK	1 mo–9 mo	12	1000 u/mL	100
Levy et al[141]	TPA	1 d–17 yr	12	0.1–0.5 mg	58
Zenz et al[129]	TPA	2 d–47 mo	17	0.5–0.25 mg	94
Ries et al[142]	TPA	14 mo–53 mo	6	0.5 mg	100

SK = streptokinase; TPA = tissue plasminogen activator; UK = urokinase.

flated and the catheter gently withdrawn. Complete evacuation of the clot usually is signaled by a pulsating gush of blood; if not, the procedure is repeated. A distal clot in discontinuity also may be present. In these patients, the catheter is passed down the superficial femoral artery, the balloon inflated, and the catheter withdrawn. When good retrograde and prograde arterial blood flow is achieved, the arteriotomy is closed.[91,143] Embolectomy should be followed by anticoagulant therapy to prevent reocclusion.

Reconstructive surgery Options for reconstructive surgery include thrombectomy with autogenous saphenous vein patch angioplasty, direct angioplasty, segmental resection with end-to-end anastomosis, and interposition-bypass grafting.[144,145] The main indication for reconstructive surgery is clinically significant claudication, which is inevitably accompanied by shortening of the limb or muscle wasting. In most cases, Doppler ultrasound and angiogram, via the contralateral femoral artery, are required to establish the vascular anatomy. Reconstructive surgery of an ischemic but viable limb in a small child probably is best deferred if possible, because future definitive surgery in larger vessels is more likely to be successful.

NON-CATHETER-RELATED ARTERIAL THROMBOEMBOLIC COMPLICATIONS

Noncatheter-related arterial TEs are relatively rare, but are problematic when present. The etiologies of noncatheter-related arterial TEs can be classified as congenital or acquired. Congenital causes of arterial TEs include familial hyperlipidemias,[146,147] hyperhomocystinuria,[148–151] and structural abnormalities.[152] Congenital causes of arterial TEs are briefly discussed subsequently, with further detail provided in Chapter 3. Acquired causes of arterial TEs include Takayasu arteritis,[153–155] Kawasaki disease,[156,157] complications of some forms of CHD or its therapy, and occlusion of specific arteries secondary to a variety of diseases.[158–162]

Congenital Predisposition to Arterial Thrombotic Disease

Congenital Hyperlipidemia in Adults Hyperlipidemia is a major risk factor for atherosclerotic vascular disease in adults. There is considerable evidence that hypercholesterolemic adults have abnormal levels during childhood,[163–167] which has led to a major effort to detect affected children, in the belief that early intervention will be of benefit. However, the age at which intervention optimally should commence remains unknown, as is the outcome of intervention therapy.

Congenital Hyperlipidemia in Children Congenital hyperlipidemic states are classified on the basis of the relative concentrations of various fractions of cholesterol, such as low-density lipoprotein (LDL), high-density lipoprotein (HDL) (inversely), and lipoprotein (a) (Lp[a]).[163,164,168] Each of the I to V types of hyperlipidemia has different genetic mechanisms, clinical presentations, and laboratory results (see Chapter 3).

Familial hypercholesterolemia (FH) is attributable to absent or defective LDL receptors, which leads to increased serum concentrations of LDL. Inheritance of FH is autosomal dominant with an incidence of 1 in 500 for heterozygotes. The incidence of homozygotes is 1 in 1 million, with affected children presenting with markedly increased serum cholesterol levels at birth, cutaneous xanthomatas, and coronary artery disease within the first decade of life. Children with homozygous FH develop a classic pattern of atherosclerosis that involves the aortic root, leading to aortic stenosis, and coronary artery ostia, leading to obstruction.[169,170] Distal coronary arteries often are pristine until adult life. Receptor-negative patients have more severe disease than receptor-defective patients,[171] and males often are more severely affected than females.[172] Death from acute myocardial infarction may occur as early as 18 months of age and survival beyond the third decade is rare.[170,173–175] Plasmapheresis and LDL apheresis are advocated as current treatments of choice, because diet and drug therapy frequently are ineffective.[172,176,177] Liver-directed gene therapy is under ongoing investigation.[178]

Although patients with heterozygous FH usually do not develop clinical evidence of ischemic heart disease until early adult life, endothelial dysfunction, identified by diminished flow-dependent dilatation, is present within the first decade of life.[179,180] Sixty-six percent of asymptomatic teenagers with a positive family history and 25% of teenagers with a negative family history have abnormal cardiac stress thallium scans.[181] Stress thallium scans show a significant correlation with angiographic abnormalities in individuals with FH.[182] Lipoprotein (a) levels also are increased in patients with abnormal thallium scans.[181] Homozygous familial defective apolipoprotein B100 has a clinical presentation similar to that of homozygous FH.[183,184]

Common Clinical Presentations of Hyperlipidemic States

Arterial TEs secondary to hyperlipidemic states can present with myocardial ischemia, cerebrovascular disease, and peripheral artery disease during childhood.

Myocardial infarction The classic hyperlipidemic state associated with myocardial infarction in childhood is homozygous FH.[169] Cerebrotendinous xanthomatosis and phytosterolemia are other rare familial sterol storage disorders associated with premature atherosclerosis and may cause myocardial infarction during childhood.[185] None of the other primary hyperlipidemic syndromes is associated with myocardial ischema in childhood.[168,171]

Cerebrovascular disease There are a number of retrospective studies that have failed to demonstrate any role for hyperlipidemia in childhood stroke.[186] Studies in homozygous FH show that atherosclerosis in the cerebral circulation lags many years behind aortic and coronary artery disease.[187–189] Postulated reasons for the lack of cerebrovascular disease include differences in shear stress, endothelial glycosaminoglycan (GAG) composition, and protection from hypertension by the universal presence of aortic stenosis in these patients.[187,188,190] Glueck et al identified a small cohort of children in whom decreased HDL levels and increased triglyceride levels were associated with otherwise unexplained stroke.[191,192] However, they

identified the same abnormalities in children with migraines.[193]

Peripheral arterial disease Arteriosclerosis is associated with spontaneous hand and digital ischemia in some teenagers and young adults.[194] However, an associated hyperlipidemic state is not necessarily present.[194] Patients with homozygous FH may develop peripheral atherosclerosis, but it rarely is clinically significant.[195]

Hyperhomocysteinemia

Homocysteine is a sulphur-containing amino acid formed by the demethylation of dietary methionine, which is dependent on the cofactors folic acid, vitamin B6 and vitamin B_{12} (Figure 6–4). Hyperhomocysteinemia is a proven independent risk factor for atherosclerotic vascular disease affecting coronary, cerebral, and peripheral arteries.[196–198] The mechanism by which homocysteine induces its prothrombotic state reflects an imbalance between procoagulant and anticoagulant properties of endothelial cell surfaces. Homocysteine also promotes vascular smooth muscle cell growth, oxidizes LDL, and may adversely affect platelet function. Hyperhomocysteinemia can have both a genetic and a nutritional basis (see Chapter 3).

Congenital Hyperhomocysteinemia

Genetic causes of hyperhomocysteinemia are cystathionine-β-synthase deficiency and 5,10-methylenetetrahydrofolate reductase (MTHFR) deficiency (see Chapter 3).[199,200] The recently identified thermolabile variant of MTHFR causes hyperhomocysteinemia and decreased plasma folate concentrations, and it occurs in 5% to 30% of the population.[201,202]

Congenital Arterial Structural Abnormalities

The occurrence of spontaneous peripheral arterial TEs are relatively common in adults and usually secondary to atherosclerosis. The occurrence of peripheral arterial TEs in children usually is secondary to intra-arterial catheters. Occurrence of spontaneous peripheral arterial TEs in children is extremely rare, with only a small number of patients identified in the literature.[152] In one 6-year-old female, narrowing of the femoral artery immediately proximal to the thrombus was identified on angiography and likely represented a congenital anatomic abnormality of the artery.[152]

Clinical presentation The clinical presentation is similar to adults and includes pallor, pain, reduced temperature, and absent pulses.[203] There frequently is a delay in diagnosis likely owing to a reduced clinical suspicion of peripheral arterial obstruction in an otherwise healthy young child. In at least one child, an initial diagnosis of reflex sympathetic dystrophy delayed the diagnosis and led to further complications. The term "reflex sympathetic dystrophy" describes a nonspecific symptom complex consisting of local pain associated with subjective motor or sensory symptoms and erratic objective vascular changes in color and temperature of the symptomatic body part.

Diagnosis Ultrasound may fail to make the diagnosis of peripheral artery TEs with certainty for several reasons, including reduced arterial blood pressure, small vessel diameters, and difficulty of obtaining optimal imaging in small children who may not remain still. Angiography remains the gold standard and should be considered to confirm or exclude the diagnosis of acute arterial obstruction when the ultrasound result is uncertain or is in conflict with the clinical picture.[203]

Treatment The management of acute peripheral arterial TEs in adults usually is local thrombolytic therapy.[204] However, the etiology of periph-

eral TEs in children is significantly different, and the likelihood of arterial damage by locally invasive catheterization probably is increased, owing to the smaller size of the affected arteries.[205] Anticoagulation with UFH followed by warfarin likely is justified, and the role of surgery should be individualized based on the threat to limb viability, growth, and potential risks of further TEs or bleeding.

Acquired Causes of Arterial Thrombosis

Secondary Hyperlipidemia Secondary causes of hyperlipidemia in childhood include poorly controlled insulin-dependent diabetes mellitus (IDDM), hypothyroidism, hepatic glycogenosis, obstructive liver disease, and nephrotic syndrome. Of these, only nephrotic syndrome is associated with arterial TEs in childhood. Cases of myocardial infarction, stroke, internal organ infarction, and peripheral artery TEs all have been documented.[27,206–209] Whether TEs are related to hyperlipidemia or coexisting coagulation defects such as antithrombin (AT) deficiency is not clear. However, the latter is more likely, given the short duration of hyperlipidemia that resolves with resolution of the primary disorder.[210,211]

Secondary Hyperhomocysteinemia Nutritional causes of hyperhomocysteinemia may occur in pa-

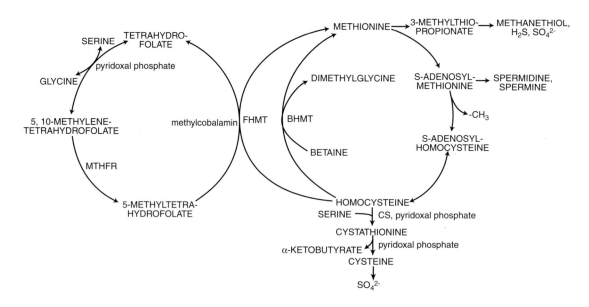

Figure 6–4 Schema of the homocysteine pathway.

tients with folate deficiency or vitamin B_{12} deficiency and in patients with chronic renal failure.[212,213] Therapeutically, supplementation with folic acid can reduce plasma concentrations of homocysteine; however, the reduction of vascular disease remains to be proven.[214] Vitamin status is a primary determinant of mild to moderate hyperhomocysteinemia, accounting for approximately two-thirds of all cases.[215] Vitamin supplementation results in near normalization of plasma homocysteine in most cases.[216,217] A meta-analysis of 38 studies evaluated the risk of hyperhomocysteinemia for arteriosclerotic vascular disease, estimated the reduction of homocysteine levels by folic acid administration, and calculated the potential reduction of coronary artery disease by increasing folic acid intake, and reduced the annual mortality by 50,000.[214] Vitamin supplementation also may reduce recurrence of venous TEs in these patients; however, at present the clinical efficacy of this approach has not been tested.[148]

Takayasu Arteritis

Takayasu arteritis is a rare chronic, idiopathic, inflammatory disease of large arteries predominantly affecting Asian females.[218] Although any artery may be involved, angiographic studies show that two-thirds of patients have aortic lesions, with the aortic arch, carotid arteries, and renal arteries being primarily affected.[219]

Clinical presentation The clinical presentation consists of limb or organ ischemia attributable to gradual stenosis of related arteries.[220,221] The physical findings frequently include a bruit in the involved area.[221]

Diagnosis The diagnosis of Takayasu arteritis frequently is delayed by several months because of diffuse clinical observations and rareness of the disease.[220] Angiography remains the gold standard for the assessment of clinical severity of the arteritis and results of specific interventions.

Treatment Glucocorticoids are the mainstay of medical therapy, with at least 60% of patients achieving remission within 1 year of treatment.[218,222] Unfortunately, 50% of patients relapse, and additional cytotoxic agents, such as methotrexate or cyclophosphamide, are required.[218,222] Stenting or arterial reconstruction is required for at least

one-third of patients.[219–221,223] Anticoagulation frequently is used to preserve flow in stenotic vessels or in vessels following stent placement or reconstructive surgery. Initial therapy usually is UFH and long-term therapy is a combination of aspirin and Oral anticoagulants (OAs) (Chapters 9, 10, and 12).

Kawasaki Disease

In 1967, a Japanese pediatrician, Tomisaku Kawasaki, described 50 children with fever for more than 5 days, cervical lymphadenopathy, rash, bilateral nonexudative conjunctivitis, inflammation of the oral mucosa, erythema, swelling of the hands and feet, and cervical adenitis.[156] During the acute phase, Kawasaki disease may cause medium- and large-vessel arteritis, arterial aneurysms, valvulitis, and myocarditis. Of particular concern are coronary artery aneurysms, which may stenose or thrombose. The incidence of coronary artery aneurysms in the absence of initial treatment is approximately 20% to 25%.[157] Coronary arterial aneurysms, or extasia, may lead to myocardial infarction, sudden death, or chronic coronary arterial insufficiency.[157] Kawasaki disease is the leading cause of acquired heart disease in children in North America.

Histopathology In Kawasaki disease, the arterial wall is affected, particularly in middle-sized and smaller muscular arteries. The histopathology shows an acute stage, characterized by an influx of polymorphonuclear leukocytes, rapidly followed by an influx of lymphocytes and cells of the mononuclear phagocytic system. At that stage of the inflammatory process, a granulomatous reaction is produced that may progress over time.

Prophylaxis for coronary artery aneurysms During the early 1980s, conventional therapy for Kawasaki disease in the acute phase was aspirin, which was used for both its anti-inflammatory and antithrombotic properties.[157] However, aspirin alone never has been shown to prevent coronary artery aneurysms or ectasia. In 1984, Furusho et al showed that intravenous gamma globulin (IgG) administered in the acute phase of the disease along with aspirin decreased the incidence of coronary arterial lesions.[224] A subsequent RCT by Newburger et al showed that a dose of 400 mg/kg per day for 4 consecutive days in addition to aspirin at a dose of 100 mg/kg per day for 14 days decreased the incidence of coronary artery aneurysms by three- to fivefold compared to aspirin alone.[225] A recent meta-analysis of 24 studies has concluded that children treated with both intravenous immune globulin (IVIG) and aspirin had a significantly lower incidence of coronary artery aneurysms compared to children were treated with aspirin alone.[157] In addition, the incidence of coronary artery aneurysms was further decreased in children who received high doses of IVIG compared to those who received low IVIG doses at both 30 and 60 days (Table 6–13).[157] Total doses less than 1 g/kg appear to be ineffective. Children who received a single high dose of IVIG (2 gm/kg) had a lower incidence of coronary artery aneurysms than those who received high multiple doses of IVIG (400 mg/kg/d for 4 days) at 30 days but not at 60 days.[157,226] Together, these studies form the bases for current recommendations for the prevention of coronary artery aneurysms in children with Kawasaki disease. These recommendations are that high-dose IVIG, preferably as a single dose (2 g/kg[157,225]), and high-dose aspirin (80 to 100 mg/kg/d for up to 14 days[225,227,228]) are initiated prior to day 10 of the illness because these interventions reduce the incidence of coronary artery abnormalities from approximately 20% to 25% to 5% by 60 days following initiation of therapy.[157] Subsequent use of low-dose aspirin, 3 to 5 mg/kg per day for 7 weeks or longer, also is recommended, because it may contribute to the prevention of coronary artery TEs.

Diagnosis of coronary artery aneurysms 2D ECHO is the primary tool for evaluation and follow-up of coronary artery abnormalities. However, there are some limitations in patients with persistent large coronary aneurysms, in which 2D ECHO may not be able to distinguish the intimal surface from the adventitial layer or detect TEs or stenosis with accuracy. Repeat 2D ECHO should be performed 6 to 8 weeks after the onset of illness. Patients with no evidence of aneurysm at 1 year likely do not require further follow-up for coronary artery aneurysms (Table 6–14).[359] Although 2D ECHO is appropriate for most patients, angiography remains the most reliable diagnostic test for coronary artery

involvement, and may be necessary in some patients.

Treatment for coronary artery aneurysm-related thrombosis The most serious complication of coronary artery aneurysms is a thrombotic occlusion that results in myocardial infarction and its associated morbidity and mortality. In this situation, prompt thrombolytic therapy should be considered, unless there is a major contraindication. Myocardial infarction should be suspected in children with a combination of chest pain, abdominal discomfort, nausea or vomiting or weakness with pallor, diaphoresis, and inconsolable crying. The diagnosis is confirmed by electrocardiographic changes and increased cardiac enzymes.[229–232] Thrombolysis should be instituted as soon as possible, ideally, within 1 to 3 hours following diagnosis. A widely used protocol of TPA for adults with myocardial infarction is suggested. General guidelines for administering thrombolytic therapy are discussed in Chapter 11. The specific protocol for the treatment of myocardial infarction differs from other protocols because of the immediate need for treatment and dosing schedule for TPA. Specifically, thrombolytic therapy should not be delayed. One approach is to give an intravenous bolus of 0.2 mg/kg (maximum of 15 mg) followed by an infusion of 0.75 mg/kg over a 30-minute period (maximum of 50 mg) and then an infusion of 0.5 mg/kg over a 60-minute period (maximum of 35 mg).[233] Unfractionated heparin should be given simultaneously, beginning with an intravenous bolus of 75 units/kg followed by 20 units/kg per hour.

In some patients, coronary artery obstruction may be severe enough to warrant surgical revascularization. Technical limitations and low graft patency rate confound surgical management of coronary artery obstruction in patients under 5 years of age. The patency rate of saphenous vein grafts generally is unsatisfactory, and bypasses using the internal thoracic (mammary) are technically problematic in the younger population.[234] In older children, internal thoracic and gastroepiploic artery grafts appear to offer better long-term patency and growth in caliber than saphenous vein grafts. Although the available data are few and anecdotal, percutaneous transluminal coronary angioplasty has

Table 6–13 Meta-analysis of Studies on the Efficacy of Aspirin and Immunoglobulin Treatment of Kawasaki Disease

Author	Design	Number	ASA	IVIG + ASA	IVIG + Low ASA	IVIG + High ASA	IVIG Dose	Incidence of CAA in Each Study Group			
								ASA at 30 d	ASA at 60 d	IVIG/ASA at 30 d	IVIG/ASA at 60 d
Hwang et al[337]	P	50	43	7			0.2 x 5 d	44.2	16.3	42.9	28.6
		49		49	49		0.4 x 5 d	`		49.0	18.4
Furosho et al[338]	P	85	45	40	40		0.4 x 5 d	42.2	31.1	15.0	7.5
		92		92	92		0.2 x 5 d			19.6	9.8
		53		53	53		0.4 x 5 d			20.8	11.3
		98	49	49	49		0.2 x 5 d	38.7	19.1	18.4	10.2
		53		53	53		0.1 x 5 d			18.9	7.8
Harada[339]	P	213	74	139	139		0.1 x 5 d	20.2	14.9	22.3	14.5
		266	95	171	171		0.1 x 5 d	31.5	22.2	9.9	8.8
		117		117	117		0.1 x 5 d			11.7	10.1
		114		114	114		0.4 x 5 d			6.1	3.4
Chung et al[340]	P	75	75					25.3			
Chung et al[341]	P	44	44					15.9			
Daniels et al[228]	R	77	77					11.6			
Engle et al[343]	P	32		32	32		1.0 x 1 d			0	0
Lee et al[344]	R	37	37					27.0			
Villian et al[345]	P	12		12	12		2.0 x 1 d			0	0
Fournier et al[346]	P	106	106					6.4			
Takahashi et al[347]	P	186	186					18.3			
Kryzer et al[348]	R	69	28	41		41	0.4 x 4 d	28.5		12.2	
Cullen et al[349]	R	11	11					27.2			
Meade et al[350]	R	25	25					16.0			
Nakashima et al[351]	P	136	67	69		69	0.4 x 3 d	31.3		13.0	
Barron et al[352]	P	22		22		22	1.0 x 1 d			9.1	9.1
Akagi et al[353]	R	493	322	171		171	0.4 x 4 d	14.9		13.4	
Beitzke et al[354]	P	31		31		31	0.4 x 4 d			32.0	
Newburger et al[225]	P	168	84	74		74	0.4 x 4 d	20.0	14.6	6.7	2.6
Newburger et al[226]	P	252		252		252	0.4 x 5 d			5.5	3.9
	P	254		254		254	2.0 x 1 d			2.3	2.3
Colloridi et al[355]	P	18		18		18	0.4 x 5 d			10.5	10.5
Ichida et al[356]	R	105	105					24.8			
Ogino et al[357]	P	113	51	62	62		0.4 x 4 d	33.3	1.9	17.7	
Schaad et al[358]	P	32	23	9		9	0.4 x 4 d	13.0		0	

ASA = aspirin; IVIG = intravenous gammaglobulin; CAA = coronary artery aneurysms; d = day; P = prospective; R = retrospective.

low ASA*— ≤ 80 mg/kg; high ASA**— > 80mg/kg.

Table 6–14 Guidelines for the Treatment of Kawasaki Disease in Children

Risk Level	Explanation Therapy	Pharmacologic Therapy	Physical Activity	Follow-up and Diagnostic Testing	Invasive Testing
I	No CA changes at any stage	None beyond initial 6–8 wk	No restrictions beyond initial 6-8 wk	None beyond first year unless cardiac disease suspected	None recommended
II	Transient CA ectasia that disappears during acute illness	None beyond initial 6–8 wk	No restrictions beyond initial 6-8 wk	None beyond first year unless cardiac disease suspected. Physician may choose to see patient at 3–5 yr intervals	None recommended
III	Small to medium solitary CAA	Aspirin 3–5 mg/kg/d, at least until abnormalities subside	<10 yr, no restrictions beyond initial 6-8 wk <20 yr, physical activity guided by ST every other year. Competitive contact athletics with endurance training discouraged.	Annual follow-up with ECHO ± ECG at 6 mo intervals <10 yr	Angiography, if ST or ECHO suggests stenosis
IV	1 or more giant CAAs, or small to medium CAAs without obstruction	Long-term aspirin (3–5 mg/kg/d) ± warfarin	< 10 yr, no restrictions beyond initial 6–8 wk < 20 yr annual ST guides recommendations. Strenuous athletics are strongly discouraged. If ST rules out ischemia, noncontact recreational sports allowed.	Annual follow-up with ECHO ± ECG ± chest x-ray ± additional ECG at 6 mo intervals. < 10 yr pharmacologic ST should be considered	Angiography, if ST or ECHO suggests stenosis. Elective catheterization may be done in certain circumstances.
V	CA obstruction	Long-term aspirin (3–5 mg/kg/d) ± warfarin. Use of calcium channel blockers should be considered to reduce myocardial oxygen consumption.	Contact sports, isometrics, and weight training should be avoided. Other physical activity recommendations guided by outcome of ST or myocardial perfusion scan.	ECHO and ECG at 6 mo intervals and annual Holter and ST	Angiography recommended for some patients to aid in selecting therapeutic options. Repeat angiography with new onset or worsening ischemia.

CA = coronary artery; CAA = coronary artery aneurysm; ECHO = echocardiography; ECG = electrocardiogram; ST = stress testing.
Reproduced with permission.[359]

not produced consistent or lasting improvement in myocardial perfusion in patients with Kawasaki disease. Coronary artery aneurysms also can cause morbidity by rupturing, which results in cardiac tamponade, as a direct consequence, and death.

Long-term follow-up Long-term management depends on the degree of coronary artery involvement. Longitudinal follow-up begins 10 to 14 days after the onset of the illness. In most children who develop coronary artery aneurysms, early signs of aneurysm formation are apparent at this time. For most patients, the coronary aneurysms regress within 1 to 2 years; however, giant coronary artery aneurysms (defined as a diameter over 8 mm) develop in approximately 1% of children with Kawasaki disease. If giant coronary aneurysms develop, more intense anticoagulation has been recommended.[231] However, the optimal use of OAs and aspirin remains unknown. Giant aneurysms almost never regress and myocardial infarction occurs in many of these patients. In contrast, small to moderate-sized aneurysms can no longer be documented by imaging techniques in 80% of affected patients within 5 years. However, there may remain prolonged abnormalities in the coronary arteries and the heart itself.[232] Late findings of decreased ventricular function and mitral and aortic regurgitation have been reported.[232] Surgical management is considered in some patients.[232]

Mechanical Heart Valves Cardiac valvular disease may be isolated or be an integral part of more complex intracardiac lesions or be the result of treatment of an underlying congenital defect. Thromboembolic events of the valve or embolization to the CNS are two of the most serious complications of mechanical heart valves.[235-249] Currently, mechanical prosthetic heart valves usually are used in the mitral and aortic position, whereas biologic prosthetic heart valves are used for tricuspid or pulmonary valve replacements in children.

Oral anticoagulant therapy is recommended for adults with mechanical prosthetic valves.[235] There are no RCTs demonstrating that OAs are necessary to prevent TEs of mechanical valves in children. Because safely monitoring OA therapy in children is problematic, some centers have not used OAs,[250,251] or they have used an antiplatelet agent alone.[251-258] In the absence of any anticoagulants, the reported rate of TEs in children is 5.7 to 27.3 per 100 patient-years (100 pt-yr).[250,251] In the presence of an antiplatelet agent alone, the reported rate of TE ranges from 1.1 to 68/100 pt-yr with three of eight studies reporting rates of TEs over 5/100 pt-yr.[251-258] Only in the studies using OAs was the incidence of TEs uniformly less than 5/100 pt-yr.[251,254-256,258-268] With one exception, the rate of major bleeding was less than 3.5/100 pt-yr. Adjuvant therapy with antiplatelet agents was used in one study.[267] The available data support the recommendation for OA therapy in children with mechanical prosthetic heart valves. Aspirin in combination with OAs may be helpful in high-risk patients, such as those with prior TEs, atrial fibrillation, and a large left atrium. Chapter 10 provides more detailed information on OA therapy in the prevention of TE related to mechanical valves.

Renal Artery Thrombosis Renal arterial thrombosis (RAT) can be classified as secondary to kidney transplantation or to other disorders. Following kidney transplantation, RAT occurs in 0.2% to 3.5% of pediatric patients. Affected patients are usually small and present with anuria, with or without clinical symptoms of rejection.[269-271] The correlation between young donor age and TE reflects the size of the transplanted vessels and anastomotic technique.[270-272] The etiology of RAT likely is multifactorial, reflecting surgical technique, preimplantation damage, immune mechanisms, hypotension or hyperperfusion, small donors and recipients, prior nephrectomy, and rejection.[270] Prophylactic therapy with low molecular weight heparin (LMWH) (0.4 mg/kg for 21 days) was reported in one case series of 70 children.[273] Randomized controlled trials are required to determine the relative efficacy and safety of prophylactic anticoagulant therapy in RAT. When TEs occur, treatment options in addition to anticoagulation include surgical embolectomy and thrombolytic therapy.[270] Renal arterial thrombosis generally is irreversible and is an important cause of renal graft loss in children, particularly those less than 6 years of age. Several case reports have described RAT not related to renal transplantation.[274-280] Other causes of RAT include UAC,[275] CC,[280] severe dehydration,[274] antiphospholipid antibody syndrome,[277] and trauma.[279]

Hepatic Artery Thrombosis Hepatic artery thrombosis (HAT), a serious complication associated with liver transplantation, usually occurs within 2 weeks of transplantation (Table 6–15).[160,281-290] Not unexpectedly, age and size of the child are the most important risk factors for HAT.[290] The reported incidence of HAT in children ranges from 3.1% to 42%,[160,281-290] which is significantly increased compared to the incidence in adults (1.5%–1.6%).[291,292] The incidence of HAT is inversely related to donor age.[288]

Early clinical symptoms of HAT often are absent or nonspecific. The clinical course usually is fulminant but can be indolent with a late onset. Serial testing with pulsed Doppler combined with real-time ultrasound of the liver parenchyma has a sensitivity of approximately 70% for the detection of HAT.[158,159,282] Because both false-positive and false-negative results occur, angiography usually is required to confirm the diagnosis. Computerized tomography (CT) of the liver may be helpful in equivocal cases. Spiral CT has been shown to be

Table 6–15 Incidence of Hepatic Artery Thrombosis in Children

Author	Design	Population	Number	HAT Number	Incidence	Time from Transplant to Diagnosis
Segel et al[281]	PC	Children	18	7	40%	NR
Dalen[282]	R	Children	53	6	11%	1 mo (1.5–8)
Todo[283]	R	NR	87	13	14.9%	NR
Esquival[285]	R	< 1 yr	26	5	25%	NR
Hoffer[284]	R	10 mo–2 yr	15	5	33%	NR
Lerut[160]	R	1 d–18 yr	136	14	10.7%	8 d (1–15)
Kaplan[286]	R	2.6 yr (0.1–9.6)	1400	10	1.1%	15 d (5–63)
Marujo[287]	R	< 10 kg > 10 kg	7169	75	9.8% 7.6%	10 d (1–36)
de Carvalho et al[288]	R	< 1 yr 1–4 yr 4–14 yr	26 112 65	3 9 4	11.5% 8.0% 6.2 %	NR NR NR
Stevens et al[289]	R	3 mo–2 yr	60 61 13	15 9 3	25% WL 15% CL 23% LRD	NR NR NR
Rela et al[290]	R	< 5 yr	73	8	11%	1mo (3 d–3 mo)

HAT = hepatic artery thrombosis; PC = prospective cohort; R = retrospective study; NR = not reported; WL = whole liver; CL = cadaveric liver; LRD = living related donor.

sensitive and specific in adults.[293] The value of magnetic resonance imaging (MRI) is yet to be fully determined.[160,294]

The prophylactic use of anticoagulants, such as UFH, LMWH, and aspirin, is controversial. The delay in occurrence of HAT and the report of a circulating dermatan sulfate (DS) proteoglycan (PG) in the first postoperative week both suggest that anticoagulation may be helpful. Mitchell et al[295] discovered the presence of three circulating anticoagulants with antithrombin activities in 24 children who underwent liver transplantation (mean age, 4.6 yr; range, 5 mo–18 yr). The primary anticoagulant was a DS PG. A lesser amount of anticoagulant activity in the form of a heparin sulfate (HS)-heparin PG also was present. Both the DS PG and the HS-heparin PG had maximal activity during the intraoperative period and disappeared during the first postoperative week. The concentrations, anticoagulant activities, and time course of these PGs suggested that they may be clinically important anticoagulants and may be protecting children from HAT in the immediate postoperative period.[295]

The mortality rate for patients with HAT ranges between 25% and 70%.[160,283,294,296,297] Anticoagulation alone is not effective. Surgical intervention or retransplantation usually is necessary, but emergency revascularization procedures may be successful in as many as 20% of children.[283,296,298–302] Thrombolytic therapy has been tried with success in a limited number of cases.[296,300–303] One report described successful thrombolytic therapy in a 9-year-old with HAT, 21 days after transplantation. A catheter was introduced into the most proximal zone of the hepatic artery and anchored in the thrombus. Urokinase, 3000 IU/kg was infused over 15 minutes and followed by 3000 IU/kg/per hour for 12 hours. The hepatic artery was patent after 24 hours of treatment and balloon dilatation.[296] A French report described the use of thrombectomy followed by locally instilled UK in three cases of HAT. Complete resolution of the TE occurred in one case and the other two showed partial resolution.[300]

Mesenteric arteries Causes of arterial TEs in the mesenteric circulation include UAC,[64] an abscess,[304] surgery,[305] Crohn's disease,[306] congenital prothrombotic disorders,[307] and congenital nephrotic syndrome.[308]

Blalock-Taussig shunts Blalock-Taussig shunts and modifications are used in children with significant cyanotic CHD who present in early infancy and cannot undergo more definitive procedures. Those shunts enhance pulmonary blood flow by redirecting subclavian arterial flow to the pulmonary artery (Figure 6–5). Gortex grafts frequently are used in modified BT shunts.[309,310]

The natural history of BT shunts has been assessed using angiography. Godart et al assessed BT shunt growth and development of stenosis and distortion in 78 patients at a mean follow-up time of 51 months.[311] They found that growth of the pulmonary arteries occurred but did not exceed the normal growth of the pulmonary arterial tree. However, a shunt procedure could cause distortion and stenosis of the pulmonary artery, which may have important implications for future corrective surgical intervention. Risk factors for patency and stenosis include the age of the patient and graft size.[312,313]

The incidence of thrombotic occlusion of BT shunts in the literature ranges from 1% to 17%.[142,312–325] There is no consistent approach to the prevention of TEs related to BT shunts. Some investigators use initial treatment with UFH followed by aspirin (1 to 10 mg/kg/d).[324] Children who develop acute BT shunt occlusion usually require some form of intervention, which may include thrombolytic therapy or stenting. Local thrombolytic therapy with TPA and SK has been

used successfully in some children.[319,326] Angioplasty, balloon dilation, stent implantation,[316,327] and repeat surgery[312,314] are other therapeutic options. The latter usually requires subsequent anticoagulation therapy.

Fontan operation The Fontan operation involves a direct right atrium-to-pulmonary artery connection for patients with univentricular hearts (Figure 6–6).[328–330] Since 1988, a modified Fontan involving a double cavopulmonary anastomosis and placement of a Gortex baffle within the right atrium has been used.[331] Potential sites for TEs include the surface of the Gortex tube (venous location) and the blind stump of the main pulmonary artery (arterial circulation).[332] There is no consensus on the optimal use of anticoagulants to prevent TE associated with a Fontan procedure (see Chapter 8).

GUIDELINES

Peripheral Artery Catheterization

1. Prophylactic UFH is recommended in doses of 1 to 3 units/kg per hour to maintain patency.

2. Unfractionated heparin, LMWH, or thrombolytic therapy may be necessary to treat peripheral artery TEs secondary to a catheter. Clinical circumstances and severity of the TE dictate the choice of therapy.

Umbilical Artery Catheterization

1. Prophylactic UFH is recommended in doses of 1 to 3 units/kg per hour to maintain patency.[11,54–58]

2. UFH, LMWH, or thrombolytic therapy may be necessary to treat a UAC-related TE. Clinical circumstances and severity of the TE dictate the choice of therapy (see Chapters 9 and 11).

Prophylaxis for Cardiac Catheterization in Children and Newborns

1. Unfractionated heparin in doses of 100 to 150 units/kg as a bolus,[118] or by a more constant supplementation,[119] is recommended to prevent TEs,

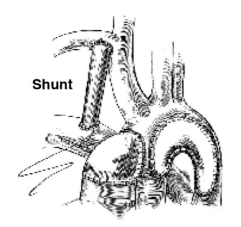

Figure 6–5 A Blalock-Taussig shunt, which connects the right subclavian artery to the pulmonary artery.

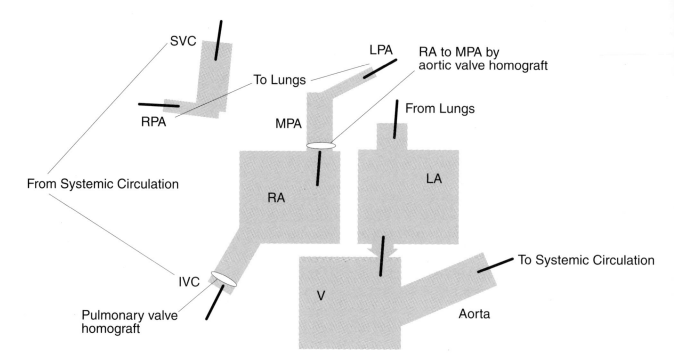

Figure 6–6 Schematic diagram of the Fontan procedure.

SVC = superior vena cava; RPA = right pulmonary artery; LPA = left pulmonary artery; RA = right atrium; LA = left atrium; V = ventricle; IVC = inferior vena cava.

particularly in small children. Aspirin alone cannot be recommended.[135]

2. Unfractionated heparin, LMWH, or thrombolytic therapy may be necessary to treat a CC-related TE. Clinical circumstances and severity of the TE dictate the initial choice of therapy (see Chapters 9 and 11). Usually, therapy is instituted with UFH (see Chapter 9), and if there is no response, thrombolytic therapy is administered (see Chapter 11).

Mechanical Prosthetic Heart Valves in Children

1. Recommended prophylactic anticoagulant therapy in children with mechanical prosthetic heart valves in the mitral valve location is OA with a target international normalized ratio (INR) range of 2.5 to 3.5.[251,254–256,259–261,263–267]

2. Children with mechanical prosthetic heart valves who suffer systemic embolism despite adequate OA therapy may benefit from the addition of aspirin at

doses of 6 to 20 mg/kg per day,[333] or Dipyridamole, (2–5 mg/kg/d), in addition to OA therapy.[334,335]

3. When full-dose OA therapy is contraindicated, long-term OA therapy sufficient to increase the INR to 2.0 to 3.0 in combination with aspirin (6–20 mg/kg/d) and dipyridamole (2–5 mg/kg/d) may be used. This recommendation is an extrapolation of one study in adults[333] and one case series in children.[267]

Kawasaki Disease in Children

1. Recommended prophylaxis for coronary artery aneurysms secondary to Kawasaki disease is an initial, single dose of IVIG (2 gm/kg) and aspirin (80–100 mg/kg/d) during the first 14 days.[157, 225,226] Subsequently, aspirin at 3 to 5 mg/kg/per day for 7 weeks or longer is recommended.[227,228]

Myocardial Infarction

1. If a child presents with myocardial infarction within 3 hours of symptoms, thrombolytic therapy

with TPA should be considered. One approach is to give an intravenous bolus of 0.2 mg/kg (maximum of 15 mg) of TPA followed by an infusion of 0.75 mg/kg over a 30-minute period (maximum of 50 mg) and then an infusion of 0.5 mg/kg over a 60-minute period (maximum of 35 mg). Unfractionated heparin should be given simultaneously, beginning with an intravenous bolus of 75 units/kg followed by 20 units/kg per hour.[233]

Blalock-Taussig Shunts

1. Further clinical investigation is needed before definitive recommendations can be made. One option is to initially treat patients with BT shunts with therapeutic amounts of UFH followed by aspirin at doses of 3 to 5 mg/kg per day indefinitely.

Fontan Operations

1. Further clinical investigation is required before recommendations for primary postoperative prophylaxis can be made. Current options include aspirin or therapeutic amounts of UFH followed by OA therapy to achieve an INR of 2 to 3. The optimal duration of prophylaxis is unknown.

REFERENCES

1. Flanigan D, Keifer T, Schuler J, et al. Experience with Iatrogenic pediatric vascular injuries. Ann Surg 1983; 198:430–9.
2. White JJ, Talbert JL, Haller JA. Peripheral arterial injuries in infants and children. Ann Surg 1968;167:757–65.
3. Formanek G, Frech RS, Amplatz K. Arterial thrombosis formation during clinical percutaneous catheterization. Circulation 1970;41:833–9.
4. Rao PS, Thapar MK,. Rogers J H J, et al. Effect of intraarterial injection of heparin on the complications of percutaneous arterial catheterization in infants and children. Cathet Cardiovasc Diagn 1981;7: 235–46.
5. Nejad MS, Klaper MA, Steggoda FR, Gianturco C. Clotting on the outer surfaces of vascular catheters. Radiology 1968;91:248–50.
6. Siegelman SS, Caplan LH, Annes GP. Complications of catheter angiography. Study with oscillometry and "pullout" angiograms. Radiology 1968;91:251–3.
7. Mortensson W, Hallbook T, Lundstrom N. Percutaneous catheterization of the femoral vessels in children. II. Thrombotic occlusion of the catheterized artery: frequency and causes. Pediatr Radiol 1975; 4:1–9.
8. Bergstrom K, Jorulf H. Reaction of femoral and common carotid arteries in infants after puncture or percutaneous catheterization. Acta Radiol [Diagn] (Stockh)1976;17:577–80.
9. Randolph AG, Cook DJ, Gonzales CA. Benefit of heparin in central venous and pulmonary artery catheters: a meta-analysis of randomized controlled trials. Chest 1998;113:165–71.
10. Bryant BG. Drugs, fluid, and blood products administered through the umbilical artery catheter: complication experiences from one NICU. Neonatal Netw 1990;9:27–46.
11. Jackson J, Truog W, Watchko J, et al. Efficacy of thromboresistant umbilical artery catheters in reducing aortic thrombosis and related complications. J Pediatr 1987;110:102–5.
12. Lindon JN, Collins REC, Coe NP. In vivo assessment of thromboresistant materials by determination of platelet survival. Circ Res 1980;46:84-90.
13. Boros SJ, Thompson TR, Reynolds JW, et al. Reduced thrombus formation with silicone elastomere (silastic) umbilical artery catheters. Pediatrics 1975; 56:981–6.
14. Bailly AL, Laurent A, Lu H, et al. Fibrinogen binding and platelet retention: relationship with the thrombogenicity of catheters. J Biomed Mater Res 1996; 30:101-8.
15. Hoar PF, Wilson RM, Mangano DT. Heparin bonding reduces thrombogenicity of pulmonary artery catheters. N Engl J Med 1980;305:993–5.
16. Mollenholt P, Eriksson I, Andersson T. Thrombogenicity of pulmonary-artery catheters. Intensive Care Med 1987;13:57–9.
17. Girod DA, Hurwitz RA, Caldwell RL. Heparinization for prevention of thrombosis following pediatric percutaneous arterial catheterization. Pediatr Cardiol 1982;3:175–80.
18. Allen EV. Thromboangiitis obliterans: methods of diagnosis of chronic occlusive arterial lesions distal to the wrist with illustrative cases. Am J Med Sci 1929;178:237–44.
19. Downs JB, Chapman RL, Hawkins F. Prolonged radial artery catheterization. An evaluation of heparinized catheters and continuous irrigation. Arch Surg 1974;108:671–3.
20. American Association of Critical Care Nurses. Evaluation of the effects of heparinized and nonheparinized flush solutions on the patency of arterial pressure monitoring lines: the AACN Thunder Project. Am J Crit Care 1993;2:3–15.

21. Butt W, Shann F, McDonnell G, Hudson. I. Effect of heparin concentration and infusion rate on the patency of arterial catheters. Crit Care Med 1987;15:230-2.

22. Kulkarni M, Elsner C, Ouellet D, Zeldin R. Heparinized saline versus normal saline in maintaining patency of the radial artery catheter. Can J Surg 1994;37:37-42.

23. Clifton GD, Branson P, Kelly HJ, et al. Comparison of normal saline and heparin solutions for maintenance of arterial catheter patency. Heart Lung 1991;20:115-18.

24. Sellden H, Nilsson K, Larsson LE, Eskstrom-Jodal B. Radial arterial catheters in children and neonates: a prospective study. Crit Care Med 1987;15:1106-9.

25. Rais-Bahrami K, Karna P, Dolanski EA. Effect of fluids on life span of peripheral arterial lines. Am J Perinatol 1990;7:122-4.

26. Heulitt MJ, Farrington EA, O'Shea M, et al. Double-blind, randomized, controlled trial of papaverine-containing infusions to prevent failure of arterial catheters in pediatric patients. Crit Care Med 1993;21:825-9.

27. Tarry S, Moser AJ, Makhoul RG. Peripheral arterial thrombosis in the nephrotic syndrome. Surgery 1993;114:618-23.

28. Mayer T, Levine ME, Thompson FA. Necrosis of the forearm following radial artery catheterization in a patient with Reye's syndrome. Pediatrics 1980; 65:141-3.

29. Martin JE, Moran JF, Cook LS, et al. Neonatal aortic thrombosis complicating umbilical artery catheterization: successful treatment with retroperitoneal aortic thrombectomy. Surgery 1989;105:793-6.

30. Fletcher MA, Brown DR, Landers S, Seguin J. Umbilical arterial catheter use: report of an audit conducted by the Study Group for Complications of Perinatal Care. Am J Perinatol 1994;11:94-9.

31. Mokrohisky ST, Levine R, Blumhagen JB, et al. Low positioning of umbilical artery catheters increases associated complications in newborn infants. N Engl J Med 1978;299:561-4.

32. Harris MS, Little GA. Umbilical artery catheters: high, low, or no. J Perinatal Med 1978;6:15-21.

33. Wesstrom G, Finnstrom O, Stenport G. Umbilical artery catheterization in newborns. I. Thrombosis in relation to catheter type and position. Acta Paediatr Scand 1979;68:575-81.

34. Neal WA, Reynolds JW, Jarvis CW, Williams HJ. Umbilical artery catheterization: demonstration of arterial thrombosis by aortography. Pediatrics 1972; 50:6-13.

35. Wesstrom G. Umbilical artery catheterization in newborns. V. A clinical follow-up study. Acta Pediatr Scand 1980;69:371-4.

36. Wesstrom G, Lassvik C. Umbilical artery catheterization in newborns. IV. Strain-gauge plethysmography for the diagnosis of catheter-related thromboembolism in the legs. Acta Paediatr Scand 1980;69: 365-70.

37. Umbilical Artery Catheter Trial Study Group. Relationship of intraventricular hemorrhage or death with the level of umbilical artery catheter placement: a multicenter randomized clinical trial. Pediatrics 1992;90:881-7.

38. Tooley WH, Myerberg DC. Should we put catheters in the umbilical artery? Pediatrics 1978;66:853-54.

39. Tooley WH. What is the risk of an umbilical artery catheter? Pediatrics 1972;50:1–2.

40. Cochran WD, Davis HT, Smith CA. Advantages and complications of umbilical artery catheterization in the newborn. Pediatrics 1968;42:769-77.

41. Gilhooly J, Lindenberg J, Reynold J. Survey of umbilical artery catheter practices. Crit Care Med 1990; 18:247.

42. Kempley ST, Loftus BG, Cooper D, Gamsu HR. 1993. Randomized trial of umbilical arterial catheter position. Acta Paediatr 1993;82:173-176.

43. Krueger TC, Neblett WW, O'Neill JA. Management of aortic thrombosis secondary to umbilical artery catheters in neonates. J Pediatr Surg 1985; 20:328-32.

44. Stringel G, Mercer S, Richler M, McMurray B. Catheterization of the umbilical artery in neonates: surgical implications. Can J Surg 1985;28:143-6.

45. Malloy MH, Cutter FR. The association of heparin exposure with intraventricular hemorrhage among very low birth weight infants. J Perinatol 1995; 15:185-91.

46. Schmidt B, Andrew M. Neonatal thrombotic disease: prevention, diagnosis, and therapy. J Pediatr 1988;113:407-10.

47. Joseph R, Chong A, Teh M, et al. Thrombotic complication of umbilical arterial catheterization and its sequelae. Ann Acad Med Sing 1985;14:576-82.

48. Vailas G, Brouillette R, Scott J, et al. Neonatal aortic thrombosis: recent experience. J Pediatr 1986; 109:101-08.

49. Alpert J, O'Donnel JA, Parsonnet V, et al. Clinically recognized limb ischemia in the neonate after umbilical artery catheterization. Am J Surg 1980; 140:413-18.

50. O'Neill JA. Neblett WWI, Born ML. Management of major thromboembolic complications of umbilical artery catheters. J Pediatr Surg 1981;16:972-8.

51. Caeton AJ, Goetzman BW. Risky business. Umbilical arterial catheterization. Am J Dis Child 1985;139: 120-1.

52. Cohen RS, Ramachandran P, Kim EH, Glasscock GF. Retrospective analysis of risks associated with an umbilical artery catheter system for continuous moni-

toring of arterial oxygen tension. J Perinatol 1995;15:195-8.

53. Hall RT, Rhodes PG. Total parenteral alimentation via indwelling umbilical catheters in the newborn period. Arch Dis Child 1976;51:929-34.

54. Rajani K, Goetzman B, Wennberg R. Effect of heparinization of fluids infused through an umbilical artery catheter on catheter patency and frequency of complications. Pediatrics 1979;63:552-6.

55. David R, Merten D, Anderson J, Gross S. Prevention of umbilical artery catheter clots with heparinized infusates. Dev Pharmacol Ther 1981;2:117-26.

56. Bosque E, Weaver L. Continuous versus intermittent heparin infusion of umbilical artery catheters in the newborn infant. J Pediatr 1986;108:141-3.

57. Horgan M, Bartoletti A, Polonsky S, et al. Effect of heparin infusates in umbilical arterial catheters on frequency of thrombotic complications. J Pediatr 1987;111:774-8.

58. Ankola P, Atakent Y. Effect of adding heparin in very low concentration to the infusate to prolong the patency of umbilical artery catheters. Am J Perinatol 1993;10:229-32.

59. Oppenheimer DA, Carroll BA, Garth KE. Ultrasonic detection of complications following umbilical arterial catheterization in the neonate. Radiology 1982;145:667-72.

60. Seibert JJ, Taylor BJ, Williamson SL, et al. Sonographic detection of neonatal umbilical-artery thrombosis. AJR Am J Roentgenol 1987;148:965-68.

61. Cook V, Weeks J, Brown J, Bendon R. Umbilical artery occlusion and fetoplacental thromboembolism. Obstet Gynecol 1995;85:870-2.

62. Goetzman BW, Stadalnik RC, Bogren HG, et al. Thrombotic complications of umbilical artery catheters: a clinical and radiographic study. Pediatrics 1975;56:374-9.

63. Payne RM, Martin TC, Bower RJ, Canter CE. Management and follow-up of arterial thrombosis in the neonatal period. J Pediatr 1989;114:853-8.

64. Shah JB, Bracero LA, Gewitz MH, et al. Umbilical artery catheters and blood flow velocities in the superior mesenteric artery: effect of insertion, removal, aspiration, and bolus infusion. J Clin Ultrasound 1998;26:73-7.

65. Glickstein JS, Rutkowski M, Schacht R, Friedman D. Renal blood flow velocity in neonates with and without umbilical artery catheters. J Clin Ultrasound 1994;22:543-50.

66. Olinsky A, Aitken FG, Isdale JM. Thrombus formation after umbilical arterial catheterization: an angiographic study. S Afr Med J 1975;49:1467-70.

67. Saia OS, Rubatelli FF, D'Elia RD, et al. Clinical and aortographic assessment of the complications of arterial catheterization. Eur J Pediatr 1978; 128:169-79.

68. Henriksson P, Wesstromg G, Hedner U. Umbilical artery catheterization in newborns. III Thrombosis: a study of some predisposing factors. Acta Paediatr Scand 1979;68:719-23.

69. Wigger H, Bransilver BR, Blanc WA. Thromboses due to catheterization in infants and children. J Pediatr 1970;76:1-11.

70. Marsh JL, King W, Barrett C, Fonkalsrud EW. Serious complications after umbilical artery catheterization for neonatal monitoring. Arch Surg 1975; 110:1203-8.

71. Lesko S, Mitchell A, Eopstein M, et al. Heparin use: a risk factor for intraventricular hemorrhage in low birth-weight infants. N Engl J Med 1986; 314:1156-60.

72. Chang G, Lueder S, DiMichele D, et al. Heparin and the risk of intraventricular hemorrhage among very low birth-weight infants. J Pediatr 1997;131:362-6.

73. Gilhooly JT, Lindenberg JA, Reynold JW. Survey of umbilical catheter practices. Clin Res 1987;34:142a.

74. Caplan MS, Cohn RA, Langman CB, et al. Favourable outcome of neonatal aortic thrombosis and renovascular hypertension. J Pediatr 1989;115:291-5.

75. Seibert JJ, Northington FJ, Miers JF, Taylor BJ. Aortic thrombosis after umbilical artery catheterization in neonates: prevalence of complications on long-term follow-up. Am J Roentgenol 1991;56:567-9.

76. Boros SJ, Nystrom JF, Thompson TR, et al. Leg growth following umbilical artery catheter-associated thrombus formation: a 4-year follow-up. J Pediatr 1975; 87:973-6.

77. Weinberg G, Brion LP, Vega-Richf CR. Dangers of arterial catheters in critically ill neonates. Pediatrics 1990;85:627-8.

78. Letts M, Blastorah B, Al-Azzam S. Neonatal gangrene of the extremities. J Pediatr Orthop 1997;17:397-401.

79. Adelman RD. Abdominal aortic aneurysm 18 years after apparent resolution of an umbilical catheter-associated thrombosis. J Pediatr 1998;132:874-5.

80. Krishnamoorthy KS, Fernandex RJ, De Long GR. Paraplegia associated with umbilical artery catheterization in the newborn. Pediatrics 1976;58:443-5.

81. Plumer LB, Kaplan GW, Mendoza SA. Hypertension in infants: a complication of umbilical arterial catheterization. J Pediatr 1976;89:802-5.

82. Bapat VM, Dinesh S, Dhaded SB, et al. Delayed presentation of false abdominal aortic aneurysm following umbilical artery catheterization. Thorac Cardiovasc Surg 1997;45:154-7.

83. Ayers A. Predictive factors for neonatal morbidity in neonates. Am J Obstet Gynecol 1998;178:872-3.

84. Haldeman S, Fowler GW, Ashwal S, Schneider S. Acute flaccid neonatal paraplegia. Neurology 1983;33: 93-5.

85. Malin SW, Baumgart S, Rosenberg HK, Foreman J. Nonsurgical management of obstructive aortic thrombosis complicated by renovascular hypertension in the neonate. J Pediatr R 1983;106:630-4.

86. Munoz ME, Roche C, Escriba et al. Flaccid paraplegia as complication of umbilical artery catheterization. Pediatr Neurol 1993;9:401-3.

87. Netz H, Madu B, Rohner G. Heparinization during percutaneous cardiac catheterization in children. Pediatr Cardiol 1987;8:167-8.

88. Celermajer DS, Robinson JTC, Taylor JFN. Vascular access in previously catheterized children and adolescents: a prospective study of 131 consecutive cases. Br Heart J 1993;70:554–7.

89. Jureidini SB, Balfour IC, Marshall D, Nouri S. Arterial approach as the sole route for cardiac catheterization in infants and children with complex congenital heart disease. Am Heart J 1991;22:1775–7.

90. Real F, Scarpelli JP, Ruttner EM, Rudolph AM. Arteriotomy and local circulation in children: the value of oscillometry. J Pediatr 1966;69:372–7.

91. Mansfield PB, Gozzaniga AB, Litwin SB. Management of arterial injuries related to cardiac catheterization in children and young adults. Circulation 1970; 42:501–7.

92. Stanger P, Heymann MA, Tarnoff H, et al. Complications of cardiac catheterization of neonates, infants, and children. Circulation 1974;50:595–608.

93. Rothman A. Arterial complications of interventional cardiac catheterization in patients with congenital heart disease. Circulation 1990;82:1868-1871.

94. Lababidi Z, Wu JR, Walls JT. Percutaneous balloon aortic valvuloplasty: results in 23 patients. Am J Cardiol 1984;53:194-7.

95. Helagason H, Keane JF, Fellows KE, et al. Balloon dilation of the aortic valve: studies in normal lambs and in children with aortic stenosis. J Am Coll Cardiol 1987;9:816-22.

96. Perry SB, Keane JF, Lock JE. Interventional catheterization in pediatric congenital and acquired heart disease. Am J Cardiol 1988;61:109G-117G.

97. Choy M, Beekman RH, Rocchini AP, et al. Percutaneous balloon valvuloplasty for valvar aortic stenosis in infants and children. Am J Cardiol 1987;59: 1010-13.

98. Beekman RH, Rocchini AP, Crowley DC, et al. Comparison of single and double balloon valvuloplasty in children with aortic stenosis. J Am Coll Cardiol 1988;12:480-5.

99. Shrivastava S, Das GS, Dev V, et al. Follow-up after percutaneous balloon valvoplasty for noncalcific aortic stenosis. Am J Cardiol 1990;65:250-2.

100. Sullivan ID, Wren C, Bain H, et al. Balloon dilation of the aortic valve for congenital aortic stenosis in childhood. Br Heart J 1989;61:186-191.

101. Rocchini AP, Beekman RH, Ben Shachar G, et al. Balloon aortic valvuloplasty: results of the Valvuloplasty and Angioplasty of Congenital Anomalies Registry. Am J Cardiol 1990;65:784-9.

102. Beekman RH, Rocchini AP, Dick M, Percutaneous balloon angioplasty for native coarctation of the aorta. J Am Coll Cardiol 1987;10:1078-84.

103. Rao PS. Balloon angioplasty of aortic coarctation: a review. Clin Cardiol 1989;12:618-28.

104. Attia IM, Lababidi ZA. Early results of balloon antioplasty of native aortic coarctation in young adults. Am J Cardiol 1988;61:930-1.

105. Suarez De Lezo J, Sancho M, Pan M, et al. Angiographic follow-up after balloon angioplasty for coarctation of the aorta. J Am Coll Cardiol 1989;3:689-95.

106. Morrow WR, Vick GW, Nihill MR, et al. Balloon dilation of unoperated coarctation of the aorta: short and intermediate term results. J Am Coll Cardiol 1988; 11:133-8.

107. Tynan M, Finley JP, Fontes V, et al. Balloon angioplasty for the treatment of native coarctation: results of Valvuloplasty and Angioplasty of Congenital Anomalies Registry. Am J Cardiol 1990;65:790-2.

108. Hellenbrand WE, Allen HD, Golinko RJ, et al. Balloon angioplasty for aortic recoarctation: results of Valvuloplasty and Angioplasty of Congenital Anomalies Registry. Am J Cardiol 1990;65:793-7.

109. Allen HD, Marx GR, Ovitt TW, Goldberg SJ. Balloon dilation angioplasty of postoperative aortic obstructions. Am J Cardiol 1986;57:828-32.

110. Saul JP, Keane JF, Fellows KE, Lock JE. Balloon dilation angioplasty of postoperative aortic obstructions. Am J Cardiol 1987;59:943-8.

111. Lababidi Z, Weinhaus L, Stoeckle H Jr, Walls JT. Transluminal balloon dilatation for discrete subaortic stenosis. Am J Cardiol 1987;59:423-5.

112. Suarez de Lezo J, Pan M, Sancho M, et al. Percutaneous transluminal balloon dilatation for discrete subaortic stenosis. Am J Cardiol 1986;58:619-21.

113. Tyagi S, Arora R, Kaul UA, Khalilullah M. Percutaneous transluminal balloon dilatation in supravalvular aortic stenosis. Am Heart J 1989;118:1041-44.

114. Marx GR, Allen HD, Ovitt TW, Hanson W. Balloon dilation angioplasty of Blalock-Taussig shunts. Am J Cardiol 1988;62:824-7.

115. Rothman A, Perry SB, Keane JF, Lock JE. Early results and follow-up of balloon angioplasty for branch pulmonary artery stenoses. J Am Coll Cardiol 1990;15: 1109-17.

116. Stefanadis C, Kourouklis C, Stratos C, et al. Percutaneous balloon mitral valvuloplasty by retrograde left atrial catheterization. Am J Cardiol 1990;65:650-4.

117. Cooper SG, Sullivan ID, Bull C, Taylor JFN. Balloon dilation of pulmonary venous pathway obstruction after Mustard repair for transposition of the great arteries. J Am Coll Cardiol 1989;14:194-8.

118. Freed M, Keane J, Rosenthal A. The use of heparinization to prevent arterial thrombosis after percutaneous cardiac catheterization in children. Circulation 1974;50:565-9.

119. Saxena A, Gupta R, Kumar RK, et al. Predictors of arterial thrombosis after diagnostic cardiac catheterization in infants and children randomized to two heparin doses. Cathet Cardiovasc Diagn 1997;41:400-3.

120. Ino T, Benson LN, Freedom RM, et al. Thrombolytic therapy for femoral artery thrombosis after pediatric cardiac catheterization. Am Heart J 1988;115:633-9.

121. McFadden PM, Ochsner JL, Mills N. Management of thrombotic complications of invasive arterial monitoring of the upper extremity. J Cardiovasc Surg 1983;24:35-9.

122. Mortensson W. Angiography of the femoral artery following percutaneous catheterization in infants and children. Acta Radiol [Diagn] (Stockh) 1976;17:581-93.

123. Vlad P, Hohn A, Lambert EC. Retrograde arterial catheterization of the left heart. Circulation 1964;29:787-8.

124. Smith C, Green RM. Pediatric vascular injuries. Surgery 1981;90:20-31.

125. Jones J, Hunter D. Consensus methods for medical and health services research. BMJ 1995;311:376-80.

126. Hurwitz RA, Franken EA, Girod DA. Angiographic determination of arterial patency after percutaneous catheterization in infants and small children. Circulation 1977;56:102-5.

127. Wessel DL, Keane JF, Fellows KE, et al. Fibrinolytic therapy for femoral arterial thrombosis after cardiac catheterization in infants and children. Am J Cardiol 1986;58:347-51.

128. Gagnon RM, Goudreau E, Joyal F, et al. The role of intravenous streptokinase in acute arterial occlusions after cardiac catheterization. Cathet Cardiovasc Diagn 1985;11:409-12.

129. Zenz W, Muntean W, Beitzke A, et al. Tissue plasminogen activator (alteplase) treatment for femoral artery thrombosis after cardiac catheterization in infants and children. Br Heart J 1993;70:382-5.

130. Brus F, Witsenburg M, Hofhuis WJD et al. Streptokinase treatment for femoral artery thrombosis after arterial cardiac catheterization in infants and children. Br Heart J 1990;63:291-4.

131. Kothari SS, Kumar RK, Varma S, Saxena A. Thrombolytic therapy in infants for femoral artery thrombosis following cardiac catheterization. Indian Heart J 1996;48:246-8.

132. Perry MO. Iatrogenic injuries of arteries in infants. Surg Gynecol Obstet 1983;157:325-31.

133. Burrows P, Benson L, Williams W, et al. Iliofemoral arterial complications of balloon angioplasty for systemic obstructions in infants and children. Circulation 1990;82:1697-704.

134. Padmanabhan J, Krovetz LJ, Varghese PJ, et al. Effect of topical papaverine in preventing thrombosis following arteriotomies. A double-blind study in infants and children. J Pediatr 1977;81:792-3.

135. Freed M, Rosenthal A, Fyler D. Attempts to reduce arterial thrombosis after cardiac catheterization in children: use of percutaneous technique and aspirin. Am Heart J 1974;87:283-6.

136. Andrew M, MacIntyre B, Williams W, et al. Heparin therapy during cardiopulmonary bypass requires ongoing quality control. Thromb Haemost 1993;70:937-41.

137. Gravlee GP, Case LD, Angert KC, et al. Variability of the activated coagulation time. Anesth Analg 1988;67:469-72.

138. Kern IB. Management of children with chronic femoral artery obstruction. J Pediatr Surg 1977;12:83-90.

139. Taylor LM, Troutman R, Filiciano P, et al. Late complications after femoral artery catheterization in children less than 5 years of age. J Vasc Surg 1990;11:297-306.

140. Kirk CR, Qureshi SA. Streptokinase in the management of arterial thrombosis in infancy. Int J Cardiol 1989;25:15-20.

141. Levy M, Benson LN, Burrows PE, et al. Tissue plasminogen activator for the treatment of thromboembolism in infants and children. J Pediatr 1991;118:467-72.

142. Ries M, Singer H, Hofbeck M. Thrombolysis of a modified Blalock-Taussig shunt with recombinant tissue plasminogen activator in a newborn infant with pulmonary atresia and ventricular septal defect. Br Heart J 1994;72:201-2.

143. Lincoln JCR, Deverall PB. The treatment of arterial thrombosis in infants and children by balloon catheters. J Pediatr Surg 1969;4:359-62.

144. Leblanc J, Wood AE, O'Shea MA, et al. Peripheral arterial trauma in children. A fifteen-year review. J Cardiovasc Surg 1985;26:325-31.

145. Chaikof EL, Dodson TF, Salam A, et al. Acute arterial thrombosis in the very young. J Vasc Surg 1992;16:428-35.

146. Broijersen A, Eriksson M, Wiman B, et al. Gemfibrozil treatment of combined hyperlipoproteinemia: no improvement of fibrinolysis despite marked reduction of plasma triglyceride levels. Arterioscler Thromb Vasc Biol 1996;16:511-6.

147. Oliver MF, Pyorala K, Shepherd J. Management of hyperlipidaemia: why, when, and how to treat. Eur Heart J 1997;18:371-5.

148. D'Angelo A, Selhub J. 1 Homocysteine and thrombotic disease. Blood 1997;90:1-11.

149. Tonstad S, Refsum H, Sivertsen M, et al. Relation of total homocysteine and lipid levels in children to premature cardiovascular death in male relatives. Pediatr Res 1996;40:47-52.

150. Malinow MR, Rajkovic A, Duell PB, et al. The relationship between maternal and neonatal umbilical cord plasma homocyst(e)ine suggests a potential role for maternal homocyst(e)ine in fetal metabolism. Am J Obstet Gynecol 1998;178:228-33.

151. de Jong SC, Stehouwer CDA, van den Berg M, et al. Endothelial marker proteins in hyperhomocysteinemia. Thromb Haemost 1997;78:1332-7.

152. Streif W, Monagle P, South M, et al. Spontaneous arterial thrombosis in children. J Pediatr 1999;134:110-2.

153. Hong C, Yun Y, Choi J, et al Takayasu arteritis in Korean children: clinical report of seventy cases. Heart Vessels 1992;7:91-6.

154. Zheng D, Fan D, Liu L. Takayasu arteritis in China: a report of 530 cases. Heart Vessels 1992;7:32-6.

155. Wiggelinkhuizen J, Cremin B, Cywes S.. Spontaneous recanalization of renal artery stenosis in childhood Takayasu arteritis: a case report. S Afr Med J 1980;57:96-8.

156. Kawasaki T. Discovery of Kawasaki disease (muco-cutaneous lymph node syndrome) and its research activities. Nippon Rinsho 1976;34:222-7.

157. Durongpisitkul K, Fururaj VJ, Park JM, Martin CF. The prevention of coronary artery aneurysm in Kawasaki disease: a meta-analysis on the efficacy of aspirin and immunoglobulin treatment. Pediatrics 1995;96:1057-61.

158. Hall T, McDiarmid S, Grant E, et al. False-negative duplex Doppler studies in children with hepatic artery thrombosis after liver transplantation. AJR Am J Roentgenol 1990;154:573-5.

159. Flint E, Sumkin J, Zajko A, Bowen A. Duplex sonography of hepatic artery thrombosis after liver transplantation. AJR Am J Roentgenol 1988;151:481-3.

160. Lerut J, Gordon R, Tzakis A, et al. The hepatic artery in orthotopic liver transplantation. Helv Chir Acta 1988;55:367-78.

161. LeBlanc J, Culham J, Chan K, et al. Treatment of grafts and major vessel thrombosis with low-dose streptokinase in children. Ann Thorac Surg 1986;41:630-5.

162. Samara E, Voss B, Pederson J. Renal artery thrombosis associated with elevated cyclosporine levels: a case report and review of the literature. Transplant Proc 1988;20:119-23.

163. Fallat RW, Tsang RC, Glueck CJ. Hypercholesterolemia and hypertriglyceridemia in children. Prev Med 1974;3:390-405.

164. Haber C, Kwiterovich PO. Dyslipoproteinemia and xanthomatosis. Pediatr Dermatol 1984;1:261-80.

165. Vilaseca MA, Moyano D, Artuch R, et al. Selective screening for hyperhomocysteinemia in pediatric patients. Clin Chem 1998;44:662-4.

166. Reddy MN. Reference ranges for total homocysteine in children. Clin Chim Acta 1997;262:153-5.

167. Stein JH, McBride PE. Hyperhomocysteinemia and atherosclerotic vascular disease: pathophysiology, screening, and treatment. Arch Intern Med 1998;158:1301-6.

168. West RJ, Lloyd JK. Hypercholesterolemia in childhood. Adv Pediatr 1979;26:1-34.

169. Haitas B, Baker SG, Meyer TE, et al. Natural history and cardiac manifestations of homozygous familial hypercholesterolaemia. QJM 1990;76:731-40.

170. Rose V, Wilson G, Steiner G. Familial hypercholesterolemia: report of coronary death at age 3 in a homozygous child and prenatal diagnosis in a heterozygous sibling. J Pediatr 1982;100:757-9.

171. Sprecher DL, Schaefer EJ, Kent KM, et al. Cardiovascular features of homozygous familial hypercholesterolemia: analysis of 16 patients. Am J Cardiol 1984;54:20-30.

172. Hoeg JM. Familial hypercholesterolemia. What the zebra can teach us about the horse. JAMA 1994;271:543-6.

173. Goldstein J, Brown M. The LDL receptor defect in familial hypercholesterolemia. Med Clin North Am 1982;66:335-62.

174. Williams ML. Death of a child as a result of familial hypercholesterolaemia. Med J Aust 1989;150:93-4 [published erratum appears in Med J Aust 1989;150:228].

175. Clemens P, Beisiegel U, Steinhagen-Thiessen E. Family study in familial hypercholesterolemia with a receptor-negative homozygous 9-year-old boy. Helv Paediat Acta 1986;41:173-82.

176. Goldstein J, Brown M. Familial hyercholesterolemia. In: Stanbury JB, ed. Metabolic basis of inherited disease. New York: McGraw Hill, 1989.

177. Leonard JV, Clarke M, Macartney FJ, Slack J. Progression of atheroma in homozygous familial hypercholesterolemia during regular plasma exchange. Lancet 1981;2:811-2.

178. Raper SE, Grossman M, Rader DJ, et al. Safety and feasibility of liver-directed ex vivo gene therapy for homozygous familial hypercholesterolemia. Ann Surg 1996;223:116-26.

179. Celermajer DS, Sorensen KE, Gooch VM, et al. Non-invasive detection of endothelial dysfunction in

children and adults at risk of atherosclerosis. Lancet 1992;340:1111-5.

180. Sorensen KE, Celemajer DS, Georgakopoulos D, et al. Impairment of endothelium-dependent dilation is an early event in children with familial hypercholesterolemia and is related to the lipoprotein(a) level. J Clin Invest 1994;93:50-5.

181. Hegele RA, Connelly PW, Cullen-Dean G, Rose V. Elevated plasma lipoprotein(a) associated with abnormal stress thallium scans in children with familial hypercholesterolemia. Am J Cardiol 1993;72:402-6.

182. Mouratidis B. Detection of silent coronary artery disease in adolescents and young adults with familial hypercholesteroemia by single-photon emission computed tomography thallium-201 scanning. Am J Cardiol 1992;70:1109-12.

183. Rubinsztein DC, Rall FJ, Seftel HC, et al. Characterization of six patients who are double heterozygotes for familial hypercholesterolemia and familial defective apo B-100. Arterioscler Thromb 1993;13:1076-81.

184. Rauh G. Familial defective apolipoprotein B100: clinical characteristics of 54 cases. Atherosclerosis 1992;92:233-41.

185. Salen G, Horak I, Rothkopf M, et al. Lethal atherosclerosis associated with abnormal plasma and tissue sterol composition in sitosterolemia with xanthomatosis. J Lipid Res 1985;26:1126-33.

186. Janaki S, Baruah JK, Jayaram SR, et al. Stroke in the young: a four-year study, 1968 to 1972. Stroke 1975;6:318-20.

187. Postiglione A, Nappi A, Brunetti A, et al. Relative protection from cerebral atherosclerosis of young patients with homozygous familial hypercholesterolemia. Atherosclerosis 1991;90:23-30.

188. Rubba A, Mercuri M, Faccenda F, et al. Premature carotid atherosclerosis: does it occur in both familial hypercholesterolemia and homocystinuria? Ultrasound assessment of arterial intima-media thickness and blood flow velocity. Stroke 1994;25:943-50.

189. Mabuchi H. Causes of death in patients with familial hypercholesterolemia. Atherosclerosis 1986;61:1-6.

190. Allen JM, Thompson GR, Myant NB, et al. Cardiovascular complications of homozygous familial hypercholesterolaemia. Br Heart J 1980;44:361-8.

191. Glueck CJ. Pediatric victims of unexplained stroke and their families: familial lipid and lipoprotein abnormalities. Pediatrics 1982;69:308-16.

192. Daniels S. Cerebrovascular arteriosclerosis and ischemic childhood stroke. Stroke 1982;13:360-4.

193. Glueck CJ, Bates SR. Migraine in children: association with primary and familial dyslipoproteinemias. Pediatrics 1986;77:316-21.

194. Guarda LA, Borrero JL. Hand and digital ischemia due to arteriosclerosis and thromboembolization in young adults: pathologic features with clinical correlations. Med Pathol 1990;3:654-8.

195. Rubba P. Extracoronary atherosclerosis in familial hypercholesterolemia. Atherosclerosis 1988;71:205-13.

196. Boers GH, Smals AG, Trijbels FJ, et al. Heterozygosity for homocystinuria in premature peripheral and cerebral occlusive arterial disease. N Engl J Med 1985;313:709-15.

197. Genest JJ. Plasma homosyteine levels in men with premature coronary artery disease. J Am Coll Cardiol 1990;16:1114-9.

198. Clarke R. Hyperhomocysteinemia: an independent risk factor for vascular disease. N Engl J Med 1991;324:1149-55.

199. Mudd SH, Skovby F, Levy HL, et al. The natural history of homocysteinuria due to cystathionine β-synthase deficiency. Am J Hum Genet 1985;37:1-31.

200. Wada Y, Narisawa K, Arakawa T. Infantile type of homocysteinuria with 5,10-methylenetetrahydrofolate reductase deficiency. Monogr Hum Genet 1978;9:140-6.

201. Jacques PF, Bostom AG, Williams RR, et al. Relation between folate status, a common mutation in methylenetetrahydrofolate reductase, and plasma homocysteine concentrations. Circulation 1996;93:7-9.

202. Kluijtmans LA, van den Heuvel LP, Boers GH, et al. Molecular genetic analysis in mild hyperhomocysteinemia: a common mutation in the methylenetetrahydrofolate reductase gene is a genetic risk factor for cardiovascular disease. Am J Hum Genet 1996;58:35-41.

203. Strandness DE, Salzman EW, Shortell CK, Marder VJ. Management of peripheral arterial disease. In: Colman W, Hirsh J, Marder VJ, eds. Hemostasis and thrombosis: basic principles and clinical practice. Philadelphia: JB Lippincott, 1994:1396-1408.

204. Ouriel K, Veith F, Sashara A. A comparison of recombinant urokinase with vascular surgery as initial treatment for acute arterial occlusion of the legs. N Engl J Med 1998;338:1105-11.

205. Monagle P, Phelan E, Downie P, Andrew M. Local thrombolytic therapy in children. Thromb Haemost 1997(suppl);504a.

206. Parrish RA, Scurry RB, Robertson AF. Recurrent arterial thrombosis in nephrosis. Am J Dis Child 1976;4:428-9.

207. Harrison BM, Wood CB. Spontaneous femoral artery thrombosis and intermittent claudication in childhood nephrotic syndrome. Am J Dis Child 1972;47:836-7.

208. Cameron JS, Ogg CS, Ellis FG, Salmon MA. 1971. Femoral artery thrombosis and intermittent claudication in childhood nephrotic syndrome. Arch Dis Child 46:215-216.

209. Zimmerman RL, Novek S, Chen JT, Roggli V. Pulmonary thrombosis in a 10-year-old child with minimal change disease and nephrotic syndrome. A clinical radiologic, and pathologic correlation with literature review. Am J Clin Pathol 1994;101:230-6.

210. Cameron J. Coagulation and thromboembolic complications in the nephrotic syndrome. In: Grunfelt B, Maxwell M, eds. Advances in nephrology. Chicago: Year Book Medical Publishers, 1984;75-114.

211. Sullivan MJ, Hough DR, Agodoa LC. Peripheral arterial thrombosis due to the nephrotic syndrome: the clinical spectrum. South Med J 1983;76:1011-16.

212. Selhub J, Jacques PF, Wilson PWF, et al. Vitamin status and intake as primary determinants of homocysteinemia in an elderly population. JAMA 1993;270:2693-8.

213. Chauveau P, Chadefaux B, Coude M, et al. Increased plasma homocysteine concentration in patients with chronic renal failure. Miner Electrolyte Metab 1992;18:196-8.

214. Boushey CJ, Beresford SAA, Omenn GS, Motulsky AG. A quantitative assessment of plasma homocysteine as a risk factor for vascular disease: probable benefits of increasing folic acid intakes. JAMA 1995;274:1049-57.

215. Naurath HJ, Joosten E, Riezler R, et al. Effects of vitamin B12, folate, and vitamin B6 supplements in elderly people with normal serum vitamin concentrations. Lancet 1995;346:85-9.

216. Franken DG, Boers FHJ, Blom HJ, et al. Treatment of mild hyperhomocysteinemia in vascular disease patients. Arterioscler Thromb 1994;14:465-70.

217. Brattstrom L, Lindgren A, Israelsson B, et al. Homocysteine and cysteine: determinants of plasma levels in middle-aged and elderly subjects. J Intern Med 1994;236:631-41.

218. Hall S, Barr W, Lie JT. Takayasu arteritis: a study of 32 North American patients. Medicine 1985;64:6489-99.

219. Tech PC, Tan LK, Chia BL. Nonspecific aorto-arteritis in Singapore with special reference to hypertension. Am Heart J 1978;95:683-65.

220. Kohrman MH, Huttenlocher PR. Takayasu's arteritis: a treatable cause of stroke in infancy. Pediatr Neurol 1986;2:154-8.

221. Lupi-Herrara E, Sanchez-Torres G, Marcushamer J. Takayasu's arteritis: clinical study of 107 cases. Am Heart J 1977;93:94-103.

222. Cupps TR, Fauci A. The vasculitides. Philadelphia: WB Saunders, 1981.

223. Gupta SK, Khanna MN, Lahiri TK. Involvement of cardiac valves in Takayasu's arteritis. Report of 7 cases. Indian Heart J 1980;32:148-55.

224. Furusho K, Nakamo H, Shinomiya K, et al. High-dose intravenous gamma globulin for Kawasaki disease. Lancet 1984;8411:1055-7.

225. Newburger J, Takahashi M, Burns J, et al. The treatment of Kawasaki syndrome with intravenous gamma globulin. N Engl J Med 1986;315:341-7.

226. Newburger JW, Takahashi M, Beiser AS. A single intravenous infusion of gamma globulin therapy as compared with four infusions in the treatment of acute Kawasaki syndrome. N Engl J Med 1991;324:1633-9.

227. Koren G, Rose V, Lavi S, Rowe R. Probable efficacy of high-dose salicylates in reducing coronary involvement in Kawasaki disease. JAMA 1985;254:767-9.

228. Daniels S, Specker P, Capannari TE, et al. Correlates of coronary artery aneurysm formation in patients with Kawasaki disease. Am J Dis Child 1987;141:205-7.

229. Suzuki A, Kamiya T, Ono Y, et al. Myocardial ischemia in Kawasaki disease: follow-up study by cardiac catherization and coronary angioplasty. Pediatr Cardiol 1988;9:1-5.

230. Kato H, Sugimura T, Akagi T, et al. Long-term consequences of Kawasaki disease. A 10 to 21 year follow-up study of 594 patients. Circulation 1996;94:1379-85.

231. Gersony WM. Kawasaki disease: clinical overview. Cardiol Young 1991;1:192-5.

232. Tatara K, Kusakawa S. Long-term prognosis of giant coronary aneurysm in Kawasaki disease: an angiographic study. J Pediatr 1987;111:705-10.

233. GUSTO Angiographic Investigators. The effects of tissue plasminogen activator, streptokinase, or both on coronary-artery patency, ventricular function, and survival after acute myocardial infarction. N Engl J Med 1993;29:1615-22.

234. Kitamura S, Kameda Y, Kawashima Y. Surgery for Kawasaki disease. Adv Card Surg 1997;9:177-94.

235. Stein PD, Alpert JS, Dalen JE, et al. Antithrombotic therapy in patients with mechanical and biological prosthetic heart valves. Chest 1998;114:602S-610S.

236. Horstkotte D, Schulte HD, Bircks W. Lower intensity anticoagulation therapy results in lower complication rates with the St. Jude Medical prosthesis. J Thorac Cardiovasc Surg 1994;107:1136-45.

237. Rodler SM, Moritz A, Schreiner W. Five-year follow-up after heart valve replacement with the CarboMedics bileaflet prosthesis. Ann Thorac Surg 1997;63:1018-25.

238. Baudet EM, Oca CC, Roques XF. A 5 1/2 year experience with the St. Jude Medical cardiac valve prosthesis. Early and late results of 737 valve replacements in 671 patients. J Thorac Cardiovasc Surg 1985;90:137-44.

239. Vogt S, Hoffman A, Roth J. Heart valve replacement with the Bjork-Shiley and St. Jude Medical prosthe-

sis: a randomized comparison in 178 patients. Eur Heart J 1990;11:583-91.

240. Acar J, Lung B, Boissel JP. AREVA: multicenter randomized comparison of low-dose versus standard-dose anticoagulation in patients with mechanical prosthetic heart valves. Circulation 1996;94: 2107-12.

241. Horstkotte D, Schulte H, Bircks W, Strauer B. Unexpected findings concerning thromboembolic complications and anticoagulation after complete 10 year follow-up of patients with St. Jude Medical protheses. J Heart Valve Dis 1993;2:291-301.

242. Cannegieter S, Rosendaal F, Wintzen A, et al. Optimal oral anticoagulant therapy in patients with mechanical heart valves. N Engl J Med 1995;333:11-17.

243. Arom KV, Emery RW, Nicoloff DM. Anticoagulant-related complications in elderly patients with St. Jude mechanical valve prostheses. J Heart Valve Dis 1996;5:505-10.

244. Skudicky D, Essop MR, Wisenbaugh T. Frequency of prosthetic valve-related complications with very low level warfarin anticoagulation combined with dipyridamole after valve replacement using St. Jude Medical prosthesis. Am J Cardiol 1994;74:1137-41.

245. Horstkotte D, Scharf RE, Schultheiss HP. Intracardiac thrombosis: patient-related and device-related factors. J Heart Valve Dis 1995;4:114-20.

246. Yamak B, Karagoz HY, Zorlutuna Y, et al. Low-dose anticoagulant management of patients with St. Jude Medical mechanical valve prostheses. Thorac Cardiovasc Surg 1993;41:38-42.

247. Hartz RS, LoCicero III J, Kucick V, et al. Comparative study of warfarin versus antiplatelet therapy in patients with a St. Jude Medical valve in the aortic position. J Thorac Cardiovasc Surg 1986;92:684-0.

248. Ribeiro PA, Al Zaibag MA, Idris M. Antiplatelet drugs and the incidence of thromboembolic complications of the St. Jude Medical aortic prosthesis in patients with rheumatic heart disease. J Thorac Cardiovasc Surg 1986;91:92-8.

249. David TE, Gott VL, Harker LA. Mechanical valves. Ann Thorac Surg 1996;62:1567-69.

250. Sade RM, Crawford FA, Fyfe DA, Stroud MR. Valve protheses in children: a reassessment of anticoagulation. J Thorac Cardiovasc Surg 1988;95:553-61.

251. Solymar L, Rao PS, Mardini MK, et al. Prosthetic valves in children and adolescents. Am Heart J 1991;121:557-68.

252. Serra A, McNicholas K, Olivier HJ, et al. The choice of anticoagulation in pediatric patients with the St. Jude Medical valve prostheses. J Cardiovasc Surg (Torino) 1987;28:588-91.

253. McGrath L, Gonzalez-Lavin L, Edlredge W, et al. Thromboembolic and other events following valve replacement in a pediatric population treated with antiplatelet agents. Ann Thorac Surg 1987;43:285-7.

254. El Makhlouf A, Friedli B, Oberhansli I, et al. Prosthetic heart valve replacement in children. J Thorac Cardiovasc Surg 1987;93:80-5.

255. Bradley LM, Midgley FM, Watson DC, et al. Anticoagulation therapy in children with mechanical prosthetic cardiac valves. Am J Cardiol 1985;56:533-5.

256. Borkon AM, Soule L, Reitz BA, et al. Five-year follow-up after valve replacement with the St. Jude Medical valve in infants and children. Circulation 1986;74(3 P†2):I-110-15.

257. LeBlanc J, Sett S, Vince D. Antiplatelet therapy in children with left-sided mechanical prostheses. Eur J Cardiothorac Surg 1993;7:211-15.

258. Bradley SM, Sade RM, Crawford FA, Stroud MR. Anticoagulation in children with mechanical valve prostheses. Ann Thorac Surg 1997;64:30-6.

259. Spevak P, Freed M, Castaneda A, et al. Valve replacement in children less than 5 years of age. J Am Cardiol 1986;8:901-8.

260. Harada Y, Imai Y, Kurosawa H, et al. Ten-year follow-up after valve replacement with the St. Jude Medical prosthesis in children. J Thorac Cardiovasc Surg 1990;100:175-80.

261. Stewart S, Cianciotta D, Alexson C, Manning J. The long-term risk of warfarin sodium therapy and the incidence of thromboembolism in children after prosthetic cardiac valves. J Thorac Cardiovasc Surg 1987;93:551-4.

262. Milano A, Vouhe PR, Baillot-Vernant F, et al. Late results after left-sided cardiac valve replacement in children. J Thorac Cardiovasc Surg 1986;92:218-25.

263. Schaffer MS, Clarke DR, Campbell DN, et al. The St. Jude Medical cardiac valve and children: role of anticoagulant therapy. J Am Coll Cardiol 1987;9: 235-9.

264. Schaff H, Danielson G, DiDonato R, et al. Late results after Starr-Edwards valve replacement in children. J Thorac Cardiovasc Surg 1984;88:583-9.

265. Human DG, Joffe HS, Fraser CB, Barnard CN. Mitral valve replacement in children. J Thorac Cardiovasc Surg 1982;83:873-7.

266. Antunes MJ, Vanderdonck KM, Sussman MJ. Mechanical valve replacement in children and teenagers. Eur J Cardiothorac Surg 1989;3:222-8.

267. Woods A, Vargas J, Berri G, et al. Antithrombotic therapy in children and adolescents. Thromb Res 1986;42: 289-301.

268. Champsaur G, Robin J, Trone F, et al. Mechanical valve in aortic position is a valid option in children and adolescents. Eur J Cardiothorac Surg 1997;11: 117-22.

269. Valdez R, Munoz R, Bracho E, et al. Surgical complications of renal transplantation in malnourished children. Transplant Proc 1994;26:50-1.

270. Harmon WE, Stablein D, Alexander SR, Tejani A. Graft thrombosis in pediatric renal transplant recipients. Transplantation 1991;51:406-12.

271. Kalicinski P, Kaminski A, Prokural A, et al. Surgical complications after kidney transplantation in children. Transplant Proc 1994;26:42-3.

272. Sheldon CA, Churchill BM, McLorie GA, Arbus GS. Evaluation of factors contributing to mortality in pediatric renal transplant recipients. J Pediatr Surg 1992;27:629-33.

273. Broyer M, Mitsioni A, Gagnadoux MF, et al. Early failures of kidney transplantation: a study of 70 cases from 801 consecutive grafts performed in children and adolescents. Adv Nephrol Necker Hosp 1993; 22:169-91.

274. Ellis D, Kaye RD, Bontemp FA. Aortic and renal artery thrombosis in a neonate: recovery with thrombolytic therapy. Pediatr Nephrol 1997;11:641-4.

275. Molteni KH, Messersmith R, Puppala BL, et al. Intrathrombic urokinase reverses neonatal renal artery thrombosis. Pediatr Nephrol 1993;7:413-5.

276. Barth RA. Fibromuscular dysplasia with clotted renal artery aneurysm. Pediatr Radiol 1993;23:296-7.

277. Ostuni PA, Lazzarin P, Pengo V, et al. Renal artery thrombosis and hypertension in a 13-year-old girl with antiphospholipid syndrome. Ann Rheum Dis 1990;49:184-7.

278. Grutmacher P, Bussmann WD, Meyer TH, et al. Non-operative revascularisation of renal artery occlusion by transluminal angioplasty. Nephrol Dial Transplant 1988;2:130-7.

279. Spirnak JP, Resnick MI. Revascularization of traumatic thrombosis of the renal artery. Surg Gynecol Obstet 1987;164: 22-6.

280. Kavalar E, Hensle TW. Renal artery thrombosis in the newborn infant. Urology 1997;50:282-4.

281. Segel MC, Zajko AB, Bowen A, et al. Doppler ultrasound as a screen for hepatic artery thrombosis after liver transplantation. Transplantation 1986;41: 539-41.

282. Dalen K, Day DL, Ascher NL, et al. Imaging of vascular complications after hepatic transplantation. Am J Roentgenol 1988;150:1285-90.

283. Todo S, Makowka L, Tzakis AG, et al. Hepatic artery in liver transplantation. Transplant Proc 1987;19: 2406-11.

284. Hoffer FA, Teele RL, Lillehei CW, Vacanti JP. Infected bilomas and hepatic artery thrombosis in infant recipients of liver transplants. Interventional radiology and medical therapy as an alternative to retransplantation. Radiology 1988;169:435-8.

285. Esquivel CO, Koneru B, Karrer F, et al. Liver transplantation before 1 year of age. J Pediatr 1987;110:545-8.

286. Kaplan SB, Zajko AB, Koneru B. Hepatic bilomas due to hepatic artery thrombosis in liver transplant recipients: percutaneous drainage and clinical outcome. Radiology 1990;174:1031-35.

287. Marujo WC. Vascular complications following orthotopic liver transplantation: outcome and the role of urgent revascularization. Transplant Proc 1991;23: 1484-86.

288. de Carvalho FB, Reding R, Falchetti D, et al. Analysis of liver graft loss in infants and children below 4 years. Transplant Proc 1991;23:1454-5.

289. Stevens L, Emond J, Piper J, et al. Hepatic artery thrombosis in infants. A comparison of whole livers, reduced-size grafts, and grafts from living-related donors. Transplantation 1992;53:396-9.

290. Rela M, Muiesan P, Baker A, et al. Hepatic artery thrombosis after liver transplantation in children under 5 years of age. Transplantation 1996;61: 1355-7.

291. Drazan K, Shaked A, Olthoff KM, et al. Etiology and management of symptomatic adult hepatic artery thrombosis after orthotopic liver transplantation (OLT). Am Surg 1996;62:237-40.

292. Esquivel CO, Jaffee R, Gordon RD et al. Liver rejection and its differentiation from other causes of graft dysfunction. Semin Liver Dis 1985;5:369-74.

293. Legmann P, Costes V, Tudoret L, et al. Hepatic artery thrombosis after liver transplantation: diagnosis with spiral CT. AJR An J Roentgenol 1995;164:97-101.

294. Sanchez-Bueno F, Robles R, Ramirez P, et al. Hepatic artery complications after liver transplantation. Clin Transpl 1994;8:399-404.

295. Mitchell L, Superina R, Delorme M, et al. Circulating dermatan sulfate and heparin sulfate/heparin proteoglycans in children undergoing liver transplantation. Thromb Haemost 1995;74:859-63.

296. Hidalgo E, Abad J, Cantarero J, et al. High-dose intra-arterial urokinase for the treatment of hepatic artery thrombosis in liver transplantation. Hepatogastroenterology 1989;36:529-32.

297. Yanaga K, Makowka L, Starzl T. Is hepatic artery thrombosis after liver transplantation really a surgical complication? Transplant Proc 1989;21:3511-13.

298. Tan KC, Yandza T, de Hemptinne B, Clapuyt PA. Hepatic artery thrombosis in pediatric liver transplantation. J Pediatr Surg 1988;23:927-30.

299. Tisone G, Gunson BK, Buckels JAC, MacMaster P. Raised hematocrit, a contributing factor to hepatic artery thrombosis following liver transplantation. Transplantation 1988;46:162-3.

300. Sarfati PO, Boillot O, Baudin F, et al. Surgical thrombectomy and in situ fibrinolysis for acute he-

patic artery thrombosis in pediatric liver transplantation. Ann Chir 1992;46:605-9.

301. Dotter CTJ, Rosch AJ, Seamen A. Selective clot lysis with low dose streptokinase. Radiology 1984;111: 31-7.

302. Katzen BT. Technique and results of 'low dose' infusion. Cardiovasc Intervent Radiol 1988;11:41-7.

303. Figueras J, Busquets J, Dominguez J, et al. Intra-arterial thrombolysis in the treatment of acute hepatic artery thrombosis after liver transplantation. Transplantation 1995;59:1356-7.

304. Al Neimi K, Boulet E, Imbaud P. Thrombosede l'artere mesenterique superieure et perforation appendiculaire chez une jeune fille. Ann Chir 1990;44:524-6.

305. Ritchey ML, Lally KP, Haase GM. Superior mesenteric artery injury during nephrectomy for Wilms' tumor. J Pediatr Surg 1992;27:612-15.

306. Talbot RW, Heppell J, Dozois RR, Beart RW Jr. Vascular complications of inflammatory bowel disease. Mayo Clin Proc 1986;61:140-5.

307. Simioni P, Zanardi S, Saracino A. Occurrence of arterial thrombosis in a cohort of patients with hereditary deficiency of clotting inhibitors. J Med 1992; 23:61-74.

308. Tsai M, Wu TJ, Teng RJ, et al. Mesenteric arterial thrombosis complicating congenital nephrotic syndrome of the Finnish type: report of a case. Chung Hua Min Kuo Hsiao Erh Ko I Hsueh Hui Tsa Chih 1995;36:445-7.

309. Taussig H. Long-time observations on the Blalock-Taussig operation IX. Single ventricle (with apex to the left). Johns Hopkins Med J 1976;139:69-76.

310. Truccone N, Bowman FJ, Malm J, Gersony W. Systemic-pulmonary arterial shunts in the first year of life. Circulation 1974;49:508-11.

311. Godart F, Qureshi SA, Simha A, et al. Effects of modified and classic Blalock-Taussig shunts on the pulmonary arterial tree. Ann Thorac Surg 1998;66: 512-18.

312. Tsai KT, Chang CH, Lin PJ. Modified Blalock-Taussig shunt: statistical analysis of potential factors influencing shunt outcome. J Cardiovasc Surg 1996; 37:149-52.

313. Gladman G, McCrindle BW, Williams WG, et al. The modified Blalock-Taussig shunt: clinical impact and morbidity in Fallot's tetralogy in the current era. J Thorac Cardiovasc Surg 1997;114:25-30.

314. Bogats G, Kertesz E, Katona M, et al. Modified Blalock-Taussig shunt using allograft saphenous vein: six years' experience. Ann Thorac Surg 1996; 61:58-61.

315. Ohuchi H, Okabe H, Nagata N, et al. Long-term patency after the Blalock-Taussig operation: comparison between classic and modified shunts. Nippon Kyobu Geka Gukkai Zasshi 1996;44:1108-13.

316. Zahn EM, Chang AC, Aldousany A, Burke R. Emergent stent placement for acute Blalock-Taussig shunt obstruction after stage 1 Norwood surgery. Cathet CardiovascDiagn 1997;42:191-4.

317. Takanashi Y, Tomizawa Y, Noishiki Y, Yoshihara K. Calcified EPTFE vascular prosthesis in the Blalock-Taussig shunt after 4 years of implantation: a case report. Jap Kyobu Goka 1997;50:71-3.

318. Berger RM, Bol-Raap G, Hop WJ, et al. Heparin as a risk factor for perigraft seroma complicating the modified Blalock-Taussig shunt. J Thorac Cardiovasc Surg 1998;116:292-3.

319. Klinge J, Hofbeck M, Ries M, et al. Thrombolysis of modified Blalock-Taussig shunts in childhood with recombinant tissue-type plasminogen activator. Z Kardio 1995;85:476-80.

320. Alcibar J, Cabrera A, Onate A, et al. Angioplasty of the stenotic Blalock-Taussig. Rev Esp Cardiol 1994;47: 819-23

321. Boulden TF, Tonkin IL, Burton EM, et al. Case of the day. Pediatric. Mycotic pseudoaneurysm and thrombosis of modified left Blalock-Taussig shunt. Radiographics 1990;10:119-21.

322. Ahmadi A, Mocellin R, Henglein D, et al. Modified Blalock-Taussig anastomosis. Its significance within the scope of surgical treatment of tetralogy of Fallot. Monatsschr Kinderheilkd 1988;136:130-40.

323. Brandt B, Camacho JA, Mahoney LT, Heintz SE. Growth of the pulmonary arteries following Blalock-Taussig shunt. Ann Thorac Surg 1986; 42:S1-4.

324. Tamisier D, Vouhe P, Vernant F, et al. Modified Blalock-Taussig shunts: results in infants less than 3 months of age. Ann Thorac Surg 1990;49:797-801.

325. Mullen JC, Lemermeyer G, Bentley MJ. Modified Blalock-Taussig shunts: to heparinize or not to heparinize. Can J Cardiol 1996;12:645-7.

326. Rajani RM, Dalvi BV, Kulkarni HL, Kale PA. Acutely blocked Blalock-Taussig shunt following cardiac catheterization: successful recanalization with intravenous streptokinase. Am Heart J 1990;20:1238-39.

327. Hijazi Z. Stenting for postoperative congenital heart disease in infants. Cathet Cardiovasc Diagn 1997;42:195-6.

328. Bjork V, Olin C, Bjarke B, Thoren C. Right atrial-right ventricular anastomosis for correction of tricuspid atresia. J Thorac Cardiovasc Surg 1979;77:452-8.

329. Breman FJ, Malm J, Hayes C, Gersony W. Physiological approach to surgery for tricuspid atresia. Circulation 1978;(Suppl 1):1-83.

330. Fontan F, Baudet E. Surgical repair of tricuspid atresia. Thorax 1971;26:240-8.

331. Jonas RA. Castaneda AR. Modified Fontan procedure: atrial baffle and systemic venous to pulmonary artery anastomotic techniques. J Card Surg 1988;3:91-6.

332. du Plessis A, Lock J, Wernovsky G, Newburger J. Cerebrovascular accidents following the Fontan operation. Pediatr Neurol 1995;12:230-6.

333. Turpie A, Gent M, Laupacis A, et al. Comparison of aspirin with placebo in patients treated with warfarin after heart valve replacement. N Engl J Med 1993;329:524-9.

334. Rajah S, Sreeharan N, Joseph A, et al. Prospective trial of dipyridamole and warfarin in heart valve patients. Acta Thera (Brussels) 1980;6:54a.

335. Turpie A, Gunstensen J, Hirsh J, et al. Randomised comparison of two intensities of oral anticoagulant therapy after tissue heart valve replacement. Lancet 1988;1:1242-5.

336. Ansell J, Patel N, Ostrovsky D, et al. Long term-patient self-management of oral anticoagulation. Arch Intern Med 1995;155:2185-9.

337. Hwang B, Lin CY, Hsieh KS, et al. High-dose intravenous gamma globulin therapy in Kawasaki disease. Acta Paediatr Scand 1989;30:15-22.

338. Furosho K, Kamiya T, Nakano H. Intravenous gamma globulin for Kawasaki disease. Acta Paediatr Jpn 1991;33:799-804.

339. Harada K. Intravenous gamma globulin in Kawasaki disease. Acta Paediatr Jpn 1991;33:805-10.

340. Chung KJ, Fulton DR, Lapp R, et al. One year follow-up of cardiac and coronary artery disease in infants and children with Kawasaki disease. Am Heart J 1988;115:1263-67.

341. Chung KJ, Brandt L, Fulton DR, Kreidberg MBI. Cardiac and coronary artery involvement in infants and children from New England with mucocutaneous lymph node syndrome (Kawasaki disease). Am J Cardiol 1982;50:136-42.

342. Bjork I, Danielsson A, Fenton JW, Jornvall H. The site in human antithrombin for functional proteolytic cleavage by human thrombin. FEBS Lett 1981;126:257–60.

343. Engle MA, Fatica NS, Bussel JB, et al. Clinical trial of single-dose intravenous gamma globulin in acute Kawasaki disease. Am J Dis Child 1989;143:1300-4.

344. Lee BW, Tay JSH, Yip WCL, et al. Kawasaki syndrome in Chinese children. Ann Trop Paediatr 1989;3:147-51.

345. Villian E, Kachaner J, Sidi D, et al. Essai de prevention des aneurisms coronaires de la maladie de Kawasaki par echanges plasmatiques pu perfusion d'immunoglobulines. Arch Fr Pediatr 1987;44:79-83.

346. Fournier PS, Doesburg V, Guerin R. La maladie de Kawasaki: aspects epidemiologiques et manifestations cardio-vasculaires. Arch Mal Coeur Vaiss 1985;78:693-8.

347. Takahashi M, Mason W, Lewis AB. Regression of coronary aneurysms in patients with Kawasaki syndrome. Circulation 1987;75:387-94.

348. Kryzer TC, Derkay CS. Kawasaki disease: five-year experience at Children's National Medical Center. Int J Pediatr Otorhinolarygol 1992;23:211-20.

349. Cullen S, Duff DF, Denham B. Cardiovascular manifestation in Kawasaki disease. Ir J Med Sci 1989;158:253-6.

350. Meade RH, Brandt L. Manifestation of Kawasaki disease in New York outbreak of 1980. J Pediatr 1982;100:558-62.

351. Nakashima M, Matsushima M, Matsuoka H, et al. High-dose gamma globulin therapy for Kawasaki disease. J Pediatr 1987;110:710-12.

352. Barron KS, Murphy DJ, Silverman BD. Treatment of Kawasaki syndrome: a comparison of two dosage regimens of intravenously administered immunoglobulin. J Pediatr 1990;117:638-44.

353. Akagi T, Rose V, Benson LN, et al. Outcome of coronary aneurysms after Kawasaki disease. J Pediatr 1992;121:689-94.

354. Beitzke A, Zobel G. Koronaraneurysm bei Kawasaki-Syndromm: Inzidenz und Prognose. Klin Padiatr 1989;201:33-9.

355. Colloridi V, Di Piero G, Colloridi G. Aspetti cardiologiel della malattia di Kawasaki. Pediatr Med Chir 1988;10:51-4.

356. Ichida F, Fatica NS, Engle MA. Coronary artery involvement in Kawasaki syndrome in Manhattan, New York: risk factors and role of aspirin. Pediatrics 1987;80:828-35.

357. Ogino H, Ogawa M, Harima Y. Clinical evaluation of gamma globulin preparation for the treatment of Kawasaki disease. Prog Clin Biol Res 1987;250:555-6.

358. Schaad UB, Odermatt K, Stocker FP, et al. Das Kawasaki-Syndrom. Schweiz Med Wochenschr 1990;120:539-47.

359. Dajani AS, Taubert KA, Takahashi M, et al. Guidelines for long-term management of patients with Kawasaki disease. Circulation 1994;89:916-22.

7

STROKE

Stroke can be defined as focal cerebral damage due to either vascular occlusion or rupture of vessels with subsequent bleeding and neurologic deficits. Only stroke due to vascular occlusion is discussed in this chapter. Stroke secondary to vascular occlusion may occur in the venous drainage of the brain, sinovenous thrombosis (SVT), or in the arterial supply to the brain, arterial ischemic stroke (AIS). Parenchymal damage or infarction of the brain occurs commonly as a sequelae of AIS and less commonly as a sequelae of SVT. For both SVT and AIS, the infarct is called "bland" if the infarct does not contain visible hemorrhage, and "hemorrhagic" if there is visible hemorrhage into the area of infarction.

The diagnosis and treatment of children with stroke differs from adults and is frequently problematic. First, stroke is common in adults, which results in rapid recognition and the potential for early intervention.[1] National Stroke Association figures in the United States estimate that approximately 730,000 strokes occur each year in the USA. In 1995, the mortality rate from stroke in the USA was 26.7 per 10,0000, which equalled 157,991 deaths due to stroke. In Canada, stroke accounts for 7% of all deaths. When the Canadian data are broken down by age, stroke is responsible for 9.5% of all male deaths above 85 years of age, yet only 0.7% of deaths in people below 34 years of age. Stroke in children is very rare with reported incidences of 0.063 to 0.12 per 10,000 children per year and a ratio of AIS to SVT of 3:1.[2-4] The infrequency of stroke in children results in delayed recognition and an inability to intervene early with medications, which may reduce subsequent neurologic deficits. Although rare, the incidence of stroke

in children is similar to the incidence of brain tumours for which a coordinated research approach has significantly decreased the mortality and morbidity. Second, vascular occlusive strokes in adults are secondary to atherosclerotic disease in the vast majority of patients, which permits a targeted approach to the diagnosis, prevention, and treatment of stroke. In contrast, vascular occlusive strokes in children are secondary to a multitude of diseases, which hinders the diagnosis, prevention, and treatment of stroke in pediatric patients. Third, there are numerous well-designed studies investigating prophylactic and therapeutic options for adults with stroke. There are no well-designed intervention trials in children, mostly reflecting a low incidence and multitude of etiologies. Fourth, the neonatal period is the time in which approximately one-third of AIS occur in children.[2,5] There are several developmental differences in the hemostatic, cerebrovascular, and neurologic systems of the young that negate the simple extrapolation of guidelines from adults to children with stroke.

The incidence of thrombotic stroke in children appears to be increasing for at least two reasons. First, the detection of thrombotic stroke in children has been significantly enhanced by the development of sensitive diagnostic tests such as computerized tomography (CT) and, particularly, magnetic resonance imaging (MRI) with angiography (MRA or MRV), as well as noninvasive tests such as cranial Doppler ultrasound in neonates.[6-9] Second, pediatric patients with previously lethal diseases, such as some forms of congenital heart disease (CHD), prematurity, sickle cell disease, and acute lymphoblastic leukemia (ALL), are surviving their primary diseases and developing serious secondary diseases, of

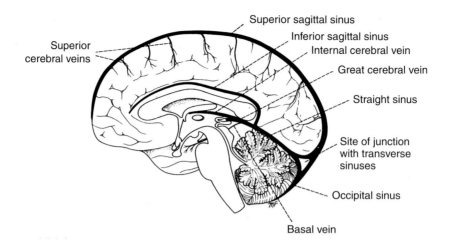

Figure 7–1 Venous drainage of the brain occurs through a network of sinuses and veins that are classified by location and considered as either "superficial" or "deep." The superficial venous system of the brain occurs through cortical veins that drain into the superior sagittal sinus.

Reproduced with permission.[16]

which thrombotic stroke is among the most serious. Thrombotic strokes, particularly in the venous system, likely remain underdiagnosed due to more subtle clinical signs and lack of use of appropriate radiographic tests.[9–13] The increasing incidence of stroke in children has contributed to a growing awareness and fostered research focused on this problem. The socioeconomic impact of stroke is considerable. In adults, the lifetime cost of a first stroke per person is estimated to be approximately $90,981.[14] The economic impact of childhood stroke has not been assessed but will be considerably more expensive than for adults reflecting the varying special needs of growing, developing children and the decades of the burden of illness.

The following chapter provides a systematic review of the literature based on Medline searches from 1966 to 1999 using combinations of key words and additional references located through the bibliographies. All articles were evaluated by study design according to previously described criteria (Chapter 1).[15] The focus of this chapter is to provide a systematic review of the epidemiology, diagnosis, prevention, and treatment of thrombotic stroke in children. SVT and AIS are considered separately.

Sinovenous Thrombosis

Anatomy and Function

Anatomy The venous drainage of the brain occurs through a network of sinuses and veins that are classified by location and considered as either "superficial" or "deep" (Figure 7–1).[16] The "superficial" venous system of the brain occurs through cortical veins that drain into the superior sagittal sinus. The superior sagittal sinus drains predominantly into the right lateral sinus (which is comprised of both a transverse and sigmoid portion) and subsequently into the jugular vein. The superficial cerebral sinuses are located outside the brain and are enclosed between two layers of fibrous dura mater with the outermost layer attached to bone through bony suture lines. The rigid attachment of sinuses results in a passive drainage of the central nervous system (CNS) venous circulation.[17] Due to a lack of valves, and lack of response to changes in systemic blood pressure, the direction of blood flow can potentially reverse. The 'deep venous system' includes the inferior sagittal sinus and the paired internal cerebral veins, which join to form the Vein of Galen and the straight sinus. Usually, the deep venous system drains predominantly into the left lateral sinus and subsequently into the jugular vein.[18] Anteriorly, there are paired cavernous sinuses that communicate with the jugular system through the petrosal sinuses.

Function The absorption of cerebrospinal fluid (CSF) is primarily through the superior sagittal sinus and occurs through 'arachnoid granulations.' Arachnoid granulations are vascular structures that extend across the walls of the superior sagittal sinus into the subarachnoid space and drain CSF into the sinus. Thromboembolic events (TEs) in the superior sagittal sinus may result in the arachnoid granulations becoming nonfunctional, which can cause a communicating hydrocephalus.[19]

Thromboembolic Events

Pathophysiology of sinovenous thrombosis SVT is a secondary complication of many different primary diseases. Historically, SVT was classified as septic and nonseptic, reflecting the importance of local head and neck infections in children. Septic SVTs are usually secondary to bacterial infections invading venous sinuses from adjacent structures such as the inner ear, thereby causing a thrombophlebitis.[20] The advent of antibiotics has significantly reduced the incidence of septic SVT in children. Nonseptic SVT is caused by several mechanisms. First, mechanical distortion that can occur during the birth process may adversely influence blood flow through the major dural sinuses, which are located along the bony suture lines.[21] Second, blood flow is relatively slow in the venous sinuses, which may, in response to a local insult, facilitate the initial formation and subsequent propagation of a thrombus. Third, dehydration may contribute to thrombus formation by causing hemoconcentration, which impairs laminar blood flow. Fourth, the physiologic absence of the endothelial cell surface receptor for thrombin, thrombomodulin in the sinovenous system, may hinder the local regulation of thrombin through the protein C/protein S inhibitory system contributing to thrombus formation (Chapter 2).[22] Fifth, certain acquired and inherited hemostatic abnormalities may contribute to SVT in specific patient populations. For example, SVT occurs in children with ALL while receiving the chemotherapeutic agent L'asparaginase (ASP).[23–31] ASP induces a variety of hemostatic abnormalities including a severe antithrombin (AT) deficiency, which may impair the regulation of thrombin with subsequent thrombus formation.[32] A second example of a hemostatic abnormality is the presence of antiphospholipid antibodies (APLA), which increase the risk of TEs in patients of all ages.[33]

Infarction secondary to sinovenous thrombosis Infarction is caused by a lack of perfusion to the afflicted area of the brain. Approximately 50% of children with SVT develop secondary infarction of the brain.[34] The mechanism by which SVT causes infarction is by increasing venous pressure, which results in increased intracranial pressure and decreased regional perfusion of the brain. The features of SVT that place children at increased risk for infarction include a rapid rate of occlusion, the size of the occlusion, and the location of the thrombus. Rapid rates of occlusion do not leave sufficient time for venous collaterals to form and commonly result in infarction.[19] Total occlusion of the sinus or vein lumen and occlusion at entry points of cerebral veins are more likely to result in venous infarction. Increased venous pressure can cause increased local extravascular fluid, which contributes to edema and hemorrhagic conversion of the infarcts.

Outcome of infarction related to sinovenous thrombosis There are variable outcomes of SVT-related infarction. First, some parenchymal lesions detected radiographically are transient and likely represent acute focal edema without infarction. Second, the low pressure and slow blood flow in the sinovenous system may predispose to extension of the thrombus and further infarction. Third, occlusion of the superior sagittal sinus, which is frequently involved in SVT, increases intracranial pressure secondary to both venous congestion and impaired CSF absorption, resulting in a communicating hydrocephalus. Recanalization of the venous drainage, even if delayed, may relieve the circulatory congestion with clinical benefit.

Location of sinovenous thrombosis-related infarction The sagittal sinus is the most common location for SVT during childhood and can cause bilateral infarcts that may be hemorrhagic (Figure 2).[35] SVT involving the internal cerebral veins, straight sinus, or Vein of Galen produce thalamic or cerebellar infarctions that may or may not be bilateral (Figure 7–3).[35]

Clinical Presentation

Age distribution Neonates and young infants predominate and account for approximately 50% of SVT during childhood.[36]

Clinical presentation As compared to AIS, the typical clinical features of SVT are subtle, diffuse, frequently associated with seizures, and may develop gradually over many hours or days. The clinical presentation of SVT is influenced by age, extent of the TE, and underlying diseases such as meningitis or hypoxia, which may cause neurologic abnormalities separate from the SVT. Neonates and young infants usually do not present with focal signs but frequently present with seizures, lethargy, and/or jitteriness.[5,11,12,37] Physical findings including a full tense fontanel, dilated scalp veins, and swelling of the eyelids may occur but are rare.[38] Older infants and preschoolers frequently present with fever, vomiting, seizures, and focal signs including hemiparesis in approximately 20%. Older

children can also present with papilledema, abducens palsy, headache, and altered levels of consciousness.[5,37]

Risk factors Risk factors are readily identifiable in most children with SVT and are age related. The majority of children (65%) have at least two risk factors with 40% having more than three risk factors.[5,39] Dehydration is especially common in neonates with SVT whereas hematologic disorders, for example, anemia, and CHD predominate in older infants and preschool children. Head and neck infections such as otitis media, mastoiditis, or sinusitis are present in nearly one-third of preschool children but only 10% of all children with SVT. Systemic lupus erythematosis (SLE), juvenile rheumatoid arthritis, and other connective tissue disorders are clustered in the older age groups.

Prothrombotic hemostatic disorders Prothrombotic disorders are discussed in detail in Chapter 3. Prothrombotic disorders can be classified as either congenital or acquired. Acquired disorders are more common than congenital disorders and consist of APLA in the form of either anticardiolipin antibodies (ACLAs) or lupus anticoagu-

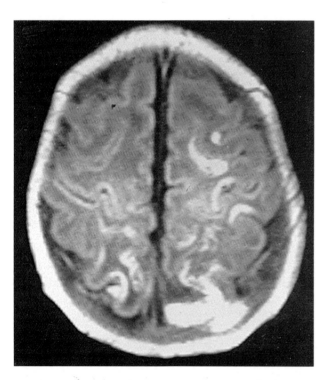

Figure 7–2 MRI showing the typical location of sinovenous thrombosis related infarctions secondary to a thrombus in the sagittal sinus, the most common location for sinovenous thrombosis. Reproduced with permission.[35]

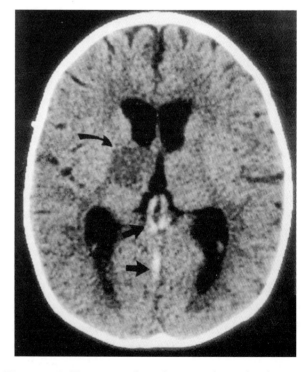

Figure 7–3 Sinovenous thrombosis involving the deep system (internal cerebral veins, straight sinus, and Vein of Galen) with thalamic infarctions (unilateral in this case). Reproduced with permision.[35]

lants (LA). Congenital disorders include activated protein C resistance (APCR) or Factor (F) V Leiden, Prothrombin gene 20210A, and deficiencies of protein C, protein S, AT, plasminogen, and dysfibrinogenemia.

Prothrombotic disorders may cause or contribute to the pathogenesis of TEs in adults and children.[40] In adults, the incidence of prothrombotic disorders in SVT has been reported as 15 to 21%.[41,42] A number of case reports and small case series have reported inherited or acquired prothrombotic disorders in children with SVT.[36,43–58]

Two recent prospective cohort studies have reported the frequency of prothrombotic disorders in children with SVT. The first study described 19 consecutive children with SVT managed at a single institution, who underwent systematic prothrombotic testing. Ten patients (52%) had at least one abnormal prothrombotic test, the presence of ACLA being the most frequent abnormality.[36] The second study reported 10 consecutive children with SVT, of whom one had inherited protein S deficiency, one APLA, and three had acquired AT deficiency secondary to L-asparaginse therapy.[44] The presence of ACLA is the single most common prothrombotic disorder in SVT during childhood. However, ACLAs are frequently transient and whether they are causal or mere associations with SVT in children remains to be shown.

Radiographic Features

General information The radiographic diagnosis of SVT can be difficult, especially for isolated cortical vein thrombosis. The availability of MRI with MRV has significantly improved the accuracy of the diagnosis of SVT.[59–62] Cerebral angiography remains the reference test if SVT cannot be confirmed by CT or MRI/MRV. SVT most commonly occurs in more than one location and usually involves the superior sagittal and lateral sinuses.[5] In one large study, 56% of patients had multiple sinuses and/or veins involved and 40% of patients had venous infarcts that were bland in two-thirds and hemorrhagic in one-third. A small number of patients had transient low-density parenchymal lesions.[5,35]

Computerized tomography Signs of SVT on a noncontrast CT include the "filled triangle" or "dense triangle" sign and the "cord sign," which reflect the presence of a thrombus in sinovenous channels (Figure 7–3).[35] On a contrast-enhanced CT, an empty triangle or "delta sign" represents bright contrast enhancement of the dura surrounding a clot in the sinovenous system (Figure 7–4).[63] Unfortunately, and not widely appreciated, CT scans cannot be relied upon to make the diagnosis of SVT in children for several reasons. First, CT scans miss the presence of SVT in 10% to 40% of children and underestimate both the extent of sinus involvement and the presence of infarcts.[13,19,37,64] Second, CT scans can yield falsely positive results in neonates due to the increased hematocrit, decreased unmyelinated brain density, and slower venous flow, which can combine to produce a high-density triangle in the torcular area mimicking the "dense triangle" sign.[63,65] Spiral CT imaging may improve the reliable diagnosis of SVT because it can delineate vascular flow, enabling noninvasive cerebral CT venography.[59] However, spiral CT imaging has not

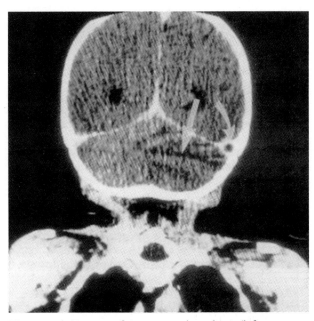

Figure 7–4 Features of sinovenous thrombosis (left transverse sinus) on a contrast-enhanced computed tomography scan. Features include an empty triangle or "delta sign," which represents bright contrast enhancement of the dura surrounding a clot in the sinovenous system. Reproduced with permission.[35]

been validated in adults for the diagnosis of SVT and has not been widely used in children.

Magnetic resonance imaging. MRI with MRV is the radiographic technique of choice for the diagnosis of SVT in children (Figure 7–5).[66–68] The excellent sensitivity and specificity of MRI/MRV reflect the capacity of these techniques to visualize flow and the presence of a thrombus and associated parenchymal lesions.[13,64,66–68] Clot progress and resolution can be readily monitored with this modality. MRI and MRV signs of SVT include an absence of flow-related signal and visualization of the thrombus, which appears as an increased signal on T1-weighted proton density and T2-weighted images in a cerebral vein or dural sinus. Signal characteristics may permit an assessment of age of the thrombus.[67] The rate and extent of recanalization following SVT in children has not been determined. Recanalization can occur as early as 2 weeks following diagnosis, or may not occur even after several years.[67]

Ultrasound Magnetic resonance imaging or venogram may not be feasible to perform in critically ill neonates. An open fontanelle offers a unique means for ultrasound detection of TEs, hemorrhagic complications, and ongoing monitoring. The development of Doppler/ultrasound offers a significant improvement over regular cranial ultrasound because it can detect normal, diminished, or absent sinovenous blood flow.[69]

Conventional angiography Conventional angiography remains the "gold standard" test for the detection of SVT in patients of all ages. Partial or complete lack of filling of cerebral veins or sinuses is diagnostic for SVT. Enlarged collateral veins, delayed venous emptying, reversal of normal venous flow direction, abnormal cortical veins (broken or corkscrew-like), and regional or global delayed venous emptying are all features of SVT.[13] However, angiography is an invasive procedure that may cause local thrombosis at the site of catheter entry, particularly in small infants with small vessels, which form the majority of children with SVT. Other problems with angiography include the need for careful scrutinization of the venous phase to detect SVT and difficulties in differentiating normal

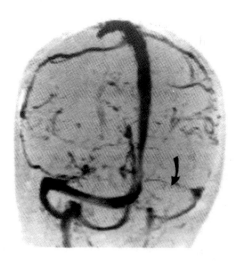

Figure 7–5 Magnetic resonance venogram (MRV) of sinovenous thrombosis in the left transverse sinus and nonvisualization of the internal sinovenous system (internal cerebral veins and straight sinus). MRI with MRV is the radiographic technique of choice for the diagnosis of sinovenous thrombosis in children. The MRI's excellent sensitivity and specificity comes from its ability to visualize flow, the presence of a thrombus, and the associated parenchymal lesions including venous infarcts. Reproduced with permission.[35]

anatomic variants from thrombotic occlusion, such as occurs with a hypoplastic left lateral sinus.[70]

Treatment Treatment of SVT can be considered as supportive therapy for the underlying disease(s), the secondary consequences of SVT, and the use of antithrombotic agents. Only the role of antithrombotic agents is discussed subsequently and readers are referred to other reviews for further information on other aspects of management of SVT.[35,71,72] Antithrombotic therapy for SVT in pediatric patients includes the use of anticoagulants and thrombolytic therapy.

Anticoagulant therapy in adults There are three randomized controlled trials (RCTs) assessing the role of anticoagulants in SVT in adults.[57,73,74] These trials show that anticoagulation in the acute situation with unfractionated heparin (UFH) clearly improves mortality and morbidity when compared to placebo, although the efficacy of LMWH remains unproven.[57,73,74] The results of these trials are supported by large cohort studies reporting an improved outcome in adults with SVT treated with UFH without an increase in hemorrhagic complications.[13,75]

Anticoagulant therapy in children As previously stated, the majority of publications describing SVT in children are case series and case reports, which are not helpful in assessing the usefulness of therapy. One recent cohort study described the use of anticoagulant therapy in children with SVT.[76] In a consecutive cohort of 30 children, 8 were ineligible for anticoagulation due to clinically significant intracranial hemorrhage (ICH) at diagnosis. However, 10 children received initial UFH and 12 initial low molecular weight heparin (LMWH). The majority of children (18) then received warfarin for 3 months. There were no extensions of the SVT and only one child who received UFH had a clinically silent ICH during therapy. The paucity of evidence for or against the use of anticoagulants has resulted in no consensus on optimal treatment of SVT in children. However, the results from the three RCTs in adults suggest that anticoagulant therapy should be considered in children with SVT and that clinical trials assessing the potential benefit of anticoagulants are urgently needed, particularly in neonates where the risk–benefit ratio of anticoagulants will likely differ from adults.[77–79] Based upon a review of the literature, approximately 50% of children with SVT are being treated with anticoagulants without major bleeding complications.[35] In the absence of clinical trials in children, several features will influence the decision to treat and the duration of treatment. Confounding variables include the severity of the clinical symptoms, extensiveness of the thrombus, presence and extent of associated hemorrhage, and the ability to monitor anticoagulant therapy. In the absence of extensive hemorrhage, one approach is to treat neonates with UFH or LMWH for 10 to 14 days and reassess. During treatment of neonates with anticoagulants, ultrasound can be used to monitor for hemorrhage and in some patients for extension of the thrombus. If anticoagulant therapy is discontinued, extension of the thrombus may again be detectable in some patients by ultrasound or power Doppler. For older infants and children, UFH or LMWH for 7 to 10 days followed by oral anticoagulants (OAs) or LMWH for 3 months should be considered.

Thrombolytic therapy Local intraclot thrombolytic therapy for the treatment of SVT has been used in a few children in situations where there is progression of the SVT in spite of maximal systemic anticoagulation.[80–83] Failure of local thrombolytic therapy has also been reported.[84] The risk–benefit ratio of thrombolytic therapy is not known in adults or children, and the hemorrhagic risks of thrombolytic therapy may be considerable. At this time thrombolytic therapy, outside of controlled trials, should in general, be discouraged.[80–84]

Outcome The long-term outcome of SVT in children is unclear and difficult to assess for several reasons, including the relatively small numbers of children with SVT at any one institution, which necessitates multicenter studies, lack of long-term follow-up of consecutive children with SVT, and the variable use of anticoagulants, which may modify the outcome. Factors that may influence outcome include the rapidity of diagnosis, extent of the TE, associated neurologic disorder, age at the time of the event, and the use of anticoagulants. There are two studies that provide some insight into the long-term outcome of SVT in children.[5,39] The first study is a single-center report of 28 consecutive patients who survived SVT and were assessed in a standard fashion.[39] The mean follow-up was 2.1 years with a range of 0.8 to 6.6 years.[39] Two-thirds of the children were normal neurologically and one-third had mild or moderate neurologic deficits.[39] The second study is a population-based prospective registry comprised of 80 consecutive pediatric patients with SVT and a mean follow-up of 1.13 years.[5] In this cohort, 53% of patients were normal, 25% had a neurologic deficit with or without seizures, 5% had seizures alone, and 9% died.[5]

Role of anticoagulants In the population-based study, approximately 50% of patients received anticoagulants without hemorrhagic complications.[5] The recent cohort study reported that three of eight nontreated children with SVT died whereas none of the 22 treated children died.[76] Whether this represents a true improved survival or indicates that the nontreated children were at the most severe end of the disease spectrum is unknown.[76] After 1 year of follow-up, 67% of patients were neurologically normal. In contrast, a pooled analysis of the literature from 1980 to 1996 identified 150 pediatric patients with SVT, with 136 without anticoagulants and 14 with anticoagulants. One hundred and thirty-six were treated supportively without anticoagulants and only 14 were anticoagulated. There was no difference in the mortality rates between treated and untreated children (14% and 16%, respectively). However, neurologic morbidity was seen in 22% of nontreated patients versus 0% of treated patients.[35]

Role of age The outcome following SVT is likely to be influenced by the age of the children at the time of the event. In the population-based study, nearly 50% of neonates had either serious neurologic impairments or died 1 year following the event.[85] In the outcome paper by deVeber et al,[39] the percentage of moderate or severe outcome was similar for infants and older children at approximately 16%.[39]

Case series have reported conflicting outcomes with some reporting disability or death in over 50%[37] and others reporting a normal outcome in over 90% of neonates with SVT.[12] However, the study reporting a normal outcome in most infants used only CT scanning without confirmatory MRI or angiogram and the follow-up interval was less than 1 year in half of the patients. Cerebral injury in the first weeks of life frequently has a late presentation due to maturational changes in the nervous system during the first year of life when myelination, neuronal pruning, and synapse modeling are occurring.[86] In the same population-based study, repeated follow-up neurologic examinations over time showed an increasing number of children with neurologic deficits of increasing seriousness.

Recurrent sinovenous thrombosis In adults with SVT, symptomatic recurrent SVT occurs in approximately 12% of patients, usually in the first year following the primary event.[71] Systemic TEs also occur in approximately 11% of adults with SVT.[71] Recurrent SVT occurs in children but the incidence or potential value of anticoagulants is unknown.[76] In the previously described cohort, 2 of 30 children suffered recurrent SVT, despite both receiving initial anticoagulation therapy.[76] DeVeber et al[39] also reported recurrent SVT in 2 of 37 children.[39]

Mortality The mortality rate associated with SVT is probably declining, reflecting earlier diagnosis and more effective treatment of underlying diseases. In the population-based study of children with SVT, the mortality rate was 10%, but not all deaths were due to SVT.[76] Other studies in adults and children report mortality rates that range from 14% to 36%.[5,3,64]

Practical Guidelines for Investigation and Treatment of Sinovenous Thrombosis in Children

History Important historical information consists of recent head/neck infection, head injury, dehydration, use of oral contraceptives, inflammatory bowel disease, autoimmune diseases, other serious primary diseases such as ALL with recent ASP therapy, and previous TEs in any location.

Family history A family history of deep vein thrombosis (DVT), pulmonary emoblism (PE), myocardial infarction, and stroke in young relatives is important to determine.

Physical examination A detailed neurologic examination is required. Special attention should be made for evidence of dehydration; papilledema; increased head circumference; head bruits; dilated facial or neck veins; facial nevus of Sturge-Weber syndrome; clinical signs of paranasal, facial, or mastoid infections; and clinical signs of cardiac disorders.

Radiologic evaluation An in-depth radiographic assessment of the CNS should be conducted, including an MRI/MRV scan if possible because a CT scan may not detect or will underestimate the extent of the SVT.

Evaluation for prothrombotic disorders A work-up for a prothrombotic disorder should be conducted and include the following: AT, protein C, protein S, plasminogen, APCR, FV Leiden, prothrombin gene 20210A, APLA including both ACLA and at least three assays testing for a lupus anticoagulant (LA), and an assay for dysfibrinogenemia. The timing of obtaining blood samples will be influenced by the immediacy of the SVT and the use of either UFH or OAs. Testing the parents provides an alternative if the child is already receiving anticoagulants.

Evaluation for other disorders Further diagnostic evaluation for the etiology may be indicated and include the following: tests for metabolic disorders predisposing to cerebral TEs including homocystinuria (serum or urine amino acids are adequate only for homozygous homocystinurea; more subtle forms require plasma homocystine levels) and hyperlipidemias (fasting serum cholesterol, triglycerides, high-density lipoprotein [HDL] and low-density lipoprotein [LDL]); CSF studies for meningitis, including bacterial meningitis, tuberculosis meningitis, and selected viral or fungal infections; assessments for SLE and other vasculitides (erythrocyte sedimentation rate), C3, C4, rheumatoid factor, anti-nuclear antibody; and sickle cell test or hemoglobin electrophoresis.

Antithrombotic medications The options for treatment of newborns include UFH or LMWH for 10 to 14 days with the duration extended depending upon individual features such as the extent of the thrombus and resolution of the insighting cause. The options for treatment of infants and children include UFH or LMWH for 5 to 10 days followed by OAs or LMWH for 3 months. The duration of anticoagulation can be assessed on an individual basis. If there is an associated significant hemorrhage, or if the patient is hypertensive or other risks for bleeding are present, anticoagulation may not be feasible. Guidelines for the use of UFH, LMWH, and OAs are provided in Chapters 9 and 10. If anticoagulation is initiated with UFH, a loading dose or 75 units/kg IV over 10 minutes is appropriate. Initial maintenance doses of UFH are age dependent: 28 units/kg/hour for infants less than 1 year of age and 20 units/kg/hour for children greater than 1 year of age. The dose of UFH is adjusted to maintain an activated partial thromboplastin time (APTT) at 60 to 85 seconds provided that that reflects a UFH concentration of either 0.30 to 0.70 anti-FXa units or 0.20 to 0.40 anti-thrombin units by a protamine sulphate assay (Chapter 13). If LMWH is selected, a loading dose is not required. The initial dose reflects the choice of LMWH. If OAs are used in the maintenance phase, an initial dose of 0.2 units/kg/day is recommended for most patients with further dose adjustments dependent on the international normalized ratio (INR) (Chapter 10).

Arterial Ischemic Stroke

Anatomy

General information The arterial supply of the brain comes from two main circulations, the "anterior" and "posterior" systems (Figure 7–6).[16] The "anterior" circulation is comprised of paired carotid arteries and the "posterior" circulation is comprised of paired vertebral arteries that join to form the basilar artery (i.e., the vertobasilar system). The anterior and posterior arterial circulations of the brain are linked by anterior and posterior communicating arteries to form the Circle of Willis. The Circle of Willis gives rise to the major cerebral arteries, which are the anterior, middle, and posterior cerebral arteries. The anterior and middle cerebral arteries are primarily supplied through the Circle of Willis by the internal carotid arteries, and the posterior cerebral arteries are the primary branches of the vertebrobasilar system. The arterial supply to the deep central structures of the brain, such as the basal ganglia, comes from small "perforator" or "lenticulostriate" branches from the stem of the anterior, middle, and posterior cerebral arteries.

Thromboembolic Complications

Pathophysiology of arterial ischemic stroke AIS is classically defined as a prolonged neurologic deficit of greater than 24 hours duration and with an infarct seen on CT or MRI. In general, AIS can be considered as embolic or due to local thrombus formation. In adults, the overwhelming majority of AIS are secondary to local atherosclerotic disease either alone or in combination with other mechanisms (Figure 7–7).[1] Embolic stroke from the heart, most commonly caused by atrial fibrillation, accounts for only a smaller percentage of AIS in adults. In marked contrast to adults, local atherosclerotic disease causing AIS does not occur during childhood and atrial fibrillation is rare. AIS in children is frequently embolic from either congenital or acquired cardiac disease or from large-caliber proximal arteries as occurs in dissection.[87,88] Examples of cardiac sources include right to left intracardiac shunts, such as occur with atrial septal defects, patent foramen ovale, and postoperative residual right to left shunt following Fontan surgery. Local abnormalities of the arterial vasculature occur in an-

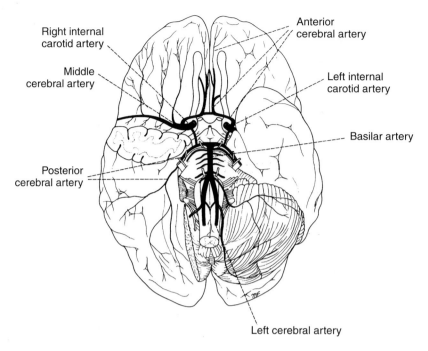

Figure 7–6 Physiologic arterial supply to the brain, which comes from two main circulations, the "anterior" and "posterior" systems. The anterior circulation is comprised of paired carotid arteries, and the posterior circulation is comprised of paired vertebral arteries that join to form the basilar artery (i.e., the vertobasilar system).

other 53% of children with AIS.[87] Local vascular abnormalities can slow blood flow and cause nonlaminar flow, which potentiates local thrombus formation. As discussed subsequently, congenital and acquired prothrombotic conditions can also cause AIS during childhood.[36,43,49,87]

Infarction secondary to arterial ischemic stroke Important functional and anatomic differ-

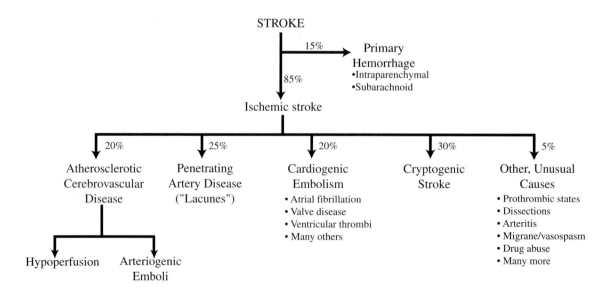

Figure 7–7 Classification of stroke by mechanisms with estimates of the frequency of various categories of abnormalities in adults. About 30% of ischemic strokes are cryptogenic. Reproduced with permission.[1]

ences between the cerebral arterial and sinovenous systems result in differing clinical presentations and location of associated infarction. The severity of the cerebral damage and type of neurologic symptoms in AIS reflect the brain structures supplied by the involved cerebral artery, availability of collateral arterial blood supply, duration of cerebral arterial occlusion, and concurrent metabolic demands of the brain. Depending on the severity of ischemia and rate of neuronal metabolic activity, neuronal damage following arterial occlusion can be reversible or irreversible. Transient ischemic attacks (TIAs) by definition result in clinical deficits that are brief, usually less than 1 hour, and do not result in permanent infarcts.[1,89,90] In contrast, for AIS there are persistent infarcts that may be permanent, in association with clinical deficits that last longer and may also be permanent. On MRI or CT, the vascular infarct is in the region of the brain that matches the type of neurologic deficit. The infarct can be considered to have two areas: the central core zone, which is comprised of irreversibly damaged brain, and a surrounding penumbra zone, which is comprised of potentially viable brain tissue. The final size of the permanent infarct depends upon several features, including the delivery of nutrients and the metabolic needs of the involved brain tissue.

Location of arterial ischemic infarcts AIS-induced infarcts can be classified as large vessel or small vessel, which are also referred to as lacunar infarcts (Figure 7–8). Large-vessel infarcts are secondary to thrombotic occlusion of major cerebral arteries and result in classic, peripheral, wedge-shaped infarcts. These infarcts involve the cerebral cortex and adjacent white matter in characteristic vascular distributions (Figure 7–9).[35] Collateral blood flow from smaller arteries in the leptomeninges or via the Circle of Willis can occur and is critically important to the ultimate size of the infarct. Small-vessel infarcts occur in peripheral areas of the brain at junctions of blood supply by the posterior, middle, and anterior cerebral arteries, commonly called the "watershed" zones. Small-vessel "lacunar" infarcts occur in the deep central brain structures such as the deep white matter, basal ganglia, and brain stem. These small infarcts are caused by occlusion of small lenticulostriate arteries, which are end-arteries arising from the proximal anterior, middle, and posterior cerebral arteries. Although the infarcts are small, the lack of vascular anastomoses result in a lack of collateral blood flow, and the dense concentration of functional pathways located in the deep structures of the brain frequently result in significant neurologic deficits. There is an

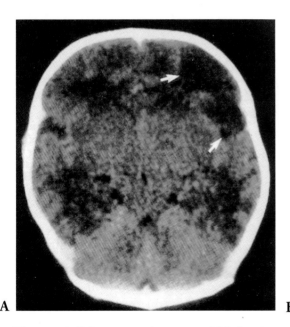

A

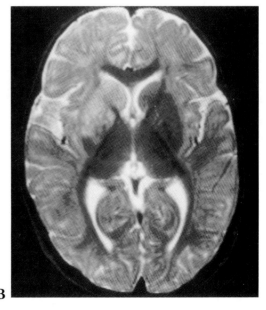

B

Figure 7–8 Infarcts secondary to arterial ischemic stroke that can be classified as large-vessel (*A*) or small-vessel (*B*). Large-vessel infarcts are secondary to thrombotic occlusion of major cerebral arteries and result in classic, peripheral, wedge-shaped infarcts.

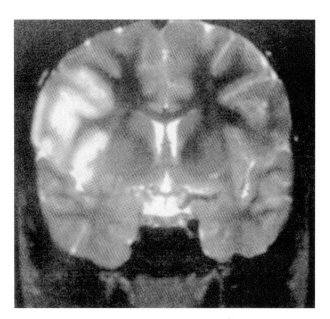

Figure 7–9 MRI showing right middle cerebral artery infarct involving cortex and subjacent white matter.

even distribution between large- and small-vessel artery infarcts in children.[34] Global hypoperfusion is the primary mechanism responsible for these infarcts.

Clinical Presentation Similar to SVT, neonates and young infants predominate and account for approximately 25% of AIS during childhood.[2,39] The predominance of neonates may be underestimated because the diagnosis of AIS is frequently delayed and may only become apparent with pathologic early hand dominance between 6 and 12 months of age.[86] Because the presentation of AIS in neonates and young infants differs from older toddlers and children, they are discussed separately.

Clinical presentation in neonates and young infants The clinical presentation of AIS in neonates is most frequently persistent acute seizures with a lack of lateralizing findings or focal neurologic deficits. Initially, neonates with persistent seizures are considered to have a focal encephalitis, migraine, or focal seizures because these disorders are more frequent in early childhood than AIS. Over the subsequent months to years, focal neurologic deficits slowly become apparent and the CT or MRI shows a vascular lesion consistent with a presumed prenatal or perinatal insult.[86,88,91,92] Many of the congenital hemiplegias described in the older literature may have been prenatal or perinatal vaso-occlusive infarcts that could not be diagnosed in the absence of CT or MRI. Seizures, fever, headache, and lethargy occur more commonly in young infants than in older children with stroke.[93] Subtle symptoms or signs are even less likely to be reported or attributed to stroke.

Clinical presentation in toddlers and older children The typical clinical presentation of AIS in toddlers and older children is an acute, prolonged neurologic deficit such as hemiparesis, with or without seizures. Seizures at the onset of stroke are relatively frequent in children compared with adults,[93,94] and only after a prolonged persistent focal deficit inconsistent with Todd's paresis is stroke considered likely. Dystonia is more common in children with basal ganglia infarction than in adults.[95]

Transient ischemic attacks In contrast to AIS, defined as prolonged neurologic deficits with an associated infarct on CT or MRI, TIAs are brief, less than 24 hours in duration, and do not produce a visible lesion on CT or MRI. Although the majority of children with AIS present with a single episode of focal neurologic deficit, TIAs followed by an AIS are increasingly recognized. The clinical differentiation between AIS and TIA is frequently difficult in children because a neurologic deficit lasting less than 24 hours may be associated with an infarct detected on CT or MRI. A careful history of the event and presence of cerebral artery pathology on MRA or conventional angiography are very helpful in making the correct diagnosis.

Risk Factors

Adults Risk factors for stroke in adults are well defined and are divided into two categories: nonmodifiable and modifiable. The nonmodifiable risk factors include the patient's age and a family history of stroke. The presence of diabetes is associated with an increased risk of stroke; however, whether this risk can be reduced by optimal diabetic control is unknown. High blood pressure is the most important modifiable risk factor for stroke. Other modifiable risk factors for stroke are smoking and physical inactivity. Pre-existing conditions such as the presence of atrial fibrillation and a previous TIA are also important risk factors for stroke.

Children Risk factors in children with AIS are definable in approximately 80% of cases,[5,7,34,96] are age related, and differ significantly from adults. Embolic stroke secondary to CHD is the most frequent cause of stroke during childhood.[97] Multiple risk factors are frequently present in individual patients.

There are a number of retrospective studies that have failed to demonstrate any role for hyperlipidemia in childhood stroke.[98] In particular, studies in homozygous familial hyperlipidemia have shown that atherosclerosis in the cerebral circulation lags many years behind aortic and coronary artery disease.[99–101] Postulated reasons for this include difference in shear stress, endothelial GAG composition, and protection from hypertension by the universal presence of aortic stenosis in these patients. The risk of stroke in homozygous familial hyperlipidemia is said to be no higher than that of the general population.[102]

Glueck and colleagues have reported a small cohort of children in whom low HDL levels and high triglyceride levels were associated with otherwise unexplained stroke. They found the same abnormalities in an increased proportion of children with migraines.[103,104]

History and physical examination The probability of identifying causes for AIS depends on the thoroughness of the investigations, including a comprehensive history and physical examination. For some children, the diagnosis is obvious such as for a radiation-induced vasculopathy, CHD, and sickle cell disease. For other children, a detailed history suggests less obvious etiologies such as recent head or neck injury, which may cause dissection, or a recent varicella infection, which may cause an angiopathy. Certain drugs are linked to AIS, including oral contraceptives, amphetamines, and cocaine. A detailed family history for stroke, myocardial infarction, hyperlipidemias, or venous TEs at an early age is important because it suggests the presence of a congenital prothrombotic condition. A detailed physical examination is important not only to define the extent of the neurologic deficit but also to detect clues as to the presence of other diseases. Important physical findings include the presence of head or neck bruits, cardiac murmurs, or cutaneous lesions typical of neurocutaneous syndromes.

Cardiac disorders Complex CHD is the single most common cause of AIS during childhood.[105] The embolism may originate from either the left or right side of the heart. Left-sided embolic sources include prosthetic valves, cardiomyopathies, and other left-sided cardiac disease. The incidence of AIS secondary to left-sided prosthetic valves is dependent on the site of the valve (mitral having an increased rate compared to aortic valves), choice of valve, and use of anticoagulant therapy (Chapter 10). In the presence of a right to left shunt, which is not uncommon in children with CHD, a venous clot can cause a paradoxical embolism. Clots on the right side of the heart may occur related to the presence of a central venous line (CVL), which is often required for intra- and postoperative care. Persistent foramen ovale (PFO) is an important cause of AIS in young adults and requires anticoagulant therapy or closure because of the risk of recurrence.[106–110] The contribution of PFO to stroke during early infancy is difficult to determine given that a PFO is present at birth in all infants and requires several months to close physiologically. Risk factors for AIS secondary to CHD include recent surgery or catheterization, the type of surgical repair, polycythemia, and anemia. The exact incidence of AIS following cardiac surgery is not known. However, in a prospective study of consecutive children with both CHD and AIS, nearly 50% of AIS occur within 72 hours of cardiac surgery or catheterization.[105] AIS may also occur at a later time and is frequently associated with a residual right to left shunt. An echocardiogram should be performed in all children with AIS and a saline study should be considered to detect a PFO.

Children with complex CHD who have had a Fontan procedure are at increased risk of stroke. Fontan procedures are described in detail in Chapter 4. Following Fontan surgery, TEs in the right side of the heart can embolize to the arterial circulation through surgical fenestrations or other right to left intracardiac communications. In addition, TEs from the left side of the atrial baffle (from the divided pulmonary artery stump) or from the ventricle (in cases with ventricular dysfunction) can embolize to the arterial system. The exact incidence of stroke following Fontan surgery is uncertain. The current literature consists of small case series.[111–114] The incidence of cerebrovascular emboli varies from 1.9% to 8.8% in larger reviews and up to 16% in smaller series. The data are all retrospective and often only assess survivors. The timing of these events again varies from less than 24 hours postoperatively to years later. Day et al[112] reported that 8.8% of 68 consecutive Fontan patients suffered a stroke, with half having evidence of multiple events on MRI.[112] All but one of these occurred later than 3 months following the operation. Du Plessias et al[114] reported that 2.6% of 645 Fontan patients suffered a focal CNS deficit. Approximately one-third of those who suffered stroke had demonstrable intracardiac TEs.[114] The Mayo Clinic reported that 1.9% of 215 survivors of Fontans prior to 1985 had strokes. The overall survival rate was 77%, with 7 brain deaths and 11 sudden and unexpected deaths.[115] Unfortunately, autopsy information was not provided so that the contribution of TEs to these adverse outcomes could not be evaluated. Frequently, a CNS infarct or stroke is the initial presentation of TEs after Fontan surgery. Presumably, there is an intracardiac or central venous TEs that are the source for the embolus. Transesophageal echocardiography should be considered to increase the sensitivity for intracardiac thrombi in children who underwent a Fontan procedure.[116,117]

Infection Although both bacterial and viral infections may cause AIS, the actual risk of AIS in children with infections is extremely low. Meningitis should be considered in children with indicative clinical features and AIS. In children with meningitis, AIS or SVT has been identified in 5% to 12% of children.[118–122] The post-varicella angiopathy is a well characterized, although rare, complication of chicken pox and usually occurs weeks to months following the primary infection.[118,121,122] The radiographic features of post-varicella angiopathy are distinctive and consist of basal ganglia infarction and stenosis of distal internal carotid or proximal anterior, middle, and posterior cerebral arteries at the Circle of Willis.[120,123]

Prothrombotic disorders Inherited or acquired coagulation disorders can predispose to AIS.[56,124–127] Reported prothrombotic abnormalities include deficiencies of protein C, protein S, AT, plasminogen, and the presence of APCR, prothrombin gene 20210A, ACLA, and LAs.[127–132] Two recent prospective cohort studies reported prothrombotic abnormalities in 34% (25 of 73) and 30% (9 of 30) of children with AIS.[36,44] Congenital prothrombotic disorders are less common in children with AIS compared to the presence of ACLAs.[36] Congenital prothrombotic states are less common.[36] Although the role of ACLAs in the pathogenesis of childhood stroke remains unclear, testing for ACLA should likely be performed in any child with AIS, including children with other identified risk factors. In children with congenital prothrombotic disorders, TEs usually occur in the setting of additional separate acquired problems that temporarily increase their risk of TEs. Therefore, children should be tested off anticoagulants if possible because transient abnormalities in many of the tests may occur for several weeks following the formation of a clot. Abnormal results on samples taken within several weeks of the stroke should be confirmed by testing parents, if the abnormality is a congenital prothrombotic disorder, and/or retesting the child several months later.

Sickle cell disease Approximately 25% of patients with sickle cell disease develop cerebrovascular complications and the vast majority occur during childhood.[133–137] Many children have asymptomatic cerebrovascular disease. Thrombotic stroke occurs as part of the thrombotic crisis and as the result of a progressive cerebral vasculopathy. Aneurysms and ICH are rare in children with sickle cell disease with an incidence of only 1.5%.[138–143] Transcranial Doppler studies are a noninvasive means of following the large-vessel vasculopathy and determining stroke risk in these patients.[144] Long-term transfusion therapy to reduce levels of hemoglobin S to below 20% to 30% reduces the risk of both primary stroke in high-risk individuals, and recurrent strokes.[145] Other therapies including hydroxyurea are under investigation.[146–148] The role of anticoagulant and antiplatelet agents are not clear but should be considered, especially when large-vessel vasculopathy or prothrombotic abnormalities and recurrent stroke co-exist.[149] Currently, exchange transfusion is the therapy of choice for acute stroke in children with sickle cell anemia.

Platelet disorders Platelet disorders including thrombocytosis can be associated with AIS. Freedman et al described two brothers with AIS who both had hyperactive platelets in aggregation studies as well as expression of P-selectin on flow cytometric analyses. Mixing experiments showed that the patient's platelets behaved normally in control plasma but that control platelets in patient's plasma were not inhibited by nitric oxide (NO), and thrombin-induced expression of platelet surface P-selectin was also not inhibited by NO. Subsequent studies showed a two- to threefold increase in plasma $H2O2$ generation in the two patients compared with control plasma. Glutathione peroxidase (GSH-Px) activity was decreased in the patients' plasmas and exogenous GSH-PX restored platelet inhibition by NO. In summary, these two patients had impaired metabolism of reactive oxygen, species that reduced the bioavailability of NO and impaired normal platelet inhibitory mechanisms. These abnormalities may have been responsible for causing thrombotic events in the CNS in these two brothers.[150]

Iron-deficiency anemia Iron-deficiency anemia has been recently associated with stroke in older infants.[151] However, the literature is limited to small numbers of case reports, and a cause and effect relationship has not been fully established. Iron-deficiency anemia affects up to 25% of the world's infants, but there are less than 20 reported cases of stroke associated with iron deficiency in the literature, suggesting that other factors are likely significant in the pathogenesis of stroke in these infants. Many of the children had other risk factors for cerebral ischemia including dehydration, PFO of other prothrombotic disorders. There are three proposed hypotheses to explain an association between iron deficiency and stroke. The first hypothesis is that the thrombocytosis that commonly occurs in children with iron deficiency is causal to stroke. However, the majority of the children with iron deficiency and stroke did not have thrombocytosis at the time of the stroke. The second hypothesis is that iron deficiency induces a hypercoaguable state related to reduced red cell deformity and subsequent

increased viscosity. However, assessment of sensitive markers of activation of the coagulation system does not support this hypothesis. The third hypothesis is that the anemia induces hypoxia due to reduced oxygen delivery and inefficient oxygen utilization. However, the lack of severe anemia in many affected children does not support this theory.[151] Further research will be required to prove a causal relationship between iron deficiency and stroke in children.

Local injury from trauma or radiation Trauma to the head and neck is the most common cause of dissection in children and usually involves the carotid or vertebral arteries.[152–154] Recurrent TIAs and recurrent AIS are characteristic of dissected cerebral arteries and provide the rationale for treatment with anticoagulants.[155] Post-radiation vasculopathy may present as a progressive large-vessel stenosis with TIAs or AIS beginning several years after irradiation of optic chiasm gliomas or other sellar or suprasellar region tumors in children.[156,157] No specific therapy halts the progression of post-radiation vasculopathy. However, anticoagulants may be helpful in preventing further AIS.

Vasculitis Noninfectious vasculitis in children is a relatively rare cause of AIS. Specific subtypes of vasculitis causing stroke are Takayasu's arteritis,[158–162] mixed connective tissue disease,[163] SLE,[164] polyarteritis nodosa,[165] and juvenile temporal arteritis.[166] Conventional angiography may be necessary to make the diagnosis of vasculitis if the MRA is normal because MRA cannot reliably detect vasculitis in medium and small vessels. Patients with noninfectious vasculitis should be evaluated for the presence of APLA. A specific vasculitis limited to cerebral vessels or CNS angiitis occurs in adults and may also occur in children, and rare cases with autopsy proof have been reported in children.[167,168]

Takayasu's arteritis Takayasu's arteritis is a rare chronic, idiopathic, inflammatory disease of large arteries predominantly affecting Asian females.[161] Although any artery can be involved, angiographic studies show that two-thirds of patients have aortic lesions, with the aortic arch, carotid arteries, and renal arteries being primarily affected.[158] The clinical presentation is limb or organ ischemia due to gradual stenosis of related arteries.[162] Clinical symptoms reflect the affected arteries[160,162] and physical findings frequently include a bruit in the involved area.[160] The diagnosis is frequently delayed by several months.[162] Angiography remains the gold standard for the assessment of clinical severity of the disease.

Glucocorticoids are the mainstay of medical therapy for Takayasu's arteritis with at least 60% of patients achieving remission within 1 year of treatment.[161,169] Unfortunately, 50% of patients relapse and additional cytotoxic agents such as methotrexate or cyclophosphamide are required.[161,169] Arterial reconstruction is required for at least one-third of patients.[158,160,162,170]

Moyamoya disease and moyamoya syndrome
Moyamoya disease occurs primarily in the Japanese population and is characterized by progressive stenosis and occlusion of the cerebral arteries at the Circle of Willis. In response to the stenosis, an abnormal network of small collateral vessels develops creating the characteristic "puff of smoke" appearance on angiogram (Figure 7–10). Children with moyamoya present with recurrent TIAs as well as AIS. In general, there is a progressive neurologic deterioration characterized by significant impairment of motor and cognitive function.[171] Hemorrhage, although common in adults with moyamoya, is relatively rare in children.[171–174] No specific medical therapy halts the progression of moyamoya disease. Moyamoya syndrome is a disorder with a similar angiographic appearance but is secondary to several slowly progressive occlusive cerebral vasculopathies, such as sickle cell disease or post-radiation vasculopathy. Although anticoagulant therapy has been used in children with Moyamoya, the efficacy and safety have not been determined. A recent report suggests that congenital prothrombotic disorders occur in some children with moyamoya disease.[175]

Metabolic vasculopathies There are several metabolic vasculopathies that may present with AIS during childhood and require specialized investigations to make the diagnosis. These include homozygous homocystinuria, Fabry disease, mitochondrial myopathy, encephalopathy, lactic acidosis and stroke-like episodes (MELAS syndrome), hyperlipidemia,[103,176] and migraine.[177,178]

Hyperhomocysteinemia Homocysteine is a sulphur-containing amino acid formed by the

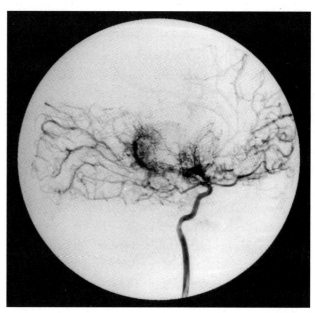

Figure 7–10 Classic picture of moyamoya disease, which is characterized by progressive stenosis and occlusion of the cerebral arteries at the Circle of Willis. In response to the stenosis, an abnormal network of small collateral vessels develops, creating the characteristic "puff of smoke" appearance on angiogram.

demethylation of dietary methionine, which is dependent on the cofactors folic acid, vitamin B_6, and vitamin B_{12}. Hyperhomocysteinemia can have both a genetic and nutritional basis. Genetic causes of hyperhomocysteinemia are cystathionine-B-synthase deficiency[179] and 5,10-methylenetetrahydrofolate reductase (MTHFR) deficiency.[180] The recently identified thermolabile variant of MTHFR causes hyperhomocysteinemia and decreased plasma concentrations of folate and occurs in 5% to 30% of the population.[181,182] Nutritional causes of hyperhomocysteinemia may occur in patients with folate deficiency, vitamin B_{12} deficiency, and patients with chronic renal failure.[183] Hyperhomocysteinemia is a proven independent risk factor for atherosclerotic vascular disease affecting the coronary, cerebral, and peripheral arteries in adults.[184–186]

Homocysteine also promotes vascular smooth muscle cells growth, oxidizes LDL, and may adversely affect platelet function.[187,188] Although hyperhomocysteinemia is unequivocally linked to vascular disease, its role in the pathogenesis of atherosclerosis remains to be elucidated. Therapeutically, supplementation with folic acid can reduce plasma concentrations of homocysteine; however, the reduction of vascular disease remains to be proven.[189]

Radiographic Features

Computerized tomography CT findings of arterial infarcts consist of bland infarcts that appear as low-density lesions in an established vascular territory. Secondary hemorrhagic infarcts have additional high-density components in the acute stage. Within the first 12 to 24 hours following an ischemic stroke, a CT of the brain is often normal.[7]

Magnetic resonance imaging/angiography MRI is more sensitive than CT for the detection of arterial infarcts, particularly for lesions in the brain stem and cerebellum. MRI is also more sensitive for hemorrhagic conversion of infarcts and avoids bone artifact.[13,190] MRA can be performed at the same time as MRI and provides further information on blood flow in the major cerebral arteries. MRA is particularly valuable in visualizing flow in the extracranial arteries (carotid, vertebral), which are the sites most frequently involved in dissection secondary to trauma.[6,8,191] MRA correlates well with conventional angiography in children with AIS and has become a noninvasive alternative to conventional angiography.[6,66,191–193]

Cerebral angiography Cerebral angiography is still considered the gold standard for visualization of the arterial vasculature of the brain; however, MRA is less invasive and usually the diagnostic test of first choice. Angiography may have some advantages over MRA for visualization of small or medium cerebral arteries, for the detection of specific features of dissection, and vasculitis (Figure 7–11). Conventional angiography should be seriously considered in children with idiopathic stroke since specific treatments that are dependent upon the correct diagnosis may be needed.

Treatment of Adults with Antithrombotic Agents

Potential use of thrombolytic therapy The rationale for thrombolytic therapy in adults is the presence of an occlusive clot in 80% of ischemic strokes. Studies in animal models[194–196] and a meta-analysis of thrombolytic therapy in 1992 suggested that further clinical trials should be conducted in

humans.[197] Over the last 6 years, a number of RCTs have assessed thrombolytic therapy given via either intravenous or intra-arterial routes.[198–207] Three placebo-controlled trials assessed intravenous streptokinase (SK) for acute stroke: the Multicenter Acute Stroke Trial–Italy (MAST-I), the Multicenter Acute Stroke Trial–Europe (MAST-E), and the Australian Streptokinase (ASK) Trial.[203–205] All trials were stopped prematurely by safety committees due to excess bleeding with SK. At this time, SK cannot be recommended for the treatment of ischemic stroke. Following initial studies to determine the optimal timing of thrombolytic therapy[204,205] and dose of tissue plasminogen activator (TPA), two large RCTs assessing the potential benefit of intravenous TPA were conducted. These were the National Institute of Neurological Disorders and Stroke (NINDS) rTPA Stroke Study Group trials and the European Cooperative Acute Stroke Study (ECASS).[207,208] Important differences existed between the NINDS and ECASS trials, including the

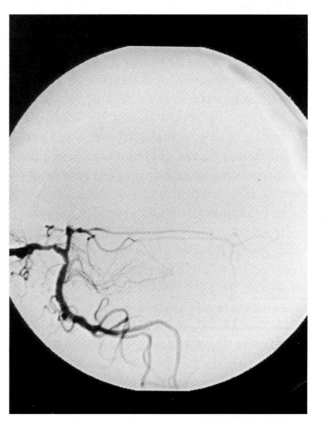

Figure 7–11 Typical appearance of vasculitis in cerebral arteries. In this anterior-posterior conventional angiogram, the left ICA and MCA are involved.

treatment window (3 hours vs 6 hours), the doses of TPA (0.9 mg/kg vs 1.1 mg/kg), and the rigid control of blood pressure required by the NINDS trial. Both trials reported a significant improvement in neurologic outcome but with an added risk of bleeding. Factors that contribute to the risk of hemorrhagic transformation secondary to thrombolytic therapy for acute stroke include time from symptom onset to treatment, diastolic blood pressure, low body mass, age, atrial fibrillation, "early signs" of ischemia, and the use of TPA.[207]

Current recommendations for thrombolytic therapy Current recommendations for the use of TPA in adults with stroke are that patients are over 18 years of age, and have a clinical diagnosis of stroke, a significant neurologic deficit, a clearly defined time of onset that must be less than 180 minutes (3 hours), and a CT showing no evidence of ICH. Several exclusion criteria must also be met and consist of minor or rapidly resolving neurologic symptoms, CNS hemorrhage on CT, a history of ICH, stroke or serious head injury within 3 months, major surgery or serious trauma within 2 weeks, gastrointestinal (GI) or urinary hemorrhage within 3 weeks, hypertension, arterial puncture at a noncompressible site or lumbar puncture within 1 week, platelet count less than 100,000, UFH within 48 hours associated with an elevated APTT, post MI pericarditis, pregnant or lactating women, and current use of OAs with an INR over 1.7. Thrombolytic therapy should also possibly be held if there is evidence of major early infarct. SK is not recommended. If TPA is used, an intravenous dose of 0.9 mg/kg (maximum of 90 mg) with 10% of the total dose given as an initial bolus and the remainder infused over 60 minutes is recommended. Strict adherence of the NINDS trial protocol is strongly recommended.[195,196,206,207,209–212]

Initial use of heparin or low molecular weight heparin The mechanism(s) by which UFH and LMWH function, dosing schedules, and monitoring are discussed in Chapter 9. The use of UFH or LMWH for the initial treatment of stroke is dependent upon the subtype of stroke, which reflects distinct pathophysiologic mechanisms.

There are only two small RCTs of intravenous UFH therapy compared to placebo for acute stroke

since 1980.[213,214] No significant benefit was demonstrated; however, the trial was small, had a relatively prolonged time to patient entry (48 hours), and excluded patients with progressing stroke.[213] Subcutaneous UFH was evaluated in the International Stroke Trial (IST).[215] The results showed that early, unmonitored subcutaneous UFH will reduce early stroke recurrence risks, but these benefits can be eliminated by increased hemorrhagic complications. The use of lower doses of UFH may provide benefits with fewer hemorrhagic side effects.

LMWH has been evaluated in a number of RCTs. However a subsequent, nearly identical trial, "FISS-bis," failed to demonstrate any benefit of Fraxiparin in acute stroke. A larger trial, the Trial of ORG 10172 in Acute Stroke treatment (TOAST), evaluated the LMWH heparinoid danaparoid (ORG 10172).[216] This multicenter, blinded, placebo-controlled trial failed to corroborate any beneficial effects from danaparoid. Overall, there was no significant difference in the proportion of patients with favorable outcomes at 3 months, although there was an improved outcome with danaparoid at 7 days. A subgroup analysis showed some benefit at 3 months for patients with acute large-artery atherosclerotic stroke. These findings were recently confirmed on further analysis of the data.[217–219] There remains considerable debate regarding the appropriate use of UFH or LMWH for the treatment of acute stroke in adults.

Early intravenous anticoagulation therapy for 3 to 5 days should be considered for adults who have acute cardioembolic strokes, or large-artery atherosclerotic ischemic strokes, and for progressing stroke when the etiology is suspected to be due to ongoing TEs.[220–222] An intravenous bolus of UFH is not recommended. Because the use of UFH is associated with a small but real risk of serious hemorrhage, patients with large infarcts, uncontrolled hypertension, or other bleeding conditions should probably not receive early anticoagulation. Because of the risk of DVT/PE in adult stroke patients, prophylactic doses of UFH or LMWH are recommended for acute stroke patients with restricted mobility.[214,223–225]

Use of aspirin There are two large RCTs assessing the early use of aspirin (less than 48 hours from the time of onset of symptoms) in adults with AIS: the IST and Chinese Acute Stroke Trial (CAST).[214,226] Both studies reported a significant reduction in recurrent stroke and mortality.[214,226] For adults who are not eligible for TPA and who are not receiving UFH or OAs, early aspirin therapy (160 to 325 mg per day) is recommended to be initiated within 48 hours of the stroke onset and may be used safely in combination with low doses of subcutaneous UFH for the prevention of DVT/PE.[1]

Treatment of Stroke in Children with Antithrombotic Agents The treatment of AIS during childhood is comprised primarily of supportive measures focused on the underlying disease and the use of antithrombotic agents. Supportive therapy is not discussed further and readers are referred to several recent reviews.[35,72] The role of antithrombotic agents is uncertain in children as there are no controlled trials assessing the risk–benefit ratio in different forms of AIS. If antithrombotic therapy is used, current guidelines are extrapolated from recommendations for adults, which may not be optimal but are useful.[227] Antithrombotic therapy for adults with AIS includes initial therapy with aspirin for most patients and less commonly with thrombolytic therapy, UFH, or LMWH and/or thrombolytic therapy, and maintenance therapy with either antiplatelet agents or OAs for secondary prevention.[228]

The use of anticoagulant therapy appears to be increasing in children with AIS. In a recent population-based study, 35% of children with AIS received one or more of UFH, LMWH, antiplatelet agents, and/or OAs. There was wide variability in indications for and choice of anticoagulants.[39] Accumulating experience with antithrombotic and anticoagulant treatment in children suggests that these agents can be safely used in children with AIS, although their efficacy and proper dose still need to be established by RCTs. The use of thrombolytic agents in children with AIS, however, has been rare and the risk–benefit ratio is completely unknown at this time. Antithrombotic treatment guidelines in childhood stroke have been published recently.[228] If AIS is associated with hemorrhage, or hypertension or other risks to anticoagulants exist, anticoagulant

therapy may not be feasible. The risks of recurrence or progression of cerebral TEs should be balanced against the risks of treatment, particularly bleeding. The subsequent sections summarize the limited information available on the use of UFH or LMWH, antiplatelet agents, OAs, and thrombolytic therapy.

Use of heparin or low molecular weight heparin In the absence of studies in children with AIS, guidelines for the use of UFH/LMWH are extrapolated from adults. Potential indications for either UFH or LMWH in children with AIS include embolism from the heart (usually complex CHD), arterial dissection, congenital prothrombotic disorders presenting with AIS, in children with progressive or additional neurologic deficits after the initial AIS, which are not caused by hemorrhagic transformation of the infarct.[80] The risk and significance of recurrent AIS must be weighed against the risk and significance of a major bleed, usually into the previously infarcted brain. Similar to adults, UFH/LMWH should be considered in children thought to have a high risk of recurrence and a low risk of secondary hemorrhage. There is increasing clinical experience that suggests that children can be treated with UFH/LMWH with reasonable safety.[80,228,229] Atherosclerotic disease, which is the usual cause of hemorrhage into the CNS in adults, is rare in children, suggesting that the risk of a CNS bleed may be less during childhood.

Antiplatelet agents The mechanism(s) by which antiplatelet agents function and dosing schedules are discussed in Chapter 12. The most commonly used antiplatelet agent in adults with AIS is aspirin. There is limited experience with ticlopidine and GPIIb/IIIA inhibitors.

Numerous clinical trials have demonstrated the benefits of aspirin as an agent for the secondary prevention of recurrent AIS following TIA or stroke in adults. The risk reduction for recurrent AIS in adults is substantial at approximately 25%.[1,220,221] Newer forms of antiplatelet agents including clopidogrel may offer improved benefit.[230] Very recent studies have reported a modest benefit of immediate aspirin therapy in acute ischemic stroke.[214,231]

In the absence of studies in children with AIS, guidelines for the use of antiplatelet agents are extrapolated from adults. However, the profound differences in pathophysiology of AIS in adults and children and the potential benefits of antiplatelet agents limit the applicability of studies performed in adults with AIS to children. Potential indications for antiplatelet agents in children include secondary prevention of recurrent AIS in the absence of cardiogenic embolism or dissection. An example is the use of aspirin to decrease the risk of recurrent AIS in the presence of cerebral arterial stenosis. Currently, most older children with AIS are placed on aspirin even when no cause is identified because of the risk of recurrent stroke in 15% to 20% of children and minimal side effects.[39,88,91,232,233] Neonates with AIS are at lower risk of recurrence and are not usually given aspirin.

Oral anticoagulants The mechanism(s) by which OAs function, dosing schedules, and monitoring are discussed in Chapter 10. OAs are used in adults with AIS for the secondary prevention of cardioembolic stroke, dissection, or when antiplatelet agents fail or are predicted to be insufficient.[1,221] OAs are used in children to prevent new or recurrent cardioembolic stroke, TEs of arterial dissection, recurrent AIS related to congenital prothrombotic disorders, and recurrent AIS or TIA while on aspirin. An INR of 2.0 to 3.0 is appropriate for most children on warfarin; for children with mechanical heart valves, the INR should be 2.5 to 3.5.[228]

Thrombolytic agents Thrombolytic agents that have been used in children include TPA, urokinase (UK), and SK. The literature consists of isolated case reports only. The mechanism(s) by which all thrombolytic agents function, dosing schedules, and monitoring are discussed in Chapter 11. Theoretically, thrombolytic therapy has the potential to be effective and lyse an acute thrombus in the CNS with short- and long-term neurologic benefit. However, there are several problematic issues with the use of thrombolytic therapy in the treatment of AIS in children. First, in the only trial that convincingly demonstrated a benefit from the use of TPA in adults with AIS, TPA was administered within 3 hours of the clinical presentation.[207] Children rarely, if ever, have AIS diagnosed within a time frame of 3 hours. Second, adults with AIS who are potential candidates for thrombolytic therapy must have a normal CT in order to avoid hemorrhage. A normal

CT in children with new focal neurologic deficits is rarely due to AIS and thrombolytic therapy would not be indicated for these other diseases. Third, the hemorrhagic risk of thrombolytic therapy into the CNS is significant in adults and essentially no information in children. Fourth, neonates have decreased plasma concentrations of plasminogen that may limit the benefits of thrombolytic therapy in the age group with the highest incidence of AIS.[77,79] Finally, the diversity of underlying causes for AIS in children likely influence the efficacy/safety ratio for thrombolytic agents. At this time, the evaluation of thrombolytic therapy in children with AIS does not appear to be feasible and further studies in adults demonstrating an improved neurologic outcome are needed. In the future, advanced MRI or nuclear medicine scanning techniques and greater clinical awareness of pediatric AIS may improve the early diagnosis of this disorder. However, until further research is available, thrombolytic therapy cannot be generally recommended as initial therapy for AIS in children.

Outcome Outcome studies of AIS in children can be grouped into prospective and retrospective studies, with prospective studies providing more reliable information. There is only one prospective study of consecutive children with AIS where neurologic outcome was assessed using a validated standardized tool.

The neurologic deficit was measured in a prospective cohort of 123 children with AIS. Neurologic deficit severity was based on the Pediatric Stroke Outcome Measure (PSOM) developed in the same study and parental response to two recovery questions. Based on the PSOM results, 37% of children were normal neurologically, 20% had a mild deficit, 26% a moderate deficit, and 16% a severe deficit. The secondary outcome based on parental response reported that 45% of children were viewed as completely recovered by their parents.

In retrospective studies of children with AIS, the prevalence of residual neurologic deficits is 75%.[3,234–237] In general, children recover more function and for longer periods of time than adults with the same type of AIS.

Variables influencing the reported outcomes of arterial ischemic stroke in children The study by DeVeber et al[39] developed a modified Euroqual as well as parental response to two questions: (1) Has your child recovered completely from his/her stroke? and (2) Does your child need extra help in day-to-day activities compared with other children his/her age?[39] There are several variables that likely influence the reported risk of adverse outcomes. In bivariate analysis of arterial stroke type, male gender, age ≤ 28 days, associated neurologic disorders, and rehabilitation therapy after stroke were predictors of poor outcome (p < .05) Multivarate analysis showed that only arterial ischemic stroke, associated neruological disorders, and presence of rehabilitation therapy were independent predictors or poor outcome (p < .02). First, a milder outcome reported in more recent studies may reflect, in part, the use of MRI, which detects more subtle forms of AIS. Second, the increasing trend to treat AIS in children with anticoagulants may have modified the outcome when compared to older case series when anticoagulant therapy was not widely used. Third, retrospective study designs have several inherent sources of bias that may overestimate abnormal outcomes. Fourth, the duration of follow-up following AIS is critically important in the assessment of the final neurologic deficit because of the later emergence of neurologic deficits in infants as the brain develops. Fifth, the depth of the follow-up outcome assessment is important as subtle learning problems may be overlooked without detailed assessment.

Predictors of outcome Factors predicting good and poor outcome in childhood AIS have recently been defined by DeVeber et al,[39] although the presence of seizures at the onset of stroke may predict later developmental delay and persistent seizures.[94,238]

Neonates Neonates with AIS are a unique group of patients because of the immaturity of their neurologic development and apparent enhanced capacity to adapt to neurologic insults. In population-based studies following neonatal AIS, a normal outcome was reported in 50% of patients at 9 months average follow-up interval. The remainder had a seizure disorder and or neurologic deficit that was usually mild in severity.[5] In retrospective studies,

motor deficits have been reported in about three-quarters, cortical sensory deficits in one-third, and seizure disorders in over one-third of neonates after AIS.[239–242] In neonates with acute hemispheric lesions, hemiparesis is rare, but focal signs frequently appear in the latter half of the first year of life as brain maturation proceeds.[92] Nearly one-third of the cohort reported by deVeber et al[39] were neonates, consistent with prior observations that neonates are at particular risk for cerebral thromboembolism.[39]

The neonates in this study had fewer poorer outcomes (31%) than older infants and children, which may reflect a relative resistence for the neonatal brain to damage or milder insults. The former view has recently been called into question.[243] An alternative explanation is that the better outcome only reflects a delay in appearance of more subtle sequelae not evident in the as yet immature brain.[86,92] This is consistent with the observation that the deficit increases over time in nearly one-third of our neonates with arterial stroke. Other studies have reported a high frequency of motor deficits (73% and 88%), cortical sensory deficits (34%), and seizure disorders (60%) after perinatal cerebral infarts and/or hemorrhage. This may reflect the inclusion of infants with delayed diagnosis and delayed onset of hemiparesis due to presumed prenatal or perinatal arterial infacts.[39]

Recurrent arterial ischemic stroke The risk of stroke recurrence in children is unknown but has been reported to be as high as 20% in one long-term series of ischemic stroke.[232] In smaller, shorter duration follow-up studies, lower recurrence rates have been found. In recent prospective studies mortality after AIS is 6%,[34] although previously mortality has been reported in up to 14%.[2,4,86] Death is usually related to the underlying cause for stroke (e.g., overwhelming sepsis or CHD) and less frequently due to the stroke itself.

SUMMARY

Stroke in children is a devastating complication with long-term ramifications. Although stroke in adults has been extensively studied, there is a paucity of information on stroke during childhood.

Understanding the epidemiology of childhood stroke is necessary in order to accurately identify potential interventions to be tested in clinical trials. The current approach of extrapolating recommendations for treatment from adults is unlikely to be optimal for children. Intervention trials are necessary in order to determine the role of antithrombotic and other therapies in pediatric patients with AIS and SVT.

REFERENCES

1. Albers GW, Easton JD, Sacco RL, Teal P. Antithrombotic and thrombolytic therapy for ischemic stroke. Chest 1998;114:683S–698S.
2. deVeber G, Adams M, Andrew M, Canadian Pediatric Neurologists. Canadian pediatric ischemic stroke registry. Analysis III [abstract]. Thromb Haemostas 1995;73.
3. Schoenberg B, Mellinger J, Schoenberg D. Cerebrovascular disease in infants and children: a study of incidence, clinical features, and survival. Neurology 1978;28:763–768.
4. Broderick J, Talbot T, Prenger E, et al. Stroke in children within a major metropolitan area: the surprising importance of intracerebral hemorrhage. J Child Neurol 1993;8:250–255.
5. deVeber G, Adams M, Andrew M, the Canadian Pediatric Ischemic Stroke Study Group. Neonatal cerebral thromboembolism: Clinical and radiographic features [abstract]. Thromb Haemostas 1997;(Suppl):725.
6. Wiznitzer M, Masaryk TJ. Cerebrovascular abnormalities in pediatric stroke: assessment using parenchymal and angiographic magnetic resonance imaging. Ann Neurol 1991;29:585–589.
7. Ball WS. Cerebrovascular occlusive disease in childhood. Neuroimaging Clin N Am 1994;4:393–421.
8. Koelfen W, Freund M, Konig S, et al. Results of parenchymal and angiographic magnetic resonance imaging and neuropsychological testing of children after stroke as neonates. Eur J Pediatr 1993;152:1030–1035.
9. Lee B, Voorhies T, Ehrlich M, et al. Digital intravenous cerebral angiography in neonates. Am J Neuroradiol 1984;5:281–286.
10. Towbin A. Central nervous system damage in the human fetus and newborn infant. Am J Dis Child Childhood 1970;119:529–542.
11. Rivkin M, Anderson M, Kaye E. Neonatal idiopathic cerebral venous thrombosis: an unrecognized cause of transient seizures or lethargy. Ann Neurol 1992;32:51–56.
12. Shevell MI, Silver K, O'Gorman AM, et al. Neonatal dural sinus thrombosis. Pediatr Neurol 1989;5:161–165.
13. Ameri A, Bousser M. Cerebral venous thrombosis. Neurologic Clinics 1992;10:87–111.
14. Taylor TN, Davis PH, Torner JC, et al. Lifetime cost of stroke in the United States. Stroke 1996;27:1459–1466.
15. Cook D, Guyatt G, Laupacis A, et al. Clinical recommendations using levels of evidence for antithrombotic agents. Chest 1995;108(Suppl):227S–230S.
16. Andrew M, deVeber G. Blood clots and strokes: a guide for parents and little folks. Hamilton: BC Decker; 1998.
17. Capra N, Anderson K. Anatomy of the cerebral venous system. In: Knapp JP, et al. editors. The cerebral venous system and its disorders, Orlando: Grune and Stratton; 1984.
18. Woodhall B. Variations of the cranial venous sinuses in the region of the torcular herophil. Arch Surg 1936;33:297–310.
19. Bousser MG, Russel RR. Pathology and pathogenesis of venous infarction. In: Cerebral venous thrombosis, London: WB Saunders; pp. 15–21.
20. deVeber G, Adams M, Andrew M, Canadian Pediatric Neurologists. Canadian Pediatric Stroke Registry. Analysis II [abstract]. Can J Neurol Sci 1995;22:S24.
21. Newton TH, Gooding CA. Compression of superior sagittal sinus by neonatal calvarial molding. Neuroradiology 1975;115:635–639.
22. Lin JH, McLean K, Morser J, et al. Modulation of glycosaminoglycan addition in naturally expressed and recombinant human thrombomodulin. J Biol Chem 1994;269:25021–25030.
23. Andrew M, Brooker L, Mitchell L. Acquired antithrombin III deficiency secondary to asparaginase therapy in childhood acute lymphoblastic leukemia. Blood Coagulation Fibrinolysis 1994;5:S24–S36.
24. Ishii H, Oh H, Ishizuka N, et al. Cerebral infarction in a patient with acute lymphoblastic leukemia after fresh-frozen plasma replacement during L-asparaginase therapy. Am J Hematol 1992;41:295–306.
25. Cairo MS, Lazarus K, Gilmore RL, Baehner RL. Intracranial hemorrhage and focal seizures secondary to use of L'asparaginase during induction therapy of acute lymphocytic leukemia. J Pediatr 1980;97:829–833.
26. Steinherz P, Miller L, Ghavimi F, et al. Dural sinus thrombosis in children with acute lymphoblastic leukemia. JAMA 1981;246:2837–2839.
27. White L, Fishman L, Shore N. Strokes and the neurotoxicity of L-asparaginase. J Pediatr 1981;101:168.
28. Priest J, Ramsay N, Latchaw R, et al. Thrombotic and haemorrhagic strokes complicating early therapy for

childhood acute lymphoblastic leukemia. Cancer 1980;46:1548–1554.

29. Packer R, Rorke L, Lange B, et al. Cerebrovascular accidents in children with cancer. Pediatrics 1985; 76:194–201.

30. Lockman L, Mastri A, Priest J, Nesbit M. Dural venous sinus thrombosis in acute lymphoblastic leukemia. Pediatrics 1980;66:943–947.

31. Ganick D, Robertson WJ, Viseskul C, Lubinsky M. Dural sinus thrombosis in leukemia. Am J Dis Child 1978;132:1040–1041.

32. Mitchell L, Hoogendoorn H, Giles A, et al. Increased endogenous thrombin generation in children with acute lymphoblastic leukemia: risk of thrombotic complications in L'Asparaginase-induced antithrombin III deficiency. Blood 1994;83:386–391.

33. Perona A, Galligani L. The clinical syndrome associated with antiphospolipid antibodies. A diagnosis to be confirmed after a long follow-up. Minerv Pediatr 1995;47:39–41.

34. deVeber G, Andrew M. Canadian pediatric ischemic stroke registry. Analysis [abstract]. Pediatr Res 1994;35:379A.

35. deVeber G. Cerebrovascular diseases in children. In: Swaiman KF, et al, editors. Pediatric neurology: principles and practice, St Louis: CV Mosby; 1999, pp. 1099–1124.

36. ..eVeber G, Monagle P, Chan A, et al. Prothrombotic disorders in infants and children with cerebral thromboembolism. Arch Neurol 1998;55: 1539–1543.

37. Barron TF, Gusnard DA, Zimmerman RA, Clancy RR. Cerebral venous thrombosis in neonates and children. Pediatr Neurol 1992;8:112–116.

38. Hartmann A, Wappenschmidt J, Solymosi L, Brassel. Clinical findings and differential diagnosis of cerebral vein thrombosis. In: Cerebral sinus thrombosis. Experimental and clinical aspects, New York: Plenum Press; 1987;pp. 171–185.

39. deVeber G, MacGregor D, Curtis R, Stephens D. Neurological outcome in survivors of childhood arterial ischemic stroke and 1. sinovenous thrombosis. J Child Neurol 1999; in press.

40. Lane DA, Mannucci PM, Bauer KA, et al. Inherited thrombophilia: part 1. Thromb Haemost 1996;76: 651–662.

41. Deschiens MA, Conard J, Horellou MH, et al. Coagulation studies, factor V Leiden, and anticardiolipin antibodies in 40 cases of cerebral venous thrombosis [comments]. Stroke 1996;27:1724–1730.

42. Zuber M, Toulon P, Marnet L, Mas JL. Factor V Leiden mutation in cerebral venous thrombosis. Stroke 1996;27:1721–1723.

43. Nowak-Gottl U, Strater R, Dubbers A, et al. Ischaemic stroke in infancy and childhood: role of Arg506 to

Gln mutation in the factor V gene. Blood Coagul Fibrinolysis 1996;7:684–688.

44. Bonduel M, Sciuccati G, Hepner M, et al. Prethrombotic disorders in children with arterial ischemic stroke and sinovenous thrombosis. Arch Neurol 1999;56:967–971.

45. Whitlock JA, Janco RL, Phillips III JA. Inherited hypercoagulable states in children. Am J Pediatr Hematol Oncol 1989;11:170–173.

46. Roddy SM, Giang DW. Antiphospholipid antibodies amd stroke in an infant. Pediatrics 1991;87: 933–935.

47. Prats J, Garaizar C, Zuazo E, et al. Superior sagittal sinus thrombosis in a child with protein S deficiency. Neurology 1992;42:2303–2304.

48. Devilat M, Toso M, Morales M. Childhood stroke associated with protein C or S deficiency and primary antiphospholipid syndrome. Pediatr Neurol 1992;9: 67–70.

49. Gobel U. Inherited or acquired disorders of blood coagulation in children with neurovascular complications. Neuropediatrics 1994;25:4–7.

50. van Kuijck MAP, Rotteveel JJ, van Oostrom CG, Novakova I. Neurological complications in children with protein C deficiency. Neuropediatrics 1994;25:16–19.

51. Uziel Y, Laxer RM, Blaser S, et al. Cerebral vein thrombosis in childhood systemic lupus erythematosus. J Pediatr 1995;126:722–727.

52. Angelini L, Zibordi F, Zorzi G, et al. Neurological disorders, other than stroke, associated with antiphospholipid antibodies in childhood. Neuropediatrics 1996;27:149–153.

53. von Scheven E, Athreya BH, Rose C, et al. Clinical characteristics of antiphospholipid antibody syndrome in children. J Pediatr 1996;129:339–345.

54. Kohlhase B, Veilhaber H, Kehl HG, et al. Thromboembolism and resistance to activated protein C in children with underlying cardiac disease. J Pediatr 1996;128:324–328.

55. Nowak-Gottl U, Koch D, Aschka B, et al. Resistance to activated rotein C (APCR) in children with venous or arterial thromboembolism. Br J Haematol 1996; 92:992–998.

56. Rich C, Cox Gill J, Wernick S, Konkol RJ. An unusual cause of cerebral venous thrombosis in a four-year-old child. Stroke 1993;24:603–605.

57. de Bruijn SFTM, Stam J. Randomized, placebo-controlled trial of anticoagulant treatment with low molecular weight heparin for cerebral sinus thrombosis. Stroke 1999;30:484–488.

58. Frey JL. Cerebral venous thrombosis: combined intrathrombus rtPA and intravenous heparin. Stroke 1999;30:489–494.

59. Casey SO, Alberico RA, Patel M, et al. Cerebral CT venography. Radiology 1996;198:163–170.

60. Dormont D, Anxionnat R, Evrard S, et al. MRI in cerebral cenous thrombosis. J Neuroradiol 1994; 21:81–99.

61. Lewin JS, Masaryk TJ, Smith AS, et al. Time-of-flight intracranial MR venography:evaluation of the sequential oblique section of technique. Am J Neuroradiol 1994;15:1657–1664.

62. Yuh WT, Simonson TM, Wang AM, et al. Venous sinus occlusive disease: MR findings. Am J Neuroradiol 1994;15:309–316.

63. Hamburger C, Villringer A, Bauer M, Lorz T. Delta (empty triangle) sign in patients without thrombosis of the superior sagittal sinus. In: Einhaupl K, et al. editors. Cerebral sinus thrombosis: experimental and clinical aspects, New York: Plenum Press; 1990.

64. Jacewicz M, Plum F. Aseptic cerebral venous thrombosis. In: Einhaupl K, editor. Cerebral sinus thrombosis. New York: Plenum Press, 1990; pp. 157–170.

65. Ludwig B, Brand M, Brockerhoff P. Postpartum CT examination of the heads of full term infants. Neuroradiology 1980;145–154.

66. Zimmerman RA, Bogdan AR, Gusnard DA. Pediatric magnetic resonance angiography: assessment of stroke. Cardiovasc Inter Radiol 1992;15:

67. Macchi PJ, Grossman RI, Gomori JM, et al. High field MR imaging of cerebral venous thrombosis. J Comput Assist Tomogr 1986;10:10–15.

68. Medlock M, Olivero W, Hanigan W, et al. Children with cerebral venous thrombosis diagnosed with magnetic resonance imaging and magnetic resonance angiography. Neurosurgery 1992;31:870–876.

69. Bezinque SL, Slovis TL, Touchette AS, et al. Characterization of superiorsagittal sinus blood flow velocity using color flow Doppler in neonates and infants. Pediatric Radiology 1995;25:175–179.

70. Hunerbein R, Reuter P, Meyer W, Kuhn FP. CT angiography of cerebral venous circulation: anatomical visualization and diagnostic pitfalls in interpretation. Rofo Fortschr Geb Rontgenstr Neuen Bildgeh Verfahr 1997;167:612–618.

71. Bousser MG, Russell RR. Cerebral venous thrombosis. Toronto: W.B. Saunders Company Ltd., 1997.

72. Roach RS, Riela AR. Pediatric cerebrovascular disorders. New York: Publishing, 1995.

73. Einhaupl KM, Villringer A, Meister W, et al. Heparin treatment in sinus venous thrombosis. Lancet 1991;338:597–600.

74. Stam J, Lensing AW, Vermeulen M, Tijssen JG.Heparin treatment for cerebral venous and sinus thrombosis. Lancet 1991;338:1154–1155.

75. Milandre L, Gueriot C, Girard N. Les thromboses veineuses cerebrales de l'adult. Annal Med Intern 1988;139:544–554.

76. deVeber G, Chan A, Monagle P, et al. Anticoagulation therapy in pediatric patients with sinovenous thrombosis: a cohort study. Arch Neurol 1998;55: 1533–1537.

77. Andrew M, Paes B, Milner R, et al. Development of the human coagulation system in the full-term infant. Blood 1987;70:165–172.

78. Andrew M, Paes B, Johnston M. Development of the hemostatic system in the neonate and young infant. Am J Pediatr Hematol Oncol 1990;12:95–104.

79. Andrew M, Paes B, Milner R, et al. Development of the human coagulation system in the healthy premature infant. Blood 1988;72:1651–1657.

80. Roach RS, Riela AR. Pediatric cerebrovascular disorders. New York: Publishing, 1995.

81. Higashida RT, Helmer E, Halbach VV, Hieshima GB. Direct thrombolytic therapy for superior sagittal sinus thrombosis. AJNR 1989;10:S4–S6.

82. Wong VK, LeMesurier J, Franseschini R, et al. Cerebral venous thrombosis as a cause of neonatal seizures. Pediatr Neurol 1987;3:235–237.

83. Griesemer DA, Theodorou AA, Berg RA, Spera TD. Local fibrinolysis in cerebral venous thrombosis. Pediatr Neurol 1994;10:78–80.

84. Monagle P, Phelan E, Downie P, Andrew M. Local thrombolytic therapy in children [abstract]. Thromb Haemostas 1997;504.

85. deVeber G, Adams M, Andrew M, Canadian Pediatric Neurologists. Canadian pediatric ischemic stroke registry Analysis III). Can J Neurol Sci 1995;22:S24.

86. Lanska M, Lanska D, Horwitz S, Aram D. Presentation, clinical course, and outcome of childhood stroke. Pediatr Neurol 1991;7:333–341.

87. Chabrier S, Rodesch G, Lasjaunias P, et al. Transient cerebral arteriopathy: a disorder recognized by serial angiograms in children with stroke. J Child Neurol 1998;13:27–32.

88. deVeber G, Adams M. Neonatal sinovenous thrombosis and arterial ischemic stroke: prospective study of clinical and radiographic features [abstract]. Can J Neurol Sci 1996;23:S16.

89. Elkind MS, Sacco RL. Stroke risk factors and stroke prevention. Semin Neurol 1998;18:429–440.

90. Tress BM. Magnetic resonance imaging and ischaemic stroke. Hosp Med 1999;60:343–347.

91. deVeber G, MacGregor D, Curtis R, et al. Infants and children with sinovenous thrombosis and arterial ischemic stroke have a high prevalence of coagulation abnormalities [abstract]. J Pediatr Hematol Oncol 1997;19:407.

92. Bouza H, Rutherford M, Acolet D, et al. Evolution of early hemiplegic signs in full term infants with unilateral brain lesions in the neonatal period: a prospective study. Neuropediatr 1994;25:201–207.

93. Trescher W. Ischemic stroke syndromes in childhood. Pediatr Ann 1992;21:374–382.

94. Yang JS, Yong DP, Hartlage P. Seizures associated with stroke in childhood. Pediatr Neurol 1995;12: 136–138.

95. Demierre B, Rondot P. Dystonia caused by putamino-capsulo-daudate vascular lesions. J Neurol Neurosurg Psych 1983;46:404–409.

96. Martin PJ, Enevoldson TP, Humphrey PRD. Causes of ischemic stroke in the young. Postgrad Med J 1997;73:8–16.

97. Kerr LM, Anderson DM, Thompson JA, et al. Ischemic stroke in the young: evaluation and age comparison of patients six months to thirty-nine years. J Child Neurol 1993;8:266–270.

98. Janaki S, Baruah JK, Jayaram SR, et al. Stroke in the young: a four year study, 1968 to 1972. Stroke 1975;6:318–320.

99. Postiglione A, Nappi A, Brunetti A, et al. Relative protection from cerebral atherosclerosis of young patients with homozygous familial hypercholesterolemia. Atherosclerosis 90:23–30.

100. Rubba A, Mercuri M, Faccenda F, et al. Premature carotid atherosclerosis: does it occur in both familial hyperchilesterolemia and homocystinuria? Ultrasound assessment of arterial intima-media thickness and blood flow velocity. Stroke 1994;25:943–950.

101. Mabuchi H. Causes of death in patients with familial hypercholesterolemia. Atherosclerosis 1986;61:1–6.

102. Allen JM, Thompson GR, Myant NB, et al. Cardiovascular complications of homozygous familial hyperholesterolaemia. Br Heart J 1980;44:361–368.

103. Glueck CJ. Pediatric victims of unexplained stroke and their families: familial lipid and lipoprotein abnormailities. Pediatr 1982;69:308–316.

104. Damasio H. A computed tomographic guide to the identification of cerebral vascular territories. Arch Neurol 1983;40:138–142.

105. Cupido C, deVeber G, Adams M, Canadian Pediatric Ischemic Stroke Study Group. A prospective clinical study of congenital heart disease in pediatric stroke [abstract]. Ann Neurol 1996;40.

106. DiTullio M, Sacco RL, Venketa N, et al. Comparison of diagnostic techniques for the detection of a patent foramen ovale in stroke patients. Stroke 1993; 24:1020–1024.

107. DiTullio M, Sacco RL, Gopal AS. Patent foramen ovale as a risk factor for cryptogenic stroke. Ann Intern Med 1992;117:461–462.

108. Hascoet JM, Hamon I, Didier F, et al. Patent foramen ovale with left to right shunt in bronchopulmonary dysplasia: coincidental or associated complication? Acta Paediatr 1994;83:258–261.

109. Besson G, Bogousslavsky J, Hommel M, et al. Patent foramen ovale in young stroke patients with mitral valve prolapse. Acta Neurol Scand 1994;89:23–26.

110. Fisher DC, Fisher EA, Budd JH, et al. The incidence of patent foramen ovale in 1,000 consecutive patients. A contrast transesophageal echocardiography study. Chest 1995;107:1504–1509.

111. Hutto RL, Williams JP, Maertens P, et al. Cerebellar infarct: late complication of the Fontan procedure? Pediatr Neurol 1991;7:161–166.

112. Day RW, Boyer RS, Tait VF, Ruttenberg HD. Factors associated with stroke following the Fontan procedure. Pediatr Cardiol 1995;16:270–275.

113. Rosenthal DN, Bulbui ZR, Friedman AH, et al. Thrombosis of the pulmonary artery stump after distal ligation. J Thorac Cardiovasc Surg 1995;110: 1563–1565.

114. du Plessis A, Lock J, Wernovsky G, Newburger J. Cerebrovascular accidents following the Fontan operation. Pediatr Neurol 1995;12:230–236.

115. Driscoll DJ, Offord KP, Feldt RH, et al. Five to fifteen year follow-up after Fontan operation. Circulation 1992;85:469–496.

116. Fyfe DA, Kline CH, Sade RM, Gillette PC. Transesophageal echocardiography detects thrombus formation not identified by transthoracic echocardiography after the Fontan operation. J Am Coll Cardiol 1991;18(7):1733–1737.

117. Stumper O, Sutherland G, Geuskens R, et al. Transesophageal echocardiography in evaluation and management after a Fontan procedure. J Am Coll Cardiol 1991;17:1152–1160.

118. Chiu CH, Lin TY, Huang YC. Cranial nerve palsies and cerebral infarction in a young infant with meningococcal meningitis. Scand J Infect Dis 1995;27: 75–76.

119. Powell LFC, Hanigan WC, McCluney KW. Subcortical infarction in children. Stroke 1994;25:117–121.

120. Silverstein FS, Brunberg JA. Postvaricella basal ganglia infarction in children. Am J Neuroradiol 1995; 16:449–452.

121. Heyderman RS, Robb SA, Kendall BE. Does computed tomography have a role in the evaluation of complicated acute bacterial meningitis in childhood. Develop Med Child Neurol 1992;34:870–875.

122. Taft TA, Chusid MJ, Sty JR. Cerebral infarction in Hemophilus influenzae type B meningitis. Clin Pediatr 1986;25:177–180.

123. Bodensteiner JB, Hille MR, Riggs JE. Clinical features of vascular thrombosis following varicella. Am J Dis Child 1992;146:100–102.

124. Hart RG, Kanter MC. Hematological disorders and ischemic stroke. Stroke 1990;21:1111–1121.

125. Gobel U. Inherited or acquired disorders of blood coagulation in children with neurovascular complications. Neuropediatrics 1994;25:4–7.

126. Vomberg PP, Breederveld C, Fleury P, et al. Cerebral thromboembolism due to antithrombin III deficiency in two children. Neuropediatrics 1987;18:42–44.

127. Ganesan V, Kelsey H, Cookson J, et al. Activated protein C resistance in childhood stroke. Lancet 1996;96:260

128. Nowak Gottl U, Strater R, Dubbers A, et al. Ischaemic stroke in infancy and childhood: role of the Arg(506) to Gln mutation in the factor V gene. Blood Coagul Fibrinolysis, 1996.

129. Vielhaber H, Ehrenforth S, Koch HG, Scharrer I, et al. Cerebral venous sinus thrombosis in infancy and childhood: role of genetic and acquired risk factors of thrombophilia. Eur J Pediatr 1998;157:555–560.

130. Nowak-Gottl U, von Eckardstein A, Junder R, et al. Lipoprotein (a) and genetic polymorphisms of MTHFR TT677, factor V G1691A, and prothrombin G20210A are risk factors of spontaneous ischaemic stroke in childhood [abstract]. Thromb Haemost (Suppl).

131. Ebert W, Schneppenheim R. Perinatal stroke in 4 newborns with FV Leiden [abstract]. Thromb Haemostas 1997;(Suppl). PS–410.

132. Poort SR, Rosendaal FR, Reitsma PH, Bertina RM. A common genetic variation in the 3'-untranslated region of the prothrombin gene is associated with elevated plasma prothrombin levels and an increase in venous thrombosis. Blood 1996;88:3698–3703.

133. Earley CJ, Kittner SJ, Feeser BR, et al. Stroke in children and sickle cell disease: Baltimore-Washington cooperative young stroke study. Neurology 1998;51:169–176.

134. Powars DR, Conti PS, Wong WU, et al. Cerebral vasculopathy in sickle cell anemia: Diagnostic contribution of positron emission tomography. Blood 1999;93:71–79.

135. Kinney TR, Sleeper LA, Wang WC, et al. Silent cerebral infarcts in sickle cell anemia: a risk factor analysis. The cooperative study of sickle cell disease. Pediatrics 1999;103:640–645.

136. Reed W, Jagust W, Al-Mateen M, Vichinsky E. Role of positron emission tomography in determining the extent of CNS ischemia in patients with sickle cell disease. Am J Hematol 1993;60:268–272.

137. Liesner R, Mackie I, Cookson J, et al. Prothrombotic changes in children with sickle cell disease: relationships to cerebrovascular disease and transfusion. Br J Haemotol 1998;103:1037–1044.

138. Anson JA, Koshy M, Ferguson L, Crowell RM. Subarachoid hemorrhage in sickle cell disease. J Neurosurg 1991;75:552–558.

139. Carey J, Numaguchi Y, Nadell J. Subarachnoid hemorrhage in sickle cell disease. Childs Nerv Syst 1990;6:47–50.

140. Van Hoff J, Ritchey AK, Shaywitz BA. Intracranial hemorrhage in children with sickle cell disease. Am J Dis Child 1985;139:1120–1123.

141. Oyesiku NM, Barrow DL, Eckman JR, et al. Intracranial aneurysms in sickle cell anemia: clinical features and pathogenesis. J Neurosurg 1991;75:356–363.

142. Balkaran B, Char G, Morris J. Stroke in a cohort of patients with homozygous sickle cell disease. J Pediatr 1992;120:360–366.

143. Love LC, Mickle JP, Sypert GW. Ruptured intracranial aneurysms in cases of sickle cell anemia. Neurosurgery 1985;16:808–812.

144. Adams R, McKie V, Nichols F, et al. The use of transcranial ultrasonography to predict stroke in sickle cell disease. N Engl J Med 1992;326:605–610.

145. Pegelow C, Adams R, McKie V, et al. Risk of recurrent stroke in patients with sickle cell disease treated with erythrocyte transfusions. J Pediatr 1995;126:896–899.

146. Maier-Redelsperger M, Labie D, Elion J. Long term hydroxyurea treatment in young sickle cell patients. Curr Opin Hematol 1999;6:115–120.

147. Koren A, Segal-Kupershmit D, Zalman L, et al. Effect of hydroxyurea in sickle cell anemia: a clinical trial in children and teenagers with severe sickle cell anemia and sickle cell beta-thalassemia. Pediatr Hematol Oncol 1999;16:221–232.

148. Kinney TR, Helms RW, O'Branski EE, et al. Safety of hydroxyurea in children with sickle cell anemia: results of the HUG-KIDS study, a phase I/II trial. Pediatric hydroxyurea group. Blood 1999;94:1550–1554.

149. Wolters HJ, ten Cate JW, Lambertus LM, et al. Low intensity oral anticoagulation in sickle cell disease reverses the prethrombotic state: promises for treatment? Br J Haematol 1995;90:715–717.

150. Kestin AS, Valeri R, Khuri SF, et al. The platelet function defect of cardiopulmonary bypass. Blood 1993;82:107–111.

151. Hartfield DS, Lowry NJ, Keene DL, Yager JV. Iron deficiency: a cause of stroke in infants and children. Pediatr Neurol 1997;16:50–53.

152. Graham CJ, Schwartz JE, Stacy T. Stroke following oral trauma in children. Ann Emerg Med 1991;20:1029–1030.

153. Garg BP, Ottinger CJ, Smith RR, Fishman MA. Strokes in children due to vertebral artery trauma. Neurology 1993;43:2555–2558.

154. Randall JM, Griffiths PD, Gardner-Medwin D, Gholkar A. Thalamic infarction in childhood due to extracranial vertebral artery abnormalities. Neuropediatr 1994;25:262–264.

155. Khurana DS, Bonnerman CG, Dooling EC, et al. Verebral artery dissection: issues in diagnosis and management. Pediatr Neurol 1996;14:255–258.

156. Mitchell WG, Fischman LS, Miller JH. Stroke as late sequala of cranial irradiation for childhood brain tumors. J Child Neurol 1991;6:128–133.

157. Nishizawa S, Ryu H, Yokoyama T. Post irradiation vasculopathy of intracranial major arteries in children. Neurologia Medico-Chirurgica 1991;31:336–341.

158. Tech PC, Tan LK, Chia BL. Nonspecific aorto-arteritis in Singapore with special reference to hypertension. Am Hrt J 1978;95:683–695.

159. Kohrman MH, Huttenlocher PR. Takayasu's arteritis; a treatable cause of stroke in infancy. Pediatr Neurol 1986;2:154–158.

160. Lupi-Herrara E, Sanchez-Torres G, Marcushamer J. Takayasu's arteritis: clinical study of 107 cases. Am Hrt J 1977;93:94–103.

161. Hall S, Barr W, Lie JT. Takayasu arteritis: a study of 32 North American patients. Medicine 1985;64:6489–6499.

162. Korhman MH, Huttenlocher PR. Takayasu arteritis: a treatable cause of stroke in infancy. Pediatr Neurol 1986;2:154–158.

163. Graf WK, Milstein JM, Sherry DD. Stroke and mixed connective tissue disease. J Child Neurol 1993;8:256–259.

164. Devinsky O, Petito CK, Alonso DR. Clinical and neuropathological findings in systemic lupus erythematosus: the role of vasculitis, heart emboli, and thrombotic thrombocytopenic purpura. Ann Neurol 1988;23:380–384.

165. Blau EB, Morris RF, Unis EJ. Polyarteritis nodosa in older children. Pediatr 1977;60:227–234.

166. Lie JT, Gordon LP, Titus JL. Juvenile temporal arteritis: biopsy study of 4 cases. JAMA 1975;234:49.

167. Matsell DG, Keene DL, Jimenez C, Humphreys P. Isolated angitis of the central nervous system in childhood. Can J Neurol Sci 1990;17:151–154.

168. Calabrese L, Furlan A, Gragg L, Ropos TJ. Primary angiitis of the central nervous system: diagnostic criteria and clinical approach. Cleve Clin J Med 1992;59:293–306.

169. Cupps TR, Fauci A. The vasculitides. Philadelphia: WB Saunders; 1981, pp. 107–115.

170. Gupta SK, Khanna MN, Lahiri TK. Involvement of cardiac valves in Takayasu's arteritis. Report of 7 cases. Indian Heart J 1980;32:148–155.

171. Suzuki J, Kodama N. Moyamoya disease. A review. Stroke 1983;14:104–109.

172. Golden G. Cerebrovascular disease. In: Swaiman K, editor. Pediatric neurologic diseases. St. Louis: CV Mosby; 1989, pp. 603–617.

173. Maki Y, Nakada Y, Nose T. Clinical and radioisotope followup study of 'moyamoya'. Childs Brain 1976;2:257–265.

174. Yoshida S, Yamamoto T, Yoshioka M, Kuroki S. Ischemic strike in children. No Shinkei Geka-Neurological Surgery 1993;21:611–616.

175. Bonduel M, Sciuccati G, Feliu Torres A, et al. Prethrombotic disorders in children with Moyamoya syndrome. Thromb Haemostas 1999;Suppl:[abstract].

176. Muhonen LA, Lauer RM. Hyperlipidemia in childhood: the United States approach. Bailliere's Clin Pediatr 1996;4:17–42.

177. Rothrock JF. Migrainous stroke. Cephalalgia 1993;13:231.

178. Feucht M, Brantner S, Scheidinger H. Migraine and stroke in childhood and adolescence. Cephalagia 1995;15:26–30.

179. Mudd SH, Skovby F, Levy HL, et a. The natural history of homocysteinuria due to cystathionine b-synthase deficiency. Am J Hum Genet 1985; 37:1–31.

180. Wada Y, Narisawa K, Arakawa T. Infantile type of homocysteinuria with 5,10-methylenetetrahydrofolate reductase deficiency. Monogr Hum Genet 1978;9:140–146.

181. Jacques PF, Bostom AG, Williams RR, et al. Relation between folate status, a common mutation in methyulenetetrahydrofolate reductase, and plasma homocysteine concentrations. Circulation 1996;93:7–9.

182. Kluijtmans LA, van den Heuvel LP, Boers GH, et al. Moleclar genetic analysis in mild hyperhomocysteinemia: a common mutation in the methylenetetrahydrofolate reductase gene is a genetic risk factor for cardiovascular disease. Am J Hum Genet 1996;58:35–41.

183. Chauveau P, Chadefaux B, Coude M, et al. Increased plasma homocysteine concentration in patients with chronic renal failure. Miner Electrol Metab 1992;18:196–198.

184. Boers GHJ. Heterozygosity for homocystinuria in premature peripheral and cerebral occlusive arterial disease. N Engl J Med 1985;313:709–715.

185. Genest JJ. Plasma homosyteine levels in men with premature coronary artery disease. J Am Coll Cardiol 1990;16:1114–1119.

186. Clarke R. Hyperhomocysteinemia: an independent risk factor for vascular disease. N Engl J Med 1991;324:1149–1155.

187. Selhub J. Homocysteine metabolism. Annu Rev Nutr 1999;19:217–246.

188. Finkelstein JD. The metabolism of homocysteine: pathways and regulation. Eur J Pediatr 1998;157:S40–S44.

189. Boushey CJ, Beresford SAA, Omenn GS, Motulsky AG. A quantitive assessment of plasma homocysteine as a

risk factor for vascular disease: probable benefits of increasing folic acid intakes. JAMA 1995; 274:1049–1057.

190. Groenendaal F, van der Ground J, Witkamp TD, de Vries LS. Proton magnetic resonance spectroscopic imaging in neonatal stroke. Neuropediatrics 1995;26:243–248.

191. Koelfen W, Wentz U, Freund M, Schulze C. Magnetic resonance angiography in 140 neuropediatrics patients. Pediatr Neurol 1995;12:31–38.

192. Vogl TJ, Balzer JO, Stemler J, et al. MR angiography in children with cerebral neurovascular diseases: findings in 31 cases. Am J Roentgen 1992;159:817–823.

193. Allison JW, Glasier CM, Stark JE, et al. Head and neck MR angiography in pediatric patients. Radiographics 1994;14:795–805.

194. Overgaard K, Sereghy T, Boysen G. Reduction of infarct volume and mortality by thrombolysis in a rat embolic stroke model. Stroke 1992;76:752–758.

195. Zivin JA, Lyden PD, DeGirolami U. Tissue plasminogen activator: reduction of neurologic damage after experimental embolic stroke. Arch Neurol 1988;45:387–391.

196. Kissel P, Chehrazi B, Seibert JA. Digital angiographic quantification of blood flow dynamics in embolic stroke treated with tissue type plasminogen activator. J Neurosurg 1987;76:399–405.

197. Wardlaw JM, Warlow CP. Thrombolysis in acute ischemic stroke: does it work? Stroke 1992;23:1826–1839.

198. del Zoppo GJ, Ferbert A, Otis S, et al. Local intra-arterial fibrinolytic therapy in acute carotid territory stroke: a pilot study. Stroke 1988;19:307–313.

199. Mori E, Tabuchi M, Yoshida T, Yamadori A. Intracarotid urokinase with thromboembolic occlusion of the middle cerebral artery. Stroke 1988;19:802–812.

200. Matsumoto K, Satoh K. Topical intraartertial urokinase infusion for acute stroke. In: Hacke W, et al, editors. Thrombolytic therapy in acute ischemic stroke, Heidelberg: Springer-Verlag; 1991, pp. 207–212.

201. Zeumer H, Freitag HJ, Zanella F, et al. Local intraarterial fibrinolytic therapy in patients with stroke: urokinase vs recombinant tissue plasminogen activator (rt-PA). Neuroradiology 1993;35:159–162.

202. del Zoppo GJ, Higashida RT, Furlan AJ, et al. PROACT: a phase II randomized trial of recombinant pro-urokinase by direct arterial delivery in acute middle cerebral artery stroke. Stroke 1998;29:4–11.

203. Hommel M, Boissel JP, Cornu C, et al. Termination of trial of streptokinase in severe acute ischemic stroke. Lancet 1995;345:578–579.

204. Donnan GA, Davis SM, Chambers BR, et al. Streptokinase for acute ischemic stroke with relationship to time of administration. JAMA 1996;276:961–966.

205. Multicentre Acute Stroke Trial-Italy (MAST-I) Group. Randomized controlled trial of stroptokinase, aspirin, and combinations of both in treatment of acute ischaemic stroke. Lancet 1995;346:1509–1514.

206. Hacke W, Kaste M, Fieschi C, ECASS Study Group. Intravenous thrombolysis with recombinant tissue plasminogen activator for acute hemispheric stroke. The European Cooperative Acute Stroke Study (ECASS). JAMA 1995;274:1017–1025.

207. The National Institute of Neurological Disorders an Stroke rt-PA Stroke Study Group. Tissue plasminogen activator for acute ischemic stroke. N Engl J Med 1995;333:1581–1587.

208. Hacke W, Kaste M, Fieschi C, et al. Randomized double-blind placebo-controlled trial of thrombolytic therapy with intravenous alteplase in acute ischaemic stroke (ECAASS II). Lancet 1998;352:1245–1251.

209. ATLANTIS: Aiteplase Thrombolysis for Acute Noninterventional Therapy in Ischemic Stroke. Major ongoing stroke trials. Stroke 1998;29:550–551.

210. del Zoppo GJ, Poeck P, Pessin MS. Recombinant tissue plasminogen activator in acute thrombotic and embolic stroke. Ann Neurol 1992;32:78–86.

211. NINDS t-PA Stroke Study Group. Generalized efficacy of t-PA for acute stroke: Subgroup analysis of the NINDS t-PA Stroke Study Group. Stroke 1997;28:2119–2125.

212. The NINDS t-PA Stroke Study Group. Intracerebral hemorrhage after intravenous t-PA therapy for ischemic stroke. Stroke 1997;28:2109–2118.

213. Duke RJ, Bloch RF, Alexander GG. Intravenous heparin for the prevention of stroke progression in acute partial stable stroke: a randomized controlled trial. Ann Intern Med 1986;105:825–828.

214. International Stroke Trial Group. The International Stroke Trial (IST): a randomised trial of aspirin, subcutaneous heparin, both, or neither among 19,435 patients with acute ischemic stroke. Lancet 1997;349:1569–1581.

215. Rothrock JF, Dittrich HC, McAllen S. Acute anticoagulation following cardioembolic stroke. Stroke 1989;20:730–734.

216. The Publications' Committee for the Trial of Org 10172 in Acute Stroke Treatment (TOAST) Investigators. Low molecular weight heparinoid, Org 10172 (danaparoid), and outcome after acute ischemic stroke: a randomized controlled trial. JAMA 1988;279:1265–1272.

217. Adams HP, Davis PH, Leira EC, et al. Baseline NIH Stroke Scale score strongly predicts outcome after stroke: a report of the Trial of Org 10172 in Acute Stroke Treatment (TOAST). Neurology 1999;53:126–131.

218. Adams HP, Bendixen BH, Leira E, et al. Antithrombotic treatment of ischemic stroke among patients with occlusion or severe stenosis of the internal carotid artery: a report of the Trial of Org 10172 in Acute Stroke Treatment (TOAST). Neurology 1999;53: 122–125.

219. Bruno A, Biller J, Adams HP, et al. Acute blood glucose level and outcome from ischemic stroke. Trial of ORG 10172 in Acute Stroke Treatment (TOAST) Investigators. Neurology 1999;52:280–284.

220. Sandercock PS, van den Belt AG, Lindley RI. Antithrombotic therapy in acute ischaemic stroke: an overview of the completed randomized trials. J Neurol Neurosurg Psychiatry 1993;56:17–25.

221. Sherman DG, Dyken ML, Gent M, et al. Antithrombotic therapy for cerebrovascular disorders. Chest 1995;108:444S–456S.

222. Kay R, Sing Wong K, Ling Yu Y, et al. Low-molecular weight heparin for the treatment of acute ischemic stroke. N Engl J Med 1995;333:1588–93.

223. Antiplatelet Trialists Collaboration. Collaborative overview of randomized trials of antiplatelet therapy: 1. Prevention of death, myocardial infarction, and stroke by prolonged antiplatelet therapy in various categories of patients. Br Med J 1994;308:81–106.

224. Sandercock PA, van den Belt AGM, Lindley RI, Slattery J. Antithrombotic therapy in acute ischemic stroke: an overview of the completed randomized trials. J Neurol Neurosurg Psych 1998;56:17–25.

225. Adams HP, Brott TG, Crowell RM. Guidelines for the management of patients with acute ischemic stroke: a statement for healthcare professionals from a special writing group of the Stroke Council, American Heart Association. Stroke 1994;25:1901–1914.

226. Chinese Acute Stroke Trial (CAST) Collaborative Group. A randomized placebo-controlled trial of early aspirin use in 20,000 patients with acute ischemic stroke. Stroke 1997;349:1641–1649.

227. Andrew M, deVeber G. Pediatric thromboembolism and stroke protocols. Hamilton: BC Decker; 1999.

228. Michelson AD, Bovill E, Monagle P, Andrew M. Antithrombotic therapy in children. Chest 1998; 114:748S–769S.

229. deVeber G, Andrew M, Adams M, et al. Treatment of pediatric sinovenous thrombosis with low molecular weight heparin [abstract]. Ann Neurol 1995;38:S32.

230. CAPRIE Steering Committee. A randomised, blinded, trial of clopidogril versus aspirin in patients at risk of ischaemic events (CAPRIE). Lancet 1996;348: 1329–1339.

231. Bousser MG. Aspirin or heparin immediately after a stroke? Lancet 1997;349:1564–1565.

232. Isler W. Stroke in childhood and adolescence. Eur Neurol 1984;23:421–424.

233. deVeber G, Curtis R, MacGregor D, et al. Neurodevelopmental outcome following pediatric arterial ischemic stroke and sinovenous thrombosis [abstract]. Ann Neurol 1997;42:519.

234. Satoh S, Shibuya H, Matsushima Y, Suzuki S. Analysis of the angiographic findings in cases of childhood moyamoya disease. Neuroradiol 1988;30:111–119.

235. Eeg-Olofsson O, Ringheim Y. Stroke in children: Clinical characteristics and prognosis. Acta Paediatr Scand 1983;72:391–395.

236. Satoh S, Reizo S, Yoshimoto T. Clinical survey of ischemic cerebrovascular disease in children in a district of Japan. Stroke 1991;33:586–589.

237. Higgins JJ, Kammerman LA, Fitz CR. Predictors of survival and characteristics of childhood stroke. Neuropediatr 1991;22:190–193.

238. Aicardi J, Amsili J, Chevrie J. Acute hemiplegia in infancy and childhood. Develop Med Child Neurol 1969;11:163–173.

239. Volpe J, Joseph J. Neurology of the newborn. Philadelphia: WB Saunders; 1995.

240. Trauner DA, Chase C, Walker P, Wulfeck B. Neurologic profiles of infants and children arter perinatal stroke. Pediatr Neurol 1993;9:383–386.

241. Wulfeck BB, Trauner DA, Tallal PA. Neurologic, cognitive, and linguistic features of infants after early stroke. Pediatr Neurol 1991;7:266

242. Koelfen W, Freund M, Varnholt V. Neonatal stroke involving the middle cerebral artery in term infants: clinical presentation and outcome. Develop Med Child Neurol 1995;37:204–212.

243. Yager JY, Thornhill JA. The effect of age on susceptibility to hypoxic ischemic brain damage. Neurosci Biobehav Rev 1997;21:167–174.

8 THROMBOEMBOLIC COMPLICATIONS IN SPECIFIC ORGAN SITES AND PEDIATRIC DISEASES

As described in previous chapters, venous thromboembolic events (VTE) are occurring with increasing frequency in children. In addition to VTE located in the venous system draining the upper and lower limbs as well as the central nervous system (CNS), thromboembolic events (TEs) also occur in vessels associated with specific organs. There also are clearly defined disease processes that are associated with an increased risk of TEs, often located in specific "target" organs. The effects of these TEs on specific organ function and the implications of individual disease processes for therapy and outcome justify discussion of these specific problematic TEs in their own right.

The following chapter discusses VTE at specific sites such as renal veins, right atrium/intracardiac and mesenteric vein, and in specific disorders such as renal and hepatic disease, systemic lupus erythematosis (SLE), acute lymphoblastic leukemia (ALL), sickle cell disease (SCD), and paroxysmal nocturnal hemoglobinuria (PNH).

Renal Disorders

Renal Vein Thrombosis

General information Renal vein thrombosis (RVT) is the most common noncatheter-related VTE during infancy and is responsible for approximately 10% of all VTE in newborns.[1] A review of the literature between 1966 and 1998 identified pediatric patients with RVT in 99 publications.[2–98]

Over 80% of publications were case reports of less than five patients and 17% were case series.

Venous drainage of the kidney Venous drainage of the cortex begins in small subcapsular veins that converge as interlobular veins draining toward the medulla into arcuate and interlobar veins. Venous drainage of the medulla begins in venulae rectae that flow into arcuate and interlobular veins.[99] Subsequently, larger intrarenal veins combine to form the main renal vein. On the left side, ureteric, gonadal, adrenal, and inferior phrenic veins join the left main renal vein at the hilus.[100] On the right side, only the ureteric vein joins the right renal vein while others drain directly into the inferior vena cava.[101]

Pathophysiologic conditions The pathophysiologic response of the kidney to VTE is dependent on the acuteness of the occlusion, the extent of the thrombus, and the development of collateral circulation. In animal models of acute complete occlusion, renal venous pressures increase and arterial blood flow diminishes or arrests, leading to destruction of the kidney or fatal retroperitoneal hemorrhage.[102] In acute partial occlusion, the renal outcome is dependent on the formation of venous collaterals.[103,104] In both acute complete and partial occlusion, the kidney initially increases in size and either returns to near prethrombotic dimensions or becomes atrophic, depending on the primary course. In contrast to acute occlusion, gradual occlusion results in extensive collateral circulation with nearly normal renal function.[105]

Age and sex distribution RVT is a disease primarily of newborns and young infants. Of the 275 evaluable cases, 79% were found to present within the first month and usually within the first week of life.[7–14,17,18,29,41,42,49,53,54,58,60,68,71,73–77,79,84,92] Some infants developed RVT in utero (Figure 8–1).[19,28,38,89] The incidence in males and females was similar, and the left and right side were affected equally. Bilateral RVT occurred in 24% of pediatric patients.[17,19,27,29,77]

Clinical presentation Presenting symptoms and clinical findings differ between neonates and older patients and are influenced by the extent and rapidity of thrombus formation. Figure 8–2 shows the common clinical presentations of RVT. Hematuria, which occurs in over 30% of patients, is macroscopic in the majority of patients. Neonates usually present with a flank mass, hematuria, proteinuria, thrombocytopenia, and nonfunction of the involved kidney. Infants less than 1 year old commonly present with diarrhea, vomiting, dehydration, and hypovolemia. The second most common association with RVT is the nephrotic syndrome.[6,46,55,79,81,88,90] Clinical findings suggestive of acute inferior vena cava thrombosis associated with RVT include cold, cyanotic, and edematous lower extremities. Chronic obstruction is characterized by dilation of collateral veins over the abdomen and upper thighs as well as bilateral postphlebitic syndrome.

Etiology of renal vein thrombosis The etiologies of RVT are diverse and reflect the prevalence of pathologic conditions in infancy. Common primary problems in neonates include perinatal asphyxia, shock, polycythemia, cyanotic congenital heart disease (CHD), diabetic mothers, dehydration, and septicemia.[21,51,65,76,78,85] These disorders result in reduced renal blood flow, increased blood viscosity, hyperosmolality, or hypercoagulability.[71] Infants of diabetic mothers are at risk because of polycythemia or increased platelet aggregability due to intrauterine hyperglycemia and relatively low extracellular fluid volume. In older children, RVT is most commonly secondary to nephrotic syndrome, burns, dehydration and fever, AT deficiency, and SLE.[6,29,46,55–58,61,67,80–82,88,90,106,107] RVT secondary to less common conditions such as hyperleukocytosis and Netherton syndrome have also been described.[4,17]

Coagulation abnormalities The most common coagulation abnormality associated with RVT is thrombocytopenia, which is usually mild with average values of 100,000 x 10^9/L.[40,71,94] Coagulation screening tests such as the prothrombin time (PT)

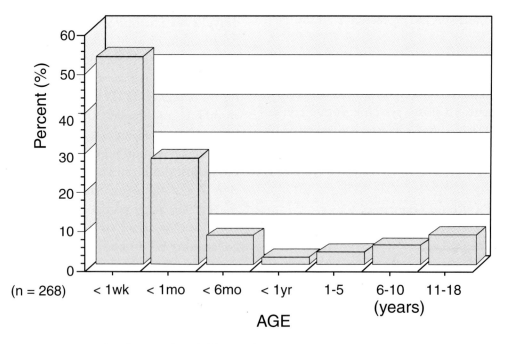

Figure 8–1 Age distribution of 28 children with renal vein thrombosis.

Reproduced with permission.[548]

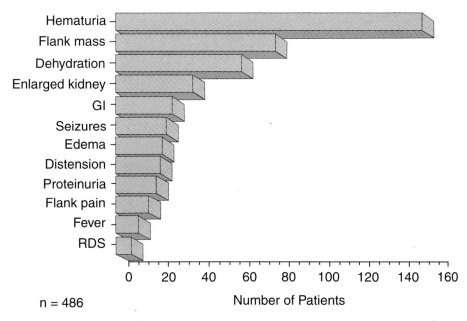

Figure 8–2 Common clinical presentations of renal vein thrombosis. GI = gastrointestinal; RDS = respiratory distress syndrome.

Reproduced with permission.[548]

and activated partial thromboplastin time (APTT) may be prolonged, and fibrin/fibrinogen degradation products (FDPs) increased. Treatment of the hemostatic abnormalities depends on the severity and associated hemostatic risk. More recently, patients have been evaluated for acquired and congenital prothrombotic disorders. Factor (F) V Leiden has been reported in a number of cases; however, the role of this abnormality in the pathogenesis of RVT remains unclear.[3,15,18] In general, children with RVT should be evaluated for an inherited predisposing etiology, since family studies, counselling, and long-term management are necessary.

Diagnosis The diagnosis of RVT has changed from an autopsy finding to an antemortem diagnosis that requires confirmation with an objective test. Prior to the mid-1980s, intravenous pylograms and contrast angiography were the most commonly used tests.[59,61] Ultrasound is currently the radiographic test of choice, because of the ease of testing in infants, its sensitivity to an enlarged kidney, and the lack of side effects.[16,26,30,32,33,38,49,57,60,62,83,89,97] The appearance on ultrasound depends on the stage at which the scan is performed and the extent of the thrombus. Initially, the interlobular and interlobar thrombus appear as highly echogenic streaks. The

echogenic streaks commence in a peripheral, focal segment of the involved kidney and persist only for a few days. In the first week, the affected kidney swells and becomes echogenic, with prominent echo-poor medullary pyramids. Subsequently, the swelling decreases and the kidney becomes heterogenous, with loss of corticomedullary differentiation. TEs are usually easily identified within the renal vein and possibly the inferior vena cava (IVC). Ultrasound may also show adrenal hemorrhage, a recognized association. In the early stages of RVT, color Doppler may demonstrate absent intrarenal and renal venous flow. Ultimately, depending on the degree of recovery, ultrasound may demonstrate focal scarring or atrophy.[2] Magnetic resonance imaging (MRI) and computed tomography (CT) have also been used.[30,60,87]

Treatment Therapeutic choices reflect both advances in tertiary care pediatrics and improved clinical status at the time of diagnosis. In the past, nephrectomy and thrombectomy were common treatment choices.[25,68,78,91,93] In the 1990s, supportive care and unfractionated heparin (UFH) are the most common treatment choices. There is agreement that supportive care that includes dialysis and effective treatment of the predisposing cause of RVT are important. Use of anticoagulants and of thrombolytic agents is highly controversial, a reflection of the absence of controlled clinical trials assessing the risk to benefit ratio of these interventions.[43] One approach is to use supportive care for unilateral RVT in the absence of uremia and no extension into the IVC.[31,47,92] UFH should be considered for unilateral RVT that does extend into the IVC and for bilateral RVT, because of the risk of pulmonary embolism (PE) and complete renal failure. Thrombolytic therapy should be considered in the presence of bilateral RVT and impending renal failure.[24,28,64] Major bleeding complications due to thrombolytic therapy may occur but in a minority of patients.

Outcome The outcome of RVT has changed from a frequently lethal complication to one in which over 85% of children survive. Unfortunately, there are no recent studies assessing long-term morbidity such as hypertension and renal atrophy. Most deaths are due to the associated disease, renal failure, and PE.

Thrombotic Complications of Access Sites for Dialysis

General information In adults, TEs of venous access for hemodialysis are the most common cause for loss of venous access. Ongoing clinical trials are assessing the usefulness of prophylactic systemic anticoagulation in prolonging vascular access in adults requiring hemodialysis. In young children, peritoneal dialysis is usually the preferred method for dialysis.[108,109] For older children, predominantly over 6 years old, hemodialysis is used, achieved through a fistula, vascular lines, or continuous arteriovenous hemofiltration (CAVH).[110–114] As for adults, local TEs are the main reason for loss of vascular access and for revision of "internal" venous access. "External" percutaneous venous access is lost due to TEs in approximately 30% of children.[108] In a consecutive series of 24 children who had failed peritoneal dialysis, the mean duration of functional dialysis available through any vascular access procedure was 7.3 months, with local TEs being the most common cause of loss of vascular access.[111] A retrospective cohort study suggested that the use of microsurgical techniques to construct atrioventricular (AV) fistulas in children may reduce the rate of TEs.[115]

A Medline search for articles concerning VTE related to dialysis in children did not reveal if UFH was used or what the dosing protocol and monitoring system was.[114] Van Biljon compared UFH (175 IU/kg) to LMWH (single bolus injection of 1 mg/kg (100 anti-FXa U/kg) in five children aged 4 to 16 years undergoing hemodialysis.[116] Clotting in the circuit occurred more often in the LMWH-treated patients. In a study of 24 pediatric patients on chronic hemodialysis, a bolus dose of 24 U/kg LMWH (Fragmin) followed by 15 U/kg Fragmin was found to be as effective as UFH in preventing clotting in the circuit.[117] Geary found that heparin-free dialysis in children resulted in an incidence of TEs of 25%. Keeping the ACT at less than 170 seconds prevented TEs in 90% of cases.[118] Zobel used a bolus of 50 IU/kg UFH and a continuous infusion of 10 IU/kg with no bleeding side effect.[110] Kjellstrand dialyzed 281 pediatric patients using low-dose UFH (clotting times less than 25% pre-dialysis determination) and had an incidence of TE of 2%.[113]

Thrombolytic therapy was used for a few patients with low-dose streptokinase (SK) with variable success.[119–121] In general, one would not advocate the use of SK, since these children may require further thrombolytic therapy and thus may develop antibodies to SK. Urokinase (UK) and tissue plasminogen activator (TPA) offer alternative forms of thrombolytic therapy.

Renal Transplantation

General information Although renal transplantation is the treatment of choice for children with end-stage renal disease,[122] it also induces important secondary causes of morbidity. Alterations in hemostasis contribute to the two most common causes of graft failures, irreversible vascular rejection and TEs of the graft artery or vein.

Thrombotic occlusion of transplanted vessels TEs in transplanted vessels are an important complication, particularly in small children.[123] Table 8–1 summarizes the information on TEs from six large case series or registries.[124–129] TEs can either be arterial or venous, with both immediate and delayed postoperative presentations.[122,124,130] Renal artery thrombosis (RAT) occurred in approximately 20% of patients, who usually presented with primary anuria or clinical symptoms of rejection. In a few cases, proteinuria and fever were also present. Similarly, RVT occurred in 2.6% to 5.2% of children

Table 8–1 Incidence of Thromboembolic Events in Children Undergoing Renal Transplantation

Author	Number of Transplants	Number of Thromboembolic Events	Incidence (%)
Sheldon et al[124]	303	15	5.2
Harmon et al[125]	1045	27	2.6
Valdez et al[126]	149	4	3.3
Broyer et al[127]	801	40	5.1
Kalicinski et al[128]	120	5	4.2
Broyer et al[129]	879	20	2.6
Total	3297	111	3.8

Reproduced with permission.[548]

who presented with anuria, reduced hemoglobin, and thrombocytopenia.[124,126–129,131]

The most complete data on TEs related to renal transplantation come from the updated North American Pediatric Renal Transplant Cooperative Study, published in 1997.[132] This study reviewed 4394 transplants (2060 living donor [LD] transplants and 2334 cadaver donor [CAD] transplants). Vascular TE rates for LD and CAD transplants were 38 of 2060 (1.8%) and 100 of 2334 (4.2%), respectively ($p < .001$). Vascular TEs accounted for 12.2% of failed index transplants and 19.2% of failed repeat transplants. The rate of graft loss due to TEs was significantly increased in children less than 2 years old compared to that of older children (2–5 years, 6–12 years, and >12 years) (9.0% vs 5.5%, 4.4%, and 3.5% for CAD transplant recipients, and 3.5% vs 3.4%, 0.7%, and 1.9% for LD graft recipients). The following factors were associated with an increased TE rate: cadaver donors less than 5 years of age; kidneys with cold ischemia time greater than 24 hours; a history of prior transplantation; and occurrence of acute tubular necrosis in recipients. Use of antilymphocyte antibody or cyclosporine on day 0 or 1 decreased the risk of local TEs.

Etiology The etiology of TEs in renal allografts has been attributed to surgical technique, perfusion or preimplantation damage, immune mechanisms, hypotension, hypoperfusion, pediatric donors, very young recipients, prior nephrectomy, rejection, and early use of cyclosporine.[130] For most patients, the causes of TEs are multifactoral. The correlation between young donor age and TEs likely reflects the ab-

solute size of the transplanted vessels and vascular anastamotic techniques required for smaller kidneys.[124,130] Conversely, Doppler ultrasound studies have demonstrated that transplantation of adult kidneys into children is associated with increased aortic blood flow in the recipient, presumably driven by the relatively reduced renal artery blood flow in the donor kidney compared to the pretransplant status. Any factors that reduce cardiac output, such as dehydration, may reduce renal arterial flow below a threshold at which RAT becomes more likely.[133] The impact of surgical technique alone is very difficult to assess. Cold storage times over 24 hours are generally correlated with delayed graft function and acute tubular necrosis, which are important risk factors.[122,130] Underlying renal disease is also important, and patients with congenital nephrotic syndrome, oxalosis, or antiphospholipid antibodies are more frequently affected than other primary diagnosis.[130,134]

Diagnosis Color Doppler ultrasound is the most useful noninvasive test for diagnosis of either RAT or RVT following transplantation. Concordance between ultrasound and angiography appears to be excellent (100% in 87 patients in one study).[135]

Prophylaxis There are no controlled trials assessing potential benefits of prophylactic anticoagulation therapy in children undergoing renal transplantation.[122,125–127,130,132,136–140] Only one study using anticoagulation therapy was identified.[136] The LMWH enoxaparin was administered at an initial dosage of 0.4 mg/kg of body weight, twice a day, over 21 days. The first dose was usually administered between 15 and 24 hours following surgery. Dosage was adjusted according to anti-FXa plasma concentrations, with target trough levels of 0.2 units/mL and peak levels of 0.4 units/mL. With this approach, the incidence of early renal failure secondary to local vascular TEs decreased from 13% in 1988 to 1.5% in 1989.[127] However, bleeding complications also increased to 24% from 4%. UFH has been recommended as prophylactic anticoagulant therapy at a dosage of 10 units/kg/hour, commencing immediately post-transplantation. However, there are no controlled data to support or reject this recommendation. Prophylactic prostacyclin (PGI₂) also has been reported.[140] Randomized controlled trials (RCTs) are required to determine the efficacy and safety of prophylactic anticoagulant therapy.

Treatment When TEs occur, treatment options include thrombolytic therapy, anticoagulation, and surgical embolectomy.[130] Graft TEs are generally irreversible. There is agreement that identification and elimination of factors predisposing to local TEs is preferable to current treatment options.

Nephrotic Syndrome

General information Nephrotic syndrome is characterized by edema, proteinuria (> 0.1 g/kg/day), and hypoalbuminemia (< 2.5 g/dL). In pediatric patients, nephrotic syndrome can be classified as congenital, steroid responsive minimal change, or secondary to other renal disorders.

Thromboembolic complications A Medline search identified 90 references describing pediatric patients with nephrotic syndrome and TEs, bleeding episodes, or abnormal coagulation parameters.[6,46,55,57,58,67,79,81,88,90,106,141–206] Etiologies of the nephrotic syndrome include minimal change (63%), congenital (18%), focal glomerulonephritis (9%), and other categories (10%).[79,157,166–168,170,171,180,182,207–210] These 90 publications described 4224 children with nephrotic syndrome; of these, 148 (3.5%) had a TE. In four large series, the incidences of TEs were 4.4%, 9.8%, 18.9%, and 27.9%, respectively.[144,145,181,182] The wide range in incidences of TEs likely reflected differences between clinical diagnoses and the systematic use of objective tests. For example, ventilation/perfusion (VQ) scans performed electively in children with steroid responsive minimal change nephrotic syndrome showed the presence of PE in

seven patients (27.9%), residual changes in 10 (38.5%), and normal findings in nine (34.9%).[181] As for most disorders, the incidence of TEs in children with nephrotic syndrome is less than that reported for adults (19% vs 50%).[211,212] Increased hypercoagulability is correlated to the degree of proteinuria and hypoalbuminema.[181,213]

Age distribution Age at the time of a TE could be determined in 57 reports.[6,46,55,57,67,79,81,88,90,141–159,161, 163,167–169,172,173,175,178,180,181,183,185,189–193,196–202,205,214,215] There was a significant relationship between age, duration of nephrotic syndrome, and presentation with a TE (Figure 8–3). Sixty-one percent of TEs occurred within 3 months of diagnosis of nephrotic syndrome, and all TEs in infants less than 1 year of age occurred within 1 month of diagnosis.

Location and diagnosis The location of TEs was reported in 85 of 148 (57%) children identified in the literature. RVT was the most common TE (30%) followed by PE (21%). Other TEs occurred in the arterial (27%) and deep venous systems (21%) including sinovenous TEs.[161,162] Prior to 1980, one-third of children were diagnosed clinically with a further third diagnosed at autopsy. More recently, objective radiologic diagnosis is more common, with ultrasound being the most frequently used test.

Renal vein thrombosis The relationship between nephrotic syndrome and RVT has been controversial.[6,142,145,216–220] In adults, the incidence of RVT in nephrotic syndrome (secondary to many causes)

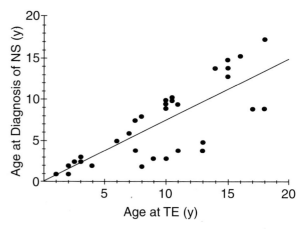

Figure 8–3 Significant relationship between age, duration of nephrotic syndrome, and presentation with a TE.

Reproduced with permission.[548]

ranges from 38% to 50%.[6,142,180,216–219,221] In situations where all patients are assessed with an objective test, the incidence is approximately 30%,[142,180,216,217,221] which is increased compared to assessment by clinical presentation alone.

Hemostatic abnormalities Thirty-three publications evaluating hemostasis in children with nephrotic syndrome reported abnormalities in plasma concentrations of almost every component of hemostasis.[88,150,152,155,160,164,165,167,173,175,177,181,183,185,] [187,188,190–195,198–200,202,203,211,212,222–224] Figure 8–4 shows the mean plasma concentrations of hemostatic parameters in children with active nephrotic syndrome. Fibrinogen, FII, FV, FVII, FVIII, FX, and FXIII are increased, with the greatest increase being for the two acute phase reactants, fibrinogen and FVIII. In contrast, plasma concentrations of FXII and antithrombin (AT) are decreased to 50% of normal values. Urinary loss of AT, protein C, and protein S is increased.[164] Components of the fibrinolytic system, TPA, urokinase plasminogen activator (UPA), and plasminogen activator inhibitor (PAI-1) are increased,[175,225] while other coagulation proteins are in the normal range (Figure 8–4). In general, platelet function studies show increased aggregability, which has been linked to arterial TEs.[211,226,227] Thrombocytosis has been reported to occur proportionally to the degree of proteinuria.[160] The significant decrease in plasma concentrations of AT has been identified as the most likely hemostatic abnormality causal to TEs in children with nephrotic syndrome.[177,181,190,195,200,203]

Treatment and outcome Modalities used to treat TEs in children with nephrotic syndrome include supportive care, dialysis, anticoagulants, and thrombolytic agents. For 63% of children, information on anticoagulant and thrombolytic therapy was not reported in the literature (Figure 8–5). For the remaining children, supportive therapy alone was the treatment of choice in 20% of children. Outcomes related to TEs were difficult to determine, again due to limited reporting (25%). Approximately one-third of children died as a direct result of progressive TEs and a minority required amputation related to an arterial TE. Children requiring amputation had not received either anticoagulants or thrombolytic therapy. The importance of anticoagulation therapy was further emphasized, based upon case reports, by the incidence of recurrent TEs when UFH or oral anticoagulants (OAs) were discontinued. Until information is available from well-designed clinical trials, children with nephrotic syndrome and TEs should be treated with anticoagulation therapy following guidelines in Chapters 9 and 10.

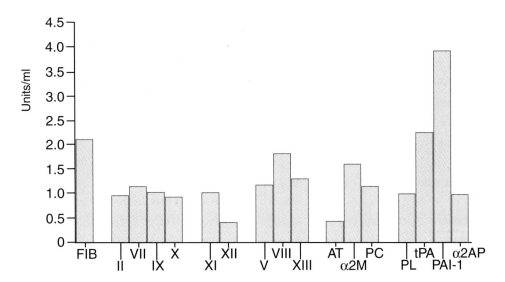

Figure 8–4 Mean plasma concentrations of hemostatic parameters in children with nephrotic syndrome. FIB = fibrinogen; AT = antithrombin; α_2M = α_2-macroglobulin; PC = protein C; PL = plasminogen; tPA = tissue plasminogen activator; PAI-1 = plasminogen activator inhibitor; α_2AP = α_2-antiplasmin.

Reproduced with permission.[548]

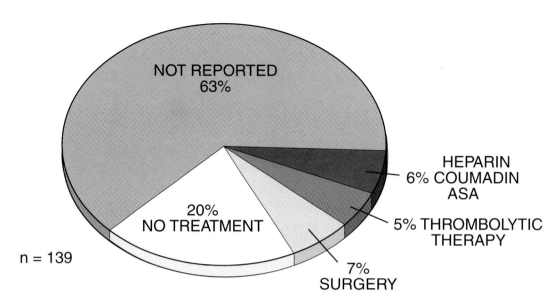

Figure 8–5 Treatment modalities for nephrotic syndrome for 63% of children. ASA = acetylsalicyclic acid (aspirin).

Reproduced with permission.[548]

Recommendations At this time, the benefit of prophylactic anticoagulation therapy in all or subpopulations of children with nephrotic syndrome is unclear. However, children with relapsed, refractory, or untreated nephrotic syndrome are at the greatest risk of TEs. Children with steroid responsive minimal change nephrotic syndrome are at relatively low risk of TEs, whereas children with nephrotic syndrome due to other causes are at increased risk. In the absence of other information, prophylactic anticoagulation therapy should be considered in children with uncontrolled nonminimal change nephrotic syndrome. Clearly, clinical trials addressing these issues are required before strong recommendations can be made.

Hepatic Thromboembolic Complications

General Information Although there are many causes of TEs related to liver disease, the majority of liver-related TEs occur secondary to liver transplantation in the postoperative period.[228,229] Most frequently, TEs are limited to the transplanted vessels and include portal vein thrombosis (PVT) and hepatic artery thrombosis (HAT). Figure 8–6 shows the hepatic to splenic and portal circulation.

Portal Vein Thrombosis

General information In newborns, portal vein thrombosis (PVT) most commonly occurs secondary to umbilical vein catheterization (UVC), with or without infection (Chapter 4).[230–232] The causes of PVTs in older children include liver transplantation, intra-abdominal sepsis, splenectomy, sickle cell anemia, and the presence of antiphospholipid antibodies (APLA).[233–240] In approximately 50% of children, an underlying etiology is not identified.[234,241,242] In contrast to adults, in whom PVT is most frequently secondary to cirrhosis, liver function is usually normal in children.[238]

Liver transplantation Following liver transplantation, PVT occurs most frequently in small children and less commonly in older children or adults. A recent composite analysis of pediatric liver transplantation reported an incidence of PVT in 2.2% of children for whom aspirin or dipyridamole was used prophylactically, and 7.8% in children for whom no prophylaxis was used;[243] A retrospective cohort study of 115 children, for whom no antiplatelet therapy was used, PVT or stenosis occurred in 15% of the children.[243] The small caliber of vessels and deficiencies of some key inhibitors of coagulation likely contribute to the occurrence of TEs in

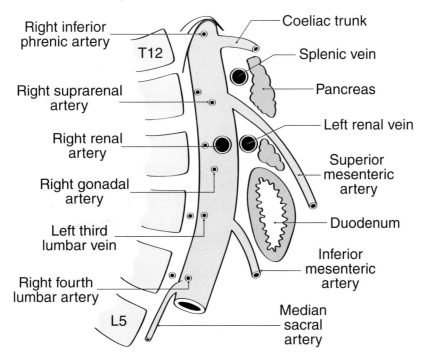

Figure 8–6 The hepatic to splenic and portal circulation.

small children.[244] The incidence of post liver transplant PVT may also be related to the type of surgical anastomosis performed.[245]

Clinical presentation The clinical presentation of PVT reflects the acuteness of the event, as well as the degree of obstruction.[246] PVT may present acutely as an acute abdomen, especially in adolescents.[236] More commonly, PVT presents with symptoms reflecting a chronic obstruction including gastrointestinal bleeding and asymptomatic splenomegaly.[238,241] If gastrointestinal bleeding occurs, it is usually recurrent.[247]

Diagnosis Radiographic tests to detect PVT include ultrasound, magnetic resonance imaging (MRI), angiography (MRA), and computed tomography (CT) scans.[248–251] Many liver transplant centers screen children for PVT in the postoperative period with ultrasound. However, the sensitivity and specificity of ultrasound remains to be proven.[252–254] Within 6 to 20 days following PVT, a sponge-like mass of collateral vessels forms. This cavernous transformation can extend, resulting in intrahepatic shunting between segmental portal veins and into the systemic circulation, resulting in portal hypertension.[255] Variceal hemorrhagic complications are an important clinical consequence of portal hyper-

tension secondary to PVT. Less commonly, portal hypertension may be associated with fatal pulmonary hypertension.[256]

Therapy Therapeutic options are, to some extent, determined by whether PVT is acute or chronic and include supportive care alone, thrombolytic therapy, anticoagulant therapy, balloon thrombectomy or dilatation, surgical thrombectomy, and revision of the anastomosis in the transplantation setting.[245,257–259] The benefits of prophylactic therapy with AT concentrates and anticoagulant therapy remain controversial. Esophageal varices, a consequence of PVT, are usually treated initially with sclerotherapy. Other therapeutic options include endoscopic variceal ligation[260] and portosystemic shunts.

Outcome Currently, the outcome of PVT is guarded, and may differ if PVT is secondary to liver transplantation or other etiologies. Of 17 children with PVT or stenosis in a cohort study of 115 patients following liver transplantation, four (25%) died, three (20%) survived with portal hypertension, and 10 had no long term-sequelae, despite varying alternative therapies.[245] In the nontransplant setting, death is common, but usually due to the underlying disease and not PVT.[246]

Hepatic Vein Thrombosis

General information Hepatic vein TEs or Budd-Chiari syndrome is rare in children, with only seven isolated case reports in the literature in the last 4 years.[261–267] Reported cases occurred secondary to the presence of CVLs in the IVC, obstruction of the IVC, protein C deficiency, PNH, and congenital membranous malformation of the IVC.[261–267]

Clinical presentation The most common clinical presentations of hepatic vein TEs include abdominal pain, abdominal distension, and symptoms of liver failure.

Treatment Treatment for hepatic vein TEs is usually focused on the associated liver disease, the underlying disease process, and on the use of antithrombotic therapy. Successful thrombolytic therapy has been reported.[265,266]

Hepatic Artery Thrombosis

General information HAT is a serious event that is usually associated with liver transplantation. It has a slightly delayed presentation, occurring approximately 1 to 2 weeks following transplantation.[268,269] The mechanisms responsible for the delay in presentation are uncertain, but include the presence of a circulating anticoagulant.[270] The anticoagulant is a dermatan sulphate proteoglycan with AT anticoagulant activities, and is present prior to and during the first days postoperatively.[270] The incidence of HAT is higher in children (3.1% to 29%)[271–273] than adults (1.5% to 1.6%).[274,275] Not unexpectedly, the age and size of the child are the most important risk factors.[276]

Clinical presentation Early clinical symptoms of HAT are often absent or nonspecific. The clinical course of HAT is usually fulminant but can be indolent with a late onset. The clinical presentation can include fulminant liver failure, biliary complications, and biliary sepsis.

Diagnosis Serial testing with pulsed Doppler combined with real-time ultrasonography of the liver parenchyma is commonly used to detect HAT; it has a sensitivity of approximately 70%.[277–281] Because both false positive and negative results may occur, angiography is usually required to confirm the diagnosis of HAT, although it may not be feasible in some critically ill patients. Angiography has also been reported to give false positive results compared to autopsy findings. Presumably, the extremely low flow that occurs in hepatic arteries of small children contributes to the diagnostic difficulty. CT of the liver may be of aid in equivocal cases. Spiral CT has been shown to be both sensitive and specific for the detection of HAT in adults.[282] The value of MRI/MRA has yet to be fully determined.[268,283]

Prophylaxis, treatment and outcome Prophylactic use of anticoagulants such as UFH, LMWH, and aspirin are unproven but attractive, given the poor outcome of HAT regardless of therapy. Therapeutic options include surgical intervention, retransplantation, and thrombolytic therapy.[284–286] Emergency surgical revascularization procedures are successful in approximately 20% of children.[286–291] Thrombolytic therapy has limited success, based upon a small number of children.[284] Because plasma plasminogen concentrations are significantly decreased in children with HAT (less than 50% of adult values), supplementation with plasminogen may be helpful prior to thrombolytic therapy.[292] The reported mortality with untreated HAT ranges from 25% to 70% in reported studies.[268,283,285,289,293]

Hepatic Veno-Occlusive Disease Following Bone Marrow Transplantation

General information Veno-occlusive disease (VOD) of the liver occurs most commonly following high-dose cytoreductive therapy prior to bone marrow transplantation.[294] Histologic features of VOD include concentric narrowing or fibrous obliteration of terminal hepatic venules and sublobular veins, dilation, and, ultimately, fibrosis of centrilobular sinusoids and necrosis of zone 3 hepatocytes.[294] Hepatic veins are frequently occluded.

Clinical presentation Clinical presentation of VOD includes three cardinal symptoms: jaundice, painful hepatomegaly, and fluid retention, which frequently can be fatal. Clinical symptoms occur early and in approximately 50% of patients.[294] The severity of VOD has been classified retrospectively, by the time to resolution of the three cardinal symptoms.[295–297]

Prophylaxis Strategies to prevent VOD include patient selection to avoid high-risk patients, UFH, prostaglandin E_1, ursodeoxycholic acid, and pentoxifylline.[295,298–311]

Six trials were identified that assessed prophylactic UFH for VOD.[298–301,312,313] Small sample size, lack of randomization, and an inability to continuously administer UFH were problems present in two of the studies.[298,301] In the only RCT, 161 patients were randomized to UFH (100 U/kg/day) or placebo. The trial showed a significant reduction in VOD without an increase in bleeding events.[300] The fourth study was a large cohort of 90 children treated with approximately 100 units/kg/day of UFH. This study reported an incidence of VOD of 5.5%,[298] similar to the UFH treatment arm in the RCT.[300]

Treatment Potential benefit of TPA for the treatment of VOD was reported in seven patients.[314–317] Although these preliminary data suggest that TPA may alter the natural history of severe VOD, further studies are required to confirm these observations.

Splenic Vein Thrombosis

General information Splenic circulation is shown in Figure 8–6. A literature review of 144 adult and pediatric patients with splenic vein TEs provides the most comprehensive information available, with little additional data since 1985.[318,319] While frequently idiopathic, splenic vein TEs can also be a complication of UVCs.[320] Patients with splenic vein TEs usually present with one or more of the following: pancreatitis in combination with gastrointestinal blood loss; splenomegaly in the absence of portal hypertension or cirrhosis; and isolated gastric/esophageal varices. The definitive tool for diagnosing splenic vein TEs is selective angiography, although ultrasound is commonly used. The differential diagnosis of splenic vein TEs includes causes of hepatic and extrahepatic portal hypertension. The treatment of choice is splenectomy. Reimplantation of splenic tissue to avoid septic complications of splenectomy in small children has been reported.[319]

Mesenteric Vessel Thrombosis TEs have been reported in both the mesenteric artery and vein. Arterial TEs in the mesenteric circulation are rare.[321–324] Possible underlying causes include an abscess, surgery, Crohn's disease, and congenital prothrombotic disorders.[321–322]

Thromboembolic Complications in Congenital Heart Disease

General Information Congenital heart disease (CHD) of a wide spectrum of severity affects approximately 1% of all live births. The majority of congenital cardiac structural abnormalities occur in otherwise healthy children, and total correction of the cardiac lesion usually results in a normal productive lifespan. One of the most frequent complications seen in survivors of CHD is TEs, which include VTE, PE, and embolism to the CNS.[325] The management of children with TEs complicating CHD is discussed in detail in Chapters 9, 10, and 11. Many TEs related to CHD occur secondary to right to left intracardiac shunts or on the arterial side of the circulation. These are discussed further in Chapter 6.

Venous Thromboembolic Disease The Canadian Childhood Thrombophilia Registry has provided the largest prospective database defining the epidemiology of VTE in children, with a mean follow-up of 2.36 years.[326] CHD was the underlying disease process in 75 of 405 children (19%) reported with VTE and had an associated mortality of 7%. Morbidity in the form of postphlebitic syndrome (PPS) and recurrent VTE occurred in 23% of children.[326] Further information on VTE is provided in Chapter 4.

Childhood Stroke The Canadian Childhood Stroke Registry identified CHD as the single most common identifiable cause of arterial ischemic stroke (AIS) in a prospective, consecutive cohort of 165 children with (AIS). Thirty-six percent of children with AIS had underlying CHD. In the entire stroke registry cohort, only 22% of children fully recovered, while two-thirds had residual neurologic defects or seizures.[327] The contribution of CHD to AIS in children is important, since this is an etiology that can likely be prevented in many children by the use of anticoagulants. Further information on childhood stroke is provided in Chapter 7.

Right Atrial Thrombosis The presence of a right atrial thrombosis is frequently clinically "asymptomatic" and identified on routine echocardiogram in

children with CHD or children receiving cardiotoxic agents for the treatment of their primary disease (e.g., acute lymphoblastic leukemia). Right atrial thrombosis also seems to occur more frequently in neonates with CVLs.[328,329] Clinically overt symptoms of right atrial thrombosis include cardiac failure, CVL malfunction, persistent sepsis, and appearance of a new cardiac murmur.[329–332] Optimal approaches to right atrial thrombosis are uncertain at this time and will likely differ, depending on the patient population. Therapeutic options consist of anticoagulation, thrombolytic therapy, and surgery. The risk of PE or obstruction to venous return is substantial, and such TEs should always be treated.[329–332]

Fontan

General information The Fontan procedure has evolved as the definitive palliative surgical treatment for most heart lesions where a biventricular circulation is not feasible.[333] The principle is to divert systemic venous return directly to the pulmonary arteries, in the setting of single ventricle physiology.[334] The single functioning ventricle, regardless of its anatomic origin, can then act as the primary pump for the systemic circulation. Fontan procedures are only sustainable when the total pulmonary vascular resistance is low. Following a Fontan procedure, pulmonary blood flow relies exclusively on systemic venous pressure, without assistance from a myocardial pump. There must be free flow of blood through the pulmonary circulation to maintain a viable circulation. The many modifications of Fontan procedures now in use were developed to reduce a variety of postoperative complications; however, the founding principle remains unchanged.[335–338]

Cardiac defects amenable to Fontan procedures The Fontan procedure was originally devised to treat tricuspid atresia. However, the Fontan or a modified Fontan procedure is now the definitive palliative surgery for any child with univentricular physiology in whom biventricular physiology is unattainable.[333] Congenital cardiac defects that may be treated with Fontan surgery are listed in Table 8–2. Other rare complex univentricular defects may also be treated with Fontan surgery.[339] Most children undergoing a Fontan procedure will have had previous surgeries, in-cluding systemic-pulmonary shunts (Blalock Taussig [BT] shunts), atrial septectomy, pulmonary artery banding, Glenn shunts, and others.[339–342]

Variations of Fontan procedures As previously described, the original Fontan procedure is rarely performed. A number of modified Fontan procedures exist in current clinical practice, and new methods are continually being described. This reflects the fact that Fontan procedures do not restore normal anatomy or physiology and, as such, are an imperfect solution.[335–338,343] Fontan procedures can be described by their anatomic relationships, the type of material used, and the presence or absence of fenestrations to provide a surgical communication between the Fontan circuit and the left atrium. Figures 8–7A to 8–7D illustrates the principles of various Fontan procedures in comparison to normal anatomy. The following discusses the anatomic relationships of Fontan procedures.

1. Direct right atrial pulmonary connections. For direct right atrial pulmonary connections, the right atrium is directly anastomosed onto the right ventricular outflow tract, main, or right pulmonary artery (Figure 8–7A). An intact pulmonary valve may be included in the circuit.

2. Total cavopulmonary connections (lateral tunnel Fontan). Total cavopulmonary connections

Table 8–2 Congenital Cardiac Defects Treatable with Fontan Surgery

A. Tricuspid atresia
 ± transposition of great vessels
 ± pulmonary atresia

B. Double inlet left ventricle
 ± transposition great vessels

C. Double inlet right ventricle

D. Double inlet ventricle of indeterminate morphology

E. Multiple ventricular septal defects

F. Double outlet right ventricle

G. Pulmonary atresia and intact ventricular septum.

H. Hypoplastic left heart

I. Unbalanced atrioventricular septal defect
 ± pulmonary valve atresia

J. Ebstein anomaly

Reproduced with permission.[363]

consist of separate anastomosis of the superior vena cava (SVC) directly and of the IVC (indirectly via an intra-atrial baffle to the terminal SVC segment) to the right pulmonary artery (Figure 8–7B). A baffle refers to an artificial wall that directs blood flow through the right atrium to the SVC inlet.

3. **Intracardiac tube grafts.** Intracardiac tube grafts are similar to a total cavopulmonary connection; however, the IVC is directed through an intra-cardiac tube (within the right atrium) to the right pulmonary artery. In some patients with tricuspid atresia, the right ventricle is used as the conduit between the right atrium and the pulmonary artery (Figure 8–7C). In these cases, the ventricle is hypoplastic and does not function as a pump but as part of an intracardiac tube to direct the systemic venous return to the pulmonary circulation.

4. **Extracardiac conduit.** For extracardiac conduits, the SVC is anastomosed directly to the right pulmonary artery, and the IVC is anastomosed via an extracardiac conduit to the right pulmonary artery, bypassing the right atrium (Figure 8–7D).

Prosthetic materials In order to complete the Fontan circuit, different materials may be required to bring together the edges of the anastomosis or to make the intracardiac baffles or tubes directing blood from the IVC. Autologous, homograft, or xenograft (usually bovine) pericardium may be used. Patches and baffles may also be made from goretex (polytetrafluoroethylene or PTFE) or Dacron. Extracardiac conduits are usually Goretex or Dacron. The use of these materials is important, since their surfaces may contribute to local TE formation.

Fenestrations Obliteration of the right ventricle frequently leads to sudden decreases in pulmonary blood flow, which can lead to cardiac failure because of inadequate preload for the left ventricle.[342] A currently popular method for avoiding this complication is creation of a surgical communication or fenestration between the Fontan circuit and the left atrium.[344] This allows right to left shunting to maintain adequate preload for the left ventricle at the expense of systemic oxygenation. Fenestrations may close spontaneously or be closed electively at a latter date, when the physiology has adapted to the reduced pulmonary blood pressure.[342] Fenestrations are one source for right to left shunts, which may result in AIS.

Mortality Fontan surgery was initially associated with a high early mortality, being over 40% in some series.[338] These early results were nevertheless encouraging, because the untreated forms of CHD were uniformly fatal.[342] Surgical mortality for the Fontan procedure is now below 10% to 15%, despite the wide range of severe cardiac defects for which Fontan surgery is offered.[334,338] Fontan surgery is now frequently performed in children less than 2 years of age, although the procedure was previously thought to be associated with an unacceptably high mortality during early infancy.[340]

Long-term outcome Long-term follow-up data are available for children operated on during the 1970s, and the outcome is generally very good. In some studies, over 75% of survivors are employed and feel well. As few as 50% of patients require any ongoing cardiac medications. Less than 15% report a physical incapacity that results in an inability to work or attend school.[334] Late complications continue to occur, including arrythemias, ventricular failure, and protein-losing enteropathy, all of which may predispose to TEs. In summary, while Fontan procedures fail to restore normal anatomy and normal cardiac physiology, the functional outcome is compatible with good long-term quality of life, provided that the secondary complications can be avoided.

Thromboembolic events A comprehensive Medline search of the English literature identified 20 publications that included information on TEs following Fontan procedures.[334,340,345–362] There were no experimental designs, case control studies, or prospective cohort designs. Four articles reported cross-sectional point surveys that directly surveyed TEs as an outcome.[345,346,361,362] In nine retrospective cohort studies, TEs were the primary outcome measure.[347–355] A further nine retrospective cohort studies reported multiple outcomes following Fontan procedures and included some details about TEs.[334,340,356–362]

Types of thromboembolic events TEs in children who have undergone Fontan procedures can be considered in two forms.[363] First, VTEs occur in the systemic venous and right atrial locations, including the Fontan circuit. These VTEs can cause local obstruction to blood flow or can extend or embolize into the pulmonary vasculature. TEs in these areas can also embolize to the arterial circulation through surgical fenestrations or other right to left intracardiac communications. Second, TEs located on the left side of the atrial baffle (from the divided pulmonary artery stump) or from the ventricle (in cases with ventricular dysfunction) can embolize to the arterial system. The most common site of arterial embolization is the cerebral circulation. Frequently, a CNS infarct or stroke is the initial presentation of TEs after Fontan surgery. Presumably, there is an intracardiac or central venous TE that is the source for the embolus.[363]

Incidence of thromboembolic events Two cross-sectional surveys used transesophageal echocardiography to assess the point prevalence of TEs following Fontan procedures, which were 17% and 20% (Table 8–3).[345,346] Details of the eight cohort studies having TEs (venous, arterial emboli, or both) as primary outcome measures are presented in Table 8–4.[347–351,354,355,364] The duration of follow-up varied considerably. The reported incidence of VTE ranged from 3% to 19% and incidence of AIS ranged from 3% to 19%.[347–351,354,355,364] The most recent of these papers describes a retrospective cohort of 16 patients undergoing extracardiac Fontan procedures. The median follow-up is 13 months and the incidence of intracardiac TE is 19%.[364] Table 8–5 outlines the available incidence data about TEs from retrospective cohort studies not primarily directed at this outcome. The reported cumulative risk of VTE ranges from 1% to 7%.[334,336,340,343,356,358–360] Only two cohort stud-

ies reported survival type analysis.[347,363] In the study by Rosenthal, the mean time from Fontan procedure to TE was greater than the mean time of follow-up,[350] suggesting that the cumulative incidence would be increased with a longer duration of follow-up.

The majority of studies used nonstandardized diagnostic tests, and many studies assessed only survivors, with no information on mortality. The incidence of TEs was increased in recent studies compared to earlier studies, reflecting increased survival, longer duration of follow-up, improved diagnostic tests, and increased awareness of TEs.[344] The retrospective nature of the studies, frequent lack of sensitive diagnostic tests, and limited follow-up not only account for variation in reported incidences, but suggest that the reported incidences of TEs following Fontan procedures are likely minimal estimations.

Timing of thromboembolic events The exact duration of time from Fontan procedure to TEs could be calculated for 109 events reported in 16 cohort studies[336,340,345,348,349,350–356,358–361] and 15 case reports.[365–379] Of 109 TEs, 54 occurred within the first 3 months following the procedure, and 55 occurred later than 3 months following the Fontan procedure. However, without the corresponding "numbers at risk" in these same time periods, these numbers are difficult to interpret. Only two series analyzed the timing of TEs. Rosenthal reported a mean time from procedure to event of 6.1 years, with a range of 6

Table 8–3 Cross-Sectional Studies Assessing Thromboembolic Events Following Fontan Procedures

Author	Mean Time Since Procedure (Years)	Number of Patients	Number (%) of Thrombosis	Comments
Stumper[346]	3.4 years	18	3 (17)	TOE* performed to globally assess results of Fontan procedures.
Fyfe[345]	Not stated	30	6 (20)	TOE performed in 30 patients over 4 months for symtomatic investigation and routine screening purposes. TTE† negative in 5 of 6 thromboses.
Cromme-Dijkhuis[361]	5 (0.75–13.5) years	37	2 (5)	Clinical thrombosis noted in 2 patients, leading to CS‡ study aimed at assessing coagulation factors.
Cromme-Dijkhuis[362]	5 (1–14) Years	66	3 (5)	Study to determine point prevalence of multiple sequelae. History of clinical thrombosis noted in 3 patients. No analysis of thrombosis.

*Transoesophageal echocardiography; †transthoracic echocardiography; ‡cross-sectional study.
Reproduced with permission.[363]

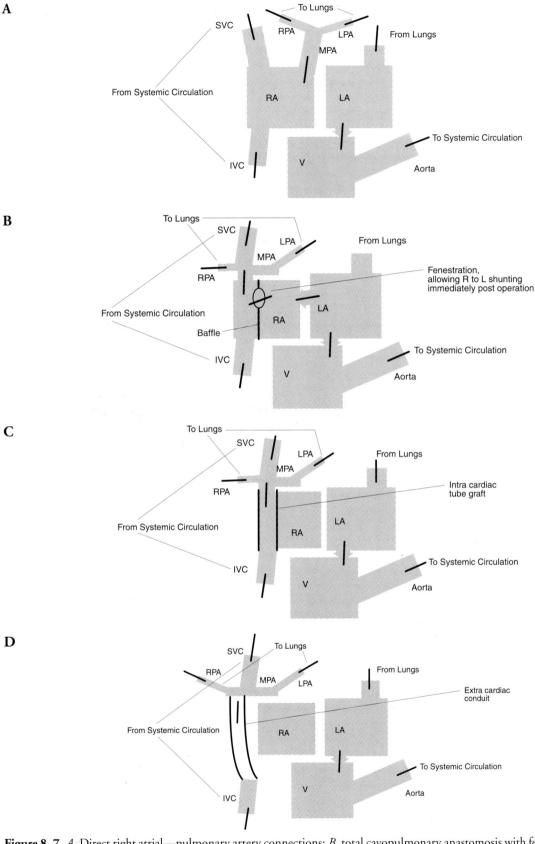

Figure 8–7 *A*, Direct right atrial—pulmonary artery connections; *B*, total cavopulmonary anastomosis with fenestration; *C*, intracardiac tube grafts; and *D*, extracardiac conduits. SVC = superior vena cava; IVC = inferior vena cava; RA = right atrium; MPA = main pulmonary artery; RPA = right pulmonary artery; LPA = left pulmonary artery V = ventricle; LA = left atrium; — = direction of blood flow.

Table 8–4   Retrospective Cohort Studies That Had Thromboembolic Events as the Primary Outcome Measure

Author	Mean Duration of Follow-up (Range)	Number in Cohort (Survivors)	Number of Thromboses (%)	Number of Strokes or Arterial Emboli (%)	Comments
Shirai[364]	(3–34 months)	16	3 (19)	NA*	Chart review; TTE† assessment for asymptomatic thrombosis, no survival analysis.
Rosenthal[347]	5.2 years (SD +/− 4.7)	70	11 (16)	3 (4)	Chart review; clinical/asymptomatic thrombosis (all patients had yearly TTE); survival analysis used.
Jahangiri[348]	24.5 months (6–55)	64 (57)	8 (14)	3 (5)	Method of data collection not stated; no uniform outcome assessment; survival analysis used.
Du Plessis[349]	Not stated	645	NA	17 (3)	Chart review and mailed questionnaire; clinical presentation only; no survival analysis.
Day [350]	4 years (0.5–15)	68	NA	6 (9)	Chart review, clinically symptomatic patients only; no survival analysis.
Matthews[351]	Not stated	25 (16)	NA	3 (19)	Clinical cases prompted review of cohort; no uniform assessment of outcome; no survival analysis.
Danielson[354]	Not stated	449	18 (4)	NA	Data collection methods not stated; method of outcome assessment not stated; no survival analysis.
Kaulitz[355]	Not stated	72	4 (5.5)	NA	No uniform outcome assessment.

*Not assessed; †transthoracic echocardiography.
Reproduced with permission.[363]

days to 13.6 years.[347] The authors performed Kaplain-Meier analysis of TE-free survival and found no plateau and a constant risk throughout the time of follow-up (mean 5.2 ± 4.7years). Jahangiri reported approximately 90% TE-free survival at 1 year following the procedure and 75% TE-free survival after 4 years (mean follow-up 24.5 ± 17 months).[348] Prophylactic anticoagulation for 3 months following Fontan procedures is frequently advocated and commonly used. However, limited duration (3 months) prophylatic anticoagulation is difficult to justify, given the current evidence that there is increased risk of TEs well beyond 3 months after Fontan surgery.

Preoperative and operative risk factors for thromboembolic complications Patient age at operation, the type of Fontan procedure performed, the type of material used for the conduit, and the use of valved versus nonvalved conduits did not affect the incidence of VTE.[348,347] Similarly, the type of

congenital abnormality and the type of Fontan procedure performed did not affect the rate of stroke. In particular, studies by Duplessis and Day assessed the role of fenestration in causing strokes, and neither found a significantly increased incidence of stroke in patients with fenestrations.[349,350]

Hemodynamic risk factors for thromboembolic events Rosenthal et al found arrhythmias in 71% of patients who subsequently developed TEs versus 43% of those who did not (p = .08).[347] However, 70% of the patients diagnosed with TEs were in sinus rhythm at the time of event. In the series by Day et al, three of eight patients who had AIS following Fontan procedures had previously documented periods of atrial or junctional arrythmias.[350] Duplessis et al found no relationship between arrythmia and stroke following Fontan procedures.[349] Day et al described a subset of patients who had cardiac catheterization (CC) following their Fontan procedure.[350] Residual right to left shunts (not surgical

Table 8–5   Studies in Which Thromboembolic Events Were Not the Primary Outcome Measure, But Which Gave Some Details of Thromboembolic Events

Author	Number in Cohort n	Mean Duration of Follow-up (Years) (Range)	Number of Thromboses (%)	Number of Strokes or Arterial Emboli (%)	Comments
Driscoll[354]	352	7.7 years (0.5–15.5)	3 (1)	4 (1)	211 of 230 survivors accounted for with mailed questionnaire; no uniform outcome assessment; survival analysis not used
Fontan[356]	100	3.66 years (0.3–14)	3 (3)	NA*	Only deaths due to thrombosis reported; no information about thrombosis in survivors collected
Prenger[336]	22	(3.75–11.75) years	2 (7)	NA	Only deaths due to thrombosis reported; no analysis thrombosis
Laks[358]	45	2.3 years (0.1–9)	1 (2)	NA	Chart review and phone contact; only deaths due to thrombosis reported; no analysis of thrombosis
Annechino[359]	38	28.8 months	1 (3)	NA	Method of follow-up and data collection not stated; no analysis related to thrombosis
Myers[340]	34	1.3 years (1 month–8.4 years)	1 (3)	NA	Chart review; no uniform outcome assessment; no survival analysis
Mair[360]	65	4 years (1–10)	1 (2)	NA	Follow-up on 65 of 79 survivors; only deaths due to thrombosis reported; no analysis of thrombosis
Quinones[344]	13	Not given	NA	1 (7)	Aspirin prophylaxis used after one of 9 patients had a stroke

*Not assessed.

Reproduced with permission.[363]

fenestrations) were present in six of seven patients with neurologic symptoms and in only 3 of 21 asymptomatic patients (p < .005). However, the true number of asymptomatic patients with residual shunts is unknown. Duplessis reported that neither polycythemia nor thrombocytosis appeared to influence the incidence of AIS.[349] Danielson reported that 16 of 18 patients who suffered TEs following Fontan procedures at the Mayo Clinic had low cardiac output.[354] However, the number with low cardiac output who did not develop TEs was not described.

Hematologic risk factors for thromboembolic complications The concept of coagulation factor abnormalities in children following Fontan procedures is not new and was originally described by Cromme-Dijkhuis et al in 1990 and 1993.[361,362] In two cross-sectional surveys of children following Fontan procedures, they described multiple coagulation factor abnormalities involving both procoag-

ulant and anticoagulant proteins. In the first study of 37 patients, they reported 63 coagulation abnormalities in 24 patients, including deficiencies of protein C, AT, FII, and FX.[362] A subsequent similar study by the same authors screened a further 66 patients.[361] In this cohort, 62% were reported to have protein C deficiency. Other abnormalities were deficiencies for protein S (6%), AT (4%), FII (36%), FVII and FIX (43%), FX (36%), and plasminogen (15%). The authors noted that these abnormalities tended to resolve as duration of follow-up lengthened. However, closer examination of the Cromme-Dijkhuis papers revealed the reference ranges used by the authors were not age-appropriate.[380] The majority of the children's plasma coagulation factor concentrations were in fact in the normal range for their ages. The apparent normalization with time reflected that, with increasing age, the children grew into the adult reference ranges, which had been inappropriately applied previously. However, 6 of 19 patients in the Cromme-Dijkhuis series had increased thrombin-antithrombin (TAT) complexes when compared to age-appropriate normal ranges. Increased TAT complexes reflect in vivo thrombin generation and suggest that a prothrombotic condition is present, although the mechanism in this instance remains unknown. In a more recent cross-sectional study, Jahangiri et al report similar conclusions.[381,382] However, the authors did not describe the source of their reference ranges, the ages of the children at time of testing, or the actual plasma concentrations of patient's protein C. The normal ranges quoted are adult reference ranges and are not applicable to the patient population in question. The lower limit of normal for children 1 to 5 years of age is as low as 0.4 units/mL, in contrast to the 0.63 units/mL used by the authors.[380] The lack of patient's preoperative protein C levels in any of the studies reported makes conclusions about the effect of Fontan surgery on protein C levels difficult to substantiate.[350,382] Normal hemostatic parameters were reported in a small number of cases in Fontan patients with TEs.[347,355,369]

Diagnosis of thromboembolic events   Diagnosis of intracardiac thrombosis following Fontan surgery can be accomplished in one of several ways. TEs may be detected on routine transthoracic or transesophageal echocardiography or at the time of angiography, which is frequently performed to assess ventricular function and pulmonary blood flow. Alternatively, echocardiography or angiography may be used to investigate clinically suspected intracardiac TEs. The majority of cohort studies, with the exception of Rosenthal et al and Shirae et al, did not indicate whether TEs were documented as a result of routine screening or as part of the investigation of new clinical symptoms.[347,364] Some TEs were diagnosed at autopsy (11 cases) and reoperation (6 cases). If children presented with AIS, CT and MRI/MRA were used to document the location of the embolus, which presumably came from an intra-cardiac source.

Two studies specifically compared transthoracic echocardiography to transesophageal echocardiography in the diagnosis of intracardiac TEs following Fontan surgery. Stumper et al, in a cross-sectional survey of 18 patients, found three intracardiac TEs

using transesophageal echocardiography, only one of which was detected by transthoracic echocardiography.[346] The sample population included children of various ages, and various durations since Fontan surgery. Eight of the 18 are described as being symptomatic at the time of investigation, although no further details were given. The three positive cases were confirmed by angiography (the gold standard), which was performed in only 11 of the 18 patients. Fyfe et al, in a similar study, found six TEs in four pediatric patients using transesophageal echocardiography, only one of which was detected by transthoracic echocardiography.[345] The cases defined as positive for TEs by transoesophageal echocardiography were confirmed by cardiac catheter (one case), direct visualization of the TE at surgery (one case), resolution of echocardiographic findings after treatment (three cases), and clinical follow-up (one case). All patients with negative transesophageal echocardiography remained clinically asymptomatic. Several other publications reported intracardiac TEs diagnosed by transesophageal echocardiography or angiography that were not detected using transthoracic echocardiography.[347-349]

Clinical symptoms   The symptoms of intra cardiac TEs are often nonspecific but include cyanosis, hypotension, reduced cardiac output, and cardiac failure. If AIS is the presenting event, then there will be accompanying neurologic deficits that reflect the site of the infarction.

Outcome of thromboembolic complications   No studies specifically assessed outcome of TEs following Fontan procedures or the relationship between method of treatment of TEs and outcome. A summary of the management approaches detailed in the literature and subsequent outcomes is provided in Table 8–6. Total resolution of TEs was achieved in only 48% of cases. Death occurred in 25% despite aggressive treatment. Follow-up duration for these patients varied from 1 month to 5 years.[345–349,352,353, 355,356,358,365–368,371,372,374,376–379]

Routine screening for intracardiac thrombosis   Six of 14 cases of TEs reported by Rosenthal et al were asymptomatic and detected by routine transthoracic echocardiography.[347] Four cases had full resolution. One TE initially resolved, but subsequently recurred. One child died of a cerebrovascular event despite treatment. Of the eight children who presented with symptoms of their TE, two died and two have residual neurologic disability. Other papers reported cases in which the treatment of asymptomatic intracardiac TE failed to prevent stroke due to embolization.[345,349]

Safety and efficacy of prophylaxis The incidence of TEs following Fontan procedures has caused the majority of authors to postulate that routine prophylactic anticoagulation with OAs or antiplatelet agents is warranted. Prenger et al used prophylactic OA therapy for 3 months following surgery in 27 patients who received porcine-valved dacron conduits for their Fontan procedure (target international normalized ratio (INR) not stated).[336] The frequency of fatal TEs in this case series, which is the only series reported in which all patients received prophylactic anticoagulation, was 7.4%. In total, from all other case series and reports, only 25 patients were documented to receive prophylactic therapy with either OAs (12 cases), aspirin (12 cases), or UFH (1 case).[344,345,347–350,355,366,377] The rationale for prophylaxing these particular patients was the presence of fenestrations (for 16), previous TEs (for 2), atrial fibrillation (in 1), and immobility (for 1). No rationale was given for a further five cases. Of the 12 patients who received OAs (target

INRs unknown), 5 had TEs during or subsequent to the prophylactic therapy. One of these patients ceased OAs due to bleeding and then had a subsequent TE.[366] Three of the patients given prophylactic aspirin and the patient given UFH had TEs while receiving their prophylactic therapy.

There is no uniform approach to the provision of prophylatic anticoagulation to children who have undergone a Fontan procedure. Wilson et al reported that of the 18 centers within the United Kingdom that performed Fontan surgery, only 12 had defined protocols for prophylatic anticoagulation. Within these 12 centers, six different protocols were in use.[377] Some centers used OAs with a target INR range of 2 to 3. Some centers used aspirin with usual doses of 5 mg/kg/day. The duration of prophylactic anticoagulation also varied from 3 months to lifelong. Many centers varied their prophylactic regimes depending on the type of Fontan procedure performed. A number of cardiologists continue to use no antithrombotic prophylaxis.

Clinical trials The incidence of TEs following Fontan surgery appears to be high enough to warrant prophylactic anticoagulation. However, the choice of agent and duration are unclear and require a clinical trial to determine. A multicenter, multinational clinical trial comparing aspirin to OAs in

Table 8–6 Outcome of Thromboembolic Events Following Fontan Procedures According to Antithrombotic Treatment

Treatment	Number Treated	Successful — Complete Resolution	Treatment Failure — Death	Subsequent Embolization, Extension, or Incomplete Resolution	Subsequent Takedown of Fontan
Surgery	4	1	2	1	–
Surgery and anticoagulation	14	7	6	–	1
Thrombolysis	6	3	1	3	–
Thrombolysis and anticoagulation	11	3	4	8	–
Heparin	5	3	1	1	–
Coumadin	23	14	2	7	1
Aspirin	2	–	–	2	–
Total	65	31	16	22	2

Reproduced with permission.[363]

children who have undergone a Fontan procedure is underway in Canada, the USA, and Australia. The outcome events will be any symptomatic TEs and any thrombus detected by transesophageal or transthoracic echocardiogram at 3 months and 2 years following the Fontan procedure. The management of TEs after Fontan surgery is discussed further in Chapters 9 and 10.

The Glenn Procedure In 1957, Glenn successfully used the classic cavopulmonary anastomosis (superior vena cavapulmonary artery shunt) as a palliative operation for tricuspid atresia.[342,383–387] The Glenn anastomosis diverts part of the systemic venous return to the lungs, while the Fontan procedure diverts the entire systemic venous circulation to the pulmonary vascular bed (in the absence of a fenestration). The bidirectional Glenn is frequently used in the staged surgical management of single ventricle patients. The potential advantages of the Glenn shunt include early reduction of volume load, minimizing reliance on other palliative procedures, and simplifying the final operative procedure at the time of the Fontan.[385,387] There is still some controversy on the optimal timing of the Glenn shunt and the interval of time until the Fontan procedure is performed. Complications of the Glenn shunt include death, effusions, impaired growth of the pulmonary arteries, pulmonary arteriovenous fistuals, and stenosis with hypoplasia of the left pulmonary artery. Thrombotic complications are rarely reported and do not appear to be a major complication following a Glenn shunt.

Thrombotic Complications of Acute Lymphoblastic Leukemia

Introduction Successful treatment of children with ALL has been achieved at the cost of significant secondary problems, including TEs. Mechanisms responsible for TEs in childhood ALL are complex and include the disease process itself, the chemotherapeutic agent, L-asparaginase, and other chemotherapeutic agents.[388,389]

Untreated Acute Lymphoblastic Leukemia The hemostatic system is significantly affected by the disease process itself, independent of the influence of

treatment (Table 8–7).[388] Plasma concentrations of some coagulation proteins are increased and others decreased.[380,390–395] Although some proteins are acute phase reactants, the reasons for abnormal plasma concentrations of the other proteins are unclear. Markers of in vivo generation of thrombin, prothrombin fragment 1.2 (F1.2), and TATs are increased in children with untreated ALL (Table 8–8).[388,392,394] Potentially responsible mechanisms include tissue factor (TF) activity, TF-FVII complexes, and cancer procoagulant.[395–398] The altered state of the coagulation system in children with untreated ALL does not affect the in vitro capacity to generate or inhibit thrombin.[390,394] The fibrinolytic

Table 8–7 Effect of Untreated Acute Lymphoblastic Leukemia on Plasma Concentrations of Coagulation Proteins

Coagulation Protein (Units/mL)	Pretreatment of ALL	Normal Controls
Prekallikrein	0.66 ± 0.18	0.96 ± 0.04
High molecular weight kinnogen	0.92 ± 0.14	0.94 ± 0.04
FXI	0.94 ± 0.10	0.87 ± 0.04
FXII	0.92 ± 0.12	0.89 ± 0.04
FII	0.82 ± 0.12	0.88 ± 0.02
FVII	0.85 ± 0.14	0.84 ± 0.04
FIX	1.04 ± 0.16	0.77 ± 0.04
FX	0.88 ± 0.12	0.81 ± 0.04
FV	0.95 ± 0.14	0.89 ± 0.04
FVIIIc	1.67 ± 0.24	0.95 ± 0.02
von Willebrand Factor	1.99 ± 0.32	0.95 ± 0.06
Fibrinogen (g/L)	3.70 ± 0.68	2.97 ± 0.14
FXIIIa	0.86 ± 0.10	1.08 ± 0.06
FXIIIs	0.95 ± 0.08	1.12 ± 0.04
Antithrombin	0.99 ± 0.06	0.91 ± 0.02
α_2-macroglobin	2.01 ± 0.18	1.66 ± 0.08
Heparin cofactor II	1.10 ± 0.16	0.88 ± 0.04
Protein C	0.60 ± 0.10	0.76 ± 0.04
Protein S	1.00 ± 0.14	0.78 ± 0.02

*Acute lymphoblastic leukemia.
Reproduced with permission.[388]

system is activated at the time of presentation with ALL (Table 8–9).[388,390,392,395] Plasma concentrations of TPA are increased resulting in a ratio of PAI₁ to TPA of approximately 2 to 1,[395] compared to 3 to 1 in healthy children and 0.75 in adults.[380] Plasma concentrations of end products of fibrinolysis including FDPs and D-dimers are also increased.[391–393,399]

L-asparaginase Alone L-asparaginase, derived from either *Escherichia coli* (*E. coli*) or *Erwinia chrysanthemi*[400,401] interferes with protein synthesis by catalyzing the hydrolysis of L-asparagine to L-aspartic acid and ammonia.[402] As a single agent, L-asparaginase significantly decreases plasma concentrations of almost all coagulation proteins and inhibitors (Figure 8–8B) versus initial levels prior to treatment (Figure 8–8A).[390–394] Why some proteins (particularly AT) are affected more than others is not clear. The content of L-asparagine does differ slightly among coagulation proteins, but there is no relationship between L-asparagine content and the magnitude of effect. For reasons that are not apparent, the effects of *E. coli* L-asparaginase are likely greater than *Erwinia* L-asparaginase.[403,404]

Combination Chemotherapy without L-asparaginase Effects of combination chemotherapy without L-asparaginase was assessed during induction and maintenance chemotherapy.[390,394,405,406] During induction without L-asparaginase, plasma concentrations of most coagulation proteins increase to levels surpassing values at presentation (Figure 8–8C).[390,394,406] A notable exception is fibrinogen, which decreases by 1.1 g/L at the completion of induction therapy.[390] During maintenance therapy, plasma concentrations of coagulation proteins cycle in a pattern that mimics the chemotherapy cycle and prednisone in particular.[399] Effects of prednisone on hemostasis have been previously reported and include hypofibrinogenemia.[407–411]

Combination Chemotherapy with L-asparaginase There were 18 reports since 1980 identified describing the effect of L-asparaginase on hemostasis, when L-asparaginase was administered as part of intensive combination chemotherapy.[390,392–395,412–424] Differences between studies reflect different chemotherapy protocols, timing of sampling, selected measurements, and concurrent therapy.[388] Despite these limitations, decreased plasma concentrations for AT,

Table 8–8   Evidence for in Vivo Generation of Thrombin in Children with Acute Lymphoblastic Leukemia

	Pretreatment at Diagnosis	Post-ASP Only	Combination Therapy without ASP	Combination Therapy with ASP	Normal Controls
F1+2 (nM)†	3.5 ± 0.91*	2.8 ± 0.68*	1.48 ± 0.34	1.67 ± 0.50	1.08 ± 0.099
TAT (pM)	134 ± 50*†	87 ± 14*	78 ± 18*	86.5 ± 16.5*	14 ± 4

*L-asparaginase; †prothrombin fragment 1+2 (nanamolar). TAT = thrombin-antithrombin complexes (picomolar).
Reproduced with permission.[388]

Table 8–9   Effect of Untreated Acute Lymphoblastic Leukemia on Components of the Fibrinolytic System

Complexes (units/mL)	Pretreatment at Diagnosis	Post ASP Only	Combination Therapy without ASP	Combination Therapy with ASP	Normal Controls
Plgn	0.96 ± 0.08	0.75 ± 0.10	0.98 ± 0.06	0.88 ± 0.12	0.93 ± 0.02
α₂AP	1.10 ± 0.08	0.93 ± 0.10	1.26 ± 0.08	1.03 ± 0.10	1.01 ± 0.02
TPA	4.6 ± 1.5	—	—	5.8 ± 1.8	4.90 ± 1.00
PAI1	8.0	—	—	8.0	3.60 ± 1.00

ASP = L-asparaginase; Plgn = plasminogen; α₂AP = α₂-antiplasmin; TPA = tissue plasminogen activator; PAI₁ = plasminogen activator inhibitor.
Reproduced with permission.[388]

fibrinogen, and plasminogen are remarkably consistent. Figure 8–8D summarizes the effects of combination chemotherapy with L-asparaginase on hemostasis in the consolidation phase of treatment.[390] Although plasma concentrations of most coagulation proteins decrease, the magnitude is less than for L-asparaginase alone (Figure 8–8B).[390,395] In one study, *Erwinia* L-asparaginase in combination with prednisone did not decrease plasma concentrations of AT.[405] The reported effects of combination chemotherapy on levels of protein C and protein S are variable.[390,392,413,416,420,424] One explanation for the lack of consistency in the literature is the use of control values from adults rather than age-matched values, which are significantly lower throughout childhood.[380] Cyclical L-asparaginase therapy during consolidation also induces a cycling pattern for

plasma concentrations of several coagulation proteins.[399,406]

L-asparaginase and Regulation of Thrombin

During the treatment of children for ALL, there is evidence for three effects: (1) there is increased endogenous generation of thrombin at presentation and for the first several months of therapy; (2) the capacity of plasmas to generate thrombin is not impaired during combination chemotherapy, despite the effects of L-asparaginase on plasma concentrations of several coagulation proteins; (3) there is an acquired (and for some protocols, intermittent) impaired capacity to inhibit thrombin primarily due to acquired AT deficiency.

L-asparaginase and Thromboembolic Events

Based on large studies from the literature, the inci-

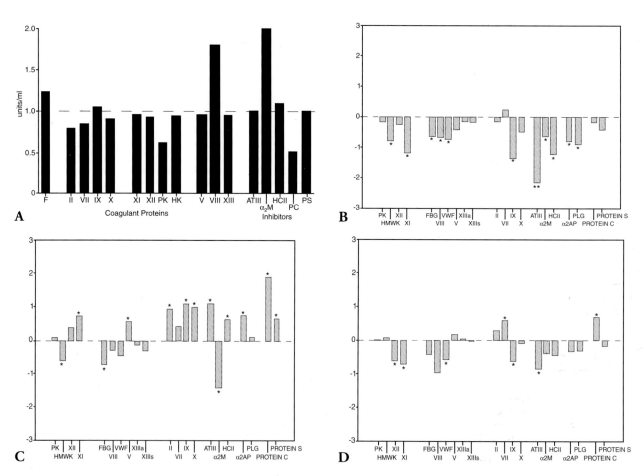

Figure 8–8 Changes in levels of components of hemostasis in children with acute lymphoblastic leukemia with treatment. *Proteins with a statistically significant decrease; **protein with most decrease. *A*, Pretreatment levels; *B*, after L-asparaginase alone; *C*, after combination chemotherapy without L-asparaginase; and *D*, at the end of combination chemotherapy. F = fibrinogen; PK = prekallikrein; HK = high molecular weight kininogen; ATIII = antithrombin; α_2M = α_2-macroglobulin; HCII = heparin cofactor II; PC = protein C; PS = protein S; PLG = plasminogen; α_2AP = α_2-antiplasmin. Reproduced with permission.[549]

dence of TEs ranged from 1.1% to 14.3% (median of 2.6%). Different chemotherapeutic protocols, varying degrees of clinical suspicion for TEs, and choice of diagnostic test contribute to the variability in reports.[425] The true incidence will almost certainly be considerably higher, since insensitive tests were used to diagnose central venous line (CVL)-related TEs when CVLs become blocked.[425] The timing of TEs was very consistent, occurring during or immediately following chemotherapy with L-asparaginase (Figure 8–9).[389,415,417,418,426–428] When L-asparaginase was given during consolidation therapy rather than induction therapy, TEs occurred during consolidation therapy.[390,394] TEs occurred most often in the CNS, two-thirds of which were thrombotic and one-third hemorrhagic. More than one documented VTE event was found in 7% of patients, and 13% had VTE in the lower or upper venous system. The interpretation of these data is limited by the potential for reporting bias of CNS events and the limited reporting of CVL-related TEs.[394,412]

Treatment Therapeutic interventions described in the literature include fresh frozen plasma (FFP), cryoprecipitate, thrombolytic therapy, UFH, OAs, aspirin, and vitamin K. UFH was used primarily for the treatment of VTE outside the CNS, whereas FFP was used primarily for VTE within the CNS. Interestingly, 20 cm^3/kg of FFP does not significantly increase plasma concentrations of coagulation components in children with ALL (Figure 8–10).[429] Two publications reporting the use of AT concentrates in children[430,431] and one in adults[432] were identified. The potential benefits of AT concentrates in children with ALL require testing in a RCT. Morbidity and mortality as a consequence of VTE in children with ALL cannot be accurately assessed.[417,426,435–437] In summary, children with ALL receiving ASP have an increased risk of TE, linked in time to ongoing endogenous generation of thrombin and intermittent but consistent decreases in the capacity to inhibit thrombin.

Current Trials PARKAA (Prophylactic Antithrombin Replacement in Kids with Acute lymphoblastic leukaemia treated with Asparaginase) is a RCT of AT replacement as TE prophylaxis for children with

ALL during L-asparaginase therapy. The trial will be completed in 1999 and form the basis of future intervention trials with AT and anticoagulants in ALL.

Systemic Lupus Erythematosus

Historic Perspective Reports of a circulating lupus anticoagulant (LA) in plasmas from some patients with SLE emerged in the early 1950s.[438,439] The anticoagulant activity was characterized by prolongation of phospholipid-dependent coagulation assays such as the APTT and did not correct with a 1:1 mix with normal plasma. The recognition that there was a strong association between a LA and false positive syphilis tests; the observation that LA activities could be absorbed from plasma by incubation with the cardiolipin portion of the syphillis test (VDRL) was also made in the 1950s.[438,439] The important observation that LA activity was associated with TEs and not bleeding was made in the 1960s.[440–442] When bleeding complications did occur in patients with SLE,[443] thrombocytopenia and acquired prothrombin deficiency were the responsible etiologies.[443] The recognition that there were other antiphospholipid antibodies in patients with SLE resulted in the broader term "antiphospholipid antibodies" (APLA).[449] APLA are a heterogenous group of antibodies that react with proteins (prothrombin, B2-Glycoprotein I) bound to phospholipids.[445,446] APLA can be separated into at least two distinct antibody types: those that interfere with clot-based assays (LA) and those detected in solid phase assays termed APLA, of which the most common is anticardiolipin antibodies (ACLA).[447,448]

Antiphospholipid Antibodies Assays Several phospholipid-dependent laboratory assays were developed or altered to detect APLAs. These assays include the APTT, kaolin clotting time (KCCT), dilute Russell's Viper Venom Test (dRVVT), and dilute PT.[449–452] For each patient, a minimum of three assays are recommended, because no single test will identify all LAs due to the heterogeneity of the antibodies.[453] If the screening test for LA is prolonged, a 1:1 mix should be performed. If the 1:1 mix does not normalize the screening test, a confirmatory assay should be performed. Either activated platelets or hexagonal phase phospholipid can be used as a

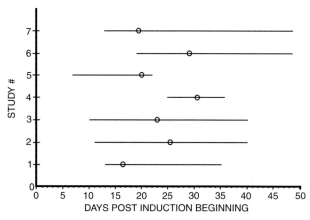

Figure 8–9 Time of occurrence of thromboembolic events following chemotherapy with L-asparaginase treatment in children with acute lymphoblastic leukemia. Reproduced with permission.[388]

confirmatory test. Activated platelets and hexagonal phase phospholipids absorb the LA, thereby permitting the phospholipid component of the coagulation test to provide a surface for coagulation factor assembly to occur.[454,455] The early observation that the APLA reacted with the cardiolipin portion in VDRL reagent led to the development of a radioimmunoassay and subsequently an ELISA for ACLA.[456,457]

Newly Detected Antiphospholipid Antibodies The known family of APLA has been expanded to include a number of other antibodies. The clinical significance of other APLA tests, including antibodies

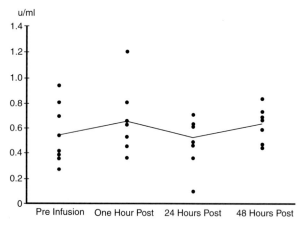

Figure 8–10 Antithrombin levels pre- and post-infusion of 20 mL/kg of fresh frozen plasma. Fresh frozen plasma does not increase the concentration of coagulation proteins in children with acute lymphoblastic leukemia. Reproduced with permission.[388]

against phosphatidylserine (aPS), phosphatidylinositol (aPI), phosphatidic acid (aPA), phosphatidylcholine (aPC), and phosphatidylethanolamine (aPE) has not been established. A recent study evaluated whether multiple APLA tests have enhanced diagnostic value for APLA syndrome. IgG, IgM, and IgA isotypes of aPS, aPI, aPA, aPC, and aPE antibodies were measured by ELISA in 26 SLE patients with clinical manifestations of APS, but negative for both ACLA and LA (group 1). The results were compared with 32 patients with SLE without any features of APLA (group 2) and 24 patients with SLE and ACLA and/or LA (group 3). In group 1, 1 of 26 (4%) was positive for IgA aPE (less frequent than in other groups) and none of the patients had any other APLAs. In group 2, 1 of 32 (3%) was positive for aPS, two (6%) for aPI, one (3%) for aPA, and four (12.5%) for aPE. None was positive for ACLA. In the third group, 13 of 24 (54%) were positive for aPS, 11 (46%) for aPI, 15 (63%) for aPA, 4 (17%) for aPC, and 7 (29%) for aPE. A further 207 SLE patients were tested for aPE. IgG/M/A aPE was found in 6 (3%), 10 (5%), and 21 (10%), respectively, but no association was found between aPE and any clinical features of APS. This study concluded that screening by multiple APLA tests does not increase the diagnostic yield in APLA.[458]

International Recommendations International recommendations for the detection of LAs are that a minimum of three sensitive phospholipid-dependent clotting assays for LA should be measured for each patient.[453,459] If one or more assays are prolonged, a 1:1 mix with normal pooled plasma should be performed. If there is evidence of inhibitory activity on normal pooled plasma, a confirmatory test with activated platelets or hexagonal phospholipids should be performed. ACLA should be measured by ELISA and other coagulopathies should be excluded.

Antiphospholipid Antibodies and Thromboembolic Events in Pediatric Patients In contrast to adults, reports of associations of TE and APLA in children with SLE are relatively rare; nine case series,[460–468] one retrospective study of 120 children in France,[464] and one cross-sectional study of 59 children in two Canadian centers.[469] The nine case reports describe a total of 10 patients ranging in ages from 5 to 17 years, with a median age of 13 years. TEs were located in the deep venous system in eight patients and in the CNS in two patients. The French retrospective study reported that 11 of 120 (9.2%) children with SLE had 16 TEs (10 DVT, 4 PE, and 2 CNS arterial events). TEs occurred early with 7 of 11 children presenting with TEs. Testing for LAs was conducted on one occasion in 111 of 120 patients using the KCCT. Thirty-eight percent of children with a LA also had a TE, compared to only 4% of children who did not have a LA or a TE; the odds ratio was 16. ACLA were not measured.

A cross-sectional study reported 59 children (ages 1 to 19 years) with SLE who had been referred to clinics at two pediatric hospitals. A history, questionnaire, and chart review were completed on all patients by a physician who had no information about the laboratory results. Only TEs that could be substantiated by review of radiographic tests were accepted. Tests for SLE and ACLA antibodies were done prospectively on two occasions at least 3 months apart. Assays to detect a LA included a KCCT, an APTT, a dRVVT, and a dPT.[469] The KCCT and APTT were performed neat and also following a 1:1 mixture with pooled normal plasma. Both dRVVT assays were initially performed with phospholipids sensitive to the LA and repeated with phospholipids insensitive to the LA. Detection and quantitation of IgG and IgM ACLA were performed by ELISA. Patients were considered to be positive if one or more tests were positive on both occasions. Thirteen TEs occurred in 10 of the 59 patients. The LA was present on one occasion in 10 of the 59 patients (17%) and on two occasions, at least 3 months apart, in a further 14 patients (24%), for a total incidence of 41% (Table 8–10). The LA was present in all 10 patients with a TE, on one occasion in 2 patients, and on two occasions in 8 patients. The two patients with TEs developed their TE after becoming positive for a LA and remained positive for a LE subsequently. The relationship between the presence of TEs and presence of LAs on one or more occasions was highly significant ($p < .001$), odds ratio of 141 (95%; confidence interval: 11.4-oo) (Table 8–10). The strength of this relationship was increased when data were analyzed for patients in whom the LA was present on two occasions ($p < .001$), odds ratio of 28.7 (95% confidence interval 4.03–138.2). The relationship between the individual LA assays and TEs is shown in Table 8–11. The dPT was the most sensitive test, detecting all 10 patients with TEs, followed by the APTT, which detected 4 of the 10 patients. The KCCT and dRVVT were the least sensitive tests. The odds ratio for ACLA antibodies and TEs was 2.12 (95%; confidence interval 0.71–22.8; $p = .08$).

Treatment with Anticoagulants General guidelines for treatment of TEs with UFH (Chapter 9)

Table 8–10 Relationship between Persistent Presence of a Lupus Anticoagulant, Anticardiolipin Antibodies, and a Combination of a Lupus Anticoagulant and Anticardiolipin Antibodies in Pediatric Patients with Systemic Lupus Erythematosus

Assay	Number of Thromboembolic Events		Odds Ratio (95% CI)	Significance (p)
	Positive	Negative		
Lupus anticoagulant				
Positive	8	6	28.7 (4.03–138.17)	< .001
Negative	2	43		
Anticardiolipin antibodies				
Positive	4	7	2.12 (0.71–22.8)	.08
Negative	6	42		
Lupus anticoagulant and Anticardiolipin antibody				
Positive	4	4	7.5 (1.16–52.1)	.022
Negative	6	45		

CI = confidence interval.

Reproduced with permission.[469]

and OAs (Chapter 10) should be followed for children with SLE and a TE. However, the LA may interfere with the coagulation tests used to monitor both UFH and OAs, and alternative strategies for monitoring may be required. First, some, but not all, APTT reagents are sensitive to LAs. Either an insensitive APTT reagent or a heparin assay should be used to monitor UFH therapy. If an APTT reagent sensitive to LA is used, it will be prolonged into the therapeutic range, when in fact the UFH concentration is subtherapeutic, and the patient is left at risk for extension of the TE. Similarly, when OAs are used, prior testing should be performed to determine if the LA interferes with the PT system. If the LA does interfere with the PT, then plasma concentrations of prothrombin can be used for monitoring OA therapy. A concentration between 0.20 and 0.30 units/mL corresponds approximately to an INR of 2 to 3. The duration of therapy is a contentious issue, even for adult patients, with mixed recommendations in the literature.[470–474] One approach to children with TE and APLA is to treat them for 6 months following the initial event, and then consider either discontinuing therapy with careful follow-up or the use of low-dose OAs, which presents a small risk for bleeding and provides some protection for recurrent disease. A child with SLE and APLA who has had two TEs should be considered for lifelong anticoagulant therapy. In summary, children with SLE and persistence of a LA have a 16- to 25-fold greater risk of TEs than children with SLE and no LA.[469] Current multicenter RCTs examining the effectiveness of primary and secondary anticoagulant prophylaxis will provide important information to improve the care of these patients.

Clinical Trials There is an ongoing, multicenter, multinational RCT assessing the role of OAs in patients (adults and children) who have SLE and a LA but have not had a TE. This trial will clarify the role of anticoagulants in these patients.

Antiphospholipid Antibody Syndrome

General Information APLA syndrome refers to patients who have APLA but do not fulfill the diagnostic criteria for SLE. The APLA syndrome is very well described in adults and is associated with recurrent TEs and recurrent fetal loss.

Antiphospholipid Antibody Syndrome in Newborns Theoretically, APLA syndrome may occur in newborns following placental transmission of IgG APLA antibodies from an affected mother. There are five cases of cerebral infarction reported in newborns in association with increased plasma concentrations of maternal ACLA.[475,476] However, recent cohort and case control studies have reported no increase in neonatal complications for infants born to APLA positive mothers, with the exception of increased risk of prematurity, 14% and 21% of infants, respectively, in the two studies.[477,478]

Neonatal SLE is characterized by persistent congenital complete heart block, often without any other structural heart defects. There is a close relation between neonatal SLE and maternal anti-Ro/La antibodies.[479] These antibodies are responsible for the destruction of the bundle of His and the AV node in the fetus, causing irreversible damage to the cardiac conduction system due to the transplacental passage of maternal antibodies to the fetus, resulting in heart failure in some newborns, while others are asymptomatic.[480,481] Total AV block is seen in 1 of 15,000 to 22,000 liveborn children, and 70% to

Table 8–11   Associations between Lupus Anticoagulant Tests and Thrombosis

Thrombosis	Dilute Prothrombin		Dilute APTT		dRVVT†		dRVVT Ionophore-Treated Platelets		Kaolin Clot	
	Positive	Negative	Positive	Negative	Positive	Negative	Positive	Negative	Positive	Negative
Positive	8	2	4	6	2	8	1	9	2	8
Negative	4	45	2	47	1	48	1	8	3	46

APPT = activated partial thromboplastin; dRVVT = dilute Russell's Viper Venom test.
Reproduced with permission.[469]

90% of these are caused by neonatal SLE. More than half of children with congenital heart block need pacemaker therapy shortly after birth. The others should be monitored for signs of incompensation.[479] One review article gave a mortality rate from complete congenital heart block at 31%.

A recent study looked at congenital heart block in patients included in a national neonatal lupus registry.[482] Isolated congenital heart block detected before birth is strongly associated with maternal autoantibodies to 49-kD SSB/La, 52-kD SSA/Ro, and 60 kD SSA/Ro ribonucleoproteins, and is a permanent manifestation of neonatal lupus syndromes. One hundred and thirteen infants were diagnosed with congenital heart block between 1970 and 1997 (56 boys and 57 girls). Bradyarrhythmia was detected before 30 weeks gestational age in 71 (82%, median 23 weeks). In no cases were major congenital cardiac anatomic defects considered causal for the development of congenital heart block. Twenty-two (19%) of the 113 children died, 16 (73%) within 3 months of birth. Cumulative probability of 3-year survival was 79%. Sixty-seven (63%) of cases required pacemakers: 35 within 9 days of life, 15 within 1 year, and 17 after 1 year of life. This large series substantiates that autoantibody-associated congenital heart block is not coincident with major structural abnormalities, is most often identified in the late second trimester, carries a substantial mortality in the neonatal period, and frequently requires pacing. Close echocardiographic monitoring of the fetal heartbeat, with heightened surveillance between 18 and 24 weeks of gestation, is required in all pregnant women in order to detect this disorder in utero.[482,483]

A case report followed an infant from the 25th week of gestation with fetal echocardiography due to heart enlargement, percardial effusion, and moderate insufficiency of the mitral and tricuspid valves. The child was delivered at 37 weeks of gestation and required pacing, supportive care, and steroid treatment.[484]

Treatment is required before heart failure develops.[480] Treatment strategies include prophylactic therapy for high-risk pregnant women and a combination of intrauterine plasmapheresis with plasma exchange or corticosteroids. Pacemaker insertion is required in most infants during the first 3 months of life.[480] Assays for anti-Ro (SSA) and anti-La (SSB)

antibodies should be performed on the sera of pregnant women with SLE.

Antiphospholipid Antibody Syndrome in Children

There are increasing numbers of case reports of children who appear to have APLA, evidenced by the presence of TEs and APLAs without the other diagnostic criteria for SLE. Some studies have reported that up to one-third of children with a TE have circulating APLAs, and up to two-thirds of children with idiopathic cerebral ischemia fulfill the criteria for the diagnosis of APLA.[485–489] However, whether APLA positivity in these children is causally related to the TEs or is an epiphenomenon is unknown. APLA positivity is also reported in children with partial epileptic seizures with normal neuroimaging studies, sickle cell anemia, idiopathic intracranial hypertension, migraine, hemolytic uremic syndrome, acute myeloid leukemia, and Tourette syndrome.[490–495]

A recent study assessed the prevalence of APLA in 203 children and adolescents aged 0.1 to 21 years (median 6 years) with a variety of medical conditions. The investigators measured IgG and IgM antibodies directed against cardiolipin, phosphatidylserine, and phosphatidic acid. The children were placed in five groups that reflected their primary diseases. Group I was comprised of 10 patients with autoimmune and autoimmune-like diseases; group II was comprised of 88 patients with infections; group III was comprised of 20 patients with metabolic diseases; group IV was comprised of 65 children with various other diseases; and group V was comprised of 20 healthy children without physical illnesses. APLAs were detected in 65 of 203 patients. In all groups of patients, the prevalence of APLAs was increased compared with healthy children. The highest prevalence of APLAs was found in patients with autoimmune or autoimmune-like diseases or infections (group I). TEs did not occur in children with increased concentrations of APLAs. Bleeding occurred in 4 of 65 patients with detectable APLAs. However, three of the four children had additional coagulation abnormalities.[502] Further well-designed studies are required to determine whether APLAs have a causal role in the pathogenesis of these childhood illnesses or are merely an epiphenomenon. Potentially, specific types of APLA may be predictive of TEs, particularly for childhood stroke. Further studies are required to determine the role of APLA in a variety of diseases that do not include SLE and APLA syndrome.

Thromboembolic Events in Sickle Cell Disease

Pertubations of Hemostasis Vascular occlusion leading to tissue ischemia and necrosis cause most of the morbidity and mortality associated with sickle cell disease (SCD).[497] There is increasing evidence that the in vivo generation of thrombin and activation of platelets may contribute to this process. The hemostatic abnormalities described in patients with SCD include moderate thrombocytosis[498,499] with decreasing platelet counts during crisis,[497] evidence for platelet activation,[498,500–504] increased plasma concentrations of both FVIII and vWF,[501,505–509] decreased plasma concentrations of FXI, FXII, protein C, the free form of protein S,[504,510–512] and increased plasma concentrations of TAT, and F1.2.[513]

Thromboembolic Events TEs likely contribute to vascular occlusion in SCD, which is characterized by stroke, acute chest syndrome,[514–516] pulmonary hypertension,[517–525] and deep vein thrombosis (DVT).[510,526] Although anticoagulants present an attractive form of therapy, there is minimal information on the efficacy or safety of anticoagulants in children with SCD.[527] The role of thrombolytic agents remains even more controversial than anticoagulants.

Stroke Ischemic stroke occurs in approximately 10% of children with SCD and is a significant cause of morbidity.[528–530] Ischemic stroke is usually a result of occlusion of large intracranial arteries, most commonly the intracranial internal carotid artery, proximal portions of the middle cerebral, and anterior cerebral arteries.[514] Pathologically, the lesions are characterized by stenotic arterial lesions with fibrotic scars, possibly from incremental thrombus formation with incorporation of sickled erythrocytes.[529] The clinical presentation reflects the site of the occlusion. Hemorrhagic stroke often occurs later and is usually related to previous occlusive vasculopathy or, less commonly, a ruptured aneurysm.[528]

Treatment of Ischemic Stroke Ischemic stroke in SCD is effectively treated by exchange transfusion[531] or simple transfusion.[532] The risk of recurrent stroke in the absence of any intervention is between 50% and 90% over 10 years.[528] Periodic long-term transfusion has reduced the risk of recurrent ischemic stroke to 10% or less.[531] Currently, there are studies assessing prevention of stroke by using transcranial Doppler ultrasound, which can detect stenosis (associated with the majority of patients at risk for cerebral infarction).[533,534]

Paroxysmal Nocturnal Hemoglobinuria

General Information PNH is an acquired disorder of hemopoietic stem cells,[535] due to a somatic mutation of the phosphatidylinositol glycan class A (PIG A) gene located on the X chromosome. To date, 84 separate mutations in the PIG A gene, mostly deletion or insertion mutations, have been described in association with PNH.[535] The PIG A gene is involved in the synthesis of the glycosyl phosphatidylinositol (GPI) anchor, to which many cell surface proteins are attached. Proteins known to be deficient on abnormal PNH cells include complement defense proteins, such as the decay-accelerating factor (DAF, CD55) and membrane inhibitor of reactive lysis (MIRL, CD59), enzymes (for example, acetylcholinesterase), receptors (for example, UK receptor), and proteins of unknown function, such as CD66.[541]

Paroxysmal Nocturnal Hemoglobinuria in Children PNH is a rare disease that usually presents in adulthood. Several large studies have reported 12% to 21% of cases occurring in children.[542–544] The diagnosis is frequently delayed, with mean time to diagnosis being 19 months in both adults and children.[543] There are significant differences in the natural history of PNH in children versus adults.[543] PNH classically presents in adults as hemolytic anemia associated with nocturnal exacerbations of hemoglobinuria (50% of cases), but this presentation is seen in only 15% of children. The most common presentation in children is bone marrow failure (50% of children versus 25% of adults). Anemia is commonly associated with macrocytosis in children.[543]

Diagnosis A positive Ham's test is required for the diagnosis of PNH.[542] The sucrose test has been used in conjunction with the Ham's test.[544] Recently, flow cytometry studies of erythrocytes or granulocytes have been found to be more specific, quantitative, and sensitive than the tests for PNH that depend on hemolysis.[545-547]

Thrombotic complications TEs are a major complication of PNH and reported incidence rates are 39% of adults and 31% of children.[542-544,548-550] The cumulative incidence increases with duration of follow-up and may be as high as 50% after 15 years.[542] The TEs are usually venous and frequently involve the hepatic veins (Budd-Chiari syndrome), CNS, portal veins, and peripheral venous systems.[542,543,548,549,551] TEs are also a common cause of death in patients with PNH. Primary prophylactic anticoagulation with OAs has been recommended, although bleeding complications are frequent.[549] No fibrinolytic or coagulation abnormalities have been documented in PNH, although increased circulating activated platelets are implicated in the TE risk.[552] Median survivals are approximately 10 to 15 years in a number of studies.[542,543,548,549] Bone marrow transplantation is the only curative treatment and may result in resolution of progressive hepatic venous TEs.[553] Spontaneous remissions occur in 15% of patients.[549]

REFERENCES

1. Schmidt B, Andrew M. Neonatal thrombosis: report of a prospective Canadian and International registry. Pediatrics 1995;96:939–43.
2. Wright N, Blanch B, Walkinshaw S, Pelling DW. Antenatal and neonatal renal vein thrombosis: new ultrasonic features with high frequency transducers. Pediatr Radiol 1996;26:686–9.
3. Haffner D, Wuhl E, Zieger B, et al. Bilateral renal venous thrombosis in a neonate associated with resistance to activated protein C. Pediatr Nephrol 1996;10:737–9.
4. Murray JC, Dorfman SR, Brandt ML, Dreyer ZE. Renal vein thrombosis complicating acute myeloid leukemia with hyperleucocytosis. J Pediatr Hematol Oncol 1996;18:327–30.
5. Formstone CJ, Hallam PJ, Tuddenham IG, et al. Severe perinatal thrombosis in double and triple heterozygous offspring of a family segregating two independent protein S mutatuions and a protein C mutation. Blood 1996;87:3731–7.

6. Tinaztepe K, Buyan N, Tinaztepe B, Akkok N. The association of nephrotic syndrome and renal vein thrombosis: a clinicopathological analysis of eight pediatric patients. Turkish J Pediatr 1989;31:1–18.
7. Nuss R, Hays T, Manco-Johnson M. Efficacy and safety of heparin anticoagulation for neonatal renal vein thrombosis. Am J Pediatr Hematol Oncol 1994;16:127–31.
8. Duncan BW, Adzick NS, Longaker MT, et al. In utero arterial embolism from renal vein thrombosis with successful postnatal thrombolytic therapy. J Pediatr Surg 1991;26:741–3.
9. Nowak-Gottl U, Schwabe D, Schneider W, et al. Thrombolysis with recombinant tissue-type plasminogen activator in renal venous thrombosis in infancy. Lancet 1992;340:1105
10. Rosenberg ER, Trought WS, Kirks DR, et al. Ultrasonic diagnosis of renal vein thrombosis in neonates. AJR 1980;134:35–8.
11. Gonzalez R, Schwartz S, Sheldon CA, Fraley EE. Bilateral renal vein thrombosis in infancy and childhood. Symposium on Urologic Emergencies 1982;9:279–83.
12. Jie KS, Bots ML, Vermeer C, et al. Vitamin K status and bone mass in women with or without aortic atherosclerosis: a population-based study. Calcif Tissue Int 1996;59:352–6.
13. Trattnig S, Frenzel K, Eilenberger M, et al. Acute renal vein thrombosis in children. Early detection with duplex and colour-coded Doppler ultrasound. Ultraschall in der Medizin 1993;14:40–3.
14. Nowak-Gottl U, von Kries R, Gobel U. Neonatal symptomatic thromboembolism in Germany: two year survey. Arch Dis Child 1997;76:F163–7.
15. Klinge J, Scharf J, Rupprecht T, et al. Selective thrombolysis in a newborn with bilateral renal venous and cerebral thrombosis and heterzygous APC resistance. Nephrol Dial Transplant 1998;13:3205–7.
16. Hibbert J, Howlett DC, Greenwood KL, et al. The ultrasound appearances of neonatal renal vein thrombosis. Br J Radiol 1997;70:1191–4.
17. Pohl M, Zimmerhackl LB, Hausser I, et al. Acute bilateral renal vein thrombosis complicating Netherton syndrome. Eur J Pediatr 1998;157:157–60.
18. Pohl M, Zimmerhackl B, Heinen F, et al. Bilateral renal vein thrombosis and venous sinus thrombosis in a neonate with FV mutation (FV Leiden). J Pediatr 1998;132:159–61.
19. Cozzolino DJ, Cendron M. Bilateral renal vein thrombosis in a newborn: a case of prenatal renal vein thrombosis. Urology 1997;50:128–31.
20. Alon U, Kodroff M, Broecker B, Kirkpatrick B. Renal tubular acidosis type 4 in neonatal unilateral kidney diseases. J Pediatr 1984;104:855–60.

21. Al-Samarrai S, Kato A, Urano Y. Renal vein thrombosis in stillborn infant of diabetic mother. Acta Pathol Jpn 1984;34:1441–7.

22. Bidgood WJ, Cuttino JJ, Clark F, Volberg F. Pyelovenous and pyelolymphatic backflow during retrograde pyelography in renal vein thrombosis. Invest Radiol 1981;16:13–9.

23. Brill P, Jagannath A, Winchester P, et al. Adrenal hemorrhage and renal vein thrombosis in the newborn: MR imaging. Radiology 1989;170:95–8.

24. Bromberg WD, Firlit CS. Fibrinolytic therapy for renal vein thrombosis in the child. J Urol 143:86–8.

25. Clark A, Saunders A, Bewick M, et al. Neonatal inferior vena cava and renal venous thrombosis treated by thrombectomy and nephrectomy. Arch Dis Child 1985;60:1076–7.

26. Cremin B, Davey H, Oleszczuk-Raszke K. Neonatal renal venous thrombosis: sequential ultrasonic appearances. Clin Radiol 1991;44:52–5.

27. Demirci A, Selcuk M, Yazicioglu I. Bilateral adrenal hemorrhage associated with bilateral renal vein and vena cava thrombosis. Pediatr Radiol 1991;21:130–1.

28. Duncan B, Adzick N, Longaker M, et al. In utero arterial embolism from renal vein thrombosis with successful postnatal thrombolytic therapy. J Pediatr Surg 1991;26:741–3.

29. Gonzalez R, Schwartz S, Sheldon C, Fraley E. Bilateral renal vein thrombosis in infancy and childhood. Urol Clin North Am 1982;9:279–83.

30. Jayogapal S, Cohen H, Brill P, et al. Calcified neonatal renal vein thrombosis demonstration by CT and US. Pediatr Radiol 1990;20:160–2.

31. Jobin J, O'Regan S, Demay G, et al. Neonatal renal vein thrombosis—long term follow-up after conservative management. Clin Nephrol 1982;17:36–40.

32. Kirks D, Rosenberg E, Johnson D, King L. Integrated imaging of neonatal renal masses. Pediatr Radiol 1985;147–56.

33. Lam A, Warren P. Ultrasonographic diagnosis of neonatal renal venous thrombosis. Ann Radiol (Paris) 1980;7–12.

34. Levine C. Intestinal obstruction in a neonate with adrenal hemorrhage and renal vein thrombosis. Pediatr Radiol 1989;19:477–8.

35. Lebowitz J, Belman A. Simultaneous idiopathic adrenal hemorrhage and renal vein thrombosis in the newborn. J Urol 1983;129:574–6.

36. Mocan H, Beattie T, Murphy A. Renal venous thrombosis in infancy: long-term follow-up. Pediatr Nephrol 1991;5:45–9.

37. Rogers P, Silva M, Carter J, Wadsworth L. Renal vein thrombosis and response to therapy in a newborn due to protein C deficiency. Eur J Pediatr 1989;149:124–5.

38. Sanders L, Jequier S. Ultrasound demonstration of prenatal renal vein thrombosis. Pediatr Radiol 1989;19:133–5.

39. Veiga P, Springate J, Brody A, et al. Coexistence of renal vein thrombosis and adrenal hemorrhage in two newborns. Clin Pediatr 1992;31:174–6.

40. Llach F, Papper S, Massry SG. The clinical spectrum of renal vein thrombosis: acute and chronic. Am J Med 1980;69:819–27.

41. Mocan H, Beattie TJ, Murphy AV. Renal venous thrombosis in infancy: long-term follow-up. Pediatr Nephrol 1991;5:45–9.

42. LeBlanc J, Culham J, Chan K, et al. Treatment of grafts and major vessel thrombosis with low-dose streptokinase in children. Ann Thorac Surg 1986;41:630–5.

43. Reimold E, Wittel R. Renal venous thrombosis in children: changes in management. South Med J 1983;76:1277–84.

44. Arneil GC, MacDonald AM, Murphy AV, Sweet EM. Renal venous thrombosis. Clin Nephrol 1973;1:119–31.

45. Evans DJ, Silverman M, Bowley NB. Congenital hypertension due to unilateral renal vein thrombosis. Arch Dis Child 1981;56:306–8.

46. Alexander F, Campbell WAB. Congenital nephrotic syndrome and renal vein thrombosis in infancy. J Clin Pathol 1971;24:27–40.

47. Miller RA, Tremann JA, Ansell JS. The conservative management of renal vein thrombosis. J Urol 1974;111:568–571.

48 Duncan RE, Evans AT, Martin LW. Natural history and treatment of renal vein thrombosis in children. J Pediatr Surg 1977;12:639–45.

49. Metreweli C, Pearson R. Echographic diagnosis of neonatal renal venous thrombosis. Pediatr Radiol 1984;14:105–8.

50. Ricci M, Lloyd D. Renal venous thrombosis in infants and children. Arch Surg 1990;125:1195–9.

51. Oppenheimer DA, Carroll BA, Garth KE, et al. Ultrasonic detection of complications following umbilical arterial catheterization in the neonate. Radiology 1982;145:667.

52. Rasoulpour M, McLean RH. Renal venous thrombosis in neonates. Initial and follow-up abnormalities. Am J Dis Child 1980;134:276–9.

53. Nazer H, Rajab AA, Qaryouti S, et al. Neonatal limb gangrene and renal vein thrombosis. Case report with review of literature. Eur J Pediatr 1987;146:429–31.

54. Munoz-Anizpe R, Walsh RF, Edge W. Obstructive aortic and renal thrombosis in the newborn-spontaneous recovery. Pediatr Nephrol 1992;6:190–1.

55. Moore HL, Katz R, McIntosh R, et al. Unilateral renal vein thrombosis and the nephrotic syndrome. Pediatrics 1972;50:598–608.

56. Waymack JP, Tweddell JS, Warden GD. Renal vein thrombosis in burned children. J Burn Care Rehabil 1988;9:472–3.

57. Trygstad CW, McCabe E, Francyk WP, Crummy AB. Renal vein thrombosis and the nephrotic syndrome: a case report with protein selectivity studies. J Pediatr 1970;76:861–6.

58. Tinaztepe K, Buyan N, Tinaztepe B, Akkok N. The association of nephrotic syndrome and renal vein thrombosis: a clinicopathological analysis of eight pediatric patients. Turk J Pediatr 1989;31:1–18.

59. Mettler FAJ, Christie JH. The scintigraphic pattern of acute renal vein thrombosis. Clin Nucl Med 1980; 5:468–70.

60. Starinsky R, Graif M, Lotan D, Kessler A. Thrombus calcification of renal vein in neonate: ultrasound and CT diagnosis. J Comput Assist Tomogr 1989;13:545–6.

61. Sfakianakis GN, Zilleruelo G, Thompson T, et al. Tc-99m glucoheptonate scintigraphy in a case of renal vein thrombosis. Clin Nucl Med 1985;10:75–9.

62. Rosenberg ER, Trought WS, Kirks DR, et al. Ultrasonic diagnosis of renal vein thrombosis in neonates. Am J Roentgenol 1980;134:35–8.

63. Touloukian RJ. Idiopathic vena caval thrombosis with renal infarction in the newborn infant: survival following nephrectomy. Surgery 1969;65:978–83.

64. Vogelzang RL, Moel DI, Cohn RA, et al. Acute renal vein thrombosis: successful treatement with intraarterial urokinase. Radiology 1988;169:681–2.

65. Tekinalp G, Oran O, Erturk G, Yetgin S. Renal and axillary thrombosis in an infant of a diabetic mother. Turk J Pediatr 1986;28:191–4.

66. Smith JA, Lee RE, Middleton RG. Hypertension in childhood from renal vein thrombosis. J Urol 1978;122:389–90.

67. Yazbeck S, Danais S, O'Regan S. Nephrosis with varicocele: probable renal vein thrombosis. Eur Urol 1985;11:215–6.

68. Thompson IM, Schneider R, Lababidi Z. Thrombectomy for neanatal renal vein thrombosis. J Urol 1975;113:396–9.

69. Valderrama E, Gribetz I, Strauss L. Peripheral gangrene in a newborn infant associated with renal and adrenal vein thrombosis. Report of a case in an offspring of a diabetic mother. J Pediatr 1972;80:101–3.

70. Sutton TJ, Leblanc A, Gauthier N, Hassan M. Radiological manifestations of neonatal renal vein thrombosis on follow-up examinations. Pediatric Radiology 1977;122:435–8.

71. Renfield ML, Kraybill EN. Consumptive coagulopathy with renal vein thrombosis. J Pediatr 1973;82:1054–6.

72. Schreier RW, Gardenswartz MH. Renal vein thrombosis. Postgrad Med 1980;67:83–93.

73. Oliver WJ, Kelsch RC. Renal venous thrombosis in infancy. Pediatr Rev 1982;4:61–6.

74. Belman AB. Renal vein thrombosis in infancy and childhood. A contemporary survey. Clin Pediatr 1976;15:1033–44.

75. Stark H. Renal vein thrombosis in infancy. Am J Dis Child 1964;108:430–5.

76. Vorlicky LN, Balfour HHJ. Cytomegalovirus and renal vein thrombosis in a newborn infant. Am J Dis Child 1974;127:742–4.

77. Seeler RA, Kapadia P, Moncado R. Nonsurgical management of thrombosis of bilateral renal veins and inferior vena cava in a newborn infant. Clin Pediatr 1970;9:543–7.

78. Lowry MF, Mann JR, Abrams LD, Chance GW. Thrombectomy for renal venous thrombosis in infant of diabetic mother. BMJ 1970;3:687.

79. Roy CC, Bedard G, Bonenfant J, Fortin R. Congental nephrosis associated with thrombosis of the inferior vena cava and of the right renal vein in a six-week-old premature infant. Can Med Assoc J 1964;90:786–9.

80. Asherson RA, Lanham JF, Hull RF, et al. Renal vein thrombosis in systemic lupus erythematosus: association with the lupus anticoagulant. Clin Exp Rheumatol 1984;2:75–9.

81. Coleman CC, Saxena K, Johnson KW. Renal vein thrombosis in a child with the nephrotic syndrome: CT diagnosis. Am J Roentgenol 1980;135:1285–6.

82. Ellis D. Recurrent renal vein thrombosis and renal failure associated with antithrombin III deficiency. Pediatr Nephrol 1992;6:131–4.

83. Bowen AD, Smazal SF. Ultrasound of coexisting right renal vein thrombosis and adrenal hemorrhage in a newborn. J Clin Ultrasound 1981;9:511–3.

84. Fielding GA, Masel J, Leditschke JF. Spontaneous neonatal renal vein thrombosis. Aust N Z J Surg 1986;56:485–8.

85. Glassock RJ, Duffy J, Kodroff MB, Chan JCM. Dehydration, renal vein thrombosis, hyperkalemic renal tubular acidosis in a newborn. Am J Nephrol 1983;3:329–37.

86. Goldman RS, Kettwich DL, Woodside JR, Borden TA. Mild unilateral proteinuria and renal vein thrombosis associated with oral contraceptive usage. Am J Kidney Dis 1983;2:471–3.

87. Greene A, Cromie WJ, Goldman M. Computerized body tomography in neonatal renal vein thrombosis. Urology 1982;20:213–5.

88. Kauffmann RH, De Fraeff J, De La Riviere GB. Unilateral renal vein thrombosis and nephrotic syndrome: report of a case with protein selectivity and antithrombin III clearance studies. Am J Med 1976; 60:1048–54.

89. Lalmand B, Avni EF, Nasr A, et al. Perinatal renal vein thrombosis. J Ultrasound Med 1990;9:437–42.

90. Lewy PR, Jao W. Nephrotic syndrome in association with renal vein thrombosis in infancy. J Pediatr 1974;85:359–65.

91. Belman AB, King LR. The pathology and treatment of renal vein thrombosis in the newborn. J Urol 1972;107:852–5.

92. Belman AB, Susmano DF, Burden JJ, Kaplan GW. Non-operative treatment of unilateral renal vein thrombosis in the newborn. JAMA 1970;211:1165–8.

93. Fraley EE, Najarian JS. Treatment of renal vein thrombosis in the newborn. JAMA 1980;212:1377a.

94. Jones JE, Reed JF. Renal vein thrombosis and thrombocytopenia in a newborn infant. J Pediatr 1965;67:691.

95. Mauer SM, Fraley EE, Fish AJ, Najarian JS. Bilateral renal vein thrombosis in infancy: report of a survivor following surgical intervention. J Pediatr 1971;78:509–12.

96. Keating MA, Althausen AF. The clinical spectrum of renal vein thrombosis. J Urol 1985;133:938–45.

97. Johannessen JV. Renal vein thrombosis: report of a case with ultrastructural findings and critical evaluation of the literature. Arch Pathol Lab Med 1974;97:277–83.

98. Hartman GE, Shochat SJ. Abdominal mass lesions in the newborn: diagnosis and treatment. Clin Perinatol 1989;16:123–35.

99. Fourman J, Moffat DB. The blood vessels of the kidney. Oxford: Blackwell Scientific Publications, 1972.

100. Hollinshead WH, McFarlane JA. The collateral venous drainage from the kidney following occlusion of the renal vein in the dog. Surg Gyn Obstet 1953;97:213.

101. Ahlberg NE, Bartley O, Chidekel N. Right and left gonadal veins. An anatomical and statistical study. Acta Radiol [Diagn] 1966;4:593.

102. Harris JD, Ehrenfeld WK, Lee JC, Wylie EJ. Experimental renal vein occlusion. Surg Gynecol Obstet 1968;126:555.

103. Koehler PR, Bowles WT, McAlister WH. Renal arteriography in experimental renal vein occlusion. Radiology 1966;86:851.

104. Crummy AB, Hipona FA. The roentgen diagnosis of renal vein thrombosis; experimental aspects. Am J Roentgenol 1965;93:898.

105. Rowntree LG, Fitz R, Geraghty JT. The effects of experimental chronic passive congestion on renal function. Arch Intern Med 1913;11:121.

106. Kanfer A, Kleinknecht D, Broyer M, Josso F. Coagulation studies in 45 cases of nephrotic syndrome without uremia. Thromb Diath Haemorrh 1970;24:562–71.

107. Said R, Hamzeh Y. Digital subtraction venography in the diagnosis of renal vein thrombosis. Am J Nephrol 1991;11:305–8.

108. Bunchman TE. Pediatric hemodialysis lessons from the past, ideas for the future. Kidney Int 1998;53:S64–S67.

109. Blowey DL, McFarland K, Alon U, et al. Peritoneal dialysis in the neonatal period: outcome data. J Perinatol 1993;13:59–64.

110. Zobel G, Trop M, Muntean W, et al. Anticoagulation for continuous arteriovenous hemofiltration in children. Blood Purif 1985;6:90–5.

111. Lumsden AB, MacDonald MJ, Allen RC, Dodson TF. Hemodialysis access in the pediatric patient population. Am J Surg 1994;168:197–201.

112. Bunchman TE. Pediatric hemodialysis: lessons from the past, ideas for the future. Kidney Int Suppl 1996;53:s64–7.

113. Kjellstrand CM, Merino GE, Mauer SM, et al. Complications of percutaneous femoral vein catheterizations for hemodialysis. Clin Nephrol 1975;4:37–40.

114. Zobel G, Rodl S, Urlesberger R, et al. Continuous renal replacement therapy in critically ill patients. Kidney Int 1998;66:S169–73.

115. Bagolan P, Spagnoli A, Ciprandi G, et al. A ten-year experience of Brescia-Ciminio arteriovenous fistulas in children: technical evolution and refinements. J Vasc Surg 1998;27:640–4.

116. van Bilijon I, van Damme-Lombaerts R, Demol A, et al. Low molecular weight heparin for anticoagulation during haemodialysis in children: a preliminary study [letter]. Eur J Radiol 1996;155:70–1.

117. Fijnvandraat K, Nurmohamed M, Peters M, et al. A cross-over dose finding study investigating a low molecular weight heparin (Fragmin®) in six children on chronic hemodialysis. Thromb Haemost 1993;69a.

118. Geary DF, Gajaria M, Fryer-Keene S, Willumsen J. Low-dose and heparin-free hemodialysis in children. Pediatr Nephrol 1991;5:220–4.

119. Rodkin RS, Bookstein JJ, Heeney DJ, Davis GB. Streptokinase and transluminal angioplasty in the treatment of acutely thrombosed hemodialysis access fistulas. Radiology 1983;149:425–8.

120. Young AT, Hunter DW, Castaneda-Zuniga WR, et al. Thrombosed synthetic hemodialysis access fistulas: failure of fibrinolytic therapy. Radiology 1985;154:639–42.

121. Abejo RC, John EG, Spigos DG. Low-dose streptokinase-induced clot lysis of an occluded arteriovenous fistula. J Pediatr 1985;106:321–3.

122. Churchill BM, Sheldon CA, McLorie GA, Arbus GS. Factors influencing patient and graft survival in 300 cadaveric pediatric renal transplants. J Urol 1988;140:1129–33.

123. Vester U, Offner G, Hayer PF, et al. End-stage renal failure in children younger than 6 years: renal transplantation is the therapy of choice. Eur J Pediatr 1998;157:239–242.

124. Sheldon CA, Churchill BM, McLorie GA, Arbus GS. Evaluation of factors contributing to mortality in pediatric renal transplant recipients. J Pediatr Surg 1992;27:629–33.

125. Harmon WE, Stablein D, Alexander SR, Tejani A. Graft thrombosis in pediatric renal transplant recipients. A report of the North American Pediatric Renal Transplant Cooperative Study. Transplantation 1991;51: 406–12.

126. Valdez R, Munoz R, Bracho E, et al. Surgical complications of renal transplantation in malnourished children. Transplant Proc 1994;26:50–1.

127. Broyer M, Mitsioni A, Gagnadoux MF, et al. Early failures of kidney transplantation: a study of 70 cases from 801 consecutive grafts performed in children and adolescents. Adv Nephrol 1993;22:169–91.

128. Kalicinski P, Kaminski A, Prokural A, et al. Surgical complications after kidney transplantation in children. Transplant Proc 1994;26:42–3.

129. Broyer M. Kidney transplantation in children-data from the EDTA registry. Transplant Proc 1989;21:1985–8.

130. Harmon WE, Stablein D, Alexander SR, Tejani A. Graft thrombosis in pediatric renal transplant recipients. Transplantation 1991;51:406–12.

131. McEnery PT, Stablein DM, Arbus G, Tejani A. Renal transplantation in children. A report of the North American Pediatric Renal Transplant Cooperative Study. N Engl J Med 1992;326:1727–32.

132. Singh A, Stablein D, Tejani A. Risk factors for vascular thrombosis in pediatric renal transplantation: a special report of the North American Renal Transplant Cooperative Study. Transplantation 1997;63:1263–7.

133. Salvatierra O, Singh T, Shifrin R, et al. Successful transplantation of adult sized kidneys into infants requires maintenance of high aortic blood flow. Transplantation 1998;66:819–23.

134. Vaidya S, Wang CC, Gugliuzza C, Fish JC. Relative risk of post transplant renal thrombosis in patients with antiphospholipid antibodies. Clin Transpl 1998;12: 439–44.

135. Mutze S, Turk I, Schonberger B, et al. Colour coded duplex sonography in the diagnostic assessment of vascular complications after kidney transplantation in children. Pediatr Radiol 1997;27:898–902.

136. Alkhunaizi AM, Olyaei AJ, Barry JM, et al. Efficacy and safety of low molecular weight heparin in renal transplantation. Transplantation 1998;66:533–4.

137. Ismail H, Kalicinski P, Drewniak T, et al. Primary vascular thrombosis after renal transplantation in children. Pediatr Transpl 1997;1:43–7.

138. Humar A, Johnson EM, Payne WD, et al. The acutely ischemic extremity after kidney transplant: an approach to management. Surgery 1998;123:344–50.

139. Hamilton H, Pontin AR, Manas D, et al. Venous thrombectomy in patients presenting with iliofemoral vein thrombosis after renal transplantation. Transpl Int 1996;9:513–6.

140. Aufricht C, Kitzmuller E, Wandl-Vergesslchk A, et al. Use of prostaglandin I2 in 3 small children at high risk of early graft thrombosis. Pediatr Nephrol 1996;10:86–7.

141. Cameron JS, Ogg CS, Ellis FG, Salmon MA. Femoral artery thrombosis and intermittent claudication in childhood nephrotic syndrome. Arch Dis Child 1971;46:215–6.

142. Cameron JS. Coagulation and thromboembolic complications in the nephrotic syndrome. In: Grunfeldt BB, Maxwell MA, eds. Advances in nephrology. Chicago: Year Book Medical Publishers, 1991.

143. Harrison BM, Wood CB. Spontaneous femoral artery thrombosis and intermittent claudication in childhood nephrotic syndrome. Am J Dis Child 1972;47: 836–7.

144. Mahan JD, Mauer SM, Sibley RK, Vernier RL. Congenital nephrotic syndrome: evolution of medical management and results of renal transplantation. J Pediatr 1984;105:549–57.

145. Mehls O, Andrassy K, Koderisch J, et al. Hemostasis and thromboembolism in children with nephrotic syndrome: differences from adults. J Pediatr 1987;110:862–7.

146. Kim MS, Stablein D, Harmon WE. Renal transplantation in children with congenital nephrotic syndrome: a report of the North American Pediatric Renal Transplant Cooperative Study (NAPRTCS). Pediatr Transpl 1998;2:305–8.

147. de Saint-Martin A, Terzic J, Christmann D, et al. Superior sagittal sinus thrombosis and nephrotic syndrome: favorable outcome with low molecular weight heparin. Arch de Pediat 1997;4:849–52.

148. Tsai M, Wu TJ, Teng RJ, et al. Mesenteric arterial thrombosis complicating congenital nephrotic syndrome of the Finnish type: report of a case. Chung Hua Min Kuo Hsiao Er h Ko i Hsueh Hui Tsa Chih 1995;36:445–7.

149. Egli F, Elminger P, Stalder G. Thrombosis as a complication of nephrotic syndrome. Helv Paediatr Acta 1973;30:20–1.

150. Yoshioka K, Miyata H, Uraoka Y, Maki S. Plasma factor XIII levels in children with renal disease. Nephron 1981;27:19–24.

151. Ueda N, Chihara M, Kawaguchi S, et al. Intermittent versus long-term tapering prednisone for initial therapy in children with idiopathic nephrotic syndrome. J Pediatr 1988;112:122–6.

152. Ueda N, Kawaguchi S, Niinomi Y, et al. Effect of corticosteroids on coagulation factors in children with nephrotic syndrome. Pediatr Nephrol 1987;1: 286–289.

153. Maffel FHA, Macedo CS, Lastoria S, et al. Arterial thrombosis following femoral venipuncture in untreated nephrotic children. J Cardiovasc Surg 1979; 20:389–91.

154. Caliskan S, Sever L, Sarioglu A, et al. Superior vena cava syndrome as a result of thrombosis in a child with nephrotic syndrome. Turk J Pediatr 1997;39:561–4.

155. Fabri D, Belangero VM, Annichino-Bizzacchi JM, Arruda VR. Inherited risk factors for thrombophilia in children with nephrotic syndrome. Eur J Pediatr 1998;157:939–42.

156. Fofah O, Roth P. Congenital nephrotic syndrome presenting with cerebral venous thrombosis, hypocalcemia, and seizures in the neonatal period. J Perinatol 1997;17:492–494.

157. Kandler C, Ries M, Rupprecht T, et al. Successful systemic low dose lysis of a caval thrombus by rt-PA in a neonate with congenital nephrotic syndrome. J Pediatr Hematol Oncol 1997;19:348–50.

158. Calishan S, Sever L, Serioglu A, et al. Superior vena cava syndrome as a result of thrombosis in a child with nephrotic syndrome. Turk J Pediatr 1997;39:561–4.

159. Hanna J, Truemper E, Burton E. Superior vena cava syndrome and chylothorax: relationship in pediatric nephrotic syndrome. Pediatr Nephrol 1997;11:20–2.

160. Anand NK, Chand G, Talib VH, et al. Hemostatic profile in nephrotic syndrome. Ind Pediatr 1996;33:1005–12.

161. Divekar AA, Ali US, Ronghe MD, et al. Superior sagittal thrombosis in a child with nephrotic syndrome. Pediatr Nephrol 1996;10:206–7.

162. Kandler C, Ries M, Ruppricht T, et al. Successful systemic low dose lysis of a caval thrombus by rt-PA in a neonate with congenital nephrotic syndrome. J Perinatol 1997;12:492–4.

163. Jarmolinski T, Maciejewski J. Intra-cardiac thrombi in nephrotic syndrome. Nephrol Dial Transplant 1997;12:1299–300.

164. Yeroniahu T, Shalev H, Landau D, Dvilansky A. Protein C and S in pediatric nephrotic patients. Sangre 1996;41:155–7.

165. Hanevold CD, Lazarchick J, Constantin MA, et al. Acquired free protein S deficiency in children with steroid resistant nephrosis. Ann Clin Lab Sci 1996;23:279–82.

166. Zimmerman RL, Novek S, Chen JTT, Roggli V. Pulmonary thrombosis in a 10-year-old child with minimal change disease and nephrotic syndrome. A clinical, radiologic, and pathologic correlation with literature review. Am J Clin Pathol 1994;101:230–6.

167. Kallen RJ, Lee S. A study of the plasma kinin-generating system in children with the minimal lesion, idiopathic nephrotic syndrome. Pediatr Res 1975;9:705–9.

168. Zimmerman RL, Novek S, Chen JT, Roggli V. Pulmonary thrombosis in a 10-year-old child with minimal change disease and nephrotic syndrome. Am J Clin Pathol 1994;101:230–6.

169. Jones GL, Hebert D. Pulmonary thrombo-embolism in the nephrotic syndrome. Pediatr Nephrol 1991;5:56–8.

170. Mahan JD, Mauer SM, Sibley RK, Vernier RL. Congenital nephrotic syndrome: evolution of medical management and results of renal transplantation. J Pediatr 1984;105:549–57.

171. Schneller M, Braga SE, Moser H, et al. Congenital nephrotic syndrome: clinicopathological heterogeneity and prenatal diagnosis. Clin Nephrol 1983;19:243–9.

172. Craig AR, Brocklebank JT. Oral anticoagulation nephrotic syndrome. Arch Dis Child 1996;75:462–3.

173. Natelson EA, Lynch EC, Hettig RA, Alfrey CP. Acquired factor IX deficiency in the nephrotic syndrome. Ann Intern Med 1970;73:373–8.

174. Garbrecht F, Gardner S, Johnson V, Grabowski E. Deep venous thrombosis in a child with nephrotic syndrome associated with a circulating anticoagulant and acquired protein S deficiency. Am J Pediatr Hematol Oncol 1991;13:330–3.

175. Thomson C, Forbes CD, Prentice CRM, Kennedy AC. Changes in blood coagulation and fibrinolysis in the nephrotic syndrome. QJM 1974;171:399–407.

176. Thrompson AR. Factor XII and other hemostatic protein abnormalities in nephrotic syndrome patients. Thromb Haemost 1982;48:27–32.

177. Mehis O, Andrassy K, Koderisch J, et al. Hemostasis and thromboembolism in children with nephrotic syndrome: differences from adults. J Pediatr 1987;110:862–7.

178. Saito S, Goodnough LT, Makker SP, Kallen R. Urinary excretion of hageman factor (factor XII) and the presence of nonfunctional hageman factor in the nephrotic syndrome. Am J Med 1981;70:531–4.

179. Wei LQ, Rong ZK, Gui L, Shan RD. CT diagnosis of renal vein thrombosis in nephrotic syndrome. J Comput Assist Tomogr 1991;15:454–7.

180. Wagoner RD, Stanson AW, Holley KE, Winter CS. Renal vein thrombosis in idiopathic membranous glomerulopathy and nephrotic syndrome: incidence and significance. Kidney Int 1983;23:368–74.

181. Hoyer PF, Gonda S, Barthels M, et al. Thromboembolic complications in children with nephrotic syndrome. Acta Paediatr Scand 1986;75:804–10.

182. Huttunen NP. Congenital nephrotic syndrome of Finnish type. Arch Dis Child 1976;51:344–8.

183. Kauffman RH, Keltkamp JJ, van Tilburg NH, van Es LA. Acquired antithrombin III deficiency and thrombosis in the nephrotic syndrome. Am J Med 1978;65:607–13.

184. de Saint-Martin A, Terzic J, Christmann D, et al. Superior sagittal sinus thrombosis and nephrotic syndrome: favorable outcome with low molecular weight heparin. Arch Pediatr 1997;4:849–52.

185. Jarmolinski T, Zachwieja J, Bortkiewicz E, et al. Thrombo-embolic disease as a complication of nephrotic syndrome in children. Pediatr Pol 1996; 71:437–41.

186. Schlegel N. Thromboembolic risks and complications in nephrotic children. Semin Thromb Hemost 1997; 23:271–80.

187. Oikawa T, Muramatsu Y, Akashi S, Usui N. A coagulation of fibrinolytic study in children with nephrotic syndrome: evaluation of hypercoagulability by measuring with plasmin-alpha$_2$ plasmin inhibitor complex and FDP D-dimer. Nippon Jinzo Gakkai Shi 1997;39:144–9.

188. Garbrecht F, Gardner S, Johnson V, Grabowski E. Deep venous thrombosis in a child with nephrotic syndrome associated with a circulating anticoagulant and acquired protien S deficiency. Am J Pediatr Hematol Oncol 1991;13:330–3.

189. Lieberman E, Heuser E, Gilchrist GS, et al. Thrombosis, nephrosis, corticosteroid therapy. J Pediatr 1968; 73:320–8.

190. Jorgensen KA, Stoffersen E. Antithrombin III and the nephrotic syndrome. Scand J Haematol 1979;22: 442–8.

191. Remuzzi G, Mecca G, Marchesi D, et al. Platelet hyper-aggregability and the nephrotic syndrome. Thromb Res 1979;16:345–54.

192. Negrier C, Delmas MC, Ranchin B, et al. Decreased factor XII activity in a child with nephrotic sydrome and thromboembolic complications. Thromb Haemost 1991;66:512–3.

193. Stuart MJ, Spitzer RE, Nelson DA, Sills RH. Nephrotic syndrome: increased platelet prostaglandin endoperoxide formation, hyperaggregability, and reduced platelet life span. Reversal following remission. Pediatr Res 1980;14:1078–81.

194. Vigano-D'Angelo S, D'Angelo A, Kaufman CE, et al. Protein S deficiency occurs in the nephrotic syndrome. Ann Intern Med 1987;107:42–7.

195. Elidrissy ATH, Gader AMA. Antithrombin III (ATIII) and fibrinogen levels in nephrotic syndrome in children. Haemostasis 1985;15:384–8.

196. Beaufils F, Schlegel N, Loirat C, et al. Urokinase treatment of pulmonary artery thrombosis complicating the pediatric nephrotic syndrome. Crit Care Med 1985;13:132–134.

197. De Mattia D, Penza R, Giordano P, et al. Thromboembolic risk in children with nephrotic syndrome. Haemostasis 1991;21:300–4.

198. Honig GR, Lindley A. Deficiency of Hageman factor (factor XII) in patients with nephrotic syndrome. J Pediatr 1971;78:633–7.

199. Adhikari M, Coovadia M, Greig HB, Christensen S. Factor VIII procoagulant activity in children with nephrotic syndrome and post-streptococcal glomerulonephritis. Nephron 1978;22:301–5.

200. Lau SO, Tkachuck JY, Haegawa DK, Edson JR. Plasminogen and antithrombin III deficiencies in the childhood nephrotic syndrome associated with plasminogenuria and antithrombinuria. J Pediatr 1980;96:390–2.

201. Tarry S, Moser AJ, Makhoul RG. Peripheral arterial thrombosis in the nephrotic syndrome. Surgery 1993;114:618–23.

202. Alkjaersig N, Fletcher AP, Narayanan M, Robson AM. Course and resolution of the coagulopathy in nephrotic children. Kidney Int 1987;31:772–80.

203. Boneu B, Bouissou F, Abbal M, et al. Comparison of progressive antithrombin activity and the concentration of three thrombin inhibitors in nephrotic syndrome. Thromb Haemost 1981;46:623.

204. Vermylen C, Levin M, Lanham J, et al. Decreased sensitivity to heparin in vitro in steroid-responsive nephrotic syndrome. Kidney Int 1987;31:1396–401.

205. Ogunbiyi OA. Renal vein thrombosis in patients with nephrotic syndrome: CT diagnosis. Afr J Med Med Sci 1995;24:33–40.

206. Yermiahu T, Shalev H, Landau D, Dvilansky A. Protein C and protein S in pediatric nephrotic patients. Sangre 1996;41:155–7.

207. Brodehl J. The treatment of minimal change nephrotic syndrome: lessons learned from multicentre cooperative studies. Pediatrics 1991;150:380–7.

208. Vernier RL, Klein DJ, Sisson SP, et al. Heparin sulfate-rich anionic sites in the human glomerular basement membrane. Decreased concentration in congenital nephrotic syndrome. N Engl J Med 1983; 309:1001–9.

209. Mahan JD, Mauer SM, Nevins TE. The Hickman catheter: a new hemodialysis access device for infants and small children. Kidney Int 1983;24:694–7.

210. Offner G, Hoyer PF, Latta K, et al. One year's experience with recombinant erythropoietin in children undergoing continuous ambulatory or cycling peritoneal dialysis. Pediatr Nephrol 1990;4:498–500.

211. Andrassy K, Ritz E, Bommer J. Hypercoagulability in the nephrotic syndrome. Klin Wochenschrift 1980; 58:1029–36.

212. Kanfer A, Kleinknecht D, Broyer M, Josso F. Coagulation studies in 45 cases of nephrotic syndrome without uremia. Thromb Diath Haemorrh 1970;24:562–71.

213. Yoshioka K, Miyata H, Uraoka Y, Maki S. Plasma factor XIII levels in children with renal disease. Nephron 1982;27:19–24.

214. Lafave MS, Decter RM. Intravesical urokinase for the management of clot retention in boys. J Urol 1993; 150:1467–8.

215. Lau SO, Bock GH, Edson JR, Michael AF. Sagittal sinus thrombosis in nephrotic syndrome. J Pediatr 1980; 97:948–50.

216. Llach F, Koffler A, Finck E, Massry SG. On the incidence of renal vein thrombosis in the nephrotic syndrome. Arch Intern Med 1977;137:333–6.

217. Kuhlmann U, Steurer J, Bollinger A, et al. Incidence and clinical significance of thromboses and thrombo-embolic complications in nephrotic syndrome patients. Schweiz Med Wochenschr 1981;111:1034–40.

218. Llach F. Thromboembolic complications in nephrotic syndrome. Coagulation abnormalities, renal vein thrombosis, other conditions. Postgrad Med J 1984; 76:111–123.

219. Chugh K, Malik N, Uberoi H, et al. Renal vein thrombosis in nephrotic syndrome—a prospective study and review. Postgrad M J 1981;57:566–70.

220. Wei LQ, Rong ZK, Gui L, Shan RD. CT diagnosis of renal vein thrombosis in nephrotic syndrome. J Comput Assist Tomogr 1991;15:454–7.

221. Liu Y, Wang HY, Pan JS. Renal vein thrombosis in nephrotic syndrome: a prospective study of 54 cases. Chung Hua Nei Tsa Chih 1989;28:250–1.

222. Thompson AR. Factor XII and other hemostatic protein abnormalities in nephrotic syndrome patients. Thromb Haemost 1982;48:28–32.

223. Hruby MA, Honig GR, Shapira E. Immunoquantitation of Hageman factor in urine and plasma of children with nephrotic syndrome. J Lab Clin Med 1980;96:501–2.

224. Asami T, Ohsawa S, Tomisawa S, et al. Glomerular deposition of alpha2-macroglobulin in a child with steriod refractory nephrotic syndrome. Nephron 1992; 61:211–3.

225. Vaziri ND. Nephrotic syndrome and coagulation and fibrinolytic abnormalities. Am J Nephrol 1983;3: 1–6.

226. Stuart MJ, Spitzer R, Nelson DA, Sills RH. Nephrotic syndrome: increased platelet prostaglandin endoperoxide formation, hyperaggregability, and reduced plateled life span. Reversal following remission. Pediatr Res 1980;14:1078–81.

227. Schieppati A, Dodesini P, Benigni A. The metabolism of arachidonic acid by platelets in nephrotic syndrome. Kidney Int 1984;25:671–6.

228. Zitelli BJ, Malatack JJ, Gartner JC, et al. Evaluation of the pediatric patient for liver transplantation. Pediatrics 1986;78:559–65.

229. Starzl TE, Esquivel C, Gordon R, Todo S. Pediatric liver transplantation. Transplant Proc 1987;19:3230–5.

230. Rehan V, Seshia MM. Complications of umbilical vein catheter. Eur J Pediatr 1994;153:141–2.

231. Kooiman AM, Kootstra G, Zwierstra RP. Portal hypertension in children due to thrombosis of the portal vein. Neth J Surg 1982;43:97–103.

232. Schwartz DS, Gettner PA, Konstantino MM, et al. Umbilical venous catheterization and the risk of portal vein thrombosis. J Pediatr 1997;131:760–2.

233. Brady L, Magilavy D, Black DD. Portal vein thrombosis associated with antiphospholipid antibodies in a child. J Pediatr Gastroenterol Nutr 1996;23:470–3.

234. Arav-Boger R, Reif S, Bujanover Y. Portal vein thrombosis caused by protein C and protein S deficiency associated with cytomegalovirus infection. J Pediatr 1995;126:586–8.

235. Skarsgard E, Doski J, Jaksic T, et al. Thrombosis of the portal venous system after splenectomy for pediatric hematologic disease. J Pediatr Surg 1993;28:1109–12.

236. Laishram H, Cramer B, Kennedy R. Idiopathic acute portal vein thrombosis: a case report. J Pediatr Surg 1993;28:1106–8.

237. Arnold KE, Char G, Serjeant GR. Portal vein thrombosis in a child with homozygous sickle-cell disease. West Ind Med J 1993;42:27–8.

238. Wilson KW, Robinson DC, Hacking PM. Portal hypertension in childhood. Br J Surg 1969;56:13–22.

239. Kowal-Vern A, Radhakrishnan J, Goldman J, et al. Mesenteric and portal vein thrombosis after splenectomy for autoimmune hemolytic anemia. J Clin Gastroenterol 1988;10:108–10.

240. Harper PL, Luddington RJ, Carrell RW, et al. Protein C deficiency and portal thrombosis in liver transplantation in children. Lancet 1988;2:924–7.

241. Macpherson AIS. Portal hypertension due to extrahepatic portal venous obstruction. J Royal Coll Surg (Edin) 1984;29:4–10.

242. Pinkerton JA, Holcomb GW, Foster JH. Portal hypertension in childhood. Ann Surg 1972;175:870–886.

243. Chardot C, Herrera JM, Debray D, et al. Portal vein complications after liver transplantation for biliary atresia. Liver Transpl Surg 1997;3:351–8.

244. Superina RA, Pearl RH, Roberts EA, et al. Liver transplantation in children: the initial Toronto experience. J Pediatr Surg 1989;24:1013–9.

245. Saad S, Tanaka K, Inomata Y, et al. Portal vein reconstruction in pediatric liver transplantation from living donors. Ann Surg 1998;227:275–81.

246. Gollin G, Ward B, Meier GB, et al. Central spanchnic venous thrombosis. Often unsuspected, usually uncomplicated. J Clin Gastroenterol 1994;18:109–13.

247. Belli L, Puttini M, Marni A. Extrahepatic portal obstruction. J Cardiovasc Surg 1980;21:439–48.

248. Harkanyi Z, Temesi M, Varga G, Weszelits V. Duplex ultrasonography in portal vein thrombosis. Surg Endo 1989;3:79–82.

249. Stringer D, Krysl J, Manson D, et al. The value of Doppler sonography in the detection of major vessel

thrombosis in the neonatal abdomen. Pediatr Radiol 1990;21:30–3.

250. Levy HM, Newhouse JH. MR imaging of portal vein thrombosis. AJR 1988;151:283–6.

251. Lee WB, Wong KP. CT demonstration of thrombosis of the portal venous system. Australas Radiol 1988; 32:360–4.

252. Burdelski M, Schmidt K, Hoyer R, et al. Liver transplantation in children: The Hannover experience. Transplant Proc 1987;19:3277–81.

253. Vacanti JP, Lillehei CW, Jenkins RL, et al. Liver transplantation in children: the Boston center experience in the first 30 months. Transplant Proc 1987;19: 3261–6.

254. Esquivel CO, Koneru B, Karrer F, et al. Liver transplantation before 1 year of age. J Pediatr 1987;110:545–8.

255. De Gaetano AM, Lafortune M, Patriquin H, et al. Cavernous transformation of the portal vein: patterns of intrahepatic and splanchnic collateral circulation detected with Doppler sonography. AJR 1995;165: 1151–5.

256. Silver MM, Bohn D, Shawn DH, et al. Association of pulmonary hypertension with congenital portal hypertension in a child. J Pediatr 1992;120:321–9.

257. Rehan VK, Cronin CM, Bowman JM. Neonatal portal vein thrombosis successfully treated by regional streptokinase infusion. Eur J Pediatr 1994;153:456–9.

258. Boles ET, Wise WE, Birken G. Extrahepatic portal hypertension in children. Am J Surg 1986;151:734–9.

259. Dilawari JB, Chawla YK. Spontaneous (natural) splenoadrenorenal shunts in extrahepatic portal venous obstruction: a series of 20 cases. Gut 1987;28:1198–200.

260. Karrer FM, Holland RM, Allshouse MJ, Lilly JR. Portal vein thrombosis: treatment of variceal hemorrhage by endoscopic variceal ligation. J Pediatr Surg 1994;29:1149–51.

261. Pieters PC, Dittrich J, Prasadu U, Berman W. Acute Budd-Chiari syndrome caused by percutaneous placement of a transhepatic inferior vena cava catheter. J Vasc Intervent Radiol 1997;8:587–90.

262. Altunas B, Yarali N, Kuyucu S, et al. Budd-Chiari syndrome in a child secondary to membranous obstruction of the hepatic vein treated by percutaneous transluminal angioplasty. Report of a case. Turk J Pediatr 1997;39:551–5.

263. Yonekura T, Kubota A, Hoki M, et al. Intermittent obstruction of the inferior vena cava by congenital anteromedial diaphragmatic hernia: an extremely rare case of Budd-Chiari syndrome in a child. Surgery 1998;124:109–111.

264. Kukner S, Altuntas B, Sasica B, Tezic T. A case of Budd-Chiari syndrome with protein C deficiency. Eur J Pediatr 1997;156:342.

265. Graham ML, Rosse WF, Halperin EC, et al. Resolution of Budd-Chiari syndrome following bone marrow transplantation for paroxysmal nocturnal haemoglobinuria. Br J Haematol 1996;92:707–10.

266. Sawamura R, Fernandes MIM, Galvao LC, Goldani HAS. Report of two cases of children with Budd-Chiari syndrome succesfully treated with streptokinase. Pediatr Gastroenterol 1996;33:179–81.

267. Saca LF, Szer IS, Henar E, et al. Budd-Chiari syndrome associated with antiphospholipid antibodies in a child: report of a case and review of the literature. J Rheumatol 1994;21:545–8.

268. Lerut J, Gordon R, Tzakis A, et al. The hepatic artery in orthotopic liver transplantation. Helv Chir Acta 1988;55:367–78.

269. Mazzaferro V, Esquivel CO, Makowka L, et al. Hepatic artery thrombosis after pediatric liver transplantation. A medical or surgical event? Transplantation 1980;47:971–7.

270. Mitchell L, Superina R, Delorme M, et al. Circulating dermatan sulphate/heparin sulfate proteoglycan(s) in children undergoing liver transplantation. Thromb Haemost 1995;74:859–63.

271. Rela M, Muiesan P, Baker A, et al. Hepatic artery thrombosis after liver transplantation in children under 5 years of age. Transplantation 1995;61:1355–7.

272. Jurim O, Csete M, Gelabert HA, et al. Reduced size grafts: The solution for hepatic artery thrombosis after pediatric liver transplantation. J Pediatr Surg 1995;30:533–55.

273. Dunn SP, Billmire DF, Falkensein K, et al. Rejection after pediatric liver transplantation is not the limiting factor to survival. J Pediatr Surg 1994;29:1141–3.

274. Drazan K, Shaked A, Olthoff KM, et al. Etiology and management of symptomatic adult hepatic artery thrombosis after orthotopic liver transplantation (OLT). Am Surg 1996;62:237–40.

275. Esquivel CO, Jaffee R, Gordon RD, et al. Liver rejection and its differentiation from other causes of graft dysfunction. Semin Liver Dis 1985;5:369–74.

276. Hashikura Y, Kawasaki S, Okumura N, et al. Prevention of hepatic artery thrombosis in pediatric liver transplantation. Transplantation 1995;60:1109–12.

277. Dalen K, Day DL, Ascher NL, et al. Imaging of vascular complications after hepatic transplantation. Am J Roentgenol 1988;150:1285–90.

278. Flint E, Sumkin J, Zajko A, Bowen A. Duplex sonography of hepatic artery thrombosis after liver transplantation. Am J Roentgenol 1988;151:481–83.

279. Hall T, McDiarmid S, Grant E, Boechat M, et al. False-negative duplex Doppler studies in children

with hepatic artery thrombosis after liver transplantation. Am J Roentgenol 1990;154:573–5.

280. Segel MC, Zajko AB, Bowen A, et al. Doppler ultrasound as a screen for hepatic artery thrombosis after liver transplantation. Transplantation 1986;41:539–41.

281. Parient D, Urvoas S, Riou JY, et al. Imaging of complications of liver transplantation in children. Ann Radiol (Paris) 1994;37:372–6.

282. Legmann P, Costes V, Tudoret L, et al. Hepatic artery thrombosis after liver transplantation: diagnosis with spiral CT. Am J Roentgenol 1995;164:97–101.

283. Sanchez-Bueno F, Robles R, Ramirez P, et al. Hepatic artery complications after liver transplantation. Clin Transpl 1994;8:399–404.

284. Figueras J, Busquets J, Dominguez J, et al. Intra-arterial thrombolysis in the treatment of acute hepatic artery thrombosis after liver transplantation. Transplantation 1995;59:1356–7.

285. Hidalgo E, Abad J, Cantarero J, et al. High-dose intra-arterial urokinase for the treatment of hepatic artery thrombosis in liver transplantation. Hepatogastroenterology 1989;36:529–32.

286. Sarfati PO, Boillot O, Baudin F, et al. Surgical thrombectomy and in situ fibrinolysis for acute hepatic artery thrombosis in pediatric liver transplantation. Ann Chir 1992;46:605–9.

287. Tan KC, Yandza T, de Hemptinne B, Clapuyt PA. Hepatic artery thrombosis in pediatric liver transplantation. J Pediatr Surg 1988;23:927–30.

288. Tisone G, Gunson BK, Buckels JAC, MacMaster P. Raised hematocrit, a contributing factor to hepatic artery thrombosis following liver transplantation. Transplantation 1988;46:162–3.

289. Todo S, Makowka L, Tzakis AG, et al. Hepatic artery in liver transplantation. Transplant Proc 1987;19:2406–11.

290. Dotter CTJ, Rosch AJ, Seamen A. Selective clot lysis with low dose streptokinase. Radiology 1984;111:31–7.

291. Katzen BT. Technique and results of 'low dose' infusion. Cardiovasc Intervent Radiol 1988;11:41–7.

292. Leaker M, Superina R, Andrew M. Fibrin clot lysis by tissue plasminogen activator (tPA) is impaired in plasma from pediatric liver transplant patients. Transplantation 1995;60:144–7.

293. Yanaga K, Makowka L, Starzl T. Is hepatic artery thrombosis after liver transplantation really a surgical complication? Transplant Proc 1989;21:3511–3.

294. Bearman S. The syndrome of hepatic veno-occlusive disease after marrow transplantation. Blood 1995;85:3005–23.

295. McDonald G, Hinds M, Fisher L, et al. Veno-occlusive disease of the liver and multiorgan failure after bone marrow transplantation: a cohort study of 355 patients. Ann Intern Med 1993;118:255–67.

296. McDonald G, Sharma P, Matthews D, et al. Venocclusive disease of the liver after bone marrow transplatation: diagnosis, incidence, and predisposing factors. Hepatology 1984;4:16–22.

297. Jones R, Lee K, Veschorner W, et al. Venocclusive desease of the liver following bone marrow transplantation. Transplantation 1987;44:778–83.

298. Bearman S, Hinds M, Wolford JL, et al. A pilot study of continuous infusion heparin for the prevention of hepatic venocclusive disease after bone marrow transplantation. Bone Marrow Transplant 1990;5:407–11.

299. Marsa-Vila L, Gorin N, Laport J, et al. Prophylactic heparin does not prevent liver veno-occlusive disease following autologous bone marrow transplantation. Eur J Haematol 1991;47:346–54.

300. Attal M, Huguet F, Rubie H, et al. Prevention of hepatic veno-occlusive disease after bone marrow transplantation by continuous infusion of low-dose heparin: a prospective, randomized trial. Blood 1992;79:2834–40.

301. Cahn J, Flesch M, Brion A, et al. Prevention of veno-occlusive disease of the liver after bone marrow transplantation: heparin or no heparin? Blood 1992;80:2149–50.

302. Gluckman E, Jolivet I, Scrobohaci M, et al. Use of prostaglandin E1 for prevention of liver veno-occlusive disease in leukaemic patients treated by allogeneic bone marrow transplantation. Br J Haematol 1990;74:277–81.

303. Bearman S, Shen D, Hinds M, et al. A phase I/II study of prostaglandin E1 for the prevention of hepatic venocclusive disease after bone marrow transplantation. Br J Haematol 1993;84:724–30.

304. Essell J, Schroeder M, Thompson J, et al. A randomized double-blind of prophylactic urosdeoxycholic acid vs placebo to prevent venocclusive disease of the liver in patients undergoing allogeneic bone marrow transplantation. Blood 1994;84(suppl 1):250a.

305. Essell J, Thompson J, Harman G, et al. Pilot trial of prophylactic ursodiol to decrease the incidence of veno-occlusive disease of the liver in allogeneic bone marrow transplant patients. Bone Marrow Transplant 1992;10:367–72.

306. Han J, Thompson P, Beutler B. Dexamethasone and pentoxifylline inhibit endotoxin-induced cachetin/tumor necrosis factor synthesis at separate points in the signaling pathway. J Exp Med 1990;172:391–4.

307. Bianco J, Appelbaum F, Nemunitis J, et al. Phase I-II trial of pentoxifylline for the prevention of transplant-related toxicities following bone marrow transplantation. Blood 1991;78:1205–11.

308. Busca A, Vivenza C, Vassalo E, et al. Continuous intravenous pentoxifylline in children undergoing bone marrow transplantation. Blood 1992;80 (suppl 1):237a.

309. Copelan E, Avalos B, Klein J, et al. Reduction in the incidence of transplant related death using methotrexate, cyclosporine and pentoxifylline compared to cyclosporine and methylprednisolone for prevention of graft versus host disease following conditioning with BuCy. Blood 1992;80 (suppl):236a.

310. Attal M, Huguet F, Rubie J, et al. Prevention of regimen-related toxicities after bone marrow transplantation by pentoxifylline: a prospective, randomized trial. Blood 1993;82:732–6.

311. Clift R, Bianco J, Appelbaum F, et al. A randomized controlled trial of pentoxifylline for the prevention of regimen-related toxicities in patients undergoing allogeneic marrow transplantation. Blood 1993;82:2025–30.

312. Hagglund H, Remberger M, Klaesson S, et al. Norethisterone treatment, a major risk factor for veno-occlusive disease in the liver after allogeneic bone marrow transplantation. Blood 1998;92:4568–72.

313. Rosenthal J, Sender L, Secola R, et al. Phase II trial of heparin prophylaxis for veno-occlusive disease of the liver in children undergoing bone marrow transplantation. Bone Marrow Transplant 1996;18:185–91.

314. Bearman S, Shuhart M, Hinds M, McDonald G. Recombinant human tissue plasminogen activator for the treatment of established severe venocclusive disease of the liver after bone marrow transplantation. Blood 1992;80:2458–62.

315. Bearman SI, Lee JL, Baron AE, McDonald GB. Treatment of hepatic veno-occlusive disease with recombinant human tissue plasminogen activator and heparin in 42 marrow transplant patients. Blood 1997;89:1501–6.

316. Patton DF, Harper JL, Wooldridge TN, et al. Treatment of veno-occlusive disease of the liver with bolus tissue plasminogen activator and continuous infusion of antithrombin III concentrate. Bone Marrow Transplant 1996;17:443–7.

317. Seibold-Weiger K, Vochem M, Mackensen-Haen S, Speer C. Fatal hepatic veno-occlusive disease in a newborn infant. Am J Perinatol 1997;14:107–11.

318. Gertsch P, Matthews J, Lerut J, et al. Acute thrombosis of the splanchic veins. Arch Surg 1993;128:341–5.

319. Simpson WG, Schwartz RW, Strodel WE. Spenic vein thrombosis. South Med J 1990;83:417–21.

320. Vos LJM, Potocky V, Broker FWL, et al. Splenic vein thrombosis with oesophageal varices. A late complication of umbilical vein catheterization. Ann Surg 1974;180:152–6.

321. Ritchey ML, Lally KP, Haase GM. Superior mesenteric artery injury during nephrectomy for Wilms' tumor. J Pediatr Surg 1992;27:612–5.

322. Al Neimi K, Boulet E, Imbaud P. Thrombosede l'artere mesenterique superieure et perforation appendiculaire chez une jeune fille. Ann Chir 1990;44:524–6.

323. Talbot RW, Heppell J, Dozois RR. Vascular complications of inflammatory bowel disease. Mayo Clin Proc 1986;61:140–5.

324. Russell JYW, Newman BM. Mesenteric vascular occlusion. JR Coll Surg Edinb 1982;27:264–8.

325. Andrew M, David M, Adams M, et al. Venous thromboembolic complications (VTE) in children: first analyses of the Canadian Registry of VTE. Blood 1994;83:1251–7.

326. Monagle P, Adams M, Mahoney M, et al. Long term outcome of pediatric thromboembolic disease: a report from the Canadian Childhood Thrombophilia Registry. Blood 1999 (in press).

327. deVeber G, Adams M, Andrew M, Canadian Pediatric Neurologists. Canadian Pediatric Ischemic Stroke Registry. Analysis III. Thromb Haemost 1995;73a.

328. Chan AKC, Coppes M, Adams M, Andrew M. Right atrial thrombosis in pediatric patients: analysis of the Canadian registry of venous thromboembolic complications. Pediatr Res 1997;39:154a.

329. Ross PJ, Ehrenkranz R, Kleinman CS, Seashore JH. Thrombus associated with central venous catheters in infants and children. J Pediatr Surg 1989;24:253–6.

330. Berman WJ, Fripp RR, Yabek SM, et al. Great vein and right atrial thrombosis in critically ill infants and children with central venous lines. Chest 1991;99:963–7.

331. Wacker P, Oberhansli I, Didier D, et al. Right atrial thrombosis associated with central venous catheters in children with cancer [review]. Med Pediatr Oncol 1994;22:53–7.

332. Korones DN, Buzzard CJ, Asselin BL, Harris JP. Right atrial thrombi in children with cancer and indwelling catheters. J Pediatr 1996;128:841–6.

333. Fontan F, Baudet E. Surgical repair of tricuspid atresia. Thorax 1971;26:240–8.

334. Driscoll DJ, Offord KP, Feldt RH, et al. Five to fifteen year follow-up after Fontan operation. Circulation 1992;85:469–96.

335. Gale AW, Danielson G, Mc Goon D, et al. Modified Fontan operation for univentricular heart and complicated congenital lesions. J Thorac Cardiovasc Surg 1979;78:831–8.

336. Prenger K, Hess J, Cromme-Dijkhuis A, Eijgelaar A. Porcine-valved dacron conduits in Fontan procedures. Ann Thorac Surg 1988;46:526–30.

337. Jonas RA. Intracardiac thrombus after the Fontan procedure. J Thorac Cardiovasc Surg 1995;110:1502–3.

338. Cetta F, Feldt RH, O'Leary PW, et al. Improved early morbidity after fontan operation: the Mayo Clinic experience, 1987 to 1992. J Am Coll Cardiol 1996;28:480–6.

339. Park MK. Pediatric cardiology for practitioners. Baltimore: Mosby, 1996.

340. Myers J, Waldhausen J, Weber H, et al. A reconsideration of risk factors for the Fontan operation. Ann Surg 1990;211:738–44.

341. Rosenthal A, Dick M. Tricuspid atresia. In: Adams F, Emmanoulides G, Riemerschreider T, eds. Heart disease in infants, children and adolescents. Baltimore: Williams and Wilkins, 1989.

342. Castaneda AR. From Glenn to Fontan. Circulation 1992;86:II-80–4.

343. Kreutzer G, Galindez E, Bono H, et al. An operation for the correction of tricuspid atresia. J Thorac Cardiovasc Surg 1973;66:613–21.

344. Quinones JA, DeLeon SY, Bell TJ, et al. Fenestrated Fontan procedure: evolution of technique and occurrence of paradoxical embolism. Pediatr Cardiol 1997;18:218–21.

345. Fyfe DA, Kline CH, Sade RM, Gillette PC. Transesophageal echocardiography detects thrombus formation not identified by transthoracic echocardiography after the Fontan operation. J Am Coll Cardiol 1991;18:1733–7.

346. Stumper O, Sutherland G, Geuskens R, et al. Transesophageal echocardiography in evaluation and management after a Fontan procedure. J Am Coll Cardiol 1991;17:1152–60.

347. Rosenthal FN, Friedman AH, Kleinman CS, et al. Thromboembolic complications after Fontan operations. Circulation 1995;92:II-287–93.

348. Jahangiri M, Ross DB, Redington AN, et al. Thromboembolism after the Fontan procedure and its modifications. Ann Thorac Surg 1995;58:1409–14.

349. du Plessis AJ, Chang AC, Wessel DL, et al. Cerebrovascular accidents following the Fontan operation. Pediatr Neurol 1995;12:230–6.

350. Day RW, Boyer RS, Tait VF, Ruttenberg HD. Factors associated with stroke following the Fontan procedure. Pediatr Cardiol 1995;16:270–5.

351. Matthews K, Bale J, Clark E, et al. Cerebral infarction complicating Fontan surgery for cyanotic congenital heart disease. Pediatr Cardiol 1986;7:161–6.

352. Fletcher SE, Case CL, Fyfe DA, Gillette PC. Clinical spectrum of venous thrombi in the Fontan patient. Am J Cardiol 1991;68:1721–2.

353. Dobell ARC, Trusler GA, Smallhorn JF, Williams WG. Atrial thrombi after the Fontan operation. Ann Thorac Surg 1986;42:664–7.

354. Danielson G. Invited commentary. Ann Thorac Surg 1994;58:1413–4.

355. Kaulitz R, Ziemer G, Bergmann F, et al. Atrial thrombus after a Fontan operation; Predisposing factors, treatment, and prophylaxis. Cardiol Young 1997;7:37–43.

356. Fontan F, Deville C, Quaegebeur J, et al. Repair of tricuspid atresia in 100 patients. J Thorac Cardiovasc Surg 1983;85:647–60.

357. Prenger KB, Hess J, Cromme-Dijkhuis AH, Eijgelaar A. Porcine-valved Dacron conduits in Fontan procedures. Ann Thorac Surg 1988;46:526–30.

358. Laks H, Milliken G, Perloff H, et al. Experience with the Fontan procedure. J Thorac Cardiovasc Surg 1984;88:939–51.

359. Annecchino F, Brunelli F, Borghi A, et al. Fontan repair for tricuspid atresia: experience with 50 consecutive patients. Ann Thorac Surg 1988;45:430–6.

360. Mair DD, Rice MJ, Hagler DJ, et al. Outcome of the Fontan procedure in patients with tricuspid atresia. Circulation 1985;72:1170–6.

361. Cromme-Dijkhuis AH, Hess J, Hahlen K, et al. Specific sequelae after Fontan operation at mid- and long-term followup. J Thorac Cardiovasc Surg 1993;106:1126–32.

362. Cromme-Dijkhuis AH, Henkens CMA, Bijleveld CMA, et al. Coagulation factor abnormalities as possible thrombotic risk factors after Fontan operations. Lancet 1990;336:1087–90.

363. Monagle P, Cochrane A, McCrindle B, et al. Editorial: thromboembolic complications after Fontan procedures: the role of prophylactic anticoagulation. J Thorac Cardiovasc Surg 1998;115:493–8.

364. Shirai LK, Rosenthal DN, Reitz BA, et al. Arrhythmias and thromboembolic complications after the extracardiac fontan operation. J Thorac Cardiovasc Surg 1998;115:499–505.

365. Downing TP, Danielson G, Ritter D, et al. Pulmonary artery thrombosis associated with anomalous pulmonary venous connection: an unusual complication following the modified Fontan procedure. J Thorac Cardiovasc Surg 1985;90:441–5.

366. Asante-Korang A, Sweeram N, McKay R, Arnold R. Thrombolysis with tissue type plasminogen activator following cardiac surgery in children. Int J Cardiol 1992;35:317–22.

367. Dajee H, Deutsch LS, Benson LN, et al. Thrombolytic therapy for superior ven caval thrombosis following superior vana cava-pulmonary anastomosis. Ann Thorac Surg 1984;38:637–9.

368. Hedrick M, Elkins RC, Knott-Craig CJ, Razook JD. Successful thrombectomy for thrombosis of the right side of the heart after the Fontan operation. J Thorac Cardiovasc Surg 1992;105:297–301.

369. Hutto RL, Williams JP, Maertens P, et al. Cerebellar infarct: late complication of the Fontan procedure? Pediatr Neurol 1991;7:161–6.

370. Galindez E, Bono H, de Palma J. An operation for the connection of tricuspid atresia. J Thorac Cardiovasc Surg 1973;66:613–21.

371. Lam J, Neirotti R, Becker AE, Planche C. Thrombosis after the Fontan procedure: transoesophageal echocardiography may replace angiocardiography. J Thorac Cardiovasc Surg 1994;108:194–5.

372. Mahony L, Nikaidohn H, Fixler D. Thrombolytic treatment with streptokinase for late intraatrial thrombosis after modified Fontan procedure. Am J Cardiol 1988;62:343–4.

373. Okita Y, Miki S, Kusuhara K, et al. Massive systemic venous thrombosis after Fontan operation: report of a case. Thorac Cardiovasc Surgeon 1988;36:335–6.

374. Putnam JB, Lemmer JH, Rocchini AP, Bove EL. Embolectomy for acute pulmonary artery occlusion following Fontan procedure. Ann Thorac Surg 1988; 45:335–6.

375. Shannon FL, Campbell DN, Clarke DR. Right atrial thrombosis: rare complication of the modified Fontan procedure. Pediatr Cardiol 1986;7:209–12.

376. Sharratt G, Lacson A, Cornel G, Virmani S. Echocardiography of intracardiac filling defects in infants and children. Pediatr Cardiol 1986;7:189–94.

377. Wilson DG, Wisheart JD, Stuart AG. Systemic thromboembolism leading to myocardial infarction and stroke after fenestrated total cavopulmonary connection. Br Heart J 1995;73:483–5.

378. Kao JM, Alejos JC, Grant PW, et al. Conversion of atriopulmonary to cavopulmonary anastomosis in management of late arrhythmias and atrial thrombosis. Ann Thorac Surg 1994;58:1510–4.

379. Beitzke A, Zobel G, Zenz W, et al. Catheter-directed thrombolysis with recombinant tissue plasminogen activator for acute pulmonary embolism after Fontan operation. Pediatr Cardiol 1996;17:410–2.

380. Andrew M, Vegh P, Johnston M, et al. Maturation of the hemostatic system during childhood. Blood 1992;80:1998–2005.

381. Jahangiri M, Shore D, Kakkar V, et al. Coagulation factor abnormalities after the fontan procedure and its modifications. J Thorac Cardiovasc Surg 1997;113: 989–93.

382. Monagle P, Andrew M. Coagulation abnormalities after Fontan procedures. J Thorac Cardiovasc Surg 1998; 115:732–3.

383. Pennington DG, Nouri S, Ho J, et al. Glenn shunt: Long term results and current role in congenital heart operations. Ann Thorac Surg 1981;31:532–9.

384. Kopf GS, Laks H, Stansel HC, et al. Thirty year followup of superior vena cava pulmonary artery (Glenn) shunts. J Thorac Cardiovasc Surg 1990;100: 662–71.

385. Mainwaring RD, Lamberti JJ, Uzark K, Spicer RL. Bidirectional Glenn. Is accessory pulmonary blood flow good or bad? Circulation 1995;92:II294–7.

386. Koutlas TC, Harrison JK, Bashore TM, et al. Late conduit occlusion after modified Fontan procedure with classic Glenn shunt. Ann Thorac Surg 1996;62: 258–61.

387. Mainwaring RD, Lamberti JJ, Uzark K. The bidirectional Glenn procedure: palliation of the univentricular heart. Adv Card Surg 1994;5:115–40.

388. Andrew M, Brooker L, Mitchell L. Acquired antithrombin III deficiency secondary to asparaginase therapy in childhood acute lymphoblastic leukemia. Blood Coagul Fibrinolysis 1994;5:S24–S36.

389. Sutor A, Ritter J. Thrombosis in children with acute lymphoblastic leukemia with special regard to asparaginase treatment. Hemostaseologie (Germany) 1992;12:35–43.

390. Mitchell L, Halton J, Vegh P, et al. Effect of disease and chemotherapy on hemostasis in children with acute lymphoid leukemia. Am J Pediatr Hematol Oncol 1994;16:120–6.

391. Abshire T, Gold S, Odom L, et al. The coagulopathy of childhood leukemia. Thrombin activation or primary fibrinolysis? Cancer 1990;66:716–21.

392. Legnani C, Palareti G, Pession A, et al. Intravascular coagulation phenomena associated with prevalent fall in fibrinogen and plasminogen during L-asparaginase treatment in leukemic children. Haemostasis 1988;18:179–86.

393. Priest J, Ramsay N, Bennett A, et al. The effect of L-asparaginase on antithrombin, plasminogen, and plasma coagulation during therapy for acute lymphoblastic leukemia. J Pediatr 1982;100:990–5.

394. Mitchell L, Hoogendoorn H, Giles A, et al. Increased endogenous thrombin generation in children with acute lymphoblastic leukemia: risk of thrombotic complications in L'Asparaginase-induced antithrombin III deficiency. Blood 1994;83:386–91.

395. Semeraro N, Montemurro P, Giordano P, et al. Unbalanced coagulation-fibrinolysis potential during L-asparaginase therapy in children with acute lymphoblastic leukemia. Thromb Haemost 1990;64: 38–40.

396. Hudig D, Bajaj S. Tissue factor-like activity of the human monocytic tumour cell line. Thromb Res 1982;27:321.

397. Kubota T, Andoh K, Sadakata H, et al. Tissue factor released from leukemic cells. Thromb Haemostas 1991;65:59–63.

398. Falanga A, Gordon S. Isolation and characterization of cancer procoagulant: a cysteine proteinase from malignant tissue. Biochem 1985;24:5558–67.

399. Andrew M, Halton J, Vegh P, Mitchell L. Coagulation proteins cycle in children on treatment for acute lymphoblastic leukaemia. Pediatr Res 1992;31: 141a.

400. Wade H, Elsworth R, Herbert E, et al. A new L-asparaginase with anti-tumor activity. Lancet 1968; 2:776–7.

401. Peterson R, Ciegler A. L-asparaginase activity by various bacteria. Appl Microbiol 1969;17:929–30.

402. Haley E, Fischer G, Welch A. The requirement for L-asparaginase of mouse leukemic cell L5178y in culture. Cancer Res 1961;21:532.

403. Eden O, Shaw M, Lilleyman J, Richards S. Non-randomised study comparing toxicity of Escherichia coli and Erwinia asparaginase in children with leukaemia. Med Pediatr Oncol 1990;18:497–502.

404. O'Meara A, Daly M, Hallinan F. Increased antithrombin III concentration in children with acute lymphatic leukaemia receiving L-asparaginase therapy. Med Pediatr Oncol 1988;16:169–74.

405. Arico M, Gamba G, Raiteri E, et al. Clotting abnormalities in children during maintenance chemotherapy for acute lymphoblastic leukemia. Haematologica 1991;76:472–4.

406. Sutor A, Niemeyer C, Sauter S, et al. Alteration of hemostasis with the treatment protocols ALL-BFM 90 and NHL-BFM 90. Klin Padiatr (Germany) 1992; 204:264–73.

407. Isacson S. The effect of predisolone on the coagulation and fibrinolytic systems. Scand J Haematol 1970; 7:212–6.

408. Jorgensen K, Sorensen P, Freund L. Effect of glucocorticosteroids on some coagulation tests. Acta Haematol 1982;68:39–42.

409. Dreyfuss F, Menczel J. The effect of corticotrophin, cortisone, and prednisone on whole blood coagulation time. J Lab Clin Med 1958;51:530–8.

410. Ozsoylu S. Corticosteroid and factor VIII. Acta Haematol 1989;81:222.

411. Menczel J, Dreyfuss F. Effect of prednisone on blood coagulation time in patients on Dicoumarol therapy. J Lab Clin Med 1960;56:14–20.

412. Kucuk O, Kwaan H, Gunnar W, Vazquez R. Thromboembolic complications associated with L-asparaginase therapy. Etiologic role of low antithrombin III and plasminogen levels and therapeutic correction by fresh frozen plasma. Cancer 1985;55:702–6.

413. Ishii H, Oh H, Ishizuka N, et al. Cerebral infarction in a patient with acute lymphoblastic leukemia after fresh-frozen plasma replacement during L-asparaginase therapy. Am J Hematol 1992;41:295–306.

414. Cairo MS, Lazarus K, Gilmore RL, Baehner RL. Intracranial hemorrhage and focal seizures secondary to use of L-asparaginase during induction therapy of acute lymphocytic leukemia. J Pediatr 1980;97: 829–33.

415. Pui C, Jackson C, Chesney C, Abildgaard C. Involvement of von Willebrand factor in thrombosis following asparaginase-prednisone-vincristine therapy for leukemia. Am J Hematol 1987;25:291–8.

416. Bezeaud A, Drouet L, Leverger G, et al. Effect of L-asparaginase therapy for acute lymphoblastic leukemia on plasma vitamin-K dependent coagulation factors and inhibitors. J Pediatr 1986;108:698–701.

417. Pui C, Chesney C, Weed J, Jackson C. Altered von Willebrand factor molecule in children with thrombosis following asparaginase-prednisone-vincristine therapy for leukemia. J Pediatr 1985;3:1266–72.

418. Priest J, Ramsay N, Latchaw R, et al. Thrombotic and haemorrhagic strokes complicating early therapy for childhood acute lymphoblastic leukemia. Cancer 1980;46:1548–54.

419. Bauer K, Teitel J, Rosenberg R. L-asparaginase induced antithrombin III deficiency: evidence against the production of a hypercoagulable state. Thromb Res 1983;29:437–42.

420. Cappellato M, Lazzaro A, Rosolen A, et al. Failure of L-asparaginase to decrease protein C—a possible rebound phenomenon. Thromb Haemostas 1986;50:238.

421. Cappellato M, Rosolen A, Zanesco L, Girolami A. Clotting complications of L-asparaginase therapy in children with ALL. Blut 1986;52:377–378.

422. Pastore G, Miniero R, Saracco R, Lange M. Thrombosis and hemorrhage during L-asparaginase therapy. J Pediatr 1983;102:639–40.

423. Pui C, Jackson C, Chesney C, et al. Sequential changes in platelet function and coagulation in leukemic children treated with L-asparaginase, prednisone, and vincristine. J Clin Oncol 1993;1:380–5.

424. Homans A, Rybak M, Baglini R, et al. Effect of L-asparaginase administration on coagulation and platelet function in children with leukemia. J Clin Oncol 1987;5:811–7.

425. David M, Andrew M. Venous thromboembolism complications in children: a critical review of the literature. J Pediatr 1993;123:337–46.

426. Ott N, Ramsay N, Priest J, et al. Sequelae of thrombotic or haemmorhagic complications following L-asparaginase therapy for childhood lymphoblastic leukemia. Am J Pediatr Hematol Oncol 1988;10:191–5.

427. Pui C, Chesney C, Bergum P, et al. Lack of pathogenetic role of proteins C and S in thrombosis associated with asparaginase-prednisone-vincristine therapy for leukaemia. Br J Haematol 1986;64:283–90.

428. Priest J, Ramsay K, Steinherz P, et al. A syndrome of thrombosis and hemorrhage complicating L-asparaginase therapy for childhood acute lymphoblastic leukemia. J Pediatr 1982;100:984–9.

429. Halton J, Mitchell L, Vegh P, et al. Fresh frozen plasma has no beneficial effect on the hemostatic system in children receiving L-asparaginase. Am J Hematol 1994;47:157–61.

430. Zaunschirm A, Muntean W. Correction of hemostatic imbalances induced by L-asparaginase therapy in children with acute lymphoblastic leukemia. Pediatr Hematol Oncol 1986;3:19–25.

431. Horigome Y, Hanada T, Inudoh M, Takita H. Cerebral thrombosis in a child with acute lymphocytic leukemia during L-asparaginase therapy. Jpn J Clin Hematol 1989;30:1284–8.

432. Gugliotta L, D'Angelo A, Mattioli Belmonte M, et al. Hypercoagulability during L-asparaginase treatment:

the effect of antithrombin III supplementation in vivo. Br J Haematol 1990;74:465–70.

433. Lockman L, Mastri A, Priest J, Nesbit M. Dural venous sinus thrombosis in acute lymphoblastic leukemia. Pediatrics 1980;66:943–7.

434. Ganick D, Robertson WJ, Viseskul C, Lubinsky M. Dural sinus thrombosis in leukemia. Am J Dis Child 1978;132:1040–1.

435. Barbui T, Rodeghiero F, Meli S, Dini E. Fatal pulmonary embolism and antithrombin III deficiency in adult lymphoblastic leukaemia during L-asparaginase therapy. Acta Haematol 1983;69:188–91.

436. Rodeghiero F, Castaman G, Dini E. Fibrinopeptide A changes during remission induction treatment with L-asparaginase in acute lymphoblastic leukemia: evidence for activation of blood coagulation. Thromb Res 1990;57:31–8.

437. Packer R, Rorke L, Lange B, et al. Cerebrovascular accidents in children with cancer. Pediatrics 1985;76:194–201.

438. Mueller J, Ratnoff O, Heinle R. Observations on the characteristics of an unusual circulating anticoagulant. J Lab Clin Med 1951;38:254–61.

439. Conley C, Hartman R. Hemorrhagic disorder caused by circulating anticoagulant in patients with disseminated lupus erythematosus. J Clin Invest 1952;150:621–2.

440. Bowie E, Thompson J, Pascuzzi C, Owen C. Thrombosis in systemic lupus erythematosus despite circulating anticoagulants. J Clin Med 1963;62:416.

441. Khamashta M, Hughes G. Antiphospholipid antibodies. A marker for thrombosis and recurrent abortion. Clin Rev Allergy 1994;12:287–96.

442. Asherson R, Hughes G. Vascular disease and thrombosis: relationship to the antiphospholipid antibodies. Contrib Nephrol 1992;99:17–25.

443. Feinstein D, Rapaport S. Aquired inhibitors of blood coagulation. Prog Haemost Thromb 1972;1:75–95.

444. Roubey R. Autoantibodies to phospholipid-binding plasma proteins: a new view of lupus anticoagulants and other "Antiphospholipid" autoantibodies. Blood 1945;84:2854–67.

445. McNeil H, Simpson R, Chesterman C, Krilis S. Anti-phospholipid antibodies are directed against a complex antigen that includes a lipid-binding inhibitor of coagulation: b2X glycoprotein I (apolipoprotein H). Proc Natl Acad Sci U S A 1990;87:4120–4.

446. Bevers EM, Galli M. Beta 2-glycoprotein I for binding of anticardiolipin antibodies to cardiolipin [letter]. Lancet 1990;336:952–3.

447. Exner T, Shaman N, Trudinger B. Separation of anti-cardiolipin antibodies from lupus anticoagulant on a phospholipid-coated polystyrene column. Biochem Biophys Res Commun 1988;155:1001–7.

448. McNeil H, Chesterman C, Krilis S. Anticardiolipin antibodies and lupus anticoagulants compromise antibody subgroups with different phospholipid binding characteristics. Br J Haematol 1989;73:506–13.

449. Exner T, Rickard K, Kronenberg H. A sensitive test demonstrating lupus anticoagulant and its behavioral patterns. Br J Haematol 1978;40:143–51.

450. Proctor R, Rapaport S. The partial thromboplastin time with kaolin. Am J Clin Pathol 1961;36:212–219.

451. Thiagarajan P, Pengo V, Shapiro S. The use of dilute Russell Viper Venom time for the diagnosis of lupus anticoagulants. Blood 1986;68:869–74.

452. Schleider MA, Nachman RL, Jaffe EA, Coleman C. A clinical study of the lupus anticoagulant. Blood 1976;48:499–509.

453. Exner T, Triplett D, Taberner D, Machin S. Guidelines for testing and revised criteria for lupus anticoagulants. SSC subcommittee for the standardization of lupus anticoagulants. Thromb Haemost 1991;65:320–2.

454. Rauch J, Tannenbaum M, Tannenbaum H, et al. Human hybridoma lupus anticoagulants distinguish between lamellar and hexagonal phase lipid systems. J Biol Chem 1986;261:9672–7.

455. Rauch J, Janoff AS. Phospholipid in the hexagonal II phase is immunogenic. Proc Natl Acad Sci U S A 1990;87:4112–5.

456. Harris E, Boey M, Mackworth-Young C, et al. Anticardiolipin antibodies: detection by radioimmunoassay and association with thrombosis in systemic lupus erythematosus. Lancet 1983;2:1211–4.

457. Loizou S, McCrea J, Rudge A, et al. Measurements of anticardiolipin antibodies by an enzyme-linked immunosorbent assay (ELISA): standardization and quantitation of results. Clin Exp Immunol 1985;62:738–45.

458. Bertolaccini ML, Roch B, Amengual O, et al. Multiple antiphospholipid tests do not increase the diagnostic yield in antiphospholipid antibodies. Br J Rheumatol 1998;37:1229–32.

459. Brandt J, Triplett D, Alving B, Scharrer I. Criteria for the diagnosis of lupus anticoagulants: an update. Thromb Haemostas 1995;74:1185–90.

460. Alarcon-Segovia D, Deleze M, Oria C, et al. Antiphospholipid antibodies and the antiphospholipid syndrome in systemic lupus erythematosus. Medicine 1989;68:353–65.

461. Dungan DD, Jay MS. Stroke in an early adolescent with systemic lupus erythematosus and coexistent antiphospholipid antibodies. Pediatrics 1992;90:96–9.

462. Pelkonen P, Simell O, Rasi V, Vaarala O. Venous thrombosis associated with lupus anticoagulant and anti-cardiolipin antibodies. Acta Paediatr Scand 1988;77:767–72.

463. Appan S, Boey M, Lim K. Multiple thromboses in systemic lupus erythematosus. Arch Dis Child 1987;62:739–41.

464. Bernstein ML, Salusinsky-Sternbach M, Bellefleur M, Esseltine DW. Thrombotic and hemorrhagic complications in children with the lupus anticoagulant. AJDC 1984;138:1132–5.

465. Olive D, Andre E, Brocard O, et al. Lupus erythemateux dissemine revele par des thrombophlebites des membres inferieurs. Arch Franc Pediatr 1979;36:807–11.

466. Ostuni PA, Lazzarin P, Pengo V, et al. Renal artery thrombosis and hypertension in a 13 year old girl with antiphospholipid syndrome. Ann Rheum Dis 1990;49:184–7.

467. Kwong T, Leonidas J, Ilowite N. Asymptomatic superior vena cava thrombosis and pulmonary embolism in an adolescent with SLE and antiphospholipid antibodies. Clin Exp Rheumatol 1994;12:215–7.

468. Rider L, Clarke W, Rutledge J. Pulmonary hypertension in a seventeen-year-old boy. J Pediatr 1992;120:149–59.

469. Berube C, Mitchell L, David M, et al. The relationship of antiphospholipid antibodies to thromboembolic disease in systemic lupus erythematosus in children: a cross-sectional study. Pediatr Res 1998;44:351–6.

470. Khamashta M, Cuadrado M, Mujic F, et al. The management of thrombosis in the antiphospholipid-antibody syndrome. N Engl J Med 1995;332:993–7.

471. Asherson RA, Baguley E, Pal C, Hughes GR. Antiphospholipid syndrome: five year follow up. Ann Rheum Dis 1991;50:805–10.

472. Lechner K, Pabinger Fasching I. Lupus anticoagulants and thrombosis. A study of 25 cases and review of the literature. Haemostasis 1985;15:254–62.

473. Derkson RH. Clinical manifestations and management of the antiphospholipid syndrome. Lupus 1996;5:167–9.

474. Rivier G, Herranz MT, Khamashta MA, Hughes GR. Thrombosis and antiphospholipid syndrome: a preliminary assessment of 3 antithrombotic treatments. Lupus 1994;3:85–90.

475. de Klerk OL, de Vries W, Sinnige LGF. An unusual case of neonatal seizures in a newborn infant. Pediatrics 1997;100:E8.

476. Akanli LF, Trasi SS, Thuraisamy K, et al. Neonatal middle cerebral artery infarction: association with elevated maternal anticardiolipin antibodies. Am J Perinatol 1998;15:399–402.

477. Botet F, Romero G, Montagut P, et al. Neonatal outcome in women treated for antiphospholipid syndrome during pregnancy. J Perinatol 1997;25:192–6.

478. Ruffatti A, Dalla Barba B, Del Ross J, et al. Outcome of 55 newborns of antiphospholipid antibody positive mothers treated with calcium heparin during pregnancy. Clin Exp Med 1998;16:605–10.

479. Johansen AS, Herlin T. Neonatal lupus syndrome. Association with complete congenital atrioventricular block. Ugeskr Laeger 1998;160:2521–5.

480. Finkelstein Y, Adler Y, Harel L, et al. Anti-Ro (SSA) and anti-La (SSB) antibodies and complete congenital heart block. Ann Med Interne 1997;148:205–8.

481. Agarwala B, Sheikh Z, Cibils LA. Congenital complete heart block. J Natl Med Assoc 1996;88:725–9.

482. Buyon JP, Hiebert R, Copel J, et al. Autoimmune-associated congenital heart block: demographics, mortality, morbidity, and recurrence rates obtained from a national neonatal lupus registry. J Am Coll Cardiol 1998;31:1658–66.

483. Falcini F, De Simone L, Donzelli G, Cerinic MM. Congenital conduction defects in children born to asymptomatic mothers with anti-SSA/SSB antibodies: report of two cases. An Ital Med Int 1998;13:169–72.

484. Ferrazzini G, Fasnacht M, Arbenz U, et al. Neonatal lupus erythematosus with congenital heart block and severe heart failure due to myocarditis and endocarditis of the mitral valve. Inten Care Med 1996;22:464–6.

485. Ravelli A, Martini A. Antiphospolipid antibody syndrome in pediatric patients. Rheum Dis Clin North Am 1997;23:657–76.

486. Schoning M, Klein R, Krageloh Mann I, et al. Antiphospholipid antibodies in cerebrovascular ischemia and stroke in childhood. Neuropediatrics 1994;25:8–14.

487. Olson JC, Konkol JR, Gill JC, et al. Childhood stroke and lupus anticoagulant. Pediatr Neurol 1994;10:54–7.

488. Takanashi J, Sugita IK, Miyazato S, et al. Antiphospholipid antibody syndrome in childhood strokes. Pediatr Neurol 1995;13:323–6.

489. deVeber G, Monagle P, Chan A, et al. Pre-thrombotic disorders in infants and children with cerebral thromboembolism. Arch Neurol 1998;55:1539–43.

490. Angelini L, Granata T, Zibordi F, et al. Neurological disorders other than stroke associated with antiphospholipid antibodies in childhood. Neuropediatrics 1998;29:249–53.

491. Nsiri B, Ghazouani E, Gritli N, et al. Antiphospholipid antibodies: lupus anticoagulants, anticardiolipin and antiphospholipid isotypes in patients with sickle cell disease. Hematol Cell Therapy 1998;40:107–12.

492. Leker RR, Steiner I. Anticardiolipin antibodies are frequently present in patients with idiopathic intracranial hypertension. Arch Neurol 1998;55:817–20.

493. Tietjen GE, Day M, Norris L, et al. Role of anticardiolipin antibodies in young patients with migraine and transient focal neurologic events: a prospective study. Neurology 1998;78:1433–40.

494. Ardiles LG, Olavarria F, Elgueta M, et al. Anticardiolipin antibodies in classic pediatric hemolytic uremic syndrome: a possible pathogenic role. Nephron 1998;78:278–83.

495. Lossos IS, Bogomolski-Yahalom V, Matzner Y. Anticardiolipin antibodies in acute myeloid leukemia: prevalence and clinical significance. Am J Hematol 1998;57:139–42.

496. Kratz C, Mauz-Korholz C, Kruck H, et al. Detection of antiphospholipid antibodies in children and adolescents. Pediatr Hematol Oncol 1998;15:325–32.

497. Francis R. Platelets, coagulation, and fibrinolysis in sickle cell disease: their possible role in vascular occlusion. Blood Coagul Fibrinolysis 1991;2:341–53.

498. Freedman M, Karpatkin S. Short communication: elevated platelet count and megathrombocyte number in sickle cell anemia. Blood 1975;46:579–82.

499. Kenny M, George A, Stuart J. Platelet hyperactivity in sickle-cell disease: a consequence of hyposplenism. J Clin Pathol 1980;33:622–5.

500. Westwick J, Watson-Williams E, Krishnamurthi S. Platelet activation during steady state sickle cell disease. J Med 1983;14:17–36.

501. Semple M, Al-Hasani S, Kioy P. A double-blind trial of ticlopidine in sickle cell disease. Thromb Haemost 1984;51:303–6.

502. Buchanan G, Holtkamp C. Evidence against enhanced platelet activity in sickle cell anemia. Br J Haematol 1983;54:595–603.

503. Mehta P. Significance of plasma beta-thromboglobulin values in patients with sickle cell disease. J Pediatr 1980;97:941–4.

504. Green D, Scott J. Is sickle cell crisis a thrombotic event? Am J Hematol 1986;23:317–21.

505. Richardson S, Matthews K, Stuart J. Serial changes in coagulation and viscosity during sickle-cell crisis. Br J Haematol 1979;41:95–103.

506. Leslie J, Langer D, Serjeant G. Coagulation changes during the steady state in homozygous sickle-cell disease in Jamaica. Br J Haematol 1975;30:159–66.

507. Famodu A. Coagulation changes in homozygous sickle cell disease in Nigeria [letter]. J Clin Pathol 1987; 40:1487.

508. Mackie I, Bull H, Brozovic M. Altered factor VIII complexes in sickle cell disease. Br J Haematol 1980;46: 499–502.

509. Abildgaard C, Simone V, Schulman I. Factor VIII (antihemophilic factor) activity in sickle-cell anaemia. Br J Haematol 1967;13:19–27.

510. Francis RBJ. Protein S deficiency in sickle cell anemia. J Lab Clin Med 1988;111:571–6.

511. Lane P, O'Connell J, Kressin DC. Spectrin-depleted erythrocyte membrane vesicles bind protein S in vitro. Am J Pediatr Hematol Oncol 1990;12:106.

512. Lane P, O'Connell J, Marlar R. Irreversibly sickled cells bind protein S: an indication of altered membrane phospholipid asymmetry. Blood 1990;76:67a.

513. Peters M, Plaat B, ten Cate H, et al. Enhanced thrombin generation in children with sickle cell disease. Thromb Haemost 1994;71:169–72.

514. Stockman J, Nigro M, Mishkin M, Oski F. Occlusion of large cerebral vessels in sickle-cell anemia. N Engl J Med 1972;287:486–9.

515. Russell M, Goldberg H, Hodson A. Effect of transfusion therapy on arteriographic abnormalities and on recurrence of stroke in sickle cell disease. Blood 1984;63:162–7.

516. Rothman S, Fulling K, Nelson JS. Sickle cell anaemia and central nervous system infarction: a neuropathological study. Ann Neurol 1986;20:684–94.

517. Walker B, Ballas S, Burka E. The diagnosis of pulmonary thromboembolism in sickle cell disease. Am J Hematol 1979;7:219–25.

518. Bashour T, Lindsay J. Haemoglobin S-C disease presenting as acute pneumonitis with pulmonary angiographic findings in two patients. Am J Med 1975;58: 559–62.

519. Yater W, Hansmann G. Sickle-cell anemia: a new cause of cor pulmonale. Report of two cases with numerous disseminated occlusions of the small pulmonary arteries. Am J Med Sci 1936;191:474–89.

520. Ende N, Pizzolato P, Ziskind J. Sicklemia. Ann Intern Med 1955;42:1065–75.

521. Clinocopathologic conference. Sickle cell anemia and pulmonary embolectomy with cardiopulmonary bypass. Am J Med 1966;41:130–6.

522. Durant J, Cortes F. Occlusive pulmonary vascular disease associated with hemoglobin SC disease. Am Heart J 1966;71:100–10.

523. Heath D, Thompson I. Bronchopulmonary anastomoses in sickle-cell anaemia. Thorax 1969;24: 232–8.

524. Collins F, Orringer E. Pulmonary hypertension and cor pulmonale in the sickle haemoglobinopathies. Am J Med 1982;73:814–20.

525. Haupt H, Moore G, Bauer T. The lung in sickle cell disease. Chest 1982;81:332–7.

526. Francis RB Jr. Elevated prothrombin F1.2 fragment in sickle cell disease: further evidence for activation of coagulation in the steady-state. Blood 1990;75:61a.

527. Salvaggio J, Arnold C, Banov C. Long-term anticoagulation in sickle-cell disease. N Engl J Med 1963; 269:182–6.

528. Powars E, Wilson B, Imbus C, et al. The natural history of stroke in sickle cell disease. Am J Med 1978; 65:461–71.

529. Adams R, Nichols F. Sickle cell anemia, sickle cell trait and thalassemia. In: Vinken P, Bruyn G, Klawans H,

eds. Vascular diseases III: handbook of clinical neurology. Netherlands: Amsterdam Elsevier, 1989:503–15.

530. Pavlakis S. Neurologic complications of sickle cell disease. Adv Pediatr 1989;36:247–76.

531. Charache S, Lubin B, Reid C. Management and therapy of sickle cell disease. NIH publication #91-2117. US Dept. of Health and Human Services 1991:22–4.

532. Balkaran B, Char G, Morris J. Stroke in a cohort of patients with homozygous sickle cell disease. J Pediatr 1992;120:360–6.

533. Aaslid R, Markwalder T, Nomes H. Non-invasive transcranial Doppler ultrasound recording of flow velosity in basal cerebral arteries. J Neurosurg 1982;57: 769–74.

534. Babikian V. Transcranial doppler evaluation of patients with ischemic cerebrovascular disease. In: Babikian V, Wechsler L, eds. Transcranial doppler ultrasonography. St. Louis: Mosby-Yearbook, 1993:87–104.

535. Rosse WF, Ware RE. The molecular basis of paroxysmal nocturnal hemoglobinuria [review]. Blood 1995;86: 3277–86.

536. Socie G, Mary JY, de Gramont A, et al. Paroxysmal nocturnal haemoglobinuria: long term followup and prognostic factors. Lancet 1996;348:573–7.

537. Ware RE, Hall SE, Rosse WF. Paroxysmal nocturnal hemoglobinuria with onset in childhood and adolescence. N Engl J Med 1991;325:991–6.

538. Tudela M, Jarque I, Perez-Sirvent ML, et al. Clinical profile and course of paroxysmal nocturnal hemoglobinuria. Sangre 1993;38:301–7.

539. Hall SE, Rosse WF. The use of monoclonal antibodies and flow cytometry in the diagnosis of paroxysmal nocturnal hemoglobinuria. Blood 1996;87: 5332–40.

540. Alfinito F, Del Vecchio L, Rocco S, et al. Blood cell flow cytometry in paroxysmal nocturnal hemoglobinuria: a tool for measuring the extent of PNH clone. Leukemia 1996;10:1326–30.

541. Fores R, Bautista G, Steegmann JL, et al. De novo smoldering paroxysmal nocturnal hemoglobinuria: A flow cytometric diagnosis. Haematologica 1997;82:695–7.

542. Bessler M, Hillmen P. Somatic mutation and clonal selection in the pathogenesis and in the control of paroxysmal nocturnal hemoglobinuria. Semin Hematol 1998;35:149–67.

543. Nafa K, Bessler M, Mason P, et al. Factor V Leiden mutation investigated by amplification created restriction enzyme site (ACRES) in paroxysmal nocturnal hemoglobinuria patients with and without thrombosis. Haematologica 1998;81:540–2.

544. Mathieu D, Rahmouni A, Villeneuve P, et al. Impact of magnetic resonance imaging on the diagnosis of abdominal complicatiosn of paroxysmal nocturnal hemoglobinuria. Blood 1995;85:3283–8.

545. Wyatt HA, Mowat AP, Layton M. Paroxysmal nocturnal haemoglobinuria and Budd-Chiari syndrome. Arch Dis Child 1995;72:241–2.

546. Gralnick HR, Vail M, McKeown LP, et al. Activated platelets in paroxysmal nocturnal haemoglobinuria. Br J Haematol 1995;91:697–702.

547. Rosse W. Epidemiology of PNH. Lancet 1996;348:560.

548. Andrew M, Brooker L. Hemostatic complications in renal disorders of the young. Pediatr Nephrol 1996;10:88–99.

549. Andrew M, Montgomery RR. Acquired disorders of hemostasis. In: Nathan DG, Orkin SH, eds. Hematology of infancy and childhood. Philadelphia: WB Saunders Company, 1998, p. 1677–1717.

9

HEPARIN AND LOW MOLECULAR WEIGHT HEPARIN THERAPY

Unfractionated heparin (UFH) is one of the most frequently prescribed drugs in pediatric tertiary care centers and is used in a diverse group of disorders such as cardiopulmonary bypass (CPB), extracorporeal membrane oxygenation (ECMO), dialysis, venous and arterial catheters, and thromboembolic events (TEs). In the past, intervention trials assessing optimal administration and monitoring of UFH were not feasible because of the relatively small number of pediatric patients requiring anticoagulation therapy. However, advances in tertiary care pediatrics have paradoxically resulted in rapidly increasing numbers of children requiring UFH, which makes intervention trials feasible. Separate clinical trials in pediatric patients are necessary because optimal use of UFH will almost certainly differ from adults due to age-dependent physiologic and pathologic differences in hemostasis that influence the activities of UFH. Until these trials are conducted, modified adult guidelines remain the primary source for recommendations in children.

Although UFH remains the recommended anticoagulant for short-term, rapid anticoagulation therapy and initial therapy for TEs, there are several limitations with UFH. Over the last 15 years, several new anticoagulant drugs that offer advantages over UFH under certain conditions have been developed. Low molecular weight heparins (LMWHs) are one class of new anticoagulants that have been tested in hundreds of trials in adults and shown to have specific advantages over UFH for the prevention and treatment of TEs. LMWHs potentially offer several advantages for pediatric patients but

require careful evaluation prior to widespread recommendation. At this time, there are two international clinical trials underway that are assessing the role of LMWH in children for prophylactic and therapeutic purposes.

This chapter discusses, for both UFH and LMWH, the following issues: (1) mechanism(s) responsible for their anticoagulant activities; (2) influence of age on their anticoagulant activities; (3) pharmacokinetics; (4) administration, monitoring, and side effects; and (5) clinical indications.

UNFRACTIONATED HEPARIN

Mechanism(s) Responsible for Heparin's Anticoagulant Activities

Unfractionated heparin was discovered in 1916 by a medical student who was looking for a coagulant made by the liver.[1] The observation that UFH required a plasma cofactor was made in 1939.[2] The antithrombin III (more recently called antithrombin [AT]) dependence of UFH was further delineated in the late 1960s.[3] UFH contains a pentasaccharide sequence that binds to AT through lysine sites causing a conformational change at the reactive center that converts AT into a rapid inhibitor of many serine proteases, including thrombin and factor (F)Xa.[4] The inhibition of thrombin requires that both AT and thrombin bind to UFH.[5-7] In contrast, the inhibition of FXa only requires the binding of AT to UFH;[8-10] thus, short polysaccharide chains containing the pentasaccharide sequence will inhibit FXa but not thrombin (Figure 9–1). In contrast, polysaccharide chains in excess of approximately 20 monosaccharide chains will inhibit either thrombin or FXa, provided the AT pentasaccharide binding sequence is present.[5–7,11,12] UFH's anticoagulant activity is primarily due to the inhibition of thrombin activation of FV and FVIII.[13]

Commercial preparations of UFH contain fragments with an average molecular weight of 15,000 daltons but with ranges from 3,000 to 30,000 daltons. Approximately two-thirds of UFH molecules do not contain pentasaccharide units that bind AT and are not active as an anticoagulant.[5,12,14–18] The anticoagulant activities of the remaining one-third of UFH molecules that bind AT are modified by plasma proteins, platelets, fibrin, and vascular surfaces. UFH binds to many proteins, including some that inhibit UFH's anticoagulant activities.[19] Increased plasma concentrations of UFH neutralizing proteins, such as histidine-rich glycoprotein (HRGP),[20–22] platelet factor 4 (PF4),[20,23,24] and vitronectin,[25] may contribute to UFH resistance in patients with inflammatory and malignant disorders. Platelets bind FXa, thereby protecting it from inactivation by UFH-AT complexes.[26,27] Activated platelets also release PF4, a protein that neutralizes UFH's anticoagulant activity.[28] Fibrin modifies UFH's anticoagulant activity by binding thrombin, thereby protecting it from inactivation by UFH-AT complexes.[29,30] The relative resistance of fibrin-bound thrombin to UFH-AT inactivation may explain why therapeutic UFH requirements are greater than prophylactic requirements for the treatment of TEs.[31] Vascular surfaces, such as the subendothelium, also protect thrombin from inactivation by UFH-AT.[32]

Unfractionated heparin influences other hemostatic activities including the fibrinolytic system and platelet function.[33] In vitro, UFH, in combination with components of the fibrinolytic system, inhibits plasmin,[34] increases the conversion of plasminogen to plasmin,[35] and impairs the activation of plasminogen by tissue plasminogen activator (TPA).[36] There is some weak evidence that UFH may increase fibrinolytic activity in vivo.[37] Unfractionated heparin also prevents rethrombosis following thrombolysis with TPA.[37] In vitro, UFH binds to platelets and may either induce or inhibit platelet aggregation depending on the experimental conditions.[38] In vivo, UFH prolongs the bleeding time in

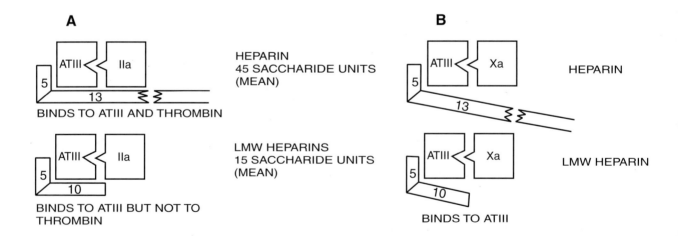

Figure 9–1 (*A*) Inactivation of thrombin. To inactivate thrombin, heparins must bind AT through an additional 13 saccharides units. Low molecular weight heparins that contain less than 18 saccharide units cannot bind to thrombin and, therefore, are unable to inactivate thrombin. (*B*) Inactivation of factor Xa. To inactivate factor Xa, heparins must bind to AT through the high affinity pentasaccharides but do not need to bind to factor Xa. Therefore, both unfractionated heparin and low molecular weight heparins are able to inactivate factor Xa.

IIa = thrombin; AT = antithrombin; Xa = factor Xa.

Reproduced with permission from Hirsch J, Levine M. Low molecular weight heparin. Blood 1992;79:1–17.

humans and increases blood loss in a rabbit model.[39–41] UFH interaction with platelets and endothelial cells may contribute to bleeding independently from its anticoagulant effect.[39]

Influence of Age on Heparin's Anticoagulant and Antithrombotic Activities

Unfractionated heparin's activities can be considered as "anticoagulant," which refers to UFH's activities in vitro, and "antithrombotic," which refers to UFH's activities in vivo. The anticoagulant activities of UFH in plasmas from infants and children have been assessed in a variety of in vitro test systems.[42–45] The antithrombotic activities of UFH in vivo have been assessed using models.[46] However, only cohort studies and case series have been used to determine UFH's antithrombotic effectiveness in pediatric patients.[47–49] The following section discusses the available information on the anticoagulant and antithrombotic activities of UFH in the young.

Anticoagulant Activities Both an increased sensitivity and resistance to UFH's anticoagulant activities have been reported in the young.[42–44,50] In-

creased UFH sensitivity is observed in systems based on assays dependent on thrombin generation, such as the activated partial thromboplastin time (APTT), activated whole blood clotting times (ACTs), and chromogenic assays of thrombin generation in the absence of fibrinogen.[44] In the absence of UFH, the capacity of plasma from newborns to generate thrombin is both significantly delayed and decreased compared to adults[42,43] and similar to plasma from adults receiving therapeutic amounts of UFH (Figure 9–2).[43] Following infancy, the capacity of plasma to generate thrombin increases but throughout childhood remains approximately 25 percent less than for adults.[45] These physiologic features of thrombin regulation influence the activities of UFH. In the presence of UFH concentrations in the therapeutic range, the capacity of plasma from newborns and children to generate thrombin is further delayed and decreased by 50 percent and 25 percent, respectively, compared to adults (see Figure 9–2).[43,45] The common feature of these assays is that they measure how UFH influences the initial rates of thrombin generation.

In contrast to results from thrombin generation assays, neonatal plasma is resistant to UFH in assays that measure the inhibition of exogenously added

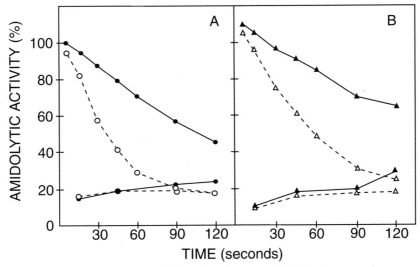

Figure 9–2 Generation of amidolytic thrombin activity in the absence and presence of heparin in defibrinated and pooled normal adult (*A*) and full-term cord plasma (*B*) after contact activation and recalcification. Solid lines, no heparin; dotted lines, 0.2 units/mL heparin; broken lines, 0.4 units/mL heparin. Newborn values are means of eight measurements performed in eight individual cord plasmas.

Reproduced with permission from Schmidt B, Ofosu F, Mitchell L, et al. Anticoagulant effects of heparin in neonatal plasma. Pediatr Res 1989;25:405–8.

FXa or thrombin (and/or protamine sulfate).[42–44,47] These UFH assays are dependent on plasma concentrations of AT and can underestimate the UFH concentration over the therapeutic range of UFH (0.2 to 0.5 units/mL by protamine sulfate assay or 0.30 to 0.70 units/mL by anti-FXa assay). Some pediatric patients requiring UFH therapy have significantly decreased plasma concentrations of AT reflecting physiologic, congenital, and/or acquired etiologies. For example, plasma concentrations of AT are physiologically decreased at birth (approximately 0.50 units/mL) and increase to adult values by 3 months of age.[52–54] Sick premature newborns, a population of children at significant risk for TEs, frequently have plasma concentrations of AT that are less than 0.30 units/mL, potentially influencing their response to UFH.[55] Fetal reference ranges are now available and show that AT levels range from 0.20 to 0.37 units/mL at gestational ages of 19 to 38 weeks.[56] In vitro studies show that the paradox of UFH sensitivity and resistance in plasma from newborns reflects the ratio of AT to thrombin (or FXa) in the assay system.[44]

Antithrombotic Activities The in vivo antithrombotic effects of UFH have been assessed in newborn piglets and show that decreased concentrations of AT limit the antithrombotic effects of UFH (Figure 9–3).[46] This relative UFH resistance can be overcome by either increasing the UFH dose or AT concentration (see Figure 9–3).[46] There is a potential risk of using high doses of UFH in newborns due to the immaturity of the hemostatic system and risk of intracranial hemorrhage (ICH).[57–59] An alternative approach is to use AT concentrates to increase plasma concentrations of AT. Clinical trials are required to assess the safety and efficacy of AT concentrates in this patient population prior to any clinical recommendations. At this time, there are no clinical studies that have focussed on the optimal use of UFH in newborns to successfully treat and/or prevent TEs.

Pharmacokinetics of Heparin

Heparin Pharmacokinetics in Adult Patients
Unfractionated heparin is administered either in-travenously or subcutaneously because it is poorly absorbed from the gastrointestinal tract. The pharmacokinetics of UFH, based on biologic activities, have been extensively studied in adults[60] and in animal models.[61] Its clearance best fits a model based on the combination of a saturable and linear nonsaturable clearance mechanism.[60,62] The initial rapid decay is the equilibration phase and the second portion of the curve is dose dependent, reflecting the elimination of UFH from the circulation.

The clearance of UFH is complex because it interacts with some cell surfaces,[19] proteins,[19,63] and proteins that neutralize its anticoagulant activities.[28]

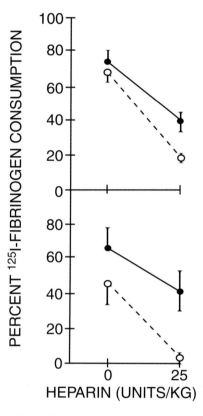

Figure 9–3 The effect of antithrombin concentrate on the antithrombotic properties of heparin in newborn piglets. Systemic consumption of ^{125}I-fibrinogen and local consumption within the occluded vein segment are shown in the upper and lower panel, respectively. Values represent means with their 95 percent confidence limits for piglets with physiologic antithrombin deficiency (●-●) and antithrombin supplemented piglets (O-O); n ≥ 16 treatment group.

kg = kilogram.

Reproduced with permission from Schmidt B, Buchanan M, Ofosu F, et al. Antithrombotic properties of heparin in a neonatal piglet model of thrombin induced thrombosis. Thromb Haemost 1988;60:289–92.

The large volume of distribution may reflect UFH binding to endothelium and subsequent internalization and depolymerization.[64] Unfractionated heparin is also taken up and desulfated by mononuclear phagocytes.[65] The precise pathway of UFH elimination is uncertain, although both liver and renal pathways are likely important. Clearance is accelerated in acute pulmonary embolism (PE) by poorly understood mechanisms.[66,67] The clearance of UFH from different sources (bovine or porcine) does not likely differ and UFH does not interact with other drugs.[68]

Heparin Pharmacokinetics in a Newborn Animal Model The influence of age on UFH pharmacokinetics has been extensively assessed in a porcine animal model,[69] and, to a lesser extent, in newborns.[70–76] The pharmacokinetics of UFH were assessed by both anti-FXa activity and radioactivity in piglets, AT supplemented piglets and adult pigs.[69] Recovery of peak anti-FXa activity was decreased in piglets compared to adult pigs[69] due to

the influence of decreased plasma concentrations of AT in piglet plasma (50% of adult values).[75] Supplementation with AT, either in vivo or in vitro, increased anti-FXa activity to values similar to adult pigs.[69] The pharmacokinetics of UFH based on anti-FXa activity were similar to radioactivity, provided AT levels were supplemented in piglets.[69] The overall clearance of UFH was twofold faster in piglets compared to pigs due to an increased volume of distribution per kilogram in piglets (Figure 9–4).[69] The half-life was similar at both ages.

Heparin Pharmacokinetics in Pediatric Patients Limited studies of UFH kinetics are available in sick premature newborns.[70,71,74] Similar to results in the porcine model,[69] the volume of distribution per kilogram for UFH is increased in premature infants compared to adults. However, half-life values are discrepant, being reported as either shorter[70,76] or similar[70,71] to adult values. The reason for the discrepant half-life measurements in newborns is not readily apparent. The porcine model suggests that

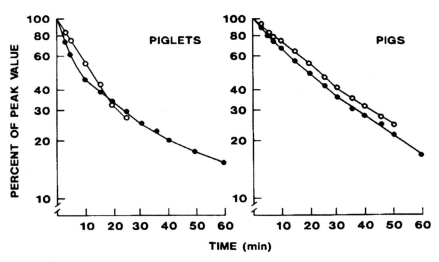

Figure 9–4 The pharmacokinetic curves of heparin in the newborn piglet and newborn piglet repleted with antithrombin after bolus intravenous injection of 100 units/kg of ^{125}I-heparin. The pharmacokinetic curves for ^{125}I-heparin (●) and anti-factor Xa activity (○) (measured with 1 volume of sample plus 1 volume adult porcine plasma) were determined. The data ware expressed as the mean of 6 to 9 experiments with all SE being less than 2 percent for radioactivity and 7 percent for anti-factor Xa activity. The anti-factor Xa clearance and ^{125}I-heparin clearance are similar in the piglet repleted with antithrombin.

AT-III = antithrombin.

Reproduced with permission from Andrew M, Ofosu F, Schmidt B, et al. Heparin clearance and ex vivo recovery in newborn piglets and adult pigs. Thromb Res 1988;52:517–27.

discrepant results for UFH clearance in newborns may be due, at least in part, to varying sensitivities of biologic assay systems used to detect the presence of UFH.[69] The responsiveness of the assay system to low concentrations of UFH is reduced in newborn plasma if sufficient AT is not exogenously added, resulting in lower anti-FXa levels.

Unfractionated heparin requirements of young children to achieve the adult therapeutic range are increased compared to adults.[48,72–74] The available information supports at least two plausible explanations for the increased UFH requirement. First, UFH is cleared more quickly in the young compared to adults in both animal models[69] and in humans.[70,71,76,77] Second, the delay in diagnosis of TEs in children may result in more extensive disease at the time of presentation, accelerating the clearance of UFH.[66,67]

Indications for Heparin Prophylaxis

Adults   In adults, numerous randomized controlled trials (RCTs) have reported the benefits of prophylactic UFH in high-risk clinical situations, which include general surgical and medical patients, patients undergoing major orthopedic surgery, or those at very high risk for venous TEs (VTE) (ie, patients with previous TEs).[13,78]

Children   In pediatric patients, prophylactic UFH is not routinely indicated in similar conditions to those in adults because the incidence of TEs is too low to warrant the risk of bleeding with UFH prophylaxis.[79] However, UFH prophylaxis is indicated in pediatric patients in certain circumstances.[79] Prophylactic UFH is most commonly used for the preservation of catheter patency, including cardiac catheterization (CC), central venous lines (CVLs), umbilical arterial catheters (UACs), and peripheral arterial catheters.[80] Frequently total parenteral nutrition (TPN) solutions have 1 to 3 units/mL of UFH added. Recent studies have confirmed the stability of UFH in 24-hour TPN infusates; however, the question of whether UFH destabilizes lipid preparations remains uncertain.[81,82] Noncatheter-related use of prophylactic UFH is rare and limited to initial prophylaxis following cardiac surgery for some forms of congenital heart disease (CHD) and short-term prophylaxis for patients with congenital prothrombotic disorders experiencing a short-term acquired risk factor for VTEs.

Treatment for Thromboembolic Events

Venous Thromboembolic Disease   In general, the initial treatment of VTEs involving the deep veins of the lower extremity, upper extremity, and pulmonary circulation is UFH. Studies in adults clearly show that initial treatment with UFH (or LMWH) is required and that initial treatment with oral anticoagulants (OAs) is insufficient, resulting in an increased risk of recurrent VTE and mortality.[13,83] Currently these guidelines are extrapolated for use in children, which is likely appropriate until studies in children provide further insight into optimal anticoagulation for VTE. However, whether all newborns with VTE require treatment with anticoagulants and what the intensity and duration should be is not clear at this time. In general, newborns with symptomatic VTE likely benefit from at least a short course of UFH (or LMWH). The necessity of using UFH (or LMWH) for the treatment of VTE in unusual locations, such as the renal vein, is unclear. If there is no contraindication and there is potential loss of organ function, initial treatment with UFH (or LMWH) should be considered. Right atrial thrombi are particularly problematic because of the risk of embolization and obstruction of the pulmonary system. If the thrombus is not interfering with function, which may necessitate a more aggressive approach with thrombolytic therapy or embolectomy, initial therapy with UFH (or LMWH) is usually indicated.

Arterial Thrombosis   Arterial TEs in children are secondary to catheters in over 90 percent of cases and most commonly occur in the aorta for neonates and femoral arteries for infants and children.[84] In general the initial treatment of arterial TEs is UFH (or LMWH). For arterial TEs that are immediately threatening limb or organ function, either thrombolytic therapy or an embolectomy may be required.[84] However, anticoagulants must be used in the initial period to avoid reocclusion following thrombolytic therapy or embolectomy. One common mistake is to continue thrombolytic therapy for 2 or 3 days without concurrent heparinization. These children become refractory to thrombolytic therapy and their clot may extend if adequate anticoagulation therapy is not being used concurrently, or at least early after thrombolytic therapy is initiated.[85,86]

Prevention of Thrombotic Disease

Children with Congenital Prothrombotic Disorders Increasing numbers of children with congenital prothrombotic disorders are being identified prior to the development of TEs, usually due to family studies because of an affected adult relative. Because most afflicted patients with congenital prothrombotic disorders do not develop TEs during childhood, routine prophylaxis for all patients can not be recommended. However, in the presence of an acquired prothrombotic situation, children with congenital prothrombotic disorders can develop VTEs and likely the benefits from short-term prophylaxis with an anticoagulant outweighs the minimal risk of bleeding. Unfractionated heparin is an option when the acquired risk factor is limited to a few days.[79] However, if the acquired risk factor will be present for several weeks or months, OAs or LMWH are preferable because of the risk of UFH-induced osteopenia.

Cardiac Catheterization In the absence of prophylactic anticoagulation, the incidence of symptomatic TEs following CC via the femoral artery is approximately 40 percent.[87] Younger children (less than 10 years of age) have an increased incidence compared to older children.[87] Prophylactic anticoagulation with aspirin does not significantly reduce the incidence of arterial TEs.[88] However, anticoagulation with 100 to 150 units/kg of UFH reduces the incidence from 40 percent to 8 percent.[87] A more recent study suggests that 50 units/kg bolus of UFH may be as efficacious as 100 units/kg when given immediately after arterial puncture. However this study was underpowered, and a recommendation for 50 units/kg as optimal prophylaxis cannot be recommended at this time.[89] Recent advances in

interventional catheterization have resulted in the use of larger catheters and sheaths that may increase the risk of TEs. Further UFH boluses are frequently used in prolonged procedures (over 60 minutes), especially during interventional catheterizations. The benefits and need for further UFH boluses have not been assessed. A short limb and claudication[90] are the long-term consequences of femoral artery TEs in children; however, the true incidence of these complications has not been assessed by any recent studies.

Blalock-Taussig Shunts Blalock-Taussig (BT) shunts are one form of palliative surgery used to enhance systemic (via the subclavian artery) to pulmonary artery blood flow in patients with severe or progressive cyanosis, usually secondary to pulmonary stenosis.[91,92] "Modified" BT shunts, where a gortex tube graft is taken from the side of the subclavian artery and anastomosed to the pulmonary artery, have been used since 1980. Because of the short length of the shunt and high flow rate, acute TEs are less common. Since 1980, there have been 238 reports involving children with BT shunts, 15 of these reported TEs.[93-107] The incidence of TEs ranged from 1 to 17 percent. Many investigators used antithrombotic therapy beginning with therapeutic doses of UFH and followed by low dose aspirin (1 to 10 mg/kg/d).[106] Other investigators used intraoperative UFH with no further anticoagulation.[107]

Fontan Operation The Fontan procedure, or a modified version, is the definitive palliative surgical treatment for most congenital univentricular heart lesions.[108-110] TEs remain a major cause of early and late morbidity and mortality. Reported incidences of VTEs and stroke ranged from 3 to 16 percent and 3 to 19 percent, respectively, in the studies where TE was the primary outcome,[111-118] and from 1 to 7 percent in studies that assessed multiple outcomes.[119-127] TEs occur at any time following Fontan procedures, but often present months to years later.[111,112] No predisposing factors have been identified with certainty, although this may be due to inadequate power and the retrospective nature of the studies. Transesophageal echocardiography is more sensitive than transthoracic echocardiography for the diagnosis of intracardiac and central venous TEs.[128,129] Despite aggressive therapy, TEs following Fontan procedures have a high mortality, and respond to therapy in less than 50 percent of cases.[111,112,116–118,120,122,128–141] There is no consensus in the literature, or in routine clinical practice, as to the optimal type or duration of anticoagulation. Consequently, a wide variety of prophylactic anticoagulant regimes are in current use. There is an urgent need for large multicenter prospective trials of prophylactic anticoagulation therapy following Fontan procedures.[142]

Endovascular Stents Endovascular stents are used increasingly to manage a number of congenital heart lesions, including branch pulmonary artery stenosis, pulmonary vein stenosis, and coarctation of the aorta, as well as postsurgical stenosis.[143] Although stents can be successfully used in infants less than one year of age, the small vessel size increases the risk of TEs. There are no studies assessing the role of anticoagulation or antiplatelet therapy to avoid stent occlusion. UFH is commonly given at the time of stent insertion, followed by aspirin therapy. Further studies are required to determine the optimal prophylactic anticoagulation required.[143–152]

Other Cardiac Disorders Other likely cardiac indications for anticoagulation in children are atrial fibrillation and myocardial infarction (MI).[153–176] There are only case reports describing antithrombotic therapy for these patients. In the absence of data, guidelines for antithrombotic therapy in adult patients are recommended.

Maintenance of Catheter Patency

Umbilical Arterial Catheters Umbilical arterial catheters are necessary for the administration of supportive care critical to the survival of sick newborns. The tips of UACs are either positioned high (level of T5-T10) or low (level of L3-L5). The optimal position to minimize TEs remains uncertain and may influence both the frequency of TEs and ICH.[177–179] A low dose continuous UFH infusion (1

to 5 units/hour) is commonly used to maintain UAC patency. The effectiveness of UFH was assessed in seven well-designed controlled trials (Table 9–1).[57,180–185] Outcomes assessed were patency, local TEs, and ICH. Patency, which is likely linked to the presence of local TE, is prolonged by the use of low dose UFH.[181–185] Local TEs, detected by ultrasound (US), were not decreased in two controlled trials. However, the power was low.[180,181]

The incidence of ICH was assessed in three trials, two of which reported an increase associated with UFH[58,59] and one of which did not.[57] In the two cohort studies, UFH was implicated as a risk factor for ICH in low birthweight infants.[58,59] One study was retrospective and the 95 percent confidence interval around the odds ratio of 3.9 was large (1.4 to 11.0) and the magnitude of the risk uncertain.[58] The other study demonstrated a positive correlation between UFH dose and frequency of ICH. However, severity of illness was also positively correlated with UFH dose and the effect could not be differentiated.[59] In the only RCT, use of UFH was not linked to an increased risk of ICH (1.49 [95% CI 0.62 -3.59]).[57] Large well-designed studies are required to determine whether low dose UFH infusion affects the incidence of ICH.

Central Venous Lines Loss of patency and associated TEs have led clinicians to use UFH flushes or infusates in an attempt to prevent these complications. A MEDLINE search identified one meta-analysis[186] and 14 clinical trials assessing the use of UFH in CVLs and 10 were included.[187–193,195,196] Three trials showed that UFH is associated with a strong trend for reducing CVL-related fibrin sheath formation.[189–191] Six trials assessed the impact of UFH on partial or total occlusion of vascular flow and that UFH decreased CVL-related TEs.[187–189,191–193] In children, patency of CVLs is frequently maintained by intermittent boluses of UFH (200 to 300 units) daily, weekly, or monthly. For infants less than 10 kg, a lower dose of 10 units/kg is frequently used to avoid transient systemic anticoagulation.

Peripheral Venous and Arterial Catheters A recent systematic review and meta-analysis reported

Table 9–1 Umbilical Artery Catheterization

Reference	Level	Intervention	Patient Number	Outcome Bleeding	Outcome Event (B or TE)
Jackson et al[180]	RCT	HB-PU	61	*	13 TE
		PVC	64	*	23 TE
Horgan et al[181]	RCT	Heparin	52	*	16 TE
		No heparin	52	*	18 TE
Rajani et al[182]	RCT	Heparin	32	*	4 B[†]
		Placebo	30	*	19 B
David et al[183]	RCT	Heparin	26	0*	3 B[†]
		No heparin	26	0*	15 B
Bosque and Weaver[184]	RCT	Heparin (C)	18	*	0 B[†]
		Heparin (I)	19	*	8 B
Horgan et al[181]	RCT	Heparin	59	*	2 B[†]
		No heparin	52	*	10 B
Ankola and Ataken[185]	RCT	Heparin	15	4 ICH	2 B[†]
		No heparin	15	5 ICH	11 B
Chang et al[57]	RCT	Heparin	5558	19 ICH	NR
		No heparin		17 ICH	NR

B = blocked; RCT = randomized controlled trial; TE = thromboembolic event; HB-PU = heparin bonded-polyurethane; PVC = polyvinyl chloride; C = continuous; I = intermittent; ICH = intracranial hemorrhage.

*No hemorrhage, *not reported, [†]p value < .05.

Reproduced with permission from Michelson AD, Bovill E, Monagle P, Andrew M. Antithrombotic therapy in children. Chest 1998;114:748S–69S.

that UFH is effective in prolonging catheter patency and reducing infusion failure in peripheral intravenous catheters when used at a concentration of 0.5 to 1 units/mL.[197–214] Intermittent UFH flushes at 10 units/mL were not beneficial; however, 100 units/mL was successful in increasing catheter patency and may decrease catheter-related phlebitis.[212,213] UFH was found to be effective in prolonging the life of peripherally placed arterial catheters, although the minimal effective dose remains to be determined.[204]

Target Range and Monitoring of Therapeutic Amounts of Heparin

The target range and monitoring of UFH administered for therapeutic purposes are dependent upon the indications, which include (a) treatment of TEs; (b) dialysis; (c) CPB; and (d) ECMO.

Treatment of Venous Thromboembolic Events In adults, the recommended therapeutic range for the treatment of VTE is an APTT that reflects a UFH level by protamine titration of 0.2 to 0.4 units/mL or an anti-FXa level of 0.3 to 0.7 units/mL.[33] Therapeutic doses of UFH in pediatric patients are the amounts of UFH required to achieve the adult therapeutic range based on UFH levels. In pediatric patients, APTT values correctly predict whether UFH concentrations are therapeutic approximately 70 percent of the time.[48] If APTT values do not accurately reflect UFH concentrations, UFH concentrations should be preferentially used as they better reflect the in vivo antithrombotic effectiveness of UFH.[48]

Doses of heparin The doses of UFH required in pediatric patients to achieve adult therapeutic APTT values have been assessed using a weight based nomogram.[48] A bolus dose of 50 units/kg was insufficient, resulting in subtherapeutic APTT values in 60 percent of children.[48] Bolus doses of 75 to 100 units/kg result in therapeutic APTT values in 90 percent of children (unpublished data). Maintenance UFH doses are age dependent, with infants having the highest requirements (28 units/kg/hr) and children over 1 year of age having lower requirements (20 units/kg/hr). The doses of UFH required for older children are similar to the weight adjusted requirements in adults (18 units/kg/hr).[215] There is tremendous variability in UFH requirements, necessitating careful monitoring and UFH dose adjustment. The duration of therapy with UFH for the treatment of VTE is a minimum of 5 days, and 7 to 10 days for extensive deep vein thrombosis (DVT) or PE.[216,217] Oral anticoagulants can be initiated on day 1 of UFH therapy except for extensive DVT or PE, in which circumstance OAs should be delayed.

Monitoring of heparin Appropriate dosage adjustment of intravenous UFH therapy can be problematic. Nomograms are convenient to use and have been successful in achieving therapeutic APTT levels in a timely manner in adults.[215,218,219] A nomogram initially used in adults was adapted, tested, and modified for children (Table 9–2).[48] UFH dosing nomograms can be adapted into pre-printed order sheets that facilitate rapid anticoagulation.

Varying sensitivities of activated partial thromboplastin times to heparin Over the past decade, hematologists have become aware that commercial reagents used to measure coagulation screening tests vary significantly in their sensitivities to anticoagulant drugs, thereby influencing patient management. One example is the differing sensitivities of prothrombin time (PT) reagents to reduced plasma concentrations of the vitamin K (VK)-dependent factors that led to the introduction of the International Normalized Ratio (INR).[220] Another example of reagent effect on assay results is the variable sensitivity of commercial APTT reagents to the presence of UFH that has led to the use of UFH assays to standardize APTT therapeutic ranges.[33,221]

Unfractionated Heparin Therapy for Dialysis

The main cause of hemorrhagic complications in uremic patients is anticoagulation for hemodialysis. Unfortunately, optimal use of UFH for hemodialysis has not been established. At least four general protocols are in use.[222–226] One common approach is

Table 9–2 Protocol for Systemic Heparin Administration and Adjustment for Pediatric Patients

I.   Loading dose: heparin 75 units/kg IV over 10 minutes.

II.   Initial maintenance dose: 28 units/kg/hour for infants less than 1 year; 20 units/kg/hour for children over 1 year.

III. Adjust heparin to maintain APTT 60-85 seconds (assuming this reflects an anti-factor Xa level of 0.30 to 0.70):

APTT (sec)	Bolus (units/kg)	Hold % (min)	Rate Change	Repeat APTT
<50	50	0	+10%	4 hrs
50–59	0	0	+10%	4 hrs
60–85	0	0	0	Next day
86–95	0	0	–10%	4 hrs
96–120	0	30	–10%	4 hrs
>120	0	60	–15%	4 hrs

IV.   Obtain blood for APTT 4 hours after administration of the heparin loading dose and 4 hours after every change in the infusion rate.

V.   When APTT values are therapeutic, a daily CBC, and APTT.

CBC = complete blood count; APTT = activated partial thromboplastin time; kg = kilogram; IV = intravenous; sec = second; min = minutes.

Reproduced with permission from Michelson AD, Bovill E, Monagle P, Andrew M. Antithrombotic therapy in children. Chest 1998;114:748S–69S.

to provide patients with a 50 unit/kg bolus dose initially and adjust a continuous infusion of UFH (initially 50 units/kg/hour) based upon the ACT.[224] Target values for ACTs vary, with some reports suggesting values over 220 seconds and others suggesting lower values between 180 and 220 seconds.[223]

Regional UFH to maintain an ACT between 180 to 200 seconds in the extracorporeal circuit has been used by some groups.[223] For this procedure, UFH is infused at 25 units/kg/hr into the arterial line, and protamine is infused at 0.25 mg/kg/hr into the venous return. The ACT is held below 120 seconds in the patient's circulation and between 180 and 200 seconds in the extracorporeal circuit.

Unfractionated heparin free dialysis has also been used for some adults with a clotting rate of 7 to 20 percent.[223] However, clotting may occur more frequently in children due to lower blood flows.[223]

A low dose UFH dialysis has been used in children. Dialysis is initiated without UFH and ACTs measured every 30 minutes. When ACTs are less than 170 seconds, a bolus of 10 units/kg of UFH is injected.[223] The thrombotic rate with this approach may be increased (7 of 21 procedures), particularly in children less than 10 kg with ACT values less than 170 seconds. Unfractionated heparin (10 units/kg/hour) is recommended for these patients.

Unfractionated Heparin Therapy During Cardiopulmonary Bypass

Cardiopulmonary bypass is an essential component of surgical procedures required to correct specific CHD. Unfractionated heparin is administered to minimize activation of the coagulation system and prevent fibrin deposition in the microvascular system as well as catastrophic occlusion of the bypass circuit.[227–229] Information, focussing on optimal dosing and monitoring of anticoagulant therapy in children during CPB, is limited to three prospective studies.[77,230,231] Both the initial bolus of UFH and concentration of UFH in the pump prime significantly influence the UFH concentration during CPB. The UFH concentration following an initial bolus of 300 to 400 units/kg is similar to adults and ranges from 3 to 5 units/mL. Following the initiation of CPB, the concentration of UFH in the pump prime significantly influences the UFH concentration because of the

extreme hemodilution in children requiring this intervention (an average of 45%).[232] For example, following an UFH bolus of 300 units/kg and a pump prime UFH concentration 1 unit/mL, UFH concentrations decrease immediately by approximately 50 percent following the initiation of CPB, resulting in an average initial UFH concentration on CPB of 1.5 units/mL (Figure 9–5).[232]

Monitoring of unfractionated heparin Monitoring UFH therapy during CPB is a critical aspect of intraoperative management because excess heparinization places patients at greater risk for bleeding complications[232] and suboptimal heparinization results in pathologic fibrin deposition.[232] ACT values are used to determine if patients are sufficiently anticoagulated to initiate CPB.[233] Target ACT values for initiation of CPB are above approximately 350 to 400 seconds.[234–239] Subsequently, ACTs are used to monitor UFH's activities and determine if further boluses are required during CPB. Following CPB, ACTs are used to ensure that UFH's activities are neutralized by protamine sulfate. Unfortunately, recent studies show that although ACT values correlate with UFH concentrations added to whole blood (Figure 9–6), there is no correlation with

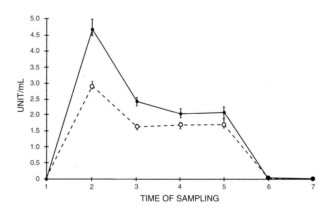

Figure 9–5 Heparin levels during cardiopulmonary bypass. Time of sampling: 1 = pre heparin bolus, 2 = post heparin bolus, 3 = beginning of cardiopulmonary bypass, 4 = during hypothermia, 5 = after hypothermia, 6 = post-protamine at the end of cardiopulmonary bypass, 7 = 24 hours after cardiopulmonary bypass.

Mean antifactor Xa (●), mean antithrombin (○).

Reproduced with permission from Chan A, Leaker M, Burrows F, et al. Coagulation profile of paediatric patients undergoing cardiopulmonary bypass. Thromb Haemost 1997; 77:270–7.

UFH concentrations during CPB in children (Figure 9–7).[230] The explanation is that ACT values also reflect the profound dilutional coagulopathy that begins immediately upon initiation of CPB in children.[230,231] Unfortunately, this means that ACT values do not reliably reflect circulating UFH concentrations and cannot be used to distinguish between a coagulopathy or UFH excess as causes of bleeding during CPB.

Reduced sensitivity of activated clotting time machines to unfractionated heparin The lack of sensitivity of ACT machines to UFH suggests that other changes in the hemostatic system must be present and detected by ACTs. Following initiation of CPB, UFH concentrations immediately decrease by approximately 50 percent and continue to decline (Figure 9–8).[230] Neither Hemochron nor HemoTec ACT values accurately reflect the minimal plasma concentrations of UFH. The timing and rapidity of the decrease in plasma UFH concentrations suggest that hemodilution (calculated at 58% at the completion of CPB) is a significant contributing feature.[230]

Variation between activated clotting time machines used during bypass A further problem with measuring ACT values in children during CPB is that results from different machines differ significantly and can be misleading.[230] In adult patients, comparisons of different ACT machines report that, although slightly different, decisions influencing UFH dosing are not changed.[240–244] A compari-

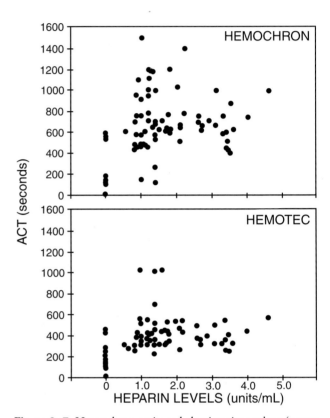

Figure 9–7 Hemochron activated clotting time values (upper panel) are compared to HemoTec activated clotting time values (lower panel) during cardiopulmonary bypass on 20 consecutive pediatric patients. Blood samples were obtained as follows: (1) prior to heparin; (2) following initial boluses of heparin (300 units/kg); (3) following institution of cardiopulmonary bypass; (4) during cardiopulmonary bypass; (5) during cardiopulmonary bypass and hypothermia; and (6) following administration of protamine sulfate. Hemochron activated clotting time values were significantly increased compared to HemoTec activated clotting time values throughout cardiopulmonary bypass. Of Hemochron activated clotting time values, 94 percent were above the threshold level of 450 seconds compared to 27 percent of HemoTec activated clotting time values.

ACT = activated clotting time.

Reproduced with permission from Andrew M, MacIntyre B, Williams W, et al. Heparin therapy during cardiopulmonary bypass requires ongoing quality control. Thromb Haemost 1993;70:937–41.

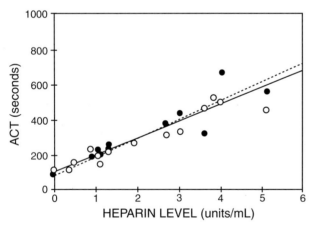

Figure 9–6 Hemochron activated clotting time values (●) are compared to HemoTec ACT values (○) on blood samples drawn from healthy individuals, directly into syringes containing increasing doses of heparin. The correlation was excellent and similar for both Hemochron activated clotting time values (Y = 98X ± 104, r² = 0.93) and HemoTec activated clotting time values (Y = 82X ± 109, r² = 0.94).

ACT = activated clotting time.

Reproduced with permission from Andrew M, MacIntyre B, Williams W, et al. Heparin therapy during cardiopulmonary bypass requires ongoing quality control. Thromb Haemost 1993;70:937–41.

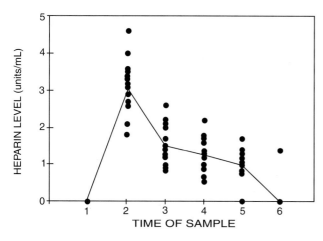

Figure 9–8 Ex vivo plasma heparin concentrations were measured by protamine sulfate neutralization in a thrombin clot based assay. Blood samples were obtained as follows: (1) prior to heparin; (2) following initial boluses of heparin (300 units/kg); (3) following institutions of cardiopulmonary bypass; (4) during cardiopulmonary bypass; (5) during cardiopulmonary bypass and hypothermia; and (6) following administration of protamine sulfate.

Reproduced with permission from Andrew M, MacIntyre B, Williams W, et al. Heparin therapy during cardiopulmonary bypass requires ongoing quality control. Thromb Haemost 1993;70: 37–41.

son of two commonly used ACT machines in children shows that ACT values differ by an average of 337 seconds (see Figure 9–7). More importantly, over 90 percent of values from one machine indicated that patients were sufficiently heparinized to initiate CPB while the second machine indicated that 63 percent of patients required further UFH.[230] In many institutions, additional UFH is administered to children during CPB if ACT values are less than 450 seconds. By switching ACT machines, clinical practice with regards to UFH therapy is significantly altered in an uncontrolled fashion.[230,231] At this time there is no good test to be substituted for ACT values. However ACT values cannot be used to distinguish excess UFH from a coagulopathy in patients who are bleeding during CPB. Operator dependent blood handling techniques such as time to placement of blood in tubes, methods of mixing blood with the activating agent, and length of mixing time can also affect ACT values.[230]

Variation between activated clotting time machines for the detection of coagulopathies
Further studies show that ACT values measured by

Hemochron and HemoTec machines differ in their sensitivity to an acquired coagulopathy.[230] Plasma concentrations of several coagulation proteins decrease by an average of 54 percent during CPB and match the calculated effect secondary to hemodilution (58%).[232] Hemodilution of the four contact factors may be particularly important because ACT values are dependent on uniform activation of the contact system. Plasma concentrations of one contact factor, FXI, decrease by 73 percent during CPB in children. When whole blood is diluted in vitro by 20 to 60 percent Hemochron ACT values are significantly longer than HemoTec ACT values, with 89 percent of Hemochron ACT values above 450 seconds compared to only 33 percent of HemoTec ACT values. These experiments confirm the important influence of hemodilution on ACT measurements made by the two machines.

Lack of interchangeability of activated clotting time machines The systematic difference between ACT results measured by two ACT machines is another example of the need for rigorous quality control in coagulation reagents (or whole blood machines). Clearly, HemoTec and Hemochron ACT machines cannot be used interchangeably in pediatric patients without significantly affecting the amounts of UFH administered, and thereby altering clinical care in an uncontrolled fashion.[230] Any new bedside UFH assays must be compared to laboratory UFH assays and to ACT values measured on machines previously used for pediatric patients.[230] In addition, new bedside UFH assays of any type must be rigorously evaluated in appropriate patient populations before being introduced into routine use in order to avoid detrimental, unplanned, and untested alterations in clinical practice.

Activation of hemostasis during bypass The adequacy of anticoagulation can be assessed to some extent by the use of biochemical markers of activation of the coagulation and fibrinolytic systems. In the past, measurement of fibrin monomer, the product of thrombin action on fibrinogen, was used to assess the adequacy of anticoagulant therapy during CPB. More sensitive markers of activation of coagulation, such as thrombin-AT (TAT) complexes and D-dimers, are available and have been assessed in children undergoing CPB.[232] Although fibrin monomers are rarely positive in children undergoing CPB, plasma concentrations of both TATs and D-dimers increase during and following surgery.[232] However, even plasma concentrations of 4 to 5 units of UFH do not suppress plasma concentrations of D-dimers in adult patients successfully undergoing CPB. The significance of increased plasma concentrations of TATs and D-dimers remains uncertain as the overall survival rate for children undergoing CPB is excellent and the reoperation rate for bleeding is minimal. Whether children would benefit from increased or decreased amounts of UFH during CPB can only be determined in clinical trials.

Unfractionated Heparin Therapy during Extracorporeal Membrane Oxygenation Extracorporeal membrane oxygenation permits the transfer of oxygen into blood across a semipermeable membrane and is currently used for infants with life-threatening severe respiratory insufficiency and children who cannot be removed from CPB.[245–247] The underlying disorders include meconium aspiration syndrome, severe respiratory distress syndrome, congenital diaphragmatic hernia, persistent pulmonary hypertension, sepsis, and CHD. The follow-up studies of survivors of ECMO are most encouraging, with a majority of infants showing normal development.[248–250] However, a significant proportion of patients suffer neurologic impairment that is frequently due to an ICH; the leading cause of death for infants on ECMO is ICH. The etiology of ICH is multifactorial, with UFH being one important contributing factor.[251–257]

Heparin dosing and monitoring Unfractionated heparin is given in full systemic doses, with a bolus of 100 to 150 units/kg followed by a continuous infusion of UFH at 20 to 70 units/kg/hr. The laboratory goal is to maintain ACT values at 2 to 3 times baseline (240 to 280 seconds).[258–261] Although anticoagulation is required for ECMO, the optimal use of UFH has never been tested in clinical trials. Whether lower doses of UFH or the use of potentially safer anticoagulant drugs, such as LMWHs, have a role in ECMO remains to be determined.

Adverse Effects of Unfractionated Heparin

Hemorrhagic Complications The most common complication of UFH is bleeding, which can be influenced by the duration of treatment, dose of UFH, route of administration, patients' response, and other patient-related features.[33] The available information suggests that major bleeding from UFH therapy is not frequent in the treatment of VTE in children.[48] However, many children were treated with suboptimal amounts of UFH.[48] The risk of bleeding may increase when therapeutic doses of UFH are used more uniformly, particularly in children with serious underlying disorders. Other identified risk factors for bleeding from UFH in adults are the presence of renal failure, concomitant use of antiplatelet agents,[262] and intermittent intravenous bolus administration of UFH.[33,263]

Treatment of unfractionated heparin-induced bleeding If anticoagulation with UFH needs to be discontinued for clinical reasons, termination of the UFH infusion will usually suffice because of the rapid clearance of UFH. If an immediate effect is required, intravenous protamine sulfate rapidly neutralizes UFH activity by virtue of its positive charge.[264] The dose of protamine sulfate required to neutralize UFH is based on the amount of UFH received in the previous two hours (Table 9–3). Protamine sulfate should be administered in a concentration of 10 mg/mL at a rate not to exceed 5 mg/minute.[264] Patients with known hypersensitivity reactions to fish, and those who have received protamine-containing insulin or previous protamine therapy, may be at risk of hypersensitivity reactions to protamine sulfate.[264]

Heparin-Induced Osteoporosis Osteoporosis is a disease characterized by decreased bone mass and microarchitectural deterioration of bone tissue, leading to enhanced bone fragility and an increase in fractures.[265] Osteoporosis may be defined in women based on bone mineral density (BMD) as measured by X-ray dual photon absorptiometry (DXA).[266] The World Health Organization (WHO) proposes three categories: (1) osteopenia—BMD 1–2.5 standard deviation (SD) below mean for young healthy adults (30 to 40 years); (2) osteo-

Table 9–3 Reversal of Heparin Therapy

Time since last heparin dose	Protamine Dose
< 30 min	1.0 mg/100 units heparin received
30–60 min	0.5–0.75 mg/100 units heparin received
60–120 min	0.375–0.5 mg/100 units heparin received
> 120 min	0.25–0.375 mg/100 units heparin received

Maximum dose of 50 mg

Infusion rate of a 10 mg/mL solution should not exceed 5 mg/min

Hypersensitivity reactions to protamine sulfate may occur in patients with known hypersensitivity reactions to fish or those previously exposed to protamine therapy or protamine-containing insulin.

min = minute; mg = milligram.

Reproduced with permission from Michelson AD, Bovill E, Monagle P, Andrew M. Antithrombotic therapy in children. Chest 1998;114:748S–69S.

porosis—BMD > 2.5 SD below mean for young adults; (3) severe osteoporosis—BMD >>2.5 SD below mean and history of nonviolent fracture.[266–269]

Incidence By definition, 15 percent of young adults have osteopenia. With age-dependent loss of BMD, one in three women will have osteoporosis by the age of 60 years. More than half of all women and one third of men will experience osteoporotic fractures during their lives.[270,271]

Mortality Most mortality of osteopenia is associated with hip fracture in the elderly.[272] However, prospective studies have reported increased mortality among men and women with low BMD.[273]

Bone mineral density The most useful risk factor for stratifying people by level of fracture risk is BMD.[273] A relationship has been shown between vertebral BMD and compressive strength.[274,275] In numerous prospective studies, the risk of vertebral fractures increases by about 2 to 2.4 times, and the risk of non-spinal fractures by 1.7 times for each 1 SD decrease in BMD from baseline.[273,276]

Measurement of bone mineral density Single photon absorptiometry (SPA) is limited to appendicular bones because the method requires a constant thickness of tissue across the measurement site.[277–279] Single photon absorptiometry measures bone mineral content (BMC) as grams of ashed bone/cm of axial length when divided by the width of bone obtained from the SPA scan, the bone min-

eral density (BMD) in units of g/cm^2. Although BMD at any skeletal site can be used for predicting all types of fractures, this may not be true for monitoring short-term changes. The spine is composed of mostly trabecular bone that is metabolically active and more likely to show effects of an insult manifesting as decreased BMD. Radial measurements reflect mostly cortical bone, with a much slower turnover, and hence effects may not show up as early.[277,280] Both axial and appendicular measurements can be used for diagnosis, but axial measures are preferred for assessment of therapy impact.

Dual x-ray absorptiometry (DXA) corrects for the effect of soft tissue on the absorption measurements, and its main application has been to measure bone mineral in lumbar spine, hip, and total body.[269,281–283] The reproducibility of such measurements, defined as the coefficient of variation, is between 1 and 3 percent. From total skeletal measurements, specific regions of interest can be defined for any desired part of the skeleton. Dual X-ray absorptiometry of the spine can be performed without specific preparation on any patient able to remain supine for about 5 minutes. The effective dose for most bone density measurements is less than 5 mSy, which is about the amount of radiation received each day from sources of natural radiation and radioactivity. The parameter measured is the BMD for DXA, the measured bone mineral content in grams divided by the projected area of the bone.[281] The units of BMD are therefore g/cm^2, which removes some of the dependence of bone mass upon body size.

Bone mineral density, developmental physiology Skeletal size and mass increase during development.[284–286] Physical activity during childhood is an important determinant of peak bone mass. After full skeletal size is attained, a period of further consolidation results in further increase of bone density.[284] This may represent the greatest opportunity for achieving maximal skeletal strength and reserves, thus reducing fracture risk in later life.[287] Peak bone mass achieved is the single most important factor that determines how much bone can be lost (with age or disease) before a critically low bone mass is reached and fractures occur.[284] The age at which peak bone mass is achieved is not certain. Estimates of peak total body BMD and BMC range from 18 to through the 20s. Specific sites may achieve peak bone mass at different times, with most studies suggesting femoral neck peak by the age of 14 to18 years.[280,288–292] However, spinal estimates vary from 14 years to the fourth decade. Recent studies suggest that 99 percent of whole body peak BMD is achieved by 22.1 years and 99 percent of BMC by 26.2 years.[284] The first 3 years of life and late puberty are critical years as these are periods of highest increase in BMD.[287] Differences in BMD exist between races and also between populations of similar race in different geographic locations. These differences may only become apparent in late adolescence.[293] Genetic factors also influence peak BMD, primarily before adulthood, and may account for up to 80 percent of population variance.[294] Other factors that can influence achieving maximal BMD are calcium (especially in prepubertal children), vitamin D intake, caffeine and alcohol intake, immobility and various medications, especially corticosteroids.[295] The major factor affecting BMD loss is aging.

Biochemical markers of bone turnover Bone formation and resorption is a continuous process that involves the formation and remodelling of collagen matrix associated with numerous other proteins.[286,296,297] Bone specific alkaline phosphatase (an enzyme used in bone formation), osteocalcin (a protein incorporated into the extracellular matrix of bone), and CICP (carboxy terminal peptide of type 1 collagen, which is cleaved and released when type 1 collagen is formed) can all be measured in human plasma as markers of bone formation.[282] The most specific and reliable marker is CICP.[296]

Fasting urinary calcium levels, hydroxyproline, pyridinoline (PYR), deoxypyridinoline (D-PYR), and cross-linked N telopeptides of type 1 collagen are all released following osteoclast-mediated bone degradation and can be measured as markers of bone resorption.[287,296] Normal ranges for the majority of these markers are established in children,[286,298] and UFH causes a marked reduction in CICP levels in children compared to age-matched normal controls and controls receiving OAs (unpublished information). A preliminary study of children on long-term warfarin (>6 months) duration shows a significant decrease in BMD for age and fractures following minimal trauma (unpublished information).

Pregnancy and lactation Normal changes in pregnancy are important, as pregnancy is one of the major indications for long-term UFH therapy. Hence many of the subsequent studies describing UFH-induced osteopenia (HIO) were performed on pregnant patients.[299–309] Pregnancy-induced osteoporosis causing spontaneous fracture is well documented.[310] The spine is frequently affected. There is some controversy over the extent of osteopenia when BMD is measured at various sites.

Goldsmith and colleagues demonstrated effects of oral contraceptive use, parity, and lactation on radial bone mineral content by SPA.[311] Wardlaw and colleagues demonstrated that duration of lactation was a significant factor (10.7 versus 2.8 months).[312] Chan and colleagues showed that adolescents may be more prone to bone loss from lactation than adults (8.1% mid-forearm after 4 months lactation).[308] The latter may be related to an inability to meet calcium requirements in the author's cohort of pregnant teens. Other authors have disputed Chan's findings, although none have performed comparable studies. In a prospective cohort, breastfeeding mothers had a 6.5 percent decrease in lumbar spine BMC in the 6 months postpartum, compared to no change in mothers who formula fed their infants (matched for age, parity, height, weight, calcium intake).[313] However, there was no difference in the mid-distal radius measurements, suggesting an effect in trabecular bone rather than cortical bone. The evidence to date suggests that these effects on bone are reversible with time.[314] The long-term fracture risk remains unknown.

Heparin-induced osteoporosis, clinical studies Clinical evidence of HIO was first reported in a cohort of 117 patients receiving long-term UFH.[315] Of the 10 who received more than 15,000 units/day, 6 suffered spontaneous vertebral fractures. None of the 107 on less than 10,000 units/day had fractures. Five of six improved dramatically on withdrawal of UFH. Since 1982, a number of series have been published of varying quality.[316,317] Hull and colleagues published a RCT of 3/12 adjusted dose UFH versus OAs for the treatment of DVT.[318] No evidence of HIO was found; however, osteoporosis was not a study endpoint and no diagnostic investigations were performed. De Swiet and colleagues reported a retrospective analysis of 20 pregnant women.[300] There were three groups: long-term (>22 weeks, n = 7), intermediate (10 to 22 weeks, n = 5), and short-term (<7 weeks, n = 8). The hands, femurs, and spines were assessed radiologically for evidence of cortical thinning. While the long-term group had significantly more thinning of the hands than the short-term group (p < .01), no differences were seen in the spine or femurs. The authors concluded that HIO was related to duration of therapy. Zimran and colleagues used histomorphometric methods to demonstrate reversibility of HIO on cessation of UFH therapy in a 23-year-old postpartum patient.[305] Dahlman and colleagues reported a prospective cohort of pregnant women.[299] Seventy patients who received long-term UFH and 30 controls were assessed with spinal x-ray postpartum. In the UFH group 17 percent were diagnosed with osteoporosis compared to none of the controls. Of these, 70 percent showed improvement within 6 months. There was no correlation between dose or UFH duration. In a separate group who had received UFH in a previous pregnancy (average of 30 months previous), none of the 18 patients had obvious osteopenia. Ginsberg and colleagues reported a prospective matched case control study, using densitometry to assess BMD in 61 patients who had received UFH for longer than 1 month in the past and in 61 control patients.[319] There was no significant difference in mean BMD (spine or wrist) between the two groups. However, the proportion with spinal BMD < 1.0 g/cm^2 was increased in the study group (p = .012). There was no association with daily or total UFH dose or duration of therapy. Possible confounders were that cases had received UFH in the past, so time-dependent reversibility would lessen any potential differences. The authors were unable to distinguish whether there was a subgroup of patients who were susceptible or whether there was a dose-dependent effect. Dahlman and colleagues published a prospective cohort of 184 pregnant women.[301] Only those with clinically suspected fractures were x-rayed. Spinal fractures were present in 2.2 percent (4 patients). Of these, 3 of 48 received high-dose UFH (mean 26,500 units/day), and 1 of 136 received low-dose UFH (mean 16,500 units/day) (p = .055). Barbour and colleagues reported a prospective matched case control study of 7 pregnant women on 12,000 to 21,000 units of UFH per day, 7 pregnant women on 23,000 to 50,000 units of UFH per day, and 14 controls matched for age, race, and smoking habits.[302] All women were on supplemental calcium. Thirty-six percent of cases had at least a 10 percent decline in proximal femur densitometry, compared to none of the controls. By 6 months postpartum, 4 of 5 had improved BMD. A dose response could not be demonstrated but the sample size was very small. In another prospective case control study, Dahlman and colleagues studied 30 controls and 39 patients on long-term UFH during pregnancy who had all received UFH for previous pregnancies (mean duration 37 weeks).[303] Single photon densitometry of the forearm showed no difference in baseline results between subjects and controls. At delivery, BMD was decreased by 4.9 percent in patients receiving UFH, compared to 2.3 percent in controls (not significant). At 7 weeks postpartum there was considerable improvement. Finally, Douketis and colleagues reported a prospective case control study of 25 pregnant women who were matched for age, weight, and smoking habits with 25 controls.[304] UFH was administered in 15 patients as a fixed dose of UFH, 5,000 units twice daily in the first trimester, and adjusted dose UFH in the second and third trimesters. Two patients received a fixed dose of UFH 5,000 units twice daily throughout the pregnancy and 8 received dose adjusted UFH throughout. Cases had lumbar spine BMD at 28 days postpartum, controls at 4 days. No fractures were found (confidence interval 0 to 13.7%); however, the mean difference in BMD was significantly different at 0.082g/cm². There was no correlation with dose (total or daily) or duration of UFH, but confidence limits were wide.

Heparin-induced osteoporosis, pediatric data There have been three case reports of HIO in children.[320-322] Murphy and colleagues reported a 14-month-old infant post liver transplant, on prednisolone, who developed DVT at day 44 post transplant.[320] After 41 days of UFH, 25 to 40 units/kg/day, he developed bilateral femoral, humeral, tibial, scapula, and rib fractures. Sackler and colleagues reported a 15-year-old boy with "pulmonary veno occlusive disease."[321] He was treated with 6,000 to 10,000 units for a total of 11 months and did not receive steroids. He developed symptomatic and radiologically proven vertebral fractures. The patient was hospitalized for 5 months, but mobility is not specifically commented upon. Avioli and colleagues[322] describe a 5 1/2-year-old child who developed fractures after 9 1/2 weeks of UFH, 10,000 units/day reported in the German literature by Schuster.[323] He was said to have hemolytic uremic syndrome (HUS) and was also treated with steroid therapy.

Conclusions from clinical studies HIO is a real clinical entity. To date no conclusive data have been able to establish the role of dose or duration of therapy. BMD as a predictor of fracture risk in this setting remains unvalidated, with no study showing correlation between decreased BMD and fracture rate.[315,316,319,322,324-328] The risk of fractures would seem to be approximately 2 to 3 percent and likely reversible on cessation of therapy. Whether peak BMD is diminished and hence risk of osteoporosis later in life is increased is unknown. Difficulties in interpreting the data arise from all studies having small numbers, lack of sensitive technique in early studies, the variation in skeletal site examined in studies utilizing BMD, and the fact that most stud-

ies occurred during pregnancy, which causes significant although perhaps variable effects on BMD.

There are only three case reports of pediatric HIO, two of which received concurrent steroid therapy.[320-322] The third received high-dose intravenous UFH therapy for a prolonged period.[321] The fact that peak BMD is not achieved until late teenage or early adult years, and studies suggesting adolescents are more prone to the effects of lactation on BMD, raise suspicions that children are at greater risk from HIO than adults. This remains to be proven in the clinical setting.

Heparin-induced osteopenia, experimental studies In the 1970s, Avioli reviewed the experimental evidence about the effect of UFH and related substances on bone.[322] The following mechanisms were proposed:

(1) Direct effect of UFH on bone cells with decreased osteoblastic or increased osteoclastic activity.
(2) Unfractionated heparin acts as a calcium chelating agent, causing secondary hyperparathyroidism.
(3) Defective ossification caused by disturbance of the matrix mucopolysaccharides of bone.

Thompson and colleagues showed that in a rats treated with subcutaneous UFH in therapeutic doses for 8 weeks, bone tensile strength was diminished compared to controls.[329] The treated animals had less new collagen present in their bones. However, whether the decreased new collagen was due to decreased production or increased breakdown was not determined. Hurley and colleagues examined collagen synthesis in 21-day fetal rat calvariae in vitro.[328] Unfractionated heparin and varying LMWHs were equally inhibitory on type 1 collagen and deoxyribonucleic acid (DNA) synthesis. The inhibitory effect was independent of the UFH's anticoagulant activity. Modification of the UFH by desulfation resulted in loss of the inhibitory effect, suggesting that the degree of sulfation contributes to the ability to inhibit collagen synthesis. In another recent study, rats were treated with subcutaneous injections of UFH. Bone was monitored by histomorphometry and by serial measurements of urinary type 1 collagen cross-linked pyridinoline (PYD) and serum alkaline phosphatase, markers of bone resorption and formation, respectively.[330] Histomorphometric analysis of the distal third of the right femur in the region proximal to the epiphyseal growth plate demonstrated that UFH induces both a time- and dose-dependent decrease in trabecular bone volume with the majority of trabecular bone loss occurring within the first 8 days of treatment. Thus, UFH doses of 1.0 units/kg/day resulted in a 32 percent loss of trabecular bone. Unfractionated heparin-treated rats also demonstrated a 37% decrease in osteoblast surface as well as a 75 percent decrease in osteoid surface. In contrast, UFH treatment had the opposite effect on osteoclast surface, which was 43 percent higher in UFH-treated rats as compared to control rats. Biochemical markers of bone turnover demonstrated that UFH treatment produced a dose-dependent decrease in serum alkaline phosphatase and a transient increase in urinary PYD, confirming the histomorphometric data. Based on these observations, UFH appears to decrease trabecular bone volume both by decreasing the rate of bone formation and increasing the rate of bone resorption.[330]

In summary, children treated with systemic UFH for prolonged periods of time are at risk of HIO. Alternative anticoagulant therapy should be considered to avoid this risk and, if prolonged therapy is unavoidable, regular BMD monitoring is recommended.

Heparin-Induced Thrombocytopenia

Heparin-induced thrombocytopenia (HIT) is a serious and relatively common complication of UFH therapy.[331–338] Typically HIT is characterized by a 50 percent or greater decrease in platelet count following 5 or more days of UFH therapy.[335] If a patient has been exposed to UFH in the recent past (less than 100 days), the presentation is frequently rapid, within the first 24 hours of re-exposure. The platelet count nadir is usually approximately 50,000, however, in some cases platelet counts do not go below 150,000.[339] In some postoperative patients, mean platelet counts may remain above 300,000.[339] The platelet nadir is not related to the risk of TEs. The discontinuation of UFH usually results in the platelet count recovering within days;[337] however, delayed recovery of platelet counts over several weeks has been observed.[339] Newer clinical syndromes associated with the development of HIT are being increasingly recognized and include OA-induced venous limb necrosis, acute systemic reactions to UFH, and UFH-induced skin lesions, which are seen in approximately 15 percent of patients with HIT secondary to subcutaneous UFH.[340,341]

The frequency of HIT is influenced by the type of UFH used, with bovine UFH having a greater risk of HIT than porcine UFH and to some extent the dose of UFH.[337,338] HIT is associated with new or extending VTE in approximately 5 percent of patients. Although arterial TEs were originally described, VTE occurs 4 times more frequently than arterial TEs.[342–345] The diagnosis of HIT can be problematic because of numerous co-existing disorders that can cause thrombocytopenia themselves.[337,338]

Laboratory assays There are, in general, two types of assays used to diagnose HIT: biologic (activation) assays and antigen or "immunoassays." The "gold standard" biologic assay is the serotonin-release assay (SRA).[346,347] However, the SRA is cumbersome to perform, and requires carefully selected control platelets and the use of radioactive markers.[346,347] Other bioassays have also been developed, including UFH-induced platelet activation (HIPA) and citrated platelet-rich plasma aggregation, which is only 30 to 70 percent sensitive.[348] All require carefully selected control platelets; a wash step in the absence of immunoglobulin (IgG), and platelet activation at low UFH concentrations but no activation at high UFH concentrations. The antigen assays include the UFH/PF4 assay, which measures the binding of patient IgG to a complex of UFH and PF4 immobilized in wells by using standard enzyme immunoassay techniques (EIA).[349,350] Alternatively a polyvinyl sulfate/PF4 EIA can also be used. Although there is good agreement between the biologic and immunologic assays for a majority of patients, there is also clear disagreement in some patients.

Natural history HIT is an intensely prothrombotic condition, with some patients developing TEs following discontinuation of UFH.[337,342] The mechanism by which HIT predisposes to TEs is by the production of platelet-derived microparticles that are released in the circulation and activate the coagulation system (Figure 9–9).[351] Patients with other acquired risk factors (such as recent surgery) are at a particularly high risk.[344] HIT is caused by an antibody that reacts with a complex of UFH and PF4. UFH appears to cause a conformational change in the PF4 molecule rendering it reactive to the IgG.

The incidence of HIT in children is not certain. There is some evidence that the onset may be delayed in neonates.[352] In the only published pediatric series, Spadone and colleagues reported a mean onset of thrombocytopenia of 22 days in 14 newborns who developed HIT.[352] Re-exposure to UFH was associated with a more rapid decrease in platelet count.[352] This group constituted 1 percent of all neonatal intensive care unit (NICU) admissions during the study period. UFH had been given as a prophylactic to maintain UAC patency, and 85 percent of neonates with HIT developed aortic TEs with a mortality of 21 percent. Of the control group without HIT, 25 percent developed aortic TEs. There have been six other case reports of pediatric HIT in the literature ranging in age from 3 months to 15 years.[353–357] Five were due to therapeutic UFH and one due to prophylactic UFH to maintain a CVL. One case resulted in extension of DVT despite thrombolytic therapy and without a significant decrease in platelet count.[355] Major bleeding

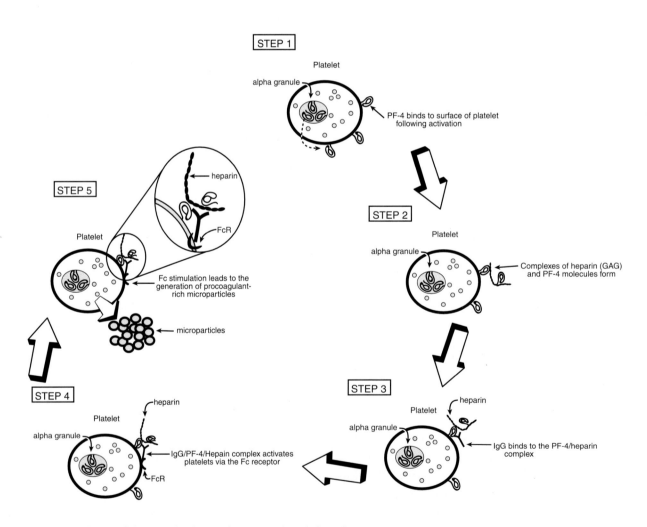

Figure 9–9 A schema of the steps leading to heparin-induced thrombocytopenia.

Reproduced with permission from Andrew M, Brooker LA, Ginsberg JS, Kelton JG. Clinical problems in anticoagulation therapy. Hematology 1997 (The Education Program of the American Society of Hematology); 8–28.

occurred in another.[356] Organan has been used successfully for treatment and to manage cardiac bypass in children with previous HIT.[353,355,358]

A high index of suspicion is required to diagnose HIT in children, especially in the setting of prophylactic UFH and multiple other risk factors for TEs. Accurate laboratory testing is essential.[346] Management consists of immediate cessation of UFH and alternative anticoagulation is recommended. Currently organan is the treatment of choice (Table 9–4).[357]

LOW MOLECULAR WEIGHT HEPARIN

Over the last two decades, several new anticoagulant drugs have been developed and offer advantages over UFH in certain disorders. LMWHs were developed as antithrombotic agents following the observation that LMWH fractions from UFH did not prolong the APTT but retained their capacity to inhibit FXa.[359] Studies in animals showed that LMWHs produce less bleeding and achieve an equivalent or superior antithrombotic effect compared to UFH.[360–362] Based upon these initial observations, LMWHs were developed commercially and underwent extensive testing in adults.

Potential Advantages

The potential advantages of LMWH for pediatric patients include consistent reproducible pharmacokinetics, subcutaneous administration, minimal need for monitoring, decreased risk of HIT, and decreased risk of osteoporosis making long-term use a feasible option instead of OAs.[359,363] However, the results of clinical trials assessing LMWHs in adults cannot be simply extrapolated to children because of age-dependent differences in the pharmacokinetics, different interaction of LMWHs with the developmentally immature hemostatic system of the young, different underlying pathologies of TEs, differences in the immune system, which influences the incidence of HIT, and the presence of growing bones, which may effect the risk of osteoporosis.[359] The issues surrounding the use of LMWHs in pediatric patients are:

(1) The influence of age on the anticoagulant and antithrombotic activities of LMWHs;
(2) The influence of age on the bioavailability and pharmacokinetics of LMWHs;
(3) The clinical use and side effects of LMWH therapy;
(4) Two ongoing international clinical trials of LMWH in children.

Table 9–4 Protocol for the Use of Organan in Pediatric Patients

Organan consists mainly of heparin sulfate, a small quantity of dermatan sulfate, and a minor amount of chondroitin sufate, and does not contain any heparin fragments. Organan has a much higher anti-Xa/anti-IIa ratio compared to heparin and low molecular weight heparin. Organan has a decreased cross reactivity rate (<10%) with heparin-induced antibody as compared to low molecular weight heparin (>90%).

Loading dose:	30 units/kg body weight/IV
Initial maintenance dose:	1.2–2.0 units/kg/hour/IV
Monitoring:	Anti-factor Xa activity can be monitored immediately following the bolus dose, every 4 hours until steady state is reached and then daily to maintain a therapeutic range of 0.4–0.8 units/mL.

Organan is predominantly removed from the circulation through the kidney. Consequently, organan is contraindicated in patients with severe impaired renal function.

kg = kilogram; IV = intravenous.

Reproduced with permission from Andrew M, deVeber G. Pediatric thromboembolism and stroke protocols. Hamilton: B.C. Decker Inc; 1997.

Influence of Age on the Anticoagulant Activities of Low Molecular Weight Heparins

Low molecular weight heparins are prepared by a variety of methods, including filtration or depolymerization of UFH to produce fractions with mean molecular weights of approximately 5,000 kDa.[364,365]

Anti-factor Xa Activities The anticoagulant activities of LMWH, similar to UFH, are dependent upon binding to AT and enhancement of AT inhibition of serine proteases. LMWHs possess increased specific activity in vitro against FXa but considerably less activity against thrombin in comparison to UFH, which has equivalent activity against both FXa and thrombin (Figure 9–1).[366] The poor inhibition of thrombin by LMWH reflects the inability of short polysaccharide chains (less than 18 saccharides) containing the AT binding site to also bind thrombin, which is necessary to inhibit its activity.[5,7] Inhibition of FXa does not require the binding of FXa to the GAG chain (see Figure 9–1).[5–7,11,12] Because of the relatively poor inhibition of thrombin, LMWHs must be monitored with an anti-FXa assay and not an APTT. APTT values are unaffected by LMWH when anti-FXa levels are less than at least 1.0 units/mL 4 to 6 hours following a subcutaneous dose. The widely varying distribution of molecular weight of LMWHs results in different antithrombin activities and, similarly, ratios of anti-FXa to antithrombin activities. International LMWH standards have been established in order to try and standardize the activities of LMWHs.[359,367,368] Although imperfect, reference preparations are likely the most practical mechanism for comparing clinical results obtained with different LMWHs.

Antithrombin Activities The antithrombin activities of LMWHs are very important to the in vivo antithrombotic effect of LMWHs.[9,10] During infancy and childhood, both AT and α_2-macroglobulin are equally important inhibitors of thrombin in the absence of UFH or LMWH.[369,370] The influence of LMWH on thrombin generation in plasma from newborns shows that newborn plasma is more sensitive to LMWH compared to adults. The sensitivity of newborn plasma to LMWH reflects the relative excess of AT compared to prothrombin (ratio of 1.5 to 1) compared to adults (ratio of 1:1 by definition) (Figure 9–10). The sensitivity of newborn plasma to LMWH can be enhanced by increasing plasma concentrations of AT.[371] In contrast, resistance to LMWH can be induced in newborn plasma by increasing plasma concentrations of prothrombin.

Influence of Age on the Bioavailability and Pharmacokinetics of Low Molecular Weight Heparin

Bioavailability The bioavailability of LMWHs is increased compared to UFH at usual therapeutic concentrations.[372] The molecular size of UFHs influences their ability to bind to plasma proteins such as HRGP, PF4, vitronectin, fibronectin, and von Willebrand Factor (vWF) with small molecular weight UFH molecules having a decreased capacity to bind to these proteins.[20,25,372–375] The reduced binding of LMWHs results in superior bioavail-

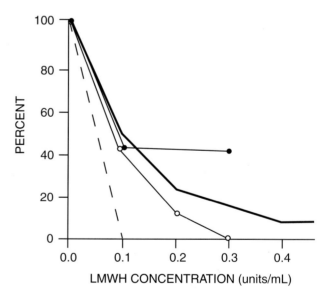

Figure 9–10 Dose response curves of thrombin activity expressed as (area under the curve) versus concentration of a low molecular weight plasma heparin (LMWH).

ATIII = antithrombin; U/mL.

Reproduced with permission from Vieira A, Ofosu F, Andrew M. Heparin sensitivity and resistance in the neonate: an explanation. Thromb Res 1991;63:85–99.

ability and a more predictable anticoagulant response. The molecular size of heparins also influences their capacity to bind to endothelial cells, with smaller molecular weights having reduced binding.[19,376,377] Thus the differing bioavailabilities and pharmacokinetics of LMWHs compared to UFHs are likely due, in part, to different capacities to bind to plasma proteins and endothelial cells.

Pharmacokinetics In contrast to UFH, the pharmacokinetics of LMWH follow a nonsaturable clearance mechanism mediated by the kidney.[378–380] Decreased binding of LMWHs to endothelial cells likely explains the lack of a saturable clearance mechanism observed for UFH.[376,377] LMWHs consistently show a longer half-life than UFHs.[378,381–386]

Pharmacokinetics in a newborn animal model In a newborn porcine model, the pharmacokinetics of LMWH CY222 (Choay Laboratories, Paris, France) follow a linear nonsaturable clearance mechanism with an overall clearance 2 to 3 times

longer than for UFH in the same model.[387] In addition, the overall clearance of LMWH in piglets was faster than for adult pigs due to a larger volume of distribution in newborns (Figure 9–11). The pharmacokinetics of CY222 based on anti-FXa activity (in the presence of in vitro supplementation with AT) were similar to the radioactivity curves in piglets and adult pigs. Increasing endogenous circulating AT concentrations did not alter the pharmacokinetics of CY222 in supplemented piglets compared to unsupplemented piglets.[387]

Pharmacokinetics in children The pharmacokinetics of LMWHs in children are available for two agents, enoxaparin (Rhone Poulenc Rorer) and reviparin (Knoll Pharma Inc).[388,389] For both LMWHs, peak anti-FXa levels occur 2 to 6 hours following an injection.[388,389] Children less than approximately 2 months of age or less than 5 kg have increased requirements per kg likely due to a larger volume of distribution, but the pharmacokinetics are similar (Figure 9–12).[388,389]

Clinical Use and Side Effects of Low Molecular Weight Heparin Therapy in Children

Therapeutic Doses Therapeutic doses of LMWH are most commonly used for the treatment of VTE in children. Two dose-finding studies have been reported for enoxaparin (Rhone Poulenc Rorer) and reviparin (Knoll Pharma Inc.).[388,390] Small infants have increased requirements compared to older children. For enoxaparin, a dose of 1.0 mg/kg subcutaneously every 12 hours achieves a therapeutic anti-FXa level of 0.50 to 1.0 units/mL for children older than 2 months of age, while a dose of 1.5 mg/kg is required for infants less than 2 months of age.[388] For reviparin, a dose of 100 units/kg subcutaneously every 12 hours will achieve a therapeutic anti-FXa level of 0.50 to 1.0 units/mL for children older than 2 months of age, while infants have increased requirements of at least 150 units/kg.[389] A nomogram is available for dose adjustments for both enoxaparin and reviparin (see Table 9–5). Subcutaneous administration of LMWH is facilitated by use of a subcutaneous catheter (Insuflon, Viggo-Spectramed, Sweden). Commercial preparations of

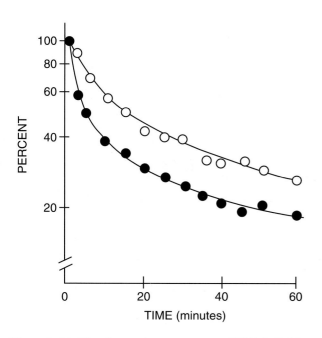

Figure 9–11 The plasma clearance curves of ^{125}I-labelled low molecular weight heparin (Choay 222) in adult pigs (○) and newborn piglets (●). The radioactivity is expressed on the y axis as a percent of the peak value.

Reproduced with permission from Andrew M, Ofosu F, Brooker L, Buchanan M. The comparison of the pharmacokinetics of a low molecular weight heparin in the newborn and adult pig. Thromb Res 1989;56:529–39.

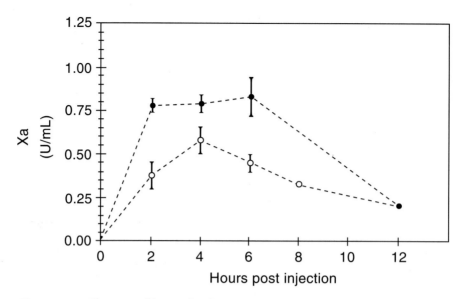

Figure 9–12 Clearance of low molecular weight heparin, based on anti-factor Xa levels after a subcutaneous injection of 1 mg/kg in children (●) and 1.64 mg/kg in newborn infants (○). The peak anti-factor Xa level at 4 hours was 0.79 units/mL in children and 0.58 in neonates.

U = unit; Xa = anti-factor Xa level.

Reproduced with permission from Massicotte P, Adams M, Leaker M, Andrew M. Low molecular weight heparin in pediatric patients with thrombotic disease: a dose finding study. J Pediatr 1996;128:313–8.

LMWHs are produced for adults and dosing is based on average adult body weights. The latter results in highly concentrated preparations that require significant dilution for small children.

Prophylactic Doses Prophylactic doses of reviparin for children greater than 5 kgs are 30 units/kg to achieve an average anti-FXa level of 0.20 units/mL. Prophylactic doses of reviparin for infants less than

Table 9–5 Nomogram for Monitoring Reviparin/Enoxaparin in Pediatric Patients

Anti-Factor Xa Level	Hold Next Dose?	Dose Change?	Repeat Anti-Factor Xa level?
< 0.35 units/mL	No	increase by 25%	4 h post next dose
0.35–0.49 units/mL	No	increase by 10%	4 h post next dose
0.5–1.0 units/mL	No	No	Next day, then one week later and monthly thereafter while receiving Reviparin-Na treatment (at 4 h post am dose)
1.1–1.5 units/mL	No	decrease by 20%	Pre next dose
1.6–2.0 units/mL	3 hrs	decrease by 30%	Pre next dose then 4 h post next dose
> 2.0 units/mL	Until anti-Xa 0.5 u/mL	decrease by 40% u/mL rpt q 12 h	Pre next dose and if not < 0.5

h = hours; u = units; Na = sodium; mL = milliliter.

Reproduced with permission from Michelson AD, Bovill E, Monagle P, Andrew M. Antithrombotic therapy in children. Chest 1998;114:748S–69S.

5 kgs are increased and currently under evaluation. For enoxaparin, doses of 0.6 mg/kg 12 hours prior to surgery achieved anti-FXa levels of 0.2 to 0.4 units/mL.[391]

Clinical Experience with Low Molecular Weight Heparin in Children In contrast to the use of LMWH in adults, there is a paucity of information in the literature about the use of LMWH in children. In one prospective cohort, 25 children with VTE and at significant risk of bleeding were treated with enoxaparin.[388] The median age was 4 years (range: newborn to 17 years) with 9 infants less than 2 months of age. Fourteen children had a DVT or PE, nine had TEs in the central nervous system (CNS), and two had complex CHD for which they received prophylactic doses at 0.5 mg/kg subcutaneously every 12 hours. The remaining 23 children received an initial dose of 1 mg/kg every 12 hours subcutaneously with subsequent doses adjusted to achieve a 4-hour anti-FXa level between 0.5 and 1.0 units/mL. Newborn infants had increased dose requirements with an average of 1.60 units/kg to achieve therapeutic levels. For children over 2 months of age, the initial dose of 1.0 mg/kg was sufficient. After the initial dose adjustment, LMWH was administered with twice-weekly monitoring. The median duration of therapy with LMWH was 14 days. Two children with previously documented gastrointestinal ulcers bled and required transfusion therapy. LMWH was continued without further events. There were no new TEs during treatment with LMWH.

The most comprehensive data on the clinical use of LMWH in children come from a consecutive cohort study at a single large pediatric institution.[390] The use of LMWH was described as either therapeutic or prophylactic.

Therapeutic low molecular weight heparin therapy in children Therapeutic doses of LMWH were received by 147 children.[390] The age distribution of patients who received therapeutic doses of enoxaparin is shown in Figure 9–13. The age range was from 1 day to 18 years (median 3.5 years; mean 6.1 years). Twenty-one patients (14.5%) were born prematurely (less than 36 weeks gestational age), and 48 patients (33.5%) were less than 3 months

chronological age at the time of initiation of treatment. Patients less than 1 year constituted the age group most frequently treated with enoxaparin. The most common underlying conditions were cancer and cardiac disease, usually CHD. Twenty-three patients (16%) were well prior to the diagnosis of the TE. Of these patients, 16 had arterial ischemic stroke (AIS) in the CNS, 4 had sinovenous thrombosis (SVT), and 3 had femoral DVT. CVL-related DVT was the reason for treatment in 73 out of 147 courses of LMWH (49.5%). The target anti-FXa range for patients receiving therapeutic doses of LMWH was 0.5 to 1.0 units/mL. Table 9–6 provides the age-dependent doses of enoxaprine. Enoxaparin was administered via a subcutaneous catheter in 128 patients (87%). Thirty-eight courses (26%) were administered at least in part in an outpatient setting. Oral anticoagulants were used as an additional part of the anticoagulation regimen in 48 courses of enoxaparin administered (33%). One-third of patients were maintained in the therapeutic range 100 percent of the time, while 65 percent were in the therapeutic range more than 70 percent of the time. Similarly, 49 percent of patients achieved therapeutic anti-FXa levels within 1 day of initiation of therapy, and 69 percent of patients achieved therapeutic anti-FXa levels within 3 days. Two patients had documented progression of their TEs while on therapy. Both patients were premature neonates (< 28 weeks gestational age), with multiple medical problems and extensive CVL-related

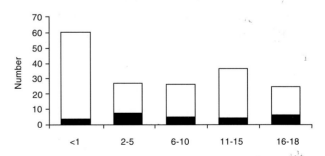

Figure 9–13 The age (years) distribution of 147 children who received therapeutic enoxaparin (▢), and 30 children who received prophylactic low molecular weight heparin (■).

Reproduced with permission from Dix D, Marzinotto V, Leaker M, et al. The use of low molecular weight heparin in pediatric patients: review of a single institution experience. J Pediatr 1998: in press.

Table 9–6 Age-Dependent Dose of Enoxaprin*

	Age	
	< 2 Months	2 Months – 18 Years
Treatment dose	1.5 mg/kg/dose q12h	1.0 mg/kg/dose q12h
Prophylactic dose	0.75 mg/kg/dose q12h	0.5 mg/kg/dose q12h

* Lovenox has 110 anti-factor Xa units/mg.

h = hours; mg = miligrams; kg = kilograms.

Reproduced with permission from Michelson AD, Bovill E, Monagle P, Andrew M. Antithrombotic therapy in children. Chest 1998;114:748

DVT. Both patients were subtherapeutic at the time of the extension of their disease and both neonates subsequently required more than 3mg/kg/dose to achieve the target anti-FXa level. Both patients did well once target anti-FXa levels were achieved. Minor bleeding occurred in 26 (17%) of the 147 study patients receiving therapeutic doses of LMWH. The most common minor bleeding complication was at the insuflon site reported in 16 patients. Other minor bleeding included oozing from CVL sites (4), gastric tubes (2), and abscess site (1). One 16-year-old boy developed melena while on chemotherapy for acute lymphoblastic leukemia (ALL). His LMWH was temporarily held and platelets were transfused for a coexistent thrombocytopenia.[390]

Major bleeds occurred in 7 (4%) of patients. Major bleeds consisted of two gastrointestinal bleeds, three ICH, and two thigh hematomas. Two of the ICH occurred in neonates with multiple medical problems including structural cerebral abnormalities, and one occurred in an infant with complex CHD who bled into the site of an old cerebral infarction site. None of the patients died as an immediate consequence of the ICH; however, all three died later of causes attributable to their underlying disease. Major bleeding in the form of thigh hematomas at the insuflon injection sites occurred in two extremely premature neonates, both of whom were less than 30 weeks gestational age.

Prophylactic low molecular weight heparin therapy in children Thirty children were treated with prophylactic doses of LMWH.[390] The age

range was from 1 week to 17 years (median 5.5 years; mean 8.2 years). Two patients (7%) were less than 3 months chronological age at the time of initiation of treatment. The most common underlying conditions were cardiac disease, usually CHD, and trauma/surgery. The indications for anticoagulant prophylaxis were for the prevention of CVL-related DVT (10), prophylaxis for prosthetic heart valves (1), cardiomyopathy (2), maintenance of shunt patency (3), and post-surgical prophylaxis (6). The target anti-FXa level for patients receiving prophylactic doses of LMWH was 0.1–0.3 units/mL. Table 9–6 provides the initial doses, the dose range required to achieve target anti-FXa levels, and the average dose that achieved target anti-FXa levels in the prophylaxis group. Enoxaparin was administered via a subcutaneous catheter in 19 patients (64%). Three courses (10%) were administered at least in part in an outpatient setting. Oral anticoagulants were used as an additional part of the anticoagulation regimen in nine courses of prophylactic enoxaparin administered (30%). One patient had a documented TE while on therapy. This patient was a sick premature neonate who required multiple CVLs and at 12 weeks of age was found on US to have a calcified nonocclusive TE extending from the left internal jugular vein to the superior vena cava (SVC). Because the TE was not deemed to be acute, only prophylactic doses of LMWH were used with anti FXa levels maintained between 0.2 and 0.4 units/mL. Unfortunately, after 136 days of prophylaxis, the patient developed clinical signs of SVC syndrome. Ultrasound examination revealed extension of the original TE, with complete occlusion of the SVC and extension into the right atrium. The patient died in congestive heart failure. Of the 30 patients who received prophylactic LMWH, 2 had minor bleeding complications presenting as oozing at the insuflon site (1) and epistaxis (1). No major bleeding complications occurred.

Monitoring Although the need for laboratory monitoring of LMWHs in adults is currently controversial, laboratory monitoring of therapeutic doses of LMWHs in children is likely to be required for several reasons. First, the pharmacokinetics of LMWHs are age and weight dependent, with enormous differences in requirements in small, growing infants. The data from the previously described study support the concept that there is considerable variation in the weight-related doses required for children, especially neonates. Second, LMWHs are being used for several months in children in place of OAs, while the data in adults are primarily for the short-term, initial use of LMWH for a few days. Third, the development of renal compromise or an acquired coagulopathy that may adversely influence the risk of bleeding is not unusual in children receiving LMWHs. Fourth, in order for long-term treatment with LMWHs to be practical, parents and/or teenage children must be trained to administer LMWHs at home. There is the potential for systematic, unintentional errors, which may be detected by intermittent monitoring.

Duration of Therapy LMWHs are increasingly being used for 3 to 6 months to treat VTE in children, replacing OAs. The reasons for this shift in practice are rapid changes in diet, use of medications, and poor venous access that all make OA therapy difficult to monitor safely. Long-term use of LMWHs raises management issues, including the stability of the pharmacokinetics of LMWHs when administered to growing children over many months, the effects of long-term LMWHs on bone development, and the safety of long-term LMWHs in children with serious primary disorders.

Invasive Procedures Based on 16 adult cases of spinal hematoma reported to the FDA in the 44 months since enoxaparin was released for general use, the FDA issued a warning that spinal hematoma complicating spinal anesthesia can occur in adult patients receiving LMWH thromboprophylaxis.[392–395] The incidence, although not known with certainty, is extremely low. For some children, lumbar punctures (LPs) are required for intra-thecal chemotherapy or for diagnostic purposes. At this time there are no reports of spinal hematomas in children while receiving LMWH. The general practice has been to skip the morning dose, perform the LP, and resume LMWH for the evening dose. Preliminary data show that in 8 of 9 patients receiving therapeutic amounts of LMWH, levels were mea-

surable at 0.2 to 0.7 units/mL.[391] Until further information is available, one approach is to omit at least two doses of LMWH, and measure an anti-FXa level prior to procedures such as LPs.

Adverse Effects The important adverse effects of LMWHs are similar to those of UFH but significantly less frequent. Potential major adverse effects include bleeding, osteoporosis, and HIT. The incidence of major bleeding secondary to therapeutic amounts of LMWH is 4%, comparable to UFH and OAs.

Low molecular weight heparin-induced osteoporosis in adults There has been one RCT assessing LMWH-induced osteoporosis. Monreal and colleagues reported 80 patients randomized to either 10,000 IU of UFH administered subcutaneously twice daily or 5,000 IU of fragmin similarly administered.[396] The mean duration of treatment was 117 days. There were seven spinal fractures, six in the UFH group and one in the LMWH group (p = .054). There was no correlation between decreased BMD and fracture rate. However, BMD measured following 3 and 6 months of treatment was decreased in both groups.

Shefras and colleagues reported a prospective case control study of patients antiphospholipid antibody (APLA) positive referred for recurrent miscarriage.[307] Spinal BMD was assessed around conception, immediately post delivery, and 6 months post delivery. Mean bone loss was 5.6% in patients treated with fragmin 5,000 IU subcutaneously daily (n = 9), 5.1% in those treated with fragmin 5,000 IU subcutaneously twice daily (n = 8) and 3.13% in the controls who did not receive UFH (n = 8). There was complete overlap of confidence intervals, suggesting that LMWH has no effect on bones over and above normal physiology.

Melissari and colleagues[306] reported a series of 11 women who received subcutaneous fragmin to maintain anti-FXa levels of 0.1 to 0.25 units/mL throughout pregnancy. Dual photon absorptiometry (DPA) of lumbar spine and hips were no different from normal age-matched non-pregnant controls. This study was extended to 21 patients with the same result. The same authors reported a case of a male with a previous vertebral fracture while on

UFH who had no radiographic or isotope bone scan evidence of osteoporosis following 3 years of LMWH at 15,000 anti-FXa units/day. In summary, initial retrospective and case control studies suggest that LMWH is safer than UFH. The only RCT showed a nonsignificant trend to decreased fracture rate, but again there was no correlation with BMD.

Low molecular weight heparin-induced osteoporosis in children There are few published data concerning LMWH-induced osteoporosis in children. Two siblings with homozygous protein C deficiency managed with prophylactic doses of subcutaneous LMWH over a three-year period were reported to have normal bone densitometry (see Figure 3–10, Chapter 3).[397] Anecdotally, spontaneous fractures have been noted in children and infants receiving LMWH (unpublished data). Further studies are required to determine the relative risk of osteoporosis during LMWH therapy.

Low molecular weight heparin-induced osteoporosis, experimental data Recent studies using histomorphometry and biochemical markers have shown that UFH decreases trabecular and cancellous bone by the combined effects of decreased formation and increased resorption.[398] Studies have shown that LMWH has a similar effect on formation of bone but does not increase bone resorption.[398] This would support the clinical data suggesting a reduced effect of LMWH on BMD in adults. However, epidemiologically, the peak ages at which children develop TEs are during infancy and their teenage years, coincidentally the years of greatest rates of bone mass accrual. The safety of medium- or long-term LMWH therapy in children needs to be determined by specific pediatric studies.

Treatment of Bleeding If the indication is urgent, protamine sulfate will completely neutralize the antithrombin activities of LMWHs but only partially neutralize the anti-FXa activities (76%).[399] Studies in animals suggest that protamine sulfate does completely reverse the bleeding consequences of LMWHs.[399] If protamine is given within 3 to 4 hours of the last dose of LMWH, then a maximal neutralizing dose is 1 mg of protamine per 100 units (1 mg) of LMWH given in the last dose over 10 minutes.

Indications for Low Molecular Weight Heparin

The indications for LMWH in children are in the process of development. At the current time there are studies reporting the use of LMWHs for the prevention and treatment of systemic VTE, as treatment for SVT, for hemodialysis, as prophylaxis following liver transplantation, and as prophylaxis following surgical procedures. The following section discusses the available information.

Venous Thromboembolic Disease

Adults In prophylactic trials, LMWHs are as or more effective than UFH for the prevention of VTEs with no detectable increase in bleeding.[13,359,363,366] Meta-analyses of clinical trials comparing UFH to LMWH in adults report somewhat conflicting results. Older meta-analyses suggest LMWHs are safer and more effective than UFH for the treatment of VTE.[400–402] However, more recent meta-analyses with larger numbers of patients suggest that they are equivalent.[400]

Children LMWHs are being used increasingly in clinical practice for the treatment and prevention of DVT in children. However, as previously discussed, there are few published studies to justify preferential LMWH use in children compared to UFH or OA therapy. From the data available one could reasonably conclude that LMWH is potentially an alternative to standard anticoagulation in children of varying ages, underlying diagnoses, and types of VTE. Subcutaneous administration of LMWH is facilitated by the use of a subcutaneous catheter and can be administered in an outpatient setting. Neonates with sparse subcutaneous tissue should probably not receive a subcutaneous catheter. Major bleeding complications occurred in less than 5 percent of patients, which compares favorably with standard anticoagulation therapy. RCTs are currently ongoing to determine the safety and efficacy of LMWH in the treatment of DVT in children. The REVIVE trial (*Revi*parin in *V*enous *Thrombo*Embolism) is an RCT comparing reviparin to UFH followed by OAs for the treatment of VTE in children. PROTEKT (*Pro*phylaxis of *Thrombo*Embolism in *K*ids *T*rial) is an RCT comparing reviparin to the standard of care for primary prophylaxis of CVL-related VTEs. The results of these and similar trials will determine the role of LMWH in the treatment and prevention of TEs in children.

Cost An important consideration for any new form of therapy is cost. Although LMWHs cost more than UFH, the reduced number of laboratory assays, nursing hours, intravenous starts, and phlebotomy time reduced the total cost of administration in initial studies. Once trials documenting safety and efficacy have been completed, cost-effectiveness analysis of LMWH in children may be required.

Treatment of Homozygous Protein C Deficiency

Homozygous type 1 protein C deficiency is rare, with only 17 cases recorded in an international database of mutations[403] and only about 20 further kindreds reported in the literature. Most commonly, homozygotes present with purpura fulminans in the neonatal period. These infants have protein C levels that are less than 0.01 units/mL. A small number of severe protein C deficient patients do not present with purpura fulminans at birth.[397,404–413] Rather, they present with severe TEs during childhood or early adult life. The protein C levels in these patients are usually measurable and range from 0.02 to 0.23 units/mL. Only nine such patients have been confirmed by DNA analysis to be true homozygotes, as distinct from compound heterozygotes.[397,407–409]

Management of homozygous protein C deficient patients is problematic.[403] Although OAs are commonly used, the target INR must be kept quite high (3 to 4.5) to avoid skin necrosis. Patients with high INRs are at considerable risk for serious bleeding.[414–416] Replacement therapy with protein C concentrate is expensive and requires intravenous access and frequent infusions due to protein C's short half-life.[417–420] On rare occasions, stanazol[421] and liver transplantation[422] have been described, each with their own limitations. LMWH has been used in a small number of patients who presented in adolescence or early adulthood with TEs.[397,405]

Recently, two sisters with protein C levels of approximately 7 percent have been treated on a long-term basis with prophylactic doses of LMWH.[397] This followed unsuccessful treatment with OA therapy and protein C replacement in the index case. In vivo markers of thrombin generation (prothrombin fragment 1.2 and thrombin inhibitor complexes) were suppressed to the same extent as during high-dose OA therapy (see Figure 3–10, Chapter 3). Neither child developed new VTE or skin necrosis. Whether this approach is applicable to infants who present with purpura fulminans is unknown.

Hemodialysis in Children

The main cause of hemorrhagic complications in uremic patients is anticoagulation for hemodialysis. Unfortunately, optimal use of UFH for hemodialysis in children has not been established and several general protocols are in use. LMWHs offer a potentially safer and effective alternative to UFH for hemodialysis in children.[423,424] One study was a small cross-over, dose-finding study in 6 children on chronic hemodialysis.[424] The authors concluded that an initial LMWH bolus dose of 24 units/kg and an infusion of 15 units/kg were safe and effective. A preliminary study of 5 children, ages 4 to 16 years, undergoing hemodialysis were given enoxaparin for a period of 4 weeks. This group was compared to a similar group of children who received UFH. There were no major hemorrhagic events; however, 0.5 anti-FXa units of LMWH was insufficient to prevent clotting in the extracorporeal circuit during dialysis.[423]

Other Rarer Indications

Liver transplantation Twenty-four children ages 5 months to 15 years received LMWH, AT concentrates, fresh frozen plasma (FFP), and a protease inhibitor during and following liver transplantation. There were no hepatic artery TEs in the treated children.[425]

Renal transplantation Forty-two children less than 5 years of age with a history of recurrent TEs and who required renal transplantation were treated with enoxaparin.[426] Only 1.5 percent lost the kidney due to TE compared historically to an incidence of 12 percent in children who did not receive enoxaparin. Non-major bleeding was present in 12 of the 42 children.

Sinovenous thrombosis There is a case report[427] and a case series of 12 children with SVT treated with LMWH.[428] The dose for the 12 children was therapeutic and anti-FXa levels between 0.50 and 1.0 units/mL were achieved.[428] There was no significant bleeding with LMWH.

REFERENCES

1. McLean J. The thromboplastic action of cephalin. Am J Physiol 1916;41:250–7.

2. Brinkhous KM, Smith HP, Warner ED, Seegers WH. The inhibition of blood clotting: an unidentified substance which acts in conjunction with heparin to prevent the conversion of prothrombin into thrombin. Am J Physiol 1939;125:683–7.

3. Abilgaard U. Highly purified antithrombin 3 with heparin cofactor activity prepared by disc electrophoresis. Scand J Clin Lab Invest 1968;21:89–91.

4. Olson ST, Shore JD. Binding of high affinity heparin to antithrombin III. Characterization of the protein fluorescence enhancement. J Biol Chem 1981;256:11065–72.

5. Rosenberg RD, Jordan RE, Favreau LV, Lam LH. Highly active heparin species with multiple binding sites for antithrombin. Biochem Biophys Res Commun 1979;86:1319–24.

6. Bjork I, Lindahl U. Mechanism of the anticoagulant action of heparin. Mol Cell Biochem 1982;48:161–82.

7. Danielsson A, Raub E, Lindahl U, Bjork I. Role of ternary complexes, in which heparin binds both antithrombin and proteinase, in the acceleration of the reactions between antithrombin and thrombin or factor Xa. J Biol Chem 1986;261:15467–73.

8. Choay J, Petitou M. The chemistry of heparin: a way to understand its mode of action. Med J Austr 1986;144:7–10.

9. Casu B, Oreste P, Torri G. The structure of heparin oligosaccharide fragments with high anti-(factor Xa) activity containing the minimal antithrombin III-binding sequence. Biochem J 1981;197:599–609.

10. Choay J, Petitou M, Lormeau J, et al. Structure-activity relationship in heparin: a synthetic pentasaccharide with high affinity for antithrombin III and eliciting high anti factor Xa activity. Biochem Biophy Res Commun 1983;116:492–9.

11. Rosenberg RD, Bauer KA. The heparin-antithrombin system: a natural anticoagulant mechanism. In: Coleman RW, Hirsh J, Marder VJ, Salzman EW, editors. Hemostasis and thrombosis: basic principles and clinical practice. Philadelphia: J.B. Lippincott Company; 1994. p. 837–60.

12. Oosta G, Gardner W, Beeler D, Rosenberg R. Multiple functional domains of the heparin molecule. Proc Natl Acad Sci U S A 1981;78:829–33.

13. Hirsh J, Warkentin TE, Raschkle, et al. Heparin and low molecular weight heparin: mechanism of action, pharmacokinetics, dosing considerations, monitoring, efficacy, and safety. Chest 1998;114:489S–510S.

14. Lindahl U, Thunberg L, Backstrom G, et al. Extension and structural variability of the antithrombin-binding sequence in heparin. J Biol Chem 1984;259:12368–76.

15. Atha DH, Lormeau JC, Petitou M. Contribution of 3-0- and 6-0-sulfated glucosamine residues in the heparin-induced conformational change in antithrombin III. Biochemistry 1987;26:6454–61.

16. Petitou M. Synthetic heparin fragments: new and efficient tools for the study of heparin and its interactions. Nouv Rev Fr Hematol 1984;26:221–6.

17. Rosenberg RD. The purification and mechanism of action of human antithrombin-heparin cofactor. J Biol Chem 1973;248:6490–505.

18. Thunberg L, Backstrom G, Lindahl U. Further characterization of antithrombin-binding sequence in heparin. Carbohydr Res 1982;100:393–410.

19. Young E, Prins M, Levine MN, Hirsh J. Heparin binding to plasma proteins, an important mechanism for heparin clearance. Thromb Haemost 1992;67:639–43.

20. Lane DA, Pijler G, Flynn AM. Neutralization of heparin related saccharides by histidine-rich glycoprotein and platelet factor 4. J Biol Chem 1986;261:3980–6.

21. Lijnen HR, Hoylaerts M, Collen D. Heparin binding properties of human histidine-rich glycoprotein: mechanism and role of heparin in plasma. J Biol Chem 1983;258:3803–8.

22. Peterson CB, Morgan WT, Blackburn MN. Histidine-rich glycoprotein modulation of the anticoagulant activity of heparin. J Biol Chem 1987;262:7567–74.

23. Holt JC, Niewiarowski S. Biochemistry of alpha-granule proteins. Semin Hematol 1985;22:151–63.

24. Lane D, Denton J, Flynn A, et al. Anticoagulant activities of heparin oligosaccharides and their neutralization by platelet factor 4. Biochem J 1984;218:725–32.

25. Preissner KT, Muller-Berghaus G. Neutralization and binding of heparin by S-protein/vitronectin in the inhibition of factor Xa by antithrombin III. J Biol Chem 1987;262:12247–53.

26. Marciniak E. Factor Xa inactivation by antithrombin III. Evidence for biological stabilization of factor Xa by factor V-phospholipid complex. Br J Haematol 1973;24:391–400.

27. Walker FJ, Esmon CT. The effects of phospholipid and factor Va on the inhibition of factor Xa by an-

tithrombin III. Biochem Biophys Res Commun 1979;90:641–7.

28. Dawes J, Smith R, Pepper D. The release, distribution and clearance of human β-thromboglobulin and platelet factor 4. Thromb Res 1978;12:851–61.

29. Weitz J, Hudoba M, Massel D, et al. Clot-bound thrombin is protected from inhibition by heparin-antithrombin III but is susceptible to inactivation by antithrombin III independent inhibitors. J Clin Invest 1990;86:385–91.

30. Hogg P, Jackson C. Fibrin monomer protects thrombin from inactivation by heparin-antithrombin III: implications for heparin efficacy. Proc Natl Acad Sci U S A 1989;86:3619–23.

31. Heras M, Chesebro JH, Penny WJ, et al. Effects of thrombin inhibition on the development of acute platelet-thrombus deposition during angioplasy in pigs: heparin versus recombinant hirudin, a specific thrombin inhibitor. Circulation 1989;79:657–65.

32. Bar-Shavit R, Eldor A, Vlodavsky I. Binding of thrombin to subendothelial extracellular matrix: protection and expression of functional properties. J Clin Invest 1989;84:1096–104.

33. Hirsh J. Heparin. N Engl J Med 1991;324:1565–74.

34. Highsmith RJ, Rosenberg RD. The inhibition of human plasmin by human antithrombin-heparin cofactor. J Biol Chem 1974;249:4335–8.

35. Edelberg JM, Pizzo SV. Kinetic analysis of the effects of heparin and lipoproteins on tissue plasminogen activator mediated plasminogen activation. Biochemistry 1990;29:5906–11.

36. Andrade-Gordon P, Strickland S. Interaction of heparin with plasminogen activators in plasminogen: effects on the activation of plasminogen. Biochemistry 1986;25:4033–40.

37. Agnelli G, Pascucci C, Cosmi B, Nenci GG. Effects of therapeutic doses of heparin on thrombolysis with tissue type plasminogen activator in rabbits. Blood 1990;76:2030–6.

38. Eika C. Inhibition of thrombin-induced aggregation of human platelets by heparin. Scand J Haematol 1971; 8:216–22.

39. Ockelford P, Carter C, Cerskus A, et al. Comparison of the in vivo hemorrhagic and antithrombotic effects of a low antithrombin III affinity heparin fraction. Thromb Res 1982;27:679–90.

40. Fernandez F, Nguyan P, Van Ryn J, et al. Hemorrhagic doses of heparin and other glycosaminoglycans induce a platelet defect. Thromb Res 1986;43:491–5.

41. Blajchman M, Young E, Ofosu F. Effects of unfractionated heparin, dermatan sulfate and low molecular weight heparin on vessel wall permeability in rabbits. Ann N Y Acad Sci 1989;556:245–54.

42. Schmidt B, Mitchell L, Ofosu F, Andrew M. Standard assays underestimate the concentration of heparin in neonatal plasma. J Lab Clin Med 1988;112:641–3.

43. Schmidt B, Ofosu F, Mitchell L, et al. Anticoagulant effects of heparin in neonatal plasma. Pediatr Res 1989;25:405–8.

44. Vieira A, Ofosu F, Andrew M. Heparin sensitivity and resistance in the neonate: an explanation. Thromb Res 1991;63:85–99.

45. Andrew M, Mitchell L, Vegh P, Ofosu F. Thrombin regulation in children differs from adults in the absence and presence of heparin. Thromb Haemost 1994;72:836–42.

46. Schmidt B, Buchanan M, Ofosu F, et al. Antithrombotic properties of heparin in a neonatal piglet model of thrombin induced thrombosis. Thromb Haemost 1988;60:289–92.

47. Andrew M, Schmidt B. The use of heparin in newborn infants. Semin Thromb Haemostas 1988;14:28–32.

48. Andrew M, Marzinotto V, Blanchette V, Ginsberg J, Burrows P, Benson L, et al. Heparin therapy in pediatric patients: a prospective cohort study. Pediatr Res 1994;35:78–83.

49. Andrew M. Developmental Hemostasis: relevance to thromboembolic complications in pediatric patients. Thromb Haemost 1995;74(1 Suppl):415–25.

50. Barnard D, Hathaway W. Neonatal thrombosis. J Pediatr Hematol Oncol 1979;1:235–44.

51. Andrew M, Schmidt B, Mitchell L, et al. Thrombin generation in newborn plasma is critically dependent on the concentration of prothrombin. Thromb Haemost 1990;63:27–30.

52. Andrew M, Paes B, Milner R, et al. Development of the human coagulation system in the full-term infant. Blood 1987;70:165–72.

53. Andrew M, Paes B, Johnston M. Development of the hemostatic system in the neonate and young infant. J Pediatr Hematol Oncol 1990;12:95–104.

54. Andrew M, Paes B, Milner R, Johnston M, Mitchell L, Tollefsen D, et al. Development of the human coagulation system in the healthy premature infant. Blood 1988;72:1651–7.

55. Shah J, Mitchell L, Paes B, et al. Thrombin inhibition is impaired in plasma of sick neonates. Pediatr Res 1992;31:391–5.

56. Reverdiau-Moalic P, Delahousse B, Bardos GBP, et al. Evolution of blood coagulation activators and inhibitors in the healthy human fetus. Blood 1996;88:900–6.

57. Chang G, Lueder S, DiMichele D, et al. Heparin and the risk of intraventricular hemorrhage among very low birth weight infants. J Pediatr 1997;131:362–6.

58. Lesko S, Mitchell A, Eopstein M, et al. Heparin use a risk factor for intraventricular hemorrhage in low

birth weight infants. N Engl J Med 1986;314: 1156–60.

59. Malloy M, Cutter G. The association of heparin exposure with intraventricular hemorrhage among very low birth weight infants. J Perinatol 1995;15:185–91.

60. De Swart CAM, Nijmeyer B, Roelofs JMM, Sixma JJ. Kinetics of intravenously administered heparin in normal humans. Blood 1982;60:1251–8.

61. Olsson P, Lagregren H, Ek S. The elimination from plasma of intravenous heparin: an experimental study on dogs and humans. Acta Med Scand 1963; 173:619–30.

62. Caranobe C, Petitou M, Dupouy D, et al. Heparin fractions with high and low affinities to antithrombin III are cleared at different rates. Thromb Res 1986;43: 635–41.

63. Lindahl U, Hook M. Glycosaminoglycans and their binding to biological macromolecules. Annu Rev Biochem 1978;47:385–417.

64. Mahadoo J, Heibert L, Jaques L. Vascular sequestration of heparin. Thromb Res 1977;12:79–90.

65. Friedman Y, Arenis C. Studies on the heparin sulfamidase activity from rat spleen: intracellular distribution and characterization of the enzyme. Biochem J 1974;139:699–708.

66. Hirsh J, van Aken W, Gallus A, et al. Heparin kinetics in venous thrombosis and pulmonary embolism. Circulation 1976;53:691–5.

67. Chiu H, van Aken W, Hirsh J, et al. Increased heparin clearance in experimental pulmonary embolism. J Lab Clin Med 1977;90:204–15.

68. Hodby ED, Hirsh J, Adeniyi-Jones C. The influence of drugs upon the anticoagulant activity of heparin. CMAJ 1972;106:562–4.

69. Andrew M, Ofosu F, Schmidt B, et al. Heparin clearance and ex vivo recovery in newborn piglets and adult pigs. Thromb Res 1988;52:517–27.

70. Yamada K, Shirahata A, Inagaki M, et al. Therapy for DIC in newborn infants. Bibl Haematol 1983;49: 329–41.

71. Domula M, Weissbach G. Heparin und Antiheparin im Kindesalter. 3. Mitteilung: Heparinspiegelmessungen und ihre bedeutung fur das heparin monitoring. Folia Haematol Int Mag Klin Morphol Blutforsh 1983;110:146–61.

72. Markarian M, Luchenco LO, Rosenblut E. Hypercoagulability in premature infants with special reference to respiratory distress syndrome and hemorrhage. II. The effect of heparin. Biol Neonate 1971;17:84–97.

73. McDonald MM, Hathaway WE. Anticoagulant therapy by continuous heparinization in newborn and older infants. J Pediatr 1982;101:451–7.

74. Rogner G. Heparin level during anticoagulant therapy in mature and premature infants. Kinderarztl Prax 1976;44:193–200.

75. Massicotte-Nolan P, Mitchell L, Andrew M. Comparative study of coagulation systems in newborn animals. Pediatr Res 1986;20:961–5.

76. McDonald MM, Jacobson LJ, Hay WW, Hathaway WE. Heparin clearance in the newborn. Pediatr Res 1981;15:1015–8.

77. Turner Gomes SO, Nitschmann E, Norman GR, et al. Effect of heparin loading during congenital heart operation on thrombin generation and blood loss. Ann Thorac Surg 1997;63:482–8.

78. Kearon C. Drug trials that have influenced our practice in the treatment of venous thromboembolism. Thromb Haemost 1997;78:553–7.

79. Michelson AD, Bovill E, Monagle P, Andrew M. Antithrombotic therapy in children. Chest 1998;114: 748S–69S.

80. Randolph AG, Cook DJ, Gonzales CA, Andrew A. Benefit of heparin use in central venous and pulmonary arterial catheters: a systematic review and meta-analysis of randomized controlled trials. Chest 1998;113:165–71.

81. Hensrud DD, Burritt MF, Hall LG. Stability of heparin anticoagulant activity over time in parenteral nutrition solutions. JPEN J Parenter Enteral Nutr 1996; 20:219–21.

82. Rattenbury JM, Timmins JG, Cawthorne EA, et al. Identification of the cause of separation (creaming) of lipid emulsions in intravenous infusion. J Pediatr Gastroenterol 1989;8:491–5.

83. Brandjes D, Heijboer H, Buller H, et al. Acenocoumarol and heparin compared with acenocoumarol alone in the initial treatment of proximal-vein thrombosis. N Engl J Med 1992;327:1485–9.

84. Andrew M, David B, deVeber G, Brooker L. Arterial thromboembolic complications in paediatric patients. Thromb Haemost 1997;78:715–25.

85. Torr SR, Nachowiak DA, Fujii S, Sobel BE. "Plasminogen steal" and clot lysis. J Am Coll Cardiol 1992;19: 1085–90.

86. Wu JH, Diamond SL. Tissue plasminogen activator (tPA) inhibits plasmin degradation of fibrin. A mechanism that slows tPA-mediated fibrinolysis but does not require alpha-2-antiplasmin or leakage of intrinsic plasminogen. J Clin Invest 1995;95: 2483–90.

87. Freed M, Keane J, Rosenthal A. The use of heparinization to prevent arterial thrombosis after percutaneous cardiac catheterization in children. Circulation 1974;50:565–9.

88. Freed M, Rosenthal A, Fyler D. Attempts to reduce arterial thrombosis after cardiac catheterization in children: use of percutaneous technique and aspirin. Am Heart J 1974;87:283–6.

89. Saxena A, Gupta R, Kumar RK, et al. Predictors of arterial thrombosis after diagnostic cardiac catheterization

in infants and children randomized to two heparin doses. Cathet Cardiovasc Diagn 1997;41:400–3.

90. Perry MO. Iatrogenic injuries of arteries in infants. Surg Gynecol Obstet 1983;157:325–31.

91. Taussig H. Long-time observations on the Blalock-Taussig operation. IX. Single ventricle (with apex to the left). Johns Hopkins Med J 1976;139(2):69–76.

92. Truccone N, Bowman FJ, Malm J, Gersony W. Systemic-pulmonary arterial shunts in the first year of life. Circulation 1974;49:508–11.

93. Tsai KT, Chang CH, Lin PJ. Modified Blalock-Taussig shunt: statistical analysis of potential factors influencing shunt outcome. J Cardiovasc Surg (Torino) 1996;37:149–52.

94. Bogats G, Kertesz E, Katona M, et al. Modified Blalock-Taussig shunt using allograft saphenous vein: six years experience. Ann Thorac Surg 1996;61:58–61.

95. Gladman G, McKrindle BW, Williams WG, et al. The modified Blalock-Taussig shunt: clinical impact and morbidity in Fallot's tetralogy in the current era. J Thorac Cardiovasc Surg 1997;114:25–30.

96. Ohuchi H, Okabe H, Nagata N, et al. Long term patency after the Blalock-Taussig operation: comparison between classic and modified shunts. Nippon Kyobu Geka Gakkai Zasshi 1996;44:1108–13.

97. Zahn EM, Chang AC, Aldousany A, Burke R. Emergent stent placement for acute Blalock-Taussig shunt obstruction after stage 1 Norwood surgery. Cathet Cardiovasc Diagn 1997;42:191–4.

98. Takanashi Y, Tomizawa Y, Noishiki Y, Yoshihara K. Calcified EPTFE vascular prosthesis in the Blalock-Taussig shunt after 4 years of implantation: a case report. Kyobu Geka 1997;50:71–3.

99. Berger RM, Bol-Raap G, Hop WJ, et al. Heparin as a risk factor for perigraft seroma complicating the modified Blalock-Taussig shunt. J Thorac Cardiovasc Surg 1998;116:292–3.

100. Klinge J, Hofbeck M, Ries M, et al. Thrombolysis of modified Blalock-Taussig shunts in childhood with recombinant tissue-type plasminogen activator. Kardiol 1995;85:476–80.

101. Alcibar J, Cabrera A, Onate A, Galdeano JM, Rumoroso JR, Pastor E, et al. Angioplasty of the stenotic Blalock-Taussig. Rev Esp Cardiol 1994;47:819–23.

102. Ries M, Singer H, Hofbeck M. Thrombolysis of a modified Blalock-Taussig shunt with recombinant tissue plasminogen activator in a newborn infant with pulmonary atresia and ventricular septal defect. Br Heart J 1994;72:201–2.

103. Boulden TF, Tonkin IL, Burton EM, et al. Case of the day. Pediatric. Mycotic pseudoaneurysm and thrombosis of modified left Blalock-Taussig shunt. Radiographics 1990;10:119–21.

104. Ahmadi A, Mocellin R, Henglein D, et al. Modified Blalock-Taussig anastomosis. Its significance within the scope of surgical treatment of tetralogy of Fallot. Monatsschr Kinderheilkd 1998;136:130–40.

105. Brandt B, Camacho JA, Mahoney LT, Heintz SE. Growth of the pulmonary arteries following Blalock-Taussig shunt. Ann Thorac Surg 1986;42:S1–S4.

106. Tamisier D, Vouhe P, Vernant F, et al. Modified Blalock-Taussig shunts: results in infants less than 3 months of age. Ann Thorac Surg 1990;49:797–801.

107. Mullen JC, Lemermeyer G, Bentley MJ. Modified Blalock-Taussig shunts: to heparinize or not to heparinize? Can J Cardiol 1996;12:645–7.

108. Bjork V, Olin C, Bjarke B, Thoren C. Right atrial-right ventricular anastomosis for correction of tricuspid atresia. J Thorac Cardiovasc Surg 1979;77:452–8.

109. Breman FJ, Malm J, Hayes C, Gersony W. Physiological approach to surgery for tricuspid atresia. Circulation 1978;(Suppl I):1–83.

110. Fontan F, Baudet E. Surgical repair of tricuspid atresia. Thorax 1971;26:240–8.

111. Rosenthal DN, Friedman AH, Kleinman CS, et al. Thromboembolic complications after Fontan operations. Circulation 1995;92:II287–293.

112. Jahangiri M, Ross DB, Redington AN, et al. Thromboembolism after the Fontan procedure and its modifications. Ann Thorac Surg 1994;58:1409–14.

113. du Plessis AJ, Chang AC, Wessel DL, et al. Cerebrovascular accidents following the Fontan operation. Pediatr Neurol 1995;12:230–6.

114. Day RW, Boyer RS, Tait VF, Ruttenberg HD. Factors associated with stroke following the Fontan procedure. Pediatr Cardiol 1995;16:270–5.

115. Matthews K, Bale J, Clark E, Marvin W, Doty D. Cerebral infarction complicating Fontan surgery for cyanotic congenital heart disease. Pediatr Cardiol 1986;7:161–6.

116. Fletcher SE, Case CL, Fyfe DA, Gillette PC. Clinical spectrum of venous thrombi in the Fontan patient. Am J Cardiol 1991;68:1721–2.

117. Dobell ARC, Trusler GA, Smallhorn JF, Williams WG. Atrial thrombi after the Fontan operation. Ann Thorac Surg 1986;42:664–7.

118. Kaulitz R, Ziemer G, Bergmann F, et al. Atrial thrombus after a Fontan operation; predisposing factors, treatment, and prophylaxis. Cardiol Young 1997;7:37–43.

119. Driscoll DJ, Offord KP, Feldt RH, et al. Five to fifteen year follow-up after Fontan operation. Circulation 1992;85:469–96.

120. Fontan F, Deville C, Quaegebeur J, et al. Repair of tricuspid atresia in 100 patients. J Thorac Cardiovasc Surg 1983;85:647–60.

121. Prenger KB, Hess J, Cromme-Dijkhuis AH, Eijgelaar A. Porcine-valved Dacron conduits in Fontan procedures. Ann Thorac Surg 1988;46:526–30.

122. Laks H, Milliken G, Perloff H, et al. Experience with the Fontan procedure. J Thorac Cardiovasc Surg 1984;88:939–51.

123. Annecchino F, Brunelli F, Borghi A, et al. Fontan repair for tricuspid atresia: experience with 50 consecutive patients. Ann Thorac Surg 1988;45:430–6.

124. Myers J, Waldhausen J, Weber H, et al. A reconsideration of risk factors for the Fontan operation. Ann Surg 1990;211:738–44.

125. Mair DD, Rice MJ, Hagler DJ, et al. Outcome of the Fontan procedure in patients with tricuspid atresia. Circulation 1985;72:1170–6.

126. Cromme-Dijkhuis AH, Hess J, Hahlen K, et al. Specific sequelae after Fontan operation at mid- and long-term followup. J Thorac Cardiovasc Surg 1993;106:1126–32.

127. Cromme-Dijkhuis AH, Henkens CMA, Bijleveld CMA, et al. Coagulation factor abnormalities as possible thrombotic risk factors after Fontan operations. Lancet 1990;336:1087–90.

128. Fyfe DA, Kline CH, Sade RM, Gillette PC. Transesophageal echocardiography detects thrombus formation not identified by transthoracic echocardiography after the Fontan operation. J Am Coll Cardiol 1991;18:1733–7.

129. Stumper O, Sutherland G, Geuskens R, et al. Transesophageal echocardiography in evaluation and management after a Fontan procedure. J Am Coll Cardiol 1991;17:1152–60.

130. Wilson DG, Wisheart JD, Stuart AG. Systemic thromboembolism leading to myocardial infarction and stroke after fenestrated total cavopulmonary connection. Br Heart J 1995;73:483–5.

131. Eijgelaar A, Hess J, Hardjowijono R, et al. Experiences with the Fontan operation. Thorac Cardiovasc Surg 1982;30:63–8.

132. Dajee H, Deutsch LS, Benson LN, et al. Thrombolytic therapy for superior vena caval thrombosis following superior vena cava-pulmonary anastomosis. Ann Thorac Surg 1984;38:637–9.

133. Downing TP, Danielson G, Ritter D, et al. Pulmonary artery thrombosis associated with anomalous pulmonary venous connection: an unusual complication following the modified Fontan procedure. J Thorac Cardiovasc Surg 1985;90:441–5.

134. Asante-Korang A, Sweeram N, McKay R, Arnold R. Thrombolysis with tissue type plasminogen activator following cardiac surgery in children. Int J Cardiol 1992;35:317–22.

135. Hedrick M, Elkins RC, Knott-Craig CJ, Razook JD. Successful thrombectomy for thrombosis of the right side of the heart after the Fontan operation. J Thorac Cardiovasc Surg 1992;105:297–301.

136. Lam J, Neirotti R, Becker AE, Planche C. Thrombosis after the Fontan procedure: transesophageal echocardiography may replace angiocardiography. J Thorac Cardiovasc Surg 1994;108:194–5.

137. Mahony L, Nikaidoh H, Fixler DE. Thrombolytic treatment with streptokinase for late intraatrial thrombosis after modified Fontan procedure. Am J Cardiol 1988;62:343–4.

138. Putnam JB, Lemmer JH, Rocchini AP, Bove EL. Embolectomy for acute pulmonary artery occlusion following Fontan procedure. Ann Thorac Surg 1988;45:335–6.

139. Sharratt G, Lacson A, Cornel G, Virmani S. Echocardiography of intracardiac filling defects in infants and children. Pediatr Cardiol 1986;7:189–94.

140. Kao JM, Alejos JC, Grant PW, et al. Conversion of atriopulmonary to cavopulmonary anastomosis in management of late arrhythmias and atrial thrombosis. Ann Thorac Surg 1994;58:1510–4.

141. Beitzke A, Zobel G, Zenz W, et al. Catheter-directed thrombolysis with recombinant tissue plasminogen activator for acute pulmonary embolism after Fontan operation. Pediatr Cardiol 1996;17:410–2.

142. Monagle P, Cochrane A, McCrindle B, et al. Thromboembolic complications after Fontan procedures: the role of prophylactic anticoagulation [editorial]. J Thorac Cardiovasc Surg 1998;115:493–8.

143. Zahn E, Lima V, Benson L, Freedom R. Use of endovascular stents to increase pulmonary blood flow in pulmonary atresia with ventricular septal defect. Am J Cardiol 1992;70:411–2.

144. Chau AKT, Leung MP. Management of branch pulmonary artery stenosis: balloon angioplasty or endovascular stenting. Clin Exp Pharmacol Physiol 1997;24:960–2.

145. Abdulhamed JM, Alyousef SA, Mullins C. Endovascular stent placement for pulmonary venous obstruction after Mustard operation for transposition of the great arteries. Heart 1996;75:210–2.

146. Hatai Y, Nykanen DG, Williams WG, et al. Endovascular stents in children under one year of age: acute impact and late results. Br Heart J 1995;74:689–95.

147. Marin ML, Veith FJ, Cynamon J, Sanchez LA, Lyon RT, Levine BA, et al. Initial experience with transluminally placed endovascular grafts for the treatment of complex vascular lesions. Ann Surg 1995;222:449–69.

148. Rome JJ. The role of catheter directed therapies in the treatment of congenital heart disease. Annu Rev Med 1995;46:159–68.

149. Mendelsohn AM, Bove EL, Lupinetti FM, et al. Intraoperative and percutaneous stenting of congenital pulmonary artery and vein stenosis. Circulation 1993;88:210–7.

150. Spijkerboer AM. Peripheral angiography and angioplasty. Curr Opin Radiol 1992;4:181–7.

151. Houde C, Zahn EM, Benson LN, et al. Intraoperative placement of endovascular stents. J Thorac Cardiovasc Surg 1992;104:530–2.
152. O'Laughlin MP, Perry SB, Lock JE, Mullins CE. Use of endovascular stents in congenital heart disease. Circulation 1991;83:1923–39.
153. Tikanoji T, Kirkinen P, Nikolajev K, et al. Familial atrial fibrillation with fetal onset. Heart 1998;79:195–7.
154. Luedtke SA, Kuhn RJ, McCaffrey FM. Pharmacologic management of supraventricular tachycardias in children. Part 2: atrial flutter, atrial fibrillation, and junctional and ectopic tachycardia. Ann Pharmacother 1997;31:1347–59.
155. Lenk M, Celiker A, Alehan D, et al. Role of adenosine in the diagnosis and treatment of tachyarrhythmias in pediatric patients. Acta Paediatr Jpn 1997;39:570–7.
156. Horowitz I, Galvis A, Gomperts E. Arterial thrombosis and protein S deficiency. J Pediatr 1992;121:934–7.
157. Ganrot P, Schersten B. Serum α_2-macroglobulin concentration and its variation with age and sex. Clin Chim Acta 1967;15:113–20.
158. Nakamura Y, Yanagawa H, Ojima T, et al. Cardiac sequelae of Kawasaki disease among recurrent cases. Arch Dis Child 1998;78:163–5.
159. Ogawa S, Fukazawa R, Ohkubo T, Zhang J, Takechi N, Kuramochi Y, et al. Silent myocardial ischemia in Kawasaki disease: evaluation of percutaneous transluminal coronary angioplasty by dobutamine stress testing. Circulation 1997;96:3384–9.
160. Bonnet D, Cormier V, Villain E, et al. Progressive left main coronary artery obstruction leading to myocardial infarction in a child with Williams disease. Eur J Pediatr 1997;156:751–3.
161. Deodhar AP, Tometzki AJ, Hudson IN, Mankad PS. Aortic valve tumor causing acute myocardial infarction in a child. Ann Thorac Surg 1997;64:1482–4.
162. Gruen DR, Winchester PH, Brill PW, Ramirez E. Magnetic resonance imaging of myocardial infarction during prothrombin complex concentrate therapy of hemophilia A. Pediatr Radiol 1997;27:271–2.
163. Saker DM, Walsh-Sukys M, Spector M, Zahka KG. Cardiac recovery and survival after neonatal myocardial infarction. Pediatr Cardiol 1997;18:139–42.
164. Iwama H, Kaneko T, Watanabe K, et al. Fatal acute myocardial infarction during general anesthesia in a 7 year old boy associated with total intramural coronary arteries. Anesthesiology 1997;87:426–9.
165. Muraskas J, Besinger R, Bell T, et al. Perinatal myocardial infarction in a newborn with a structurally normal heart. Am J Perinatol 1997;14:93–7.
166. Fogelman R, Gow RM, Casey F, Hamilton RM. Pseudoinfarction pattern in an infant. Pediatr Cardiol 1997;18:312–7.
167. Kececioglu D, Deng MC, Schmid C, Kehl HG, Baba HA, Yelbuz M, et al. Anomalus origin of the left coronary artery from the pulmonary artery with large anterior myocardial infarction and ischemia: successful tunnel repair and concomitant heterotopic heart transplantation as biological bridge to recovery. Transpl Int 1997;10:161–3.
168. Martins VP, Macedo AJ, Kaku S, Pinto F, Pinto E, Nunes MA, et al. Acute myocardial infarct in infants. Acta Med Port 1997;9:341–6.
169. Romero IC, Bueno CM, Bariuso LM, et al. Acute myocardial infarction in a 5 year old boy. Rev Espl Cardiol 1996;49:855–7.
170. Patel CR, Judge NE, Muise KL, Levine MM. Prenatal myocardial infarction suspected by fetal echocardiography. J Am Soc Echocardiogr 1996;9:721–3.
171. de Silva MV, de Silva GD, Lamabadusuriya SP. Myocardial infarction in an infant due to anomalous origin of the left coronary artery. Ceylon Med J 1996;41:115–7.
172. Kato H, Sugimura T, Akagi T, et al. Long term consequences of Kawasaki disease. A 10 to 21 year follow up study of 594 patients. Circulation 1996;94:1379–85.
173. Miyamoto T, Horigome H, Sato H, Yamada M, Inai K, Takeda T, et al. Anomalous origin of the left coronary artery from the pulmonary trunk with myocardial infarction and severe left ventricular dysfunction in infancy: assessment of myocardial damage using SPECT studies with 201TICI and 123I-BMIPP. Kaku Igaku 1996;33:169–74.
174. Tometzki AJ, Pollock JC, Wilson N, Davis CF. Role of ECMO in neonatal myocardial infarction. Arch Dis Child Fetal Neonatal Ed 1996;74:F143–4.
175. Ogawa S, Nagai Y, Zhang J, Yuge K, Hino Y, Jimbo O, et al. Evaluation of myocardial ischemia and infarction by signal-averaged electrocardiographic late potentials in children with Kawasaki disease. Am J Cardiol 1996;78:175–81.
176. de Caro E, Ribaldone D. Acute myocardial infarction and residual impairment of coronary perfusion: unusual complications of mitral endocarditis in a paediatric patient. G Ital Cardiol 1996;26:427–9.
177. Fletcher MA, Brown DR, Landers S, Seguin J. Umbilical arterial catheter use: report of an audit conducted by the study group for complications of perinatal care. Am J Perinatol 1994;11:94–9.
178. Lott J, Connor G, Phillips J. Umbilical artery catheter blood sampling alters cerebral blood flow velocity in preterm infants. J Perinatol 1996;16:341–5.
179. Rand T, Weninger M, Kohlhauser C, Bischof S, Heinz-Peer G, Trattig S, et al. Effect of umbilical artery catheterization in mesenteric hemodynamics. Pediatr Radiol 1996;26:435–8.
180. Jackson J, Truog W, Watchko J, et al. Efficacy of thromboresistant umbilical artery catheters in reducing

aortic thrombosis and related complications. J Pediatr 1987;110:102–5.

181. Horgan M, Bartoletti A, Polonsky S, et al. Effect of heparin infusates in umbilical arterial catheters on frequency of thrombotic complications. J Pediatr 1987;111:774–8.

182. Rajani K, Goetzman B, Wennberg R, et al. Effect of heparinization of fluids infused through an umbilical artery catheter on catheter patency and frequency of complications. Pediatrics 1979;63:552–6.

183. David R, Merten D, Anderson J, Gross S. Prevention of umbilical artery catheter clots with heparinized infusates. Dev Pharmacol Ther 1981;2:117–26.

184. Bosque E, Weaver L. Continuous versus intermittent heparin infusion of umbilical artery catheters in the newborn infant. J Pediatr 1986;108:141–3.

185. Ankola P, Atakent Y. Effect of adding heparin in very low concentration to the infusate to prolong the patency of umbilical artery catheters. Am J Perinatol 1993;10:229–32.

186. Randolph AG, Cook DJ, Gonzales CA. Benefit of heparin in central venous and pulmonary artery catheters: a meta-analysis of randomized controlled trials. Chest 1998;113:165–71.

187. Fassolt A, Brandli F, Braun U. Antothrombotika zur prophylaxe der begleitthrombosen bei infraklavikularen vena-cava-kathetern. Infusionsth Klin Ernahr 1979;6:50–4.

188. Fabri PJ, Mirtallo JM, Ruberg RL. Incidence and prevention of thrombosis of the subclavian vein during total parenteral nutrition. Surg Gynecol Obstet 1982;155:238–40.

189. Brismar B, et al. Reduction of catheter-associated thrombosis in parental nutrition by intravenous heparin therapy. Arch Surg 1982;117:1196–9.

190. Ruggiero RP, Aisenstein TJ. Central catheter fibrin sleeve - heparin effect. JPEN J Parenter Enteral Nutr 1983;7:270–3.

191. Macoviak JA, Melnik G, McLean G, et al. The effect of low dose heparin on the prevention of venous thrombosis in patients receiving short-term parenteral nutrition. Curr Surg 1984;41:98–100.

192. Fabri PJ, Mirtallo JM, Evvert ML, et al. Incidence and prevention of thrombosis of the subclavian vein during total parenteral nutrition. JPEN J Parenter Enteral Nutr 1984;8:705–7.

193. Efsing HO, Lindblad B, Mark J, Wolff T. Thromboembolic complications from central venous catheters: a comparision of three catheter materials. World J Surg 1983;7:419–23.

194. Smith PK, Miller DA, Lail S, Mehta AV. Urokinase treatment of neonatal aortoiliac thrombosis caused by umbilical artery catheterization: a case report. J Vasc Surg 1991;14:684–7.

195. Bailey MJ. Reduction of catheter-associated sepsis in parenteral nutrition using low dose intravenous heparin. BMJ 1979;1:1671–3.

196. Appelgren, Ransjo U, Bindslev L, Larm O. Does surface heparinisation reduce bacterial colonisation of central venous catheters. Lancet 1995;345:130–1.

197. Brown K, Uyboco JST, McMillan DD. Heparin is not required for peripheral intravenous locks in neonates. Paediatr Child Health 1999;4:39–42.

198. Alpan G, Eyal F, Springer C, et al. Heparinization of alimentation solutions administered through peripheral veins in premature infants. A controlled study. Pediatrics 1984;74:375–8.

199. Treas LS, Latinis-Bridges B. Efficacy of heparin in peripheral venous infusion in neonates. Obstet Gynecol Neonatal Nurs 1991;21:214–9.

200. Wright A, Hecker J, McDonald G. Effects of low dose heparin on failure of intravenous infusions in children. Heart Lung 1995;24:79–82.

201. Moclair AE, Moselhi M, Benjamin IS, Hecker JF. Total parenteral nutrition via a peripheral vein: a comparison of heparinized and non-heparinized regimens. Int J Pharm Pract 1991;1:38–40.

202. Sketch MH, Cale M, Mohiuddin SM, Booth RW. Use of percutaneously inserted venous catheters in coronary care units. Chest 1972;62:684–9.

203. Stradling JR. Heparin and infusion phlebitis. Br Med J 1978;2:1195–6.

204. Randolph AG, Cook DJ, Gonzalez CA, Andrew M. Benefit of heparin in peripheral venous and arterial catheters: systematic review and meta-analysis of randomized controlled trials. BMJ 1998;316:969–75.

205. Maddox RR, Rush DR, Rapp RP, et al. Double-blind study to investigate methods to prevent cephalothin-induced phlebitis. Am J Hosp Pharm 1977;34:29–34.

206. Bassan MM, Moselhi M, Benjamin IS, Hecker JF. Prevention of lidocaine-infusion phlebitis by heparin and hydrocortisone. Chest 1983;84:439–41.

207. Dunn DL, Lenihan SF. The case for the saline flush. Am J Nurs 1987;6:798–9.

208. Holford NHG, Vozeh S, Coates P, Porvell JR. More on heparin locks. N Engl J Med 1977;296:1300–1.

209. Kleiber C, Hanrahan K, Fagan CL, Zittergruen MA. Heparin vs saline peripheral i.v. locks in children. Pediatr Nurs 1993;19:405–9.

210. Shoaf J, Oliver S. Efficacy of normal saline injection with and without heparin for maintaining intermittent intravenous site. Appl Nurs Res 1992;5:9–12.

211. Ashton J, Gibson V, Summers S. Effects of heparin versus saline solution on intermittent infusion device irrigation. Heart Lung 1990;19:608–12.

212. Hamilton RA, Plia JM, Clay C, Sylvan L. Heparin sodium versus 0.9% sodium chloride injection for

maintaining patency of indwelling intermittent infusion devices. Clin Pharm 1988;7:439–43.

213. Meyer BA, Little CJ, Thorp JA, et al. Heparin versus normal saline as a peripheral line flush in maintenance of intermittent intravenous lines in obstetric patients. Obstet Gynecol 1995;85:433–6.

214. Daniell HW. Heparin in the prevention of infusion phlebitis. A double blind controlled study. JAMA 1973;226:1317–21.

215. Raschke R, Reilly B, Guidry J, et al. The weight-based heparin dosing nomogram compared with a "standard care" nomogram. Ann Intern Med 1993;119:874–81.

216. Gallus A, Jackaman J, Tillett J, et al. Safety and efficacy of warfarin started early after submassive venous thrombosis or pulmonary embolism. Lancet 1986;2:1293–6.

217. Hull R, Raskob G, Rosenbloom D. Heparin for 5 days as compared with 10 days in the initial treatment of proximal venous thrombosis. N Engl J Med 1990;322:1260–4.

218. Cruickshank M, Levine M, Hirsh J, et al. A standard heparin nomogram for the management of heparin therapy. Arch Intern Med 1991;151:333–7.

219. Elliot G, Hiltunen S, Suchyta M, et al. Physician-guided treatment compared with a heparin protocol for deep vein thrombosis. Arch Intern Med 1994;154:999–1004.

220. Hirsh J. Oral anticoagulant drugs. Review article. N Engl J Med 1991;324:1865–75.

221. Shojania A, Tetreault J, Turnbull G. The variations between heparin sensitivity of different lots of activated partial thromboplastin time reagent produced by the same manufacturer. Am J Clin Pathol 1988;89:19–23.

222. Leone M, Jenkins R, Golper T, Alexander S. Early experience with continuous arteriovenous hemofiltration in critically ill pediatric patients. Crit Care Med 1986;14:1058–63.

223. Geary DF, Gajaria M, Fryer-Keene S, Willumsen J. Low-dose and heparin-free hemodialysis in children. Pediatr Nephrol 1991;5:220–4.

224. Zobel G, Trop M, Muntean W, et al. Anticoagulation for continuous arteriovenous hemofiltration in children. Blood Purif 1988;6:90–5.

225. Pourchez T, Moriniere P, Fournier A, Pietri J. Use of Permcath (Quinton) catheter in uraemic patients in whom the creation of conventional vascular access for haemodialysis is difficult. Nephron 1989;53:297–302.

226. Burger H, Koostra G, de Charro F, Leffers P. A survey of vascular access for haemodialysis in the Netherlands. Nephrol Dial Transplant 1991;6:5–10.

227. Woodman RC, Harker LA. Bleeding complications associated with cardiopulmonary bypass. Blood 1990;76:1680–97.

228. Mammen EF, Koets MH, Washington BC, Wolk LW, Brown JM, Burdick M, et al. Hemostasis changes during cardiopulmonary bypass surgery. Semin Thromb Hemost 1985;11:281–92.

229. Bick RL. Hemostasis defects associated with cardiac surgery, prosthetic devices, and other extracorporeal circuits. Semin Thromb Hemost 1985;11:249–80.

230. Andrew M, MacIntyre B, Williams W, Gruenwald C, Johnston M, Burrows F, et al. Heparin therapy during cardiopulmonary bypass requires ongoing quality control. Thromb Haemost 1993;70:937–41.

231. Horkay F, Martin P, Rajah S, Walker D. Response to heparinization in adults and children undergoing cardiac operations. Ann Thorac Surg 1992;53:822–6.

232. Chan A, Leaker M, Burrows F, Williams W, Gruenwald C, White L, et al. Coagulation profile of paediatric patients undergoing cardiopulmonary bypass. Thromb Haemost 1997;77:270–7.

233. Hattersley P. Activated coagulation time of whole blood. JAMA 1966;196(5):150–4.

234. Babka R, Colby C, El-Etr A, Pifarre R. Monitoring of intraoperative heparinization and blood loss following cardiopulmonary bypass surgery. J Thorac Cardiovasc Surg 1977;73:780–2.

235. Dennis LH, Stewart JL, Conrad ME. Heparin treatment of haemorrhagic diathesis in cyanotic congenital heart-disease. Lancet 1967;1:1088–9.

236. Bull BS, Korpman RA, Huse WM, Briggs BD. Heparin therapy during extracorporeal circulation. I. Problems inherent in existing heparin protocols. J Thorac Cardiovasc Surg 1975;69:674–84.

237. Young JA, Kisker CT, Doty DB. Adequate anticoagulation during cardiopulmonary bypass determined by activated clotting time and the appearance of fibrin monomer. Ann Thorac Surg 1978;26:231–40.

238. Culliford AT, Gitel SN, Starr N, et al. Lack of correlation between activated clotting time and plasma heparin during cardiopulmonary bypass. Ann Surg 1980;193:105–11.

239. Bode A, Lust RM. Masking of heparin activity in the activated coagulation time (ACT) by platelet procoagulant activity. Thromb Res 1994;73:285–300.

240. Keeth J, Trickey T, King E, et al. A clinical evaluation of the hemotec ACT. Proc Am Acad Cardio Perf 1988;9:22–5.

241. Schriever H, Epstein S, Mintz M. Statistical correlation and heparin sensitivity of activated partial thromboplastin time, whole blood coagulation time, and an automated coagulation time. Am J Clin Pathol 1973;60:323–9.

242. Papaconstantinou C, Radegran K. Use of the activated coagulation time in cardiac surgery. Scand J Thorac Cardiovasc Surg 1981;15:213–5.

243. Mabry C, Thompson B, Read R, Campbell G. Activated clotting time monitoring of intraoperative heparinization: our experience and comparison of two techniques. Surgery 1981;90:889–95.

244. Kesteven P, Pasaoglu I, Williams B, Savidge G. Significance of the whole blood activated clotting time in cardiopulmonary bypass. J Cardiovasc Surg (Torino) 1986;27:85–9.

245. Kanto WP. A decade of experience with neonatal extracorporeal membrane oxygenation. J Pediatr 1994;124:335–47.

246. Bui KC, LaClair P, Vanderkerhove J, Bartlett RH. ECMO in premature infants. Review of factors associated with mortality. ASAIO Trans 1991;37:54–9.

247. Meliones JN, Custer JR, Snedecor S, et al. Extracorporeal life support for cardiac assist in pediatric patients. Review of the ELSO registry data. Circulation 1991;84:III168–72.

248. Davis FB. Long-term follow up of survivors of neonatal ECMO: what do we really know? Pediatr Nurs 1998;24:343–7.

249. Kanto WP, Bunyapen C. Extracorporeal membrane oxygenation. Controversies in selection of patients and management. Clin Perinatol 1998;25:159–75.

250. Trittenwein G, Furst G, Golej J, et al. Extracorporeal membrane oxygenation in neonates. Acta Anaesthesiol Scand 1997;111:143–4.

251. Hardart GE, Fackler JC. Predictors of intracranial hemorrhage during neonatal extracorporeal membrane oxygenation. J Pediatr 1999;134:156–9.

252. Horwitz JR, Cofer BR, Warner BW, et al. A multicenter trial of 6-aminocaproic acid (Amicar) in the prevention of bleeding in infants on ECMO. J Pediatr Surg 1998;33:1610–3.

253. Khan AM, Shabarek FM, Zwischenberger JB, Warner BW, Cheu HA, Jaksic T, et al. Utility of daily head ultrasonography for infants on extracorporeal membrane oxygenation. J Pediatr Surg 1998;33:1229–32.

254. Dela Cruz TV, Stewart DL, Winston SJ, et al. Risk factors for intracranial hemorrhage in the extracorporeal membrane oxygenation patient. J Perinatol 1997;17:18–23.

255. De Sanctis JT, Branson RT, Blickman JG. Can clinical parameters help reliably predict the onset of acute intracranial hemorrhage in infants receiving extracorporeal membrane oxygenation. Radiology 1996;199:429–32.

256. Bulas DI, Taylor GA, O'Donnell RM, et al. Intracranial abnormalities in infants treated with extracorporeal membrane oxygenation: update on sonographic and CT findings. AJNR Am J Neuroradiol 1996;17:287–94.

257. Gravck xtracorporeal circulatory support in neonatal respiratory failure: a prospective randomized study. Pediatrics 1985;76:479–87.

260. Seay RE, Uden DL, Kriesmer PJ, Payne NR. Predictive performance of three methods of activated clotting time measurement in neonatal ECMO patients. ASAIO J 1993;39:39–42.

261. Nagaya M, Futamura M, Kato J, et al. Application of a new anticoagulant (Nafamostat Mesilate) to control hemorrhagic complications during extracorporeal membrane oxygenation: a preliminary report. J Pediatr Surg 1997;32:531–5.

262. Yett HS, Skillman JJ, Salzman EW. The hazards of heparin plus aspirin. N Engl J Med 1978;298:1092–3.

263. Levine M, Raskob GE, Landefeld S, Kearon C. Hemorrhagic complications of anticoagulant treatment. Chest 1998;114:511S–23S.

264. Carr MJ, Carr S. At high heparin concentrations, protamine concentrations which reverse heparin anticoagulant effects are insufficient to reverse heparin antiplatelet effects. Thromb Res 1994;75:617–30.

265. Consensus Development Conference. Diagnosis, prophylaxis, and treatment of osteoporosis. Am J Med 1993;94:646–50.

266. Kanis JA. Assessment of fracture risk and its application to screening for menopausal osteoporosis: synopsis of a WHO report. Osteoporos Int 1994;4:368–81.

267. Looker AC, Johnston CC, Wahner HW, Dunn WL, Calvo MS, Harris TB, et al. Prevalences of low femoral bone density in older U.S. women from NHANES III. J Bone Miner Res 1995;10:796–802.

268. World Health Organization. Assessment of fracture risk and its application to screening for postmenopausal osteoporosis. Report of a WHO study group. World Health Organ Tech Rep Ser 1994;843:1–129.

269. World Health Organization. Standardization of proximal femur bone mineral density (BMD) measurements by DXA. International Committee for Standards in Bone Measurement. Bone 1997;21:369–70.

270. Smith DM, Khairi MRA, Johnston CC. The loss of bone mineral with aging and its relationship to risk fracture. J Clin Invest 1975;56:311–5.

271. De Laet CEDH, Van Hout BA, Burger H, et al. Hip fracture in elderly men and women: validation in the Rotterdam study. J Bone Min Res 1998;13:1587–93.

272. Melton LJ. Hip fracture: a worldwide problem today and tomorrow. Bone 1993;14:S1–8.

273. Marshall D, Johnell O, Wedel H. Meta-analysis of how well measure of bone mineral density predict occurrence of osteoporotic fractures. BMJ 1996;312:1254–9.

274. Edmonston SJ, Singer KP, Day RE, et al. Ex vivo estimation of thoracolumbar vertebral body compressive strength: the relative contributions of bone densito-

metry and vertebral morphometry. Osteoporos Int 1997;7:142–8.

275. Singer K, Edmonston S, Day R, et al. Prediction of thoracic and lumbar vertebral body compressive strength: correlations with bone mineral density and vertebral region. Bone 1995;17:167–74.

276. Bauer DC, Gluer CC, Genant HK, et al. Quantitative ultrasound and vertebral fracture in postmenopausal women. J Bone Min Res 1995;10:353–8.

277. Genant HK, Enfelke K, Fuerst T, et al. Noninvasive assessment of bone mineral and structure: state of the art. J Bone Min Res 1996;11:707–30.

278. Cameron JR, Sorenson JA. Measurement of bone mineral in vivo: an improved method. Science 1963;142:230–2.

279. Kelly TL, Crane G, Baran DT. Single X-ray absorptiometry of the forearm: precision, correlation, and reference data. Calcif Tissue Int 1994;54:212–8.

280. Sowers M, Clark MK, Hollis B, et al. Radial bone mineral density in pre- and preimenopausal women: a prospective study of rates and risk factors for loss. J Bone Miner Res 1992;7:647–57.

281. Lewis MK, Blake GM, Fogelman I. Patient dose in dual X-ray absorptiometry. Osteoporos Int 1994;4:11–5.

282. Akesson K. Biochemical markers of bone turnover: a review. Acta Orthop Scand 1995;66:376–86.

283. Mazess RB, Barden HS, Bisek JP, Hanson J. Dual energy X-ray absorptiometry for total body and regional bone mineral and soft-tissue composition. Am J Clin Nutr 1990;51:1106–12.

284. Teegarden D, Proulx WR, Martin BR, et al. Peak bone mass in young women. J Bone Min Res 1995;10:711–5.

285. Gilsanz V, Gibbens DT, Roe TF, et al. Vertebral bone density in children: effect of puberty. Radiology 1988;166:847–50.

286. Tommasi M, Bacciottini L, Benucci A, et al. Serum biochemical markers of bone turnover in healthy infants and children. Int J Biol Markers 1996;11:159–64.

287. del Rio L, Carrascosa A, Pons F, et al. Bone mineral density of the lumbar spine in white Mediterranean spanish children and adolescents: changes related to age, sex, and puberty. Pediatr Res 1994;35:362–6.

288. Recker RR, Davies KM, Hinders SM, et al. Bone gain in young adult women. JAMA 1992;268:2403–8.

289. Gilsanz V, Gibbens DT, Carlson M, et al. Peak trabecular vertebral density: a comparison of adolescent and adult females. Calcif Tissue Int 1988;43:260–2.

290. Thomas KA, Cook SD, Bennett JT, et al. Femoral neck and lumbar spine bone mineral densities in a normal population 3-20 years of age. J Ped Orthop 1991;11:48–58.

291. Theintz G. Longitudinal monitoring of bone mass accumulation in healthy adolescents: evidence for a marked reduction after 16 years of age at the levels of lumbar spine and femoral neck in female subjects. J Clin Endocrinol Metab 1992;43:1060–5.

292. Bonjour JP, Theintz G, Buchs B, et al. Critical years and stages of puberty for spinal and femoral bone mass accumulation during adolescence. J Clin Endocrinol Metab 1991;73:555–63.

293. Gilsanz V, Roe TF, Mora S, et al. Changes in vertebral bone density in black girls and white girls during childhood and puberty. N Engl J Med 1991;325:1597–600.

294. Gilsanz V, Skaggs DL, Kovanlikaya A, et al. Differential effect of race on the axial and appendicular skeletons of children. J Clin Endocrinol Metab 1998;83:1420–7.

295. Johnston CC, Miller JZ, Slemenda CW, et al. Calcium supplementation and increases in bone mineral density in children. N Engl J Med 1992;327:82–7.

296. Chestnut C. Theoretical overview: bone development, peak bone mass, bone loss, and fracture risk. Am J Med 1991;91:2S–4S.

297. Delmas PD. Biochemical markers of bone turnover: methodology and clinical use in osteoporosis. Am J Med 1991;91:59S–63S.

298. Alatas O, Colak O, Alatas E, et al. Osteocalcin metabolism in late fetal life: fetal and maternal osteocalcin levels. Clin Chim Acta 1995;239:179–83.

299. Dahlman T, Lindvall N, Hellgren M. Osteopenia in pregnancy during longterm heparin treatment: a radiological study post partum. Br J Obstet Gynaecol 1990;97:221–8.

300. De Sweit M, Ward PD, Fidler J, et al. Prolonged heparin therapy in pregnancy causes bone demineralization. Br J Obstet Gynaecol 1983;90:1129–34.

301. Dahlman TC. Osteoporotic fractures and the recurrence of thromboembolism during pregnancy and the puerperium in 184 women undergoing thromboprophylaxis with heparin. Am J Obstet Gynecol 1993;168:1265–70.

302. Barbour LA, Kick SD, Steiner JF, et al. A prospective study of heparin-induced osteoporosis in pregnancy using bone densitometry. Am J Obstet Gynecol 1994;170:862–9.

303. Dahlman TC, Sjoberg HE, Ringertz H. Bone mineral density during long-term prophylaxis with heparin in pregnancy. Am J Obstet Gynecol 1994;170:1315–20.

304. Douketis JD, Ginsberg JS, Burrows RF, et al. The effects on longterm heparin therapy during pregnancy on bone density. Thromb Haemost 1996;75:254–7.

305. Zimran A, Shilo S, Fisher D, Bab I. Histomorphometric evaluation of reversible heparin-induced osteoporosis in pregnancy. Arch Intern Med 1986;146:386–8.

306. Melissari E, Parker CJ, Wilson NV, et al. Use of low molecular weight heparin in pregnancy. Thromb Haemost 1992;68:652–6.

307. Shefras J, Farquharson RG. Bone density studies in pregnant women receiving heparin. Obstet Gynecol 1996;65:171–4.

308. Chan GM, Ronald N, Slater P, et al. Decreased bone mineral status in lactating adolescent mothers. J Pediatr 1990;101:767–70.

309. De Swiet M, Dorrington Ward P, Fidler J, et al. Prolonged heparin therapy in pregnancy causes bone demineralization. Br J Obstet Gynaecol 1983;90:1129–34.

310. Smith R, Stevenson JC, Winearls CG, et al. Osteoporosis of pregnancy. Lancet 1985;1178–80.

311. Goldsmith NF, Johnston JO. Bone mineral: effects of oral contraceptives, pregnancy, and lactation. J Bone Joint Surg 1975;57A:657–68.

312. Wardlow GM, Pike AM. The effect of lactation on peak adult shaft and ultra-distal forearm bone mass in women. Am J Clin Nutr 1986;44:283–6.

313. Hayslip CC, Klein TA, Wray HL, Duncan WE. The effects of lactation on bone mineral content in healthy postpartum women. Obstet Gynecol 1989;73:588–92.

314. Smith R, Athanasou NA, Ostlere SJ, Vipond SE. Pregnancy-associated osteoporosis. QJM 1995;88:865–78.

315. Griffith GC, Nichols G, Asher JD, Flanagan B. Heparin osteoporosis. JAMA 1965;193:85.

316. Jaffe MD, Willis PW. Multiple fractures associated with long term sodium heparin therapy. JAMA 1965;193:158–60.

317. Squires JW, Pinch LW. Heparin-induced spinal fractures. JAMA 1979;241:2417–8.

318. Hull R, Delmore T, Carter C, et al. Adjusted subcutaneous heparin versus warfarin sodium in the long-term treatment of venous thrombosis. N Engl J Med 1982;306:189–94.

319. Ginsberg J, Kowalchuk G, Hirsh J, et al. Heparin effect on bone density. Thromb Haemost 1990;64(2):286–9.

320. Murphy M. Heparin therapy and bone fractures. Lancet 1992;340:1098–9.

321. Sackler JP. Heparin induced osteoporosis. Br J Radiol 1973;46:548–50.

322. Avioli L. Heparin induced osteoporosis: an appraisal. Adv Exp Med Biol 1975;52:375–87.

323. Schuster J. Pathology of osteopathy following heparin therapy. Dtsch Med Wochenschr 1969;2334–8.

324. Matzsch T, Bergqvist D, Hedner U, et al. Effects of low molecular weight heparin and unfragmented heparin on induction of osteoporosis in rats. Thromb Haemost 1990;63(3):505–9.

325. Monreal M, Vinas L, Monreal L, et al. Heparin-related osteoporosis in rats. Haemostasis 1990;20:204–7.

326. Lenaers-Claeys G, Vaes G. Collagenase, procollaginase, and bone resorption effects of heparin, parathyroid hormone and calcitonin. Biochim Biophys Acta 1979;584:375–88.

327. Shaughnessy SG, Young E, Deschamps P, Hirsh J. The effects of low molecular weight and standard heparin on calcium loss from fetal rat calvaria. Blood 1995;86:1368–73.

328. Hurley M. Structural determinants of the capacity of heparin to inhibit collagen synthesis in 21 day fetal rat calvarie. J Bone Min Res 1990;1127–33.

329. Thompson RC. Heparin osteoporosis: an experimental model using rats. J Bone Joint Surg 1973;55A:606–12.

330. Muir JM, Andrew M, Hirsh J, et al. Histomorphometric analysis of the effects of standard heparin on trabecular bone in vivo. Blood 1996;88:1314–20.

331. Kelton J, Smith J, Warkentin T, et al. Immunoglobulin G from patients with heparin induced thrombocytopenia binds to a complex of heparin and platelet factor 4. Blood 1994;83:3232–9.

332. Kelton J. Heparin-induced thrombocytopenia. Haemostasis 1986;16:173–86.

333. Kelton J, Powers P. Heparin-associated thrombocytopenia: an immune disorder. New York: Elsevier Science; 1981.

334. Kelton J, Sheridan D, Santos A, et al. Heparin-associated thrombocytopenia: laboratory studies. Blood 1988;72:925–30.

335. Warkentin T, Kelton J. Heparin-induced thrombocytopenia. Prog Hemost Thromb 1991;10:1–34.

336. Andrew M, Brooker LA, Ginsberg JS, Kelton JG. Clinical problems in anticoagulation therapy. Hematology 1997 (The Education Program of the American Society of Hematology) 8–28.

337. Warkentin T, Kelton J. Heparin-induced thrombocytopenia. Annu Rev Med 1989;40:31–44.

338. King D, Kelton J. Heparin-associated thrombocytopenia. Ann Intern Med 1984;100:535–40.

339. Warkentin T, Kelton J. Interaction of heparin with platelets, including heparin-induced thrombocytopenia. In: Goldhaber S, Bounameaux H, editors. Low molecular weight heparins in prophylaxis and therapy of thromboembolic diseases. Series: "Fundamental and Clinical Cardiology." New York: Marcel Dekker Inc; 1994. p. 75–127.

340. Warkentin TE. Heparin-induced skin lesions. Br J Haematol 1996;92:494–7.

341. Warkentin TE, Chong BH, Greinacher A. Heparin-induced thrombocytopenia: towards consensus. Thromb Haemost 1998;79:1–7.

342. Warkentin TE, Kelton JG. A 14 year study of heparin induced thrombocytopenia. Am J Med 1996;101: 502–7.

343. Boshkov L, Warkentin T, Hayward C, et al. Heparin-induced thrombocytopenia and thrombosis: clinical and laboratory studies. Br J Haematol 1993;84(2): 322–8.

344. Warkentin TE. Heparin-induced thrombocytopenia in patients treated with low molecular weight or unfractionated heparin. N Engl J Med 1995;332: 1330–5.

345. Warkentin TE, Kelton JG. Heparin-induced thrombocytopenia. Prog Hemost Thromb 1991;10:1–34.

346. Sheridan D, Carter C, Kelton J. A diagnostic test for heparin-induced thrombocytopenia. Blood 1986;67: 27–30.

347. Kelton J, Sheridan D, Brain M, et al. Clinical usefulness of testing for a heparin-dependent platelet-aggregating factor in patients with suspected heparin-associated thrombocytopenia. J Lab Clin Med 1984;103: 606–12.

348. Look KA, Sahud M, Flaherty S, Zehender JL. Heparin-induced platelet aggregation versus platelet factor 4 enzyme linked immunosorbent assay in the diagnosis of heparin-induced thrombocytopenia-thrombosis. Am J Clin Pathol 1997;108:78–82.

349. Arepally G, Reynolds C, Tomaski A, et al. Comparison of PF4/heparin ELISA assay with the 14C-serotonin release assay in the diagnosis of heparin-induced thrombocytopenia. Am J Clin Pathol 1995;104: 648–54.

350. Kelton JG, Warkentin TE. Heparin-induced thrombocytopenia: what the serologists have taught us. J Lab Clin Med 1996;128:346–8.

351. Warkentin TE, Hayward CPM, Boshkow LK, et al. Sera from patients with heparin-induced thrombocytopenia generate platelet-derived microparticles with procoagulant activity: an explanation for the thrombotic complications of heparin-induced thrombocytopenia. Blood 1994;84:3691–9.

352. Spadone D, Clark F, James E, et al. Heparin-induced thrombocytopenia in the newborn. J Vasc Surg 1996;15:306–11.

353. Wilhelm M. Cardiopulmonary bypass in patients with heparin induced thrombocytopenia using Organon 10172. Ann Thorac Surg 1996;61:920–4.

354. Potter C. Heparin induced thrombocytopenia in a child. J Pediatr 1992;121:135–8.

355. Klement D, Rammos S, von Kries R, et al. Heparin as a cause of thrombus progression. Heparin-associated thrombocytopenia is an important differential diagnosis in paediatric patients even with normal platelet counts. Eur J Pediatr 1996;155:11–4.

356. Murdoch IA. Heparin induced thrombocytopenia in children. Acta Paediatr 1993;82:495–7.

357. Magnani HN. Heparin-induced thrombocytopenia (HIT); an overview of 230 patients treated with Orgaran (Org 10172). Thromb Haemost 1993;70: 554–61.

358. Leaker M, Saxon BR. Heparin induced thrombocytopenia in a young child managed with Orgaran for cardiopulmonary bypass surgery. Blood 1998(abstract);204a.

359. Weitz JI. Low molecular weight heparins. N Engl J Med 1997;337:688–98.

360. Carter C, Kelton J, Hirsh J, et al. The relationship between the hemorrhagic and antithrombotic properties of a low molecular weight heparin in rabbits. Blood 1982;59:1239–45.

361. Thomas DP, Merton RE, Lewis WE, Barrowcliffe TW. Studies in man and experimental animals of a low molecular weight heparin fraction. Thromb Haemost 1981;45:214–8.

362. Andriuoli G, Mastacchi R, Barbanti M, Sarret M. Comparison of the antithrombotic and haemorrhagic effects of heparin and a new low molecular weight heparin in rats. Haemostasis 1985;15:324–30.

363. Kuijer PMM, Prins MH, Buller HR. Low molecular weight heparins: treatment of venous thromboembolism. In: Sashara AA, Loscalzo J, editors. Advances in therapeutic agents in thrombosis and thrombolysis. New York: M Dekker Inc.; 1997. p. 129–47.

364. Linker A, Hovingh P. Isolation and characterization of oligosaccharides obtained from heparin by the action of heparinase. Biochemistry 1972;11:563–7.

365. Cade JF, Buchanan MR, Boneu B. A comparison of the antithrombotic and hemorrhagic effects of low molecular weight heparin fractions: the influence of the method of preparation. Thromb Res 1984;35: 613–25.

366. Hirsh J, Levine M. Low molecular weight heparin. Blood 1992;79:1–17.

367. Gray EW, Heath AB, Mulloy B, et al. A collaborative study of proposed European Pharmacopoeia reference preparations of low molecular mass heparin. Thromb Haemost 1995;74:893–9.

368. Ahsan A, Jeske W, Mardiguian J, Fareed J. Feasibility study of heparin mass calibrator as a GPC calibrator for heparins and low molecular weight heparins. J Pharm Sci 1994;83:197–201.

369. Schmidt B, Mitchell L, Ofosu F, Andrew M. Alpha-2-macroglobulin is an important progressive inhibitor of thrombin in neonatal and infant plasma. Thromb Haemost 1989;62:1074–7.

370. Mitchell L, Piovella F, Ofosu F, Andrew M. Alpha-2-macroglobulin may provide protection from thromboembolic events in antithrombin III deficient children. Blood 1991;78:2299–304.

371. Vieira A, Ofosu F, Andrew M. The activity of a low molecular weight heparin (CY222) in neonatal plasma. Thromb Haemost 1991;63:85–98.

372. Young E, Wells P, Holloway S, et al. Ex vivo and in vitro evidence that low molecular weight heparins exhibit less binding to plasma protein than unfractionated heparin. Thromb Haemost 1994;71:300–4.

373. Sobel M, McNeill PM, Carlson PL. Heparin inhibition of von Willebrand factor dependent platelet function in vitro and in vivo. J Clin Invest 1991;87:1787–93.

374. Andersson LO, Barrowcliffe TW, Holmer E. Molecular weight dependency of the heparin potentiated inhibition of thrombin and activated factor X: effect of heparin neutralization in plasma. Thromb Res 1979;15:531–41.

375. Dawes J, Pavuk N. Sequestration of therapeutic glycosaminoglycans by plasma fibronectin. Thromb Haemost 1991;65:829a.

376. Barzu I, Molho P, Tobelem G, et al. Binding of heparin and low molecular weight heparin fragments to human vascular endothelial cells in culture. Nouv Rev Fr Hematol 1984;26:243–7.

377. Barzu T, van Rijn JLML, Petitou M, et al. Heparin degradation in the endothelial cells. Thromb Res 1987;47:601–9.

378. Boneu B, Caranobe C, Cadroy Y, et al. Pharmacokinetics of standard and unfractionated heparins, and low molecular weight heparins in the rabbit. Semin Thromb Hemost 1988;14:18–27.

379. Canarobe C, Barret A, Gabaig AM. Disappearance of circulating anti-Xa activity after intravenous injection of unfractionated heparin an of low molecular weight heparin (CY216) in normal and nephrectomized rabbits. Thromb Res 1985;40:129–33.

380. Palm M, Mattsson C. Pharmacokinetics of heparin and low molecular weight fragment (fragmin) in rabbits with impaired renal or metabolic clearance. Thromb Haemost 1987;58:932–5.

381. Briant L, Caranobe C, Saivin S, et al. Unfractionated heparin and CY 216: pharmacokinetics and bioavailabilities of the antifactor Xa and IIa effects after intravenous and subcutaneous injection in the rabbit. Thromb Haemost 1989;61:348–53.

382. Frydman A. Low molecular weight heparins: an overview of their pharmacodynamics, pharmacokinetics and metabolism in humans. Haemostasis 1996;26:24–38.

383. Matzsch T, Bergquist D, Hedner U, Ostergaard P. Effects of an enzymatically depolymerized heparin as compared with conventional heparin in healthy volunteers. Thromb Haemost 1987;57:97–101.

384. Bradbrook ID, Magnani HN, Moilker HC. ORG 10172: a low molecular weight heparinoid anticoagulant with a long half life in man. Br J Clin Pharmacol 1987;23:667–75.

385. Bratt G, Tornebohm E, Widlund L. Low molecular weight heparin (KABI 2165, FRAGMIN): pharmacokinetics after intravenous and subcutaneous administration in human volunteers. Thromb Res 1986;42:613–20.

386. Frydman A, Bara L, Leroux Y. The antithrombotic activity and pharmacokinetics of enoxaparin, a low molecular weight heparin, in man given single subcutaneous doses of 20 up to 80 mg. J Clin Pharmacol 1988;28:608–18.

387. Andrew M, Ofosu F, Brooker L, Buchanan M. The comparison of the pharmacokinetics of a low molecular weight heparin in the newborn and adult pig. Thromb Res 1989;56:529–39.

388. Massicotte P, Adams M, Marzinotto V, et al. Low molecular weight heparin in pediatric patients with thrombotic disease: a dose finding study. J Pediatr 1996;128:313–8.

389. Massicotte MP, Adams M, Leaker M, Andrew M. A nomogram to establish therapeutic levels of the low molecular weight heparin (LMWH), clivarine in children requiring treatment for venous thromboembolism (VTE). Thromb Haemost 1997;Suppl: 282(Abstr.)

390. Dix D, Marzinotto V, Leaker M, et al. The use of low molecular weight heparin in pediatric patients: review of a single institution experience. J Pediatr 1999; in press.

391. Dix D, Charpentier K, Sparling C, Massicotte MP. Determination of trough anti-factor Xa levels in pediatric patients on low molecular weight heparin (LMWH). J Pediatr Hematol Oncol 1998;(Abstr.)

392. Lumpkin MM. Food and Drug Administration public health advisory: low molecular weight heparin and spinal/epidural anesthesia or spinal puncture. Int J Trauma Nurs 1998;4:56–7.

393. Lumpkin MM. Food and Drug Administration public health advisory. Anesthesiology 1998;88:27A–28A.

394. Massie BM. News from the Food and Drug Administration Cardio-Renal Advisory Committee meeting 26 June, 1997. Circulation 1997;96:2483.

395. Reports prompt new warnings on low molecular weight heparins, heparinoids. Am J Health Syst Pharm 1998;55:210–

396. Monreal M, Lafoz E, Olive A, et al. Comparision of subcutaneous unfractionated heparin with a low molecular weight heparin (Fragmin) in patients with venous thromboembolism and contraindications to coumarin. Thromb Haemost 1994;71:7–11.

397. Monagle P, Andrew M, Halton J, et al. Homozygous protein C deficiency: description of a new mutation and successful treatment with low molecular weight heparin. Thromb Haemost 1998;79:756–61.

398. Muir JM, Hirsh J, Weitz J, et al. A histomorphometric comparison of the effects of heparin and low molecular weight heparin on cancellous bone in rats. Blood 1997;9:3236–42.

399. Van Ryn-McKenna J, Cai L, Ofosu F, et al. Neutralization of enoxaparine induced bleeding by protamine sulfate. Thromb Haemost 1990;63:271–4.

400. Siragusa S, Cosmi B, Piovella F, et al. Low molecular weight heparins and unfractionated heparin in the treatment of patients with acute venous thromboembolism: results of a meta-analysis. Am J Med 1996;100:1–9.

401. Lensing AWA, Prins MH, Davidson BL, et al. Treatment of deep venous thrombosis with low molecular weight heparins. A meta-analysis. Arch Intern Med 1995;155:601–7.

402. Leizorovicz A, Simmonneau G, Decousus H, Boissel JP. Comparison of efficacy and safety of low molecular weight heparins and unfractionated heparin in initial treatment of deep venous thrombosis: a meta-analysis. BMJ 1994;309:299–304.

403. Reitsma P, Bernardi F, Doing R, et al. Protein C deficiency: a database of mutations,1995 update on behalf of the subcomitee on plasma coagulation inhibitors of the scientific and standardization committee of the ISTH. Thromb Haemost 1995; 73:876–9.

404. Melissari E, Kakkar V. Congenital severe protein C deficiency in adults. Br J Haematol 1989;72:222–8.

405. Pescatore P, Horellou J, Conard J, et al. Problems of oral anticoagulation in an adult with homozygous protein C deficiency and late onset of thrombosis. Thromb Haemost 1993;69(4):311–5.

406. Tripodi A, Franchi F, Krachmalnicoff A, Mannucci P. Asymptomatic homozygous protein C deficiency. Acta Haematol 1990;83(3):152–5.

407. Yamamoto K, Matsushita T, Sugiura I, et al. Homozygous protein C deficiency: identification of a novel missuse mutation that causes impaired secretion of the mutant protein C. J Lab Clin Med 1992;119(6): 682–9.

408. Conard J. Homozygous protein C deficiency with late onset and recurrent coumarin induced skin necrosis. Lancet 1992;339:743–4.

409. Grundy C, Melissari E, Lindo V, et al. Late-onset homozygous protein C deficiency. Lancet 1991; 338(8766):575–6.

410. Tuddenham E, Takase T, Thomas A, et al. Homozygous protein C deficiency with delayed onset of symptoms at 7 to 10 months. Thromb Res 1989;53(5):475–84.

411. Sharon C. Homozygous protein C deficiency with moderately severe clinical symptoms. Thromb Res 1986; 41:483–8.

412. Manabe S, Matsuda M. Homozygous protein C deficiency combined with heterozygous dysplasmino-

413. genemia in a 21 year old thrombophilic male. Thromb Res 1985;39:333–41.

413. Samama M. Successful progressive anticoagulation in a severe protein C deficiency and previous skin necrosis at the initiation of oral anticoagulant treatment. Thromb Haemost 1984;51:132–3.

414. Dreyfus M, Masterson M, David M, et al. Replacement Therapy with a Monoclonal Antibody Purified Protein C concentrate in newborns with severe congenital Protein C deficiency. Semin Thromb Hemost 1995;21:371–81.

415. Hylek EM, Singer DE. Risk factors for intracranial hemorrhage in outpatients taking warfarin. Ann Intern Med 1994;120:897–902.

416. Hirsh J, Dalen JE, Anderson DR, et al. Oral anticoagulants: mechanism of action, clinical effectiveness, and optimal therapeutic range. Chest 1998;114: 445S–469S.

417. Baliga V, Thwaites R, Tillyer ML, et al. Homozygous protein C deficiency- management with protein C concentrate. Eur J Pediatr 1995;154:534–8.

418. Dreyfus M, Magny J, Bridey F, et al. Treatment of homozygous protein C deficiency and neonatal purpura fulminans with a purified protein C concentrate. N Engl J Med 1991;325:1565–8.

419. De Stefano V, Mastrangelo S, Schwarz H, et al. Replacement therapy with a purified protein C concentrate during initiation of oral anticoagulation in severe protein C congenital deficiency. Thromb Haemost 1993;70:247–9.

420. Gerson W, Dickerman J, Bovill E, Golden E. Severe acquired protein C deficiency in purpura fulminans associated with disseminated intravascular coagulation: treatment with protein C concentrate. Pediatrics 1993;91:418–22.

421. Broekmans A. Treatment of hereditary protein C deficiency with stanazol. Thromb Haemost 1987;57: 20–4.

422. Casella J, Bontempo F, Markel J, et al. Successful treatment of homozygous protein C deficiency by hepatic transplantation. Lancet 1988;1(8583):435–8.

423. van Bilijon I, van Damme-Lombaerts R, Demol A, et al. Low molecular weight heparin for anticoagulation during haemodialysis in children: a preliminary study [letter]. Eur J Radiol 1996;155:70–1.

424. Fijnvandraat K, Nurmohamed M, Peters M, et al. A cross-over dose finding study investigating a low molecular weight heparin (Fragminæ) in six children on chronic hemodialysis. Thromb Haemost 1993; 69:1134a.

425. Hashikura Y, Kawasaki S, Okumura N, et al. Prevention of hepatic artery thrombosis in pediatric liver transplantation. Transplantation 1995;60:1109–12.

426. Broyer M, Gagnadoux MF, Sierro A, et al. Preventive treatment of vascular thrombosis after kidney trans-

plantation in children with low molecular weight heparin. Transplant Proc 1991;23:1384–5.

427. de Saint-Martin A, Terzic J, Christmann D, et al. Superior sagittal sinus thrombosis and nephrotic syndrome: favorable outcome with low molecular weight heparin. Arch Pediat 1997;4:849–52.

428. deVeber G, Chan A, Monagle P, et al. Anticoagulation therapy in pediatric patients with sinovenous thrombosis: a cohort study. Arch Neurol 1998;55:1533–7.

429. Andrew M, deVeber G. Pediatric thrombembolism and stroke protocols. Hamilton: B.C. Decker Inc; 1997.

10   ORAL ANTICOAGULATION THERAPY IN PEDIATRIC PATIENTS

In the early 1900s, sweet clover was planted in the Dakota plains and Canada because it flourished in the poor soil and was an alternative for corn in silage. In 1924, Schofield described a previously unreported hemorrhagic disorder in cattle who fed on spoiled sweet clover silage.[1] The cause was shown to be reduced prothrombin levels and eventually the hemorrhagic agent was identified as bishydroxycoumarin (dicumarol) in 1943.[2] A number of analogues were then synthesized, the most useful of which was racemic warfarin. (Warfarin is an acronym for the patent holder, *W*isconsin *A*lumni *R*esearch *F*oundation, plus the coum*arin*-derived suffix.) Warfarin became a widely used rodenticide; however, use in humans was not considered safe until a man survived attempted suicide with repeated doses of warfarin in 1951. Clinical trials quickly followed, and oral anticoagulants (OAs) have been in widespread clinical use ever since.[3]

Oral anticoagulants are used for the treatment and primary of secondary prevention of thromboembolic events (TEs). Current recommendations for adult patients are based upon well-designed clinical trials that have addressed the issue of optimal use of OAs.[3] At the present time, guidelines for the use of OAs in children[4] are extrapolated from recommendations for adults, which may not be an optimal approach given the profound age-related differences in blood coagulation.[5-8] There is an urgency to the establishment of optimal age appropriate guidelines for the use of OAs because increasing numbers of children require treatment, and recent studies show that there are significant differences in the response of children to OAs compared to adults.[9-11]

The objectives of this section are to discuss:

(1) The activities of OAs.

(2) The influence of age on vitamin K (VK)-dependent proteins and OAs.

(3) The relationship between VK status, OAs, and bone structure.

(4) Indications for OAs.

(5) Target range for OAs.

(6) Factors influencing dose response relationships.

(7) Monitoring of OAs.

(8) Complications of OAs.

(9) The future of OAs in pediatric patients.

A MEDLINE search was conducted of the literature from 1966 to June 1998 and supplemented with references from the listed articles. A total of 43 publications were identified that described OAs in children: 40 case reports or case series,[12-49] 1 national survey,[50] and 2 prospective cohort studies.[9,11] The national survey was based upon a questionnaire mailed to 407 British hematologists, pediatric cardiologists, and cardiac surgeons, with a response rate of 58 percent.[50] The cohort studies assessed consecutive children (ages 1 month to 18 years) attending an outpatient pediatric anticoagulation clinic at a large tertiary care children's hospital.[9,11]

ACTIVITIES OF ORAL ANTICOAGULANTS

The essential substance of OAs is coumarin, a VK antagonist. The chemical characteristics of the coumarin derivatives required for anticoagulant activity are an intact 4-hydroxycoumarin residue with a carbon substitute at the 3 position.[49] Aceno-coumarol, phenprocoumon, and warfarin all have an asymmetrical carbon atom in the substituent at the 3 position.[49] Warfarin (3-[α-Phenyl-β-Acetyl ethyl]-4-hydroxycoumarin) is the OA used in North America, whereas both warfarin and phen-procoumon (3-[α-Phenyl-β-propyl]-4-hydroxy-coumarin) are used in Europe. Acenocoumarol is used in South America and other parts of the world. Their mode of action is identical; however, they differ by their metabolism. Warfarin and aceno-coumarol are relatively short-acting anticoagulants compared to phenprocoumon, which is a long acting agent.[51–58] Oral anticoagulants function by competitively interfering with VK metabolism.[57–59] VK is an essential cofactor for the post-translational carboxylation of glutamic acid (Gla) residues on specific coagulant proteins (factor (F) II, FVII, FIX, and FX).[54,60,61] Gla residues serve as calcium-binding sites that are essential for VK-dependent coagulant proteins to bind to phospholipid surfaces and thrombin generation to occur.[54,60,61] Oral anticoagulants competitively inhibit two enzymes involved in VK metabolism resulting in decreased plasma concentrations of active forms of FII, FVII, FIX and FX[55–57,59] (Figure 10–1). Specifically, the post-translational carboxylation of glutamate residues on the N-terminal regions of VK-dependent proteins to γ-carboxyglutamates (Gla)[54–57,59–63] are catalyzed by the reduced form of VK (VKH$_2$). VKH$_2$ is oxidized to form VK epoxide and Gla residues are formed. Vitamin K epoxide is then cycled back to VK by VK epoxide reductase and the VK is reduced to VKH$_2$ by VK reductase.[55–57] Oral anticoagulants lead to increasing concentrations of VK epoxide in the liver and plasma by inhibiting VK epoxide reductase and possibly VK reductase.[55–57,59] The lack of VKH$_2$ limits the γ-carboxylation of VK coagulant proteins (FII, FVII, FIX, FX) and inhibitors (protein C and protein S). For prothrombin, less

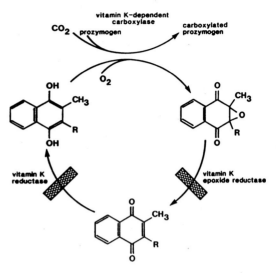

Figure 10–1 Warfarin inhibits vitamin K epoxide reductase and vitamin K reductase (hatched box), thereby blocking the conversion of vitamin K epoxide to vitamin KH$_2$. Vitamin KH$_2$ is a cofactor for the carboxylation of inactive proenzymes (factors II, VII, IX, X) to the carboxylated proenzyme in a reaction that is catalyzed by vitamin K-dependent γ-carboxylase and requires carbon dioxide and oxygen.

K(VK) = vitamin; O$_2$ = oxygen; CO$_2$ = carbon dioxide.

Reproduced with permission from Furie B, Furie B. Molecular basis of vitamin K-dependent γ-carboxylation. Blood 1990;75:1753–62.

than 6 Gla domains, as compared to 10 to 13 physiologically, reduces activity to less than 2 percent.[60]

Pharmacodynamics

Oral anticoagulants are usually administered orally although available and active in a parenteral form. Warfarin is rapidly and nearly completely absorbed, reaching a peak plasma concentration in adults within 90 minutes,[62,64] and has a half-life of 36 to 42 hours.[49,51,53,59,62,64–66] Warfarin binds to many plasma proteins and also accumulates in the liver.[67] Commercial preparations of OAs consist of racemic mixtures of two optically active isomers, the R and S forms, which are metabolized by different routes.[52,53,66,68,69] The S-isomer is a more potent anticoagulant than the R-isomer in warfarin and phenprocoumon; however, the reverse is true for acenocoumarol. Some drug interactions may be more prominent with the S-isomer of warfarin. There is considerable variation in patient response to warfarin.[51] The absorption of phenprocoumon is similar to that of warfarin but, due to the delayed metabolization of phenprocoumon, the elimination half-life is much longer, with a mean of 157 hours and a large individual variation of between 76 and 274 hours.[67-69] Acenocoumarol has a half-life of 8 hours in man; however, the ongoing activity of metabolites prolongs the anticoagulant effect. Potential biologic explanations for some of the variability in response are differing plasma concentrations of the VK coagulant proteins, pharmacokinetics, and other comorbid conditions. As discussed subsequently, there are numerous patient-related factors that also influence the activity of OAs.

Hereditary Resistance to Oral Anticoagulants

Patients resistant to OAs often require 5 to 20 times the usual dose for their age. The responsible mechanism is thought to be a reduced affinity for the receptor for OAs.[70-72]

Laboratory Monitoring of Oral Anticoagulants

The prothrombin time (PT) is sensitive to reductions of FII, FVII, and FX, and is the most commonly used test for monitoring OAs in North America.[73] Unfortunately thromboplastin reagents for PT assays have widely varying sensitivities to decreased plasma concentrations of VK-dependent proteins.[74-77] Prior to the recognition of this problem, when targeting the same PT ratio, patients in North America were receiving excessive amounts of OA compared to patients in Europe, with unnecessary hemorrhagic side effects.[65,78-80] The International Normalized Ratio (INR) was developed and is accepted internationally as a mechanism for standardizing variations in PT values due to thromboplastin reagents.[65,77,80] The INR is calculated as the ratio of the patient's PT value to the control PT value to the power of the International Sensitivity Index (ISI):

$$\left(\frac{PT[patient]}{PT[control]}\right)^{ISI}$$

where the ISI is a measure of the responsiveness of thromboplastin reagents to decreased activity of VK-dependent coagulant proteins. The introduction of the INR has significantly reduced the incidence of bleeding in adult patients receiving OAs in North America.[3,81] Unfortunately most pediatric studies have not reported their results as INR values, which hinders the interpretation and generalizability of their results. Laboratories involved in monitoring OAs need to provide INR values to clinicians to facilitate optimal management.

INFLUENCE OF AGE ON VITAMIN K-DEPENDENT PROTEINS AND RESPONSE TO ORAL ANTICOAGULANTS

Vitamin K-Dependent Coagulant Proteins

Figure 10–2 shows the gestational age (GA) dependency of plasma concentrations of the VK-dependent coagulant proteins. In 19 to 29 week old fetuses, plasma concentrations of the VK-dependent coagulant factors (FII, FVII, FIX, FX) are approximately 9.9 to 33.8 percent of adults values.[82] Between 30 and 40 weeks GA, levels of the VK coag-

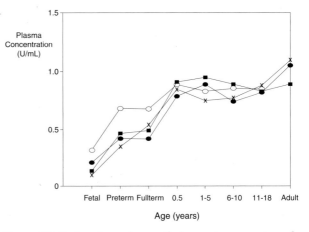

Figure 10–2 Age dependency of plasma concentrations for the vitamin K coagulant proteins. With permission from Marzinotto V, Leaker M, Massicotte MP, Andrew M. Childhood thrombophilia programs: an approach to the prevention and treatment of thromboembolic disease in pediatric patients. In: Ansell JE, Oertel LB, Wittkowsky AK, editors. Managing oral anticoagulation. Gaithersburg: Aspen Publishers Inc.; 1996.

factor II (■), factor VII (O), factor IX (x), factor X(●).

U/mL = units/mL; mo = months.

ulant factors continue to increase and are approximately 50 percent of adult values at birth.[5-7] These levels are similar to those found in adults receiving OAs for the treatment of venous thromboembolic events (VTE).[3,81] Following the neonatal period, plasma concentrations of FII, FVII, FIX, and FX rapidly increase and are within the adult normal range by 6 months of age[5-7] (see Figure 10–2). However, average values of the VK-dependent coagulant proteins remain approximately 20 percent lower than adult values until the late teenage years.[8] A small number of newborns also have evidence of functional VK deficiency state, indicated by significant levels of descarboxy VK-dependent proteins at birth.[83] The presence of VK deficiency significantly increases the sensitivity to OAs and, potentially, the risk of bleeding. The physiologic reductions in plasma concentrations of prothrombin reduce the quantity and rate of thrombin generation in vitro in neonates and children compared to adults.[84,85] The pattern of thrombin generation in newborns is similar to plasma from adults receiving therapeutic amounts of OAs.[10,85] Supplementation with prothrombin increases thrombin generation to amounts similar to adults for both neonates (Figure 10–3) and children[84,86] (Figure 10–4).

Vitamin K-Dependent Inhibitors

The two VK-dependent inhibitors are protein C and protein S. Protein C is activated by thrombin complexed to an endothelial cell surface receptor, thrombomodulin (TM). Activated protein C (APC) inactivates FVa and FVIIIa by enzymatic degradation. At birth, protein C levels are significantly decreased compared to adult values[5-7,87] and protein C is present in a fetal form.[87,88] Plasma concentrations of protein C remain mildly but significantly decreased throughout childhood. Protein S is a cofactor that promotes the APC inactivation of FVa and FVIIIa. Protein S circulates in plasma in both a free (active) and complexed form (with C4b binding protein).[89,90] Plasma concentrations of free

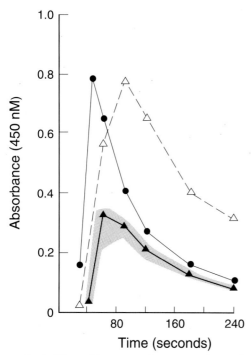

Figure 10–3 Thrombin generation curves in cord plasma (▲-▲), which is significantly decreased compared to adults (●-●). Only the addition of prothrombin (△-△) increases the amount of thrombin generated to adult values. Increasing plasma concentrations of other coagulation factors did not increase the amount of thrombin generated (▒▒▒).

nM = nanomolar.

Reproduced with permission from Andrew M, Schmidt B, Mitchell L, et al. Thrombin generation in newborn plasma is critically dependent on the concentration of prothrombin. Thromb Haemost 1990;63:27–30.

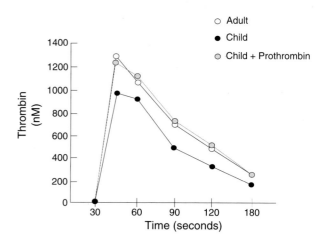

Figure 10–4 Thrombin generation is reduced by 20 percent in healthy children (●) compared with adults (○). The addition of prothrombin increased thrombin generation to values equivalent to adults (◐).

nM = nanomolar.

Reproduced with permission from Andrew M, Mitchell L, Vegh P, Ofosu F. Thrombin regulation in children differs from adults in the absence and presence of heparin. Thromb Haemost 1994;72:836–42.

protein S are similar to adult values throughout childhood.[8]

Age Dependency of Anticoagulant Activities of Oral Anticoagulants

The effects of OAs on thrombin regulation have been compared in pediatric and adult patients. In vitro, the capacity to generate thrombin is significantly delayed in plasmas from pediatric as compared to adult patients with similar INR values (Figure 10–5).[10] Thrombin generation in plasmas from children receiving OAs is also dependent on the intensity of anticoagulation (Figure 10–6).[10] Plasma concentrations of the VK-dependent coagulation proteins are similar (Table 10–1) and do not provide an explanation for the difference in thrombin regulation in pediatric and adult patients receiving OAs.[10] In vivo, a marker of endogenous thrombin generation, prothrombin fragment 1.2 (F1.2), is significantly decreased in children compared to adults receiving OAs and with similar INR values (children: 0.30 ± 0.03 nM, adult: 0.45 ± 0.04, $p < 0.05$). Concentrations of F1.2 are also dependent on INR values (Figure 10–7).[10] The re-

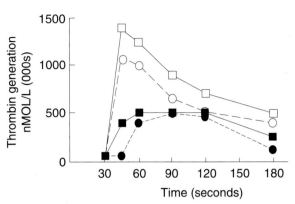

Figure 10–5 Thrombin generation is reduced by approximately 20 percent in plasmas from children receiving warfarin and achieving International Normalized Ratios of approximately 2.5 (●) compared to adults with similar International Normalized Ratios (■). The magnitude of the difference is similar to plasmas from healthy children (○) and adults (□).

nMOL/L = nanomoles/L.

Reproduced with permission from Massicotte P, Marzinotto V, Adams M, et al. Enhanced thrombin regulation during warfarin therapy in children compared to adults. Thromb Haemost 1998;80:570–4.

sponsible mechanisms for these in vivo and ex vivo differences in thrombin regulation in children are not completely understood. Plasma concentrations

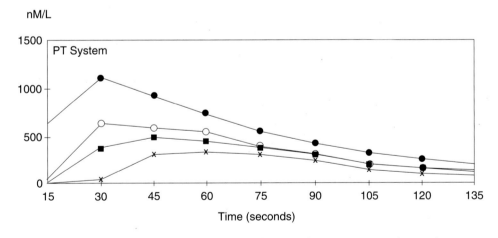

Figure 10–6 Thrombin generation in plasma from children receiving warfarin is dependent on the intensity of anticoagulation as indicated by increasing International Normalized Ratios. (Neat (●), International Normalized Ratios less than 2 (○), International Normalized Ratios between 2 and 3 (■), and International Normalized Ratios greater than 3 (X).

PT system = prothrombin time system; nM/L = nanomoles/litre.

Reproduced with permission from Massicotte P, Marzinotto V, Adams M, et al. Enhanced thrombin regulation during warfarin therapy in children compared to adults. Thromb Haemost 1998;80:570–4.

Table 10–1 Plasma Concentrations of Six Vitamin K-Dependent Proteins in Children and Adults Receiving Warfarin

	Children	Adults
INR	2.58 ± 0.160	2.40 ± 0.14
Factor II (U/mL)	0.42 ± 0.036	0.36 ± 0.036
Factor VII (U/mL)	0.47 ± 0.038	0.51 ± 0.045
Factor IX (U/mL)	0.58 ± 0.037	0.65 ± 0.058
Factor X (U/mL)	0.28 ± 0.032	0.25 ± 0.026
Protein C (U/mL)	0.68 ± 0.044	0.65 ± 0.031
Free Protein S (U/mL)	0.60 ± 0.046	0.51 ± 0.034

INR = International Normalized Ratio; U/mL = units/mL.

Reproduced with permission from Massicotte P, Marzinotto V, Adams M, et al. Enhanced thrombin regulation during warfarin therapy in children compared to adults. Thromb Haemost 1998;80:570–4.

of the inhibitor α_2-macroglobulin (α_2M) are increased during childhood and contribute to an enhanced regulation of thrombin physiologically.[8,91] Recent studies show that α_2M also contributes to an enhanced regulation of thrombin in children receiving OAs.[10] Together these observations suggest that children may require a less intense regimen with OAs than adults, which only well-designed clinical trials can determine.

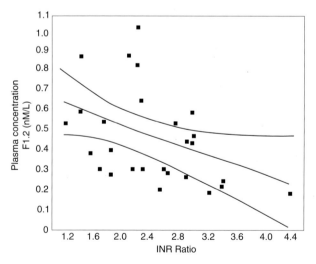

Figure 10–7 Plasma concentrations of in vivo marker for thrombin generation (prothrombin fragment 1.2) is also dependent on International Normalized Ratios.

F1.2 = prothrombin fragment; 1.2nM/L = nanomoles/ litre.

Reproduced with permission from Massicotte P, Marzinotto V, Adams M, et al. Enhanced thrombin regulation during warfarin therapy in children compared to adults. Thromb Haemost 1998;80: 570–4.

RELATIONSHIP BETWEEN VITAMIN K STATUS, ORAL ANTICOAGULANTS, AND BONE STRUCTURE

In humans, two clearly distinct groups of Gla-containing proteins have been identified: those that play a role in blood coagulation and those that predominantly occur in calcified tissues. Examples of the latter category include osteocalcin[92–96] and matrix Gla protein,[95–97] both of which are found in bone, as well as plaque Gla protein, which has been identified in calcified vessel walls and arteriosclerotic plaques.[98]

Vitamin K Dependence of Osteocalcin

Osteocalcin, also known as bone Gla protein (BGP), is a noncollagenous protein that must be γ-carboxylated to be incorporated into bone.[92,93,95,99] γ-carboxylated osteocalcin binds to hydroxyapatite and may be important for bone mineralization.[92,95,100] The exact function of osteocalcin remains unclear, but there is evidence to suggest it has a role in regulating bone formation and is a marker of this process.[92,95,96] There is also evidence that osteocalcin may have a role in bone resorption.[96,100] A small fraction of denovo synthesized osteocalcin is not incorporated into the matrix of bone but is set free into the blood stream where it may be detected by a radioimmunoassay.[96,101,102] During childhood, osteocalcin levels are age dependent and increased by several fold compared to adults.[103–105] Plasma concentrations of osteocalcin may also vary with the VK status in some individuals.[106,107]

Relationship between Vitamin K Status and Osteoporosis

The relationship between VK status and osteoporosis remains controversial. Based on biochemical indicators, a reduced VK status is associated with reduced bone mineral density (BMD) at the hip,[108–110] lumbar spine,[111] second metacarpal,[112] and increased risk of fracture[113] in healthy adults. In adults who already have sustained a fracture, especially at the hip, serum VK concentrations are less than in age-matched controls. Plasma concentrations of osteocalcin have been proposed as a potential marker for osteoporosis.[95,104,114] Oral anticoagulants decrease both the total plasma concentrations of osteocalcin and degree of carboxylation to levels similar to that in women with osteoporosis.[115–117] Predictably, OAs inhibit binding of osteocalcin to hydroxyapatite and cause an accumulation of free osteocalcin in bone.[118]

Relationship between Oral Anticoagulation and Bone Disease

Warfarin is known to have major effects on fetal bones, with bone abnormalities being an integral part of the warfarin embryopathy. There is a variable but definite incidence of teratogenesis associated with the use of OAs in the first trimester of pregnancy. From 1966 to 1998 there were 43 publications identified in a MEDLINE search describing the association between OAs and a fetal embryopathy. Chondrodysplasia punctata, the most common syndrome associated with warfarin use in pregnancy, consists of abnormal cartilage and bone formation occurring as nasal hypoplasia and excessive irregular calcifications in the epiphyses and vertebrae.[43,119–122] The long bone epiphysis, calcaneus, terminal phalanges, and even nasal bones may also be involved. Broad hands and skull abnormalities have also been described (Figure 10–8). With growth and ossification, the stippled areas are incorporated into normal bone and asymmetric growth has not been reported.[43,119,120] Animal experiments provide further evidence for an adverse effect of warfarin on bone. Young rats treated with sublethal doses of warfarin developed excessive calcification with growth plate closure and reduced growth of the long bones,[118,123] masillonasal hypoplasia, reduced length of the nasal bones, and massive calcification of the cartilage of the nasal septum. Lambs treated with OAs for 3 months had a 30 percent decrease in bone mass compared to control animals, irregular calcium deposition, and remodelling abnormalities.[124] Bone formation was reduced significantly, while bone resorption was only mildly affected. There are no-placebo controlled prospective trials investigating the effects of OAs in adults. Increased urinary excretion of calcium in men ages 30 to 39 years on long-term warfarin therapy (>1 year) versus controls and older men (ages 40 to 45 years) on long-term warfarin therapy may indicate increased bone resorption.[125] The clinical evidence for an effect of warfarin on bone density is conflicting.[110,112,126–130] A number of cross-sectional studies have found conflicting results ranging from no effect[128,129] to a reduction in BMD.[110,112,126,130,131] While difficult to compare across studies, the results suggest that the adverse effect of OA was increased in younger patients (25 to 59 years).[110] There have been no prospective studies in children and only one case report of warfarin-induced osteoporosis.[132] Clinically, children on long-term OA therapy may present with spontaneous fractures and have reduced BMD.[133] The increased rate of bone formation in children suggests they may be at increased risk compared to adults, but this remains to be proven. Importantly, the first 3 years of life and late puberty are normally the periods of highest increase in BMD.[134] These ages coincide with the peaks in age distribution of TEs and hence OA administration in children.

INDICATIONS FOR ORAL ANTICOAGULANTS

Indications for OAs in adults can be grouped as primary and secondary prevention of VTE, 1 to 2 percent of myocardial infarction, and prevention of

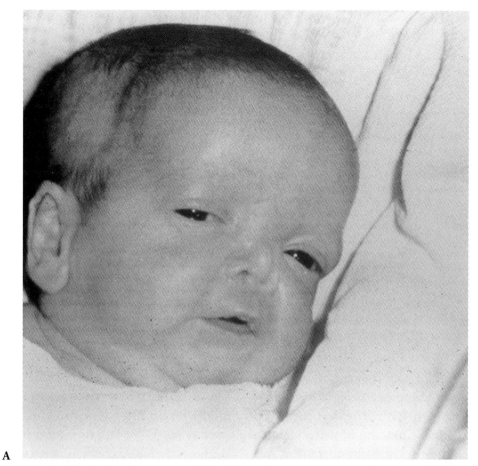

A

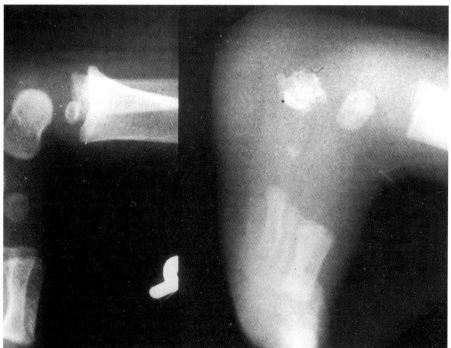

B

Figure 10–8 *A,* A child with warfarin embryopathy. *B,* A radiogram of the stippled bone apophysis in warfarin fetal embryopathy.

Reproduced with permission from Hall JG. Embryopathy associated with oral anticoagulant therapy. Birth Defects. Orig Artic Ser 1976;12:33–7.

Table 10–2 Indications for Oral Anticoagulants in Adults

I Venous Thromboembolism Prophylaxis

- High-risk surgery for venous thromboembolism

II Venous Thromboembolism Treatment

- Venous thromboembolism
- Pulmonary embolism

III Prevention of Systemic Embolism

- Tissue heart valves
- Acute myocardial infarction (to prevent systemic embolism)
- Valvular heart disease
- Atrial fibrillation
- Mechanical prosthetic heart valves
- Bileaflet mechanical valve in aortic position

Table 10–4 Underlying Disorders in Pediatric Patients Treated with Oral Anticoagulants

Number of patients	319
Consecutive courses with OAs	352
Number of females	139
Number of males	180
Congenital heart disease	164
Mechanical heart valves	37
Renal disease	23
Stroke/sinus venous thrombosis	19
Malignancy	18
Systemic lupus erythematosus	11
Infectious disease	10
Prothrombotic disorders	5
Idiopathic thrombosis	3
Others	29

OAs = oral anticoagulants (OAs).

Reproduced with permission from Streif W, Andrew M, Marzinotto V, et al. Analysis of warfarin therapy in pediatric patients: a prospective cohort study. Blood 1999 (in press).

systemic embolism in patients with prosthetic heart valves or atrial fibrillation (Table 10–2).[3] Indications for OAs in pediatric patients differ from adults because diseases such as myocardial infarction and embolic stroke are very rare and the underlying pathology is profoundly different.[3] Indications for OAs in pediatric patients are evenly distributed between secondary prevention (41%) and primary prevention for VTE (59%)[4,9,11] (Table 10–3). Table 10–4 provides information on the underlying diseases in 319 consecutive pediatric patients treated with OAs.[11] Indications for OA are rapidly increasing in pediatrics and reflect advances made in the treatment of congenital heart disease (CHD), use of stents, and organ transplantation.

Table 10–3 Indications for Oral Anticoagulants in Pediatric Patients

I Treatment: Definite

- Venous thromboembolic complications

II Treatment: Probable

- Myocardial infarction
- Some forms of stroke

III Prophylaxis: Definite

- Mechanical prosthetic heart valves
- Biological prosthetic heart valves
- Atrial fibrillation

IV Prophylaxis: Possibly

- Fontans
- Central venous catheters
- Kawasaki disease
- Other forms of congenital heart disease

Reproduced with permission from Michelson AD, Bovill E, Monagle P, Andrew M. Antithrombotic therapy in children. Chest 1998;114:748S–69S.

Prevention of Venous Thromboembolic Events

Several randomized controlled trials (RCTs) in adults show that OAs with target INR values between 1.5 and 3.0 effectively prevents VTE in high-risk situations such as orthopedic surgery[135–139] and gynecologic surgery.[140] For comparable surgical procedures, prophylactic anticoagulation is not indicated in children, at least prior to puberty, due to the very low incidence of VTE. However, there are groups of children at significant risk for VTE from either congenital or acquired prothrombotic disorders in whom the benefits of short-term anticoagulation prophylaxis with OAs or other agents likely outweigh the risks. For example, children with heterozygous deficiencies of antithrombin (AT), protein C, protein S, activated protein C resistance (APCR), or prothrombin gene 20210 G, and an acquired risk factor such as immobilization (eg, due to a cast), central venous line (CVL), recurrent VTE, or antiphospholipid antibodies, would likely benefit from intermittent prophylaxis with anticoagulants, of which OAs provide one option.

Treatment of Venous Thromboembolic Events in Adults

Randomized controlled trials in adults show that OAs are required for a minimum of 3 months for the treatment of proximal deep vein thrombosis (DVT) and symptomatic calf vein thrombosis.[141–143] A large study performed by the British Thoracic Society reported that rates of recurrent VTE doubled if the duration of OA therapy was reduced from 3 months to 4 weeks.[144] These findings were confirmed by 2 further studies,[145,146] the largest of which compared 6 weeks to 6 months of OA therapy. A recent double blind study by Kearon and colleagues[147] looked at the benefit of extended anticoagulation. Patients in both arms of the study received 3 months of OA therapy for a first idiopathic VTE. Subsequently, one arm continued to receive OA therapy for a further 12 months, while the patients in the other arm received a placebo. The study was terminated after 162 patients were entered and approximately 10 months of therapy. Of the 83 patients who received a placebo, 17 had a recurrent VTE (27.4% per patient-year) compared with 1 of 79 patients (1.3% per patient-year) who continued to receive OAs.[147] These and other studies also suggest that the risk for late recurrent VTE in adult patients with a transient risk factor, such as surgery, is significantly reduced compared to

the risk for late recurrent VTE in patients with idiopathic VTE or a persistent risk factor (Table 10–5).[144–146,148,149] Current recommendations for the treatment of VTE in adults are at least 5 days of adjusted dose unfractionated heparin (UFH), or fixed dose low molecular weight heparin (LMWH), without discontinuation until therapeutic OA therapy is established (2 days of a therapeutic INR). If there is an extensive proximal DVT or significant pulmonary embolism (PE), initiation of OAs should be delayed and longer initial therapy with UFH used. A moderate dose regimen (INR of 2.0 to 3.0) is as effective as the more intense regimen (INR of 3.0 to 4.5) but is associated with a significantly decreased incidence of bleeding.[150] In general, OAs with an INR of 2 to 3 should be continued for 3 to 6 months. The optimal duration of OAs may differ between patients who have VTE associated with transient or continuing risk factors however, this remains to be defined.[150] Following a second episode of VTE, indefinite OA greatly reduces the risk of further VTE.[151] The reduced incidence of recurrent VTE is, however, achieved at the cost of an increase in major bleeding (8.6% versus 2.7% over 4 years).[151] The optimal duration of OA in adults following VTE is likely influenced by individual risk factors for recurrent VTE and bleeding.[150]

Treatment of Venous Thromboembolic Events in Children

There are no RCTs assessing the optimal use of OAs in children. Recommendations for adults provide

Table 10–5 Risk of Late Thrombotic Recurrences

Study	Mo. of Observation	Idiopathic (# Patients)	DVT (% Recurrences)	Post Op (# Patients)	DVT (% Recurrences)	p
Prandoni 1992[148]	15	145	24	105	5	< .001
British Thoracic Society 1992[144]	12	596	14	116	3	0
Pini 1994[149]	9	117	11	70	1	.03
Levine 1995[145]	9	212	12	89	0	< .001
Schulman 1995[146]	24	553	18	344	7	< .001

Mo = months; # = number; DVT = deep vein thrombosis; Post Op = postoperative.

Reproduced with permission from Pini M. Prevention of recurrences after deep venous thrombosis: role of low molecular weight heparin. Semin Thromb Haemost 1997;23:51–4.

useful initial guidelines for children but may not reflect optimal therapy as the target ranges and duration of therapy may differ. Oral anticoagulants are particularly problematic in newborns and in general should be avoided when possible. Short courses of UFH or longer courses of LMWH are alternative approaches to the treatment of VTE with OAs in newborns. In some instances, such as homozygous protein C or protein S, OAs cannot be avoided. In these circumstances, very frequent monitoring is advised.

Cardiac Disease

Oral anticoagulants are commonly used in several cardiac conditions that are relatively uncommon but present a significant risk of VTE, including valvular heart disease,[152] biologic prosthetic valves,[12,158,163] mechanical prosthetic valves,[9,11,13–18,50,155–157] endovascular stents,[157–162] Fontan surgery,[19–21,164–171] giant coronary aneurysms in Kawasaki's disease,[172–183] cardioembolic stroke,[183] Takayasu's arteritis,[22,23,184–187] myocarditis, and myocardial infarction.[188–208]

Valvular Heart Disease in Children

Valvular heart diseases in childhood encompass a wide variety of abnormalities with variable presentations. The valve lesion may be isolated, or an integral part of more complex intracardiac lesions, or the result of treatment of the underlying CHD. VTE, either of the valve or embolization to the central nervous system (CNS), are some of the most serious complications of successful cardiac valve replacement. Artificial valves are either made of biologic materials (frequently porcine) or are mechanical prosthetics. The failure of biologic prosthetic heart valves in children poignantly illustrates the fallacy of extrapolating recommendations for adults to children without evaluation in clinical trials. Commercially prepared biologic prosthetic heart valves became available in 1971 and achieved excellent early results in adult patients. Biologic prosthetic heart valves rapidly became the "valve of choice" for children. Subsequently, premature degeneration and calcification of biologic prosthetic valves occurred in the majority of children, resulting

in replacement by mechanical prosthetic heart valves.[208–214] Current recommendations for children are that, in general, mechanical prosthetic heart valves be used in the mitral position and biologic prosthetic heart valves reserved for the tricuspid and pulmonary positions.

Biologic Prosthetic Heart Valves

In the absence of any controlled trials in children, recommendations for adults are used.[151] For bioprosthetic heart valves in the mitral position, OAs with a target INR of 2.0 to 3.0 for a period of 3 months are recommended.[154,216–219] For patients with atrial fibrillation, a history of previous VTE, or a left atrial thrombus at surgery, long-term treatment with OAs should be considered with the same target INR range.[153] For bioprosthetic heart valves in the aortic position (and sinus rhythm), OAs are optional.[154,220–224] However, increased rates of VTE occur during the first 3 months following placement of bioprosthetic valves in the aortic position.[221–223] Patients with bioprosthetic heart valves and previous VTE should be treated long term with OAs. The optimal INR and duration of therapy are still uncertain.[152] Adults with bioprosthetic valves who have a permanent pacemaker are also at high risk for VTE.[221] Although the benefits of OAs have not been demonstrated in a well-designed clinical trial, one approach is to use OAs with a target INR of 2.0 to 3.0.[152,221] For adults with bioprosthetic valves who are in sinus rhythm, long-term therapy with aspirin, 325 mg/day, may offer some protection against VTE.[152,217]

Mechanical Prosthetic Heart Valves in Adults

In general, OA therapy with a target INR range of 2.5 to 3.5 is recommended for adults with mechanical prosthetic heart valves.[152,224,225] A target INR range to 3.5 to 4.5 may be considered for patients with caged-ball or caged-disk valves. A target INR range of 2.0 to 3.0 may be considered for patients with a St Jude Medical valve in the aortic position, provided the left atrium is normal size, the patient is in sinus rhythm, and the ejection fraction is normal.[224,225] Aspirin at a dose of 80 mg/day in combination with OAs provides extra protection without a substantially increased risk of bleeding.[226–229] Increased doses of aspirin in combination with an INR of 2.5 to 3.5 may increase the risk of bleeding.[228] Some studies show that dipyridamole (400 mg/day) and OAs provide effective prophylaxis and provide an alternative.[231] Patients with mechanical prosthetic heart valves who suffer systemic VTE, despite adequate therapy with OAs, may benefit from additional aspirin, 80 mg/day,[232] or dipyridamole, 400 mg/day.[152,226,232]

Mechanical Prosthetic Heart Valves in Children

The outcomes for pediatric patients with mechanical prosthetic heart valves who received no prophylactic anticoagulation therapy were described in two case series.[28,37] In the absence of anticoagulation therapy, TE occurs at a rate of 5.7 percent per year with St Jude Medical valves[28] and at rates of 6.8 to 27.3 percent per year[4] for other types of valves (Table 10–6).[37] In the presence of empiric low doses of aspirin (6 to 20 mg/kg/day) and/or dipyridamole (2 to 5 mg/kg/day), and the absence of OA, VTE occurs at rates of 1.1 to 6.8 percent per year[13,17,29,30,33,34,37,233,234] with three of eight studies reporting VTE rates of over 5 percent per year (Table 10–7).[30,34,233] Patients with VTE have a significant mortality rate.[28] With OAs, the incidence of VTE is uniformly less than 5 percent per year

(Table 10–8).[13–15,17,33–39,154,234–235] There were three deaths due to VTEs and two due to bleeding.[15,17,37,235,237] One of the three patients had discontinued OAs and the anticoagulant status of the other two could not be determined. With one exception, the rate of major bleeding was less than 3.5 percent per year (Table 10–8). In one study, two patients required blood transfusions (rate of 8.2%/year) and recovered uneventfully.[34] Adjuvant therapy with antiplatelet agents was used in one study.[39] Based on information available for adults and children, aspirin in combination with OAs should be considered for high-risk patients, including those with prior VTEs, atrial fibrillation, large left atrium, left atrial TEs, ball valves, and mitral valves. The available data support the recommendation for OAs in children with mechanical prosthetic heart valves. Problems of effectively monitoring OAs can be addressed through anticoagulation clinics for children[9,11] and the use of whole blood monitors in the clinic and at home.[10,40,238]

Endovascular Stents

Endovascular stents are used increasingly to manage a number of congenital heart lesions, including branch pulmonary artery stenosis, pulmonary vein stenosis, and coarctation of the aorta, and to treat post-surgical stenosis.[157–162] Stents can be successfully used in infants less than one year of age. However, the small vessel size likely increases the risk of

Table 10–6 Thromboembolic and Hemorrhagic Complications of Mechanical Prosthetic Heart Valves with No Antithrombotic Therapy

Reference	Level	Number	Age	Valve Type	Position	TE %/yr	HEM %/yr	Death
Sade et al[28]	V	48	5 mo-21 yr	St Jude	Ao,M	**	0	1M[†]
					Ao+M	**		
					overall	5.7		
Solymar et al[37‡]	V	(186)*	1-19 yr	St Jude	Ao	6.8	0	0
					M	20.0		
					≥ 2	27.3		

TE = thromboembolic event; HEM = hemorrhage; Ao = aortic; M = mitral; CS = case series. The presence of 2 or more valves is indicated at ≥.

**Not reported. [†]The death was secondary to a mitral valve thrombosis. *The number of patients treated with no antithrombotic therapy could not be determined. ‡This is an updated version of Rao 1989.[29]

(186) refers to the entire patient population of the study.[37]

Reproduced with permission from Michelson AD, Bovill E, Monagle P, Andrew M. Antithrombotic therapy in children. Chest 1998;114:748S–69S.

Table 10–7 Thromboembolic and Hemorrhage Complications of Mechanical Prosthetic Heart Valves Treated with Antiplatelet Agents

Reference	Level	Number	Dose	Ages	Valve Type	Position	TE/ % pt yr	HEM/ % pt yr	Death
Serra et al[30]	CS	24	ASA 6 mg/kg/d DIP 25 mg/kg/d	5–20 yr	St Jude	Ao	68	•	0
						M	19	•	0
McGrath et al[233]	CS	30	ASA 900 mg/kg/d DIP 150 mg/kg/d	4–20 yr	St Jude	Ao,M	32	0*	0
						≥ 2	•	•	Ao+M
El Makhlouf et al[33]	CS	150	ASA 20 mg/kg/d DIP 5 mg/kg/d	2–16 yr	Various	Ao,M	•	•	0
						≥ 2	•	•	0
						Overall 2	2.3	1	0
Bradley et al[34]	CS	10	ASA 6.1 mg/kg/d DIP 1.9 mg/kg/d	<19 yr	Various	Ao	0	0*	0
						M	12	0*	0
Solymar et al‡ [37]	CS	(186)	ASA 12 mg/kg/d DIP 3 mg/kg/d	1–20 yr	Various	Ao	1.8	•	0
						M	2.5	•	2 CVA
						≥ 2	•	•	0
Borkon et al[13]	CS	8	Not provided	3 wk–17 yr	Various	Ao	0	0*	0
						M 1	1.1	0*	1M†
LeBlanc et al[234]	CS	20	ASA 10 mg/kg/d DIP 3 mg/kg/d	1–17 yr	Various	Ao	0	0*	0*
						M	1.7	0*	0*
Bradley et al[17]	C	16	ASA 10 mg/kg/d DIP 6 mg/kg/d	3–16 yr	St Jude	Ao,M ≥2	1.7	0	2

yr = year; wk = week; ASA = acetylsalicylic acid; DIP = dipyridamole; Ao = aortic; M = mitral; TE = thromboembolic event; HEM = hemorrhage; CVA = cerebral vascular accident; CS = case series; C = cohort.

≥The presence of 2 or more valves. *No hemorrhage. •Not reported. †1M was secondary to a mitral valve thrombosis. ‡This is an updated version of Rao, 1989.[29]

The number of patients treated with antiplatelet agents could not be determined. (186) refers to the entire patient population of the study.[37]

Reproduced with permission from Michelson AD, Bovill E, Monagle P, Andrew M. Antithrombotic therapy in children. Chest 1998;114:748S–69S.

TE. There are no studies assessing the role of OAs to avoid stent occlusion in children. Unfractionated heparin is commonly given at the time of stent insertion, followed by aspirin therapy. A subset of patients with small stents (4 mm or less), with stents in the superior vena cava (SVC), or with pulmonary vein stents likely benefit from initial UFH therapy followed by OAs with a target INR range of 2 to 3. Further studies are required to determine the optimal dose and duration of prophylactic OAs.

Fontan Operation

The Fontan procedure is discussed in detail in Chapter 8. Prophylactic anticoagulation with OAs or antiplatelet agents following Fontan procedures is frequently recommended but there is no consensus on optimal therapy, which has resulted in a wide variety of prophylactic regimes.[20,21,169,170] All published studies of anticoagulation therapy in Fontan patients are case series, which provide the weakest form of evidence and prevent any firm recommendations. An international controlled trial is currently underway. The study compares aspirin to OAs with a target INR of 2 to 3 for 3 years, with outcome TE being assessed following 3 months and 2 years of therapy. This trial should result in more definitive recommendations on optimal anticoagulation therapy for children who require Fontan surgery.

Kawasaki Disease

Kawasaki disease (mucocutaneous lymph node syndrome) is characterized by fever of more than 5 days duration, cervical lymphadenopathy, bilateral nonexudative conjunctivitis, rash, and mucus membrane and peripheral extremity changes that are not

Table 10–8 Thromboembolic and Hemorrhagic Complications of Mechanical Heart Valves Treated with Oral Anticoagulants

Reference	Level	Number	Ages	Valve Type	Position	TE %/yr	HEM %/yr	Deaths
Spevak et al[14]	CS	56	< 5 yr	Various	Ao,M	1.6	0.8	—
El Maklouf et al[33]	CS	83	2–16 yr	Various	Ao,M	2.3	0	(4)‡
Harada et al[15]	CS	40	4 mo–15 yr	St Jude	Ao		0	
					M	1.3		1M†
Stewart et al[35]	CS	30	6–17 yr	Various	Ao,M	2.3	0.5	—
					≥ 2			
Bradley et al[34]	CS	20	< 19 yr	Various	AoM	0	8.2	—
Milano et al[235]	CS	71	≤ 15 yr	Various	Ao	0.7	0	
					M	4.0		1 M†
					≥ 2	1.4		
Schaffer et al[36]	CS	33	9–48 mo	St Jude	Ao	0.13	0	—
					M	0.38		
Solymar et al[37]	CS	(186)	1–20 yr	Various	Ao	2.1	2.1	
					M	3.2	3.2	1 M†
					≥ 2	5.0	2.6	
Schaff et al[155]	CS	48	6 mo–18 yr	Starr-Edwards	Ao	5.3	—	—
					M	2.0	—	
Borkon et al[13]	CS	22	3 wk–17 yr	St Jude	Ao	—	0	—
					M	1.1		
					Pulm	—		
Human et al[236]	CS	56	2–12 yr	Various	M	n = 3	0	—
Antunes et al[38]	CS	352	≤ 20 yr	Various	Ao	0.8	—	—
					M	0.5	—	
					≥ 2	1.7	—	
Woods et al[39]	CS	20+	5 mo–16 yr	Various	Ao,M	1.8	0.9	1
					≥			
Champsaur et al[237]	CS	54	1–17 yr	Various	Ao>2	0.3	0.3	1 bleeding 1 valve TE
Bradley et al[17]	C	48	6 mo–18 yr	St Jude	Ao,M	2.6	1.5	1 bleeding 1 valve TE

yr = year; mo = month; wk = week; Ao = aortic; M = mitral; Pulm = pulmonary; Tri = tricuspid; TE = thromboembolic event; Hem = hemorrhage; CS = case series; C = cohort.

≥The presence of 2 or more valves. +patients were treated with a combination of warfarin and ASA. †The death was due to a mitral valve thrombosis. ‡The anticoagulant used could not be determined.

Reproduced with permission from Michelson AD, Bovill E, Monagle P, Andrew M. Antithrombotic therapy in children. Chest 1998;114:748S–69S.

explained by any other disease process.[172,173] Coronary artery aneurysms (CAAs) occur in 20 percent of children who receive no therapy,[174,180] but can be prevented in most children by the early use of high dose aspirin (80 to 100 mg/kg/d for up to 14 days[175,179]) and intravenous gamma globulin (IgG) (see Table 6–13, Chapter 6).[177–179] Subsequent use of low dose aspirin, 3 to 5 mg/kg/d for 7 weeks or longer, is indicated to prevent coronary aneurysm TEs. If giant CAAs develop, anticoagulation is recommended;[179,180] however, the relative benefits of OAs versus aspirin are unknown. Surgical management is considered in some patients.[181] Myocardial infarction due to TE of a CAA remains the major cause of death in Kawasaki disease. The seriousness of the consequences of TEs of the CAAs likely justify prophylactic anticoagulation therapy. One approach is to use a combination of OAs with a target INR of 2 to 3 in combination with an antiplatelet agent.[4,176,177,239–260]

Cardioembolic Stroke in Adults

Cardiogenic embolism to the CNS occurs in adults with atrial fibrillation, following cardioversion, valvular disease, ventricular thrombi, and other cardiac disorders.[182] For atrial fibrillation in high-risk patients, long-term OAs with a target INR of 2.0 to 3.0 is recommended.[182,262,263] High-risk patients are defined as those with a previous transient ischemic attack or stroke, poor left ventricular function, hypertension, or a constellation of other risk factors.[182,262,264–269] Oral anticoagulants are recommended instead of aspirin because of the greater reduction in stroke provided by OAs. For low-risk patients in whom the annual risk of stroke on aspirin is 2 percent or less, aspirin should be considered.[183] Patients requiring elective cardioversion should be administered effective OAs with a target INR of 2.0 to 3.0 for 3 weeks prior to cardioversion and a subsequent 4 weeks.[183] Standard heparin followed by OAs with a target INR of 2.0 to 3.0 is recommended in nonhypertensive patients with small- to moderate-sized embolic strokes in whom a computed tomography scan (CT scan) or magnetic resonance imaging (MRI) done 48 hours or more after onset documents the absence of spontaneous hemorrhagic transformation.[182] Anticoagulant therapy should be postponed 5 to 14 days in patients with large, embolic strokes or uncontrolled hypertension because of the predisposition of these patients to hemorrhagic transformation. These recommendations for adults provide useful guidelines for children in whom there is minimal information on cardioembolic stroke not due to prosthetic heart valves.

Takayasu's Arteritis

Takayasu's arteritis is a rare chronic, idiopathic, inflammatory disease of large arteries predominantly affecting Asian females.[22,23,183–186,272–274] Although any artery can be involved, angiographic studies show that two-thirds of patients have aortic lesions, with the aortic arch, carotid arteries, and renal arteries being primarily affected. The clinical presentation is limb or organ ischemia due to gradual stenosis of related arteries. Clinical symptoms reflect the affected arteries. Physical findings frequently include a bruit in the involved area and the diagnosis is frequently delayed by several months.[183] Angiography remains the gold standard for the assessment of clinical severity of the disease. Glucocorticoids are the mainstay of medical therapy, with at least 60 percent of patients achieving remission within 1 year of treatment. Unfortunately 50 percent of patients relapse and additional cytotoxic agents such as methotrexate or cyclophosphamide are required.[272,275] Arterial reconstruction is required for at least one-third of patients.[272–276] Oral anticoagulants are frequently used in combination with antiplatelet agents to preserve blood flow prior to and following arterial reconstruction.

TARGET RANGE FOR ORAL ANTICOAGULANTS

The desired INR ranges for children are directly extrapolated from recommendations for adult patients. There are no clinical trials that have assessed the optimal INR ranges for children based upon clinical outcomes. The usual recommended therapeutic range for children is a target INR of 2.0 to 3.0.[4] Children with prosthetic heart valves or recurrent VTEs are usually treated to achieve a target INR range of 2.5 and 3.5.[4] More recently, selected children are being treated with a target INR range between 1.4 and 1.9 for prophylactic purposes.[4,9,277] In general, dosing requirements for OAs can be considered as initial (or loading) and maintenance.

Loading Dose

Eight publications provide information on loading doses for OA therapy in children (Table 10-9).[9,11,24,25,34,39,50,278] An initial dose of 0.2 mg/kg, with subsequent dose adjustments made according to a nomogram using INR values, was evaluated in a prospective cohort study.[9,11] With this dosing regimen, all patients achieve their target INR range and 79 percent attain their target INR in less than 7 days. The length of time required to achieve a minimal INR of 2.0 is age dependent, ranging from a median of 5 days in infants to 3 days in teenagers. The overlap with UFH is approximately 5 days. Because of the length of time required to achieve a therapeutic range, higher loading doses of 0.3 and 0.4 mg/kg were tested but resulted in excessively high INR values on days 3 to 5 in at least 50 percent of children and cannot be generally recommended.[11] There should be two consecutive INR values in the target range before discontinuing UFH or LMWH therapy. A nomogram may be helpful in the loading phase of OAs (Table 10–10). For phenprocoumon the loading dose is extrapolated from adult values and adapted for pediatric use.[26]

Maintenance Dose

Maintenance Dose to Achieve INR Values between 2 and 3 Eight publications provide information on maintenance dose requirements for OAs to achieve INR values between 2.0 and 3.0 in chil-

dren (Table 10–9).[9,11,24,25,34,39,278] Maintenance doses for OAs are age dependent, with infants having the highest and teenagers having the lowest requirements. The published age-specific weight-adjusted doses for children vary due to the different study designs, patient populations, and possibly the small number of children studied. The largest cohort study (n = 319) found infants required an average of 0.32 mg/kg and teenagers 0.09 mg/kg of warfarin.[11] For adults, OA requirements/kg are not precisely known but are in the range of 0.04 to 0.08 mg/kg for an INR of 2 to 3.[81] The increased requirement for OAs in the young is further evident when one considers the decreased plasma concentrations of prothrombin (20% of adult values) and decreased capacity to generate thrombin throughout childhood.[8,10] The latter should decrease OA requirements in children for any target INR value. The mechanisms responsible for the age dependency of OAs are not completely clear. The increased content of VK in infant formulas increases their dose requirements.[11] A nomogram has also proved helpful for adjusting maintenance OA doses (Table 10–10). For phenprocoumon, the maintenance dose is an average 1.4 mg/m^2/day with wide variations.

Table 10–9 Comparison of Published Oral Anticoagulant Protocols

Study	Number	Loading Dose (mg/kg/day)	Maintenance Dose (mg/kg/day)		Laboratory Test
Carpentieri et al[24]	19	0.5–0.7	0.08–0.18PT (15–25 % of load)		(1.5–2 x control)
Hathaway[278]	8	N/A	0.16		N/A
Bradley et al[34]	20	N/A	0.16 (0.05–0.34)		PTR (1.2–3.3)
Woods et al[39]	31	1.5 mg/day	2.33 mg/day		INR (2.0–3.0)
Doyle et al[25]	26	0.21	0.10		PT
Evans et al[50]	137	0.1–1.0	Based on INR on day 4		INR (2.6-3.8)
Andrew et al[9]	115	0.20	age dependent		INR (2.0–3.0)
			< 1 yr	0.31	
			1–5	0.16	
			6–10	0.13	
			1–18	0.08	
Streif 1998[11]	319	0.20	< 1	0.33	INR (2.0–3.0)
			> 1< 6	0.15	
			≥ 6 < 13	0.13	
			> 13	0.09	

INR = International Normalized Ratio; PT = prothrombin time; PTR = prothrombin to control ratio; PI = prothrombin index; N/A = information not available; mg = milligrams; kg = kilograms.

Table 10–10 Protocol for Oral Anticoagulation Therapy to Maintain an INR btween 2 and 3 for Pediatric Patients

I. Day 1: If the baseline INR is 1.0 to 1.3:

Dose = 0.2 mg/kg orally

II. Loading days 2–4: If the INR is:

1.1–1.3	Repeat initial loading dose
1.4–1.9	50% of initial loading dose
2.0–3.0	50% of initial loading dose
3.1–3.5	25% of loading dose
>3.5	Hold until INR <3.5 then restart at 50% less than the previous dose

III. Maintenance oral anticoagulation dose guidelines:

INR	ACTION
1.1–1.4	Increase by 20% of dose
1.5–1.9	Increase by 10% of dose
2.0–3.0	No change
3.1–3.5	Decrease by 10% of dose
>3.5	Hold until INR <3.5 then restart at 20% less than the previous dose

INR = International Normalized Ratio; mg = milligrams; kg = kilograms.

Reproduced with permission from Michelson AD, Bovill E, Monagle P, Andrew M. Antithrombotic therapy in children. Chest 1998;114:748S–69S.

Maintenance Doses to Achieve INR Values between 1.4 and 1.9 In some adult patients, low-dose OA offers a safe and effective alternative to full-dose OA.[279,280] Low-dose OA is currently used in pediatric patients for two reasons. First, children with a new thrombus and a long-term predisposing cause for recurrent TEs are treated with therapeutic doses of OA for 3 months followed by a low-dose regimen. Second, children with an old thrombus or significant risk for TE are treated initially with a low-dose regimen. The average dose requirement of OAs is 0.08 mg/kg with a range of 0.03 to 0.17 mg/kg.[11] These initial results suggest that low-dose OA may provide an effective treatment strategy in selected children but require further evaluation before being widely recommended.

Maintenance Doses to Achieve INR Values between 3.0 and 4.5 A small group of pediatric patients likely benefit from OAs with a target INR range of 3.0 to 4.5. These children have recurrent VTE in the presence of OAs that achieve a target INR range of 2.0 to 3.0 or children with homozygous protein C or S deficiency.[281] When patients have recurrent VTE while receiving OAs, the actual previous INR values are critically important to determine if INR values were less than 2.0. Patients with recurrent VTE and a markedly subtherapeutic INR do not require a target INR range of 3.0 to 4.5.[27]

Duration of Oral Anticoagulant Therapy

The duration of therapy with OAs in children reflects recommendations for adults and the underlying disorders. Children requiring short-term treatment (3 to 6 months) are the minority in the literature review and two cohort studies.[9,11] Approximately one-third of pediatric patients require OAs on a lifelong basis because of mechanical prosthetic heart valves or recurrent VTE. Patients with long-term but not lifelong requirements for OAs are most frequently children with VTE secondary to CVLs. Following an initial 3 months of full-dose therapy with OAs, children with VTE secondary to CVLs may benefit from low doses of OAs until the CVL is removed. However, the need for long-term prophylactic OAs is uncertain.

Optimal Therapeutic INR Ranges for Children

Although current recommendations for OAs in children are essentially the same as for adults, this approach may not be optimal. The suppression of thrombin generation in vitro and in vivo is significantly greater in pediatric patients compared to adults.[10] There may be age-dependent differences in the optimal intensity of OAs within the pediatric population, with neonates requiring less intense therapy compared to older children.[11] Clinical trials addressing optimal intensity of OAs in pediatric patients are required.

FACTORS INFLUENCING DOSE RESPONSE RELATIONSHIPS

One of the frustrating aspects of safely monitoring OAs is the effect of many other variables on OA activities. This necessitates both close monitoring and frequent dose changes. In children, adjustments of the OA dose are most frequently precipitated by the introduction of drugs, changes in dose, changes in diet, and concurrent illnesses.[9,11] Educating parents about these issues is important so that changes in INR values can be anticipated and frequency of monitoring increased.

Age Distribution of Children Requiring Oral Anticoagulants

Age has a significant effect on dose requirements for OAs. The age distribution of children requiring OAs is skewed, with the two largest groups comprised of children less than one year of age and teenagers (Figure 10–9).[11] Teenagers are not necessarily compliant with their medication and infants are a difficult group of patients to monitor due to poor venous access as well as complicated medical problems.[9,11]

Concurrent Use of Other Drugs

The majority of children requiring OA therapy are also receiving multiple medications, both on a long-term basis to treat their primary problems or intermittently to treat acquired problems (eg, infection) (Figure 10–10).[9] These medications influence dose requirements for OAs in a fashion similar to adults. The most commonly used drugs are those to en-

hance cardiac function, antibiotics, anticonvulsants, and chemotherapy (particularly 6-mercaptopurine and prednisone) (Table 10–11). Drugs administered intermittently, particularly chemotherapy and antibiotics, necessitate frequent monitoring and dose adjustments. In some children repeatedly exposed to drugs on a cyclical basis, dose changes of OAs can be anticipated and instituted to prevent nontherapeutic INR values.

Drugs can influence the pharmacokinetics of OAs by altering its metabolic clearance and rate of absorption, by inhibiting the synthesis of VK-dependent coagulation proteins, or by affecting other hemostatic pathways. Drug interaction with the S- or R-warfarin isomer may be differential and of some clinical significance. The activity of S-warfarin is five times more potent as a VK antagonist compared to R-warfarin.[68,69] Differential effects of drugs on clearance of the S-isomer and R-isomer can profoundly influence the overall anticoagulant effect. Drugs that inhibit the metabolic clearance of the S-isomer[282–285] have the potential to prolong the PT much more than drugs that inhibit the metabolic clearance of the R-isomer.

Numerous antiplatelet agents can increase the risk of bleeding by interfering with platelet function and, in the case of high-dose aspirin, by damaging the intestinal mucosa. There are numerous case reports of other possible drug interactions. When feasible, concurrent use of drugs that influence hemostasis should be avoided.

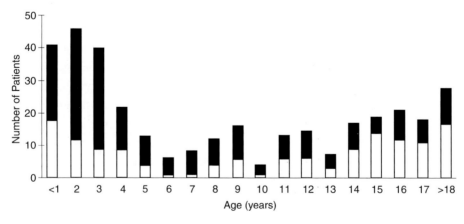

Figure 10–9 Age distribution of children receiving warfarin therapy for primary (☐) and secondary (■) prophylaxis. With permission from Streif W, Andrew M, Marzinotto V, et al. Analysis of warfarin therapy in pediatric patients: a prospective cohort study. Blood 1999; in press.

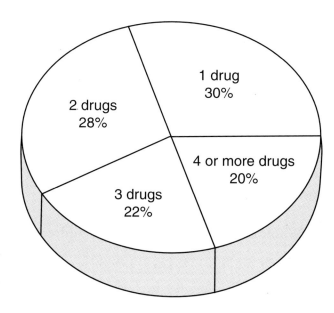

Figure 10–10 Distribution of the number of other drugs received concurrently by children on warfarin.

Reproduced with permission from Massicotte P, Brooker L, Marzinotto V, Andrew M. Oral anticoagulation therapy in children. In: Poller, Hirsh, editors. Oral anticoagulants. London: Arnold; 1996: 216–217.

Table 10–11 Commonly Used Drugs in Children that Affect their INR Value

Drug	Effect on INR
Amiodarone	Increase
Acetylsalicylic acid	Increase or no change
Amoxil	Slight increase
Ceclor	Increase
Tegretol	Decrease
Dilantin	Decrease
Phenobarbital	Decrease
Cloxacillin	Increase
Prednisone	Increase
Trimethoprim-Sulfamethoxazole	Increase
Ranitidine	Increase
6-Mercaptopurine	Decrease

INR = International Normalized Ratio.

Reproduced with permission from Michelson AD, Bovill E, Monagle P, Andrew M. Antithrombotic therapy in children. Chest 1998;114:748S–69S.

Diet

There are several circumstances in which diet profoundly influences OAs in children. First, breastfed infants are very sensitive to OAs due to decreased concentrations of VK in breast milk.[288–291] Second, infants fed with nutrient formulas are resistant to OAs due to increased concentrations of VK (55 to 110 μg/litre) to protect against hemorrhagic disease of the newborn.[288] Third, children with short-gut syndrome may have impaired absorption of OAs.[292] Fourth, children with serious primary disorders frequently require total parenteral nutrition (TPN), which is routinely supplemented with VK, increasing OA requirements. Fifth, both TPN and nutrient formulas may sequestrate warfarin in the macromolecular fraction, decreasing the availability.[293]

The dietary influences on OAs in children can be compensated for in some circumstances. A steady intake of VK in breast-fed infants can be insured by daily supplementation with a few ounces of formula. Vitamin K can be removed from TPN, thereby reducing OA requirements. Children requiring high doses of OAs require frequent monitoring, particularly if their dietary intake is compromised by an intercurrent illnesses.

Presence of Coagulopathies

Impaired liver function and presence of the lupus anticoagulant are the most frequent concurrent coagulopathies in children that affect OAs. Baseline values for the PT/INR are important as they may be abnormal. Patients with Fontans are particularly sensitive to OAs, likely due to the increased right-sided pressure, which results in some hepatic dysfunction.[11] One approach to the initiation of OA therapy in children with liver dysfunction is to reduce the initial dose of OAs from 0.2 mg/kg to 0.1 mg/kg. For children with an antiphospholipid antibody that interferes with the PT, plasma concentrations of prothrombin can be used to monitor OAs. INR values between 2.0 and 3.0 usually result in prothrombin concentrations of approximately 0.20 to 0.40 units/mL.[10,294]

Intermittent Illness

Most children experience several viral infections accompanied by fever and frequent use of antibiotics for ear, nose, and throat infections. Requirements for OAs may change rapidly and close monitoring is again required.

MONITORING ORAL ANTICOAGULATION THERAPY

Monitoring OAs in children is difficult and requires close supervision for several reasons. First, most children have serious primary problems that influence the biologic effect and clearance of OAs, as well as the risk of bleeding. Second, most children are receiving several other drugs, either on a long-term basis to treat their primary problems or intermittently to treat acquired infections. Most drugs affect requirements for OA through a variety of mechanisms.[4,81] Third, the age distribution of children requiring OA is skewed with the two largest groups comprised of children less than one year of age and teenagers.[11,27] Monitoring OAs is problematic in both age groups.[14,15,27–30,33,35,39,233] Fourth, on average children require INR measurements every 2 weeks because of frequent changes in their clinical status.[9,11] In contrast to adults, only 10 to 20 percent of children can be safely monitored monthly.[11] Fifth, many children do not live near tertiary care pediatric centers and rely on community laboratories for blood sampling. Understandably, phlebotomy teams in community laboratories are not as skilled at obtaining blood samples from small children with poor venous access. The difficulty of safely monitoring OA therapy has served as a deterrent to its use, even in children with a high risk of TEs or stroke. Potential solutions for optimizing OA therapy in children include pediatric anticoagulation clinics and the use of whole blood monitors in clinics and/or at home.

Anticoagulation Clinics

There are convincing reports supporting the benefits of anticoagulation clinics in adults.[295,296] The combination of increased complexity of monitoring OAs in children and the increasing numbers of children requiring OA therapy provide a strong rationale for pediatric anticoagulation clinics based in tertiary care centers. A combination of community and hospital laboratories can be used for the actual testing, provided the results are expressed as INRs. However, medical decisions are ideally made by a centralized program that is coordinated by nursing (or pharmacy) and physician personnel with expertise in pediatric anticoagulation.

Whole Blood PT Monitors for Children

The correlation between whole blood monitor and laboratory INR values has been evaluated in adult populations, with correlation coefficients greater than 0.89 in all studies.[297–304] The difficulties in monitoring OA therapy in children led to studies of whole blood monitors in both an anticoagulation clinic and at home.[31,238] There are currently two whole blood monitors for PT/INR values that are available in North America and tested extensively in children. These monitors are the ProTime® Microcoagulation System (International Technidyne Corp., Edison, NJ) (Figure 10–11)[304] and the CoaguChek (Boehringer Mannheim) (Figure 10–12).[238] Each instrument is based on similar, although slightly different technology.

The ProTime system consists of a monitor and a disposable reagent cuvette. Each cuvette has five channels for triplicate testing of the PT and the simultaneous analysis of two levels of controls with each test. The cuvette is warmed to 37°C and one drop of fresh whole blood is placed in the small reservoir. The instrument draws a precise volume of blood into the channels in the cuvette, which contain a high sensitivity thromboplastin (ISI approximately 1.0). The control channels contain thromboplastin reagent plus purified plasma-extracted coagulation factors and biologic anticoagulants. The blood sample in each channel is pumped back and forth through a precision restriction until a clot begins to form, obstructing blood flow. Cessation of blood flow below a predetermined rate is detected using an optical method, monitored by a series of LEDs. The INR is calculated from the median of

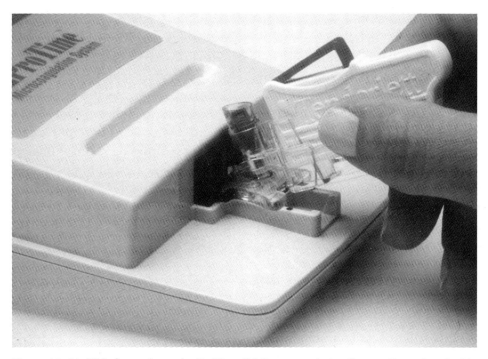

Figure 10–11 This figure shows the ProTime® Micro coagulation System. Reproduced with permission.[45]

the three patient PTs measured via a conversion equation in the microprocessor.

For the CoagUChek monitor, a test strip containing a reaction zone of iron oxide particles and rabbit brain thromboplastin (lot specific ISI between 1.9 and 2.2) is inserted into the monitor and warmed to 37°C. A drop of capillary blood is applied to the test strip application zone. Capillary forces draw the blood to the reaction zone where the thromboplastin activates the coagulation cascade.

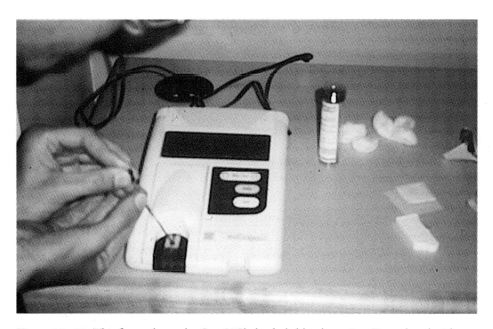

Figure 10– 12 This figure shows the CoagUChek whole blood monitor. Reproduced with permission.[45]

Two magnets are directly below the reaction zone within the CoaguUChek. The iron oxide particles are aligned horizontally by a permanent magnet and are forced into vertical alignment by a pulsating electromagnet at a frequency of 2 Hz. A photocell, situated above the test strip, records the regular pulsation pattern by reflectance photometry. As a fibrin matrix is formed the iron oxide particle movement is inhibited and eventually stopped. The time from the first contact of blood with the thromboplastin to the cessation of movement (clot formation) is measured and calculated into an INR using a calibration code stored in the lot specific code chip.

In the pediatric studies to date, all patients' self-tested results were highly correlated to the ProTime system used in the clinic (r = 0.92) (Figure 10–13).[304] The correlation of home results to the laboratory results by site ranged from r = 0.81 to 0.93 depending on the PT reagent employed. The reference INR predicted within 0.5 INR units equally well by home (77%) and laboratory (70%) tests. Similarly, all patients' self-tested results were highly correlated to the CoaguUChek monitor in the clinic (r = 0.96) (Figure 10–14).[238] The correlation of home results to the laboratory results was slightly reduced (r = 0.76); however, this had no impact on clinical care. The INR obtained from CoaguUChek

was within 0.5 of the laboratory INR for 71 percent of paired patient samples and within 0.9 in 92 percent of paired patient samples.[238] There was no correlation between increasing INR and † INR. In summary, whole blood PT/INR monitors are safe and accurate for children requiring anticoagulation. Parents and patients have proven that they are capable of performing accurate fingerprick INR tests at home, allowing for prompt and convenient monitoring with greater flexibility in testing. Figure 10–15 shows a typical pattern of INR values in a small patients using a whole blood monitor at home for over a year.

COMPLICATIONS OF ORAL ANTICOAGULANTS

Thrombotic Complications

The risk of TE in children treated with OAs is dependent on the underlying reason for the use of OAs and the intensity of therapy. Preceding sections have provided detailed risks of recurrent TE. In general, for children with mechanical prosthetic valves, the risk of TE with an INR in the target range of 2.5

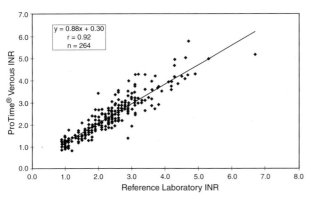

Figure 10–13 Correlation between laboratory International Normalized Ratios and ProTime® Microcoagulation System International Normalized Ratios (r = 0.92).

INR = International Normalized Ratio; n = number.

Reproduced with permission from Becker D, Andrew M, Triplett D. Continued accurate patient prothrombin time self-testing over prolonged duration using the ProTime Microcoagulation System [abstract]. Thromb Haemost 1997 Suppl:PS–2862.

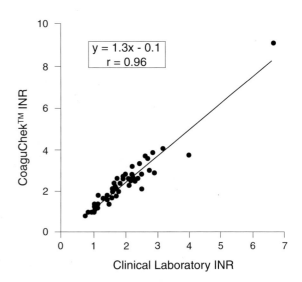

Figure 10–14 Correlation between laboratory International Normalized Ratios and the CoaguUChek whole blood monitor International Normalized Ratios (r = 0.96).

INR = International Normalized Ratio.

Reproduced with permission from Marzinotto V, Monagle P, Chan AKC, et al. Capillary whole blood monitoring of anticoagulants in children in outpatient clinics and home setting. Pediatr Cardiol. 1999, in press.

to 3.5 is less than 5 percent per year.[4] The risk of re-current TE in children with a previous DVT and a target INR range of 2.0 to 3.0 is approximately 5 percent.[4] The risk of VTE in many other disorders treated with OAs in children is unknown. Children with subtherapeutic INR values are likely at greater risk for VTE than those with therapeutic values (Figure 10–16).

Hemorrhagic Complications

The risk of bleeding in children treated with OAs is dependent on the underlying disease, presence of a concurrent coagulopathy, and intensity of therapy. Within the target INR range of 2.0 to 3.5, minor bleeding complications of no clinical consequence (bruising, nosebleeds, heavy menses, microscopic hematuria, bleeding from cuts and loose teeth, ileostomy) occur in approximately 20 percent of children receiving OAs.[9,11] The risk of serious bleed-ing in children receiving OAs for prophylaxis for mechanical prosthetic valves ranges from no events to 8.2/100 patient-years[4] and is similar to the risk of bleeding in adults, 1.6 to 7.9/100 patient-years.[151] The risk of serious bleeding in children receiving

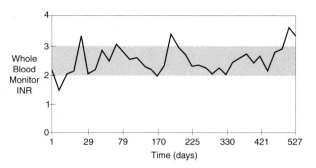

Figure 10–15 Typical pattern of International Normalized Ratios measured by a whole blood prothrombin time moni-tor in a child receiving warfarin and requiring International Normalized Ratios between 2 and 3.

INR = International Normalized Ratio.

Reproduced with permission from Andrew M, Michelson AD, Bovill T, et al. The prevention and treatment of throm-boembolic disease in children: a need for thrombophilia pro-grams. J Pediatr Hematol Oncol 1997;7–22.

OAs for the treatment of VTE is approximately 1.7 percent.[9,11] The risk of serious bleeding in children treated with a target INR of 3.0 to 4.0 is approxi-mately 4.8 percent.[42] In the literature, 54 pediatric patients were identified with significant hemor-rhagic events. For 21 of these children the INR was supratherapeutic. These data suggest that children

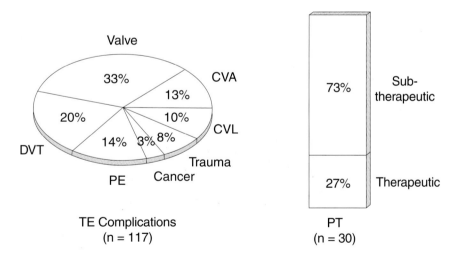

Figure 10–16 Underlying diagnosis of thromboembolic events in 117 pediatric pa-tients reported in the literature. Of the 30 evaluable patients, 73% had International Normalized Ratios that were subtherapeutic at the time of event.

% = percent; DVT = deep vein thrombosis; PE = pulmonary embolism; CVL = cen-tral venous line; CVA = cerebral vascular attack; n = number; PT = prothrombin time TE = thromboembolic event; PT = prothrombin time.

Reproduced with permission from Massicotte P, Brooker L, Marzinotto V, Andrew M. Oral anticoagulation therapy in children. In: Poller, Hirsh, editors. Oral antico-agulants. London: Arnold; 1996:216–227.

with supratherapeutic INR values are at greater risk for hemorrhagic complications than those with INR values within the target range (Figure 10–17).

Emergent Reversal of Oral Anticoagulants due to Excessively "High" INRs

The strategies to reverse OAs are dependent on the presence of bleeding and the ongoing requirement for OAs. In the absence of bleeding but the presence of an ongoing requirement for OAs, VK can be administered at doses of 0.5 to 2 mg subcutaneously but not intramuscularly. In the absence of bleeding and with no requirement for ongoing OAs, VK can be administered at doses of 2 to 10 mg subcutaneously. In the presence of clinically significant but not life threatening bleeding, VK can be administered at doses of 0.5 to 2 mg subcutaneously (not intramuscularly) and plasma at doses of approximately 20cc/kg. In the presence of clinically significant bleeding that is life threatening or will cause significant morbidity, VK can be administered in-

travenously (5 to 10 mg) by slow infusion over 10 to 20 minutes because of the risk of anaphylactic shock. Plasma and/or prothrombin complex concentrates that contain FII, FVII, FIX, and FX should be considered.

Elective Reversal of Oral Anticoagulant Therapy

Reversal of OAs is required in a variety of situations.[305] For patients receiving low doses of OAs with a target INR less than 1.5, no reversal is necessary for most surgeries or procedures. Exceptions include high-risk surgeries for bleeding such as eye surgery and neurosurgery, which require complete reversal of OA activities with a normal INR. Usually these surgeries are planned and OAs can be discontinued approximately 72 hours (3 doses) prior to the procedure. An INR should be measured prior to the procedure to confirm that it is within the normal range. For patients receiving OAs with a target INR greater than 2, the risk of significant hemor-

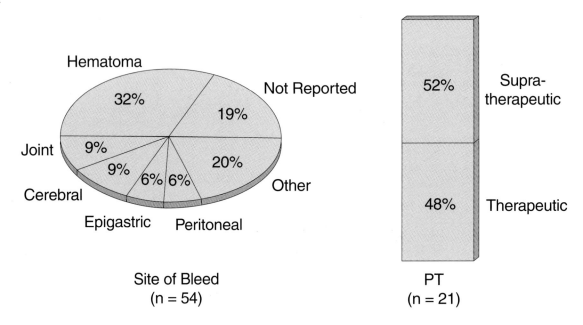

Figure 10–17 Proportion and location of hemorrhagic complications in 54 pediatric patients reported in the literature. Of the 21 evaluable patients, 52% had International Normalized Ratios that were supratherapeutic at the time of event.

n = number; PT = prothrombin time.

Reproduced with permission from Massicotte P, Brooker L, Marzinotto V, Andrew M. Oral anticoagulation therapy in children. In: Poller, Hirsh, editors. Oral anticoagulation. London: Arnold; 1996.

rhage for most surgeries or procedures is significant, necessitating reversal (Table 10–12). The clinical strategy depends on the risk of significant TEs. Where the risk of TE is significant and reversal of OAs for even a short period of time leaves patients vulnerable to TE, interim strategies for anticoagulant therapy are required. One approach is to discontinue OA therapy 72 hours (3 doses) prior to surgery and then either admit 24 hours prior to surgery and initiate UFH therapy without a bolus at an appropriate dose for age (Chapter 9) or train parents to administer subcutaneous UFH (or LMWH) at home (Chapter 9). If INR values are greater than 1.5 12 hours prior to surgery, low doses of VK (0.5 mg) can be administered subcutaneously and the INR rechecked approximately 6 hours later. If intravenous UFH is being administered, it should be discontinued approximately 6 hours prior to surgery and a PT and activated partial thromboplastin time (APTT) measured approximately 3 hours prior to surgery. The preoperative PT and APTT should be within normal limits. Postoperatively, and in consultation with the surgical team, anticoagulant therapy can be resumed with UFH without a bolus and with a target APTT in the usual therapeutic range (chapter 9). Oral anticoagulant therapy can be resumed postoperatively on the evening of day 1 or later depending on the surgical procedures. The UFH infusion can be discontinued when a therapeutic INR is reached (for DVT/PE an INR value of 2.0 to 3.0, and for mechanical valves an INR of 2.5 to 3.5). For patients receiving full-dose OA therapy with a target INR greater than 2 and where the risk of recurrent TE is minimal, OA therapy can be discontinued 72 hours (3 doses) prior to surgery. The patient can be admitted on the day of or the evening before surgery according to usual clinical practice. The PT should be measured prior to surgery and be within the normal range. Depending upon the nature of the surgery, maintenance doses of OAs can be initiated on the evening of the day of surgery.

Other Complications

Nonhemorrhagic complications, such as tracheal calcification or hair loss, occur only rarely in young children.[32,41] Although OA therapy does not appear to affect bone density in adults,[127,128,306] but may affect children. At this time, there are no other serious complications reported in the pediatric population.

CONCLUSION

Increasing numbers of children are requiring OA therapy. The complexity of their underlying problems and the numerous difficulties in safely and effectively monitoring OA therapy in children provide a strong rationale for anticoagulation clinics located in tertiary care pediatric centers staffed by a nurse (or pharmacist) and physician with experience in pediatric thrombophilia. Community laboratory services and whole blood PT/INR monitors can be used effectively to enhance the quality of OA monitoring and the quality of life for these young patients. Although these measures will improve the safety and efficacy of OA therapy in children, intervention clinical trials are urgently needed to address the issue of optimal anticoagulation therapy in children. Available data suggest that lower intensities of OA may be effective in pediatric patients.

Table 10–12 Reversal of Oral Anticoagulation Therapy

1. No Bleeding

   A) Rapid reversal of oral anticoagulants is necessary and the patient **will** require oral anticoagulants again in the near future: give vitamin K 0.5 to 2 mg subcutaneously or intravenously (not intramuscularly), depending upon the patient's size.

   B) Rapid reversal of oral anticoagulants is necessary and the patient **will not** require oral anticoagulants again: vitamin K 2 to 5 mg subcutaneously or intravenously (not intramuscularly).

2. Significant Bleeding

   A) Significant bleeding that is not life threatening and will not cause morbidity: treat with vitamin K as in #1A plus fresh frozen plasma (20 cc/kg/intravenously).

   B) Significant bleeding that is life threatening and will cause morbidity: treat with vitamin K intravenously (5 mg) by slow infusion over 10 to 20 minutes because of the risk of anaphylactic shock. Consider giving prothrombin concentrate (containing factors II, VII, IX, X) 50 units per kg intravenously rather than fresh frozen plasma (20 cc/kg intravenously).

Reproduced with permission from Michelson AD, Bovill E, Monagle P, Andrew M. Antithrombotic therapy in children. Chest 1998;114:748S–69S.

REFERENCES

1. Schofield FW. Damaged sweet clover. The cause of a new disease in cattle simulating hemorrhagic septicemia and blackleg. J Am Vet Med Assoc 1924; 64:553–75.

2. Campbell HA, Link KP. Studies on the hemorrhagic sweet clover disease. IV. The isolation and crystallization of the hemorrhagic agent. J Biol Chem 1941;138:21–33.

3. Hirsh J, Dalen JE, Anderson DR, et al. Oral anticoagulants: mechanism of action, clinical effectiveness, and optimal therapeutic range. Chest 1998;114: 445S–69S.

4. Michelson AD, Bovill E, Monagle P, Andrew M. Antithrombotic therapy in children. Chest 1998; 114:748S–69S.

5. Andrew M, Paes B, Milner R, et al. Development of the human coagulation system in the full-term infant. Blood 1987;70:165–72.

6. Andrew M, Paes B, Milner R, et al. Development of the human coagulation system in the healthy premature infant. Blood 1988;72:1651–7.

7. Andrew M, Paes B, Johnston M. Development of the hemostatic system in the neonate and young infant. J Pediatr Hematol Oncol 1990;12:95–104.

8. Andrew M, Vegh P, Johnston M, et al. Maturation of the hemostatic system during childhood. Blood 1992; 80:1998–2005.

9. Andrew M, Marzinotto V, Brooker L, et al. Oral anticoagulant therapy in pediatric patients: a prospective study. Thromb Haemost 1994;71:265–9.

10. Massicotte P, Marzinotto V, Adams M, et al. Enhanced thrombin regulation during warfarin therapy in children compared to adults. Thromb Haemost 1998; 80:570–4.

11. Streif W, Andrew M, Marzinotto V, et al. Analysis of warfarin therapy in pediatric patients: a prospective cohort study. Blood 1999 (in press).

12. Stein PD, Alpert JS, Copeland JG, et al. Antithrombotic therapy in patients with mechanical and biological prosthetic heart valves. Chest 1995;108: 371S–9S.

13. Borkon AM, Soule L, Reitz BA, et al. Five year follow-up after valve replacement with the St Jude Medical valve in infants and children. Circulation 1986; 74(supp I):I-110–5.

14. Spevak P, Freed M, Castaneda A, et al. Valve replacement in children less than 5 years of age. J Am Coll Cardiol 1986;8:901–8.

15. Harada Y, Imai Y, Kurosawa H, et al. Ten-year follow-up after valve replacement with the St Jude Medical prosthesis in children. J Thorac Cardiovasc Surg 1990;100:175–80.

16. Fiane AE, Seem E, Geiran O, Lindberg HL. Carbomedics valve in congenital heart disease. Scand J Thor Cardiovasc Surg 1994;28:123–6.

17. Bradley SM, Sade RM, Crawford FA, Stroud MR. Anticoagulation in children with mechanical valve prostheses. Ann Thorac Surg 1997;64:30–6.

18. Vosa C, Renzulli A, Lombardi PF, Damiani G. Mechanical valve replacement under 12 years of age: 15 years of experience. J Heart Valve Dis 1995;4: 279–83.

19. Rosenthal D, Friedman A, Kleinman S, et al. Thromboembolic complications after Fontan operations. Circulation 1995;92:II287–93.

20. Jahangiri M, Ross DB, Redington AN, et al. Thromboembolism after the Fontan procedure and its modifications. Ann Thorac Surg 1994;58:1409–14.

21. Monagle P, Cochrane A, McCrindle B, et al. Thromboembolic complications after Fontan procedures: the role of prophylactic anticoagulation [Editorial]. J Thorac Cardiovasc Surg 1998;115:493–8.

22. Brunette MG, Bonny Y, Spigelblatt L, Barrette G. Long term immunosuppressive treatment of a children with Takayasu's arteritis and high IgE immunoglobulins. Pediatr Nephrol 1996;10:67–9.

23. Vanoli M, Miani S, Amft N, et al. Takayasu's arteritis in Italian patients. Clin Exp Rheumatol 1995;13: 45–50.

24. Carpentieri U, Nghiem QX, Harris LC. Clinical experience with an oral anticoagulant in children. Arch Dis Child 1976;51:445–8.

25. Doyle JJ, Koren G, Chen MY, Blanchette VS. Anticoagulation with sodium warfarin in children: effect of a loading regimen. J Pediatr 1988;113:1095–7.

26. Sutor AH. Oral anticoagulation in children. Semin Thromb Hemost 1999 (in press).

27. Kumar S, Haigh J, Rhodes L, et al. Poor compliance is a major factor in unstable outpatient control of anticoagulant therapy. Thromb Haemost 1989;62: 729–32.

28. Sade R, Crawford FJ, Fyfe D, Stroud M. Valve prostheses in children: a reassessment of anticoagulation. J Thorac Cardiovasc Surg 1988;95:553–61.

29. Rao S, Solymar L, Mardini M, et al. Anticoagulant therapy in children with prosthetic valves. Ann Thorac Surg 1989;47:589–92.

30. Serra A, McNicholas K, Olivier HJ, et al. The choice of anticoagulation in pediatric patients with the St Jude Medical valve prostheses. J Cardiovasc Surg 1987;28: 588–91.

31. Massicotte P, Marzinotto V, Vegh P, et al. Home monitoring of warfarin therapy in children with a whole blood prothrombin time monitor. J Pediatr 1995; 127:389–94.

32. Hooshang T, Capitanio M. Tracheobronchial calcification: an observation in three children after mitral

valve replacement and warfarin sodium therapy. Radiology 1990;176:728–30.

33. El Makhlouf A, Friedli B, Oberhansli I, et al. Prosthetic heart valve replacement in children. J Thorac Cardiovasc Surg 1987;93:80–5.

34. Bradley LM, Midgley FM, Watson DC, et al. Anticoagulation therapy in children with mechanical prosthetic cardiac valves. Am J Cardiol 1985;56:533–5.

35. Stewart S, Cianciotta D, Alexson C, Manning J. The long-term risk of warfarin sodium therapy and the incidence of thromboembolism in children after prosthetic cardiac valves. J Thorac Cardiovasc Surg 1987;93:551–4.

36. Schaffer MS, Clarke DR, Campbell DN, et al. The St Jude Medical cardiac valve and children: role of anticoagulant therapy. J Am Coll Cardiol 1987;9: 235–9.

37. Solymar L, Rao PS, Mardini MK, et al. Prosthetic valves in children and adolescents. Am Heart J 1991;121: 557–68.

38. Antunes MJ, Vanderdonck KM, Sussman MJ. Mechanical valve replacement in children and teenagers. Eur J Cardiothorac Surg 1989;3:222–8.

39. Woods A, Vargas J, Berri G, et al. Antithrombotic therapy in children and adolescents. Thromb Res 1986;42:289–301.

40. Massicotte P, Marzinotto V, Vegh P, et al. Home monitoring of warfarin therapy in children with a whole blood prothrombin time monitor. J Pediatr 1995; 127:389–94.

41. Ries M, Klinge J, Rauch R. Erfahrungen mit der antikoagulatientherapie bei 10 patienten an der Univ Kinderklinik Erlangen. In: Sutor AH, editor. Thrombosen im Kindesalter. Basel: Editiones Roche; 1992.

42. Tait RC, Ladusans EJ, El-Metaal M, et al. Oral anticoagulation in paediatric patients: dose requirements and complications. Thromb Haemost 1996;74: 228–31.

43. Hall JG. Embryopathy associated with oral anticoagulant therapy. Birth Defects Orig Artic Ser 1976;12:33–7.

44. Massicotte P, Brooker L, Marzinotto V, Andrew M. Oral anticoagulation therapy in children. In: Poller, Hirsh, editors. Oral anticoagulants. London: Arnold; 1996. p. 216–227.

45. Andrew M, deVeber G. Blood clots and strokes: a guide for parents and little folks. Hamilton: B.C. Decker Inc; 1998.

46. Andrew M, Michelson AD, Bovill T, et al. The prevention and treatment of thromboembolic disease in children: a need for thrombophilia programs. J Pediatr Hematol Oncol 1997;19:7–22.

47. Uziel Y, Laxer RM, Blaser S, et al. Cerebral vein thrombosis in childhood systemic lupus erythematosus. J Pediatr 1995;126:722–7.

48. Andrew M, David M, Adams M, et al. Venous thromboembolic complications (VTE) in children: first analyses of the Canadian Registry of VTE. Blood 1994;83:1251–7.

49. O'Reilly R. Anticoagulant, antithrombotic, and thrombolytic drugs. In: Goodman-Gilman A, Goodman L, Gilman A, editors. The pharmacological basis of therapeutics. New York: MacMillan Publishing Co Inc; 1980.

50. Evans D, Rowlands M, Poller L. Survey of oral anticoagulant treatment in children. J Clin Pathol 1992;45:707–8.

51. O'Reilly RA, Aggeler PM. Determinants of the response to oral anticoagulant drugs in man. Pharmacol Rev 1970;22:35–96.

52. Hewick D, McEwan J. Plasma half-lives, plasma metabilites and anticoagulant efficacies of the enantiomers of warfarin in man. J Pharm Pharmacol 1983;25:458–65.

53. Lewis RJ, Trager W. Warfarin metabolism in man: identification of metabolites in urine. J Clin Invest 1970;49:907–13.

54. Furie B, Furie B. Molecular basis of vitaminK-dependent γ-carboxylation. Blood 1990;75: 1753–62.

55. Whitlon DS, Sadowski JA, Suttie JW. Mechanisms of coumarin action: significance of viamin K epoxide reductase inhibition. Biochemistry 1978;17:1371–7.

56. Fasco MJ, Hildebrandt EF, Suttie JW. Evidence that warfarin anticoagulant action involves two distinct reductase activities. J Biol Chem 1982;257:11210–2.

57. Choonara IA, Malia RG, Haynes BP. The relationship between inhibition of vitamin K1 2,3-epoxide reductase and reduction of clotting factor activity with warfarin. Br J Clin Pharmacol 1988;25:1–7.

58. Trivedi LS, Rhee M, Galvan JH, Fasco MJ. Normal and warfarin-resistant rat hepatocyte metabolism of vitamin K1 2,3 epoxide: evidence for multiple pathways of hydroxyvitamin K formation. Arch Biochem Biophys 1988;264:67–73.

59. Shearer MJ, McBurney A, Breckenridge AM, Barkhan P. Effect of warfarin on the metabolism of phylloquinone (vitamin K1): dose response relationship in man. Clin Sci Mol Med 1977;52:621–30.

60. Stenflo J, Fernlund P, Egan W, Roepstorff P. Vitamin K-dependent modifications of glutamic acid residues in prothrombin. Proc Natl Acad Sci U S A 1974;71: 2730–3.

61. Nelsestuen G, Zytkovicz T, Howard J. The mode of action of vitamin K. Identification of γ-carboxyglutamic acid as a component of prothrombin. J Biol Chem 1974;249:6347–50.

62. Breckenridge A. Oral anticoagulant drugs: pharmacokinetic aspects. Semin Hematol 1978;15:19–26.

63. O'Reilly R. Vitamin K and the oral anticoagulant drugs. Annu Rev Med 1976;27:245–61.

64. Kelly JG, O'Malley K. Clinical pharmacokinetics of oral anticoagulants. Clin Pharmacokinet 1979;4:1–15.

65. Poller L, Taberner DA. Dosage and control of oral anticoagulants: an international collaborative study. Br J Haematol 1982;51:479–85.

66. O'Reilly R. Warfarin metabolism and drug-drug interactions. In: Wessler S, Becker C, Nemerson Y, editors. The new dimensions of warfarin prophylaxis. New York: Plenum Press; 1987. p. 205–12.

67. Sutcliffe FA, MacNicoll AD, Gibson GG. Aspects of anticoagulant action: a review of the pharmacology, metabolism and toxicology of warfarin and congeners. Rev Drug Metabol Drug Interact 1987; 5:225–72.

68. Breckenridge A, Orme M, Wesseling H. Pharmacokinetics and pharmacodynamics of the enantiomers of warfarin in man. Clin Pharmacol Ther 1974; 15:424–30.

69. O'Reilly RA. Studies on the optical enantiomorphs of warfarin in man. Clin Pharmacol Ther 1974;16: 348–54.

70. O'Reilly RA, Aggeler PM, Hoag MS, et al. Hereditary transmission of exceptional resistance to coumarin anticoagulant drugs: the first reported kindred. N Engl J Med 1964;271:809–15.

71. Alving BM, Strickler MP, Knight RD, et al. Hereditary warfarin resistance. Arch Intern Med 1985;145: 499–501.

72. O'Reilly R, Rytand D. 'Resistance' to warfarin due to unrecognized vitamin K supplementation. N Engl J Med 1980;303:160–1.

73. Quick A. The prothrombin time in haemophilia and in obstructive jaundice. J Biol Chem 1935;109:73–4.

74. Loeliger E, van den Besselaar A, Lewis S. Reliability and clinical impact of the normalization of the prothrombin times in oral anticoagulant control. Thromb Haemost 1985;54:148–54.

75. Loeliger E, van den Besselaar A, Broekmans A. Intensity of oral anticoagulation in patients monitored with various thromboplastins. N Engl J Med 1983;308: 1228–9.

76. Zucker S, Cathey MH, Sox PJ, Hall EC. Standardization of laboratory tests for controlling anticoagulant therapy. Am J Clin Pathol 1970;53:348–54.

77. Poller L. Thromboplastin and oral coagulant control. Br J Haematol 1987;67(1):116–7.

78. Poller L, Thomson J. The interpretation of prothrombin results: a national survey. Br J Haematol 1969;16: 31–7.

79. Poller L. Laboratory control of oral anticoagulants. Br Med J (Clin Res Ed) 1987;294:1184.

80. International Committee for Standardization in Haematology, International Committee on Thrombosis and Haemostasis. ICSH/ICTH Recommendations for reporting prothrombin time in oral anticoagulant control. Thromb Haemost 1985;53:155–6.

81. Hirsh J. Oral anticoagulant drugs. [Review]. N Engl J Med 1991;324:1865–75.

82. Reverdiau-Moalic P, Delahousse B, Bardos GBP, et al. Evolution of blood coagulation activators and inhibitors in the healthy human fetus. Blood 1996; 88:900–6.

83. Bovill E, Soll R, Lynch M, et al. Vitamin K1 metabolism and the production of des-carboxy prothrombin and protein C in the term and premature neonate. Blood 1993;81:77–83.

84. Andrew M, Schmidt B, Mitchell L, et al. Thrombin generation in newborn plasma is critically dependent on the concentration of prothrombin. Thromb Haemost 1990;63:27–30.

85. Schmidt B, Ofosu F, Mitchell L, et al. Anticoagulant effects of heparin in neonatal plasma. Pediatr Res 1989;25:405–8.

86. Andrew M, Mitchell L, Vegh P, Ofosu F. Thrombin regulation in children differs from adults in the absence and presence of heparin. Thromb Haemost 1994; 72:836–42.

87. Greffe BS, Marlar RA, Manco-Johnson M. Neonatal protein C: molecular composition and distribution in normal term infants. Thromb Res 1989;56:91–8.

88. Manco-Johnson MJ, Spedale S, Peters M, et al. Identification of a unique form of protein C in the ovine fetus: developmentally linked transition to the adult form. Pediatr Res 1995;37:365–72.

89. Moalic P, Gruel Y, Body G, et al. Levels and plasma distribution of free and C4b-BP-bound Protein S in human fetuses and fullterm newborns. Thromb Res 1988;49:471–80.

90. Schwartz HP, Muntean W, Watzke H, Richter B, Griffin JH. Low total protein S antigen but high protein S activity due to decreased C4b-binding protein in neonates. Blood 1988;71:562–5.

91. Schmidt B, Mitchell L, Ofosu F, Andrew M. Alpha-2-macroglobulin is an important progressive inhibitor of thrombin in neonatal and infant plasma. Thromb Haemost 1989;62:1074–7.

92. Price PA. Vitamin K dependent formation of bone Gla protein (osteocalcin) and its function. Vitam Horm 1985;42:65–108.

93. Slovik DM, Gundberg CM, Neer RM, Lian JB. Clinical evaluation of bone turnover by serum osteocalcin measurements in a hospital setting. J Clin Endocrinol Metab 1984;58:228–30.

94. Delmas PD. Biochemical markers of bone turnover: methodology and clinical use in osteoporosis. Am J Med 1991;91:59S–63S.

95. Akesson K. Biochemical markers of bone turnover: a review. Acta Orthop Scand 1995;66:376–86.

96. Hauschka PV, Lian JB, Cole DE, Gundberg CM. Osteocalcin and matrix Gla protein: vitamin K-dependent proteins in bone. Physiol Rev 1989;69: 990–1047.

97. Price PA, Urist MR, Otawara Y. Matrix Gla protein, a new gamma-carboxyglutamic acid containing protein which is associated with the organic matrix of bone. Biochem Biophys Res Commun 1983;117: 765–71.

98. van Haarlem LJ, Soute BA, Hemker HC, Vermeer C. Characterization of Gla-containing proteins from calcified human atherosclerotic plaques. In: Suttie JW, editor. Current Advances in Vitamin K Research. New York: Elsevier; 1988. p. 287–92.

99. Vermeer C. Gamma-carboxyglutamate-containing proteins and the vitamin K dependent carboxylase. Biochem J 1990;266:625–36.

100. Lian JB, Tassinari M, Glowacki JM. Resorption of implanted bone prepared from normal and warfarin treated rats. J Clin Invest 1984;73:1223–6.

101. Lian JB, Friedman PA. The vitamin K dependent synthesis of gamma-carboxyglutamic acid by bone microsomes. J Biol Chem 1978;253:6623–6.

102. Price PA, Williamson MK, Lothringer JW. Origin of the vitamin K dependent bone protein found in plasma and its clearance by kidney and bone. J Biol Chem 1981;256:12760–6.

103. Magnusson P, Hager A, Larsson L. Serum osteocalcin and bone and liver alkaline phosphatase isoforms in healthy children and adolescents. Pediatr Res 1995;38:955–61.

104. Tommasi M, Bacciottini L, Benucci A, et al. Serum biochemical markers of bone turnover in healthy infants and children. Int J Biol Markers 1996;11:159–64.

105. Alatas O, Colak O, Alatas E, et al. Osteocalcin metabolism in late fetal life: fetal and maternal osteocalcin levels. Clin Chim Acta 1995;239:179–83.

106. Knapen MHJ, Hamulyak K, Vermeer C. The effect of vitamin K supplementation on circulating osteocalcin (bone gla protein) and urinary calcium excretion. Ann Intern Med 1989;111:1001–5.

107. Vermeer C, Hamulyak K. Pathophysiology of vitamin K deficiency and oral anticoagulants. Thromb Haemost 1991;66:153–9.

108. Szulc P, Arlot M, Chapuy MC, et al. Serum undercarboxylated osteocalcin correlates with hip bone mineral density in elderly women. J Bone Miner Res 1994;9:1591–5.

109. Szulc P, Chapuy MC, Meunier PJ, Delman PD. Serum undercarboxylated osteocalcin is a marker of the risk of hip fracture in elderly women. J Clin Invest 1993;91:1769–74.

110. Fiore CE, Tamburino C, Foti R, Grimaldi D. Reduced axial bone mineral content in patients taking an oral anticoagulant. South Med J 1990;83:538–42.

111. Kanai T, Takagi T, Masuhiro K, et al. Serum vitamin K level and bone mineral density in post menopausal women. Int J Gynaecol Obstet 1997;56:25–30.

112. Resch H, Pietschmann P, Krexner E, Willvonseder R. Decreased peripheral bone mineral content in patients under anticoagulant therapy with phenprocoumon. Eur Heart J 1991;12:439–41.

113. Jie KS, Bots ML, Vermeer C, et al. Vitamin K status and bone mass in women with or without aortic atherosclerosis: a population based study. Calcif Tissue Int 1996;59:352–6.

114. Sower M, Willing M, Burns TP, et al. Genetic markers, bone mineral density, and serum osteocalcin levels. J Bone Min Res 1999;14:114–9.

115. Menon RK, Gill DS, Thomas M, et al. Impaired carboxylation of osteocalcin in warfarin-treated patients. J Clin Endocrinol Metab 1987;64:59–61.

116. Pietschmann P, Woloszczuk W, Panzer S, et al. Decreased serum osteocalcin levels in phenprocoumon treated patients. J Clin Endocrinol Metab 1988;66: 1071–4.

117. Plantalech L, Guillaumont M, Vergaud P, et al. Impairment of gamma carboxylation of circulating osteocalcin (Bone Gla protein) in elderly women. J Bone Miner Res 1991;6:1211–6.

118. Price PA, Williamson MK. Effects of warfarin on bone. J Biol Chem 1981;256:12754–9.

119. Becker MH, Fenieser NB, Finegold M. Chondrodysplasia punctata: is maternal warfarin therapy a factor. Am J Dis Child 1975;129:356–9.

120. Pettifor JM, Benson R. Congenital malformations associated with the administration of oral anticoagulants during pregnancy. J Pediatr 1975;86:459–62.

121. Shaul W, Emery H, Hall JG. Chondrodysplasia punctata and maternal warfarin use during pregnancy. Am J Dis Child 1975;129:360–2.

122. Hall JAG, Pauli RM, Wilson KM. Maternal and fetal sequelae of anticoagulation during pregnancy. Am J Med 1980;68:122–40.

123. Price PA, Williamson MK, Haba T, et al. Excessive mineralization with growth plate closure in rats on chronic warfarin treatment. Proc Natl Acad Sci U S A 1982;79:7734–8.

124. Pastoureau P, Vergnaud P, Meunier PJ, Delmas PD. Osteopenia and bone remodeling abnormalities in warfarin-treated lambs. J Bone Miner Res 1993;8: 1417–26.

125. Jie KS, Gijsbers BL, Knapen MH, et al. Effects of vitamin K and oral anticoagulants on urinary calcium excretion. Br J Haematol 1993;83:100–4.

126. Philip WJ, Martin JC, Richardson JM, et al. Decreased axial and peripheral bone density in patients taking long-term warfarin. QJM 1995;88:635–40.

127. Piro L, Whyte M, Murphy W, Birge S. Normal cortical bone mass in patients after long term Coumadin therapy. J Clin Endocrinol Metab 1982;54:470–3.

128. Rosen H, Maitland L, Suttie J, et al. Vitamin K and maintenance of skeletal integrity in adults. Am J Med 1993;94:62–8.

129. Houvenagel E, Leloire O, Vanderlinden T, et al. The level of osteocalcin and bone mass in patients receiving anti-vitamin K agents. Rev Rhum Mal Osteoartic 1989;56:677–9.

130. Sato Y, Honda Y, Kunoh H, Oizumi K. Long-term oral anticoagulation reduced bone mass in patients with previous hemispheric infarction and nonrheumatic atrial fibrillation. Stroke 1997;28:2390–4.

131. Monreal M, Olive A, Lafoz E. Heparins, coumarin and bone density [letter]. Lancet 1991;338:706.

132. Dreyfus M, Magny J, Bridey F, et al. Treatment of homozygous protein C deficiency and neonatal purpura fulminans with a purified protein C concentrate. N Engl J Med 1991;325(22):1565–8.

133. Massicotte P, Julian J, Webber C, Charpentier K. Osteoporosis. A potential complication of long term warfarin therapy. Thromb Haemost 1999;Suppl: 1333a.

134. del Rio L, Carrascosa A, Pons F, et al. Bone mineral den sity of the lumbar spine in white mediterranean spanish children and adolescents: changes related to age, sex, and puberty. Pediatr Res 1994;35:362–6.

135. Francis C, Marder V, Evarts C, Yaukookbodi S. Two-step warfarin therapy: prevention of postoperative venous thrombosis without excessive bleeding. JAMA 1983;249:374–8.

136. Powers P, Gent M, Jay R, et al. A randomized trial of less intense postoperative warfarin or aspirin therapy in the prevention of venous thromboembolism after surgery for fractured hip. Arch Intern Med 1989;149:771–4.

137. Sevitt S, Gallagher N. Prevention of venous thrombosis and pulmonary embolism in injured patients. Lancet 1959;ii:981.

138. Taberner DA, Poller L, Burslem RW, Jones JB. Oral anticoagulants controlled by the British comparatice thromboplastin versus low dose heparin in prophylaxis of deep vein thrombosis. Br Med J 1978; 1:272–4.

139. Poller L, McKernan A, Thomson J, et al. Fixed minidose warfarin: a new approach to prophylaxis against venous thrombosis after major surgery. BMJ 1987;295:1309–12.

140. Stentella P, Frega A, Cipriano L, et al. Prevention of thromboembolic complications in women undergoing gynecologic surgery. Clin Exp Obstet Gynecol 1997;24:58–60.

141. Hull R, Delmore T, Genton E. Warfarin sodium versus low-dose heparin in the long-term treatment of venous thrombosis. N Engl J Med 1979;301:855–8.

142. Hull R, Delmore T, Carter C, et al. Adjusted subcutaneous heparin versus warfarin sodium in the long-term treatment of venous thrombosis. N Engl J Med 1982;306:189–94.

143. Hyers TM, Agnelli G, Hull RD, et al. Antithrombotic therapy for venous thromboembolic disease. Chest 1998;114:561S–7S.

144. Research Committee of the British Thoracic Society. Optimum duration of anticoagulation for deep-vein thrombosis and pulmonary embolism. Lancet 1992;340:873–6.

145. Levine M, Hirsh J, Gent M, et al. Optimal duration of oral anticoagulant therapy: a randomized trial comparing four weeks with three months of warfarin in patients with proximal vein thrombosis. Thromb Haemost 1995;74:606–11.

146. Schulman S, Rhedin A, Lindmarker P, et al. A comparison of six weeks with six months of oral anticoagulant therapy after a first episode of venous thromboembolism. N Engl J Med 1995;332:1661–5.

147. Kearon C, Gent M, Hirsh J, et al. A comparison of three months of anticoagulation with extending anticoagulation for a first episode of idiopathic venous thromboembolism. N Engl J Med 1999;340:955–6.

148. Prandoni P, Lensing A, Buller H, et al. Deep-vein thrombosis and the incidence of subsequent symptomatic cancer. N Engl J Med 1992;327:1128–33.

149. Pini M, Aiello S, Manotti C, et al. Low molecular weight heparin versus warfarin in the prevention of recurrences after deep vein thrombosis. Thromb Haemost 1994;72:191–7.

150. Kearon C. Drug trials that have influenced our practice in the treatment of venous thromboembolism. Thromb Haemost 1997;78:553–7.

151. Schulman S, Granqvist S, Holmstrom M, et al. The duration of oral anticoagulation therapy after a second episode of venous thromboembolism. N Engl J Med 1997;336:393–8.

152. Stein PD, Alpert JS, Dalen JE, et al. Antithrombotic therapy in patients with mechanical and biological prosthetic heart valves. Chest 1998;114:602S–10S.

153. Turpie A, Gunstensen J, Hirsh J, et al. Randomised comparison of two intensities of oral anticoagulant therapy after tissue heart valve replacement. Lancet 1988;1:1242–5.

154. Heras M, Chesbro JH, Fuster VB. High risk of early thromboemboli after bioprosthetic cardiac valve replacement. J Am Coll Cardiol 1995;25:1111–9.

155. Schaff H, Danielson G, DiDonato R, et al. Late results after Starr-Edwards valve replacement in children. J Thorac Cardiovasc Surg 1984;88:583–9.

156. Ibrahim M, Cleland J, O'Kane H, et al. St Jude medical prosthesis in children. J Thorac Cardiovasc Surg 1994;108:52–6.

157. Cabalka AD, Emery RW, Petersen RJ, et al. Long term followup of the St Jude medical prosthesis in pediatric patients. Ann Thorac Surg 1995;60:S618–23.

158. Zahn E, Lima V, Benson L, Freedom R. Use of endovascular stents to increase pulmonary blood flow in pulmonary atresia with ventricular septal defect. Am J Cardiol 1992;70:411–2.

159. Zahn EM, Chang AC, Aldousany A, Burke R. Emergent stent placement for acute Blalock-Taussig shunt obstruction after stage 1 Norwood surgery. Cathet Cardiovasc Diagn 1997;42:191–4.

160. Hijazi Z. Stenting for postoperative congenital heart disease in infants. Cathet Cardiovasc Diagn 1997;42:195.

161. Abdulhamed JM, Alyousef SA, Mullins C. Endovascular stent placement for pulmonary venous obstruction after Mustard operation for transposition of the great arteries. Heart 1996;75:210–2.

162. Chau AKT, Leung MP. Management of branch pulmonary artery stenosis: balloon angioplasty or endovascular stenting. Clin Exp Pharmacol Physiol 1997;24:960–2.

163. Mendelsohn AM, Bove EL, Lupinetti FM, et al. Intraoperative and percutaneous stenting of congenital pulmonary artery and vein stenosis. Circulation 1993; 88:210–7.

164. Fontan F, Paudet E. Surgical repair of tricuspid atresia. Thorax 1971;26:240–8.

165. Driscoll DJ, Offord KP, Feldt RH, et al. Five to fifteen year follow-up after Fontan operation. Circulation 1992;85:469–96.

166. Gale AW, Danielson G, Mc Goon D, et al. Modified Fontan operation for univentricular heart and complicated congenital lesions. J Thorac Cardiovasc Surg 1979;78:831–8.

167. Prenger K, Hess J, Cromme-Dijkhuis A, Eijgelaar A. Porcine-valved dacron conduits in Fontan procedures. Ann Thorac Surg 1988;46:526–30.

168. Jonas RA. Intracardiac thrombus after the Fontan procedure. J Thorac Cardiovasc Surg 1995;110:1502–3.

169. Cetta F, Feldt RH, O'Leary PW, et al. Improved early morbidity after fontan operation: the Mayo clinic experience, 1987 to 1992. J Am Coll Cardiol 1996; 28:480–6.

170. Okita Y, Miki S, Kusuhara K, et al. Massive systemic venous thrombosis after Fontan operation: report of a case. Thorac Cardiovasc Surg 1988;36:335–6.

171. Shannon FL, Campbell DN, Clarke DR. Right atrial thrombosis: rare complication of the modified Fontan procedure. Pediatr Cardiol 1986;7:209–12.

172. Ogawa S, Nagai Y, Zhang J, et al. Evaluation of myocardial ischemia and infarction by signal-averaged electrocardiographic late potentials in children with Kawasaki disease. Am J Cardiol 1996;78:175–81.

173. Dajani AS, Bison AL, Chung KL, et al. Diagnostic guidelines for Kawasaki disease. Am J Dis Child 1990;144:1218–9.

174. Centre for Disease Control. Kawasaki disease-New York. MMWR Morb Mortal Wkly Rep 1980; 29:61–3.

175. Kato H, Koike S, Yokoyama T. Kawasaki disease: effect of treatment on coronary artery involvement. Pediatrics 1979;63:175–9.

176. Koren G, Rose V, Lavi S, Rowe R. Probable efficacy of high-dose salicylates in reducing coronary involvement in Kawasaki disease. JAMA 1985;254:767–9.

177. Daniels S, Specker P, Capannari TE, et al. Correlates of coronary artery aneurysm formation in patients with Kawasaki disease. Am J Dis Child 1987;141:205–7.

178. Newburger J, Takahashi M, Burns J, et al. The treatment of Kawasaki syndrome with intravenous gamma globulin. N Engl J Med 1986;315:341–7.

179. Durongpisitkul K, Fururaj VJ, Park JM, Martin CF. The prevention of coronary artery aneurysm in Kawasaki disease: a meta-analysis on the efficacy of aspirin and immunoglobulin treatment. Pediatrics 1995;96: 1057–61.

180. Gersony WM. Kawasaki disease: clinical overview. Cardiol Young 1991;1:192–5.

181. Tatara K, Kusakawa S. Long term prognosis of giant coronary aneurysm in Kawasaki disease: an angiographic study. J Pediatr 1987;111:705–10.

182. Albers GW, Easton JD, Sacco RL, Teal P. Antithrombotic and thrombolytic therapy for ischemic stroke. Chest 1998;114:683S–98S.

183. Kohrman MH, Huttenlocher PR. Takayasu's arteritis; a treatable cause of stroke in infancy. Pediatr Neurol 1986;2:154–8.

184. Yokio K, Hosoi E, Akaike M, et al. Takayasu's arteritis associated with antiphospholipid antibodies. Report of 2 cases. Angiology 1996;47:315–9.

185. Akazawa H, Ikeda U, Yamamoto K, et al. Hypercoagulable state in patients with Takayasu's arteritis. Thromb Haemost 1996;75:701–864.

186. Kerr GS, Hallahan CW, Giordano J, et al. Takayasu arteritis. Ann Intern Med 1994;120:919–20.

187. Hu WL, Lu JH, Meng CC, Hwang B. Neonatal myocardial infarction: a case. Chung Hua I Hsueh Tsa Chih (Taipei) 1988;61:110–5.

188. Nakamura Y, Yanagawa H, Ojima T, et al. Cardiac sequelae of Kawasaki disease among recurrent cases. Arch Dis Child 1998;78:163–5.

189. Fukuda T, Akagi T, Ishibashi M, et al. Noninvasive evaluation of myocardial ischemia in Kawasaki disease: comparison between dipyridamole stress thallium imaging and exercise stress testing. Am Heart J 1998;135:482–7.

190. Ogawa S, Fukazawa R, Ohkubo T, et al. Silent myocardial ischemia in Kawasaki disease: evaluation of percutaneous transluminal coronary angioplasty by dobutamine stress testing. Circulation 1997;96:3384–9.

191. Bonnet D, Cormier V, Villain E, et al. Progressive left main coronary artery obstruction leading to myocardial infarction in a child with Williams disease. Eur J Pediatr 1997;156:751–3.

192. Deodhar AP, Tometzki AJ, Hudson IN, Mankad PS. Aortic valve tumor causing acute myocardial infarction in a child. Ann Thorac Surg 1997;64:1482–4.

193. Gruen DR, Winchester PH, Brill PW, Ramirez E. Magnetic resonance imaging of myocardial infarction during prothrombin complex concentrate therapy of hemophilia A. Pediatr Radiol 1997;27:271–2.

194. Saker DM, Walsh-Sukys M, Spector M, Zahka KG. Cardiac recovery and survival after neonatal myocardial infarction. Pediatr Cardiol 1997;18:139–42.

195. Iwama H, Kaneko T, Watanabe K, et al. Fatal acute myocardial infarction during general anesthesia in a 7-year-old boy associated with total intramural coronary arteries. Anesthesiology 1997;87:426–9.

196. Muraskas J, Besinger R, Bell T, et al. Perinatal myocardial infarction in a newborn with a structurally normal heart. Am J Perinatol 1997;14:93–7.

197. Fogelman R, Gow RM, Casey F, Hamilton RM. Pseudoinfarction pattern in an infant. Pediatr Cardiol 1997;18:312–7.

198. Kececioglu D, Deng MC, Schmid C, et al. Anomalous origin of the left coronary artery from the pulmonary artery with large anterior myocardial infarction and ischemia: successful tunnel repair and concomitant heterotopic heart transplantation as biological bridge to recovery. Transpl Int 1997;10:161–3.

199. Martins VP, Macedo AJ, Kaku S, et al. Acute myocardial infarct in infants. Acta Med Port 1997;9:341–6.

200. Romero IC, Bueno CM, Bariuso LM, et al. Acute myocardial infarction in a 5-year-old boy. Rev Esp Cardiol 1996;49:855–7.

201. Patel CR, Judge NE, Muise KL, Levine MM. Prenatal myocardial infarction suspected by fetal echocardiography. J Am Soc Echocardiogr 1996;9:721–3.

202. de Silva MV, de Silva GD, Lamabadusuriya SP. Myocardial infarction in an infant due to anomalous origin of the left coronary artery. Ceylon Med J 1996;41:115–7.

203. Kato H, Sugimura T, Akagi T, et al. Long term consequences of Kawasaki disease. A 10 to 21 year follow-up study of 594 patients. Circulation 1996;94:1379–85.

204. Miyamoto T, Horigome H, Sato H, et al. Anomalous origin of the left coronary artery from the pulmonary trunk with myocardial infarction and severe left ventricular dysfunction in infancy: assessment of my-ocardial damage using SPECT studies with 201TICI and BMIPP. Kaku Igaku 1996;33:169–74.

205. Tometzki AJ, Pollock JC, Wilson N, Davis CF. Role of ECMO in neonatal myocardial infarction. Arch Dis Child Fetal Neonatal Ed 1996;74:F143–4.

206. de Caro E, Ribaldone D. Acute myocardial infarction and residual impairment of coronary perfusion: unusual complications of mitral endocarditis in a paediatric patient. G Ital Cardiol 1996;26:427–9.

207. Kaminer S, Truemper E. Hemopericardium and cardiac tamponade as presenting findings of anomalous left coronary artery syndrome complicated by transmural myocardial infarction. Pediatr Cardiol 1996;17:198–200.

208. Brown J, Dunn J, Spooner E, Kirsh M. Late spontaneous disruption of a porcine xenograft mitral valve: clinical, hemodynamic, echocardiographic, and pathologic findings. J Thorac Cardiovasc Surg 1978;75:606–11.

209. Geha A, Laks H, Stansel HJ, et al. Late failure of porcine valve heterografts in children. J Thorac Cardiovasc Surg 1979;78:351–64.

210. Silver M, Pollock J, Silver M, et al. Calcification in porcine xenograft valves in children. Am J Cardiol 1980;45:685–9.

211. Dunn J. Porcine valve durability in children. Ann Thorac Surg 1981;32(4):357–68.

212. Miller D, Stinson E, Oyer P, et al. The durability of porcine xenograft valves and conduits in children. Circulation 1982;66(2 Pt.2):I172–85.

213. Odell J. Calcification of porcine bioprostheses in children. In: Cohn L, Gallucci V, editors. Cardiac bioprostheses: proceedings of the Second International Symposium. New York: Yorke Medical Books; 1982. p. 231.

214. Williams D, Danielson G, McGoon D, et al. Porcine heterograft valve replacement in children. J Thorac Cardiovasc Surg 1982;84(3):446–50.

215. Fiore L, Brophy M, Deykin D. The efficacy and safety of the addition of aspirin in patients treated with oral anticoagulation after heart valve replacement: a meta-analysis. Blood 1993;82:409a.

216. Nunez L, Aguado GM, Larrea JL. Prevention of thromboembolism using aspirin after mitral valve replacement with porcine bioprosthesis. Ann Thorac Surg 1984;37:84–7.

217. Ionescu MI, Smith DR, Hasan SS. Clinical durability of the pericardial xenograft valve: ten years experience with mitral replacement. Ann Thorac Surg 1982;34:212–4.

218. Gonzales-Lavin L, Chi S, Blair TC. Thromboembolism and bleeding after mitral valve replacement with porcine valves: influence of thromboembolic risk factors. J Surg Res 1984;36:508–15.

219. Horstkotte D, Schulte HD, Bircks W. Lower intensity anticoagulation therapy results in lower complication rates with the St Jude medical prostheses. J Thorac Cardiovasc Surg 1994;107:1136–45.

220. Louagie YA, Jamart J, Eucher P. Mitral valve Carpentier-Edwards bioprosthetic replacement, thromboembolism, and anticoagulants. Ann Thorac Surg 1993;56:931–7.

221. Cohn LH, Allred EN, DiSesa VJ. Early and late risk of aortic valve replacement: a 12 year concomitant comparison of the porcine bioprosthetic and tilting disc prosthetic aortic valves. J Thorac Cardiovasc Surg 1984;88:695–705.

222. Bolooki H, Kaiser GA, Mallon SM. Comparison of long term results of Carpentier-Edwards and Hancock bioprosthetic valves. Ann Thorac Surg 1986;42:494–9.

223. Bloomfield P, Kitchin AJ, Wheatley DJ. A prospective evaluation of the Bjork-Shiley, Hancock, and Carpentier-Edwards heart valve prostheses. Circulation 1986;73:1213–22.

224. Acar J, Iung B, Boissel JP. AREVA: multicenter randomized comparison of low dose versus standard dose anticoagulation in patients with mechanical prosthetic heart valves. Circulation 1996;94:2107–12.

225. Horstkotte D, Schulte H, Bircks W, Strauer B. Unexpected findings concerning thromboembolic complications and anticoagulation after complete 10 year followup of patients with St. Jude medical protheses. J Heart Valve Dis 1993;2:291–301.

226. Cappelleri JC, Fiore L, Brophy M. Efficacy and safety of combined anticoagulant and antiplatelet therapy versus anticoagulant monotherapy after mechanical heart-valve replacement: a meta-analysis. Am Heart J 1995;130:547–52.

227. Altman P, Rouvier J, Garfinkel E, et al. Comparison of two levels of anticoagulant therapy in patients with substitute heart valves. J Thorac Cardiovasc Surg 1991;101:427–31.

228. Albertal J, Sutton M, Pereyra D. Experience with moderate intensity anticoagulation and aspirin after mechanical valve replacement. A retrospective, non-randomized study. J Heart Valve Dis 1993;2:302–7.

229. Meschengieser SS, Carlos GF, Santarelli MT. Low intensity oral anticoagulation plus low dose aspirin versus high intensity oral anticoagulation alone: a randomized trial in patients with mechanical prosthetic heart valves. J Thorac Cardiovasc Surg 1997;113:910–6.

230. Chesbro JH, Fuster V, Elveback LR. Trial of combined warfarin plus dipyridamole or aspirin therapy in prosthetic heart valve replacement: danger of aspirin compared with dipyridamole. Am J Cardiol 1983;51:1537–41.

231. Turpie A, Gent M, Laupacis A, et al. Comparison of aspirin with placebo in patients treated with warfarin after heart valve replacement. N Engl J Med 1993;329:524–9.

232. Sullivan JM, Harken DE, Gorlin R. Effect of dipyridamole on the incidence of arterial emboli after cardiac valve replacement. Circulation 1969;39(Suppl):I149–53.

233. McGrath L, Gonzalez-Lavin L, Edlredge W, et al. Thromboembolic and other events following valve replacement in a pediatric population treated with antiplatelet agents. Ann Thorac Surg 1987;43:285–7.

234. LeBlanc J, Sett S, Vince D. Antiplatelet therapy in children with left-sided mechanical prostheses. Eur J Cardiothorac Surg 1993;7:211–5.

235. Milano A, Vouhe PR, Baillot-Vernant F, et al. Late results after left-sided cardiac valve replacement in children. J Thorac Cardiovasc Surg 1986;92:218–25.

236. Human DG, Joffe HS, Fraser CB, Barnard CN. Mitral valve replacement in children. J Thorac Cardiovasc Surg 1982;83:873–7.

237. Champsaur G, Robin J, Trone F, et al. Mechanical valve in aortic position is a valid option in children and adolescents. Eur J Cardiothorac Surg 1997;11:117–22.

238. Marzinotto V, Monagle P, Chan AKC, et al. Capillary whole blood monitoring of oral anticoagulants in children in outpatient clinics and home setting. Pediatr Cardiol. In press 1999.

239. Hwang B, Lin CY, Hsieh KS, et al. High-dose intravenous gammaglobulin therapy in Kawasaki disease. Acta Paediat 1989;30:15–22.

240. Furosho K, Kamiya T, Nakano H. Intravenous gamma globulin for Kawasaki disease. Acta Paediatr Jpn 1991;33:799–804.

241. Harada K. Intravenous gamma globulin in Kawasaki disease. Acta Paediatr Jpn 1991;33:805–10.

242. Chung KJ, Fulton DR, Lapp R, et al. One year followup of cardiac and coronary artery disease in infants and children with Kawasaki disease. Am Heart J 1988;115:1263–7.

243. Chung KJ, Brandt L, Fulton DR, Kreidberg MBI. Cardiac and coronary artery involvement in infants and children from New England with mucocutaneous lymph node syndrome (Kawasaki disease). Am J Cardiol 1982;50:136–42.

244. Engle MA, Fatica NS, Bussel JB, et al. Clinical trial of single-dose intravenous gamma globulin in acute Kawasaki disease. Am J Dis Child 1989;143:1300–4.

245. Lee BW, Tay JSH, Yip WCL, et al. Kawasaki syndrome in Chinese children. Ann Trop Paediatr 1989;3:147–51.

246. Villain E, Kachaner J, Sidi D, et al. Essai de prevention des anevrismes coronaires de la maladie de Kawasaki

par echanges plasmatiques ou perfusion d'immunoglobulines. Arch Fr Pediatr 1987;44:79–83.

247. Fournier PS, Doesburg V, Guerin R. La maladie de Kawasaki: Aspects epidemiologiques et manifestations cardio-vasculaires. Arch Mal Coeur Vaiss 1985;78:693–8.

248. Takahashi M, Mason W, Lewis AB. Regression of coronary aneurysms in patients with Kawasaki syndrome. Circulation 1987;75:387–94.

249. Kryzer TC, Derkay CS. Kawasaki disease: five year experience at Children's National Medical Center. Int J Pediatr Otorhinolaryngol 1992;23:211–20.

250. Cullen S, Duff DF, Denham B. Cardiovascular manifestation in Kawasaki disease. Ir J Med Sci 1989;158:253–6.

251. Meade RH, Brandt L. Manifestation of Kawasaki disease in New York outbreak of 1980. J Pediatr 1982;100:558–62.

252. Nakashima M, Matsushima M, Matsuoka H, et al. High-dose gammaglobulin therapy for Kawasaki disease. J Pediatr 1987;110:710–2.

253. Barron KS, Murphy DJ, Silverman BD. Treatment of Kawasaki syndrome: a comparison of two dosage regimens of intravenously administered immunoglobulin. J Pediatr 1990;117:638–44.

254. Akagi T, Rose V, Benson LN, et al. Outcome of coronary aneurysms after Kawasaki disease. J Pediatr 1992;121:689–94.

255. Beitzke A, Zobel G. Koronaraneurysm bei Kawasaki-Syndromm: Inzidenz und prognose. Klin Padiatr 1989;201:33–9.

256. Newburger JW, Takashashi M, Beiser AS. A single intravenous infusion of gamma globulin therapy as compared with four infusion in the treatment of acute Kawasaki syndrome. N Engl J Med 1991;324:1633–9.

257. Colloridi V, Di Piero G, Colloridi G. Aspetti cardiogiel della malattia di Kawasaki. Pediatr Med Chir 1988;10:51–4.

258. Ichida F, Fatica NS, Engle MA. Coronary artery involvement in Kawasaki syndrome in Manhattan, New York: risk factors and role of aspirin. Pediatrics 1987;80:828–35.

259. Ogino H, Ogawa M, Harima Y. Clinical evaluation of gammaglobulin preparation for the treatment of Kawasaki disease. Prog Clin Biol Res 1987;250:555–6.

260. Schaad UB, Odermatt K, Stocker FP, et al. Das Kawasaki-Syndrom. Schweiz Med Wochenschr 1990;120:539–47.

261. Eckman MH, Levine HJ, Deeb N, Pauker SC. Making decisions about antithrombotic therapy in heart disease: decision analytic and cost-effectiveness issues. Chest 1998;114:699S–714S.

262. Laupacis A, Albers G, Dalen JE, et al. Antithrombotic therapy in atrial fibrillation. Chest 1998;114:579S–89S.

263. Cerebral Embolism Study Group. Immediate anticoagulantion of embolic stroke: brain hemorrhage and management options. Stroke 1983;14:668–76.

264. Hylek EM, Singer DE. Risk factors for intracranial hemorrhage in outpatients taking warfarin. Ann Intern Med 1994;120:897–902.

265. The European Atrial Fibrillation Trial Study Group. Optimal oral anticoagulant therapy in patients with nonrheumatic atrial fibrillation and recent cerebral ischemia. N Engl J Med 1995;333:5–10.

266. The Stroke Prevention in Atrial Fibrillation Investigators. Bleeding during antithrombotic therapy in patients with atrial fibrillation. Arch Intern Med 1996;156:409–16.

267. van der Meer FJM, Rosendaal FR, Vandenbroucke JP, and Briet E. 1993. Bleeding complications in oral anticoagulant therapy. An analysis of risk factors. Arch Int Med 153:1557–62.

268. Palareti G, Leali N, Coccheri S, Poggi M. Bleeding complications of oral anticoagulant treatment: an inception-cohort, prospective collaborative study (IS-COAT). Lancet 1996;348:423–8.

269. Fihn SD, Callahan CM, Martin DC, et al. The risk for and severity of bleeding complications in elderly patients treated with warfarin. Ann Intern Med 1996;124:970–9.

270. Stroke Prevention in Atrial Fibrillation Investigators. Patients with nonvalvular atrial fibrillation at low risk of stroke during treatment with aspirin: stroke prevention in atrial fibrillation III study. JAMA 1998;279:1273–6.

271. Manning WJ, Leeman DE, Gotch P. Pulsed doppler evaluation of atrial mechanical function after electrical cardioversion of atrial fibrillation. J Am Coll Cardiol 1989;13:617–23.

272. Hall S, Barr W, Lie JT. Takayasu arteritis: a study of 32 North American patients. Medicine 1985;64:6489–99.

273. Lupi-Herrara E, Sanchez-Torres G, Marcushamer J. Takayasu's arteritis: clinical study of 107 cases. Am Heart J 1977;93:94–103.

274. Tech PC, Tan LK, Chia BL. Nonspecific aorto-arteritis in Singapore with special reference to hypertension. Am Heart J 1978;95:683–95.

275. Cupps TR, Fauci A. The vasculitides. Anonymous W.B. Saunders, Philadelphia. 107–15.

276. Gupta SK, Khanna MN, Lahiri TK. Involvement of cardiac valves in Takayasu's arteritis. Report of 7 cases. Indian Heart J 1980;32:148–55.

277. Andrew M, Marzinotto V, Pencharz P, et al. A cross-sectional study of catheter-related thrombosis in chil-

dren receiving total parenteral nutrition at home. J Pediatr 1995;126:358–63.

278. Hathaway WE. Use of antiplatelet agents in pediatric hypercoagulable states. Am J Dis Child 1984;138: 301–4.

279. Bern MM, Lokich JJ, Wallach SR, et al. Very low doses of warfarin can prevent thrombosis in central venous catheters. A randomized prospective trial. Ann Intern Med 1990;112:423–8.

280. Fordyce M, Baker A, Staddon G. Efficacy of fixed minidose warfarin prophylaxis in total hip replacement. BMJ 1991;303:219–20.

281. Marlar R, Montgomery R, Broekmans A, et al. Diagnosis and treatment of homozygous protein C deficiency: report of the Working Party on Homozygous Protein C and Protein S, International Committee on Thrombosis and Haemostasis. J Pediatr 1989; 114:528–34.

282. O'Reilly RA, Trager WF. Stereoselective interaction of phenylbutazone with 13C/12C-labelled racemates of warfarin in man. Fed Proc 1978;37:545.

283. Lewis RJ, Trager WF, Chan KK. Warfarin: stereochemical aspects of its metabolism and the interaction with phenylbutazone. J Clin Invest 1974;53: 1607–17.

284. Toon S, Low LK, Gibaldi M. The warfarin-sulfinpyrazone interaction: stereochemcial considerations. Clin Pharmacol Ther 1986;39:15–24.

285. O'Reilly RA. The stereoselective interaction of warfarin and metronidazole in man. N Engl J Med 1976; 295:354–7.

286. Toon S, Hopkins KJ, Garstang FM, et al. The warfarin-cimetidine interaction: stereochemical considerations. Br J Clin Pharmacol 1986;21:245–6.

287. Graham DY, Smith JL. Aspirin and the stomach. Ann Intern Med 1986;104:390–8.

288. Haroon Y, Shearer MJ, Rahim S, et al. The content of phylloquinone (vitamin K_1) in human milk, cow's milk and infant formula foods determined by high-performance liquid chromatography. J Nutr 1982;112:1105–17.

289. Greer FR, Mummah-Schendel LL, Marshall S, Suttie JW. Vitamin K_1 (phylloquinone) and Vitamin K_2 (menaquinone) status in newborns during the first week of life. Pediatrics 1988;81:137–40.

290. Shearer MJ, Barkhan P, Rahim S, Stimmler L. Plasma vitamin K_1 in mothers and their newborn babies. Lancet 1982;2:460–3.

291. Von Kries R, Shearer MJ, McCarthy PT, et al. Vitamin K_1 content of maternal milk: Influence of the stage of lactation, lipid composition, and vitamin K_1 supplements given to the mother. Pediatr Res 1987; 22:513–7.

292. Lehman M, Kolb K, Barnhart G, et al. Warfarin absorption in a patient with short-bowel syndrome. Clin Pharm 1985;4:325–6.

293. Kuhn T, Garnett W, Wells B, Karnes H. Recovery of warfarin from an enteral nutrient formula. Am J Hosp Pharm 1989;46:1395–9.

294. Lind SE, Callas PW, Golden EA, et al. Plasma levels of factors II, VII, and X and their relationship to the international normalized ratio during chronic warfarin therapy. Blood Coagul Fibrinolysis 1997;8:48–53.

295. Cortelazzo S, Finazzi G, Viero P, et al. Thrombotic and hemorrhagic complications in patients with mechanical heart valve prosthesis attending an anticoagulation clinic. Thromb Haemost 1993;69(4): 316–20.

296. Ellis R, Stephens M, Sharp G. Evaluation of a pharmacy-managed warfarin-monitoring service to coordinate inpatient and outpatient therapy. Am J Hosp Pharm 1992;49:387–94.

297. Ansell J, Holden A, Knapic N. Patient self-management of oral anticoagulation guided by capillary (finger stick) whole blood prothrombin times. Arch Intern Med 1989;149:2509–11.

298. Lucas F, Duncan A, Jay R, et al. A novel whole blood capillary technique for measuring the prothrombin time. Am J Clin Pathol 1987;88(4):442–6.

299. Jennings I, Luddington R, Baglin T. Evaluation of the Ciba Corning Biotrack 512 coagulation monitor for the control of oral anticoagulation. J Clin Pathol 1991;44:950–3.

300. Weibert R, Adler D. Evaluation of a capillary whole-blood prothrombin time measurement system. Clin Pharm 1989;8:864–7.

301. White R, McCurdy S, von Marensdorff H, et al. Home prothrombin time monitoring after the initiation of warfarin therapy. Ann Intern Med 1989;111:730–7.

302. McCurdy S, White R. Accuracy and precision of a portable anticoagulation monitor in a clinical setting. Arch Intern Med 1992;152:589–92.

303. Belsey R, Fischer P, Baer D. An evaluation of a whole blood prothrombin analyzer designed for use by individuals without formal laboratory training. J Fam Pract 1991;33:266–71.

304. Becker D, Andrew M, Triplett D. Continued accurate patient prothrombin time self-testing over prolonged duration using the ProTime Microcoagulation system [abstract]. Thromb Haemost 1997;Suppl: PS–2862.

305. Kearon C, Hirsh J. Management of anticoagulation before and after elective surgery. N Engl J Med 1997;336:1506–11.

11

THROMBOLYTIC THERAPY

Thrombolytic therapy has been used in almost every clinical disorder in which intravascular obstruction of blood flow is thought to be pathogenic. The classic clinical scenario is acute myocardial infarction (MI). Since the first use of thrombolytic therapy for this indication in 1958, there have been numerous well-designed randomized controlled trials (RCTs) involving well over 200,000 adults documenting the efficacy and safety of a variety of thrombolytic agents and regimes.[1-4] Other clinical situations in which well-designed RCTs have been performed in adults include massive pulmonary embolism (PE) and some arterial and deep vein thrombosis (DVT).[5-7] Corresponding studies in infants and children have not been conducted for a variety of reasons (Chapter 1), resulting in the extrapolation of adult guidelines. This approach is not likely optimal because of age-dependent differences in the pathophysiology of underlying disorders and overall activity of the fibrinolytic system, which influences the response to thrombolytic agents.[8,9] As well, risk factors for hemorrhagic complications of thrombolytic agents are also age dependent. The aims of this chapter are to discuss (1) available thrombolytic agents and their mechanisms of activity; (2) the effect of developmental hemostasis on thrombolysis; (3) the therapeutic options when using thrombolytic agents; (4) adverse effects and contraindications to thrombolytic therapy; and (5) current guidelines for the use of thrombolytic agents in children. The content of this chapter is based on a comprehensive review of the pediatric literature,[10] a 10-year review of thrombolytic therapy at a single pediatric institution, and, when relevant, information on the use of thrombolytic therapy in adults.

AVAILABLE THROMBOLYTIC AGENTS AND THEIR MECHANISMS OF ACTIVITY

General Information

The in vivo activities of all thrombolytic agents are dependent on the pharmacologic conversion of endogenous plasminogen to plasmin.[11] Plasminogen is present in blood at a 2:1 molar excess over its natural inhibitor, $\alpha_2$antiplasmin (α_2AP). Nonselective activation of plasminogen likely generates enough plasmin to deplete α_2AP, resulting in unregulated plasmin activities. Plasmin, a serine protease with broad substrate specificity, degrades several plasma proteins including fibrinogen, factor (F) V, and FVIII. Plasmin also binds to fibrin via lysine binding sites, which are required for optimal inhibition by α_2AP. Therefore, fibrin-bound plasmin is relatively resistant to degradation, but upon disassociation from fibrin, is rapidly inactivated. Physiologically, plasminogen bound to fibrin is activated by tissue plasminogen activator (TPA), resulting in fibrinolysis without systemic depletion of fibrinogen or α_2AP.

In general, thrombolytic agents may be considered as nonselective plasminogen activators, which include streptokinase (SK), urokinase (UK), and acylated plasminogen-streptokinase complex (APSAC), or more specific fibrin-bound plasminogen activators, which include TPA or its recombinant variants (reteplase, ianoteplase, TNK-rTPA), and single-chain UK-type plasminogen activator (scu-PA), staphylokinase, and vampire bat plasminogen activator (b-PA). The production of fibrin-specific thrombolytic agents is an attempt to mimic the natural fibrinolytic process and achieve maximum fibrinolysis with minimal depletion of fibrinogen and hence reduced clinical bleeding. Alternatively, thrombolytic agents may be classified chronologically. First-generation agents are SK and UK. Second-generation agents include TPA, APSAC, and scu-PA. Third-generation agents include reteplase, TNK-TPA, ianoteplase, staphylokinase, and b-PA. Several of these thrombolytic agents are approved for clinical use.[11,12]

Nonselective Thrombolytic Agents

Streptokinase SK was the first thrombolytic agent to be used in children. SK was isolated in 1933 and characterized as a single-chain polypeptide with a molecular weight of 46 kD (Table 1).[12–15] SK is a proteolytic enzyme produced by β-hemolytic streptococci with an amino terminal sequence homology to trypsin-like serine proteases. Paradoxically, SK has no catalytic sites and cannot cleave peptide bonds. SK is unique among plasminogen activators because the plasminogen-SK complex has plasmin-like activity without plasminogen proteolysis. Stoichiometric amounts of SK and plasminogen (Lys or Glu) combine to form a complex that has plasmin-like activity. The SK-plasminogen complex then converts plasminogen to plasmin directly. The efficiency of this conversion relates to whether Lys or Glu-plasminogen is in the complex because Lys-plasminogen is converted five-fold more effectively than Glu-plasminogen. Proteolytic cleavage of SK and plasminogen within the complex, or exposure of free SK to plasmin, leads to the formation of SK-plasmin complexes. SK-plasmin complexes have increased catalytic activity compared to free plasmin. In addition, SK-plasmin complexes can convert plasminogen directly to plasmin, whereas free plasmin can only convert Glu-plasminogen to Lys-plasminogen. SK-plasmin complexes are relatively resistant to inhibition by $\alpha_2 AP$ and α_2 macroglobulin (α_2M). SK-plasmin(ogen) complexes bind fibrin via the kringle domains of plasmin, leading to activation of fibrin-bound plasminogen and generation of fibrinogen/fibrin degradation products (FDPs), which further enhance SK plasminogen activity. SK has a monophasic half-life in plasma of 18 to 30 minutes. However, the half-life of the lytic effects of SK is 82 to 184 minutes.

In addition, SK plasmin(ogen) complexes activate plasminogen, which degrades circulating fibrinogen, causing a systemic lytic state.

Compared to other thrombolytic agents, SK has several disadvantages.[11] First, patients with recent streptococcal infections or previous exposure to the therapeutic use of SK can develop antibodies that bind to SK, significantly reducing bioavailability. Within days of a dose, concentrations of neutralizing antibodies may increase to levels that are sufficient to completely inactivate a subsequent standard dose of SK. The antibodies persist for up to 1 year in 80% of patients and 2 to 4 years in 50% of patients.[16–18] Second, patients can develop allergic reactions to SK, which include fever, hypotension, urticaria, and bronchospasm and occur with increased frequency on second or subsequent exposures to the drug.[19,20] Hypotensive responses occur in 6% to 8% of patients.[20–23] Third, SK appears to be less efficient at lyzing thrombi in vitro[24] and in vivo compared to other available agents.[25] The only advantage of SK over other currently available thrombolytic agents is cost. If cost were not an issue, SK would not likely continue to be used as a thrombolytic agent.

Urokinase UK was the second thrombolytic agent to be used in children. Human UK, located on chromosome 10, is a single-chain glycoprotein

Table 11–1 Nonselective and Selective Thrombolytic Agents

	MW(kD)	Half-life (Min)	Source
Nonselective			
Streptokinase	46	82–184	β-hemolytic streptococcus
Urokinase	54	61	Fetal kidney
APSAC	131	94	Modified from SK
Selective			
TPA	68	46	Endothelial cells
Reteplase	40	15	Mutant from TPA
TNK-rTPA	58	20	Mutant from TPA
Staphylokinase	15	6	*Staphylococcus aureus*

MW = molecular weight; KD = kilodaltons; APSAC = acylated plasminogen-streptokinase complex; SK = streptokinase; TPA = tissue plasminogen activator.

with a molecular weight of 54 kD (see Table 11–1).[26,27] Single-chain UK (Scu-PA) undergoes limited hydrolysis by plasmin or kallikrein to form double-chain UK. The double-chain configuration of UK consists of a heavy-chain, which contains the serine protease active site, and a light chain.[28] UK has no fibrin specificity. UK was initially purified from human urine and subsequently from fetal kidney cell cultures.[29,30] Purified UK preparations are nonantigenic and nonpyrogenic and may be associated with reduced coagulation abnormalities compared to SK, although clinical bleeding occurs at a similar rate. Recombinant UK is currently available, but limited by cost.[31]

In 1999, the Federal Drug Administration (FDA) issued a drug warning about UK (Abbokinase, Abbott Laboratories). Abbokinase is produced from primary cell cultures of kidney cells harvested postmortem from human neonates. The kidney cells used in manufacture were harvested postmortem from neonates from populations at high risk for a variety of infectious diseases. The FDA warned that the screening of potential donors was inadequate, both in terms of questions to determine infectious status and viral serology tests performed. Further, the storage and handling may have permitted infectious contamination, and the viral inactivation procedures were unvalidated. Although the

FDA was unaware of any cases of infectious diseases attributed to the use of UK, they recommended "that Abbokinase be reserved for only those situations where a physician has considered the alternatives and has determined that the use of Abbokinase is critical to the care of a specific patient in a specific situation." Prior to the FDA warning, UK was the agent most widely used to unblock central venous lines (CVLs) in children. The use of UK has declined dramatically since the FDA warning, and the future of the harvested preparation is yet to be determined.

The initial and terminal half-lives of UK are 12 and 61 minutes, respectively, with pharmacokinetics following a two compartmental model involving intravascular and interstitial compartments. Hepatic clearance is the main mechanism of removal of UK from blood.[32] UK is more efficient than SK at lysing thrombi in vitro in plasmas with decreased concentrations of plasminogen, such as occur in many pediatric patients (Figure 11–1).[24] UK is approximately seven times more expensive than SK.

Acylated plasminogen-streptokinase complex Rapid inactivation and clearance from blood was recognized as a limiting factor in the efficiency of SK-plasmin(ogen) complex catalytic activities. APSAC is a chemically modified derivative in which SK is noncovalently associated with plasminogen,

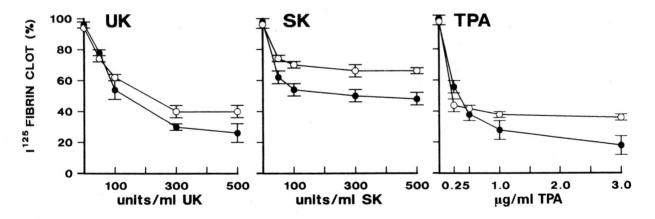

Figure 11–1 Remaining ^{125}I-fibrin in the presence of increasing amounts of UK, SK, and TPA in a fibrin clot system (washed cord[125]I-fibrin clots in cord plasma: C/C, [o-o]) and similar adult system (A/A, [•-•]). The cord system was resistant to the effects of all three thrombolytic agents compared to the adult system (mean ± SEM, p < .01).

UK = urokinase; SK = streptokinase; TPA = tissue plasminogen activator; SEM = standard error of mean.

Reproduced with permission.[24]

and the active site of plasminogen is covalently modified with a *p*-anisoyl group (see Table 11–1).[12,14,33] APSAC binds fibrin through the plasminogen kringle domains. The molecular mass of APSAC is 131 kD. In contrast to SK, APSAC can be given as a rapid intravenous bolus without causing significant hypotension. APSAC has a considerably prolonged plasma half-life (94 minutes) compared to SK, although the exact mechanism is unknown. Unfortunately, APSAC remains antigenic, has a similar potential to cause allergic reactions as SK, and is no more efficient clinically.[34] APSAC has been assessed in an in vitro model of clot lysis in adults[35–37] but there are no publications describing its use in children.

Selective Thrombolytic Agents

Tissue plasminogen activator TPA was the third thrombolytic agent to be used in children starting in the late 1980s. Human TPA, which is located on chromosome 8, is a single-chain glycoprotein with a molecular weight of 68 kD (see Table 11–1).[12,14,38–40] TPA is produced by endothelial cells as a single-chain polypeptide that can be cleaved by plasmin, kallikrein, and FXa to form a two-chain molecule. Two-chain TPA has reduced catalytic activity compared to single-chain TPA in the absence of fibrin but has equivalent catalytic activity in the presence of fibrin. The TPA molecule contains five distinct domains: a fibrinonectin finger-like domain, an epidermal growth factor-like domain, two kringle-like domains, and a serine protease domain. The functions of these domains have been determined by the use of deletion and inclusion mutants, and specific domains are responsible for fibrin binding, plasma clearance, cell surface binding, and stimulation of plasminogen activation by fibrin.[11,41] Fibrin binding increases the catalytic activity of TPA several hundredfold.[42–44] Clearance of TPA from the blood is by specific hepatic receptors. Using a two-compartment model, the initial half-life is 4 to 5 minutes, with a terminal half-life of 46 minutes.[45] TPA is not immunogenic and no serious allergic reactions have been reported. TPA was initially thought to be a superior thrombolytic agent because of fibrin specificity, avoidance of systemic fibrinogenolysis, and rapid lysis of thrombi.[46] How-

ever, these benefits were not consistently confirmed in clinical trials and TPA can result in a systemic lytic state. The likely explanation for the generalized lytic state is that TPA also activates plasminogen bound to the (DD)E fibrin complexes, which are the major degradation products of cross-linked fibrin. Activation of (DD)E-bound plasminogen generates free plasmin, causing a systemic lytic state. TPA is more efficient than SK and similar to UK at lyzing thrombi in vitro in plasmas with decreased concentrations of plasminogen such as in newborns (see Figure 11–1).[24]

Reteplase Reteplase (40 kD), a recombinant mutant of TPA, lacks the finger, growth factor, and kringle domains of the parent molecule, which reduces the affinity for fibrin and endothelial cells and increases the half-life (see Table 11–1).[12,14,47] The prolonged half-life enables reteplase to be given as a double bolus rather than an infusion.[48,49] Studies in animals suggest that reteplase results in a more rapid and complete thrombolysis of clots compared to TPA. However, in clinical trials, reteplase is no more effective than TPA and there is no significant experience of reteplase in children.

TNK-rTPA TNK-rTPA is another mutant of the parent TPA molecule with a molecular weight of 58 kD (see Table 11–1).[50] Alteration of the plasminogen activator inhibitor (PAI) binding site and manipulation of the glycosylation sites reduce plasma clearance and increase fibrin specificity. The plasma half-life is approximately 20 minutes.[51–53] Clinical studies are in progress in adults and there is no experience of TNKI-rTPA in children.

Staphylokinase Staphylokinase is a 15 kD protein produced by *Staphylococcus aureus,* which forms a stoichiometric complex with plasminogen and has a plasma half-life of 6 minutes.[54,55] In contrast to SK, this complex can be inhibited by α_2AP, and has significantly increased fibrin specificity (see Table 11–1).[56,57] However, relatively little clinical work has been performed to date and there is no information in children.

Recombinant single-chain urokinase type plasminogen activator Recombinant scu-PA can be obtained from *Eschericha coli.*[58] While the molecule is converted by hydrolysis to two-chain UK, there is evidence that scu-PA has intrinsic plasminogen-activating activity, and that for in vivo thrombolysis conversion of scu-PA to UK is less important. Scu-PA has significant fibrin specificity, although the exact mechanism for this is unknown. The pharmacokinetics and plasma clearance are similar to UK.[11] There is no experience of scu-PA in children.

Influence of Developmental Hemostasis on Thrombolytic Therapy

Neonates Physiologic plasma concentrations of components of the fibrinolytic system (TPA, PAI-1, α_2AP, plasminogen, and histidine-rich glycoprotein (HRGP)) are profoundly age dependent with the most significant differences occurring during the neonatal period (Chapter 2).[59–73] At birth, plasma concentrations of plasminogen are decreased to 50% of adult values, α_2AP to 80% of adult values, and both TPA and PAI-1 are increased to almost twice adult values. Plasma concentrations of TPA and PAI-1 in cord blood are less than those in samples from newborns, likely reflecting release of TPA and PAI-1 from endothelial cells during the birth process.[59,60,71,73] PAI-2 levels are detectable in cord blood but at concentrations that are significantly less than for pregnant women.[74] Plasminogen, like fibrinogen, exists in a fetal form at birth and is characterized by two glycoforms with an increased amount of sialic acid and mannose.[75,76] The latter does not seem to interfere with the catalytic activities of plasmin but may interfere with cell surface activation of plasminogen to plasmin.[75] The overall effect is that the physiologic concentrations and activities of components of the fibrinolytic system at birth result in a decreased capacity to generate plasmin.[24,71,75]

Childhood During childhood, plasma concentrations of plasminogen and α_2AP are similar to adults while concentrations of TPA are decreased by almost twofold and PAI-1 increased twofold.[77] The latter result in a decreased ratio of TPA to PAI-1 in children (0.37) compared to adults (1.36). In addition, there is a poor response to venous occlusion in children compared to adults, suggesting that the overall capacity of the fibrinolytic system to respond is decreased during childhood.[77,78]

Response to Thrombolytic Agents Endogenous plasma concentrations of plasminogen are critically important to the overall effect of exogenous thrombolytic agents because the activities of thrombolytic agents are mediated by converting endogenous plasminogen to plasmin. At birth, plasma concentrations of plasminogen are reduced to 50% of adult values (21 mg/100 mL) in healthy term infants and to a greater extent in premature infants.[59,61] Plasma concentrations of plasminogen gradually increase during childhood (Figure 11–2).

Decreased plasma concentrations of plasminogen in newborns slow the generation of plasmin[71] and reduce the thrombolytic effects of SK, UK, TPA, and APSAC as assessed in an in vitro fibrin clot system (Figure 11–1).[24,35–37,79] A similar response occurs in children with acquired plasminogen deficiency.[79] Ries et al[80] studied the kinetics of in vitro fibrinolysis in a microtitre clot lysis assay following the addition of different concentrations of SK, UK, and recombinant (r)TPA to plasmas from children and adults. Following clot formation,

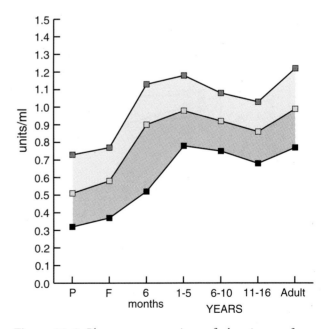

Figure 11–2 Plasma concentrations of plasminogen from fetal to adult life. P and F data are taken from day 1 of life. Data are mean ± 2 SD.

P= premature; F = full term.

a rapid lysis was observed with all thrombolytic agents. The 50% lysis time correlated to the plasminogen activator dose and showed no differences among normal adults, children aged 1 to 6 years, and children aged 7 to 14 years. Newborns demonstrated a significantly prolonged lysis time (50%) with all UK concentrations. The 50% lysis time with rTPA and SK was significantly prolonged only at high concentrations, whereas there were no differences at lower concentrations. Supplementation of deficient plasmas with plasminogen increases the thrombolytic effect of SK, UK, and TPA (Figure 11–3).[24,35,79] Although there are other age-dependent differences in the fibrinolytic system, they are not likely to influence the response to pharmacologic amounts of thrombolytic agents.

Therapeutic Options

Choice of Thrombolytic Agents   There are no studies that compare the cost, efficacy, and safety of different thrombolytic agents in children. The comparative costs of SK, UK, and TPA are shown in Table 11–2. Although SK is the cheapest of the three agents, SK has the potential for allergic reactions and is likely less effective in children with physiologic or acquired deficiencies of plasminogen. UK was widely used for pediatric patients, but the

FDA warning has substantially diminished the use of UK in North America. TPA has become the agent of choice in children for several reasons, including the FDA warning regarding UK, experimental evidence of improved clot lysis in vitro compared to UK and SK, fibrin specificity, and low immunogenicity.[24] However, TPA is considerably more expensive than either SK or UK, and the increased in vitro clot lysis by TPA has not been extended into clinical trials in children. There is minimal or no experience with other thrombolytic agents in children.

Administration of Thrombolytic Therapy

The administration of thrombolytic therapy can be considered as either systemic, infused through a peripheral venous access site, or local, infused through a catheter with its tip located in close proximity to the thrombus. Catheter-directed infusions may be given through either multilumen or single-lumen catheters. There are numerous dosing schedules for children, which include bolus dosing, continuous infusion, or pulse spray infusions.

Route of Administration
Adults   The rationale for the choice of route of administration for thrombolytic agents in adults is

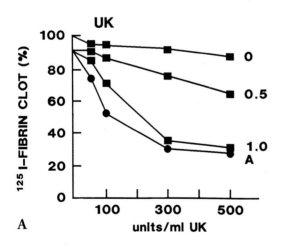
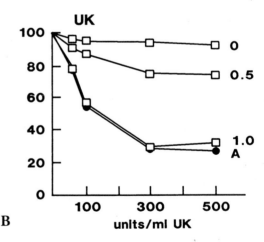

Figure 11–3 Percent remaining fibrin clot. *A,* washed ^{125}I-fibrin clots in plasminogen-depleted adult plasma. Increasing amounts of exogenous purified adult Glu-plasminogen was added in doses of 0, 0.5, and 1.0 units/mL (■—■). Original adult system (●—●). *B,* washed cord ^{125}I-fibrin clot in plasminogen-depleted cord plasma. Increasing amounts of exogenous purified cord Glu-plasminogen was added in doses of 0, 0.5, and 1.0 units/mL (□—□). Original adult system (●—●).

Reproduced with permission.[24]

Table 11–2 Comparative Costs of Recombinant Tissue Plasminogen Activator, Streptokinase, and Urokinase

	Vial Size	Approximate Cost (Canadian Dollars)
UK	5000 units	45
SK	1.5 million units	360
	0.75 million units	180
rTPA	100 mg	2700
	50 mg	1350

rTPA = recombinant tissue plasminogen activator; SK= streptokinase; UK = urokinase (UK).

relevant to the treatment of children. Initial trials in adults with MI showed that intracoronary administration of thrombolytic agents into coronary arteries improved reperfusion and overall survival.[25] Subsequent studies confirmed the effectiveness of intracoronary thrombolytic therapy, and suggested that lower local doses may have had a decreased risk of bleeding compared to systemic doses.[81–89] However, there were several potential advantages for systemically administered thrombolytic therapy that led to further studies. These advantages included shorter time to maximize myocardial rescue; removal of the access site for catheterization, which is a major site for bleeding; and generalizability of the benefits of thrombolytic therapy to hospitals where cardiac catheterization (CC) facilities are not available, which constitutes the vast majority of patients. Currently, thrombolytic therapy for adults with MI and massive PE is administered via peripheral veins.

In contrast, thrombolytic therapy for adults with acute peripheral arterial obstruction is usually administered locally via a catheter inserted at a site distant from the occlusion, usually through the contralateral femoral artery.[90] In contrast to patients with MI, time is not as crucial in determining outcome. The tip of the catheter is placed within the thrombus, and a guide wire passed through the thrombus to determine the likelihood of thrombolysis and to create channels to enhance the delivery of the thrombolytic agent within the clot. Thrombolytic therapy is terminated when successful lysis of the clot is demonstrated angiographically, usually

after 4 to 8 hours of therapy. Perfusion thrombolytic therapy is rarely continued for longer than 12 to 24 hours due to an increasing resistance to thrombolytic therapy due to consumption of endogenous plasminogen or the "plasminogen steal."[91] A number of recent large prospective trials support the use of catheter-directed thrombolytic therapy over surgery as initial treatment for acute lower limb ischemia. These studies confirm reduced mortality rates, improved limb salvage, and cost effectiveness for catheter-directed thrombolysis compared to primary surgical intervention.[90,92,93] The only studies that have directly compared catheter-directed to systemic thrombolysis have reported similar revascularization and bleeding rates.[94]

Children Children rarely suffer from MI, except in rare circumstances such as congenital defects compromising the circulation to the coronary arteries or occlusion of coronary artery aneurysms due to Kawasaki[95–101] or Takayasu's disease.[102,103] Clinical trials assessing the benefits of local versus systemic thrombolytic therapy are not likely feasible in children with MI, even with multicenter international participation. However, there is no obvious reason that conclusions of trials in adults with MI cannot be extrapolated to children. Short high-dose peripheral administration of a thrombolytic agent would likely be similarly effective in children with MI as for adults except for the risk of bleeding.

In contrast to MI, the approach for adults with acute peripheral arterial occlusion is not likely optimal for children. The majority of peripheral arterial occlusions are secondary to femoral artery catheters in small patients. In this scenario, the catheter has usually been removed prior to the decision to treat with thrombolytic therapy. Inserting a catheter from the contralateral femoral artery may in fact induce more thromboembolic events (TEs). The risk of damage to the vessel is likely increased in children due to small vessel size and the relatively large size of catheters. In addition, bleeding from a fresh puncture site is frequent and can be life threatening due to the small blood volume in small infants. Even if the catheter remained in situ, the tip of the catheter would likely be proximal to the thrombus and thrombolytic therapy given through the catheter could just as effectively be administered systemically. The majority of papers reporting successful thrombolysis for femoral artery TEs following CC in children are based upon systemic, not local, thrombolytic therapy.

Thrombolytic therapy is used occasionally for venous TEs in children. From 1966 to 1997, there were 70 cases reported in the English literature of local thrombolytic therapy in children, excluding femoral artery TEs following CC and low-dose thrombolysis to unblock CVLs.[104–139] Complete or partial lysis was achieved in 70% of cases, with major bleeding occurring in 11% of children. A recent level IV study reported successful lysis in only one of seven patients and five major complications in three patients.[140]

At this time, there is no evidence to suggest that there is an advantage of local over systemic thrombolytic therapy in children. Local therapy may be appropriate for catheter-related TEs when the catheter is already in situ; however, the site of the TE in relation to the catheter tip should be considered.

Catheter-directed thrombolysis Catheter-directed thrombolysis for adult peripheral vascular disease usually involves placement of catheters such that the tip is situated within the thrombus. With effective lysis of the clot, a single-lumen catheter frequently needs repositioning with the aid of a guidewire. The procedure is time consuming, and frequent manipulation of the catheter potentially increases the complication rate. Recently, multiple side hole multilumen catheters have been developed. Catheters are placed via a guidewire across the entire length of the thrombus. Thrombolytic agents can then be infused simultaneously over the whole length of a thrombosed vessel, eliminating the need for repeated catheter manipulations. Cohort studies report equivocal lysis rates with conventional catheter-directed lysis. A potential problem is that the extremely small caliber of the multiple lumens makes injection of contrast for follow-up angiography more difficult. There are isolated case reports of thrombolysis via multi-lumen catheter use in children.[141]

Infusion techniques Conventional thrombolytic therapy is given as a continuous infusion, with or without an initial bolus. A variety of dosage regimes are used and the details discussed subsequently. Alternatively, single large bolus doses of thrombolytics have been advocated by some authors. Recent experimental evidence suggests that mechanical methods of thrombolysis can be used to augment pharmacologic thrombolysis. Application of 0.5 to 1 MHz ultrasound at greater than 0.5 W/cm^2 is known to accelerate fibrinolysis in vitro and in animal models, but unacceptable tissue heating occurs and tissue penetration is limited. Use of 40 kHz at greater than 25 W/cm^2 improves fibrinolysis in vitro with little heating and good tissue penetration in initial animal studies.[142,143] Clinical data at this time remain sparse. One method of combining physical and pharmacologic therapy is pulse spray thrombolysis.[144–146] Pulse spray pharmacomechanical thrombolysis consists of brief high-pressure pulsed injections of concentrated fibrinolytic agent throughout the length of a clot via a multiside hole catheter. The high-pressure pulses macerate the thrombus, increasing the contact area available for effective thrombolysis to occur. The advantages of pulse spray therapy are said to be rapid thrombolysis, regardless of the age of the TE. However, no comparative trials have been performed with other thrombolytic regimes. The technique is currently not in widespread clinical use and there are no reported cases in children.

Table 11–3 Bolus and Maintenance Doses and Thrombolytic Therapy Duration for Femoral Artery Thromboembolic Events in Children

	Bolus	*Maintenance*	*Median Duration (Range)*
UK	0–15,000 U/kg	440–50,000 U/kg/hr	48 hours (10 hours–3 weeks)
SK	0–10,000 U/kg	50–3,000 U/kg/hr	24 hours (2 hours–6 days)
TPA	0–2 mg	0.06–0.6 mg/kg/hr	4 hours (2 hours–6 days)

UK = urokinase; SK = streptokinase; TPA = tissue plasminogen activator.

Dose and Duration of Therapy

There are no studies in children comparing the efficacy, safety, and dose schedules of currently available thrombolytic agents in the treatment of either venous or arterial TEs. Consequently, there is a wide range of dose schedules reported for each thrombolytic agent. In general, these are extrapolations of adult doses, based on weight. The administration of thrombolytic agents in children can be classified as (1) "low-dose" regimes administered locally to restore patency to blocked CVLs; (2) "systemic" dose therapy administered peripherally to treat large-vessel TEs; and (3) "catheter-directed" therapy with low doses of thrombolytic therapy.

Low-Dose Thrombolytic Therapy for Restoration of Central Venous Line Patency
Low-dose thrombolytic therapy is frequently instilled into CVLs that are no longer patent for the purpose of restoring CVL patency and salvaging venous access. Classically, the CVL will no longer bleed back or flush, and a small volume of thrombolytic agent, often approximately equal to the dead space of the CVL, is forced into the CVL and left for a period of time prior to being aspirated or flushed. Historically, the most commonly used drug for this purpose was UK, with reports described in at least five case series and 220 patients.[147–151] Doses reported in the literature vary from 1500 to 10,000 units per CVL lumen diluted in approximately 2 mL. Usually, the UK is left in the CVL for 2 to 4 hours with reported ranges of 5 minutes to 12 hours. Most reports suggest an attempt at aspiration following the installation time of UK. However, other protocols suggest flushing of the CVL following the period of time of local instillation. The success rate of local UK for the re-establishment of CVL patency varies from 59% to 92%, but with most studies reporting a patency restoration rate of over 80%. Since the FDA warning about the potential viral contamination of human UK preparations, the use of UK has become almost nonexistent in North America.

An alternative to UK for the purpose of restoration of CVL patency is TPA. However, there is limited clinical experience with TPA for this purpose and only adults have been studied. The dose of TPA studied for the purpose of restoration of CVL patency is 2 mg in 2 mL instilled into the CVL for 2 to 4 hours. In one cohort study, TPA was successful in five of six patients at re-establishing patency after UK had failed in all patients.[152] The only RCT of thrombolytic therapy in patients compared 2 mg of TPA to 10,000 units of UK, with both agents left in situ for 2 hours. Patency was restored in 89% of CVLs treated with TPA compared to 59% of those treated with UK.[153]

SK is not recommended for the purpose of restoring CVL patency because children often require multiple treatments, and the risk of an allergic reaction is significant. If SK is used, the usual dose is 10,000 units/3 mL instilled into the CVL for a period of 2 hours prior to withdrawal.

Systemic Thrombolytic Therapy
Over 340 children have been described in the literature who have received systemic doses of thrombolytic therapy.[80,101,104,107,113,117,125,128,154–182] The most common indication is femoral artery thrombi following CC. The doses are described in Table 11–3.

The average duration of therapy differed between the different thrombolytic agents. The median duration of therapy for TPA was 4 hours, whereas the median durations for SK and UK were 24 and 48 hours, respectively (Figure 11–4). The current trend for thrombolytic therapy in adult

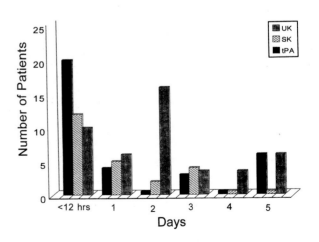

Figure 11–4 Duration of therapy for children treated with either urokinase, streptokinase, or tissue plasminogen activator.

Reproduced with permission.[10]

Table 11–4 Systemic Thrombolytic Therapy for Pediatric Patients*

	Bolus	Maintenance	Duration	Monitoring
UK	4400 U/kg	4400 U/kg/hr	6–12 hours	Fibrinogen, TCT, PT, APTT
SK	2000 U/kg	2000 U/kg/hr	6–12 hours	Same
TPA	None	0.1–0.6 mg/kg/hr	6–12 hours	Same

*Start heparin therapy either during or immediately upon completion of thrombolytic therapy. A loading dose of heparin may be omitted. The length of time for optimal maintenance is uncertain. Values provided are starting suggestions; some patients may respond to longer or shorter courses of therapy.

UK = urokinase; TCT = thrombin clothing time; PT = prothrombin time; APTT = activated partial thromboplastin time; SK = streptokinase; TPA = tissue plasminogen activator.

populations is towards short-term therapy, often administered as an initial bolus followed by a 3-hour infusion. A significant limitation of thrombolytic agents beyond 24 hours is a depletion of plasminogen, known as the "plasminogen steal."[91] The latter results in a refractory state that limits the response to all thrombolytic agents. The latter is particularly relevant in children with extensive venous TEs where thrombolytic therapy is frequently prolonged for several days. There are no studies that compare the efficacy and safety of the various regimes of thrombolytic therapy in children. Currently recommended guidelines for thrombolytic therapy in children are in Table 11–4.[8]

Catheter-Directed Thrombolytic Therapy

Catheter-directed thrombolytic therapy in children has been reported in just over 100 patients, with the largest series describing 11 patients.[106,111,114,118–120,124,125,127,128,133,134,136,183–185] Many of these papers reported the infusion of thrombolytic therapy through an umbilical artery catheter or CVL that was already in situ, although in some cases, new catheters were inserted specifically for the purpose of local thrombolytic therapy. Approximately 50% of cases used UK, 35% SK, and 15% TPA. The range of doses used is described in Table 11–5. These studies, in the context of the entire literature, do not support the use of specific catheter-directed thrombolysis in children. Rather, the available evidence suggests that the systemic activation of the fibrinolytic system is dose dependent, not site dependent.

Monitoring Thrombolytic Therapy

General Information There are no therapeutic ranges of specific tests that can be used to measure the effects of thrombolytic agents and their clinical efficacy. The correlation between specific hemostatic parameters and the efficacy and safety of thrombolytic therapy is too weak to have useful clinical predictive value. For adult patients being treated for MI or massive PE, laboratory monitoring of thrombolytic activity is not generally used since the dose of thrombolytic agent will not be modified according to laboratory data and the duration of treatment is very short. However, when longer courses of thrombolytic therapy are used, a variety of coagulation tests can be used to monitor the systemic effects and ensure that a fibrinogen/fibrinolytic effect is present. These tests include fibrinogen concentration, thrombin clotting time (TCT), FDPs, and D-dimer.

The fibrinogen concentration usually decreases by at least 25% to 50% in response to systemic doses of thrombolytic therapy. Plasma concentrations of D-dimers and FDPs increase, indicating that there is a response to the thrombolytic agent. If

Table 11–5 Bolus and Infusion Doses and Thrombolytic Therapy Duration for Catheter-Directed Thrombolytic Therapy in Children

	Bolus	Maintenance	Duration
UK	0–4400 U/kg	200–10,000 U/kg/hr	1 hour–9 days
SK	0–2000 U/kg	50–4000 U/kg/hr	24 hours–11 days
TPA	0–0.5 mg/kg	0.01–0.5 mg/kg/hr	3 hours–10 days

UK = urokinase; SK = streptokinase; TPA = tissue plasminogen activator.

fibrinogen concentrations are less than 1.0 g/L, then dose reductions of the thrombolytic agent and infusion of replacement therapy in the form of cryoprecipitate or fresh frozen plasma should be considered. As part of supportive therapy, platelet counts should be maintained over 50,000 x 10⁹/L, and ideally over 100 x 10⁹/L. Measurement of plasma concentrations of plasminogen are useful if prolonged or repeat thrombolysis is being considered.[71,186]

Supportive Care during Thrombolytic Therapy

There are several precautions that should be in place for children receiving thrombolytic therapy in order to minimize the risk of clinically important bleeding, and enhance the chances of successful thrombolysis of the clot. These precautions include (1) no intramuscular injections; (2) minimal manipulation (i.e., physiotherapy, bathing); (3) avoidance of concurrent use of oral anticoagulants or antiplatelet agents; (4) no urinary catheterization, rectal temperatures, or arterial punctures; (5) if venous access is problematic, an indwelling catheter for blood sampling should be placed prior to the initiation of thrombolytic therapy; (6) patients should be located in either an intensive care unit or a designated site where the staff has experience in the use of thrombolytic therapy; (7) sedation should be considered depending on the child and clinical circumstances; (8) there should be clear designation at the bedside that the patient is receiving thrombolytic therapy; and (9) in case of bleeding, compresses, topical thrombin, cryoprecipitate, amicar, and packed red blood cells (PRBCs) should be readily available.[186–188]

Role of Adjuvant Therapy

Unfractionated Heparin

Adults In adult trials of thrombolytic therapy, the relatively high risk of reocclusion provided a rationale for the investigation of adjuvant anticoagulant therapy to improve the success of thrombolysis. In vitro or in animal models, thrombolytic therapy induces a procoagulant state characterized by activation of the coagulation system, generation of thrombin, and reocclusion or extension of the TE in the absence of anticoagulant therapy. The addition of thrombolytic agents to whole blood or recalcified citrated plasma results in accelerated generation of thrombin. The latter result in the generation of fibrinopeptide A, which can be prevented by the concurrent presence of unfractionated heparin (UFH) or plasmin inhibitors.

There are several large trials in adults, including GISSI-2, ISIS 3, and GUSTO, that have addressed the role of adjuvant UFH in vivo.[23,189–191] A systematic review of the data showed that adjuvant UFH led to a modest reduction in death, reinfarction, and PE, but an increased risk of bleeding.[192] Mortality rates in trials of thrombolytic therapy in adults are predominantly confined to trials focused on MI.

Children The crucial issues for adjuvant anticoagulant therapy in children are the probability of reocclusion and bleeding. The risk of reocclusion in children may be similar to adults, given that plasminogen activator-induced thrombin generation is the same in plasminogen-depleted plasma as it is in normal plasma. The effect of adjuvant UFH on the bleeding risk, particularly intracranial hemorrhage (ICH), may be reduced in children compared to adults due to the lack of atheromatous vascular disease. Although ICH may be reduced, major bleeding at other sites may be increased due to the increased frequency of recent invasive procedures performed in children requiring thrombolytic therapy. There are no studies in children that determine the potential benefits or risks of adjuvant UFH therapy during thrombolytic therapy. One approach is to use UFH at doses of 10 to 20 U/kg/hr throughout thrombolytic therapy, particularly if TPA is used because of the increased risk of reocclusion.

Antiplatelet Agents

Adults Concurrent anticoagulant therapy with aspirin has been assessed in some adult trials, particularly those trials assessing mortality following MI (ISIS-2).[20,193] The benefit of aspirin in this patient population likely reflects the improved mortality following MI with aspirin therapy regardless of thrombolytic therapy. A theoretical basis for adjuvant aspirin therapy is the evidence of platelet activation secondary to thrombin generation during thrombolytic therapy.

Children There are no data to support or refute the use of concurrent or subsequent aspirin therapy in association with thrombolytic therapy in children. The only randomized controlled trial in which aspirin was assessed in children was in the prevention of arterial TEs following CC.[194] Aspirin was not shown to have any benefit for these events, which are the most common reason for the use of thrombolytic therapy during childhood. In general, aspirin is not commonly used in children for the prevention or treatment of TEs.

Supplemenation with Plasminogen

Adults The critical importance of the plasminogen concentration in the bathing milieu to the degree of thrombolysis of fibrin clots achieved in adult plasma and whole blood systems has been shown previously.[36,37]

Children As described previously, plasma concentrations of plasminogen are reduced physiologically to approximately 58% of adult values in healthy term infants at birth and 51% of healthy premature infants. Plasma concentrations of plasminogen are likely further reduced in sick infants who require thrombolytic therapy. These populations are important to consider because they constitute the majority of children receiving thrombolytic therapy. Figure 11–1 shows the decreased response to thrombolytic therapy using an in vitro system with cord plasma that mimics the in vivo fibrinolytic system during infancy.[24] Figure 11–3 shows that supplementation with plasminogen increases the response to thrombolytic therapy.[24]

Available sources of plasminogen Plasminogen concentrates are available in Europe but not in North America. The sources available for plasminogen supplementation in North America are fresh frozen plasma (FFP) and cryoprecipitate. The limitation of FFP and cryoprecipitate for replacement therapy is, primarily, the volume of product that is required to increase plasma concentrations of plasminogen to clinically important levels.

Guidelines In the absence of clinical trials in children, the available information suggests that plasminogen supplementation should be considered in two clinical scenarios. First, FFP supplementation should be considered prior or during thrombolytic therapy in neonates to ensure adequate substrate to enable a fibrinolytic response. Second, prolonged thrombolytic therapy is likely to exhaust plasminogen supplies in children more readily than in adults. Although short courses of thrombolytic therapy are the standard of care for adults, prolonged infusions of thrombolytic therapy are commonly used in children. With infusions of thrombolytic therapy over 24 hours, consideration should be given to either monitoring plasminogen concentrations or empiric infusion of FFP (10–20 mL/kg) to optimize effective thrombolysis. Together these observations provide the rationale for clinical trials assessing the potential benefits of plasminogen supplementation in vivo.

Few reports describe the use of plasminogen concentrates in children with plasminogen deficiency.[195,196] One infant with ligneous conjunctivitis was found to be homozygous for the deficiency.[196] Mingers reported three unrelated female children with ligneous conjunctivitis who were found to be homozygous for type I plasminogen deficiency.[195] Infusion of Lys-plasminogen resulted in prompt and adequate plasminogen recovery in all three patients. The infused plasminogen had a short half-life and increased amounts of plasmin-antiplasmin complexes and D-dimer.[195]

Effectiveness of Thrombolytic Therapy

Study Design The majority of the pediatric literature describing thrombolytic therapy in children consists of case reports and small series. These study designs make the assessment of efficacy of thrombolytic therapy difficult because of a strong selection bias with reporting of only successful cases and a lack of uniform evaluation of clot lysis.

Monitoring with Objective Tests Frequently the original diagnosis and the follow-up is clinical, without any objective documentation. For venous TEs, ultrasound is the most commonly used objective test to establish the effectiveness of thrombolytic therapy. Unfortunately, ultrasound is not sensitive for the presence of TEs in the upper central system, which is the location of the majority of venous thrombi in children. For arterial thrombosis, the commonly used objective tests include absent pulses assessed by hand-held Doppler, decreased blood pressure in excess of 10 mmHg compared to the contralateral limb, and, less frequently, assessment by angiography. Only 53% of cases reported in the literature had subsequent objective testing, 24% had outcome assessed only clinically, and in 23% the method of assessment was unable to be determined.

Classification of Outcome for Arterial Thrombosis

Another difficult issue with regard to assessing the effectiveness of thrombolytic therapy is the classification of outcome assessment. For the purposes of this chapter, resolution of symptoms of arterial TEs were classified as none, partial, or complete based upon resolution of the same criteria used to diagnose an arterial thrombus. The classification of complete resolution of arterial thrombosis was dependent on the return of pulse, perfusion, temperature, and blood pressure in the affected limb compared to the contralateral limb. Partial resolution was dependent on some response of pulse, temperature, and perfusion but a persistent blood pressure differential of greater than or equal to 10mmHg between the affected and contralateral limb. Patients failing to meet the criteria for full or partial resolution were considered as treatment failures.

Using these criteria, 81% of reported cases had full resolution, 14% partial resolution, and 5% no resolution.[10] However, these results are likely overly optimistic due to the reporting bias discussed previously. In a 10-year review of thrombolytic therapy at Hospital for Sick Children, Toronto, 88 patients were identified as having received systemic dose thrombolytic therapy for vessel occlusion during the study period. Of 59 patients treated with SK, 33 (59.9%) achieved total clot resolution compared to 23 of 29 with TPA (79.3%) was significantly decreased. Figure 11–4 shows the duration of therapy for each thrombolytic agent. Eighty percent of patients treated with TPA achieved full resolution of symptoms in less than 12 hours of therapy (median duration 4.9 hours). Patients treated with SK required a longer course of treatment with only 37% achieving full resolution within 12 hours, with a median duration of therapy of 17 hours. Further,

prospective appropriately designed studies will be required to more accurately determine the effectiveness of thrombolytic therapy in children.

Bleeding Complications of Thrombolytic Therapy

Mechanisms The major and most serious complication of all thrombolytic agents is bleeding. There are likely several mechanisms that contribute to bleeding during and following thrombolytic therapy. Thrombolytic therapy is associated with hemorrhagic risks that depend on the method of administration, duration, dose, and type of agent used.[197] Commonly, bleeding occurs during treatment as a result of fibrinogenolysis due to nonselective activation of plasminogen by plasminogen activators (SK and UK).[198] Plasminogen activators that selectively activate fibrin-bound plasminogen (TPA) lead to reduced fibrinogenolysis and at least theoretically have decreased bleeding side effects.[197,199] However, large clinical trials have not shown consistent safety from bleeding with fibrin-selective thrombolytic agents (such as alteplase), possibly due to differences in duration or route of administration[198] and effects on platelets within the thrombus.[200] Furthermore, once formed, plasmin can cause vessel wall permeability by damaging endothelial cell membranes, resulting in detachment of cells from the matrix and induced cell lysis.[201] Finally, bleeding may result from effects on platelet IIb/IIIa receptors by aspirin or heparin that are used as adjuvants to the thrombolytic agents.[202]

Incidence and Type

Adults Major bleeding in adults is frequently defined as a decrease in hemoglobin of 2 g/dL over 24 hours, the need for transfusion therapy with PRBCs, and may also be described by site, which includes bleeds in the retroperitoneum and central nervous system (CNS). Bleeding requiring transfusion therapy occurs in approximately 5% of adults, with some variation that mostly reflects the number of invasive procedures performed.[203–209] ICH occurs in 0.4% to 0.8% of adults.[20,23,189,190,204,210–213] Patients with recent surgery, injury, or other vessel damage are at particular risk for major bleeding during thrombolytic therapy. Unfortunately, the increased fibrin specificity of some thrombolytic agents such as TPA has not reduced the incidence of major bleeding. In fact, some trials of TPA, such as the GUSTO-I, reported an increased risk of ICH in adults treated with TPA (0.72%) compared to patients treated with SK (0.54%).

Children The accepted definition of major bleeding in adults has little meaning in children. Hemoglobin values often decrease by more than 2 g/dL in 24 hours due to frequent blood sampling and a small blood volume. Similarly, transfusions of PRBCs are a frequent form of supportive therapy for sick infants and children with marrow suppression, such as secondary to chemotherapy. The importance of the site of major bleeding in adults equally applies to children, with ICH and retroperitoneal bleeds being clinically important.

The incidence of major bleeding secondary to thrombolytic therapy in children is uncertain. The majority of data comes from case reports and case series, which are inherently biased. Based upon a composite review of the literature and two level IV studies, the incidence of bleeding occurs in approximately 30% of pediatric patients.[10] The most frequent problem is bleeding at sites of invasive procedures, which required treatment with blood products. Minor bleeding at local sites was frequent and occurred in 54% of children. The increased incidence of bleeding in children receiving thrombolytic therapy, compared to adults, in part represents different underlying diseases and risks for bleeding. The largest proportion of children to receive thrombolytic therapy have femoral artery TEs following femoral artery catheterization. The catheter access site provides a frequent source of bleeding, which often requires transfusion therapy due to the small blood volume of these infants. In contrast, the majority of adults who receive thrombolytic therapy have not had a recent invasive procedure.

Intracranial hemorrhage A recent review of the literature specifically examined the incidence of ICH during thrombolytic therapy in children.[214] There was no information about concurrent UFH administration in this study. In total, ICH was found in 14 of 929 (1.5%) patients analyzed. When subdivided according to age, ICH was identified in 2 of 468 (0.4%) children after the neonatal period, 1 of 83 (1.2%) term infants, and 11 of 86 (13.8%) preterm infants. However, in the largest study of premature infants included in this review, the incidence of ICH was the same in the control arm, which did not receive thrombolytic therapy. There was no evidence to support a difference in bleeding risk between different thrombolytic agents.

Treatment of bleeding due to thrombolytic therapy Before thrombolytic therapy is used, other concurrent hemostatic problems such as thrombocytopenia or vitamin K deficiency should be corrected when possible. Clinically mild bleeding, which is usually oozing from a wound or puncture site, can be treated with local pressure and supportive care. In patients with clinically significant bleeding, the choice and doses of blood products can be guided by appropriate hemostatic monitoring. The most useful single assay is plasma concentrations of fibrinogen, which can usually be obtained rapidly and helps to determine the need for replacement therapy with either cryoprecipitate or plasma. A commonly used lower hemostatic plasma concentration for fibrinogen is 100 mg/dL or less. The activated partial thromboplastin time (APTT) may not be helpful in the presence of decreased fibrinogen concentrations, concurrent UFH therapy, and presence of FDPs. Major hemorrhagic complications from a local site can be treated by stopping the infusion of the thrombolytic agent, and the administration of cryoprecipitate (usual dose of 1 bag/5kg) and other blood products as indicated. If the hemorrhagic complication is life threatening, an antifibrinolytic agent can also be used, with one option being a bolus of Amicar (100 mg/kg [max dose 5 mg] followed by 30 mg/kg/hr [max 1.25 g/hr]) until the bleeding stops. If concomitant UFH therapy is being administered, cessation and possible reversal of UFH with protamine sulphate should be considered. Treatment of mild hemorrhagic complications secondary to thrombolytic therapy consists of local measures (pressure, topical thrombin preparations) and transfusion of PRBCs if necessary.[186]

Failure of Thrombolytic Therapy

Failure of thrombolytic therapy can be considered as either a lack of response or recurrent TEs.

Lack of Response to Thrombolytic Therapy

Mechanisms Despite aggressive thrombolytic therapy with or without adjunctive anticoagulant therapy, thrombi may be resistant to thrombolytic therapy.[12] The factors related to this resistance remain uncertain, and in some instances may relate to the age of the thrombus.

Adults In adults, the most accurate estimates for a lack of response to thrombolytic therapy are for acute coronary occlusion, in which case 25% of patients are resistant to thrombolytic therapy at 60 to 90 minutes.

Children The frequency of true resistance to thrombolytic therapy in pediatric patients is uncertain. The available information based upon a literature review suggests that complete re-establishment of flow with thrombolytic therapy was accomplished in 81% of patients, partial resolution in 14% of children, and no resolution in the remaining 5% of children. The frequency of resistance to thrombolysis was similar for SK, UK, and TPA. However, the duration of therapy required to achieve successful thrombolysis differed significantly between thrombolytic agents. The duration of TPA therapy was 12 hours or less in 91% of children, compared to a minimum of 48 hours in 66% of children treated with UK, and a median of 24 hours for SK therapy in 78% of children (Figure 11–4).[10]

Reocclusion

Mechanisms The reason for our current understanding of vascular reocclusion following thrombolytic therapy is the paradoxical prothrombotic effects of plasmin.[215] In buffer systems, plasmin activates prothrombin, FXII, FVII, and transiently FV.[216] Plasmin at high concentrations can activate platelets ex vivo and result in platelet activation in vivo.[217] The presence of ongoing thrombin generation in vivo can contribute to local reocclusion from new thrombi.

Adults The incidence of reocclusion in adults with arterial thrombotic disorders is determined by the need for additional interventional procedures, which are in the order of 30% to 40%.

Children There are no reliable data on the incidence of reocclusion in children treated with thrombolytic therapy.

Contraindications to Thrombolytic Therapy

Adults

General information There are well-defined contraindications to thrombolytic therapy in adults, which can be classified as absolute or relative contraindications.[218] Almost all clinically significant complications of thrombolytic therapy are related to local or distant hemorrhage, particularly in the CNS or retroperitonium.

Absolute contraindications Absolute contraindications for thrombolytic therapy include children with sites of recent internal or noncompressible hemorrhage (6 weeks), major gastrointestinal hemorrhage, and major surgical procedures. Patients with CNS lesions, including cerebrovascular accidents within the previous year, head trauma, or brain surgery within the previous 6 months, or known intracranial neoplasms should also be excluded when possible.[12–14,25] Clinical circumstances may necessitate thrombolytic therapy despite these risks.

Relative contraindications Relative contraindications include patients with bacterial endocarditis due to the risk of septic embolization, uncontrolled hypertension, acute pancreatitis, and active peptic ulceration. Pregnancy is also a relative contraindication due to the risk of placental separation.[218]

Catheter-directed therapy In patients with significant bleeding risks, local (catheter-directed) thrombolytic therapy is frequently advocated as a safer alternative to systemic thrombolytic administration. However, life-threatening bleeding has been reported in many cases of catheter-directed lytic therapy, and the same contraindications as apply for systemic therapy should apply for local therapy. Bleeding complications are more likely related to dose and duration of therapy than site of administration.

Age of the thrombus Extended time since thrombus formation is often considered to be a relative contraindication to thrombolytic therapy. In part, this concept originates from the fact that the major clinical use of thrombolytic therapy is for coronary reperfusion following acute MI. Early reperfusion results in preservation of myocardial tissue, which improves cardiac function and hence outcome. Once myocardium is necrotic, reperfusion is no longer beneficial. In animal models, myocardial necrosis commences at the endocardium 15 minutes after acute coronary occlusion, and is 85% complete by 24 hours.[218] However, even apart from the issues of potential myocardial salvage, "old" thrombus is thought to respond less well than "fresh" thrombus to thrombolytic therapy. This is a major reason cited for the reduced response rate of venous TEs to thrombolytic therapy compared to arterial TEs. The relationship between duration of TEs and presentation of clinical symptoms is not always clear, and in general venous TEs are thought to accumulate over a more prolonged time period. A retrospective review of 85 patients with iliac and femoral vein TEs treated with either SK or UK reported that response rates deteriorated progressively, with increasing duration of symptoms. Patients presenting within 3 days had a 94% complete or partial resolution compared to 82% for 1 to 2 weeks of symptoms and 69% for 3 to 4 weeks of symptoms. In this review, only one of the seven patients who presented with symptoms of 5 to 8 weeks duration achieved even a partial response.[219]

Children

General information In the absence of specific pediatric guidelines, adult guidelines for "absolute" and "relative" contraindications to thrombolytic therapy should be considered for children. However, thrombolytic therapy in adults is most commonly used for acute coronary thrombolysis in previously well patients. In contrast, thrombolytic therapy in children is frequently required for major arterial or venous TEs that have complicated interventional procedures or surgery. The decision to use thrombolytic therapy in children is usually a diffi-

cult balance between aggressive treatment of a life- or limb-threatening TE and potentially life-threatening bleeding complications. Frank discussion between physician and parents with regard to potential risks and benefits of thrombolysis is required prior to the use of thrombolytic therapy in children and neonates.

Catheter-directed therapy As discussed previously, if there is a catheter in place, catheter-directed therapy should be considered. However, the placement of a catheter for the purposes of administering thrombolytic therapy may not have an advantage, and further clot formation may occur in the vessels in which the catheter is placed.[140] The risk of catheter-induced thrombosis is likely increased in children compared to adults due to the small vessels involved in children and the increased ratio of the diameter of the catheter to vessel wall.

Age of the thrombus There is minimal information available on the influence of age of the thrombus and response to thrombolytic therapy in children. However, there is no biologically obvious reason to suspect that an old thrombus in children would be any more responsive to thrombolytic therapy than for adults. Although most arterial thrombi in children are diagnosed in a timely fashion, most venous TEs require several days to weeks of age before they are diagnosed. A case series of four children with extensive venous TEs, estimated to be of 3 to 4 weeks duration, reported failure of thrombolytic therapy in all patients.[128] The decision to use thrombolytic therapy in children with a delayed presentation must be individualized, based on the anticipated benefits of successful therapy, balanced against the potential risks.

Clinical Use of Thrombolytic Therapy in Children

General Information A review of the literature provides epidemiologic details of children who have received thrombolytic therapy.[10] The age distribution of children receiving thrombolytic agents is similar, with newborns and infants less than 1 year of age composing 21% and 35% of pediatric patients treated with thrombolytic agents.[10] Children with congenital heart disease comprise the largest patient group at 51% of patients. Catheterization, on a short- or long-term basis, was the single most frequent cause of TE treated with thrombolytic therapy. Catheterizations could be grouped as CCs, CVLs, or umbilical artery catheters (UACs). Of these, CC was the single most frequent indication for thrombolytic therapy. UK and TPA had similar distributions and were used to treat thrombi in all locations. In contrast, SK was used primarily for arterial occlusion in the lower system secondary to CC. The following briefly summarizes the clinical situations in which thrombolytic therapy is used in children. Further details of the management of each condition are described in the relevant chapters.

Venous Thrombosis In general, the goal of thrombolytic therapy for the treatment of venous disease (Chapter 4) is the prevention of postphlebitic syndrome (PPS). Although thrombolytic therapy frequently removes the thrombus more quickly than anticoagulants alone, there is no convincing evidence that PPS is prevented or limited by early removal of the thrombus.[220] The reason for this discrepancy is that PPS is caused not only by the presence of a thrombus but permanent impairment of valves in the venous system. The early removal of the thrombus may not result in restoration of venous valve function. Similar to adults, there is little rationale for thrombolysis of venous TEs in the majority of children. However, there are some exceptions. First, bilateral renal vein thrombosis with impaired renal function has a uniformly dismal prognosis if complete renal failure occurs. Although there are no comparative studies, rapid resolution of the TE may be life saving in this situation.[121,221,222] Second, thrombolytic therapy that successfully removes thrombi from vessels essential for future

organ transplantation is likely indicated in the absence of absolute contraindications. Third, the presentation of a relatively acute superior venae cava syndrome, which is usually due to new clot extension of old thrombi present for many weeks, may respond to thrombolytic therapy with enhanced venous flow from the head. Successful salvage of arteriovenous fistulas has also been reported.[223,224] In other clinical scenarios, individual consideration should be given in cases where venous gangrene is impending or limb viability is threatened.[130,159,225]

Central Venous Lines

Loss of patency Low-dose thrombolytic therapy is frequently used to restore patency to dysfunctional CVLs. The doses and indications for this purpose were discussed previously. In general, if more than one or two doses of thrombolytic therapy are used to restore CVL patency, further investigation for large-vessel TEs should be considered.

Associated venous thrombosis CVL-related DVT is common in children (Chapter 4). While there are several single case reports documenting successful lysis of CVL-related DVT, failure of thrombolytic therapy is the more likely outcome. The main reason for failure of thrombolytic therapy is the age of the thrombus, which is usually several days to weeks old and only detected when new clot extension occurs. There are no data to support a concept of improved outcome with thrombolytic therapy compared to standard anticoagulation therapy for CVL–related DVT. The exception to this may be acute superior vena cava syndrome with cardiovascular compromise.[107,109,111,148–151,169–174,184, 226–232]

Prevention of sepsis Three reports have described low-dose UK as prophylaxis or treatment

Table 11–6 Low-Dose Urokinase as Prophylaxis or Treatment for Central Venous Line-Related Sepsis

Author	Design	Number	Dose Schedule	Outcome
Fishbein et al[233]C	1		200 IU/kg/hr UK for 24 hr	Sepsis resolved
Jones et al[234]	P	224	5000 IU/mL UK (1–2 mL) 1 hr dwell	All sepsis resolved; 12 (32%) had a recurrence
Haffar et al[235]	R	8	5000 IU/mL UK (2.5–3 mL) 3–4 hr dwell	One of 8 sepsis resolved; antibiotic therapy was concurrent

UK = urokinase; C = case report; PC = prospective cohort; R = retrospective review.

for CVL-related sepsis (Table 11–6).[233–235] Doses were similar to those used to restore patency to a dysfunctional CVL. The results did not support the use of thrombolytic agents for either prevention or treatment for CVL-related bacteremia.

Arterial Thrombosis Arterial TEs in children are almost exclusively related to intravascular catheters, the most common being femoral artery catheters for cardiac angiography.[24,80,109,116,157,164–166,185,194,236–242] Interventional catheter procedures, especially in young children, are commonly associated with femoral artery TEs. The indications for thrombolysis are threatened limb viability or impending gangrene and reduced pulses with diminished distal circulation despite adequate UFH therapy.

Intracardiac

Right atrial, right ventricular, Fontan circuit, and prosthetic heart valve (see Chapter 6). There are isolated case reports describing the use of thrombolytic therapy for intracardiac TEs that may occur in the right atrium, right ventricular, a Fontan circuit, and associated with a prosthetic heart valve. In each of these situations, there is a risk of embolization during thrombolytic therapy. If the lesions are valvular and considered infective in origin (i.e., endocarditis), thrombolytic therapy is in general contraindicated. Attempted thrombolysis of intracardiac TE does not preclude subsequent surgical intervention in the presence of supportive care. If the cardiovascular status is stable, thrombolytic therapy is a reasonable first option in the presence of an intracardiac thrombus.[120,136,160,176,181–183,243–249]

Arterial Ischemic Stroke and Cerebral Sinus Thrombosis Isolated case reports of thrombolysis for arterial ischemic stroke and cerebral venous TEs have described both successful lysis and treatment failure. There are minimal data on the use of thrombolysis in arterial ischemic stroke in children. Data from adult studies would suggest a critical therapeutic window during which therapy must be commenced if any benefit is to be achieved.[250] The diagnostic process for children with acute neurologic events is considerably more complex than for adults. There are likely few cases in which throm-

bolysis is appropriate in these situations; however, each case deserves individual consideration.[131,137,139,251–253]

Other Diseases Thrombolytic therapy has been used in a number of diseases, which did not involve intravascular TEs.

Intraventricular thrombolysis In 1992, Whitelaw et al reported intraventricular infusion of SK in nine preterm infants with progressive posthemorrhagic ventricular dilatation. SK (20 to 25000 units) was infused via a 20-gauge needle inserted through the lambdoid suture over 48 to 72 hours.[254] All of the infants survived, and surgical shunting was required in only one case, compared to 60% of historic controls. A 200% increase in fibrinolytic activity of spinal fluid was noted during therapy.[255]

Intravessical thrombolysis In 1993, LaFave et al reported intravessical infusion of UK to resolve urinary obstruction due to clot retention in two young boys.[256] UK was instilled through the urethra via a small Foley catheter, which was then clamped for 2 hours before the bladder was drained. Urinary retention was resolved without further intervention in both boys. There was no evidence of systemic anticoagulation. SK bladder installation had previously been described in adults.[256]

Purpura fulminans In 1995, Zenz et al described the administration of TPA to two infants with life-threatening septic shock and purpura fulminans caused by meningococcal sepsis.[257] Both children had evidence of skin necrosis associated with severe persistent hypotension and disseminated intravascular coagulation (DIC). In addition to antibiotics, inotrope support, and replacement with antithrombin (AT) and protein C concentrates, the children were treated with 0.5 mg/kg/hr of TPA (this was later reduced to 0.25 mg/kg/hr). Duration of therapy was approximately 4 hours, during which time dramatic clinical improvement occurred. Both children recovered fully.[257]

CONCLUSIONS

Thrombolytic therapy is the therapeutic application of a physiologic process, which remains incompletely understood. Over recent years, there has been a rapid expansion of the number of thrombolytic agents available for clinical use. Despite these advances, there has been a paucity of research on their optimal use in children. Differences in developmental hemostasis would suggest that the response to thrombolytic agents will differ in children compared to adults.

Conclusions based on the limited pediatric literature are guarded because they reflect data from case series and case reports. However, some observations are striking and worthy of highlighting: (1) children less than 1 year old are the single largest group requiring thrombolytic therapy; (2) CC is the most common indication for thrombolytic therapy in pediatric patients; (3) there is no apparent rationale for the choice of thrombolytic agents for use in the distinct clinical categories; (4) there is no uniformity in dosing, although certain minimal doses can be established; (5) the effectiveness of TPA appears to be more rapid than that for either UK or SK, but this observation requires confirmation in clinical trials; (6) at least partial lysis of thrombi occurs in approximately 80% of children; and (7) bleeding from local sites is common and may require transfusion therapy. Major bleeding is relatively rare.

Only through well-designed RCTs can optimal use of thrombolytic therapy be determined for children. Such trials will need to be large, multicenter studies and will therefore be expensive, which raises questions about their feasibility. In the interim, standard thrombolytic therapy guidelines are recommended based on the available data and extrapolation from adult trials.

REFERENCES

1. TIMI Study Group. The thrombolysis in myocardial infarction trial. N Engl J Med 1985;312:932–6.
2. Verstraete M, Bernard R, Bory B, et al. Randomized trial of intravenous recombinant human tissue-type plasminogen activator versus intravenous streptokinase in acute myocardial infarction. Lancet 1985;1:842–8.
3. Collen D, Topal E, Tiefenbrun A, et al. Coronary thrombolysis with recombinant human tissue-type plasminogen activator: a prospective, randomized placebo controlled trial. Circulation 1984;70:1012–7.
4. Anglo-Scandinavian Study of Thrombolysis (ASSET). Trial of tissue plasminogen activator or mortality reduction in acute myocardial infarction. Lancet 1988;2:525–30.
5. Goldhaber S, Kessler C, Heit J, et al. Randomized controlled trial of recombinant tissue plasminogen activator versus urokinase in the treatment of acute pulmonary embolism. Lancet 1988;2:293–8.
6. Verstraete M, Miller G, Bounameaux H, et al. Intravenous and intrapulmonary recombinant tissue-type plasminogen activator in the treatment of acute massive pulmonary embolism. Circulation 1988;77:353–360.
7. Turpie A. Thrombolytic therapy in venous thromboembolism. In: Sobel B, Collen D, Grossbard E, eds. Tissue plasminogen activator in thrombolytic therapy. New York: Marcel Dekker,1987:131–46.
8. Michelson AD, Bovill E, Monagle P, Andrew M. Antithrombotic therapy in children. Chest 1998;114:748S–769S.
9. Andrew M. Developmental hemostasis: relevance to newborns and infants. In: Nathan DG, Oski FA, eds. Hematology of infancy and childhood. Philadelphia: WB Saunders, 1998:114–57.
10. Leaker M, Massicotte MP, Brooker L, Andrew M. Thrombolytic therapy in pediatric patients: a comprehensive review of the literature. Thromb Haemost 1996;76:132–4.
11. Weitz JI, Stewart RJ, Fredenburgh JC. Mechanism of action of plasminogen activators. Thromb Haemost 1999;82:974–82.
12. Loscalzo J. Fibrinolytic therapy. In: Beulter E, Lichtinan M, Collen B, Kipps T, eds. Williams hematology. New York: McGraw Hill, 1995:1585–91.
13. Martindale W. Martindale: the extra pharmacopoeia. London: Pharmaceutical Press, 1989.
14. Avery GS, Speight TM, Holford NHG. Avery's drug treatment: a guide to the properties, choice, therapeutic use and economic value. Auckland: Adis International, 1997.
15. Castellino FJ. A unique enzyme-protein substrate modifier reaction: plasmin/streptokinase interaction. Trends Biochem Sci 1979;5:1–5.
16. Massel D. Clinical use of coronary thrombolytic therapy: previous streptokinase therapy. Can J Cardiol 1993;9:518–20.
17. Elliot JM, Cross DB, Cederholm-Williams S. Streptokinase titers 1 to 4 years after intravenous streptokinase. Circulation 1991;84:116–7.
18. Massel D, Turpie AGG, Oberhardt BJ. Estimation of resistance to streptokinase: a preliminary report of a rapid bedside test. Can J Cardiol 1993;9:134E–5E.

19. Gruppo Italiano per lo studio della streptokinase nell infarcto miocardico (GISSI). Effectiveness of intravenous thrombolytic treatment in acute myocardial infarction. Lancet 1986;1:397–402.

20. ISIS-2 (Second International Study of Infarct Survival). Randomized trial of intravenous streptokinase, oral aspirin, both or neither among 17,187 cases of suspected acute myocardial infarction. Lancet 1988;2:349–60.

21. Lew AS, Laramee P, Cercek B. The hypotensive effect of intravenous streptokinase in patients with myocardial infarction. Circulation 1985;72:1321–6.

22. Wei JY, Markis JE, Malagold M. Cardiovascular reflexes stimulated by reperfusion of eschemic myocardium in acute myocardial infarction. Circulation 1983;67:796–801.

23. ISIS-3 Collaborative Group. ISIS-3: A randomized comparison of streptokinase vs tissue plasminogen activator vs anistrplase and of aspirin plus heparin vs aspirin alone among 41,299 cases of suspected actue myocardial infarction. Lancet 1992;339:753–70.

24. Andrew M, Brooker L, Paes B, Weitz J. Fibrin clot lysis by thrombolytic agents is impaired in newborns due to a low plasminogen concentration. Thromb Haemost 1992;68:325–30.

25. Cairns JA, Kennedy JW, Fuster V. Coronary thrombolysis. Chest 1998;114:634–57.

26. Longstaff C, Clough AM, Gaffney PJ. Kinetics of plasmin activation of single chain urinary-type plasminogen activator a (scu-PA) and demonstration of a high affinity interaction between scu-PA and plasminogen. J Biol Chem 1992;267:173–9.

27. Ichinose A, Fujikawa K, Suyama T. The activation of pro-urokinase by plasma kallikrein and its inactivation by thrombin. J Biol Chem 1986;261:3486–9.

28. Behrendt N, Ronne E, Dano K. The structure and function of the urokinase receptor, a membrane protein governing plasminogen activation on the cell surface. Biol Chem Hoppe Seyler 1995;376:269–79.

29. Stump DC, Thienpont M, Collen D. Urokinase-related proteins in human urine. Isolation and characterization of single-chain urokinase (pro-urokinase) and urokinase-inhibitor complex. J Biol Chem 1986; 261:1267–73.

30. Rijken DC, Binnema DJ, Los P. Specific fibrinolytic properties of different molecular forms of pro- urokinase from a monkey kidney cell culture. Thromb Res 1986;42:761–8.

31. Weaver WD, Hartmann JR, Anderson JL, et al. New recombinant glycosylated prourokinase for treatment of patients with acute myocardial infarction. Prourokinase study group. J Am Coll Cardiol 1994;24:1242–8.

32. Stump DC, Kieckens L, De Cock F, Collen D. Pharmacokinetics of single chain forms of urokinase-type plasminogen activator. Pharmacol Exp Ther 1987;242:245–50.

33. Smith RA, Dupe RJ, English PD, Green J. Fibrinolysis with acyl-enzymes: a new approach to thrombolytic therapy. Nature 1981;290:505–8.

34. Marder VJ, Hirsh J, Bell WR. Rationale and practical basis of thrombolytic therapy. In: Colman RW, Hirsh J, Marder VJ, Salzman EW, eds. Hemostasis and thrombosis: basic principles and clinical practice. Philadelphia: Lippincott, 1994:1514–40.

35. Leaker M, Brooker L, Ofosu K, et al. Anisoylated streptokinase-plasminogen activator complex offers no advantage over streptokinase for fibrin clot lysis in cord plasma. Biol Neonate 1999 (submitted).

36. Sabovic M, Lijnen HR, Keber D, Collen D. Correlation between progressive adsorption of plasminogen to blood clots and their sensitivity to lysis. Thromb Haemost 1990;64:450–4.

37. Sabovic M, Lijnen H, Keber D, Collen D. Effect of retraction on the lysis of human clots with fibrin specific and non-fibrin specific plasminogen activators. Thromb Haemost 1989;62:1083–7.

38. Lijnen HR, Collen D. Molecular and cellular basis of fibrinolysis. In: Hoffman R, Benz EK, Shattil SJ, et al, eds. Hematology. Basic principles and practice. New York: Churchill Livingstone Inc., 1995: 1588–96.

39. Madison EL, Sambrook JF. Probing structure-function relationships of tissue-type plasminogen activator by oligonucleotide-mediated site specific mutagenesis. Methods Enzymol 1993;223:249–71.

40. Lijnen HR, Collen D. Strategies for the improvement of thrombolytic agents. Thromb Haemostas 1991;66: 88–110.

41. Stewart RJ, Fredenburgh JC, Weitz JI. Characterization of the interactions of plasminogen and tissue and vampire bat plasminogen activators with fibrinogen, fibrin, and the complex of D-dimer noncovalently linked to fragment E. J Biol Chem 1998;273: 18292–9.

42. Hoylaerts M, Rijken D, Lijnen H, Collen D. Kinetics of the activation of plasminogen by human tissue plasminogen activator. Role of fibrin. J Biol Chem 1982;257:2912–9.

43. Horrevoets AJ, Pannekoek H, Nesheim ME. A steady-state template model that describes the kinetics of fibrin-stimulated (Glu) and (Lys78) plasminogen activation by native tissue type plasminogen activator and variants that lack either the finger or kringle-2 domain. J Biol Chem 1997;272:2183–91.

44. Bringmann P, Gruber D, Liese A, et al. Structural features mediating fibrin selectivity of vampire bat plasminogen activators. J Biol Chem 1995;270: 25596–603.

45. Rijken DC, Otter M, Kuiper J, van Berkel TJ. Receptor-mediated endocytosis of tissue-type plasminogen activator (t-PA) by liver cells. Thromb Res 1990;10:63–71.

46. Collen D, Gold HK. Fibrin specific thrombolytic agents and new approaches to coronary arterial thrombolysis. In: Julian D, Kubler W, Norris RM, et al, editors. Thrombolysis in cardiovascular disease. New York: Marcel Decker Inc., 1990:45–67.

47. Kohnert U, Rudolph R, Verheijen JH, et al. Biochemical properties of the kringle 2 and protease domains are maintained in the refolded t-PA deletion variant BM 06.022. Protein Eng 1992;5:93–100.

48. Camani C, Kruithof EKO. The role of the finger and growth factor domains in the clearance of tissue-type plasminogen activator by hepatocytes. J Biol Chem 1995;270:26053–6.

49. Smalling RW, Bode C, Kalfleisch J. More rapid, complete, and stable coronary thrombolysis with bolus administration of reteplase compared with alteplase infusion in acute myocardial infarction. Circulation 1995;91:2725–32.

50. Keyt BA, Paoni NF, Refino CJ, et al. A faster acting and more potent form of tissue plasminogen activator. Proc Natl Acad Sci U S A 1994;91:3670–4.

51. Paoni NF, Keyt BA, Refino CJ, et al. A slow clearing, fibrin-specific, PAI-1 resistant variant of t-PA (T103N, KHRR 296-299, AAAA). Thromb Haemost 1993;70:307–12.

52. Refino CJ, Paoni NF, Keyt BA, et al. A variants t-PA (T103N, KHRR 296-299 AAAA) that, by bolus, has increased potency and decreased systemic activation of plasminogen. Thromb Haemost 1993;70:313–319.

53. Stewart RJ, Fredenburgh JC, Keyt BA, Weitz JI. The fibrin-specificities of tissue type plasminogen activator and, to a lesser extent, the TNK variant are compromised by kringle-dependent interactions with (DD)E. Blood 1997;40:144a.

54. Collen D. Thrombolytic therapy. Thromb Haemost 1997;78:742–6.

55. Collen D, Schlott B, Engelborghs Y, et al. On the mechanism of activation of human plasminogen by recombinant staphylokinase. J Biol Chem 1993;268:8284–9.

56. Silence K, Collen D, Lijnen HR. Regulation by alpha-2-antiplasmin and fibrin of the activation of plasminogen with recombinant staphylokinase in plasma. Blood 1993;82:1175–83.

57. Lijnen HR, Van Hoef B, De Cock F, et al. On the mechanism of fibrin-specific plasminogen activation by staphylokinase. J Biol Chem 1991;266:11826–32.

58. Winkler ME, Blaber M. 1986. Purification and characterization of recombinant single-chain urokinase produced in *Escherichia coli*. Biochem 1986;25:4041–4045.

59. Andrew M, Paes B, Milner R, et al. Development of the human coagulation system in the full-term infant. Blood 1987;70:165–72.

60. Andrew M, Paes B, Milner R, et al. Development of the human coagulation system in the healthy premature infant. Blood 1988;72:1651–7.

61. Andrew M, Paes B, Johnston B. Development of the hemostatic system in the neonate and young infant. Am J Pediatr Hematol Oncol 1990;12:95–104.

62. Aballi A, de Lamerens S. Coagulation changes in the neonatal period and in early infancy. Pediatr Clin North Am 1962;9:785–817.

63. Bleyer W, Hakami N, Shepard T. The development of hemostasis in the human fetus and newborn infant. J Pediatr 1971;79:838–53.

64. Hathaway WE, Bonnar J. Bleeding disorders in the newborn infant. In: Oliver TKJ, ed. Perinatal coagulation. Monographs in neonatology. New York: Grune and Stratton, 1978:115–169.

65. Buchanan G. Coagulation disorders in the neonate. Pediatr Clin North Am 1986;33:203–20.

66. Montgomery RR, Marlar RA, Gill JC. Newborn haemostasis. Clin Hematol 1985;14:443–60.

67. Gobel U, Voss HC, Petrich C, et al. Etiopathology and classification of acquired coagulation disorders in the newborn infant. Klin Wochenschr 1979;57:81–6.

68. McDonald M, Hathaway W. Neonatal haemorrhage and thrombosis. Semin Perinatol 1983;7:213–25.

69. Bahakim H, Gader AGMA, Galil A, et al. Coagulation parameters in maternal and cord blood at delivery. Ann Saudi Med 1990;10:149–55.

70. Corrigan J. Neonatal thrombosis and the thrombolytic system. Pathophysiology and therapy. Am J Pediatr Hematol Oncol 1988;10:83–91.

71. Corrigan J, Sluth J, Jeter M, Lox C. Newborn's fibrinolytic mechanism: components and plasmin generation. Am J Hematol 1989;32:273–8.

72. Kolindewala JK, Das BK, Dube B, Bhargava B. Blood fibrinolytic activity in neonates: effect of period of gestation, birth weight, anoxia and sepsis. Indian Pediatr 1987;24:1029–33.

73. Runnebaum IB, Maurer SM, Daly L, Bonnar J. Inhibitors and activators of fibrinolysis during and after childbirth in maternal and cord blood. J Perinatal Med 1989;17:113–9.

74. Lecander I, Astedt B. Specific plasminogen activator inhibitor of placental type PAI 2 occurring in amniotic fluid and cord blood. J Lab Clin Med 1987;110:602–5.

75. Edelberg JM, Enghild JJ, Pizzo SV, Gonzalez-Gronow M. Neonatal plasminogen displays altered cell surface binding and activation kinetics. Correlation

with increased glycosylation of the protein. J Clin Invest 1990;86:107–12.

76. Summaria L. Comparison of human normal, full-term, fetal and adult plasminogen by physical and chemical analyses. Haemostasis 1989;19:266–73.

77. Siegbahn A, Ruusuvaara L. Age dependence of blood fibrinolytic components and the effects of low-dose oral contraceptives on coagulation and fibrinolysis in teenagers. Thromb Haemost 1988;60:361–364.

78. Andrew M, Vegh P, Johnston M, et al. Maturation of the hemostatic system during childhood. Blood 1992;80:1998–2005.

79. Leaker M, Superina R, Andrew M. Fibrin clot lysis by tissue plasminogen activator (tPA) is impaired in plasma from pediatric liver transplant patients. Transplantation 1995;60:144–7.

80. Ries M, Singer H, Hofbeck M, Klinge J. Tissue plasminogen activator (alteplase) treatment for femoral artery thrombosis after cardiac catheterization in infants and children. Br Heart J 1993;70:382–5.

81. Kennedy JW, Ritchie JL, Davis KB. Western Washington randomized trial of intracoronary streptokinase in acute myocardial infarction. N Engl J Med 1983;304:1477–82.

82. Simoons ML, Serruys PW, Brand M. Improved survival after early thrombolysis in acute myocardial infarction: a randomized trial by the Interuniversity Cardiology Institute in The Netherlands. Lancet 1985;2:578–81.

83. Khaja F, Walton JA, Brymer JF. Intracoronary fibrinolytic therapy in acute myocardial infarction: report of a prospective randomized trial. N Engl J Med 1983;308:1305–11.

84. Leiboff RH, Katz RJ, Wasserman AG. A randomized, angiographically controlled trial of intracoronary streptokinase in acute myocardial infarction. Am J Cardiol 1984;53:404–7.

85. Rentrop KP, Feit F, Blanke H. Effects of intracoronary streptokinase and intracoronary nitroglycerin infusion on coronary angiographic patterns and mortality in patients with acute myocadial infarction. N Engl J Med 1984;311:1457–63.

86. Anderson JL, Marshal HW, Bray BE. A randomized trial of intracoronary streptokinase in the treatment of acute myocardial infarction. N Engl J Med 1983;308:1312–8.

87. Raizner AE, Tortoledo FA, Verani MS. Intracoronary thrombolytic therapy in acute myocardial infarction: a prospective randomized controlled trial. Am J Cardiol 1985;55:301–8.

88. Alderman EL, Jutzy KR, Berte LE. Randomized comparison of intravenous versus intracoronary streptokinase for myocardial infaction. Am J Cardiol 1984;54:14–5.

89. Rogers WJ, Mantle JA, Hood WP. Prospective randomized trial of intravenous and intracoronary streptokinase in acute myocardial infarction. Circulation 1983;68:1051–61.

90. Kandarpa K. Catheter directed thrombolysis of peripheral arterial occlusions and deep vein thrombosis. Thromb Haemost 1999;82:987–96.

91. Torr SR, Nachowiak DA, Fujii S, Sobel BE. "Plasminogen steal" and clot lysis. J Am Coll Cardiol 1992;19:1085–90.

92. Diffin DC, Kandarpa K. Assessment of peripheral intraarterial thrombolysis versus surgical revascularization in acute lower limb ischemia: a review of the limb salvage and mortality statistics. J Vasc Interv Radiol 1996;7:57–63.

93. Ouriel K, Kolassa M, DeWeese JA, Green RM. Economic implications of thrombolysis or operation as the initial treatment modality in acute peripheral arterial occlusion. Surgery 1995;118:810–4.

94. Schwieder G, Grimm W, Siemens HJ, et al. Intermittent regional therapy with rt-PA is not superior to systemic thrombolysis in deep venous thrombosis (DVT)-a German multicentre trial. Thromb Haemost 1995;74:1240–3.

95. Ogawa S, Nagai Y, Zhang J, et al. Evaluation of myocardial ischemia and infarction by signal-averaged electrocardiographic late potentials in children with Kawasaki disease. Am J Cardiol 1996;78:175–81.

96. Suzuki A, Kamiya T, Ono Y, et al. Myocardial ischemia in Kawasaki disease: followup study by cardiac catherization and coronary angioplasty. Pediatr Cardiol 1988;9:1–5.

97. Nakamura Y, Yanagawa H, Ojima T, et al. Cardiac sequelae of Kawasaki disease among recurrent cases. Arch Dis Child 1988;78:163–5.

98. Chung KJ, Fulton DR, Lapp R, et al.One year followup of cardiac and coronary artery disease in infants and children with Kawasaki disease. Am Heart J 1988;115:1263–7.

99. Ogawa S, Fukazawa R, Ohkubo T, et al. Silent myocardial ischemia in Kawasaki disease: evaluation of percutaneous transluminal coronary angioplasty by dobutamine stress testing. Circulation 1997;96:3384–9.

100. Kato H, Sugimura T, Akagi T, et al. Long term consequences of Kawasaki disease. A 10 to 21 year followup study of 594 patients. Circulation 1996;94:1379–85.

101. Burtt DM, Pollack P, Bianco JA. Intravenous streptokinase in an infant with Kawasaki's disease complicated by acute myocardial infarction. Pediatr Cardiol 1986;6:307–311.

102. Basso C, Baracca E, Zonzin P, Thiene G. Sudden cardiac arrest in a teenager as first manifestation of Takayasu's disease. Int J Cardiol 1994;43:87–9.

103. Vos GD, van der Blij JF, van Leeuwen TM, Losekoot G. Takayasu's disease as the cause of myocardial infarct in an infant. Ned Tijdschr Geneeskd 1987;131:1355–7.

104. Pongiglione G, Marsini M, Ribaldone D. Right atrial thrombosis in two premature infants: successful treatment with urokinase and heparin. Eur Heart J 1986;7:1086–1089.

105. Higashida RT, Helmer E, Halbach VV, Hieshima GB. Direct thrombolytic therapy for superior sagittal sinus thrombosis. Am J Neuroradiol 1989;10:S4–6.

106. Corrigan JJ, Allen HD, Jeter M, et al. Aortic thrombosis in a neonate: failure of urokinase thrombolytic therapy. Am J Pediatr Hemostas Oncol 1982;4:243–7.

107. Caglar MK, Tolboon J. The successful treatment of superior vena cava syndrome with urokinase in an infant with a central venous catheter. Helv Paediat Acta 1988;43:483–6.

108. Deeg K, Wolfel D, Rupprecht T. Diagnosis of neonatal aortic thrombosis by colour coded Doppler sonography. Pediatr Radiol 1992;22:62–3.

109. Anderson BJ, Keeley SR, Johnson ND. Prothrombinex-induced thrombosis and its management with regional plasminogen activator in hepatic failure. Med J Aust 1990;153:352–6.

110. Gamba P, Pettenazzo A, Kalapurackal M, et al. Primary occlusion of the iliac and femoral artery in two newborn infants: efficacy of medical treatment. J Pediatr Surg 1993;28:735–7.

111. Delaplane D, Scott P, Riggs TW, et al. Urokinase therapy for a catheter-related right atrial thrombus. J Pediatr 1982;100:149–52.

112. Giacoia G. High-dose urokinase therapy in newborn infants with major vessel thrombosis. Clin Pediatr 1993;32:231–7.

113. Kirk CR, Bhrolchain CN, Qureshi SA. Streptokinase for aortic thrombosis. Arch Dis Child 1988;63:1086–7.

114. Strife J, Ball WS Jr, Towbin R, et al. Arterial occlusion in neonates: use of fibrinolytic therapy. Radiology 1988;166:395–400.

115. Hoffer FA, Fellows KE. Local streptokinase infusion in children. Am J Roentgenol 1984;143:695a.

116. Molteni KH, Messersmith R, Puppala BL, et al. Intrathrombic urokinase reverses neonatal renal artery thrombosis. Pediatr Nephrol 1993;7:413–5.

117. Wilson C, Merritt R, Thomas D. Successful treatment of superior vena cava syndrome with urokinase in an infant. J Parent Ent Nutr 1988;12:81–3.

118. Vogelzang RL, Moel DI, Cohn RA, et al. Acute renal vein thrombosis: successful treatement with intraarterial urokinase. Radiology 1988;169:681–2.

119. Pritchard SL, Culham JAG, Rodgers PCJ. Low-dose fibrinolytic therapy in infants. J Pediatr 1985;106:594–8.

120. Olsen MM, Blumer JL, Gauderer MW, Izant RJJ. Streptokinase dissolution of a right atrial thrombus. J Pediatr Surg 1985;20:19–21.

121. Bromberg WD, Firlit CS. Fibrinolytic therapy for renal vein thrombosis in the child. J Urol 1990;143:86–8.

122. Hidalgo E, Abad J, Cantarero J, et al. High-dose intra-arterial urokinase for the treatment of hepatic artery thrombosis in liver transplantation. Hepato-gastroenterol 1989;36:529–32.

123. Richardson R, Applebaum H, Touran T, et al. Effective thrombolytic therapy of aortic thrombosis in the small premature infant. J Pediatr Surg 1988;23:1198–200.

124. Pyles L, Pierpont M, Steiner M, et al. Fibrinolysis by tissue plasminogen activator in a child with pulmonary embolism. J Pediatr 1990;116:801–4.

125. Levy M, Benson LN, Burrows PE, et al. Tissue plasminogen activator for the treatment of thromboembolism in infants and children. J Pediatr 1991;118:467–72.

126. Dillon PW, Fox PS, Berg CJ, et al. Recombinant tissue plasminogen activator for neonatal and pediatric vascular thrombolytic therapy. J Pediatr Surg 1993;28:1264–9.

127. Goldberg RE, Cohen AM, Bryan PJ, et al. Neonatal aortic thrombosis treated with intra-arterial urokinase therapy. J Can Assoc Radiol 1989;40:55–6.

128. Ryan C, Andrew M. Failure of thrombolytic therapy in four children with extensive thromboses. Am J Dis Child 1992;146:187–93.

129. Young AT, Hunter DW, Castaneda-Zuniga WR, et al. Thrombosed synthetic hemodialysis access fistulas: failure of fibrinolytic therapy. Radiology 1985;154:639–42.

130. Doyle E, Britto J, Freeman J, et al. Thrombolysis with low dose tissue plasminogen activator. Arch Dis Child 1992;67:1483–4.

131. Horowitz M, Purdy P, Unwin H, et al. Treatment of dural sinus thrombois using selective catheterization and urokinase. Ann Neurol 1995;38:58–67.

132. Anderson BJ, Keeley SR, Johnson ND. Caval thrombolysis in neonates using low doses of recombinant human tissue-type plasminogen activator. Anaesth Intensive Care 1991;19:22–7.

133. Leblanc JG, Culham JAG, Chan K, et al. Treatment of grafts and major vessel thrombosis with low-dose streptokinase in children. Ann Thorac Surg 1986;41:630–3.

134. Suarez CR, Ow EP, Lambert GH, et al. Urokinase therapy for a central venous catheter thrombus. Am J Hematol 1989;31:269–72.

135. Abejo RC, John EG, Spigos DG. Low-dose streptokinase-induced clot lysis of an occluded arteriovenous fistula. J Pediatr 1985;106:321–3.

136. Zureikat GY, Martin GR, Silverman NH, Newth CJL. Urokinase therapy for a catheter-related right atrial thrombus and pulmonary embolism in a 2 month old infant. Pediatr Pulmonol 1986;2:303–6.

137. Gebara BM, Goetting MG, Wany AM. Dural sinus thrombosis complicating subclavian vein catheterization: treatment with local thrombolysis. Pediatr 1995;95:138–40.

138. Cairns RA, MacKenzie WG, Culham JAG. Urokinase treatment of forearm ischemia complicating supracondylar fracture of the humerus in three children. Pediatr Radiol 1993;23:391–4.

139. Griesemer DA, Theodorou AA, Berg RA, Spera TD. Local fibrinolysis in cerebral venous thrombosis. Pediatr Neurol 1994;10:78–80.

140. Monagle P, Phelan E, Downie P, Andrew M. Local thrombolytic therapy in children. Thromb Haemost 1997;(suppl);504a.

141. Kaufman SL, Martin LG, Gilarsky BP, et al. Urokinase thrombolysis using a multiple side hole multilumen infusion catheter. Cardiovasc Intervent Radiol 1991;14:334–7.

142. Suchkova V, Baggs R, Francis CW. 40 kHz ultrasound accelerates thrombolysis and improves muscle perfusion and acidosis in a rabbit femoral artery thrombosis model. Thromb Haemost 1999;(suppl)11–2a.

143. Diamond S. Ultrasound enhances plasmin activity on fibrin. Thromb Haemost 1999;(suppl):360a.

144. Bookstein JJ, Valji K. Pulse-spray pharmacomechanical thrombolysis. Cardiovasc Intervent Radiol 1992;15:228–33.

145. Valji K, Bookstein JJ. Efficacy of intrathrombic heparin with pulse spray thrombolysis in rabbit inferior vena cava thrombosis. Invest Radiol 1992;27:912–7.

146. Valji K, Bookstein JJ. Effects of intrathrombic administration of prostaglandin E1 during pulse-spray thrombolysis with tissue-type plasminogen activator in experimental thrombosis. Radiology 1993;186:873–6.

147. La Quaglia MP, Caldwell C, Lucas A, et al. A prospective randomized double-blind trial of bolus urokinase in the treatment of established Hickman catheter sepsis in children. J Pediatr Surg 1994;29:742–5.

148. Wachs T. Urokinase administration in pediatric patients with occluded central venous catheters. J Intraven Nurs 1989;13:100–3.

149. Winthrop AL, Wesson DE. Urokinase in the treatment of occluded central venous catheters in children. J Pediatr Surg 1984;19:536–8.

150. Kellam B, Fraze D, Kanarek K. Clot lysis for thrombosed central venous catheters in pediatric patients. J Perinatol 1987;VII:242–4.

151. Bagnall HA, Gomperts E, Atkinson JB. Continuous infusion of low-dose urokinase in the treatment of central venous catheter thrombosis in infants and children. Pediatrics 1989;83:963–6.

152. Atkinson JB, Bagnall HA, Gomperts E. Investigational use of tissue plasminogen activator (t-PA) for occluded central venous catheters. J Parent Ent Nutr 1990;14:310–1.

153. Haire WD, Atkinson JB, Stephens LC, Kotulak GD. Urokinase versus recombinant tissue plasminogen activator in thrombosed central venous catheters: a double-blinded, randomized trial. Thromb Haemost 1994;72:543–7.

154. Griffin M, Casta A. Successful urokinase therapy for superior vena cava syndrome in premature infant. Am J Dis Child 1988;142:1267–8.

155. Marsh D, Wilkerson S, Cook L, Pietsch J. Right atrial thrombus formation screening using two-dimensional echocardiograms in neonates with central venous catheters. Pediatrics 1988;81:284–6.

156. Rao S, Chow-thung E, Flanigan D. Urokinase therapy in newborn infants with aorto-iliac thrombosis. In: Mannucci PM, D'Angelo A, eds. Urokinase: basic and clinical aspects. Orlando, FL: Academic Press Inc., 1982:215–21.

157. Reznik VM, Anderson J, Griswold WR, et al. Successful fibrinolytic treatment of arterial thrombosis and hypertension in a cocaine-exposed neonate. Pediatrics 1989;84:735–8.

158. Vailas G, Brouillette R, Scott J, et al. Neonatal aortic thrombosis: recent experience. J Pediatr 1986;109:101–8.

159. Beaufils F, Schlegel N, Loirat C, et al. Urokinase treatment of pulmonary artery thrombosis complicating the pediatric nephrotic syndrome. Crit Care Med 1985;13:132–4.

160. Joyce LD, Boucek M, McGough EC. Urokinase therapy for thrombosis of tricuspid prosthetic valve. J Cardiovas Surg 1983;85:935–7.

161. Kennedy LA, Drummond WH, Knight ME, et al. Successful treatment of neonatal aortic thrombosis with tissue plasminogen activator. J Pediatr 1990;116:798–801.

162. Bhat R, Fisher E, Doshi U, et al. Neonatal abdominal aortic thrombosis. Crit Care Med 1981;9:858–861.

163. Emami A, Saldanha R, Knupp C, Kodroff M. Failure of systemic thrombolytic and heparin therapy in the treatment of neonatal aortic thrombosis. Pediatrics 1987;79:773–7.

164. Wessel DL, Keane JF, Fellows KE, et al. Fibrinolytic therapy for femoral arterial thrombosis after cardiac

catheterization in infants and children. Am J Cardiol 1986;58:347–51.

165. Ino T, Benson LN, Freedom RM, et al. Thrombolytic therapy for femoral artery thrombosis after pediatric cardiac catheterization. Am Heart J 1988;115: 633–9.

166. Brus F, Witsenburg M, Hofhuis WJD, et al. Streptokinase treatment for femoral artery thrombosis after arterial cardiac catheterization in infants and children. Br Heart J 1990;63:291–4.

167. Kothari SS, Kumar RK, Varma S, Saxena A. Thrombolytic therapy in infants for femoral artery thrombosis following cardiac catheterization. Indian Heart J 1996;48:246–8.

168. Zenz W, Muntean W, Beitzke A, et al. Tissue plasminogen activator (alteplase) treatment for femoral artery thrombosis after cardiac catheterization in infants and children. Br Heart J 1994;72:403–4.

169. Wever M, Liem K, Geven W, Tanke R. Urokinase therapy in neonates with catheter related central venous thrombosis. Thromb Haemost 1995;73:180–5.

170. Alkalay AL, Mazkereth R, Santulli T, Pomerance JJ. Central venous line thrombosis in premature infants: a case management and literature review. Am J Perinatol 1993;10:323–6.

171. Berman WJ, Fripp RR, Yabek SM, et al. Great vein and right atrial thrombosis in critically ill infants and children with central venous lines. Chest 1991;99:963–7.

172. Rodenhuis S, van't Hek LG, Vlasveld LT, et al. Central venous catheter associated thrombosis of major veins: thrombolytic treatment with recombinant tissue plasminogen activator. Thorax 1993;48: 558–559.

173. Ross PJ, Ehrenkranz R, Kleinman CS, Seashore JH. Thrombus associated with central venous catheters in infants and children. J Pediatr Surg 1989; 24:253–6.

174. Barzaghi A, Dell'Orto M, Rovelli A, et al. Central venous catheter clots: incidence, clinical significance and catheter care in patients with hematologic malignancies. Pediatr Hematol Oncol 1995;12:243–50.

175. Weinberg G, Brion LP, Vega-Richf CR. Dangers of arterial catheters in critically ill neonates. Pediatrics 1990;85:627–8.

176. Krogmann ON, Kries RV, Rammos S, et al. Left ventricular thrombus in a 2-year-old boy with cardiomyopathy: lysis with recombinant tissue-type plasminogen activator. Eur J Pediatr 1991;150: 829–31.

177. Gal P, Ransom JL. Neonatal thrombosis: treatment with heparin and thrombolytics. Ann Pharmacother 1991;25:853–6.

178. Torkington J, Hitchcock R, Wilkinson K, Kiely E. Successful use of recombinant tissue plasminogen activator in the treatment of aortic thrombosis in a premature neonate. Eur J Endovasc Surg 1997;13: 515–6.

179. Smith PK, Miller DA, Lail S, Mehta AV. Urokinase treatment of neonatal aortoiliac thrombosis caused by umbilical artery catheterization: a case report. J Vasc Surg 1991;14:684–7.

180. Ahluwalia JS, Kelsall AW, Diedericj S, Rennie JM. Successful treatment of aortic thrombosis after umbilibal catheterization with tissue plasminogen activator. Acta Paediatr 1994;83:1215–7.

181. Di Sessa T, Yeatman LA Jr, Williams RG, et al. Thrombosis of complicating balloon angioplasty of left pulmonary artery stenosis after Fontan's procedure: successful treatment with intravenous streptokinase. JAMA 1985;253:791–5.

182. Rajani RM, Dalvi BV, Kulkarni HL, Kale PA. Acutely blocked Blalock-Taussig shunt following cardiac catheterization: successful recanalization with intravenous streptokinase. Am Heart J 1990;120:1238–9.

183. Hassall E, Ulich T, Ament ME. Pulmonary embolus and Malassezia pulmonary infection related to urokinase therapy. J Pediatr 1983;102:722–725.

184. Curnow A, Idowu J, Behrens E, et al. Urokinase therapy for silastic catheter-induced intravascular thrombi in infants and children. Arch Surg 1985;120:1237–40.

185. Abdurrahman L, Aditia I, Mayer JE, et al. Acute pulmonary embolism in a neonate: precipitation during cardiac catheterization and successful treatment. Pediatr Cardiol 1998;19:431–5.

186. Andrew M, deVeber G. Pediatric thromboembolism and stroke protocols. Hamilton, ON: B.C. Decker Inc., 1997.

187. Brueggemeyer A, Kenner C. Use of thrombolytic medications in the neonate. Neonatal Netw 1985,Dec; 4(3)34–7.

188. Reidy SJ, O'Hara PA, O'Brien P. Streptokinase use in children undergoing cardiac catheterization. J Cardiovasc Nurs 1989;4:46–56.

189. The International Study Group. In-hospital mortality and clinical course of 20,891 patients with suspected acute myocardial infarction randomized between alteplase and streptokinase with or without heparin. Lancet 1990;336:71–5.

190. The GUSTO Investigators. An international randomized trial comparing four thrombolytic strategies for acute myocardial infarction. N Engl J Med 1993; 329:673–82.

191. O'Connor CM, Meese R, Carney R. A randomized trial of intravenous heparin in conjuction with anistreplase (anisoylated plasminogen atreptokinase activator complex) in acute myocardial infarction: the Duke University Clinical Cardiology Study (DUCCS). J Am Coll Cardiol 1994;29:11–8.

192. Collins R, MacMahon S, Flather M. Clinical effects of anticoagulant therapy in suspected acute myocardial infarction: systematic overview of randomized trials. BMJ 1996;313:652–9.

193. Antiplatelet Trialists' Collaboration. Collaborative overview of randomized trials of antiplatelet therapy: I. Prevention of death, myocardial infarction, and stroke, by prolonged antiplatelet therapy in various categories of patients. BMJ 1994;308:81–106.

194. Freed M, Rosenthal A, Fyler D. Attempts to reduce arterial thrombosis after cardiac catheterization in children: use of percutaneous technique and aspirin. Am Heart J 1974;87:283–6.

195. Mingers AM, Heimburger N, Zeithler P, et al. Homozygous type I plasminogen deficiency. Semin Thromb Hemostas 1997;23:259–69.

196. Schott D, Dempfle CE, Beck P, et al. Therapy with a purified plasminogen concentrate in an infant with ligneous conjunctivitis and homozygous plasminogen deficiency. N Engl J Med 1998;339:1679–86.

197. Thomas GR, Thibodeaux H, Errett CJ, et al. Limiting systemic plasminogenolysis reduces the bleeding potential for tissue-type plasminogen activators but not for streptokinase. Thromb Haemost 1996;75:915–20.

198. Bell WR. Evaluation of thrombolytic agents. Drugs 1997;54:11–7.

199. Marci M, Panzini E, Lozzi A, Russo F. Systemic venous thrombolysis with rt-PA in arterial embolism of the legs in the elderly. Clin Ter 1996;147:371–6.

200. Ferguson JJ, Taqi K. IIb/IIIa receptor blockade in acute myocardial infarction. Am Heart J 1999;138:164–70.

201. Okajima K, Abe H, Binder HR. Endothelial cell injury induced by plasmin in vitro. J Lab Clin Med 1995;126:377–84.

202. Wheeldon N, Cumberland D. Pharmacologic prevention of acute ischemic complications of coronary angioplasty. Cathet Cardiovasc Diagn 1997;42:249–56.

203. Cheseboro JH, Knaterud G, Roberts R. Thrombolysis in myocardial infarction (TIMI) trial, phase 1: a comparison between intravenous plasminogen activator and intravenous streptokinase. Circulation 1987;76:142–54.

204. Verstraete M, Bleifeld W, Bory M. Randomized trial of intravenous recombinant tissue-type plasminogen activator versus intravenous streptokinase in acute myocardial infarction. Lancet 1985;1:842–7.

205. Gore JM, Granger CB, Simoons ML. Stroke after thrombolysis: mortality and functional outcomes in the GUSTO-I Trial. Circulation 1995;92:2811–8.

206. Berkowitz SD, Granger CB, Pieper KS. Incidence and predictors of bleeding after contemporary thrombolytic therapy for myocardial infarction. Circulation 1997;95:2508–16.

207. Simoons ML, Maggioni AP, Knatterud G, et al. Individual risk assessment for intracranial haemorrhage during thrombolytic therapy. Lancet 1993;342:1523–8.

208. Selker HP, Bechansky JR, Schmid CH. Presenting pulse pressure predicts thrombolytic therapy-related intracranial hemorrhage: thrombolytic predictive instrument (TPI) project results. Circulation 1994;90:1657–61.

209. Maggioni AP, Franzosi MG, Santoro E. The risk of stroke in patients with acute myocardial infarction after thrombolytic and antithrombotic treatment. N Engl J Med 1992;327:1–6.

210. Wilcox RG, ven der Lippe G, Olsson CG. Trial of tissue plasminogen activator or mortality reduction in acute myocardial infarction: Anglo-Scandinavian Study of Early Thrombolysis (ASSET). Lancet 1988;2:525–30.

211. International Joint Efficiency Comparison of Thrombolytics. Randomized, double-blind comparison of reteplase double-bolus administration with streptokinase in acute myocardial infarction (INJECT): trial to investigate equivalence. Lancet 1995;346:329–36.

212. The Global Use of Strategies to Open Occluded Coronary Arteries (GUSTO III) Investigators. A comparison of reteplase with alteplase for acute myocardial infarction. N Engl J Med 1997;337:1118–23.

213. The Continuous Infusion versus Double-Bolus Administration of Alteplase (COBALT) Investigators. A comparison of continuous infusion of alteplase with double-bolus administration for acute myocardial infarction. N Engl J Med 1997;337:1124–30.

214. Zenz W, Arlt F, Sodia S, Berghold A. Intracerebral hemorrhage during fibrinolytic therapy in children: a review of the literature of the last thirty years. Semin Thromb Haemost 1997;23:321–32.

215. Merlini PA, Ardissino D, Bauer KA, et al. Activation of the hemostatic mechanism during thrombolysis in patients with unstable angina pectoris. Blood 1995;86:3327–32.

216. Weitz JI. Elevated fibrinopeptide A and B levels during thrombolytic therapy: real or artefactual? Thromb Haemost 1996;75:529–35.

217. Puri RN, Colman RW. Reocclusion after thrombolytic therapy: strategies for inhibiting thrombin-induced platelet aggregation. Blood Coagul Fibrinolysis 1993;4:465–78.

218. White HD, van de Werf F. Thrombolysis for acute myocardial infarction. Circulation 1998;97:1632–46.

219. Theiss W, Wirtzfeld A, Fink U, Maubach P. The success rate of fibrinolytic therapy in fresh and old thrombosis of the iliac and femoral veins. Angiology 1983;34:61–9.

220. Hirsh J, Salzman EW, Marder VJ. Treatment of venous thromboembolism. In: Colman RW, Hirsh J, Marder VJ, Salzman EW, eds. Hemostasis and thrombosis: basic principles and clinical practise. Philadelphia: JB Lippincott Company, 1994:1346–66.

221. Vogelzang RL, Moel DI, Cohn RA, et al. Acute renal vein thrombosis: successful treatment with intraarterial urokinase. Radiology 1988;169:681–2.

222. Crowley JJ, Pereira JK, Harris LS, Becker CJ. Peripherally inserted central catheters: experience in 523 children. Radiology 1997;204:617–21.

223. Poulain F, Raynaud A, Bouquelot P, et al. Local thrombolysis and thromboaspiration in the treatment of acutely thrombosed arteriovenous hemodialysis fistulas. Cardiovasc Intervent Radiol 1991;14:98–101.

224. Rodkin RS, Bookstein JJ, Heeney DJ, Davis GB. Streptokinase and transluminal angioplasty in the treatment of acutely thrombosed hemodialysis access fistulas. Radiology 1983;149:425–8.

225. Pyles LA, Pierpont ME, Steiner ME, et al. Fibrinolysis by tissue plasminogen activator in a child with pulmonary embolism. J Pediatr 1990;116:801–4.

226. Robinson LA, Wright BT. Central venous catheter occlusion caused by body-heat-mediated calcium phosphate precipitation. Am J Hosp Pharm 1982;39:120–1.

227. Hinson RM, Naulty C. Letter. J Perinatol 1995;16:519–20.

228. Mulvihill SJ, Fonkalsrud EW. Complications of superior versus inferior vena cava occlusion in infants receiving central total parenteral nutrition. J Pediatr Surg 1984;19:752–7.

229. Haire WD, Lieberman RP, Lund GB, et al. Obstructed central venous catheters. Restoring function with a 12-hour infusion of low-dose urokinase. Cancer 1990;66:2279–85.

230. Backeljauw PF, Moodie DS, Murphy DJJ. High-dose urokinase therapy for the lysis of a central venous catheter-related thrombus in a young patient with Hodgkin's disease. Clin Pediatr 1991;30:274–7.

231. Haire WD, Lieberman RP, Edney J, et al. Hickman catheter-induced thoracic vein thrombosis. Cancer 1990;66:900–8.

232. Suarez CR, Gonzalez J, Menendez C, et al. Neonatal and maternal platelets: activation at time of birth. Am J Hematol 1988;29:18–21.

233. Fishbein JD, Friedman HS, Bennett BB, Falletta JM. Catheter-related sepsis refractory to antibiotics treated successfully with adjunctive urokinase infusion. Pediatr Infect Dis J 1990;9:676–8.

234. Jones GR, Konsler GK, Dunaway RP, et al. Prospective analysis of urokinase in the treatment of catheter sepsis in pediatric hematology-oncology patients. J Pediatr Surg 1993;28:350–7.

235. Haffar AA, Rench MA, Ferry GD, et al. Failure of urokinase to resolve Broviac catheter-related bacteremia in children. J Pediatr 1984;104:256–8.

236. Rodriguez M, Sosenko I. Catheter-induced aortic thrombus masquerading as coarctation of the aorta. Clin Pediatr 1989;28:581–4.

237. Mortensson W. Angiography of the femoral artery following percutaneous catheterization in infants and children. Acta Radiol [Diagn] 1976;17:581–93.

238. Burrows P, Benson L, Williams W, et al. Iliofemoral arterial complications of balloon angioplasty for systemic obstructions in infants and children. Circulation 1990;82:1697–704.

239. Zenz W, Muntean W, Beitzke A, et al. Tissue plasminogen activator (alteplase) treatment for femoral artery thrombosis after cardiac catheterization in infants and children. Br Heart J 1993;70:382–5.

240. Rothman A. Arterial complications of interventional cardiac catheterization in patients with congenital heart disease. Circulation 1990;82:1868–71.

241. Hohn AR, Craenen J, Lambert EC. Arterial pulses following percutaneous catheterization in children. Pediatrics 1969;43:617–20.

242. Kern IB. Management of children with chronic femoral artery obstruction. J Pediatr Surg 1977;12:83–90.

243. Besse P, Ledain L, Chayon J, et al. Acute thrombosis of disc valve prostheses: fibrinolytic treatment-diagnosis. Haemostasis 1986;16:90–101.

244. Kemennu L, Riggs TW. Tissue plasminogen activator lysis of a right ventricular thrombus. Am Heart J 1992;123:1057–8.

245. Koska J, Kunichika ET, Pepine CJ, Wagman AJ. Successful use of low dose tissue plasminogen activator for treatment of thrombosed prosthetic valve in a 22 month old child. Am Heart J 1992;124:783–5.

246. Mahony L, Nikaidoh H, Fixler DE. Thrombolytic therapy with streptokinase for late intraatrial thrombosis after modified Fontan procedure. Am J Cardiol 1988;62:343–4.

247. Martinez-Tallo E, Campo F, Delgado M, et al. Thrombus in right atrium in two infants successfully treated with tissue plasminogen activator. Pediatr Emerg Care 1997;13:37–9.

248. Puleo JA, Fontanet HL, Schocken DD. The role of prolonged thrombolytic infusions and transesophageal echocardiography in thrombosed prosthetic heart valves: case report and review of the literature. Clin Cardiol 1995;18:679–84.

249. Jost C, Yancy C, Ring S. Combined thrombolytic therapy for prosthetic mitral valve thrombosis. Ann Thorac Surg 1993;55:159–61.

250. Hacke W, Ringleb P, Stingele R. Thrombolysis in acute cerebrovascular disease: indications and limitations. Thromb Haemost 1999;82:983–6.

251. DeWitte T, Cross I, Moran CJ, et al. Relationship between clot location and outcome after basilar artery thrombolysis. Am J Neuroradiol 1997;18:1221–8.

252. Lindley RI. Thrombolytic treatment for acute ischaemic stroke: consent can be ethical. BMJ 1998;316:1005–7.

253. DiRocco C, Iannelli A, Leone G, et al. Heparin-urokinase treatment in aseptic dural sinus thrombosis. Arch Neurol 1981;38:431–5.

254. Whitelaw A, Rivers RP, Creighton L, Gaffney P. Low dose intraventricular fibrinolytic treatment to prevent posthaemorrhagic hydrocephalus. Arch Dis Child 1992;67:12–4.

255. Whitelaw A. Endogenous fibrinolysis in neonatal cerebrospinal fluid. Eur J Pediatr 1993;152:928–30.

256. Lafave MS, Decter RM. Intravesical urokinase for the management of clot retention in boys. J Urol 1993;150:1467–8.

257. Zenz W, Muntean W, Gallistl S, et al. Recombinant tissue plasminogen activator treatment in two infants with fulminant meningococcemia. Pediatrics 1995;96:44–8.

12 ANTIPLATELET AGENTS AND ALTERNATIVES TO STANDARD ANTICOAGULANT THERAPY

Over recent years there has been a tremendous increase in the number of antiplatelet agents in clinical use. In addition to drugs that inhibit platelet biochemical reactions, newer agents that target the glycoprotein IIb/IIIa (GP IIb/IIIa) receptor have been developed. While many of these newer drugs have been extensively tested in various adult populations, there have as yet been no reports on their use in children. Despite these new advances, aspirin, the prototypical antiplatelet drug, remains the cheapest, most widely studied, and most frequently used antiplatelet agent. Aspirin is increasingly used as primary and secondary prophylaxis in children with thromboembolic events (TEs). The following section discusses (1) the relevant age-dependent platelet factors that may influence therapy, (2) pharmacology, (3) indications for antiplatelet therapy, (4) doses, and (5) adverse effects.

Age-Dependent Features

Compared to adult controls, neonatal platelets are hyporeactive to thrombin, adenosine diphosphate (ADP)/epinephrine, and thromboxane A_2 (TXA_2) but show increased reactivity to ristocetin.[1,2] The hyperactivity of neonatal platelets is the result of a defect intrinsic to neonatal platelets.[1] Paradoxically, the bleeding time (BT) is short in newborns due to increased red blood cell size, increased hematocrit, and increased concentrations of von Willebrand factor (vWF) with disproportionately increased high molecular weight multimers.[3–5] No studies of platelet function in healthy children were identified except for the BT that, relative to adults, is prolonged throughout childhood in two of three studies (Figure 12–1).[6–8] These physiologic differences suggest that the optimal dosage of antiplatelet

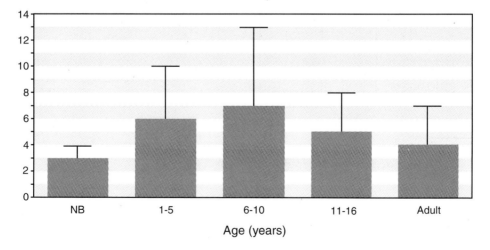

Bleeding Time (mins)

Age (years)

Figure 12–1 The effect of age on bleeding times.

agents in newborns and children may also differ from adults.

Aspirin Aspirin irreversibly inactivates the enzyme cyclooxygenase (Figure 12–2).[9–12] In platelets this inhibition prevents the conversion of arachidonic acid to the prostaglandin endoperoxide G_2, thus preventing TXA_2 production. Aspirin is rapidly absorbed from the gastrointestinal (GI) tract, such that the antiplatelet effect is demonstrable within an hour of ingestion.[13] The effect is dose dependent and cumulative.[14] When aspirin therapy is ceased, cyclooxygenase activity returns only as new platelets are added to the circulation, which takes 7 to 10 days.[15,16]

Pharmacology of Antiplatelet Agents

Dipyridamole Dipyridamole probably derives its antiplatelet effects from both inhibition of cyclic nucleotide phosphoesterase and blocking the uptake of adenosine.[17] Direct stimulation of prostaglandin I_2 (PGI_2) has also been suggested, but the relevance of this mechanism at in vivo pharmacologic doses is doubtful. The absorption of dipyridamole from the GI tract is variable and the drug is metabolized in the liver with biliary excretion.[18] Enterohepatic recirculation may occur.[18]

Thienopyridines Ticlopidine and clopidogrel are related compounds. Both drugs selectively inhibit ADP-induced platelet aggregation.[19–21] The exact mechanism of action remains uncertain.[22] Both drugs lack antiplatelet activity in vitro, suggesting in vivo transformation to active metabolites is required.[22] The target of the active metabolites within the platelet is also unknown and is thought to be a receptor mediating the activity of ADP.[20,21]

Ticlopidine Ticlopidine is rapidly absorbed from the GI tract, with peak plasma concentrations achieved 1 to 3 hours after a single oral dose.[19] The apparent elimination half-life is 24 to 36 hours; however, there is substantial drug accumulation after bid dosing. Ticlopidine is reversibly bound to plasma proteins.[19] The antiplatelet effect of ticlopidine is additive to that of aspirin.[23]

Clopidogrel Clopidogrel does not achieve measurable plasma levels after single oral doses.[21] Clopi-

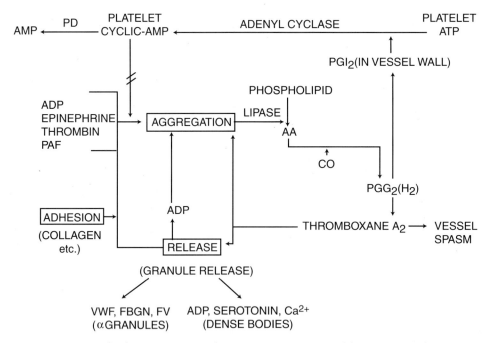

Figure 12–2 Platelet activation mechanisms. Aspirin irreversibly inactivates the enzyme cyclo-oxygenase.

AA = arachadonic acid; CO = cyclo-oxygenase; PD = phosphodiesterase.

Reproduced with permission.[145]

dogrel is probably rapidly absorbed and extensively metabolized by the liver, with the main systemic metabolite being SR26334. SR26334 has an elimination half-life of approximately 8 hours.[21] The active metabolites of clopidogrel likely cause cumulative irreversible platelet inhibition similar to that seen with aspirin.[24] This observation leads to the once daily dosing regimen usually used for clopidogrel.[20,21] The antiplatelet effects of clopidogrel and aspirin are probably additive; however, further studies are required to confirm this.

Glycoprotein IIb-IIIa Antagonists   GPIIb-IIIa antagonists are a new class of antiplatelet drugs that are now available in intravenous form (ReoPro™, Aggrastat™, Intregelin™) and will soon be available in oral form.[25–29] These drugs, which are either chimeric antibodies (ReoPro™) or peptides (Aggrastat™ and Intregelin™), act by binding to the platelet surface GPIIb-IIIa complex, thereby inhibiting fibrinogen-mediated platelet aggregation.[25–27,30–32] Because fibrinogen binding to the platelet GPIIb/IIIa complex is the final common pathway of platelet aggregation, these drugs are powerful antiplatelet agents.[33] However, there are as yet no reports of their use in children.

Therapeutic Range, Dose Response, and Monitoring of Antiplatelet Agents

Aspirin   There is no therapeutic range or need to monitor aspirin. In adults, well-designed randomized trials have shown that the antiplatelet effects of aspirin are effective in doses ranging from 50 to 100 mg/day, and further studies have suggested that doses as low as 30 mg/day may be adequate.[34–38] In children, there are no studies that compare different doses of aspirin. Empiric low doses of 1 to 5 mg/kg/day have been proposed as adjuvant therapy for Blalock-Taussig shunts, some endovascular stents, and some cerebrovascular events.[39] For mechanical prosthetic heart valves, aspirin doses of 6 to 20 mg/kg/day were used in eight studies,[40–47] either alone or in combination with 6 mg/kg/day of dipyridamole in three divided doses.[47] High dose aspirin, 80 to 100 mg/kg/day, is used in Kawasaki's disease during the acute phase (up to 14 days), then

3 to 5 mg/kg/day for 7 weeks or longer if there is echocardiographic evidence of coronary artery abnormalities.[48–50]

Dipyridamole   In children, the second most commonly used antiplatelet agent for mechanical prosthetic heart valves is dipyridamole in doses of 2 to 5 mg/kg/day.[47,51] Adult doses are generally 100 to 400 mg/day. No monitoring is required.[17]

Ticlopidine   Studies in adults have used ticlopidine at doses of 250 mg bid and clopidogrel at 75 mg daily.[18,52–55] There appears no difference in the antiplatelet effect when 50, 75 or 100 mg/day of clopidogrel is used.[21] There is no reported use in children and dosage recommendations are unknown. No monitoring of dose effect is required.

Glycoprotein IIb-IIIa Antagonists   There is no information on dosage for GPIIb-IIIa antagonists in children. Although GPIIb-IIIa antagonist therapy may need to be monitored, the optimal assays are still under investigation.[56] The appropriate therapeutic ranges for these assays may prove to be different in children, because of the agent-dependent differences in platelet function described above.

Adverse Effects of Antiplatelet Agents

Aspirin   Newborns may be exposed to antiplatelet agents due to maternal ingestion (aspirin as treatment for preeclampsia in clinical trials aimed at reducing intracranial bleeding, or therapeutically, indomethacin as medical therapy for patent ductus arteriosus).[57,58] Clearance of both salicylate and indomethacin is slower in newborns, potentially placing them at risk for longer periods of time. However, in vitro studies have not demonstrated an additive effect of aspirin on the hypofunction of newborn platelets, and evidence linking maternal aspirin ingestion to clinically important bleeding in newborns is weak (level V). Indomethacin does prolong the bleeding time in newborns, but the evidence linking indomethacin to intracranial hemorrhage (ICH) is weak.[59,60]

In older children, aspirin rarely causes clinically important hemorrhage, except in the presence of an underlying hemostatic defect or in children also treated with anticoagulants or thrombolytic therapy. The relatively low doses of aspirin used as antiplatelet therapy, as compared to the much higher doses used for anti-inflammatory therapy, seldom cause other side effects. GI tract side effects (abdominal discomfort, heartburn, nausea, GI tract bleeding) from aspirin occur with increasing frequency with higher doses and are less likely to occur at low doses.[61] In adults, clinically important complications are less likely at daily doses less than 325 mg/day.[62] Overt upper GI tract bleeding may occur with long-term therapy at doses of 75 to 250 mg/day. In the absence of concomitant nonsteroidal anti-inflammatory drugs or intrinsic GI tract disease the risk of peptic ulceration is small. If symptoms of gastric irritation develop, older, larger children may benefit by using enteric coated aspirin, although enteric coated aspirin may be no less harmful to the GI tract.[62] A second approach is the commencement of an H_2 antagonist or antacid.[62,63]

Reye's syndrome is a rare acute encephalopathy complicated by hepatic dysfunction that occurs mostly in children.[64–68] A strong association between development of Reye's syndrome and aspirin use has been reported in case control studies. However, a causal relationship has not been proven and the association appears to be a dose-dependent effect of aspirin.[69–75] With antiplatelet doses of aspirin (1 to 5 mg/kg/day) Reye's syndrome rarely if ever is involved. However, as a precautionary measure, parents should be educated to stop aspirin use in the presence of fever and/or if their child has chickenpox or influenza.

Dipyridamole   Headache is a frequently reported side effect in adults taking dipyridamole. There are few pediatric data available.

Thienopyridines   Ticlopidine is associated with significant neutropenia (< 1 x 10^9/L) in approximately 2 percent of patients.[76] Other adverse effects include thrombocytopenia, aplastic anemia,[77] and thrombotic thrombocytopenic purpura (TTP),[78] which usually respond to plasmapheresis. Skin rashes, diarrhea, and cholestatic jaundice have also been noted. In the CAPRIE study, clopidogrel was

associated with increased frequency of severe rash and severe diarrhea compared to aspirin but with reduced gastrointestinal discomfort.[55] Neutropenia was not increased in the clopidogrel arm.

Glycoprotein IIb-IIIa Antagonists   GPIIb-IIIa antagonists can induce antigenicity and thrombocytopenia.[79–85] Further studies are required to determine the clinical significance of these side effects in children.

Treatment of Bleeding Due to Antiplatelet Agents   It is unusual for aspirin or dipyrimadole alone to cause serious bleeding. More frequently, antiplatelet agents are one of several other causes of bleeding such as an underlying coagulopathy and antithrombotic agents.[86] Transfusions of platelet concentrates and/or the use of products that enhance platelet adhesion (plasma products containing high concentrations of vWF, or D-des amino arginine vasopressin [DDAVP]) may be helpful.

ALTERNATIVES TO UNFRACTIONATED HEPARIN AND LOW MOLECULAR WEIGHT HEPARIN THERAPY

Occasionally, alternative second line therapy to unfractionated heparin (UFH) or low molecular weight heparin (LMWH) may be required in children. A common situation is the treatment of heparin induced thrombocytopenia (HIT), in which the most commonly used drug is orgaran (danaproid). Other options include hirudin or lepirudin. Less commonly, one is faced with failure of UFH or LMWH in the treatment of acute TEs. In this situation, apart from increasing the intensity of anticoagulation or using an alternative anticoagulant, one sometimes needs to consider the use of an intravenous filter or interruption device.

Orgaran

Orgaran is prepared from animal intestinal mucosa and is a mixture of anticoagulant glycosaminoglycans (GAGs).[87] Orgaran has an anti-factor(F)Xa/anti-FIIa activity of 28:1, which is significantly different from most LMWHs.[87] Orgaran is given intravenously or subcutaneously and has a half-life based on anti-FXa activity of approximately 24 hours.[88–91] Plasma clearance is predominantly renal and so dose reduction may be required in renal failure. Bleeding complications are infrequently reported; however, there is no known antidote for orgaran as protamine is ineffective in reversing the anti-FXa activity.[91] Organ does not affect the International Normalized Ratio (INR), which simplifies the conversion to oral anticoagulant (OA) therapy when the acute HIT is resolved.[92]

Clinical Indications While orgaran is approved in the United States for thromboprophylaxis in surgical patients, the primary clinical use is as an immediate substitute for UFH in patients suspected of having acute HIT.[89,92–94] In vitro cross reactivity with HIT antibodies is low, at less than 5 percent, as compared to over 90 percent for LMWH.[95] However, even in the presence of cross reactive antibodies, the platelet recovery in patients with HIT treated with orgaran is unimpaired.[96,97] There appears to be no reason to perform in vitro testing for cross reactive antibodies to orgaran.[92] A randomized controlled trial (RCT) has shown the effectiveness of orgaran in the treatment of HIT.[94] In addition, there is a retrospective analysis of 338 patients with acute HIT treated with orgaran.[93] Organ was successful in achieving platelet recovery without new or progressive TEs, and without complications that required drug interruption in 91 percent of patients.[93,94]

Pediatric Patients The published literature on the use of orgaran in children is sparse, with only isolated case reports.[98–100] Current dose recommendations for the treatment of HIT in children are a loading dose of 30 units/kg followed by a maintenance dose of 1.2 to 2.0 units/kg/hour. Organ can be monitored using an anti-factor Xa assay, providing that orgaran is used to make the standard curve.[92] The therapeutic range is 0.4 to 0.8 units/mL. Two case reports described the use of orgaran in cardiopulmonary bypass (CPB) in children.[99,100] Further studies will be required to optimize the management of this clinical scenario, which is complicated by the long half-life of orgaran and the irreversible anti-FXa effect. Children re-

quiring CPB and who have a past history of HIT occurring greater than 100 days previously may benefit from UFH therapy for CPB because of the ease of monitoring and reversibility with protamine. Subsequently, orgaran would be immediately initiated following completion of the CPB and neutralization of UFH.

Hirudin and Lepirudin

Hirudin is a naturally occurring direct thrombin inhibitor produced in the salivary gland of the medicinal leech.[101] Lepirudin is the synthetic analogue.[102] Both molecules are 65 amino acids; however, lepirudin has a leucine instead of an isoleucine in the amino terminal end and lacks sulfonation of the tyrosine at position 63.[102] Lepirudin is given intravenously and the half-life is 1.5 hours.[92,103–105] Plasma clearance is via the kidneys, and drug accumulation with resultant bleeding is commonly seen in patients with renal failure.[106] There is no known antidote. Hirudin and lepirudin are monitored using the activated partial thromboplastin time (APTT) with a recommended target range being 1.5 to 2.5 times the baseline value.[92] The prothrombin time (PT) is also prolonged during treatment with hirudin or lepirudin, making conversion to OA therapy more difficult. Approximately half the patients treated with lepirudin for HIT develop IgG antihirudin antibodies, which are associated with an unexpected increase in anticoagulant effect in a small number of patients.[107]

Clinical Indications Lepirudin is approved for the treatment of HIT in a number of countries.[92] In studies comparing lepirudin to historical controls, lepirudin was associated with a 50 percent reduction in mortality, limb amputation, and new TEs.[108] Lepirudin may be better suited to patients with HIT who require surgical intervention due to the short half-life.[92] There are no published data on the use of hirudin or lepirudin in children.

Argatroban

Argatroban is an arginine-based synthetic direct thrombin inhibitor.[109–111] The half-life is 40 minutes, although excretion is hepatic and prolonged in liver failure.[109–111] Argatroban can be monitored using the APTT, with the recommended target range of 1.5 to 3 times baseline.[109–111] There is no antidote for the anticoagulant effect, and argatroban prolongs the INR, similarly to hirudin, again making conversion to OA therapy difficult.[92] There is limited experience in adults with HIT, and no published data on the use of argatroban in children.

Ancrod

Ancrod is derived from a snake venom, extracted from the Russel pit viper.[112] Ancrod cleaves fibrinopeptide A but not fibrinopeptide B from fibrinogen.

Clinical Indications Ancrod was previously commonly used in Canada for the management of HIT.[113–116] However, ancrod does not reduce thrombin generation, which may lead to TE extension. Orgaran has almost totally replaced the use of ancrod as a first-line therapy for HIT. Ancrod is given as a loading dose of 1 to 2 units/kg infused over 6 hours, followed by a maintainence dose of 1 to 2 units/kg/24 hours. During therapy with ancrod, fibrinogen should be monitored and maintained between 0.5 and 1.0 g/L.

INTRAVENOUS FILTER DEVICES

Prior to the discovery of anticoagulant drugs, the only therapy available for the prevention of fatal pulmonary embolism (PE) in patients with lower limb deep vein thrombosis (DVT) was inferior vena cava (IVC) ligation or plication. Unfortunately the immediate and delayed complication rate associated with the procedure was significant, and mortality high. Intraluminal venous interruption devices were first introduced in the early 1970s. There are now a number of different types of intravenous interruption devices; however, the Greenfield and bird's nest filters are the most widely used.[117–123] Filters are usually inserted via the internal jugular or femoral veins and advanced into position in the IVC under fluoroscopic control.[124–127]

Clinical Indications The most common indication for the use of IVC interruption is to prevent PE in the presence of a contraindication to anticoagulant therapy in a patient with, or a high risk of, proximal DVT.[124] The contraindication may be transient, such as urgent surgery, or more long term, such as coexistent illness that increases the risk of bleeding. Other indications include recurrent TE despite adequate anticoagulation, for example in patients with cancer, trauma, and elective surgery.[127–136] Depending on the indication, simultaneous use of anticoagulants is frequently advocated.[117] The evidence for the efficacy of intravenous filters is based on uncontrolled case series. The majority of studies poorly described inclusion and exclusion criteria and follow up was often incomplete. In the only randomized trial of filter placement, the rate of PE was reduced. However, the reduced rate of PE was associated with an increase in DVT in the group receiving filters. The overall survival was not different in the two groups.[137]

Complications Potential complications of intravenous filters include perforation of the IVC, migration of the filter, infection, filter tilting (leading to loss of filtering ability), insertion site DVT, IVC obstruction, and recurrent PE.[118]

Pediatric Patients Intravenous interruption devices are rarely used in children. Only a handful of anecdotal reports of successful and failed IVC filters in children have been published.[138,139] In contrast to adults, temporary filters are often used in children and removed when the source of PE is no longer present.[138] The majority of DVT in children is associated with central venous lines (CVLs) and occurs in the upper venous system, in contrast to adults in whom the majority of DVT occurs in the lower limbs. Thus, there is limited ability to place a filter between the thrombus and the right side of the heart. In addition, reduced size of veins makes filter insertion considerably more difficult, and requires smaller size filters that may not be available for very small infants. There are no specific guidelines for the use of filters in children and the risk/benefit ratio needs to be considered in each case.

Embolectomy

Adult Patients In adults, surgical embolectomy in the venous system is usually only considered for massive PE.[124] The embolectomy may be performed as an open procedure or by a transvenous catheter approach.[140] Neither treatment has been compared to anticoagulant or lytic treatment in a prospective trial. In general, the procedure is reserved for patients with massive PE for whom death is imminent or for whom conservative therapy has failed. Not surprisingly, mortality in this group is high.[136,141]

Pediatric Patients Open surgical embolectomy is reported as successful therapy in premature neonates and children as young as 6 days old.[142,143] Embolectomy is often used following major cardiac surgery.[144] For example, embolectomy following Fontan surgery, when the cause of obstructed pulmonary blood flow is not clear, and exploratory surgery is required. Embolectomy should always be followed by an appropriate period of anticoagulation.

REFERENCES

1. Rajasekhar D, Kestin A, Bednarek F, et al. Neonatal platelets are less reactive than adult platelets to physiological agonists in whole blood. Thromb Haemost 1994;72:957–63.
2. Nossel HL, Lanzkowsky P, Levy S, et al. A study of coagulation factor levels in women during labour and in their newborn infants. Thromb Diath Haemorrh 1966;16:185–97.
3. Katz JA, Moake JL, McPherson PD, et al. Relationship between human development and disappearance of unusually large von Willebrand factor multimers from plasma. Blood 1989;73:1851–8.
4. Weinstein M, Blanchard R, Moake J, et al. Fetal and neonatal von Willebrand factor (vWf) is unusually large and similar to the vWf in patients with thrombotic thrombocytopenia purpura. Br J Haematol 1989;72:68–72.
5. Gerrard J, Docherty J, Israels S, et al. A reassessment of the bleeding time: association of age, hematocrit, platelet function, von Willebrand factor, and bleeding time thromboxane B_2 with the length of the bleeding time. Clin Invest Med 1989;12:165–71.
6. Andrew M, Vegh P, Johnston M, et al. Maturation of the hemostatic system during childhood. Blood 1992;80:1998–2005.
7. Sanders J, Holtkamp C, Buchanan G. The bleeding time may be longer in children than in adults. J Pediatr Hematol Oncol 1990;12:314–8.
8. Aversa L, Vasquez A, Penalver J, et al. Bleeding time in normal children. J Pediatr Hematol Oncol 1995;17:25–8.
9. Roth G, Majerus P. The mechanism of the effect of aspirin on human platelets. I. Acetylation of a particulate fraction protein. J Clin Invest 1975;56:624–32.
10. Roth GJ, Stanford N, Majerus PW. Acetylation of prostaglandin synthase by aspirin. Proc Natl Acad Sci U S A 1975;72:3073–7.
11. Burch JW, Stanford PW, Majerus PW. Inhibition of platelet prostaglandin synthetase by oral aspirin. J Clin Invest 1979;61:314–9.
12. Majerus PW. Arachadonate metabolism in vascular disorders. J Clin Invest 1983;72:1521–5.
13. Pederson AK, FitzGerald GA. Dose-related kinetics of aspirin: presystemic acetylation of platelet cyclooxygenase. N Engl J Med 1984;311:1206–11.
14. Patrono C. Aspirin as an antiplatelet drug. N Engl J Med 1994;330:1287–94.
15. Cerskus AL, Ali M, Davies BJ. Possible significance of small numbers of functional platelets in a population of aspirin-treated platelets in vitro and in vivo. Thromb Res 1980;18:389–97.
16. O'Brien JR. Effects of salicylates on human platelets. Lancet 1968;1:779–83.
17. FitzGerald GA. Dipyridamole. N Engl J Med 1987;316:1247–57.
18. Patrono C, Coller B, Dalen JE, et al. Platelet active drugs: the relationships among dose, effectiveness, and side effects. Chest 1998;114:470S–88S.
19. Ito MK, Smith AR, Lee ML. Ticlopidine: a new platelet aggregation inhibitor. Clin Pharm 1992;11:603–17.
20. Savi P, Heilmann E, Nurden P. Clopidogrel: an antithrombotic drug acting on the ADP-dependent activation pathway of human platelets. Clin Appl Thromb/Hemost 1996;2:35–42.
21. Herbert JM, Frehel D, Vallee E. Clopidogrel, a novel antiplatelet and antithrombotic agent. Cardiovasc Drug Rev 1993;11:180–98.
22. Schror K. Antiplatelet drugs. A comparative review. Drugs 1995;50:7–28.
23. Lecompte TP, Lecrubier C, Bouloux C. Antiplatelet effects of the addition of acetylsalicylic acid 40 mg daily to ticlopidine in human healthy volunteers. Clin Appl Thromb/Hemostas 1997;3:245–50.
24. FitzGerald GA, Patrono C. Antiplatelet drugs. In: Verstraete M, Fuster V, Topol E, editors. Cardiovascular thrombosis-thrombocardiology, thromboneurology. Philadelphia: Lippincott-Raven; 1998. p. 121–39.
25. Coller BS. A new murine monoclonal antibody reports an activation-dependent change in the conformation

and/or microenvironment of the platelet glycoprotein IIb-IIIa. J Clin Invest 1985;76:101–8.

26. Philips DR, Scarborough RM. Clinical pharmacology of eptifibatide. Am J Cardiol 1997;80:11B–20B.

27. Hartman GD, Efbertson MS, Halczenko W. Non-peptide fibrinogen receptor antagonists. 1. Discovery and design of exosite inhibitors. J Med Chem 1992;35:4640–2.

28. Simpfendorfer C, Kottke-Marchant K, Lowrie M. First chronic platelet glycoprotein IIb/IIIa integrin blockade: a randomized, placebo-controlled study of xemilofiban in unstable angina with percutaneous coronary interventions. Circulation 1997;96:76–81.

29. Cannon CP, McCabe CH, Borzak S. Randomized trial of an oral platelet glycoprotein IIb/IIIa antagonist, sibrafiban, in patients after an acute coronary syndrome: results of the TIMI 12 trial. Circulation 1998;97:340–9.

30. Egbertson MS, Chang CT, Duggan ME. Non-peptide fibrinogen receptor antagonists. 2. Optimization of a tyrosine template as a mimic for Arg-Gly-Asp. J Med Chem 1994;37:2537–51.

31. Harrington RA, Kleiman NS, Kottke-Marchant K. Immediate and reversible platelet inhibition after intravenous administration of a peptide glycoprotein IIb/IIIa inhibitor during percutaneous coronary intervention. Am J Cardiol 1995;76:1222–7.

32. Gold HK, Gimple LS, Yasuda T. Pharmacodynamic study of F(ab')2 fragments of murine monoclonal antibody 7E3 directed against human platelet glycoprotein IIb/IIIa in patients with unstable angina pectoris. J Clin Invest 1990;86:651–9.

33. Coller BS. Blockade of platelet GPIIb/IIIa receptors as an antithrombotic strategy. Circulation 1995;92:2373–80.

34. The RISC Group. Risk of myocardial infarction and death during treatment with low dose aspirin and intravenous heparin in men with unstable coronary artery disease. Lancet 1992;336:827–30.

35. Juul-Moller S, Edvardsson N, Jahnmatz B. Double-blind trial of aspirin in primary prevention of myocardial infarction in patients with stable chronic angina pectoris. Lancet 1992;340:1421–5.

36. The SALT Collaborative Group. Swedish Aspirin Low-Dose Trial (SALT) of 75 mg aspirin as secondary prophylaxis after cerebrovascular ischaemic events. Lancet 1991;338:1345–491.

37. Lindblad B, Persson NH, Takolander R. Does low dose acetylsalicylic acid prevent stroke after carotid surgery? A double-blind, placebo-controlled randomized trial. Stroke 1993;24:1125–8.

38. The Dutch TIA Trial Study Group. A comparison of two doses of aspirin (30 mg vs 283 mg a day) in patients after a transient ischemic attack or minor ischemic stroke. N Engl J Med 1991;325:1261–6.

39. Hathaway WE. Use of antiplatelet agents in pediatric hypercoagulable states. Am J Dis Child 1984;138:301–4.

40. Serra A, McNicholas K, Olivier HJ, et al. The choice of anticoagulation in pediatric patients with the St. Jude Medical valve prostheses. J Cardiovasc Surg 1987;28:588–91.

41. Bradley LM, Midgley FM, Watson DC, et al. Anticoagulation therapy in children with mechanical prosthetic cardiac valves. Am J Cardiol 1985;56:533–5.

42. McGrath L, Gonzalez-Lavin L, Edlredge W, et al. Thromboembolic and other events following valve replacement in a pediatric population treated with antiplatelet agents. Ann Thorac Surg 1987;43:285–7.

43. El Makhlouf A, Friedli B, Oberhansli I, et al. Prosthetic heart valve replacement in children. J Thorac Cardiovasc Surg 1987;93:80–5.

44. Solymar L, Rao PS, Mardini MK, et al. Prosthetic valves in children and adolescents. Am Heart J 1991;121:557–68.

45. Borkon AM, Soule L, Reitz BA, et al. Five year follow-up after valve replacement with the St. Jude Medical valve in infants and children. Circulation 1986;74(Supp I):I-110–5.

46. LeBlanc J, Sett S, Vince D. Antiplatelet therapy in children with left-sided mechanical prostheses. Eur J Cardiothorac Surg 1993;7:211–5.

47. Bradley SM, Sade RM, Crawford FA, Stroud MR. Anticoagulation in children with mechanical valve prostheses. Ann Thorac Surg 1997;64:30–6.

48. Newburger J, Takahashi M, Burns J, et al. The treatment of Kawasaki syndrome with intravenous gamma globulin. N Engl J Med 1986;315:341–7.

49. Durongpisitkul K, Fururaj VJ, Park JM, Martin CF. The prevention of coronary artery aneurysm in Kawasaki disease: a meta-analysis on the efficacy of aspirin and immunoglobulin treatment. Pediatrics 1995;96:1057–61.

50. American Heart Association. Guidelines for long term management of patients with Kawasaki Disease. Committee on Rheumatic Fever, Endocarditis, and Kawasaki disease, Council on Cardiovascular Disease in the Young. Heart Dis Stroke 1994;3:169–70.

51. Katircioglu SF, Yamak B, Ulus AT, et al. Aortic valve replacement with the St Jude Medical prosthesis and fixed dose anticoagulation. J Cardiac Surg 1998;12:363–70.

52. Hass WK, Easton JD, Adams HP. A randomized trial comparing ticlopidine hydrochloride with aspirin for the prevention of stroke in high risk patients. N Engl J Med 1989;321:501–7.

53. Becquemin JP. Effect of ticlopidine on the long term patency of saphenous vein bypass grafts in the legs. Étude de la Ticlopidine après Pontage Femoro-

Poplite and the Association Universitaire de Recherche en Chirurgie. N Engl J Med 1997; 337:1726–31.

54. Gershlick AH. Antiplatelet therapy following stent deployment. Heart 1997;78:24–6.

55. CAPRIE Steering Committee. A randomised, blinded, trial of clopidogrel versus aspirin in patients at risk of ischaemic events (CAPRIE). Lancet 1996; 348:1329–39.

56. Coller BS. Monitoring platelet GPIIb/IIIa antagonist therapy. Circulation 1997;96:3828–32.

57. van Overmeire B, Brus F, van Acker KJ, et al. Aspirin versus indomethacin treatment of patent ductus arteriosus in preterm infants with respiratory distress syndrome. Pediatr Res 1995;38:886–91.

58. Davis J, Hendricks-Munoz K, Hagberg D, Manning J. The effects of indomethacin on renal function and intracranial hemorrhage in infants with patent ductus arteriosus. Dev Pharmacol Ther 1990;14:15–9.

59. Friedman Z, Whitman V, Maisels MJ, et al. Indomethacin disposition and indomethacin-induced platelet dysfunction in premature infants. J Clin Pharmacol 1978;18:272–9.

60. Corazza MS, Davis RF, Meritt A, et al. Prolonged bleeding time in preterm infants receiving indomethacin for patent ductus arteriosus. J Pediatr 1984; 105:292–6.

61. Roderick PJ, Wilkes HC, Meade TW. The gastrointestinal toxicity of aspirin: an overview of randomized controlled trials. Br J Clin Pharmacol 1993;35: 219–26.

62. Kelly JP, Kaufman DW, Jurgelon JM. Risk of aspirin-associated major upper gastrointestinal bleeding with enteric-coated or buffered product. Lancet 1996;348:1413–6.

63. Hawkey CJ, Karrasch JA, Szczepanski L. Omeprazole compared with misoprostol for ulcers associated with non-steroidal anti-inflammatory drugs. N Engl J Med 1998;338:727–34.

64. Hurwitz ES, Barrett MJ, Bregman D, et al. Public health service study of Reye's syndrome and medications: report of a main study. JAMA 1987;257:1905–11.

65. Prescott LF. Effects of non-narcotic analgesics on the liver. Drugs 1986;32:129–47.

66. Arrowsmith JB, Kennedy DL, Kuritsky JN, Faich GA. National patterns of aspirin use and Reye's syndrome reporting, United States, 1980 to 1985. Pediatrics 1987;79:858–63.

67. Hall S. Reye's syndrome and aspirin: a review. Br J Clin Pract Suppl 1990;70:4–11.

68. Public Health Laboratory Service Communicable Disease Surveillance Centre, London. Reye's syndrome and aspirin. Br J Clin Pract Suppl 1990;70:4–11.

69. Porter J, Robinson P, Glasgow J, et al. Trends in the incidence of Reye's syndrome and the use of aspirin. Arch Dis Child 1990;65:826–9.

70. Remington P, Shabino C, McGee H, et al. Reye's syndrome and juvenile rheumatoid arthritis in Michigan. Am J Dis Child 1985;139:870–2.

71. Makela A, Lang H, Korpela P. Toxic encephalopathy with hyperammonaemia during high-dose salicylate therapy. Acta Neurol Scand 1980;61:146–51.

72. Starko K, Ray C, Dominguez L, et al. Reye's syndrome and salicylate use. Pediatrics 1980;66:859–64.

73. Halpin T, Holtzhauer F, Campbell R, et al. Reye's syndrome and medication use. JAMA 1982;248: 687–91.

74. Young R, Toretti D, Williams R, et al. Reye's syndrome associated with long-term aspirin therapy. JAMA 1984;251:754–6.

75. Baum J. Aspirin in the treatment of juvenile arthritis. Am J Med 1983;74(6A):10–5.

76. FitzGerald GA. Ticlopidine in unstable angina: a more expensive aspirin? Circulation 1990;82:296–8.

77. Yeh SP, Hsueh EJ, Wu H. Ticlopidine-associated aplastic anemia: a case report and review of the literature. Ann Hematol 1998;76:87–90.

78. Bennett CL, Weinberg PD, Rozenberg-Ben-Dror K. Thrombotic thrombocytopenic purpura associated with ticlopidine: a review of 60 cases. Ann Intern Med 1998;128:541–4.

79. EPIC Investigators. Use of a monoclonal antibody directed against the platelet glycoprotein IIb/IIIa receptor in high risk coronary angioplasty. N Engl J Med 1994;330:956–61.

80. EPILOG Investigators. Platelet glycoprotein IIb/IIIa receptor blockade and low dose heparin during percutaneous coronary revascularization. N Engl J Med 1997;336:1689–96.

81. Kereiakes DJ, Essel JH, Abbottsmith CW. Abciximab-associated profound thrombocytopenia: therapy with immunoglobulin and platelet transfusion. Am J Cardiol 1996;78:1161–3.

82. Berkowitz SD, Harrington RA, Rund MM. Acute profound thrombocytopenia following c7E3 Fab (abciximab) therapy. Circulation 1997;95:809–13.

83. Tcheng JE, Kereiakas DJ, George BS. Safety of readministration of abciximab: interim results of the ReoPro readministration registry (R3). J Am Coll Cardiol 1998;31:238A.

84. IMPACT-II Investigators. Randomized placebo controlled trial of effect of eptifibatide on complications of percutaneous coronary intervention: IMPACT-IIa. Lancet 1997;349:1422–8.

85. RESTORE Investigators. Effects of platelet glycoprotein IIb/IIIa blockade with tirofiban on adverse cardiac events in patients with unstable angina or acute

myocardial infarction undergoing coronary angio-plasty. Circulation 1997;96:1445–53.

86. American Society of Hospital Pharmacists. AHFS Drug Information. Bethesda, MD. American Society of Hospital Pharmacists. 1992;1055–6.

87. Danhof M, de Boer A, Magnani H, Stiekma J. Pharmacokinetic considerations on orgaran (ORG 10172) therapy. Haemostasis 1992;22:73–84.

88. Bradbrook ID, Magnani HN, Moilker HC. ORG 10172: a low molecular weight heparinoid anticoagulant with a long half life in man. Br J Clin Pharmacol 1987;23:667–75.

89. Wilde M, Markham A. Danaparoid. A review of its pharmacological and clinical use in the management of heparin induced thrombocytopenia. Drugs 1997;54:903–24.

90. Stiekema J, Wijnand H, Van Dinther T, et al. Safety and pharmacokinetics of the low molecular weight heparinoid Org 10172 administered to healthy elderly volunteers. Br J Clin Pharmacol 1989;27:39–48.

91. Hoek J, Nurmohamed M, Hamelynck K, et al. Prevention of deep vein thrombosis following total hip replacement by low molecular weight heparinoid. Thromb Haemost 1992;67:28–32.

92. Hirsh J, Warkentin TE, Raschkle R, et al. Heparin and low molecular weight heparin: mechanism of action, pharmacokinetics, dosing considerations, monitoring, efficacy, and safety. Chest 1998;114:489S–510S.

93. Chong BH, Magnani HN. Organan in Heparin-induced thrombocytopenia. Haemostasis 1992;22:85–91.

94. Magnani HN. Heparin-induced thrombocytopenia (HIT): an overview of 230 patients treated with orgaran (Org 10172). Thromb Haemost 1993;70:554–61.

95. Warkentin TE. Danaparoid (orgaran) for the treatment of heparin-induced thrombocytopenia (HIT) and thrombosis: effects on in vivo thrombin and cross-linked fibrin generation, and evaluation of the clinical significance of in vitro cross-reactivity (XR) of danaparoid for HIT-IgG. Blood 1996;88:626a.

96. Warkentin TE. Limitations of conventional treatment options for heparin induced thrombocytopenia. Semin Hematol 1998;35:17–25.

97. Warkentin TE. Heparin induced thrombocytopenia. Pathogenesis, frequency, avoidance, and management. Drug Saf 1997;17:325–41.

98. Klement D, Rammos S, von Kries R, et al. Heparin as a cause of thrombus progression. Heparin-associated thrombocytopenia is an important differential diagnosis in paediatric patients even with normal platelet counts. Eur J Pediatr 1996;155:11–4.

99. Wilhelm M. Cardiopulmonary bypass in patients with heparin induced thrombocytopenia using Orgaran 10172. Ann Thorac Surg 1996;61:920–4.

100. Leaker M, Saxon BR. Heparin induced thrombocytopenia in a young child managed with Orgaran for cardiopulmonary bypass surgery [abstract]. Blood 1998;(suppl).

101. Harvey RP, Degryse E, Sefani L. Cloning and expression of cDNA coding for the anticoagulant hirudin from blood sucking leech. Proc Natl Acad Sci USA 1986;83:1084–8.

102. Hofsteenge J, Stone ST, Donnela-Deane A. The effect of substituting phosphotyrosine for sulphotyrosine activity of hirudin. Eur J Biochem 1990;188:55–9.

103. Esslinger HU, Haas S, Maurer R, et al. Pharmacodynamic and safety results of PEG-hirudin in healthy volunteers. Thromb Haemost 1997;77:911–9.

104. Schenk JF, Glusa E, Radziwon P, et al. A recombinant hirudin (IK-HIR02) in healthy volunteers I. Effects on coagulation parameters and bleeding time. Haemostasis 1997;26:140–9.

105. Pineo GF, Hull RD. Hirudin and hirudin analogues as new anticoagulant agents. Curr Opin Hematol 1995;2:380–5.

106. Vanholder R, Camez A, Veys N, et al. Pharmacokinetics of recombinant hirudin in hemodialyzed end-stage renal failure patients. Thromb Haemost 1997;77:650–5.

107. Eichler P, Greinacher A. Anti-hirudin antibodies induced by recombinant hirudin in the treatment of patients with heparin-induced thrombocytopenia (HIT). Ann Hematol 1996;72:A4.

108. Greinacher A, Volpe H, Janssens U, et al. Recombinant hirudin (lepirudin) provides safe and effective anticoagulation in patients with heparin-induced thrombocytopenia: a prospective study. Circulation 1999;99:73–80.

109. Kikumoto R, Tamao Y, Tesuka T. Selective inhibition of thrombin by (2R,4R)-4methyl-1-[N2- [(3-methyl-1,2,3,4-tetrahydro-8-quinolinyl+++) sulfonyl]-1-arginyl)]-2-piperidin-ecarboxylic acid. Biochemistry 1984;23:85–90.

110. Yasuda T, Gold HK, Yaoita H. Comparative effects of aspirin, a synthetic thrombin inhibitor, and a monoclonal antiplatelet glycoprotein IIb/IIIa antibody on coronary artery reperfusion, reocclusion, and bleeding with recombinant tissue-type plasminogen activator in a canine preparation. J Am Coll Cardiol 1990;16:714–22.

111. Gold HK, Torres FW, Garabedian HD. Evidence for a rebound coagulation phenomenon after cessation of a 4 hour infusion of a specific thrombin inhibitor in patients with unstable angina pectoris. J Am Coll Cardiol 1993;21:1039–47.

112. Marsh NA. Snake venoms affecting the haemostatic system: a consideration of their mechanisms, practical applications and biological significance. Blood Coagul Fibrinolysis 1994;5:399–400.

113. Demers C, Ginsberg J, Brill-Edwards P, et al. Rapid anticoagulantion using ancrod for heparin-induced thrombocytopenia. Blood 1991;78:2194–7.

114. Soutar RL, Ginsberg JS. Anticoagulant therapy with ancrod. Crit Rev Oncol Hematol 1993;15:23–33.

115. Cole CW, Fournier L, Bormanis J. Heparin-associated thrombocytopenia and thrombosis: optimal therapy with ancrod. Can J Surg 1990;33(3):207–10.

116. Cole CW, Shea B, Bormanis J. Ancrod as prophylaxis or treatment for thromboembolism in patients with multiple trauma. Can J Surg 1995;38:249–65.

117. Greenfield LJ, Michna BA. Twelve year clinical experience with the Greenfield vena cava filter. Surgery 1988;104:706–12.

118. Dorfman GS. Percutaneous inferior vena caval filters. Radiology 1990;174:987–92.

119. Hubbard KP, Roehm JO, Abbruzzese JL. The bird's nest filter: an alternative to long term oral anticoagulation in patients with advanced malignancies. Am J Clin Oncol 1994;17:115–7.

120. Lord RS, Benn I. Early and late results after bird's nest filter placement in the inferior vena cava: clinical and duplex ultrasound followup. Aust N Z J Surg 1994;64:106–14.

121. Murphy SF, Dorfman GS, Yedlicka JW. LGM vena cava filter: objective evaluation of early results. J Vasc Interv Radiol 1991;2:107–15.

122. Millward SF, Peterson RA, Moher D. LGM (Vena Tech) vena caval filter: experience at a single institution. J Vasc Interv Radiol 1994;5:351–6.

123. Bull PG, Mendel H, Schlegl A. Gunther vena caval filter: clinical appraisal. J Vasc Interv Radiol 1992; 34:395–9.

124. Hyers TM, Agnelli G, Hull RD, et al. Antithrombotic therapy for venous thromboembolic disease. Chest 1998;114:561S–7S.

125. Greenfield LJ, Cho KJ, Proctor M. Results of a multicenter study of the modified hook-titanium Greenfield filter. J Vasc Surg 1991;14:253–7.

126. Greenfield LJ, Cho KJ. Late results of suprarenal Greenfield vena cava filter placement. Arch Surg 1992;127:969–73.

127. Rohrer MJ, Scheidler MG, Wheeler Brownell H. Extended indications for placement of an inferior vena cava filter. J Vasc Surg 1989;10:44–50.

128. Golneke PJ, Garrett WV, Thompson JE. Interruption of the vena cava by means of the Greenfield filter: expanding the indications. Surgery 1988;103:111–7.

129. Cohen JH, Tenenbaum N, Citron M. Greenfield filter as primary therapy for deep venous thrombosis and/or pulmonary embolism in patients with cancer. Surgery 1991;109:12–5.

130. Calligaro KD, Bergen WS, Hant MJ. Thromboembolic complications in patients with advanced cancer: anticoagulation versus Greenfield filter placement. Ann Vasc Surg 1991;5:186–9.

131. Emerson RH, Cross R, Head WC. Prophylactic and early therapeutic use of the Greenfield filter in hip and knee joint arthroplasty. J Arthroplasty 1991; 6:129–35.

132. Sarasin FP, Eckman MH. Management and prevention of thromboembolic events in patients with cancer related hypercoagulable states: a risky business. J Gen Intern Med 1993;8:476–86.

133. Rogers FB, Shackford SR, Wilson J. Prophylactic vena cava filter insertion in severely injured trauma patients: indications and preliminary results. J Trauma 1993;35:637–41.

134. Rosethal D, McKinsey JF, Levy AM. Use of the Greenfield filter in patients with major trauma. Cardiovasc Surg 1994;2:52–5.

135. Webb LX, Rush PT, Fuller SB. Greenfield filter prophylaxis of pulmonary embolism in patients undergoing surgery for acetabular fracture. J Orthop Trauma 1992;6:139–45.

136. Timsit JF, Reynaud P, Meyer G. Pulmonary embolectomy by catheter device in massive pulmonary embolism. Chest 1991;100:655–8.

137. Decousus H, Leizorovicz A, Parent F, et al. A clinical forum of vena caval filters in the prevention of pulmonary embolism in patients with proximal deep vein thrombosis. N Engl J Med 1998;338:409–15.

138. Khong PL, John PR. Technical aspects of insertion and removal of an inferior vena cava IVC filter for prophylactic treatment of pulmonary embolus. Pediatr Radiol 1997;27:239–41.

139. McBride WJ, Gadowski GR, Keller MS, Vane DW. Pulmonary embolism in pediatric trauma patients. J Trauma 1996;37:913–5.

140. Stewart JR, Greenfield LJ. Transvenous vena caval filtration and pulmonary embolectomy. Surg Clin North Am 1982;62:411–30.

141. Greenfield LJ, Langham MR. Surgical approaches to thromboembolism. Br J Surg 1984;71:968–70.

142. Moreno-Cabral RJ, Breitweser JA. Pulmonary embolectomy in the neonate. Chest 1983;84:502–4.

143. Gorlach G, Hager K, Mulch J, et al. Surgical therapy of pulmonary thrombosis due to candidiasis in a premature infant. J Cardiovasc Surg 1986;27:341–3.

144. Putnam JB, Lemmer JH, Rocchini AP, Bove EL. Embolectomy for acute pulmonary artery occlusion following Fontan procedure. Ann Thorac Surg 1988; 45:335–6.

LABORATORY APPROACH TO CHILDREN WITH THROMBOEMBOLIC COMPLICATIONS

Laboratory evaluation and management of pediatric patients with, or at risk for, thromboembolic events (TEs) present unique challenges for several reasons. First, the dynamic physiologic state of the hemostatic system, particularly during the first weeks and months of life, necessitates multiple reference ranges of normal that reflect the age of the patient. Age-appropriate reference ranges are particularly important for the diagnosis of congenital prothrombotic disorders, since young children routinely have plasma concentrations for antithrombin (AT), protein C, and protein S that are decreased and within the range for adults with heterozygote deficiencies.[1–4] Second, although acquired hemostatic problems are considerably more common than congenital problems, the latter needs to be considered, since the most severe forms frequently present first during the first weeks to months of life. Third, the responsiveness of the child's hemostatic system to unfractionated heparin (UFH), oral anticoagulants (OAs), and thrombolytic agents differs markedly from adults, often requiring a variety of tests to be certain that these agents are achieving the desired effect. Fourth, the risk of bleeding is frequently increased in children with TEs requiring anticoagulants, due to other coexisting coagulopathies such as liver disease, vitamin K (VK) deficiency, disseminated intravascular coagulation (DIC), and thrombocytopenia. Fifth, the small size of pediatric patients frequently presents a technical

challenge, since large volumes of blood cannot be obtained for testing and microtechniques may be necessary.

This chapter provides a practical laboratory approach for the investigation, diagnosis, and management of pediatric patients with TEs. The laboratory assays described are those most frequently used by the authors, with details of adaptation for limited sample size. Age-appropriate reference ranges are provided in Chapter 2 and target therapeutic ranges for anticoagulant therapy are provided in Chapters 9, 10, and 11. Readers requiring more detailed information are referred to comprehensive laboratory texts that focus on coagulation assays.[5]

GENERAL PRINCIPLES OF COMMON COAGULATION ASSAYS

Clot-Based Assays Clot-based assays remain the most commonly used type of assay for measurement of specific coagulant factors and some inhibitors of the coagulation system. In general, plasma samples with a deficiency of a coagulant protein result in prolongation of the prothrombin time (PT) and/or the activated partial thromboplastin time (APTT). When a patient's plasma is mixed with a plasma deficient for a specific coagulant factor, the degree of correction of either the PT or APTT is proportional to the plasma concentrations of that factor in the patient's plasma, because all other factors are present at physiologic concentrations. The concentration of the coagulant factor is determined from a reference curve prepared with the coagulant factor-deficient plasma and varying dilutions of standard human plasma. Figure 13–1 provides two examples of clot-based factor assays for FVIII and FII, one based on the APTT system (Figure 13–1A) and one on the PT system (Figure 13–1B), respectively.

Chromogenic Assays In general, chromogenic assays are carried out in two steps. First, the test plasma is prepared for the particular assay. For example, for the measurement of plasminogen, plasma samples are incubated with an excess of streptokinase (SK) to activate plasminogen to plasmin. For the measurement of α_2-antiplasmin (α_2AP), the test plasma is incubated with an excess of added plasmin under conditions where α_2AP is the predominant inhibitor of the added plasmin. Second, a synthetic chromogenic substrate with a peptide sequence sensitive to the enzyme in question is added to the assay mixture. The generated enzyme or added enzyme in excess cleaves the chromogenic substrate, releasing *p*-nitroaniline and resulting in a color change that is measured photometrically at 405 nm. The release of *p*-nitroaniline is directly proportional to the concentration of generated enzyme and inversely proportional to the concentration of an inhibitor in the presence of added enzyme (i.e., plasmin). Figure 13–2 provides two examples of chromogenic assays, one used to measure plasminogen (Figure 13–2A) and one for α_2AP (Figure 13–2B).

Immunological Assays

General information Immunologic assays are most frequently used to measure concentrations of inhibitors of coagulation. The most commonly used assays are radial immunodiffusion (RID),[6] Laurell rocket electrophoresis,[7] and enzyme-linked immunoabsorbent assay (ELISA).[8]

Radial immunodiffusion The principle of RID is that an antigen will passively diffuse from a well in an agarose gel that contains an antibody directed at the antigen in question. A circular precipitation line will form, and the diameter of the circle is directly proportional to the antigen concentration. To perform RID, an appropriate concentration of antibody is added to dissolved agarose, and the agarose is then poured between two glass plates separated by a 1-mm brass plate. After solidification of the agarose, 2-mm wells are punched into the agarose, and appropriate dilutions of an antigen dilution are placed in the wells. Following a set time of incubation, rings are formed and their diameters measured. The radius of each ring is plotted on linear graph paper against the percentage concentration of a normal pooled plasma. A standard line is run on each plate, prepared by diluting normal pooled plasma in barbital buffer.

Laurell rocket electrophoresis Laurell rocket electrophoresis is an adaption of RID, performed in an agarose gel medium containing an antibody specific for the protein of interest.[7] After plasma specimens containing the protein are applied to wells in the agarose, electrophoresis is used to migrate the proteins into the antibody field. A rocket-shaped

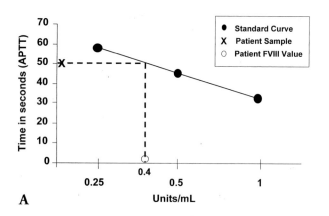
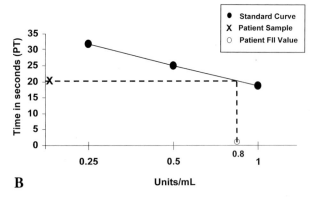

Figure 13–1 Two examples of clot-based factor assays: *A*, based on the activated partial thromboplastin time (APTT) system; and *B*, based on the prothrombin time (PT) assay.

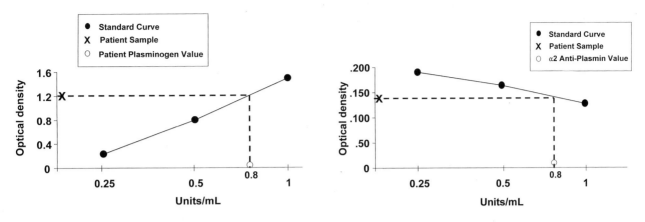

Figure 13–2 Two examples of chromogenic assays: *A*, to measure plasminogen; *B*, to measure the inhibitor, α2-antiplasmin.

precipitin pattern forms along the axis of migration. The length of the rocket pattern is proportional to the antigen concentration. A standard line is run on each plate, prepared by diluting normal pooled plasma in tricine buffer.

Enzyme-linked immunoabsorbent assay (ELISA) The principle behind ELISA is that a specific protein of interest can be measured by capturing it on a microtitre plate coated with an antibody. The antibody binds the protein of interest,[8] which is then detected with an anti-human antibody conjugated to horseradish peroxidase (HRP). The bound anti-human antibody-conjugate activity is expressed by incubation with an HRP substrate. The intensity of the color generated is proportional to the concentration of the protein of interest present in the sample.

Coagulation Screening Tests

General Information All pediatric patients being evaluated for TEs should have taken a detailed history, a physical examination, and an evaluation with coagulation screening tests for any underlying hemostatic problem that might influence diagnostic tests or tests used to monitor antithrombotic therapy. The PT, APTT, thrombin clotting time (TCT), and fibrinogen concentration are the four most commonly used screening tests of coagulation and have important functions in the monitoring of antithrombotic therapy.

Collection of Small Blood Volumes for Assay Adaption of coagulation assays by decreasing the volume of blood required for an assay is frequently necessary for children.[9] The following screening assays require 0.9 mL of whole blood. Plastic tubes containing the correct amount of anticoagulant (usually 9 parts blood to 1 part 0.105 M sodium citrate) are pre-prepared in the laboratory. Following collection of blood samples from an indwelling catheter or venipuncture, the plasma is obtained by centrifugation of blood samples at 1700 x g for 15 minutes. Plasma is removed, placed in clean plastic tubes, and recentrifuged again for a further 5 minutes at the same speed. Plasma is again removed and aliquoted for immediate and future testing.

For patients who have hematocrit values above 0.55 (55%), the citrate concentration should be adjusted. The National Committee for Clinical Laboratory Standards (NCCLS) provides a nomogram for determining the amounts of anticoagulant and blood for hematocrit values above 0.55 (NCCLS document H21-A). Another alternative is to use a formula to determine the correct amount of citrate for hematocrit values above 55%; x = (100 – packed cell volume [PCV]/(595 – PCV) mL, where x is the volume of anticoagulant required to prepare a unit volume of anticoagulated blood and PCV is the packed cell volume in percent. If a patient is receiving thrombolytic therapy, the blood sample should be collected into the same anticoagulant mixture, but it should contain a plasmin inhibitor such as εamino caproic acid (AMICAR), with a final concentration of 0.2 trypsin inhibitor (TIU) per mL of blood.

If blood samples are from inpatients, the plasmas may require screening for contamination with UFH. One method is to use a sensitive TCT and repeat the TCT following the addition of protamine sulphate (PSO$_4$). If the TCT becomes normal, a repeat sample without contamination with UFH should be obtained if possible. However, this is frequently not feasible for small infants and newborns. A second alternative is to add appropriate concentrations of PSO$_4$ to neutralize the UFH prior to measurement of the PT and APTT. One way is to add 5 µL of 50 units per mL PSO$_4$ solution into 100 µL of plasma, where 2.5 units of PSO$_4$ per mL of plasma (25 µg PSO$_4$/mL plasma) are used to neutralize the UFH. For example, 2.5 µL of a 1000 u PSO$_4$/mL stock (10 mg PSO$_4$/mL, Fujisawa Canada Inc. ON, CA) is added to 999 µL of the UFH-containing plasma and the resultant mixture analyzed.

Prothrombin Time and Activated Partial Thromboplastin Time   The methods used to measure PT and APTT values are dependent on the volume of plasma and the equipment available. The manual method is time-consuming and not necessary for most pediatric patients. However, the manual method, in addition to the automated method, is described, because it permits the use of very small amounts of plasma. The manual method is performed in a water bath with a transparent front panel, using a stainless steel hook.

Manual Methods
Reagents
Sample used: 20 µL
- Calcium thromboplastin
- APTT reagent
- CaCl$_2$ (0.02 M or 0.025 M solution)

Prothrombin time
Sample used: 20 µL
- 6 x 50 mm glass tube
- Add 20 µL of plasma
- Incubate at 37° C for 1 minute

- Add 20 µL of prewarmed calcium thromboplastin
- Start timer

The endpoint is the first strand of fibrin formation.

Activated partial thromboplastin time
Sample used: 20 µL
- 6 x 50 mm glass tube
- Add 20 µL of plasma
- Add 20 µL of APTT reagent
- Mix and incubate at 37°C for the appropriate time for the reagent
- Add 20 µL of pre-incubated CaCl$_2$ (0.02 M or 0.025 M solution)
- Start timer
- Record the time of first formation of fibrin strand

Automated Methods   Automated methods are for an Automated Coagulation Laboratory (ACL, Instrumentation Laboratory, Milan, Italy). Other automated instruments capable of using reduced plasma volumes can be used, and the protocols for the particular instrument followed. To measure PT and APTT values using an ACL, 160 µL of plasma is placed in a micro sample cup (Kodak micro tube #1213115; Johnson & Johnson, Raritan NY).

Prothrombin time
Sample used: 50 µL
- Automatically pipette 50 µL of plasma into cuvette rotor
- Add 100 µL of calcium thromboplastin

Clot formation is measured automatically.

Activated partial thromboplastin time
Sample used: 50 µL
- Automatically pipette 50 µL into cuvette rotor
- Add 50 µL of reagent
- Mix plasma and APTT reagent together
- Incubate 5 minutes
- Add 50 µL of CaCl$_2$

Clot formation is measured automatically.

Thrombin Clotting Time   The TCT described here is used to screen for UFH contamination in samples and for decreased plasma concentrations of fibrinogen. The method described is a calcium (Ca^{++})dependent TCT, which makes it relatively insensitive to fibrin/fibrinogen degradation products (FDPs) and to fetal fibrinogen.

Reagents
- Dilute bovine thrombin to 100 u/mL in normal saline
- Aliquote and freeze bovine thrombin at 70 °C
- Dilute bovine thrombin to 2 u/mL in 0.15M NaCl
- Seegers buffer (0.112 M NaCl, 0.0037 M $CaCl_2$, 1.66% Acacia, 0.0277M imidazole, pH 7.3)

Manual method
Sample used: 20 µL
- 6 x 50 mm glass tube
- Add 60 µL of Seegers titration mixture
- Add 20 µL of plasma
- Add 20 µL of 2 u/mL thrombin
- Start timer

The endpoint is at the first appearance of fibrin.

The normal control plasma time for a 2 u/mL TCT must be 23 to 27 seconds. If the patient's TCT is prolonged, 1 µL of PSO_4 (1 u/mL) is added to 20 µL of plasma and the TCT repeated. If the test is now normal, an appropriate amount of PSO_4 (5 µL PSO_4/100 µL plasma (50 µg PSO_4/mL)) is added to plasma for subsequent measurement of the PT and APTT. The test may be performed on a semi-automated device such as the ST4 (Diagnostica Stago, Asnieres-Sur-Seine, France) with the ratio of Seegers buffer to plasma remaining the same.

Fibrinogen The measurement of fibrinogen is a useful screening test, particularly for patients requiring thrombolytic therapy. Three different methods are described. Method 1 is the classic TCT described by Clauss.[10] Method 2 is a capillary fibrinogen method based on the Clauss assay. Method 3 is an automated fibrinogen assay using the ACL.

Reagents
- Veronal buffer (0.0071 M sodium acetate, 0.0071 M sodium diethylbarbiturate, 0.131 M NaCl, pH 7.3)
- Dilute bovine thrombin to 100 u/mL in 0.15 M NaCl

Method 1
Sample used: 15 µL
Dilutions of the fibrinogen standard are prepared in a test tube or reaction cup depending on the instrumentation available. (ST4, Diagnostica Stago, Asnieres-Sur-Seine, France).

Dilution	Plasma Volume (µL)	Buffer Volume (µL)
1/10	10	90
1/15	10	140
1/20	5	95
1/30	5	145
1/40	5	195

- Incubate 100 µL of the diluted plasma at 37°C for 2–3 minutes
- Add 50 µL of thrombin (100 u/mL)
- Start timer
- Measure each dilution in duplicate
- Plot results (concentration versus time) on log-log paper
- Make 2 dilutions for both the control and patient plasma at 1/10 and 1/20 and assayed as above

For samples from newborn the first dilution made is 1/10; the second is dependent on the result obtained with the first dilution and is either a 1/5 or 1/20 dilution.

Method 2
Sample used: 100 µL (whole blood)
This is a capillary fibrinogen method based on the Clauss assay. Micropipettes are prepared by diluting a standard preparation of UFH to 50 u/mL in water. A standard glass 100 µL micropipette is rinsed with the UFH solution, the residual liquid blown out, and the tubes dried.

Preparation of blood collecting tube
- 12 x 75 mm plastic tube
- Pipette 400 µL of veronal buffer and 10 µL of buffered sodium citrate

Obtaining the blood sample
- Draw 100 µL of capillary blood into a heparinized tube
- Immediately rinse into the citrate/buffer tube
- Centrifuge blood at 1500 g for 10 minutes

The diluted plasma is removed from the cells.
- Following method 1 for fibrinogens, pipette 100 µL of diluted plasma into the reaction tube
- Add 50 µL of thrombin (100 u/mL)

The timed endpoint is read from the standard line. The dilution of plasma used is calculated from the hematocrit, as plasma volume per 100 µL of blood divided by buffer/anticoagulant and plasma volume.

Method 3

Sample used: 50 µL

Fibrinogen concentrations can be accurately calculated by the ACL in normal plasmas using the PT/fibrinogen program with calcium thromboplastin. However, an over-estimation of fibrinogen is obtained in patients receiving thrombolytic therapy and in some cases of DIC.[11,12]

Discussion Reference values for PT, APTT, TCT, and fibrinogen values during infancy and childhood are age-dependent and provided in Chapter 2. Values for PT and APTT are prolonged at birth, primarily due to decreased plasma concentrations of the contact factors (F), FXII, FXI, prekallikrein (PK), and high molecular weight kininogen (HMWK), as well as the VK-dependent coagulant proteins. Values for PTs and APTTs are also influenced by the laboratory reagents used in their measurement.

Within the last two decades, the widely varying sensitivities of differing PT reagents to decreased plasma concentrations of VK-dependent proteins has been recognized.[13,14] Different reagents can re-

sult in several-second discrepancies for PT values, which can adversely bias patient management, particularly for patients requiring OAs. A mechanism for adjusting to differing sensitivities of PT reagents, the International Normalized Ratio (INR), was introduced during the 1980s. INRs are calculated as the patient's PT divided by the control PT in seconds to the power of the ISI, where the ISI is the international sensitivity index. The ISI specifically corrects for differing sensitivities of various reagents to decreased plasma concentrations of VK-dependent coagulant factors. The variability in published PT values in newborns reflects, in part, the use of different reagents.

APTT reagents and different lot numbers of the same reagent have widely varying sensitivities to concentrations of UFH.[15,16] Recommendations for therapeutic APTT values are based upon clinical trials in adults, in which therapeutic APTT values are equivalent to UFH concentrations of 0.2 to 0.4 u/mL by PSO_4, or 0.3 to 0.6 u/mL by anti-FXa activity.[17] Current recommendations are that laboratories validate their therapeutic APTT values for UFH by either a PSO_4 titration or anti-FXa heparin assay.[17] Laboratories involved in the evaluation of children, particularly newborns, must be aware of the effects of differing reagents on APTT values.

The third screening test frequently used in pediatric patients is the TCT. Depending upon how the TCT is measured, it can be prolonged by decreased plasma concentrations of fibrinogen, a dysfibrinogenemia, the presence of UFH, and/or FDPs.[18] The sensitivity of the TCT to each of these variables is influenced by the presence or absence of Ca^{++}, use of a buffer, and concentration of thrombin in the assay system.[18] The reference ranges for TCTs provided in Chapter 2 are based upon a two-unit TCT performed in a buffer containing Ca^{++}. This form of TCT is very sensitive to UFH and fibrinogen concentration, but is not sensitive to FDPs or dysfibrinogenemias. These characteristics are particularly helpful in newborns, in whom there is no need to detect a uniformly present fetal dysfibrinogenemia or the presence of FDPs, which are better measured separately using sensitive assays (see subsequent section), or UFH contamination from indwelling lines through which blood samples are obtained. Both TCT values and fibrinogen concentrations, when measured using the assays described, give similar values for infants, children, and adults.

COAGULATION FACTOR ASSAYS

General Information Patients with TEs and abnormal screening test results require further evaluation to determine the nature of the underlying coagulopathy, which may be related to the thrombotic process or will affect the monitoring of anticoagulant or thrombolytic therapy.

Assay Details for Factors VIII, IX, XI, XII, and High Molecular Weight Kininogen (HMWK) FVIII, FIX, FXI, FXII, and HMWK are each assayed in an identical manner, with the variable being the particular factor-deficient plasma. The method, based on the one-stage assay of Biggs et al,[19] can be modified for use on semi-automated and automated instruments.

Reagents
- Veronal buffer (0.0071 M sodium acetate, 0.0071 M sodium diethylbarbiturate, 0.131 M NaCl, pH 7.4)
- APTT reagent
- Deficient plasma
- CaCl$_2$ (0.02 or 0.025 M solution)

Preparation of standard plasma
Dilute standard plasma in either 12 x 75 mm plastic test tube or reaction cuvette of the instrument.

Dilution	Plasma Volume (µL)	Veronal Buffer (µL)
1/10	10	90
1/20	5	95
1/40	5	195
1/80	5	395
1/100	5	495

Manual micro method
Sample used: 15 µL
- 6 x 50 mm glass tube
- Pipette 20 µL of diluted plasma
- 20 µL of deficient plasma
- 20 µL of APTT reagent
- Mix and incubate for the specific reagent time
- Add 20 µL of pre-warmed CaCl$_2$
- Start timer
- Record time of first fibrin strand formation

Semi-automated instrument method
Sample used: 15 µL
(Stago ST4)
- Reaction cuvette pipette
- Add 50 µL of each dilution of diluted plasma
- 50 µL of a deficient plasma
- 50 µL of APTT reagent
- Mix and incubate for the specific reagent time
- Add 50 µL of pre-warmed CaCl$_2$ (0.02 or 0.025 M CaCl$_2$)
- Start timer and measure time of clot formation

Automated method
Sample used: 15 µL
(ACL)
- Use a 1/10 dilution of normal plasma
- Place in factor diluent (IL, Milan, Italy) to generate a standard line
- Run controls and samples individually at 1/10 and 1/20 in factor diluent

Results are reported automatically.

For the manual and semi-automated methods, the clotting times are determined and results plotted against u/mL concentration on semi-log paper. The patient's plasma is diluted 1/10 and 1/20 in buffer, and the results are read off the standard curve. By making the plasma dilution directly into the reaction well or test tube, only 15 µL of patient plasma is required for each assay. If manual testing is done, all four factor assays will use only 15 µL of plasma. Figure 1A provides an example of the curves for one of these assays.

Assay Details for Factors II, V, VII, and X FII, FV, FVII, and FX are assayed in an identical manner, using plasma deficient in the factor of interest. Deficient plasmas are available from most all diagnostic companies, and a thromboplastin reagent is used instead of an APTT reagent and $CaCl_2$.

Semi-automated instrument method

Sample used: 15 μL
(Stago ST4)

- 12 x 75 mm test tube or reaction cup
- Pipette 25 μL of diluted plasma
- Pipette 25 μL of deficient plasma
- Mix and add 100 μL of prewarmed thromboplastin

The clotting times are plotted on semi-log paper against the concentration of the factor of interest. The four extrinsic assays can be measured using a total of 30 μL of plasma. Figure 1B shows a typical example.

Assay Details for Prekallikrein PK is measured using a chromogenic assay based on the method of Klugt et al.[20]

Reagents

- PK-deficient plasma
- Substrate S2302, Chromogenix (Molndal, Sweden)
- Dilute substrate to 6 mM in Tris buffer
- Dilute dextran sulphate 25 mg/L in buffer
- Tris buffer (50 mM Tris, 12 mM NaCl, pH 7.8)
- 50% acetic acid

Chromogenic assay for prekallikrein

Sample used: 10 μL

- Prepare dilutions in a plastic test tube

Concentration (μ/mL)	Plasma Volume (μL)	PK Deficient (μL)
0	0	100
0.1	10	90
0.25	25	75
0.50	50	50
0.75	75	25
1.01	100	0

- Dilute control and patient plasmas in duplicate at 0.50 u/mL concentration
- 20 μL plasma in 20 μL PK-deficient plasma
- Mix 10 μL plasma dilution in 10 μL dextran sulphate buffer at 0°C (wet ice)
- Incubate on ice 15 minutes
- Add 90 μL prewarmed buffer (37°C)
- Subsample at timed intervals:

50 μL of the above mixture into prewarmed (37°C) microtitre plate containing 200 μL 6 mM S2302

- Incubate exactly 3.5 minutes
- Stop the reaction, following the above timing, with 40 μL of acetic acid
- Read the optical density (OD) at 405 nM

The OD versus concentration of the reference samples is then plotted on linear graph paper, and results for the unknown test samples are read off this line.

Discussion Reference values for FV, FVIII, FIX, FX, FXI, FXII, and HMWK are provided in Chapter 2. At birth, plasma concentrations of the four VK-dependent coagulant factors and the four contact factors are physiologically decreased. Gradually during childhood, they increase to adult values. For children being investigated or treated for TEs, decreased plasma concentrations of these factors can indicate a concurrent problem such as liver disease, VK deficiency, or DIC. In addition, the age-dependent differences in hemostasis during early life may influence the response of APTT or PT values to UFH and OAs.

THE FIBRINOLYTIC SYSTEM

General Information Measurements of the fibrinolytic system are valuable in the assessment of children with potential abnormalities that may predispose them to TEs, and for the monitoring of thrombolytic therapy. The global potential of the fibrinolytic system can be measured in vitro by the euglobulin lysis time (ELT) or whole blood clot lysis time (WBCLT). The overall in vivo activity of the fibrinolytic system can be measured by the concentration of FDPs, and D-dimers. Finally, there are specific assays for components of the fibrinolytic system including tissue plasminogen activator

(TPA), plasminogen activator inhibitor-1 (PAI-1), α_2AP, and plasminogen.

Assay Details Plasma samples can be prepared in a fashion similar to the assessment of the coagulation system, except in the measurement of TPA or PAI. Both of these assays require an acidified citrate tube such as Stabilyte (American Diagnostica, Greenwich, CT™, USA) or Diatube (Becton Dickinson, ON™, CA). The reduction of blood pH by acidified citrate increases the stability of TPA and prevents platelet activation without causing hemolysis. Whole blood should be spun and plasma removed from the cells within 30 minutes. The sample must be processed within 4 hours of blood taking.

Euglobulin Lysis Time
Reagents
- Glass conical tube
- Add 9 mL of distilled water with 0.1 mL of 1% glacial acetic acid (0.174M acetic acid)
- Borate buffer (0.154 M NaCl, 0.0026 M $Na_2B_4O_7 \cdot 10H_2O$, pH 9.0)
- $CaCl_2$ (0.025 M)

Method for the euglobin lysis time
Sample used: 0.5 mL
- Dilute 0.5 mL of plasma in 9 mL of chilled acetic water
- Place at 4°C for 30 minutes
- Centrifuge at 4°C for 5 minutes at 365 g
- Discard the supernatant
- Add 0.5 mL of borate buffer
- Dissolve the precipitate and place at 37°C
- Add 0.5 mL of $CaCl_2$ (0.025 M) and mix gently
- Note the clotting time and observe for clot lysis

The normal reference range for adults is 1.5 to 5 hours.[22]

Dilute Whole Blood Clot Lysis Time
Sample used:0.2 mL (whole blood)

Reagents
- Phosphate saline buffer (0.02 M Phosphate, 0.15 M NaCl, pH 7.4)
- Dilute bovine thrombin to 50 u/mL in normal saline

Method
- Dilute 0.2 mL of whole blood in 1.8 mL of phosphate saline buffer containing 0.1 mL of 50 u/mL thrombin
- Incubate the clotted sample at 37°C and observe clot lysis[23]

Tissue Plasminogen Activator TPA can be measured with a chromogenic method, Spectrolyse® TPA/PAI (American Diagnostica, Greenwich, CT USA), based on a functional parabolic rate assay.[24,25] Blood is collected in Stabilite™ tubes as described earlier; the acidification preserves TPA activity and destroys the inhibitory capacity of α_2AP. TPA activity is measured by adding Glu-plasminogen, chromogenic substrate sensitive to plasmin, and fibrin at a neutral pH. In the presence of fibrin, TPA converts plasminogen to plasmin, which cleaves the chromogenic substrate. The amount of color developed is proportional to the amount of TPA activity in the sample.

A quantitative determination of TPA in plasma can be measured using an ELISA method. (Diagnostica Stago, Asnieres-Sur-Seine, France; Biopool, Umea, Sweden) and Imubind™ (American Diagnostica Greenwich, CT, USA).[26]

Plasma is added to a microplate well coated with anti-TPA IgG that binds the plasma TPA to this coating antibody; HRP labelled anti-TPA IgG fragments are added and react with the bound TPA. Peroxidase substrate is added and the developed color is proportional to the amount of TPA present.

α_2 Antiplasmin α_2AP is usually measured by chromogenic assays, which are available through several diagnostic companies. Measurement of α_2AP activity is carried out in two steps. First, the test plasma is incubated with an excess of plasmin under conditions where the influence of other PK inhibitors are minimized. Second, residual plasmin activity is measured using a specific chromogenic substrate.[27]

Plasminogen Activator-1 PAI-1 can be measured by antigenic or activity assays (Diagnostica Stago, Asnieres-Sur-Seine, France; Biopool, Umea, Sweden; Dade Behring, Marburg, Germany). All of the available functional assays vary. The Diagnostica

Stago kit (Asnieres-Sur-Seine, France) measures the concentration of PAI-1 by adding urokinase (UK) to the test plasma, which forms a PAI-1/plasmin complex that reduces the generation of plasmin. The Spectrolyse™ PAI (American Diagnostics, Greenwich, CT, USA) is a two-stage assay, in which TPA is added to the sample and allowed to complex with PAI-1 in the patient's sample. The patient's sample is acidified to destroy α_2AP activity, and then diluted in water. Residual TPA activity is measured by adding the patient's sample to a mixture of Glu-plasminogen, poly-D-lysine, and chromogenic substrate. Residual TPA converts plasminogen to plasmin, which hydrolyzes the chromogenic substrate. The amount of color produced is proportional to the amount of TPA activity in the sample. Poly-D-lysine acts as a stimulator of the TPA-catalyzed conversion of plasminogen to plasmin. PAI is measured as the difference between TPA added and the amount of TPA recovered.[28]

EVALUATION FOR IN VIVO GENERATION OF THROMBIN AND PLASMIN

General Information When the coagulation system is activated, thrombin is generated and fibrinogen converted to fibrin. Associated with this central event, several markers of thrombin generation and activities are formed. Sensitive assays that detect the conversion of prothrombin to thrombin and thrombin action on fibrinogen are available for clinical use. These assays include prothrombin fragment 1.2 (F1.2), thrombin-antithrombin complexes (TATs), fibrinopeptide A (FPA), and fibrin monomer. Similarly, when the fibrinolytic system is activated, plasmin is generated and proteolyzes many substrates, including both fibrinogen and fibrin. There are numerous assays available for detecting plasmin-derived products of fibrin and fibrinogen. The two most frequently used assays are D-dimer and FDPs. D-dimer is specific to plasmin degradation of cross-linked fibrin, not fibrinogen. In contrast, most FDP assays detect plasmin proteolysis of either fibrinogen or fibrin.

Assay Details for In Vivo Thrombin Generation
Thrombin-antithrombin complexes TATs are assayed using commercially available kits from Dade-Behring (Marburg, Germany) and Affinity Biologicals (Hamilton, ON, CA). The assay is an ELISA that utilizes anti-human thrombin antibodies (sheep or rabbit) for the capture and detecting antibodies conjugated with HRP as the second antibody. Obtaining the blood sample must be atraumatic to avoid falsely increased values. The method used is as described by the manufacturer.[29]

Prothrombin fragment 1.2 F1.2 is assayed using commercially available kits from either Dade-Behring (Marburg, Germany) or Organon Teknica, (Durham, NC, USA). The assay is an ELISA that binds the F1.2 antigen in the sample to anti-F1.2 antibodies (capture), and then peroxidase-conjugated antibodies are added that bind to the free F1.2. The bound enzyme activity is determined by the addition of a chromogenic substrate with hydrogen peroxide. The manufacturer's protocol is followed.[30]

Fibrinopeptide A There are no commercial kits available at this time that measure FPA.

Soluble fibrin There are several commercial kits available for the measurement of soluble fibrin (SF). Immunologic measurement of SF by ELISAs are available from Enzymun-Test (Boehringer Mannheim, Tutzing, Germany), Thrombus Precursor Protein (TpP™), (Corgenix, Westminister, CO, USA), and Fibrinostika (Organon Teknica, Durham, NC, USA). The methods used are as described by the manufacturers. Two functional assays for SF are also available, and consist of a fibrin monomer test called Berichrom FM (Dade Behring, Marburg, Germany) and Coa-Set fibrin monomer (DiaPharma, Franklin, OH, USA)

Assay for In Vivo Plasmin Generation: D-dimer There are several D-dimer assays available. The ELISA assays include Asserachrom D-dimer (Diagnostica Stago, Asnieres-Sur-Seine, France); Fibronesticon (Organon Teknika, Durham, NC, USA); and Dimertest Gold (American Diagnostics, Greenwich, CT, USA). Latex agglutination assays include Data-Fi Dimertest (Dade Behring, Marburg, Germany); Accuclot D-dimer (Sigma Diagnostics, St. Louis, MO, USA); Dimertest Latex, (Ortho Clinical Diagnostic, Raritan, NY, USA); Fibronosticon D-dimer, (Organon Teknika, Durham, NC, USA) and Dimertest (American Diagnostics, Greenwich, CT, USA). SimpliRED, a whole blood agglutination test designed for bedside testing, is commercially available from American Diagnostics, Greenwich, CT, USA and Dade Behring, Marburg, Germany. The following is a typical example of the methods for measurement of D-dimer.

Latex agglutination method (Dade Behring) Pipette 25 µL of latex beads coated with monoclonal D-dimer antibody onto a black coated glass slide. Add 10 µL of plasma and mix. The slide gently rocked for 3 minutes. Observe for agglutination. Depending on the degree of agglutination, either a 1/2 or 1/8 dilution is made. If the sample is positive at a 1/8 dilution, further dilutions may be made or a result of > 2000 ng/mL reported. Positive and negative controls are run.

Fibrinogen/fibrin degradation products
Sample used: 25 µL
(Dade Behring)

Preparation of serum samples
- Pipette 25 µL of plasma into a 6 x 50 mm glass tube
- Add 25 µL of a mixture of 0.1 M Epsilon-amino-n-caproic acid in 0.025 M $CaCl_2$
- Mix and add 1 µL of 5000 u/mL thrombin
- Mix and leave for 30 minutes at room temperature

The tube is centrifuged to obtain serum.

Method
Sample used: 25 µL
- Dilute the serum sample 1/2 in saline glycine buffer (0.1 M glycine, 0.145 M NaCl, pH 8.2)
- Ringed glass slide
- Pipette 10 µL of latex particles coated with an anti-human fibrinogen or anti-human E and E fibrinogen fragments
- Add 10 µL of each dilution of serum
- Mix gently and rock for 2 minutes
- Observe for agglutination of the latex particles

Discussion Coagulation tests that detect the generation and activities of thrombin and plasmin are generally reserved for patients in whom DIC is suspected. However, some of these tests (TATs, F1.2) can be useful in monitoring therapy with UFH in pediatric patients with TEs and a poor response to UFH. Other tests are helpful in documenting that thrombolytic therapy is having at least a biochemical effect (FDPs, D-dimer). Reference levels for TATs, F1.2, and for D-dimer are available in Chapter 2.

EVALUATION FOR VITAMIN K DEFICIENCY

General Information VK deficiency is important to diagnose in children who develop or are at risk for TEs, because of the risk of bleeding with anticoagulants as well as for accurate monitoring during therapy with OAs. There are several types of assays available for detection of VK deficiency. The following describes two of the most commonly used assays, the Echis assay and PIVKA II assay (protein induced in the absence of VK).

The Echis assay To distinguish between liver disease and VK deficiency, two rapid assays for prothrombin are available.[31] One is a standard Ca^{++}-dependent biologic assay using thromboplastin as the activator, and the second uses the snake venom Echis Carinatus as the activator (Figure 13–3). The Echis Carinatus venom is specific for activation of prothrombin without a Ca^{++} requirement, and therefore activates decarboxylated forms of prothrombin. Ratios of the results for prothrombin activity based on the Echis assay divided by the Ca^{++}-dependent prothrombin assay over 1.0 are diagnostic of VK deficiency

Reagents
- Ecarin (Diagnostica Stago) diluted with 1 mL H_2O and 1 mL 0.15 M NaCl
- Veronal buffer (0.0071 M sodium acetate, 0.0071 M sodium diethylbarbiturate, 0.131 M NaCl, pH 7.4)
- FII-deficient plasma

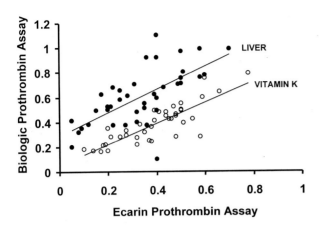

Figure 13–3 Relationship between the Ca^{++}dependent prothrombin assay and the Echis assay in normal and vitamin K deficient patients.

Method

Sample used: 30 μL

Dilutions of standard plasma are made in veronal buffer in a glass test tube or reaction cup, depending on the instrument available.

Dilution	Plasma Volume (μL)	Veronal Buffer (μL)
1/5	40	160
1/10	20	180
1/20	10	190
1/40	5	195
1/80	5	395
1/100	5	495

- Glass tube or instrument reaction cuvette
- Pipette 50 μL of diluted plasma
- 50 μL FII deficient plasma
- 50 μL of reconstituted Ecarin
- Start timer

A standard curve is constructed with u/mL versus time in seconds on log-log paper. Patient and control plasma are diluted 1/5 and 1/10 and assayed as above. The values are read off the standard line or, when using an automated method, the results are reported automatically. The biologic assay for FII is described under coagulation factor assays.

PIVKA II Assay VK-dependent proteins produced in the absence of VK (PIVKA) can be measured by specific ELISA assays. Most commonly, prothrombin (FII) is the selected VK-dependent coagulant protein for measurement. The PIVKA II assay consists of a solid support microplate coated with mouse monoclonal antibodies specific for PIVKA II and without reactivity with native prothrombin. Both test samples and calibration samples are pipetted into coated microwells. If PIVKA II is present, it is recognized and captured to the surface. Anti-prothrombin rabbit immunoglobulin coupled to HRP is added, and binds to remaining antigenic determinants on prothrombin. Activity of the bound antibody-enzyme conjugate is then detected by o-phenylenediamine (OPD) in the presence of urea peroxide, with absorbance measured at 492 nM. The degree of color change is directly related to the concentration of PIVKA II. PIVKA II concentration in the normal population is less than 2 ng/mL.[32]

Discussion VK deficiency is an important and relatively common coagulopathy in children with serious primary diseases. Many children who will require treatment with OAs are ill with serious primary disorders that, in combination with the use of antibiotics, places them at risk for VK deficiency. The clinical usefulness of the Echis assay is that it is specific and rapid. The measurement of PIVKA II or other PIVKA coagulant proteins is also specific and rapid.

CONGENITAL PROTHROMBOTIC DISORDERS

General Information An increasing number of congenital prothrombotic states have been identified over the past decade. Not infrequently, children from families with a positive history of TEs are being referred for evaluation. Congenital prothrombotic disorders that are clearly causal to TEs in children and adults include the presence of activated protein C resistance (APCR), prothrombin gene 20210; deficiencies of AT, protein C, protein S, and plasminogen; and dysfibrinogenemia. Other potential but less well-defined congenital prothrombotic disorders include hyperhomocysteinemia, methylenetetrahydrofolate reductase (MTHFR) mutation, lipoprotein (a) (LP[a], heparin cofactor II (HCII), and PAI.[33-35] In general, pediatric patients with TEs should be evaluated for clearly causal congenital prothrombotic disorders even in the presence of an identifiable acquired risk factor for TEs.[36-39]

AT, protein C, protein S, HCII, and plasminogen can be measured both functionally and immunologically. In clinical practice, the most expeditious approach is to initially measure functional levels and, if these are abnormal, measure immunologic levels. The latter is important to distinguish between quantitative (Type I) and qualitative (Type II) defects. Functional assays for inhibitors and plasminogen are measured using commercially available kits and, additionally, for a clot-based protein C assay. The following provides assays for both activity and immunologic assessment of the congenital prothrombotic disorders.

CLEARLY CAUSAL RISK FACTORS FOR THROMBOEMBOLIC EVENTS

Activated Protein C Resistance

Laboratory testing for activated protein C resistance The original functional test for APCR was a modified APTT that measured the anticoagulant response to the addition of a standard amount of activated protein C (APC) (Chromogenix, Molndal, Sweden).[40] Results were expressed as a ratio, calculated by dividing APTT values obtained in the presence of added APC by APTT values obtained in the absence of added APC.[40] Abnormal results were usually considered to be ratios less than 2.0.[40] The original APTT-based assay for APCR had some limitations, which included a dependence on plasma concentrations of FV and FVIII, and the age of the patient.[41] The recent modification of the original APC assay by using 1:5 dilutions of patients' plasma in FV-deficient plasma instead of undiluted plasma adjusts the APC ratios to those of adults.[36] A chromogenic assay that measures the capacity of APC to limit the generation of FXa by inactivating FVIIIa in plasma is also available.[42]

Laboratory DNA analysis for factor V Leiden Screening for the FV Leiden mutation involves iso-

lation of DNA from peripheral blood lymphocytes, amplification by means of the polymerase chain reaction (PCR) of a region (220 bp) of the FV gene that spans the mutation, and then digesting the amplified DNA with the restriction endonuclease MnlI. The digested fragments are then electrophoresed on an agarose gel containing ethidium bromide, and the number and sizes of the resulting separated fragments indicate whether an individual is normal (116 bp, 67 bp, and 37 bp fragment bands), heterozygous (153 bp, 116 bp, 67 bp, and 37 bp bands), or homozygous (153 bp and 67 bp bands) for the abnormality.[43]

Prothrombin Gene The prothrombin gene in humans is organized in 14 exons separated by 13 introns. The untranslated 5' upstream and 3' downstream regions may possibly play regulatory roles in prothrombin gene expression. Individuals containing alleles with a G to A mutation at the 20210 nucleotide position within the 3' untranslated region have increased prothrombin levels leading to increased risk of TEs.[44] This mutation occurs in 18% of patients with personal and family histories of TEs, 6.2% of all patients with TEs, and 1% of healthy individuals.[44] Screening for the 20210 AG genotype requires extraction of DNA from peripheral blood lymphocytes using BioRad InstaGene Kit (Mississauga, ON, CA), PCR amplification of the sequence (345 bp) that contains the mutation by use of the appropriate primers, and digestion of the amplified DNA with restriction endonuclease Hind III. The resultant fragments are electrophoresed on an agarose gel containing ethidium bromide, and the number and sizes of the separated fragment bands indicate whether an individual is normal (345 bp band only), heterozygous (345 bp, 322 bp and 23 bp bands), or homozygous (322 bp and 23 bp bands) for the abnormality.[44,45]

Antithrombin Deficiency

Assay details AT activity can be measured by clot-based or chromogenic assays that assess the inhibition of either thrombin or FXa. There are two commercially available kits that measure AT concentrations based upon anti-FXa activity: Coamate Antithrombin (Chromogenix, Molndal, Sweden) distributed by diaPharma (Franklin, OH, USA), and Actichrome AT anti-FXa, (American Diagnostics, Greenwich, CT, USA). There are at least six commercially available kits that measure AT concentrations based upon anti-FIIa activity: American Diagnostics, Greenwich, CT, USA; Organon Teknika, Durham, NC, USA; Diagnostica Stago, Asnieres-Sur-Seine, France; Instrumentation Laboratories, Lexington, MA, USA; Ortho Clinical Diagnostic, Raritan, NY, USA; and Dade Behring, Marburg, Germany. For all AT assays, the manufacturer's protocols are followed.[46] The following summarizes the principle components for all assays.

Antithrombin activity assay
Sample used: 15 µL
- Dilute plasma in a buffer containing UFH
- Add an excess of either FXa or FIIa
- Incubate for 1 minute
- Add either an anti-FXa or anti-FIIa substrate
- Measure the change in delta absorbance

The plasma concentration is determined by reading the patient's results from a reference curve generated using the same method.

Plasma concentrations of AT can be measured immunologically using a commercial kit that provides an ELISA assay from Affinity Biologicals, Hamilton, ON, CA. Antibodies to AT can also be purchased from many different companies, and in-house Mancini radial immunoassays developed.

Protein C Deficiency
Assay details Protein C can be measured by chromogenic assays, functional clot-based assays, and antigenic assays. There are six functional clot-based assays available in commercial kits: ProClot (Instrumentation Laboratories, Lexington, MA, USA); Protein C Clotting Time (Dade Behring, Marburg, Germany); Acticlot C (American Diagnostics, Greenwich, CT, USA); Accuclot Protein C (Sigma Diagnostics, St. Louis, MO, USA); Staclot Protein C (Diagnostica Stago, Asnieres-Sur-Seine, France); and Protein C Assay (Ortho-Clinical Diagnostic, Raritan, NY, USA). There are seven chromogenic assays available in commercial kits: IL Protein C (Lexington, MA, USA); Actichrome Protein

C (American Diagnostics, Greenwich, CT, USA); Accucolor Protein C (Sigma Diagnostics, St. Louis, MO, USA); Stachrom Protein C (Diagnostica Stago, Asnieres-Sur-Seine, France); Berichrom Protein C (Dade Behring, Marburg, Germany); Protein C (Organon Teknika, Durham, NC, USA); and Electrachrome Protein C (Ortho-Clinical Diagnostic, Raritan, NY, USA). There are three commercially available kits that measure the plasma concentration of protein C with ELISAs: Asserachrom Protein C (Diagnostica Stago, Asnieres-Sur-Seine, France); Protein C (Affinity Biologicals, Hamilton, ON, CA); and Thrombonostika Protein C (Organon Teknika, Durham, NC, USA). There are two commercially available kits for the determination of the plasma concentration of protein C by Laurell Rocket EID plates: Relliplate C (American Diagnostics, Greenwich, CT, USA); and Acculor protein C (Sigma Diagnostics, St. Louis, MO, USA). The manufacturer's specific protocols are followed for each of the assay kits. The following summarizes the principal components for protein C functional clot-based assays.

Plasma is first diluted in either buffer or protein C-deficient plasma. If plasma is diluted in buffer, then protein C-deficient plasma is subsequently added, followed by the snake venom Agkistrodon contortrix. APTT reagent is then added and the mixture is incubated for a specific time. $CaCl_2$ is added, and the clotting time measured. Activated protein C will inhibit both FVIIIa and FVa resulting in an inverse relationship in which longer clotting times reflect increased plasma concentrations of protein C in plasma.

Protein S Deficiency
Assay details Protein S can be measured by functional clot-based assays and antigenic assays. There are four functional clot-based assays available: Protein S (Instrumentation Laboratories, Lexington, MA, USA); (Dade Behring, Marburg, Germany); Acticlot S (American Diagnostics, Greenwich, CT, USA); and Staclot S (Diagnostica Sago, Asnieres-Sur-Seine, France). The manufacturer's protocol is followed for specific assay kits. There are three antigenic assays for protein S: Asserachrom (Diagnostica Stago, Asnieres-Sur-Seine,

France); Protein S (Affinity Biologicals, Hamilton, ON, CA); and (Organon Teknika, NC, USA). There are two assays for free, unbound protein S: Protein S ELISA (Affinity Biologicals, Hamilton, ON, CA); and Thrombonostika (Organon Teknika, Durham, NC, USA). Protein S requires the separation of free protein S from bound protein S using a polyethylene glycol precipitation (PEG) method. Laurell Rocket EID are available from American Diagnostics, Greenwich, CT, USA (Relliplate S) and Sigma Diagnostics, St. Louis, MO, USA (Accuclor Protein S). To measure free protein S, PEG precipitation is also required with these methods. The specific manufacturer's protocols are used. The typical features of a protein S functional clot-based assay are reviewed below.

Protein S functional clot-based assay
Sample used: 10 µL
- Dilute plasma in buffer or protein S-deficient plasma
- Add agkistrodon contortrix (a snake venom) to maximally activate protein C
- Add a thromboplastin/$CaCl_2$ reagent
- Measure the inhibition of Fva

The results are plotted on linear graph paper with time in seconds on the Y axis versus u/mL on the X axis. The manufacturer's protocol is followed for the specific assay kits.

LESS WELL-DEFINED CONGENITAL RISK FACTORS FOR THROMBOEMBOLIC EVENTS

Other potential but less well-defined congenital prothrombotic disorders include hyperhomocysteinemia, MTHFR mutation, Lp(a), HCII, and PAI.[47]

Hyperhomocysteinemia Homocysteine is an amino acid that is essential in the pathway converting methionine to cysteine. The causes of hyperhomocysteinemia can be classified as either acquired or congenital. Acquired hyperhomocysteinemia is caused by deficiencies of one of two vitamins, cobalamin or folate. These acquired causes of hyperhomocysteinemia are resolved by replacement of the deficient vitamin. The genetic causes of hyperhomocysteinemia are abnormalities of either cystathionine-α-synthase or MTHFR genes.

Plasma concentrations of homocysteine are measured by high performance liquid chromatography (HPLC).[48] In brief, the reduction of disulfide bonds and deproteinization by sulfhydryl groups with ammonium 7-fluorobenzo-2-oxa-1,3-diazole-4-sulfonate (SBD-F) is followed by HPLC separation, utilizing fluorescence detection.

Methylenetetrahydrofolate Reductase Genotyping
MTHFR is an enzyme in the homocysteine remethylation pathway that catalyzes the reduction of 5,10-methylenetetrahydrofolate to 5-methyltetrahydrofolate. MTHFR deficiency results in increased plasma concentrations of homocysteine, a risk factor for cardiovascular disease. The C to T transition in the MTHFR gene at position 677 changes a highly conserved alanine residue to valine. Homozygosity for this mutation results in the production of a thermolabile variant of MTHFR, which is an increased risk for cardiovascular disease. Analysis for the MTHFR mutation uses a method similar to those employed for detection of FV Leiden and prothrombin gene abnormalities. Screening for the MTHFR mutation requires extraction of DNA from peripheral blood lymphocytes (white cell [buffycoat] fraction extracted using lysis buffer from BioRad InstaGene Kit [Mississauga, ON, CA]), PCR amplification of a region (198 bp) of the sequence that contains the mutation (by use of the appropriate primers), and digestion of the amplified DNA with *Hin*fI restriction endonuclease. The resultant fragments are electrophoresed on an agarose gel containing ethidium bromide, and the number and sizes of the separated fragment bands indicate whether an individual is normal (198 bp band only), heterozygous (198 bp, 175 bp, and 23 bp bands), or homozygous (175 bp and 23 bp bands) for the abnormality.[49]

Lipoprotein (a) Lp(a) was first discovered in 1963 by Kare Berg as a genetic trait in human plasma.[50] Since its discovery, the Lp(a) structure has been determined to be a dimer consisting of one low density lipoprotein (LDL) molecule joined by a disulfide bond to an apolipoprotein (a) molecule. Recent interest has been placed on the physiologic role of the apolipoprotein (a) portion of the Lp(a) molecule, as it has been shown to be highly homologous to plasminogen although not possessing identical biologic activity.

Similar to LDL cholesterol, Lp(a) is synthesized in the liver. Although Lp(a) shows some homology to LDL cholesterol in structure, physiologic circulating levels of Lp(a) do not appear to be regulated by the same mechanisms as LDL cholesterol. Likewise, cholesterol feeding does not appear to increase levels of Lp(a) in plasma, although it does increase levels of LDL cholesterol. Most pharmacologic agents that do have an effect on lowering LDL cholesterol levels have little effect on levels of Lp(a), suggesting that in vivo regulation differs.

Human Lp(a) can be quantified by an automated immunoprecipitin analysis.[51] One of the more than 40 kits available that measure Lp(a) is the Lp(a) SPQ Test System (Diasorin, Stillwater, MN, USA). A polymeric enhancer is added to the sample and, after an initial incubation time and measurement of the sample blank, undiluted antibody is added and mixed. Insoluble antigen-antibody complexes begin to form immediately, producing turbidity in the mixture and increases in the amount of light scattered by the solution. After an incubation period of approximately 10 minutes, the absorbance of the solution is measured at the analytical wavelength (340 nM). A calibration curve is generated by assaying a series of standards with known Lp(a) concentrations. Concentrations for the controls and samples are interpolated from the calibration curve. Patients must fast for at least 12 hours. The sample is an EDTA sample processed for serum. Only 0.5 mL (minimum) is required for analysis.

Heparin Cofactor II   A commercial kit from Diagnostica Stago (Asnieres-Sur-Seine, France) is available to assay HCII. The method has been adapted for use on a ACL 300 analyzer from Instrumentation Laboratories. The assay is carried out in two stages. First the plasma is diluted in buffer (1/80) containing dermatan sulfate, and an excess of thrombin is added. The reference plasma is diluted 1/40 (100%). The instrument will make serial dilutions of this plasma, thus generating a reference curve. The mixture is allowed to incubate for 60 seconds and a chromogenic substrate is added; the change in delta absorbance is read. The ACL will automatically add the prediluted plasma and thrombin to the measuring rotor. After the incubation period, substrate is added and change in delta absorbance recorded. The assay can be done using microtitre plates and read as an endpoint method on a microtitre plate reader, or in test tubes, transferring to a cuvette for reading at 405 nM in a spectrophotometer.

Plasminogen Deficiency   There are seven commercially available kits that measure the functional activity of plasminogen: Actichrome PLG (American Diagnostics, Greenwich, CT, USA); Accucolor™ Plasminogen (Sigma Diagnostics, St. Louis, MO, USA); Stachrom PLG (Diagnostica Stago, Asnieres-Sur-Seine, France); Berichrom Plasminogen (Dade Behring, Marburg, Germany); Electrachrome Plasminogen (Ortho-Clinical Diagnostic, Raritan, NY, USA); Plasminogen kit (Instrumentation Laboratories, Lexington, MA, USA); and plasminogen(Organon Teknika, Durham, NC, USA). Manufacturers' protocols are used for adaptation to different instruments.

Plasminogen Activity Assay
Sample used: 15 μL
- Dilute plasma in buffer in which excess streptokinase is added
- Complexes of SK and plasminogen form, which convert a second plasminogen molecule to plasmin
- Add a chromogenic substrate

The amount of *p*-nitroanaline released is measured at 405 nM.

There are two commercial antigen assay (ELISA) kits available, either from Affinity Biologicals, Hamilton, ON, CA, or American Diagnostics, Greenwich, CT, USA. Antibodies to human plasminogen are also available from Affinity Biologicals, Hamilton, ON, CA.

Discussion   All known congenital prothrombotic disorders are autosomal in inheritance, with clinical expression in the heterozygous state, usually as adults. Increasing numbers of children are being referred for evaluation for congenital prothrombotic conditions, due to the recent identification of these disorders and referrals for family studies, usually when a young adult develops a TE. Although individuals with congenital prothrombotic disorders rarely develop TEs during childhood, early diagnosis is important, so that relatively simple, yet effective preventative measures can be taken in the presence of an acquired prothrombotic risk factor. Common acquired risk factors during childhood consist of immobilization, trauma, sepsis, and dehydration, while less common risk factors include cancer, central venous lines, and others.

In order to accurately diagnose the presence of congenital prothrombotic disorders, valid age-dependent reference ranges must be used. Comprehensive studies of healthy premature infants, full-term infants, and children ages 1 to 16 years are available (Chapter 2).[2-4] At birth, plasma concentrations of AT, protein C, protein S, plasminogen, and HCII are decreased; fibrinogen is present as a "fetal" or "dys" fibrinogen; and APCR ratios are increased (Chapter 2).[2-4,52] During childhood, only plasma concentrations of protein C remain decreased (Chapter 2).[4] If adult ranges of protein C concentrations are used, as many as 30% of children would be mistakenly identified as being heterozygous. All abnormal test results should be repeated on at least one further occasion to confirm the diagnosis and family studies performed. Tests performed during the acute presentation of a TE may be artificially abnormal and the results should be repeated at a subsequent time.

ANTIPHOSPHOLIPID ANTIBODIES

General Information Several phospholipid-dependent laboratory assays were developed or altered to detect the presence of antiphospholipid antibodies (APLAs). APLAs can be divided into two groups: lupus anticoagulants (LAs) and anticardiolipin antibodies (ACLAs). Assays for LAs include APTTs, kaolin clotting times (KCCT), dilute Russell Viper Venom Test (dRVVT), and dilute PTs.[53-55] For each patient, two or more assays are recommended, because no single test will identify all LAs due to the heterogeneity of the antibodies

(Table 13–1).[56,57] If a screening test for a LA is prolonged, a 1:1 mix should be performed. If the 1:1 mix does not normalize the screening test, a confirmatory assay should be performed. Either activated platelets or hexagonal phase phospholipids can be used as confirmatory tests. Activated platelets and hexagonal phase phospholipids absorb LAs, thereby permitting the phospholipid component of the coagulation test to provide a surface for coagulation factor assembly to occur.[58,59] Normal ranges for these assays in children aged 1 to 16 years are provided in Table 13–2.

Assays for Lupus Anticoagulants
Activated partial thromboplastin time APTTs may be performed in microtubes as described previously, or assayed on any coagulation analyzer using LA sensitive APTT reagents (PTT-LA, Diagnostica Stago, Asnieres-Sur-Seine, France).

Reagents
- APTT reagent
- $CaCl_2$ (0.02 M or 0.025 M)
- Normal pooled plasma filtered through a 0.22 mµ filter
- Confirm reagent containing hexagonal phase phospholipid

Automated method
Sample used: 50 µL
- Automatically pipette 50 µl plasma
- Add 50 µl of reagent
- Incubate for 5 minutes
- Add 50 µl of $CaCl_2$
- Measure the clotting time

Results greater than 3 standard deviations are abnormal. When abnormal values are obtained, the abnormal plasma is then mixed 1:1 with filtered plasma and the assay repeated. If there is no correction into the normal reference range, a confirmatory APTT is performed, using a reagent containing hexagonal phase phospholipid (Staclot LA, Diagnostica Stago, Asnieres-Sur-Seine, France).

Dilute Russell's viper venom The reagents are commercially available: Dilute Russell Viper Venom and DRVVT Confirm (American Diagnostics, Greenwich, CT, USA), Viperquik Test and

Table 13–1 Associations between Individual Lupus Anticoagulant Tests and Thrombosis

	Dilute PT		Dilute APTT		Dilute RVVT Confirm Reagent		Ionophore-treated Platelets		Kaolin Clot Time	
Positive	8	2	4	6	2	8	1	9	2	8
Negative	4	45	2	47	1	48	1	48	3	46

PT = prothrombin time; APTT =activated partial thromboplastin time; RVVT = Russel's viper venom time.

Reproduced with permission.[68]

Table 13–2 Normal Ranges for Screening Tests in Children Aged 1 to 16 Years

Assay	Normal Range
Prothrombin time (sec)	29–58
Activated partial thromboplasmin time (sec)	24–56
Kaolin clotting time (sec)	60–180
Dilute Russell's viper venom time (sec)	22–44
IgG (IG units)	0–16
IgM (IM units)	0–30

Viperquik Check (Organon Teknika, Durham, NC, USA), and LA 1 and LA 2 (Dade Behring, Marburg, Germany). The manufacturers' protocols are followed.

Reagents
- Russell's viper venom reagent
- Russell's viper venom reagent confirm

Automated method
Sample used: 50 µL
- Thrombin clotting time program
- Automatically pipette 50 µL of plasma
- Add 50 µL of RVV reagent
- Measure clot formation

The test can be adapted to automated instruments or done in a microtube by adding 40 µL of plasma to 40 µL of prewarmed dRVV. If the clotting time is greater than 2 standard deviations (SD) from the mean normal reference interval, a confirmatory test is run. The confirmatory test reagent is a high phospholipid reagent that overwhelms the LA effect in the in vitro test system, thus giving a normal result in an LA positive plasma using the same procedure as dRVV. The final result is expressed as a ratio of the test time to the confirmatory test time. A ratio

equal to or greater than 1.3 is considered positive for the presence of LA.

Dilute prothrombin time The assay is a modification of the tissue thromboplastin inhibition test.[60] It was adapted for use on an ACL (Instrumentation Laboratories, Milan, Italy).

Reagents
- Veronal buffer (0.0071 M sodium acetate, 0.0071 M sodium diethylbarbiturate, 0.131 M NaCl, pH 7.4)
- Normal pooled plasma filtered through a 0.22 mu filter
- PT reagent (Recombiplastin, Ortho-Clinical Diagnostics, Raritan, NY, USA)
- $CaCl_2$ (0.02 M)

Method
Sample used: 50 µL
- APTT program
- Dilute PT reagent 1/200 with veronal buffer
- Pipette 50 µL of plasma into the cuvette rotor
- Add 50 µL of diluted PT reagent
- Incubate for 5 minutes
- Add 50 µL of $CaCl_2$

Clot formation is automatically measured.

Results equal to or greater than 3 SD from the mean reference interval are considered abnormal. The test is repeated, mixing the test plasma with normal pooled plasma prepared as above. A lack of correction indicates the presence of a lupus anticoagulant.

Anticardiolipin antibody The early observation that the APLA reacted with the cardiolipin portion in venereal disease research laboratory reagent (VDRL serologic test for syphilis) led to the development of a radioimmunoassay and subsequently an ELISA for ACLA.[61,62] More recently, ELISAs have been developed for many other phospholipid antigens.[63] Some of the ELISAs use the protein co-factors that bind distinctive subgroups of APLAs (such as α2-glycoprotein-I and prothrombin) for detection.[64,65] Most authors have reported normal values for ACLAs in children that are similar to those found in adults.[66-68] One study, however, found significantly increased ACLA IgG values in a large group of healthy children.[69] ACLAs should be measured by ELISA and other coagulopathies should be excluded

STANDARD HEPARIN ASSAYS

General Information Assays for UFH are important for the safe monitoring of UFH in patients of all ages. International recommendations are that laboratories standardized their APTT values against UFH levels because APTT reagents are not standardized for their sensitivity to UFH. Different reagents and even different lot numbers of the same reagent have widely differing sensitivities to UFH.[70] The two most commonly used assays for UFH are an anti-thrombin assay using PSO$_4$[71] and an anti-FXa assay.[72] Recommended therapeutic ranges for the PSO$_4$ UFH assay are 0.2 to 0.5 u/ml and for the anti-FXa heparin assay 0.35 to 0.70 u/mL. The details of these two assays are provided subsequently.

Protamine heparin assay

Reagents
- Veronal buffer (0.0071 M sodium acetate, 0.0071 M sodium diethylbarbiturate, 0.131 M NaCl, pH 7.40)
- PSO$_4$: serial diluted from 1u/mL down to 0.05 u/mL in veronal buffer
- Seegers (1.66% Acacia, 0.0037 M CaCl$_2$, 0.112 M NaCl, 0.0277 M imidazole, pH 7.3)
- Bovine thrombin diluted to 2 u/mL in 0.15 M NaCl

Manual micro method
Sample used: 100 µL
- 6 x 50 mm glass tube
- Add 20 µL Seegers buffer
- 20 µL standard plasma
- 20 µL diluted thrombin
- Start timer and record the clotting time (adjust thrombin to 20 seconds)

This will give a baseline time for normal plasma. Repeat the assay using different PSO$_4$ dilutions with patient plasma
- 20 µL Seegers buffer
- 20 µL standard plasma
- 1 µL PSO$_4$ dilution
- 20 µL diluted thrombin
- Start timer and record the clotting time

The first concentration of PSO$_4$ will be dependent on the initial TCT of the sample. The longer the TCT, the greater concentration of PSO$_4$ added to the sample. The procedure is repeated 4 to 5 times with differing PSO$_4$ dilutions, and the clotting times are plotted on semi-log paper versus the PSO$_4$ concentrations. A straight line should be obtained, and the point at which the line crosses the normal baseline is equal to the UFH concentration (Figure 13–4). The therapeutic range established for adults and used in pediatrics is 0.20 to 0.40 u/mL.[71]

Anti-Factor Xa Heparin Assay There are two types of anti-FXa assays, a clot-based assay and a chromogenic assay. Both are available as commercial kits and the manufacturer's method is followed. The following outlines the chromogenic assay, the most commonly used anti-FXa assay.

Chromogenic heparin assay
Sample used: 10 µ
- Add FXa to plasma
- Dilute in a buffer containing AT
- Incubate for 1 minute
- Add an Xa specific substrate
- Measure the delta absorbance

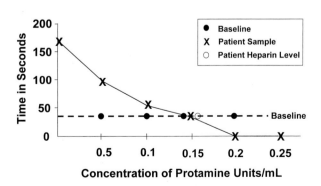

Figure 13–4 Example of a manual micro protamine sulphate heparin thrombin clotting time standard line.

The amount of Xa inhibited is inversely proportional to the concentration of UFH in the plasma (Figure 13–5). The chromogenic anti-FXa assays uses 10 μL of plasma compared to the PSO$_4$ heparin assay, which requires a minimum of 100 μL of plasma. The therapeutic range established for adults and used in pediatrics is 0.35 to 0.70 u/mL.

When low molecular weight heparin (LMWH) is used for the treatment of TEs, this assay is a useful monitoring tool. Calibration plasmas for LMWH are adaptable to all automated methods and are available from Diagnostica Stago, Asnieres-Sur-Seine, France, and American Diagnostics, Greenwich, CT, USA. The therapeutic range for LMWH is 0.5 to 1.0 u/mL.

Discussion Currently, pediatric patients being treated with therapeutic amounts of UFH are monitored in a fashion similar to adults. Because APTT reagents have widely varying sensitivities to UFH, current recommendations are that the therapeutic range for APTT values reflect the therapeutic range based on one of the two heparin assays discussed above. Further, if APTT values for an individual pediatric patient are not increasing as expected, measuring a UFH level should be considered. Discrepancies between APTT values and UFH concentrations can be due to increased levels of

FVIII, which is an acute phase reactant; prolonged baseline APTT values that reflect physiologically low concentrations of the contact and/or VK-dependent factors; the presence of a LA that can also prolong the baseline APTT; and decreased plasma concentrations of the inhibitor AT. There is increasing evidence that plasma concentrations of UFH better reflect the in vivo antithrombotic effectiveness of UFH than APTT values when their results are discordant.

BLEEDING TIME

General Information Bleeding times currently remain the only available test of in vivo platelet function. In the past, bleeding times in newborns and children were performed with adult automated devices, modified template devices, or Ivy bleeding times.[73–76] More recently, modified automated devices have been made specifically for infants and children: Surgicutt® Newborn and Surgicutt® Jr. (International Technidyne, Edison, NJ, USA).[75,76] These automated devices have been tested in large populations of healthy children and provide good reproducibility with less discomfort.[75] The following section provides the method for using an automated device to determine the bleeding time in newborns and children.

Bleeding Times in Newborns
- Adjust the blood pressure cuff according to the baby's weight:

  - 30 mm Hg in infants greater than 2 kg
  - 25 mm Hg in infants weighing 1–2 kg
  - 20 mm Hg in infants weighing < 1 kg

- Make a single vertical incision of 2.5 mm in length and 0.5 mm in depth on the cleansed skin of the forearm with an automated device
- Absorb blood from the incision every 15 seconds with filter paper until the bleeding stops.

Vertical incisions are chosen because of the very small arms and superficial location of veins in premature infants. The upper limit of normal for the automated device is 135 seconds.[75]

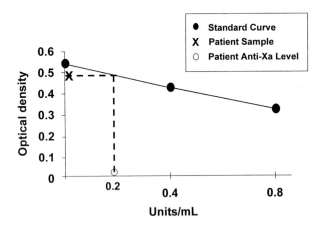

Figure 13–5 Chromogenic heparin assay. The amount of Xa inhibited is inversely proportional to the concentration of heparin in the plasma.

Bleeding Times in Children

- Inflate pediatric blood pressure cuff to 40 mm Hg
- Make a horizontal incision 3.5 mm by 1 mm in depth on the forearm
- Absorb blood from the incision every 15 seconds with filter paper until the blood stops

Beyond the first 2 months of life, bleeding times have been measured in large numbers of healthy children using an automated pediatric device (Surgicutt, International Technidyne, Edison, NJ, USA).[4] The pediatric automated device cuts the skin with a swiping action with a retractable blade. Age-dependent normal values are provided in Chapter 2.

Acknowledgements The authors would like to thank Patsy Vegh, Lesley Berry, and Marilyn Johnston in the preparation of this manuscript.

REFERENCES

1. Reverdiau-Moalic P, Delahousse B, Bardos GBP, et al. Evolution of blood coagulation activators and inhibitors in the healthy human fetus. Blood 1996;88:900–906.
2. Andrew M, Paes B, Milner R, et al. Development of the human coagulation system in the full-term infant. Blood 1987;70:165–172.
3. Andrew M, Paes B, Milner R, et al. Development of the human coagulation system in the healthy premature infant. Blood 1988;72:1651–1657.
4. Andrew M, Vegh P, Johnston M, et al. Maturation of the hemostatic system during childhood. Blood 1992;80:1998–2005.
5. Thomson JM. Blood coagulation and haemostasis. London: Churchill Livingstone, 1991.
6. Mancini G, Carbonara O, Heremans JF. Immunochemical quantitation of antigens by single radial immunodiffusion. J Immunochem 1965;2:235–254.
7. Laurell CB. Antigen-antibody crossed electrophoresis. Anal Biochem 1965;10:358–361.
8. Amiral J, Adalbert B, Adam M. Application of enzyme immunoassays to coagulation testing. Clin Chem 1984;30:1512–1516.
9. Johnston M, Zipursky A. Microtechnology for the study of the blood coagulation system in newborn infants. Can J Med Tech 1980;42:159–164.
10. Clauss A. Gerinnungsphysiologishe Schnell Method zue best immungoles Fibrinogen. Acta Haematol 1957;17:237–246.
11. Bick RL, Wheeler A, Campasano N. A comparative study of the DuPont antithrombin III and fibrinogen assay systems. Am J Clin Pathol 1985;83:541–546.
12. Hoffman M, Greenberg C. The effect of fibrin polymerization inhibitors on quantitative measurements of plasma fibrinogen. Am J Clin Pathol 1987;88:490–493.
13. Hirsh J. Oral anticoagulant drugs. Review article. N Engl J Med 1991;324:1865–1875.
14. Hull R, Hirsh J, Jay R, et al. Different intensities of oral anticoagulant therapy in the treatment of proximal-vein thrombosis. N Engl J Med 1982;307:1676–1681.
15. Stevenson KJ, Easton AC, Curry A. The reliability of activated partial thromboplastin time methods and the relationship to lipid composition and ultrastructure. Thromb Haemost 1986;55:250–258.
16. D'Angelo A, Seveso MP, D'Angelo SV. Effect of clot-detection methods and reagents on activated partial thromboplastin time (APTT): implications in heparin monitoring by APTT. Am J Clin Pathol 1990;94:297–306.
17. Hirsh J, Warkentin TE, Raschkle, et al. Heparin and low molecular weight heparin: mechanism of action, pharmacokinetics, dosing considerations, monitoring, efficacy, and safety. Chest 1998;114:489S–510S.
18. Ockelford P, Carter C. Disseminated intravascular coagulation: the application and utility of diagnostic tests. Semin Thromb Haemost 1982;8:198–216.
19. Biggs R. Human blood coagulation. In: Biggs R, ed. Haemostasis and thrombosis. Philadelphia: Blackwell Scientific Publications, 1972:614.
20. Kluft C. Determination of prekallikrein in human plasma: optimal conditions for activating prekallikrein. J Lab Clin Med 1978;91:83–95.
21. Monagle P, Vegh P, Mitchell L, Andrew M. Investigation of fibrinolytic response to venous stress testing in children [abstract]. Thromb Haemost 1999;Suppl:2494a.
22. Bucknell M. The effect of citrate on euglobin methods of estimating fibrinolytic activity. J Clin Pathol 1958;11:403–405.
23. Fearnley G, Balmford G, Fearnley E. Evidence of a diurnal fibrinolytic rhythm, with a simple method of measuring natural fibrinolysis. Clin Sci 1957;16:645–650.
24. Ranby M, Norrman B, Wallen P. A sensitive assay for tissue plasminogen activator. Thromb Res 1982;27:743–749.
25. Wiman B, Mellbring G, Ranby M. Plasminogen activator release during venous stasis and exercise as determined by a new specific assay. Clin Chim Acta 1983;127:279–288.

26. Korninger C, Speiser W, Wojta J, Binder BR. Sandwich ELISA for tissue plasminogen activator antigen employing a monoclonal antibody. Thromb Res 1986;41:527–535.

27. Whol RC, Sino L, Robbins KC. Methods for studying fibrinolytic pathway components in human plasma. Thromb Res 1982;27:520–535.

28. Eriksson E, Ranby M, Gyzand E. Determination of plasminogen activator inhibitor in plasma using tissue plasminogen activator and a chromogenic single point poly-D-lysine stimulated assay. Thromb Res 1988;50:91–101.

29. Pelzer H, Schartz A, Heimburger N. Determination of human thrombin-antithrombin III complex in plasma with an enzyme-linked immunosorbent assay. Thromb Haemost 1988;59:101–106.

30. Pelzer H, Schwarz A, Stuber W. Determination of human prothrombin activation Fragment 1+2 in plasma with an antibody against a synthetic peptide. Thromb Haemost 1991;65:153–159.

31. Corrigan JJ, Earnst D. Factor II antigen in liver disease and warfarin induced vitamin K deficiency: correlation with coagulation activity using echis venom. Am J Haem 1980;8:249–55.

32. Grosley BM, Hirschauer C, Chambrette B, et al. Specific measurement of hypocarboxylated prothrombin in plasma or serum and application to the diagnosis of hepatocellular carcinoma. J Lab Clin Med 1996; 127:553–564.

33. van den Belt A, Prins M, Huisman M, Hirsh J. Familial thrombophilia: a review analysis. Clin Appl Thromb Hemost 1996;2:227–236.

34. Ramaker J, Goerdt S, Zouboulis C, et al. Recurrent thrombophlebitis and ulcera crurum as manifestations of hereditary blood coagulation disorders and Klinefelter syndrome. Discussion based on 4 case examples. Hautarzt 1997;48:634–639.

35. Blaisdell F. Acquired and congenital clotting syndromes. World J Surg 1990;14:664–669.

36. Nowak-Gottl U, Kohlhase B, Vielhaber H, et al. APC resistance in neonates and infants: adjustment of the APTT-based method. Thromb Res 1996;81:665–670.

37. Miletich J, Prescott S, White R, et al. Inherited predisposition to thrombosis. Cell 1993;72:477–480.

38. Seligsohn U, Zivelin A. Thrombophilia as a multigenic disorder. Thromb Haemost 1997;78:297–301.

39. Nuss R, Hays T, Manco Johnson M. Childhood thrombosis. Pediatrics 1995;96:291–294.

40. Dahlback B, Carlsson M, Svensson PJ. Familial thrombophilia due to a previously unrecognized mechanism characterized by poor anticoagulant response to activated protein C: prediction of a cofactor to activated protein C. Proc Natl Acad Sci U S A 1993; 90:1004–1008.

41. Laffan MA, Manning R. The influence of factor VIII on measurement of activated protein C resistance. Blood Coagul Fibrinol 1996;7:761–765.

42. Montaruli B, Schinco P, Pannocchia A, et al. Use of modified functional assays for activated protein C resistance in patients with basally prolonged APTT. Thromb Haemost 1997;78:1042–1048.

43. Perry DJ, Pasi KJ. Resistance to activated protein C and factor V Leiden. QJM 1997;90:379–385.

44. Poort SR, Rosendaal FR, Reitsma PH, Bertina RM. A common genetic variation in the 3'-untranslated region of the prothrombin gene is associated with elevated plasma prothrombin levels and an increase in venous thrombosis. Blood 1996;88:3698–3703.

45. Poort S, Michiels J, Rietsma P, Bertina R. Homozygosity for a novel missense mutation of the prothrombin gene causing a severe bleeding disorder. Thromb Haemost 1994;72:819–824.

46. Odegard OR, Lie M, Abilgaard U. Heparin cofactor activity measured with an amidolytic method. Thromb Res 1975;6:287–294.

47. Iijima H, Iida T, Murayama K, et al. Plasminogen activator inhibitor-1 in central serous chorioretinopathy. Am J Ophthalmol 1999;127:477–478.

48. Fortin LJ, Genest J. Measurement of homocyst(e)ine in the prediction of arteriosclerosis. Clin Biochem 1995;28:155–162.

49. Frosst P, Blom H, Milos R, et al. A candidate genetic risk factor for vascular disease: a common mutation methylenetetrahydrofolate reductase. Nat Genet 1995;10:111–113.

50. Berg K. A new serum type in man: the LP system. Vox Sang 1965;10:513–527.

51. Tate JR, Riffai N, Berg K, et al. International Federation of Clinical Chemistry standardization project for the measurement of lipoprotein (a). Phase I. Evaluation of the analytical performance of lipoprotein (a) assay systems and commercial calibrators. Clin Chem 1998;8:1629–1640.

52. Uttenreuther-Fisher MM, Ziemer S, Gaedicke G. Resistance to activated protein C (APCR): reference values of APC-ratios for children. Thromb Haemost 1996;76:813–821.

53. Exner T, Rickard K, Kronenberg H. A sensitive test demonstrating lupus anticoagulant and its behavioral patterns. Br J Haematol 1978;40:143–151.

54. Thiagarajan P, Pengo V, Shapiro S. The use of dilute Russell Viper Venom time for the diagnosis of lupus anticoagulants. Blood 1986;68:869–874.

55. Proctor R, Rapaport S. The partial thromboplastin time with kaolin. Am J Clin Pathol 1961;36:212–219.

56. Exner T, Triplett D, Taberner D, Machin S. Guidelines for testing and revised criteria for lupus anticoagulants. SSC Subcommittee for the Standardization of

Lupus Anticoagulants. Thromb Haemost 1991;65: 320–322.

57. Brandt J, Triplett D, Alving B, Scharrer I. Criteria for the diagnosis of lupus anticoagulants: an update. Thromb Haemost 1995;74:1185–1190.

58. Rauch J, Tannenbaum M, Tannenbaum H, et al. Human hybridoma lupus anticoagulants distinguish between lamellar and hexagonal phase lipid systems. J Biol Chem 1986;261:9672–9677.

59. Rauch J, Janoff AS. Phospholipid in the hexagonal II phase is immunogenic. Proc Natl Acad Sci U S A 1990;87:4112–4115.

60. Schleiden MA, Nachman RL, Jaffe EA, Coleman M. A clinical study of the lupus anticoagulant. Blood 1976;48:499–509.

61. Harris E, Boey M, Mackworth-Young C, et al. Anticardiolipin antibodies: detection by radioimmunoassay and association with thrombosis in systemic lupus erythematosus. Lancet 1983;2:1211–1214.

62. Loizou S, McCrea J, Rudge A, et al. Measurements of anticardiolipin antibodies by an enzyme-linked immunosorbent assay (ELISA): standardization and quantitation of results. Clin Exp Immunol 1985;62:738–745.

63. Amiral J, Minard F, Chambrette B. Development of standardized immunoassays for identification, characterization, and quantification of antiphospholipid antibodies. Biol Clin Haematol 1991;13:81–88.

64. Arvieux J, Roussel B, Jacob MC, Colomb MG. Measurement of anti-phospholipid antibodies by ELISA using beta 2-glycoprotein I as an antigen. J Immunol Methods 1991;143:223–229.

65. Arvieux J, Darnige L, Caron C, et al. Development of an ELISA for autoantibodies to prothrombin showing their prevalence in patients with lupus anticoagulants. Thromb Haemost 1995;74:1120–1125.

66. Ravelli A, Caporali R, Di Fuccia G, et al. Anticardiolipin antibodies in pediatric systemic lupus erythematosus. Arch Pediatr Adolesc Med 1994;148: 398–402.

67. Gattorno M, Buoncompagni A, Molinari AC, et al. Antiphospholipid antibodies in paediatric systemic lupus erythematosus, juvenile chronic arthritis and overlap syndromes: SLE patients with both lupus anticoagulant and high-titre anticardiolipin antibodies are at risk for clinical manifestations related to the antiphospholipid syndrome. Br J Rheumatol 1995;34:873–881.

68. Berube C, Mitchell L, David M, et al. The relationship of antiphospholipid antibodies to thromboembolic disease in systemic lupus erythematosus in children: a cross-sectional study. Pediatr Res 1998;44: 351–356.

69. Kontiainen S, Miettinen A, Seppala I, et al. Antiphospholipid antibodies in children. Acta Paediatr 1996;85:614–615.

70. van den Beseelaar AM, Neuteboom J, Meeuwisse-Braun J, Bertina RM. Preparation of lyophilized partial thromboplastin time reagent: composed of synthetic phospholipids: usefulness for monitoring heparin therapy. Clin Chem 1997;43:1215–1222.

71. Vestergaard L. The titration of heparin with protamine. Scand J Clin Lab Invest 1954;6:284–287.

72. Teien AN, Lie M. Evaluation of amidolytic heparin assay method. Increased sensitivity by adding purified antithrombin III. Thromb Res 1977;10: 399–410.

73. Feusner JH. Normal and abnormal bleeding times in neonates and young children utilizing a fully standardized template technique. Am J Clin Pathol 1980;74:73–77.

74. Andrew M, Castle V, Mitchell L, Paes B. A modified bleeding time in the infant. Am J Hematol 1989;30:190–191.

75. Andrew M, Paes B, Bowker J, Vegh P. Evaluation of an automated bleeding time device in the newborn. Am J Hematol 1990;35:275–277.

76. Andrew M, Castle V, Saigal S, et al. Clinical impact of neonatal thrombocytopenia. J Pediatr 1987;110: 457–464.

INDEX